Personnel and Human Resource Management

THE WEST SERIES IN MANAGEMENT

Consulting Editors
DON HELLRIEGEL, Texas A & M
JOHN W. SLOCUM, JR., Southern Methodist University

I wish to express my deepest gratitude and appreciation to my parents for their unconditional support throughout the preparation of this book and all my other undertakings.

Contents

Personnel and Human Resource Management

Randall S. Schuler
UNIVERSITY OF MARYLAND

WEST PUBLISHING COMPANY
St. Paul New York Los Angeles San Francisco

Written to accompany this textbook is a book of
applied readings in human resource management.
The readings provide additional real-life examples
illustrating the application of personnel activities
discussed in this textbook. The readings book is
available from your local bookstore under the title
*Applied Readings in Personnel and Human
Resource Management,* by Schuler, McFillen, and
Dalton.

If you cannot locate it in the bookstore, ask your
bookstore manager to order it for you.

Copy Editor: Rebecca Smith Randolph
Designer: Louis P. Neiheisel II
Production Coordination: Del Mar Associates
Composition: Graphic Typesetting Service

Printed in the United States of America

Library of Congress Cataloging in Publication Data

Schuler, Randall S
  Personnel and human resource management.

  (The West series in management)
  Bibliography: p.
  Includes index.
  1. Personnel management.   I. Title.
HF5549.S249   658.3   80-26541
ISBN O-8299-0406-9

Preface

The effective management of human resources has become increasingly important to organizations. In a growing number of them, the personnel and human resource department has taken an expanded role. Today, personnel departments are involved in the strategic planning of top management. They help interpret an extensive set of state and federal regulations and help ensure that the organization complies with them. They develop innovative ways to attract and retain qualified employees, by such methods as alternative work schedules. Personnel departments are also concerned about the quality of work life and employee health. Personnel departments engage in the more traditional personnel activities as well, such as staffing, appraisal, compensation, training and development, and labor relations.

Since organizational effectiveness is becoming more imperative, organizations are now demanding that personnel departments prove *their* effectiveness. As a consequence, personnel departments collect, interpret, and use personnel data. This process not only helps the personnel department prove its effectiveness but also increases the likelihood that the organization's human resources will be used more effectively.

This book discusses personnel functions and activities in the framework of a life cycle model of personnel and human resource management. This theoretical perspective is spiced with numerous real-life examples from such sources as *Fortune* and *Business Week,* with cases, illustrations, "slices of life," and scenarios that show how theory can be applied. These supplements are also meant to stimulate your interest in this vital area of organizational management. For example, there is an extensive discussion of career management in which you are asked to define your own goals and objectives. At other points, you are asked to solve problems that confront personnel managers

on a regular basis. All in all, this book was written to enable you to meet the challenge of managing human resources and to demonstrate the worth and vitality of personnel and human resource management.

This book was written with the aid, cooperation, and counsel of many individuals. Among those I particularly wish to thank are Rick Braschel and Jim Thomas at Nationwide Insurance Companies; Barney Offerman, Stu Klein, and Jan P. Muczyk at Cleveland State University; Tony Campagna, Jim McFillen, Bob Miljus, and Nan Weiner at The Ohio State University; Robert Kerr and Olga Crocker at the University of Windsor; James Rush at Western Ontario University; Ray Aldag at the University of Wisconsin-Madison; Todd Jick, Vic Murray, and Dave Demick of York University; Frank E. Kuzmits at the University of Missouri; and Judy Olian of the University of Maryland.

The following people helped shape this book by reviewing the manuscript prior to publication: Floyd A. Patrick, Eastern Michigan University; Stephen Rubenfeld, Texas Tech University; Richard J. Ward, Bowling Green State University; Lena B. Prewitt, University of Alabama; Cynthia D. Fischer, Texas A & M University; John Dickson, University of Arizona; Hubert S. Field, Auburn University; James L. Bowditch, Boston College; Donald Schwab, University of Wisconsin-Madison; George Stevens, Arizona State University; Don Hellriegel, Texas A & M University; and John Slocum, Southern Methodist University.

Special thanks go to several people who were especially helpful in the writing of this book. Among them are Tom Milburn, who provided a great deal of insightful commentary and social support along the way, and my brother Ed, who provided a great deal of commentary, social support, critical evaluation, and real-life examples. Dan Dalton of Indiana University played an invaluable role as the writer of the Slices of Life and the personnel problems in each chapter and served as a sounding board for many of the ideas that later were incorporated into the book. Margaret Watman saved me near the end of the process by working many long and tedious hours to obtain permission for use of all the quoted material. The book is much livelier because of these quotes. She also wrote Appendix C and contributed greatly to the Instructor's Manual. Eddie Roberts was extremely helpful in preparing this manuscript. Without her support and patience, as well as that of Donald Walker and Maria Brown, this book could never have been written.

A very special word of thanks goes to my close friend and colleague Bill Todor. Bill, in addition to writing Section Six (Establishing and Maintaining Effective Labor Relations), provided many valuable ideas for the rest of the book. He was also the one who was always there to hear me out. To him I extend my sincere appreciation and gratitude.

I wish also to express my appreciation for support provided by the College of Administrative Science and the Mershon Center at the Ohio State University. The cooperation of the several publishers, authors, and permissions editors who granted me permission to use their materials was extremely valuable in making this a lively and practical textbook. Finally, I wish to thank Don Hellriegel of Texas A & M and John W. Slocum, Jr., who as friends and consulting editors really helped make the whole effort very worthwhile.

Randall S. Schuler
College Park, Maryland

Personnel and Human Resource Management

SECTION ONE

Understanding Personnel and Human Resource Management

CHAPTER OUTLINE

PERSONNEL AND HUMAN RESOURCE MANAGEMENT

Purposes of Personnel and Human Resource Management

Productivity and Quality of Working Life

Employee Performance, Satisfaction, Health, Turnover, and Absenteeism

Nondiscrimination

The Importance of Personnel and Human Resource Management

Human Resource Costs

The Productivity Crisis

The Pace and Complexity of Change

Symptoms at the Workplace

Who's Responsible for Personnel and Human Resource Management?

The Managers

The Employees

FUNCTIONS AND ACTIVITIES OF PERSONNEL MANAGEMENT

Planning for Human Resource Management

Staffing the Organization

Appraising and Compensating Employees

Training and Developing Employees

Establishing and Maintaining Effective Labor Relations

Improving and Analyzing the Work Environment

THE ROLES OF THE PERSONNEL AND HUMAN RESOURCE DEPARTMENT

Personnel Policy Formulation

Personnel Policy Implementation

Audit and Control of Personnel Policies

Innovation

ORGANIZING THE PERSONNEL AND HUMAN RESOURCE DEPARTMENT

Personnel Department Climates

Personnel in the Hierarchy

Centralization versus Decentralization

STAFFING THE PERSONNEL DEPARTMENT

Line Managers and Personnel Specialists and Generalists

Qualities of the Personnel Manager and Personnel Staff

The Personnel Manager

Personnel Generalists

Personnel Specialists

Choosing a Personnel Department That's Right for You

WHAT THIS BOOK IS ABOUT

Purposes of this Book

A Model of Personnel and Human Resource Management

Themes of This Book

Practical Realities

Theory and Research

For Whom Is This Book Written?

OBJECTIVES

● To discuss the importance of personnel and human resource management

● To explain the functions and activities of personnel and human resource management

● To identify and discuss the purposes of personnel and human resource management

● To discuss the four roles of a personnel and human resource department

THOUGHT STARTERS

● How can the effectiveness of a personnel and human resource department be determined?

● What criteria should be used in evaluating organizations?

● Why do organizations have a personnel and human resource department?

● Which personnel and human resource department should you work in?

CHAPTER ONE
Some Basic Concepts

It is so commonplace now for chief executives to deliver speeches extolling "people" as their companies' most important resource that one tends to dismiss the phrase as cant. For some chief executives, of course, it may be. But a growing number of them really do realize that the quality and morale of their employees can make the difference between success and failure for their companies. One chief executive who is especially articulate on the importance of a company's human resources is Delta Airlines' Tom Beebe. "The name of the game in business today is personnel," he says emphatically. "You can't hope to show a good financial or operating report unless your personnel relations are in order, and I don't care what kind of a company you're running. A chief executive is nothing without his people. You've got to have the right ones in the right jobs for them, and you've got to be sure employees at every level are being paid fairly and being given opportunities for promotion. You can't fool them, and any chief executive who tries is going to hurt himself and his company."

Companies eager to increase their workers' productivity—and which were not?—discovered that an alert personnel director was in a unique position to contribute to the companies' welfare. For example, George Sherman, the vice president of industrial relations at Cleveland's Midland-Ross Corp., got to wondering just why productivity rates in Japanese factories were so high. He flew to Japan, visited some factories, and concluded that part of the answer lay in the use of committees, made up of both workers and supervisors, that met regularly to hear suggestions for meeting production goals. On his return to the U.S., Sherman got clearance to form Japanese-style committees of workers and supervisors at the company's electrical-equipment plant in Athens, Tennessee. One modification of the Japanese plan involved the offer of a cash bonus to both workers and managers if productivity really did increase beyond the goal set by Midland-Ross. One year and 400 suggestions later, productivity at the Athens plant was up by 15 percent. The company was able to cancel plans to invest $250,000 in added manufacturing capacity, because output increased without it. Now Sherman expects to set up similar committees at other plants.

Pressure on American corporations from their not-so-silent partner, Uncle Sam, has done a great deal to add luster to the job of personnel director. In the last twenty years, there have been more than a hundred individual pieces of federal legislation directly affecting the relationship between corporations and their employees—e.g., the Work Hours Act of 1962, the Occupational Safety and Health Act of 1970, and the Employees' Retirement Income Security Act of 1974. There has been a whole basket of laws and regulations to outlaw discrimination, including the Civil Rights Act of 1960, the Equal Pay Act of 1963, and the Age Discrimination in Employment Act of 1967.

Furthermore, many companies that had expanded geometrically during the 1960's discovered that their acquisition programs had left them with a tangle of incompatible compensation plans, and with scores of highly paid executives who now seemed to be in the wrong jobs, or worse, were superfluous. And with the stock market remaining in the doldrums, stock-option plans that had looked like money machines during the 1960's suddenly seemed most unsatisfactory; new compensation plans had to be devised to keep key executives contented. The job of personnel director took on new dimensions—especially as chief executives began scrambling to minimize the adverse effects of the recession.

From Herbert E. Meyer, "Personnel Directors Are New Corporate Heroes," Fortune, *February 1976, pp. 84–88. Courtesy of* Fortune *Magazine, ©1976 Time, Inc.*

These few paragraphs illustrate the growing importance of personnel and human resource management in organizations and provide several reasons for it. Although there may be some disagreement over how important personnel and human resource management really is, there is a great deal of agreement that now is the time to more effectively manage and care for human resources. But how can this be done? Furthermore, who is to do it? There are many answers to the question of what to do, but there is growing agreement that those with specialized knowledge in personnel and human resource management should be the doers. Thus personnel and human resource departments in organizations are becoming increasingly concerned with questions of how best to manage human resources. In addition, these questions are primary concerns of this book.

In order to effectively address these concerns, you need to know the "what" and the "how" of personnel and human resource departments in organizations. Describing and examining in detail the "what" and the "how" (along with the "should") are what this book is about. But first the essence of what personnel and human resource departments do must be defined. After that, this chapter briefly examines the functions and activities of personnel and human resource management and the people who perform them. Another focus is the relationship of those people, functions, and activities to the rest of the organization. The chapter ends with a discussion of this book's plan, its themes and philosophy, and what it intends to accomplish.

PERSONNEL AND HUMAN RESOURCE MANAGEMENT

Personnel and human resource management is a set of functions and activities to be used in the management of human resources in a nondiscriminatory, affirmative, and effective manner for the benefit of the organization, the individual, and society in a given organizational and environmental context.

Purposes of Personnel and Human Resource Management

Productivity and Quality of Work Life. The two major purposes of personnel and human resource management are to enhance productivity and the quality of work life.[1] Some organizations may value productivity more than quality of work life; others may value the quality of work life more than productivity. In either case, their relative importance and definition often flows from the strategies and policies of the total organization. Increasingly, personnel functions and activities are becoming directly tied to corporate strategies.[2]

Edwin Land of Polaroid Corporation has described the basic purposes of his organization in terms of both the product (hence productivity) and the quality of work life for employees:

We have two basic aims. One is to make products that are genuinely new and useful to the public, products of the highest quality and at reasonable cost. In this way we assure the financial success of the company and each of us has the satisfaction of helping to make a creative contribution to the society.

The other is to give everyone working for the company a personal opportunity within the company for full exercise of his talents—to express his opinions, to share in the progress of the company as far as his capacities permit, and to earn enough money, so that the need for earning more will not always be the first thing on his mind. The opportunity, in short, to make his work here a fully rewarding and important part of his life.[3]

From these two aims, particularly the second, flow all Polaroid's strategies related to personnel and human resource management. The better Polaroid is at attaining these aims, the more effective their personnel and human resource functions and activities are.

Employee Performance, Satisfaction, Health, Turnover, and Absenteeism. The personnel and human resource department can improve the organization's productivity and the quality of work life for employees by using selected indicators, or **personnel criteria,** related to them. There are many criteria associated with productivity and quality of work life, but in evaluating the effectiveness of the personnel functions and activities, the criteria most frequently used are employee performance, satisfaction, and health. Symptoms of malfunction are high turnover and absenteeism. There are other criteria used in evaluating specific functions and activities. For example, the staffing function can be evaluated by its ability to attract good job applicants and by how well the people actually hired do in terms of performance, absenteeism, turnover, and satisfaction.

Nondiscrimination. Although productivity and quality of work life and their related criteria are laudable purposes and useful measures for determining the effectiveness of personnel and human resource management, they primarily represent the concerns of the organization and the employee. They omit a concern for the environmental context in which the organization exists. Two important purposes of personnel and human resource management related to concern for the environment (as well as for the individual and the organization) are to act without discrimination and affirmatively (with respect to age, sex, race, national origin, and religion). In addition, the personnel manager should also be concerned with acting legally. Acting without discrimination and affirmatively are legal requirements for many organizations, but organizations face numerous other laws and regulations too. For example, organizations must meet occupational safety and health standards and must abide by the regulations or laws pertaining to union organizing and collective bargaining.

As with performance, satisfaction, health, turnover, and absenteeism, the effectiveness of personnel and human resource management can be evaluated according to how well the organization avoids discrimination and other violations of laws and regulations pertaining to personnel management.

The Importance of Personnel and Human Resource Management

Although there are many reasons for providing personnel and human resource management, four major ones are (1) the costs associated with human resources, (2) the productivity crisis, (3) the increasing pace and complexity of social, cultural, legal, and educational changes, and (4) the symptoms of dysfunction in the workplace.

Human Resource Costs.   Today, corporations realize that it pays to be concerned with how they manage their human resources.

Top management has finally realized that the people costs are as important as other costs. Management realizes that its important assets are not simply financial resources but having the people on hand at the right time and the right place to make a thing go.[5]

(By the way, for those of you who can "make a thing go," the rewards are attractive. A recent study by Heidrick & Struggles, Inc., a Chicago-based executive search firm, indicates that the average salary of top-level human-resource executives is approximately $80,000.)

The positive results from personnel activities designed to manage and develop human resources effectively are significant reductions in accidents, absenteeism, and error rates and significant increases in morale, quality of the product or service, and productivity and profits, their important byproduct.[6] For example:

After running several surveys to measure employee attitudes and morale, Ruben Krigsman, manager of personnel research at Union Carbide Corporation, instituted several new training programs and reorganized the workplace which gave the blue-collar workers more responsibility. The result? In just three months, productivity soared by 25%; the amount of finished goods passing inspection jumped from 50% to 80% and absenteeism dropped from 5% to 3%.[7]

The Productivity Crisis.   During the 1960s, productivity in the United States increased at an annual rate of about 3 percent. By 1973 it was nearly zero. It fell sharply in 1974, resulting in a decline in the rate of productivity.[8] From 1973 to 1978, the increase in the annual rate of productivity in major industrial states averaged 3.1 percent in Japan, 3.2 percent in West Germany, and 0.4 percent in the United States. In addition, the average Japanese auto worker produces between forty and fifty cars a year, compared with twenty-five in the United States and eleven in West Germany. This productivity crisis is not only a real threat to the U.S. economy but also underlines the importance of human resource management.

This is so, because to date the more effective management of human resources seems to be the best hope for stopping the slide in productivity. Human resource managers will have an unprecedented opportunity to have the ear of top management if they can propose concrete solutions to these real problems.[9]

The Pace and Complexity of Change.   Several ongoing changes in the cultural and educational levels and social order of the United States have contributed to the concerns of human resource management. For example, because midlife career changes are becoming more common and most occupations require increased knowledge, training and development programs for all employees have developed rapidly.

In 1940 the U.S. Department of Labor was enforcing 16 statutes and executive orders affecting personnel practices. By 1960 the number had grown to 40, and by 1980 there were no fewer than 130.[10]

In 1952 women made up less than 33 percent of the work force. Today they make up approximately 45 percent. The change in the percentage of women in the work force is even more dramatic when 1920 is compared with 1980.

The current work force is generally becoming more knowledgeable and better informed. Whereas in 1970 only one of eight workers had a college degree, in 1980 one of every four workers who entered the labor force had one. These high-quality human resources are potentially more productive. However, this opportunity presents a real challenge to organizations: "As society becomes better informed, it also tends to become more critical, less accepting of authority and more cynical."[11] Young workers appear to be particularly cynical about decisions made by supervisors and correspondingly more resistant to authority. Older workers, however, still tend to "reflect earlier values of society and are, therefore, more inclined to be organization people, to accept authority and to seek primarily the satisfaction of lower level needs at work."[12] Thus the effective management of human resources requires not only knowing how to manage and channel the skills of the young workers but also knowing how to manage a work force with a mixed set of values.

Symptoms at the Workplace.   Rapid social change has been accompanied by changes in the relationship between the worker and the job. Some of the terms used to describe what is happening in the workplace include *worker alienation, boredom,* and *job dissatisfaction.*[13] These symptoms are often associated with decreasing motivation and increasing counterproductive behavior and worker demands on the workplace. Although these symptoms can certainly be found in most workplaces, whether they are factories or offices, public or private organizations, the extent to which they are reported to exist in the workplace varies greatly.[14]

Who's Responsible for Personnel and Human Resource Management?

The Managers.   Personnel and human resource management is the task of individuals who have specialized in and who are primarily responsible for personnel and human resource management (personnel managers) and of individuals not specialized in but often responsible for the day-to-day implementation of personnel functions and activities (line supervisors and line managers). This is not meant to imply that the personnel manager never implements personnel functions and activities or that the line manager does not get involved in their development and administration. Indeed, these two managers are interdependent in the effective management of human resources. Nor can the effective management of human resources occur without the support and direction of top management. Top management influences the number and execution of personnel functions and activities in an organization. This influence is best shown by the role that top management allows the personnel manager and department to play in the organization.

The Employees.   Increasingly, employees are taking a role in personnel and human resource management. For example, employees may be asked to appraise their own performance or the performance of their colleagues. Employees may also help determine their own performance standards and goals. It is no longer uncommon for employees to write their own job descriptions. Perhaps most significantly, employees are taking a more active role in managing their own careers, assessing their own needs and values, and designing their own jobs.

The term *personnel manager* (or executive) or *personnel and human resource manager* refers to the person or position heading up the personnel and human resource department. In organizations, this position may also be labeled the vice president of personnel or the vice president of employee relations.

The term *personnel and human resource department* can be used interchangeably with the term *personnel department* or just *personnel*. These different names are used in different organizations. Nevertheless, all the functions and activities of personnel and human resource management relate to any of the terms. The term *staff* or *personnel staff* refers to the employees in the personnel department (either generalists or specialists) working for the personnel manager.

Line manager (or *supervisor*) refers to the person in charge of the employees who are working directly on the product that the organization produces. The terms *individual, person*, and *worker* refer to anyone in the organization. The term *employee* generally refers to the person who works for the line manager or the personnel manager; this person may also be called a nonmanagerial employee. *White-collar worker* refers to managerial, professional, and technical employees—or those who work in offices. *Blue-collar worker* refers to the nonmanagerial employee. Use of the term *subordinate* is avoided—except in Chapter 9, where the terms *subordinate* and *superior* are explained.

FUNCTIONS AND ACTIVITIES OF PERSONNEL MANAGEMENT

Six personnel and human resource management **functions and activities** are described in this book:
- Planning the organization's human resource needs
- Staffing the organization's human resource needs
- Appraising and compensating the organization's human resources
- Training and developing the human resources of the organization
- Establishing and maintaining effective labor relations
- Improving and analyzing the organizational environment

These functions represent the essence of personnel management. Although the personnel departments of many organizations may not currently be performing all these functions, the trend is clearly in the direction of performing them all.

Planning for Human Resource Management

The two major activities in this function are
● Planning and forecasting the organization's short-term and long-term human resource requirements
● Analyzing the jobs in the organization and determining the skills and abilities that are needed
These two activities are essential for effectively performing many of the personnel management activities. For example, they help indicate (1) what types of employees and how many the organization needs today as well as tomorrow, (2) how the employees will be obtained (for example, from outside recruiting or by internal transfers and promotions), and (3) the training needs the organization will have. In fact, these two activities can be viewed as the major factors influencing the staffing and development functions of the entire organization.

Although these two activities are so vital in the management of human resources, most organizations have only recently incorporated them into personnel departments. Today, in almost all of the nation's 500 largest industrial companies, personnel managers have responsibility for human resource planning; this was true for only a handful of companies five years ago.[15] Organizations are increasingly relating human resource planning to corporate goals or strategies. Typical of the trend is Tenneco's requirement that vice presidents submit five-year "executive resources" plans along with five-year business plans:

If a division, for example, is planning to shift from a marketing to a production orientation, the company vice-president of employee relations must make certain that it is planning not only to develop a large enough production staff to meet the new demands in that area but also to make a suitable reduction of marketing specialists.[16]

Staffing the Organization

Once the organization's human resource needs have been determined, they have to be filled. Thus staffing activities become necessary. These include
● Recruiting job applicants (candidates)
● Selecting from among the job applicants those most appropriate for the available jobs
● Socializing and accommodating newly selected employees
The organization must cast a wide net for potential employees in order to ensure a full and fair search for job candidates.

Time was when the organization could rely on "walk-ins" to provide the major source of supply for nonexempt employees; it could choose exempt employees

*from traditional sources. If a comer was spotted, the organization might carefully
tailor the job description so that the requisite experience fit him—and probably
only him—to the job. Now, however, the organization must prepare job
descriptions and specify requisite experience and training with care and publicize
its openings.*[17]

These recruiting procedures apply to external candidates (those not currently employed by the organization) as well as to internal candidates (those who are currently
employed by the organization).

After the candidates have been identified, they must be selected. Common procedures used in selection include obtaining completed application forms or resumes;
interviewing the candidates; checking education, background, experience, and references; and various forms of testing. Regardless of the exact procedures used,
however,

*Selection procedures must be based on job-related standards. In other words,
any criteria a manager chooses to use—from candidate's experience or education
to performance on any preemployment test—must be demonstrably related to job
performance.*[18]

In other words, selection procedures must result in a match between a candidate's
ability and the abilities required by the job.

Although this match assures the organization of getting someone who can do the
job, it does not always ensure that the new employee will stay. One consequence
of this is an increased concern for providing a match between the candidate's needs
and the rewards associated with the job. Another consequence is greater attention
to the process of bringing the new employee into the organization. The organization
must not only convey its expectations (socialization) to the new employee (the
traditional orientation session being one means to do this) but must also adapt to
the employee's expectations (accommodation).

Appraising and Compensating Employees

After employees are on the job, it becomes necessary to determine how well they
are doing and to reward them if they are doing well. If they are not doing well, it
becomes necessary to determine why. This determination may indicate that the
reward structure needs to be changed. It may also indicate that employee training
is necessary or that disciplinary action must be taken.

Employees are generally rewarded on the basis of the value of the job, their
personal contributions and their performance. Although providing rewards based on
level of performance can increase an employee's motivation to perform, many rewards are more generally given on the basis of the value of the job the employee is
doing. However, rewards based solely on the employee's personal contributions—
those provided just for being a member of the organization—are rapidly increasing.

Which form of compensation is most fair? Which form is most effective for the

organization? By what methods can jobs fairly be evaluated to determine their value? These questions and others are part of the appraising and compensating function which includes
- Appraising employee performance
- Administering direct compensation on the basis of job evaluation
- Providing incentive compensation on the basis of performance level
- Administering indirect compensation benefits to employees of the organization

None of these activities is easy, but all must be done to ensure the effective use of human resources. They must be done not only to get employees to join the organization, to participate, and to perform but also to determine possible training and development needs.

Training and Developing Employees

Training and developing activities include training employees, developing management, and helping to develop careers. These activities are designed to increase the abilities of the employees of the organization in order to facilitate employee performance. The training and development function includes
- Determining, designing, and implementing employee training and development programs to increase employee ability and employee performance

Employee training and development programs may be seen as activities meant to increase employee performance in the short run, whereas career management can be seen as a way for the employee and the organization jointly to increase employee performance and long-run satisfaction.

It is very true, though seemingly trite, to say that the continuity and success of any organization depend to a great extent on its ability to attract, evaluate, develop, utilize and retain well-qualified people at professional and managerial levels. Translated into fewer words, this merely means that a successful organization must have well organized and well administered human resource and career planning programs?[19]

Thus the second activity in the training and developing function is
- Designing and providing opportunities for managing careers

Establishing and Maintaining Effective Labor Relations

This function is composed of two sets of activities that relate to how employees organize themselves in dealing with the organization and how the organization bargains and negotiates with its organized employees. Specifically, the activities are
- Understanding the reasons and methods used by employees in organizing
- Bargaining and settling grievances with employees and the organizations representing them

This function is particularly important for organizations that have unionized employees. On one hand, the formal union-management relationship can effectively define the extent to which other personnel functions can be applied to the work force. On the other hand, the union-management relationship can be instrumental in developing new programs for the improvement of human resources.

Improving and Analyzing the Work Environment

Two activities in which the union-management relationship has been crucial for personnel management are

● Improving the physical work environment to maximize employee safety and health

● Improving the sociopsychological work environment, especially in regard to the quality of work life and employee job stress

The federal regulations specified in the Occupational Safety and Health Act of 1970 have special influence in improving the work environment of employees. These improvements directly and positively influence the physical safety and security of employees and their sociopsychological well-being.

Remember that the primary purpose of the improvement activities is employee well-being (physical and mental), whereas the primary purpose of the training and development activities is employee performance. In practice as well as theory, however, there is some overlap. For example, in many programs designed to improve the sociopsychological work environment, employee performance may increase along with satisfaction, responsibility, and self-control.[20]

In order to effectively improve the quality of the work environment, one must first know what the work environment is like. This means that the personnel and human resource department must collect information on existing conditions and employees. These data can then be used to develop and implement programs for improvements. After the programs have been implemented, additional data are collected. The two sets of data are then compared, using such techniques as correlation coefficients and subgroup analysis. Many of these techniques are also useful in the evaluation of such employment decisions as hiring and firing and in the evaluation of the other personnel functions. These techniques will grow more important as it becomes increasingly necessary to use human resources more effectively and to justify the existence and credibility of the personnel department.[21] Hence the third and final activity in improving and analyzing the work environment:

● Collecting and using personnel data for effective human resource management

THE ROLES OF THE PERSONNEL AND HUMAN RESOURCE DEPARTMENT

Not all organizations consider the personnel and human resource department to fulfill important functions. In fact,

There was a time when the personnel director was primarily concerned with only blue-collar workers: he had little effect on company policy(s). He was viewed as little more than a record keeper and director of recreation, one chief duty being to preside at retirement parties.[22]

In part because of this recordkeeping, flag-waving role played by the personnel department in the past, and in some organizations in the present, comments like the following became common:

The image of personnel is zero, though some gripes are unjustified. Personnel is reluctant to get rid of its obvious nonperformers. The image of personnel in the community is poor.[23]

But in many organizations and communities today the role and the image of the personnel department are changing.[24] The quotes from *Fortune* at the beginning of this chapter are becoming more and more representative. Even the change in title to personnel *and* human resource department reflects the expanding roles and growth in importance.

Personnel Policy Formulation

The second aim of the Polaroid Corporation stated in the quote on page 6 is an example of an organization's personnel policy. The question is, What role should the personnel and human resource department play in the formulation of personnel policy? The answer for any given organization will most likely depend on top management. One role the personnel department could play is that of providing information to be used by top management. The specific types of information could include the concerns of the employees and the impact of the external environment, particularly federal.and state regulations, on the use of human resources.

Personnel staff can also provide advice in the process of policy formulation. The chief executive may still make policy statements, but these could be regarded as drafts of policy. Formal adoption of a final policy can then take place after others, such as the personnel manager and line managers, have had a chance to provide their comments. At Honeywell there is an executive employee-relations committee, composed of five operating group vice presidents and five staff vice presidents, that is the senior policy board for employee-relations issues. This committee not only helps ensure extensive informational input into personnel policies but also increases their likelihood of being accepted. This acceptance then eases the way for the implementation of personnel policy, the next personnel role.

Personnel Policy Implementation

"In reality, personnel programs succeed because line managers make them succeed."[25] The "bread-and-butter" job of the personnel department, therefore, is to enable line managers to make things happen. Thus in the more traditional personnel activities, such as selecting, interviewing, training, evaluating, rewarding, couseling, promoting, and firing, the personnel department is basically providing a service to line managers. In addition, the personnel department administers direct and indirect compensation programs. Since the line managers are ultimately responsible for their employees, many of them see these services as useful. The personnel department can also assist line managers by providing information on and interpretation of equal employment opportunity legislation and safety and health standards.

The responsibility of the personnel department in personnel policy implementation is to provide the services needed by the line managers on a day-to-day basis, to keep them informed of regulations and legislation regarding human resource management, and to provide an adequate supply of job candidates for the line managers to select from. But to fulfill these responsibilities, the personnel department must be accessible. When the department is not accessible, the personnel manager loses touch with the needs of line managers. Consider this typical statement made by a line manager: "If only the personnel people would visit us sometime, they might better understand what it is we do."[26] The personnel staff should be as close to where the people and the problems are as possible. This is an organizing concern, so getting the personnel staff close to the action will be discussed in the section on organizing later in the chapter. One comment on organizing relevant here, however, is that getting the personnel staff close to the action involves decentralizing. But since the personnel functions and activities must be implemented with organizational consistency and integrity (to maintain fairness), the personnel and human resource department has to have a centralized auditing and controlling role.

Audit and Control of Personnel Policies

This role is one of the most critical today because of fair employment legislation. Various state and federal regulations are making increasingly sophisticated demands on organizations. Responses to these regulations can best be made by a central group supplied with accurate information, the needed expertise, and the blessing of top management.

Expertise is also needed for implementing many personnel activities, such as, distributing employee benefits. And since having personnel experts is costly, organizations hire as few as possible and centralize them. Their expertise then filters to other areas of the organization.

In organizations that have several locations and several divisions or units, there is often tension between the need to implement policy at the point of action (decentralization) and the need to implement it fairly across several divisions of an organization. There is also tension between the need for decentralization and the need for having the expertise necessary to comply with complex regulations and advising on the best methods for personnel activities. The audit and control role will be discussed at greater length in the section on organizing the personnel and human resource department.

Innovation

A final important and ever-expanding role for the personnel and human resource department is that of providing up-to-date application of current techniques and of developing and exploring innovative approaches to personnel problems and concerns.

Naturally, the innovative role must be in tune with the times and the set of issues confronting a particular company. In periods of rising inflation and escalating wage and salary demands, the emphasis may be on compensation issues. In times of retrenchment and falling profits, creative work sharing and lay-off plans may be needed.[27]

Today there are many issues confronting the personnel department that require it to actively fulfill its innovation role. It might be said that the personnel department stands between an irresistible force and an immovable object. The irresistible force is the desire of a growing proportion of the employed population for emancipation from repetitive work, authoritarian bosses, and all sorts of job stresses. The immovable object is the necessity of getting people to work harder and smarter in order to survive in an increasingly competitive and unpredictable environment.[28] Thus the personnel manager has to devise methods for satisfying the needs of the employees, who are preoccupied with getting the most out of the system, while getting them to contribute their best.

Times have changed since the days of the laissez-faire approach to personnel management, when the personnel manager was the one who arranged the Christmas party and the retirement parties. From the perspective of using an organization's human resources, all the easy yards have been gained; the yards ahead will be increasingly tough.[29] A purpose of this book, therefore, is to help smooth those yards for you—whether you are a line manager, a personnel manager, or a student preparing for a career in organizations.

ORGANIZING THE PERSONNEL AND HUMAN RESOURCE DEPARTMENT

Several issues related to the organization of personnel and human resources have already been introduced:
● The need for the personnel and human resource staff to be where the action is and to identify with the organization they are a part of
● The need for a fair and consistent application of personnel policies in the organization, regardless of how small or large and diversified it is
● The need for the views of the personnel department to be an integral part of personnel policy
● The need for the personnel department to have sufficient power and authority to help ensure that personnel policies will be implemented without discrimination, legally and affirmatively
● The need for the personnel department not just to react to personnel crises but to be active and innovative in dealing with human resource management
These five issues, which are the essence of the roles that personnel departments can play, affect the *organization* of personnel and human resources. For example, the personnel department can be organized so that it effectively plays only one of the four roles. Or it can be organized so that it plays two or more roles. The number of roles played often depends on the way top management views personnel and human resource activities and what it is willing to let the personnel department do. As a result, top management creates personnel department climates.

Personnel Department Climates

Four distinctly different **personnel department climates** that top management can create are described in Exhibit 1.1. The four climates are the "full partner," "showcase," "show me," and "routine service" departments. They can be identified by the extent to which the personnel department fills its possible roles. For example, all four personnel roles would probably be filled in the "full partner" department. Fewer roles are filled in the "showcase" department and fewer still in the "show me" department and the "routine service" department.

Since it is becoming more necessary for personnel departments to play all four roles in order to be effective, the remaining issues related to organizing the personnel department will be considered from the "full partner" perspective.

Personnel in the Hierarchy

The person who has explicit responsibility for human resource problems should be positioned at a high level in the organization's hierarchy and should not, because of disrespect for the function, be deprived of the status that will make him or her effective.[30]

Exhibit 1.1 The Four Personnel Department Climates

Type of Department	Attitude of Top Management	Attitude of Middle Management	Effectiveness of Personnel Department
Full Partner	High level of support and influence in company policies and plans	High level of cooperation and respect	High benefits-to-cost ratio; good employee morale and productivity; low absenteeism and turnover
Showcase	High level of support and influence; personnel is its "eyes and ears" in dealing with lower management	Lack of genuine or widespread cooperation and support	Low benefits-to-cost ratio because of superficial programs and frills; heavier emphasis on auditing and control roles, including studies and reports
Show Me	Low level of support	Must be "sold" on personnel services; good support from some departments, in which personnel may carry out counseling, advice, and service roles reasonably well	At best, moderate benefits-to-cost ratio (vary by department); departments vary considerably in morale, turnover, absenteeism; more politicking by personnel staff
Routine Service	Limited influence and support; may perceive personnel department as adequate	Limited influence and support; may view personnel department as necessary evil	Modest benefits and costs; emphasis on routine clerical and service roles (recruiting, employment screening, orientation, record keeping, overseeing cafeteria or plant facilities, employee benefits)

Adapted from R. A. Harschnek Jr., D. J. Peterson, and R. L. Malone, "Which Personnel Department Is Right for You?" *Personnel Administrator*, April 1978, p. 59.

This indicates the importance of a "full partner" status for personnel, a status echoed by James Henderson, president and chief operating officer of Cummins Engine Company:

I have always viewed top management and the personnel function as a partnership. Management is, after all, people. At Cummins the personnel head has always reported to the senior operating officer and has been a part of all major decisions.[31]

Other major organizations also reflect this "full partner" status and the associated power and respect necessary to fulfill the four roles effectively. At the United California Bank, the top personnel manager is titled the senior vice president of personnel, and at RCA, the executive vice president for industrial relations. In both organizations, the top personnel manager reports to the president.

Because effective labor-management relations can be such an important part of effective human resource management, several large organizations with a large unionized work force have organized personnel activities to reflect this importance. General Motors, Weyerhaeuser, AT&T, and Burlington Industries all have a vice president of personnel and a vice president of labor relations.

For the effective fulfillment of the four personnel roles, the personnel and human resource department should have its top manager at the top of the organizational hierarchy. Being at the top allows this person to play a part in personnel policy formulation and to have the power necessary for its fair and consistent implementation. Yet being at the top of the hierarchy does not address the need for personnel to be where the action is.

Centralization versus Decentralization

The organizing concept of centralization versus decentralization relates to the issue of the balance between getting personnel to where the action is and fairly and consistently applying personnel policies. It is also related to the balance between the benefits of having personnel generalists and of having personnel specialists. **Centralization** means that essential decision making and policy formulation is done at one location (at headquarters); **decentralization** means that the essential decision making and policy formulation is done at several locations (in the divisions or departments of the organization).

With the recent increases in regulatory requirements for use of human resources and the increased expertise necessary to deal with complex personnel functions, organizations are moving away from personnel generalists and toward personnel specialists. And at the same time, organizations, especially larger ones, are moving personnel staff into the organization's divisions. As a result, there are trends to centralize some aspects of personnel and to decentralize others. Paul Corballis, director of corporate employee relations at Pitney Bowes, Inc., describes these events at his company:

We have been slowly divisionalizing, putting the day-to-day work [personnel] out into the operating divisions. And as we have divisionalized, at the corporate level we have created a group of individual specialties, a pension group, an insurance group, compensation and benefits, and so forth.[32]

For the personnel activities that require expertise, organizations generally hire specialists. But because of the expense, as few specialists as possible are hired. If an organization is large and has several plants or offices or divisions, the specialists are located in one place (at corporate headquarters) but serve all the divisions. The personnel activities requiring less-specialized expertise are staffed by people at the divisional level, thereby increasing the autonomy of the divisions. Thus in a large, multidivision organization (which describes most of the largest industrial, retailing, and financial organizations), there is generally a corporate personnel and human resource department staffed largely with specialists and several divisional personnel departments staffed largely with generalists. The personnel and human resource department at headquarters then has two purposes:

• To develop and coordinate personnel policy for the personnel staff in all locations, including headquarters

• To execute the personnel functions and activities for all the employees at headquarters

As the divisions grow, they begin to hire their own specialists and to administer almost all their own personnel functions and activities. The result is almost a complete personnel and human resource department, similar to what would be found in most organizations without divisions. An illustration of such a department is shown in Exhibit 1.2. The chart shows that a rather complete set of personnel activities is conducted in the Information Group division of Xerox; however, specialists in many of these activities may still be located at corporate headquarters. These specialists help ensure some fairness and consistency in the administration of personnel activities in all of the divisions.

Note what can happen if some central control and auditing is not maintained. When divisional managers are held responsible for the performance of their divisions, they naturally want as much control over their divisions as possible, including the personnel activities. Since managers often have different styles and preferences, their personnel activities may differ greatly from one division to the next. For example, divisions may use different performance evaluation forms or use the same ones differently. Suppose you're in one of the divisions and want to transfer to a better job in another division. Assume that past performance is being used to select the candidate for the better job. Also assume that there is another candidate for the job currently working in the division where the job is located. Although you have received the highest performance ratings possible since you joined the division, all the other divisions "know" that everybody in your division gets the highest performance ratings possible. Assuming that the other candidate has a good performance record, who do you think would be more likely to be offered the better job?

Regardless of whether organizations are large or small, when personnel activities become decentralized there must be some uniformity in their administration. If not, activities may be administered differently to the detriment of the organization and the individual, as well as society. But centralization of activities is not always the answer. For one thing, centralization reduces local autonomy; for another, it removes personnel staff from the action. Thus centralization often results in a somewhat

Exhibit 1.2 Personnel Organization of Xerox Corporation's Information Group*

Reprinted, by permission of the publisher, from "Organizing and Staffing the Human Resources Function: A Personnel Symposium," *Personnel*, January/February 1978, p. 19, © 1978 by AMACOM, a division of American Management Associations. All rights reserved.

*This chart shows reporting relationships only and is in no way intended to reflect relative importance.

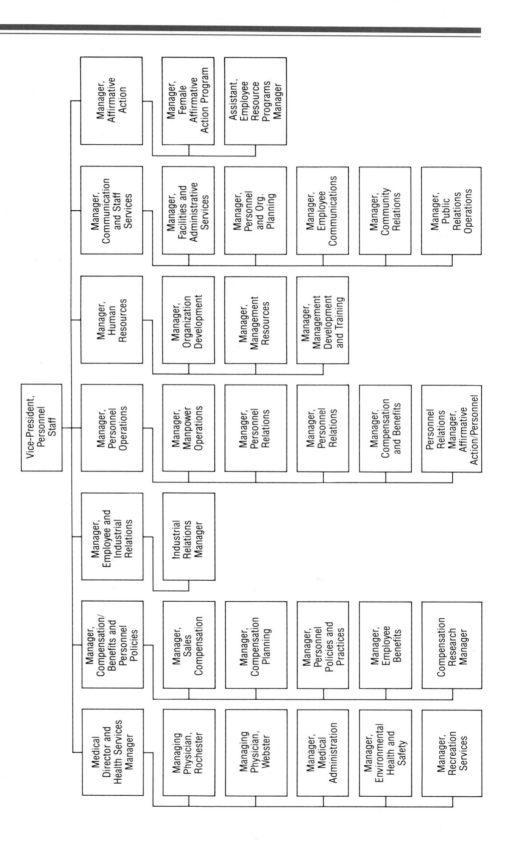

unavoidable tension. The challenge is for the tension to be managed effectively. The extent to which tension, and the entire personnel department, are managed effectively depends in large part on how the department is staffed.

STAFFING THE PERSONNEL DEPARTMENT

Earlier it was stated that comments like "The image of personnel is zero" and "The image of personnel in the community is poor" were due in part to the recordkeeping, flag-waving role formerly played by the personnel department. But this image was also due in part to the people who staffed personnel positions. "Too often, personnel members have been called incompetent. Too often, other departments have used personnel as a dumping ground for their failures."[33] A transfer to personnel, therefore, was rarely seen as a step up the experience or promotion ladder. Little wonder, then, that the personnel department could only keep records, wave flags, and arrange parties.

Adding to the general incompetence of those in personnel was their general lack of interest in or naivete about what the organization did and how it was run:

A majority of major corporation personnel directors couldn't state the dollar volume of sales for their company, didn't know the profit level and had little idea of the rate of return.[34]

In other words, the personnel staff had no idea what was happening in the organization.

As indicated in the quotations at the beginning of this chapter, however, the image, status, and importance of personnel and human resource management have increased dramatically in many organizations. And it is often in those organizations that the personnel department performs all four personnel and human resource roles. This is in part because top management now pays greater attention to who heads the personnel department. It is important to know who to select to fill positions in the personnel department.

Line Managers and Personnel Specialists and Generalists

Perhaps the most effective person who can head the personnel department is a superstar from the line organization. Since attracting the superstar means paying a higher salary than the person has been receiving, the effect of the superstar accepting the position is to increase the personnel department's credibility and prestige in the organization. However, even if the person is not a superstar, line experience gives the personnel manager influence over the other line managers. To understand just how far some companies have gone in this area, consider IBM's policy of assigning line managers to work in the corporate personnel and human resource department for up to two or three years.

In addition, the well-trained personnel specialist often gains influence by becoming a personnel generalist through training and experience. The personnel specialist who wants to reach the top may benefit greatly by rotating through a line job in order to increase his or her ability to understand and deal with the entire organization.[35]

Qualities of the Personnel Manager and Personnel Staff

The Personnel Manager.   Now that you know where to look for the person to head the personnel and human resource department, you need to know what to look for. What qualities should personnel managers possess? Remember that they are to head departments that fill all four personnel roles and perform all six personnel and human resource management functions.

To begin with, personnel managers need to be effective managers. They must be able to identify problems, develop alternative solutions, and then select and implement the most effective one. In addition, they must develop and maintain an integrated and effective management information system for helping to identify problems and implement policy. They must be innovative and aggressive and be willing to take such risks as serving as the conscience of the organization. Furthermore, they must be effective at selecting, building, and developing an entire personnel staff to carry out the six functions and activities.

Personnel Generalists.   What qualities do the rest of the personnel staff need, and where do they come from? Line positions are one important source. A brief tour by a line supervisor in a personnel position, usually as a personnel generalist, can convey to the personnel department the knowledge, language, needs, and requirements of the line. As a result, the personnel department can more effectively fill its service role. Another source of personnel talent is current nonmanagerial employees. In many organizations personnel positions are staffed with former hourly employees. Like line managers, these people bring with them information about the needs and attitudes of employees. In many cases they are particularly effective in their personnel positions.

Personnel generalists should possess many of the same qualities as personnel specialists, but it is apparent that the generalist's level of expertise in a personnel specialty generally need not be at the same depth as the specialist's. The generalist, however, needs to have a moderate level of expertise in many personnel activities and must be able to get more specialized knowledge when it is needed.

Personnel Specialists.   Personnel staff specialists should have skills related to the specialty, an awareness of the relationship of that specialty to other personnel activities, and a knowledge of the organization and where the personnel and human resource department fits. Individuals joining an organization for the first time should also have an appreciation for the political realities of organizations.[36] Another thing is for individuals in personnel to "guard against the development of 'them' and 'us' situations and remember that they are not in business to promote the latest fads—and companies are not in business to perpetuate personnel departments."[37] Universities are an important source of personnel specialists. Since specialists may work at almost any personnel and human resource activity, qualified applicants can come from specialized programs in law, personnel psychology, labor and industrial relations, personnel management, counseling, organizational development, and medical and health sciences.

Perhaps the most overriding quality required by both generalists and specialists, and one that improves the overall image of the personnel department, is the attitude and behavior of "doers and good doers" rather than "do gooders."

Choosing a Personnel Department That's Right for You

Now that you are aware of what personnel and human resource management is, what its functions and activities are, its current importance, the roles the personnel department can play in organizations, and some of the organizing and staffing issues, reading and studying the rest of this book can provide you with the skills necessary to use much of this awareness—which, by the way, should be useful whether you end up in a personnel department or not. (See Appendix A for the types of jobs available in the personnel and human resource area). Remember that a good part of being a successful line manager is managing human resources effectively, which is what this book is all about. If you anticipate ending up in a personnel department, however, an important question to think about is, Which personnel department is right for you?[38] Of course, your decision depends on many factors unique to each organization, such as its location, friends who may already be employed by the organization, the person who would be your supervisor, and how much the organization would pay you.

Your analysis can also depend on several factors that you can use to evaluate any personnel job. These general factors, related to the four climates of the personnel department, are described in Exhibit 1.3. Depending on the answers you get to questions like the ones listed in Exhibit 1.3, you can decide what type of climate the organization has and choose the one with the most appealing characteristics. The department's climate is important, because it helps determine many aspects of your job—including how much variety, responsibility, and challenge you will most likely have and how you will feel about working in the department. Such feelings include your satisfaction with your boss and co-workers, your enthusiasm (whether you really want to get up in the morning and go to work), and even how you feel outside of work.

It is equally important for you to know what your needs and goals, likes and dislikes, skills and abilities really are to ensure that your selection is the right one. You will have several opportunities throughout this book to begin identifying your own qualities.

WHAT THIS BOOK IS ABOUT

This book has several purposes, one of which is helping you to identify your personal qualities and the aspects of organizations that may assist you in choosing the right job, whether in personnel or not. Other purposes include

● Increasing your expertise in the functions and activities of personnel and human resource management

● Increasing your awareness of how these functions and activities are applied in organizations

Exhibit 1.3 Interview Responses by Type of Personnel Department

Key Questions	Full Partner Department	Showcase Department	Show Me Department	Routine Service Department
"I was wondering if you would care to fill me in on your plans for the personnel department this year?"	"Review the pay structure from top to bottom. Set up personnel policies and procedures and manpower planning for the new division."	"Finish the cafeteria. It's a hotfood line and decorated similar to a restaurant in the 1920s. The products we make will fit right in."	"Conduct an attitude survey to find out the reasons for problems that exist in some of the departments."	"Review pay and benefits, because costs are too high. Move the department to another location in the building."
"Could you fill me in a bit about the educational and professional background of the other people in your personnel department?"	"All the professionals have at least a college degree. Myself, I have an MBA."	"All the professionals on the staff, including myself, have a master's degree."	"Another person and I have a college degree. The others have been brought through the ranks with training."	"We have over thirty years of experience."
"Could you give me an idea of the reporting relationships in the personnel department here?"	"To the chief executive officer."	"To the chief executive officer."	"To the vice president for finance or plant manager."	"To the vice president for finance or plant manager."
"What challenges and improvements would you say you are most concerned with making next?"	"We are maintaining an annual update of the equal employment opportunity plan. Despite all the hullabaloo raised by the government's concern for equality, it is only telling companies what they should have been doing all along."	"Complete a long overdue (last done five years ago) update of the equal opportunity plan. We've hired a top pro from one of the Fortune 500 firms to do it and have allocated a sizable budget."	"Getting top management to accept the fact that a foreman training program and an updated benefits package is necessary."	"The personnel records are pretty disorganized, so we plan to convert to a computer format."
"Could you give me some idea of the kind of effort to maintain or build operational support from first-line supervision here?"	"We've always received good cooperation. They enforce the personnel policies and procedures well."	"All in all, it's OK, but they are a funny group. When we are in personnel meetings, they talk a good line. When they are back in their departments, it's frequently a whole different story."	"There's pretty good cooperation from lower-level managers, although some tend to run their departments the way they please."	"I think, in general, they meet your demands. They'll come to you when they have a real problem."

Adapted from R. A. Harschnek Jr., D. J. Petersen, and R. L. Malone, "Which Personnel Department Is Right for You?" p. 60. Reprinted with permission from the April 1978 issue of the *Personnel Administrator* copyright 1978, The American Society for Personnel Administration, 30 Park Drive, Berea, OH 44017.

● Assisting you in being an effective manager of human resources

● Presenting the complexities, challenges, and tradeoffs involved in being an effective manager of human resources

● Sharing with you a concern for effective human resource management

A Model of Personnel and Human Resource Management

The model of personnel and human resource management used in this book represents a "life cycle" of personnel functions and activities. The life cycle describes the general order in which the personnel functions and activities would be applied. It begins with the *planning* of who to get, when, and where, then moves to actually *getting* them, *appraising and compensating* their performance, *training and developing* them, *establishing and maintaining* effective relationships with them, *improving* work conditions for them, and finally *collecting and using* personnel data for improving and evaluating personnel activities.

The life cycle model also takes into account the impact of the external and internal environment on these functions and activities. The external environment is composed of the organization's competitors, regulators, and suppliers and of the broader political, social, and cultural makeup of the society the organization is embedded in. The internal environment is made of the qualities of individuals, tasks, and interpersonal relationships and of the characteristics of the organization.

Finally, the life cycle model depicts the outcomes of the personnel functions and activities—against which their effectiveness can be determined. In keeping with the influence of the internal and external environments on the management of human resources, the outcomes against which effectiveness is determined are those valued by society and the employees as well as by the organization.

These three features of the life cycle model—the sequential flow of functions and activities, the influence of the internal and external environments and the suggested outcomes—are illustrated in Exhibit 1.4.

The life cycle model reflects several other important features:

● The functions and activities included in this model are those that would be undertaken by a personnel and human resource department performing all four major personnel roles: policy formulation, policy implementation, audit and control, and innovation.

● The inclusion of collecting personnel data on the work environment as a personnel and human resource function reflects the growing concern for employee safety and health and for the quality of the employee's work environment. Chapter 19 presents data-gathering techniques and statistical methods for analyzing the data. These techniques are becoming more important to personnel managers as they seek ways to show the effectiveness of their department and demonstrate the usefulness of its many activities.

● The impact of environmental factors is integrated with the personnel functions and activities they are most relevant to. Thus the rules and regulations of such agencies as the Equal Employment Opportunity Commission and the Occupational Safety and Health Administration are discussed throughout the book. An important

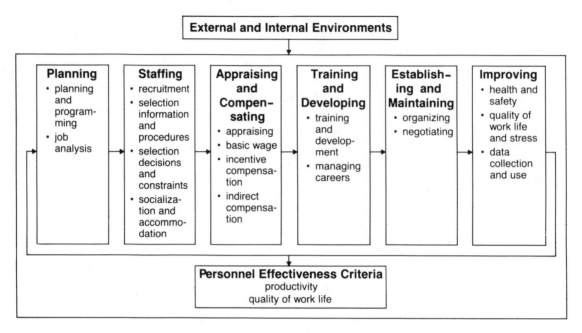

Exhibit 1.4   The Life Cycle Model of Personnel and Human Resource Management

reason for discussing their impact throughout the book rather than in one specific chapter is that equal employment and affirmative action represent a philosophy of personnel management even more than they represent a set of rules and techniques.
● It has been suggested that personnel managers must become more professional if the personnel field (or department) is to survive as a part of management.[39]

Another aspect of this growing trend to professionalism is the certification of individuals as knowledgeable in personnel and human resource functions and activities. The personnel functions and activities covered in this book, including personnel research, cover the six functional areas associated with the specialist and general accreditation exams.[40] Thus familiarization with the functions covered in this book help prepare an individual for professional certification.

Themes of This Book

Practical Realities.   A major theme of this book is the practical realities of personnel and human resource management. Examples from organizations and personnel managers are used to illustrate the application, and the difficulties in that application, of the personnel activities being examined. Thus each chapter begins with a scenario or quotation, and more short scenarios and quotations are provided throughout the chapter. In addition, there is an insert in each chapter called A Slice of Life, which highlights a particular application or problem that is often found in organizations. However, this is not a book of unconnected examples and experiences, because another theme complements this one.

Theory and Research. The other major theme is to provide the most current and useful information related to personnel and human resource management. Thus extensive use is also made of current research and theory related to the effective use and management of human resources. Consequently, you will receive not only an extensive description of all the current personnel functions and activities but also an understanding of why personnel functions and activities should work and how they actually work.

To increase your understanding, a case study is provided at the end of each chapter. After each case study are a few questions that you should be able to answer after reading the chapter. Remember in answering to draw on your knowledge of both why and how the personnel activity works.

For Whom Is This Book Written?

This book is written for you who will one day work in organizations or are already working in an organization. Knowledge of effective personnel functions and activities is vital for anyone working in organizations but particularly for managers and especially for personnel staff (specialist or generalists) and managers. This is true whether you work in a private or public organization, a large or small organization, a slow-growing or fast-growing organization. Although the type and size of the organization may influence the size of the personnel department, the functions and activities that are performed, and even the roles that are played, there is generally a personnel department in any organization—and effective management of human resources is always necessary. This is not to say, however, that human resources are managed in the same way in different types and sizes of organizations. To the contrary, there are several important differences in personnel management between public and private organizations, between slow-growing and fast-growing organizations, and between large and small organizations.[41] These differences are highlighted in Chapter 2, along with other internal and external environmental influences on personnel and human resource management.

SUMMARY

This chapter examines the growing importance of the functions and activities of personnel and human resource management, defines what personnel management is, and lists its purposes. Because of the increasing complexity of personnel management, nearly all organizations have established a department for it. However, not all of these departments perform all of the personnel functions and activities. Which ones a department actually performs and the way it does depend greatly on the roles that the department plays in the organization. There are four roles that a personnel and human resource department can play, and all of them are played in the organizations that are most concerned with the effective management and use of human resources.

Personnel and human resource departments also have climates. The four basic climates are essentially associated with the roles played by different departments.

You can use the concept of departmental climates to help identify the personnel department you want to work in.

After determining the roles and hence the functions and activities that a personnel and human resource department will perform, the organization is in a position to organize and staff the department. The organization must decide whether to centralize or decentralize personnel functions and activities and what sources to tap in staffing the department.

This book is for everyone who is or will be working in an organization but especially for those who are responsible for the management and use of human resources—line managers and personnel managers and staff. And in order to make this book as useful (and enjoyable) as possible, it has been written around the major themes of why personnel functions and activities should work and how they work in practice.

The remaining chapters will expose you to a great deal of information about personnel and human resource management. You will also be asked to consider many questions, some of which are not answered in this book. That's because only you can provide the answers. Try to answer them all. By the end of the book, you will not only know a great deal about personnel and human resource management but also a great deal about yourself and your life in organizations.

KEY CONCEPTS

centralization	functions and activities	personnel department climates
decentralization	personnel and human resource management	personnel criteria

DISCUSSION QUESTIONS

1. Why are personnel and human resource departments becoming so important?

2. How can the effectiveness of a personnel department be determined?

3. What is the relationship between the roles played by the personnel department and the functions and activities it performs?

4. What are the advantages and disadvantages of centralizing personnel functions and activities?

Of decentralizing them?

5. What is the relationship between the personnel manager and the line manager?

6. What issues arise in staffing the personnel department?

7. What are the four climates describing personnel and human resource departments?

8. How can you determine what type of personnel department you want to work in?

ENDNOTES

1. F. E. Schuster, "Human Resources Management: Key to the Future," *Personnel Administrator*, December 1978, p. 68.

2. "Personnel Widens Its Franchise," *Business Week*, February 26, 1979, p. 116.

3. Reprinted by permission of the *Harvard Business Review*. Excerpt from "Organizing and Staffing the Personnel Function" by Fred K. Foulkes (May/June 1977), p. 144. Copyright © 1977 by the President and Fellows of Harvard College; all rights reserved.

4. J. Farley, *Affirmative Action and the Woman Worker* (New York: AMACOM, 1979).

5. "Personnel Widens Its Franchise," p. 116. Reprinted from the February 26, 1979 issue of *Business Week* © 1979 by McGraw-Hill, Inc., 1221 Avenue of the Americas, New York, NY 10020. All rights reserved.

6. T. Mills, "Human Resources: Why the New Concern?" *Harvard Business Review*, March/April 1975, p. 133.

7. "Personnel Widens Its Franchise," p. 121.

8. Schuster, p. 68.

9. Schuster, p. 34. Reprinted with permission from the December 1978 issue of the *Personnel Administrator* copyright 1978, The American Society for Personnel Administration, 30 Park Dr., Berea, OH 44017.

10. Foulkes, 1977, p. 144.

11. Schuster, p. 34.

12. Schuster, p. 35.

13. U.S. Department of Health, Education, and Welfare, *Work in America*, report of a special task force to the Secretary (Cambridge, Mass.: MIT Press, 1973).

14. See Mills and Department of Health, Education, and Welfare.

15. "Personnel Widens Its Franchise," p. 116.

16. "Personnel Widens Its Franchise," p. 116.

17. Farley, p. 33.

18. Farley, p. 33.

19. "Toward a More Comprehensive Career Planning Program" by Stephen L. Cohen and Herbert H. Meyer, p. 611. Reprinted with permission *Personnel Journal*, Costa Mesa, CA, copyright September 1979.

20. R. E. Walton, "Work Innovations in the United States," *Harvard Business Review*, July/August 1979, pp. 88–98.

21. J. A. Fitz-enz, "The Measurement Imperative," *Personnel Journal*, April 1978, pp. 193–195.
    R. L. Malone and D. J. Petersen, "Personnel Effectiveness: Its Dimensions and Development," *Personnel Journal*, October 1977, pp. 498–501.

22. Reprinted by permission of the *Harvard Business Review*. Excerpt from "The Expanding Role of the Personnel Function" by Fred K. Foulkes (March/April 1975), p. 73. Copyright © 1975 by the President and Fellows of Harvard College; all rights reserved.

23. Foulkes, 1977, p. 142.

24. E. J. Gilbin, "The Evolution of Personnel," *Human Resource Management*, Fall 1978, pp. 25–30.

25. Foulkes, 1977, p. 146.

26. Foulkes, 1977, p. 147.

27. Foulkes, 1977, p. 149.

28. R. C. Hodgson, "Where the Action Is: A Perspective on the Future of Personnel Management," *Business Quarterly,* Spring 1977, pp. 92–95.

29. Hodgson, p. 92–95.

30. Foulkes, 1975, p. 77.

31. J. A. Henderson, "What the Chief Executive Expects of the Personnel Function," p. 42. Reprinted with permission from the May 1977 issue of the *Personnel Administrator*, copyright 1977, The American Society for Personnel Administration, 30 Park Dr., Berea, OH 44017.

32. "Organizing and Staffing the Human Resources Function: A Personnel Symposium," *Personnel*, January/February 1978, pp. 11–20.

33. Foulkes, 1977, p. 151.

34. G. Odiorne, *Management by Objectives Newsletter,* July 1974. Cited in Foulkes, p. 73.

35. This section is a summary of Foulkes, 1977, pp. 152–153.

36. P. J. Frost, V. F. Mitchell, and W. R. Nord (eds.), *Organizational Reality* (Santa Monica, Calif.: Goodyear, 1978).
R. R. Ritti and G. R. Funkhouser, *The Ropes to Skip and the Ropes to Know* (Columbus, Ohio: Grid, 1977).

37. Foulkes, 1975, p. 73.

38. R. A. Harschnek Jr., D. J. Petersen, and R. L. Malone, "Which Personnel Department Is Right for You?" *Personnel Administrator*, April 1978, pp. 58–66.

39. H. G. Heneman Jr., "The Changing Role of the Personnel Function," paper presented at the Silver Anniversary and Annual Conference of the American Society for Personnel Administration, San Juan, Puerto Rico, June 1973.

40. *Accreditation for Personnel and Human Resource Professional* (Berea, Ohio: Personnel Accreditation Institute, July 1979).

41. R. C. Gruver, "Personnel Management in the Small Organization," *Personnel Administrator*, March 1978, pp. 38–44.
J. Klee, "Personnel Practices of the United Nations," *Public Personnel Management*, January/February 1979, pp. 47–55.
J. Kotter and V. Sathe, "Problems of Human Resource Management in Rapidly Growing Companies," *California Management Review*, Winter 1978, pp. 29–36.
E. L. Loen, *Personnel Management Guides for Small Business* (Washington, D.C.: Small Business Administration, 1974).
J. M. Rosow, "Human Dignity in the Public-Sector Workplace," *Public Personnel Management*, January/February 1979, pp. 7–14.

CHAPTER OUTLINE

PERSONNEL MANAGEMENT AND ITS ENVIRONMENTS

The Importance of Organizational Environments

Environmental Relationships with Personnel Management
  Internal Environment
  External Environment

THE INTERNAL ENVIRONMENT

Individual Qualities
  Needs and Values
  Expectations
  Perceptions
  Motivation
  Ability
  Performance and Satisfaction
  Individual Stress

Job Qualities
  Job Security
  Job Load
  Task Characteristics
  Task Conditions

Interpersonal Relationships
  Groups
  Leadership

Organizational Characteristics
  Top Management of the Organization
  Organizational Policies and Practices
  Size of Organization
  Type of Industry
  Organizational Growth
  Diversity of Structure
  Employee Abilities Needed

THE EXTERNAL ENVIRONMENT

Suppliers

Regulators

Competitors

Labor Force
  Who's in the Labor Force?
  Labor Force Characteristics
  Who Does What?

PERSONNEL PROBLEM Expansion: Production, Yes; Personnel, ???

OBJECTIVES

● To describe the environment for personnel and human resource management

● To discuss the relationships between the environment and personnel management

● To explain the individual qualities important to the personnel manager

● To describe the components of the external environment

THOUGHT STARTERS

● What motivates you? What are your important needs and values?

● What do you expect from your job and the organization you work in?

● Which has more influence on the individual— the group or the supervisor?

● What is your ideal job, supervisor, and organization?

CHAPTER TWO

The Environment for Personnel and Human Resource Management

During the past generation, social and cultural changes in the United States have led to rising expectations and demands about life and work. Modes of work and life styles that were acceptable in the past are increasingly felt as oppressive by young workers in factories, offices, and development labs. It is no longer considered sufficient to have a "decent" job that pays enough to provide adequate food and shelter. The goal of comfort and security is still central for the majority of production workers, employees, and service workers. However, . . . for many workers the quality of the job is as important and after reaching a certain level of income or safety even more important than increases in wages. . . . management, and even union officials, tend to overestimate the workers' satisfaction with work conditions and to underestimate a growing consciousness that the quality of work needs to be improved.

What is meant by improving the quality of work? Most workers have never been stimulated to evaluate their work in broad human terms, and less to consider alternative ways of designing tasks. In those few companies where workers

have been encouraged to critically analyze their jobs, a general consensus emerges of negative and positive work attributes. In general, workers want to avoid jobs that are monotonous, repetitive, over-controlled, and isolated from interaction with others. In contrast, they seek jobs that require activeness—planning and judgment—autonomy on the job, variety, and that are demanding enough to stimulate learning. Beyond these psychological factors, workers are also concerned with the dignity associated with the job and with opportunities for career development. They are also increasingly concerned that the work be "meaningful," that it involve clearly useful tasks and require sufficient skill to be worthy of respect.

Taken together, these requirements move in the direction of humanizing work. In contrast, dehumanized work is a job which makes the worker into a machine part, totally controlled, fully predictable, and easily replaceable. For quite a while, there has been evidence that, when work is less dehumanized, most workers are more satisfied and there is less absenteeism and turnover. In the recent past, however, Americans appeared more willing to adapt themselves to mechanized work. Many appeared to have been satisfied by such jobs, as long as they paid a decent wage. There are a number of reasons for this.

1. Some industrial workers, such as the ones described by Frederick Winslow Taylor, were immigrants, for whom the pay and standard of living were superior to what they had known before. Indeed, before the wave of immigration in the 1880s, there was a growing movement to democratize the workplace. The immigrants generally came from traditional cultures where one accepted his place in society. Furthermore, the worker might gain satisfaction from his role in the subculture rather than in the factory. At home, he might have headed a patriarchal family. There, he was respected by his wife and children, and he could feel compensated for the dreary work.

2. Other factory workers, including early union organizers, considered the first priority for workers to be decent wages, health and unemployment benefits, and the establishment of collective bargaining principles. In return for security and benefits, management retained control of design and organization of work. Many people accepted the notion that work had

to be organized so that human considerations would be sacrificed for maximal efficiency. It was generally taken for granted that the requirements of advanced technology should determine the work, and that maximum specialization and repetitiveness, combined with minimal training, was the most profitable approach. Even many humanists accepted this idea and aimed for a shorter work week as the main relief from dehumanization, ignoring the probability that to be creative in leisure while mindless and passive in work demands a schizoid attitude.

Today, these attitudes of workers are changing, and industrial experiments indicate possibilities for modifying technology and the organization work. . . . younger workers are more democratic and less authoritarian. Members of the new generation are more self-affirmative and expect to be treated with respect by their employers. They seek work that allows them to be more active and autonomous. [However,] many are resentful and rebellious, and [there have been] incidents of industrial sabotage as protests against dehumanized work.

Reprinted with permission of Macmillan Publishing Co., Inc. from M. Maccoby's "Introduction" to Where Have All the Robots Gone? *by H. Sheppard and N. Herrick, Copyright © 1972 by The Free Press, a division of Macmillan Publishing Co., Inc., p. xxv–xxvi.*

T his is an excellent analysis of how the internal and external environments of organizations influence personnel and human resource management. Qualities of the job and characteristics of the organization influence employee satisfaction, absenteeism, and turnover; society's values and standards influence employee expectations of what the workplace should offer. Three important lessons for personnel managers are (1) that employees' expectations have been changing; (2) that if organizations fail to respond to these changes, use of human resources will be less than effective: but (3) that organizations can change. By changing, organizations can avoid industrial sabotage, satisfy employees, and attain high performance. The critical question is, How can these conditions be attained, and how can the personnel manager help in attaining them? The major way the personnel manager helps is by performing the personnel and human resource functions and activities, but an understanding of how, when, and why these functions work is necessary for performing them effectively.

A major purpose of this chapter is to answer this critical question. To provide an understanding of how, when, and why these functions and activities work, it is necessary to examine an organization's complete environment—internal and external. But before examining it in detail, the internal and external environments for personnel management must be defined. Then the importance of these environments and their relationships with the personnel functions and activities can be explained.

PERSONNEL MANAGEMENT AND ITS ENVIRONMENTS

The **internal environment** is made up of the organizational characteristics, individual qualities, interpersonal relationships, and task qualities that are related to the effective management of an organization's human resources. Exhibit 2.1 shows how these elements of the internal environment interact with personnel functions and

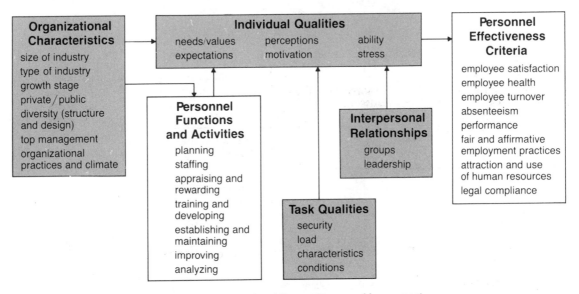

Exhibit 2.1 The Internal Environment for Personnel and Human Resource Management

activities and with the criteria for determining a personnel department's effectiveness. The arrows between the components in Exhibit 2.1 indicate the flow of impact—what causes what. However, over time all the components influence and are influenced by personnel and human resource management.

The **external environment** consists of the labor force available to the organization and the human-resource suppliers, competitors, and regulators, that may somehow affect personnel management. As shown in Exhibit 2.2, there are two major components of the external environment. The component made up of suppliers, competitors, and regulators has direct relationships with the internal environmental factors consisting of organizational characteristics, personnel functions and activities, and personnel effectiveness criteria. The component made up of the qualities of the labor force is directly associated with organizational characteristics, individual qualities, and personnel functions and activities.

The Importance of Organizational Environments

The quote at the beginning of this chapter, as well as the one at the beginning of Chapter 1, illustrates the growing importance of the internal and external environments in personnel and human resource management. These environments have

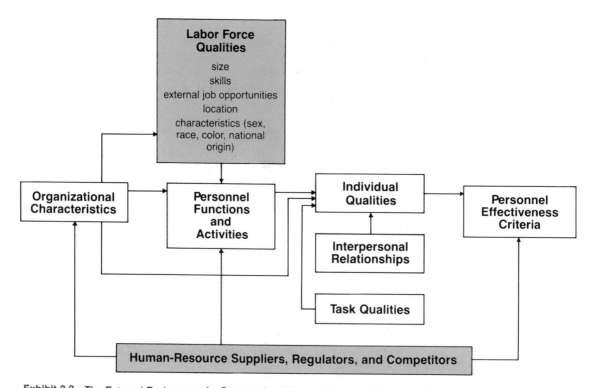

Exhibit 2.2   The External Environment for Personnel and Human Resource Management

always been important, but recently they have become much more extensive and powerful than ever before. For one thing, their impact is more widely recognized today. For another, organizational environments, which were once relatively stable, are now changing. The number of statutes enforced by the Department of Labor has increased almost fourfold in the past twenty years, and they have required fundamental changes in employment systems. "Previous employment legislation, such as wage and hour laws, required relatively simple changes in policies and careful and extensive recordkeeping."[1] Now, however, changes are more complicated.

Even the larger social and economic context in which organizations operate has increased the importance of personnel management. Senator Charles H. Percy, commenting on issues related to the quality of work life and the fulfillment of employee needs and values, suggested that this concern is an "idea whose time has come in the particular social and economic history of the United States, and perhaps in the whole industrialized world."[2]

In sum, the internal and external environments for personnel management have always been important. Today, however, they are even more important.

Environmental Relationships with Personnel Management

The components of the organization's internal and external environments have extensive relationships with personnel management. Only selected relationships are briefly reviewed here. Additional relationships are discussed later in this chapter.

Internal Environment. Organizational characteristics have both direct and indirect effects on personnel functions and activities. The indirect relationship is through top management's statement of personnel policy, which establishes the roles the personnel department will play and the general tone of the personnel department's relationship with the rest of the organization. These then influence the personnel department's functions and activities.

Personnel functions and activities can more directly be influenced by size of the organization. For example, in smaller organizations you are much less likely to find personnel staff dealing with career development or even human resource planning.[3] And you are likely to find fewer personnel staff members in small organizations than in large organizations, although personnel staffs tend to vary in size depending on the type of industry. As Exhibit 2.3 shows, banks and small manufacturing organizations have the largest personnel staffs; large manufacturing organizations have the smallest.

Individual qualities are extremely important in personnel management, because they make personnel functions and activities more or less effective. Furthermore, it is because of these qualities that certain personnel activities exist. For example, if all employees always had sufficient ability to perform their jobs, there would be no need for employee training and development. If employees were attracted to the organization, were satisfied, performed well, and were rarely absent, there would be no need for evaluating and rewarding them. In fact, there would be no real need for the personnel department.

Exhibit 2.3 Personnel Staff Sizes

Industry	Personnel Staff Ratio*	Number on Personnel Staff†
Manufacturing (under 500 employees)	1:96	1–12 (300)
Manufacturing (500–999)	1:116	1–20 (800)
Manufacturing (1,000–4,999)	1:130	2–90 (4,900)
Manufacturing (over 5,000)	1:352	7–126 (22,000)
Research and development	1:102	1–60 (5,000)
Public utilities	1:154	1–110 (22,339)
Hospitals	1:180	1–28 (4,000)
Retail stores	1:228	1–31 (5,800)
Banks	1:98	1–72 (9,000)
Insurance companies	1:101	1–142 (30,000)
Transportation and distribution	1:272	1–75 (26,000)
Government agencies	1:272	2–104 (68,000)
Education	1:161	1–46 (11,300)
Nonprofit organizations	1:76	1–12 (1,955)
Other firms	1:194	1–120 (35,000)

From *The Personnel Executive's Job* (Englewood Cliffs, N.J.: Prentice Hall/ASPA, 1977).

*Average number of employees on the payroll for each person on the personnel staff.

†Smallest and largest personnel staff reported for each industry. The numbers in parentheses indicate the total number of employees on the payroll for firms reporting the largest personnel staffs. The firms represented here do not necessarily have the lowest or highest ratio of personnel staffers relative to the total work force.

External Environment.   The qualities of the labor pool have a direct influence on the individual qualities of the employees in the organization and thus on personnel functions and activities. For example, the lack of trained workers in the external labor supply has a direct effect on an organization's training and development activities.

It is also true that organizational characteristics influence qualities of the labor supply. For example, the type of industry and the diversity of the organization determine the skills it needs and attracts to a given location. Thus the manager-scientist-professional-nonmanager mix of an area's work force depends on the type of organizations based there. This in turn influences personnel functions and activities.

The type of industry also determines the competitors of the organization and its regulation by local, state, and federal governments. An organization in a competitive environment may have to offer at least the same number and quality of personnel services—compensation levels and career-management programs, for example—as its rivals. This component of the external environment also has an especially big influence on the criteria used for judging the personnel department's effectiveness. Because of society's concern and increased government regulation, employee health and the fair and affirmative use of employees are legitimate criteria for evaluating a personnel department.

THE INTERNAL ENVIRONMENT

So far, the relationships among the internal environment, the external environment, and personnel management have been presented in a rather simple framework. In organizations, however, the relationships are rather complex. It is important for you to understand some of these complex relationships, but only the most important of them are presented here, in the interests of saving space and time.

The four components of the internal environment that are most critical for personnel and human resource management are individual qualities, interpersonal relationships, task qualities, and organizational characteristics. Certainly, an organization's internal environment has other qualities. But these four are most relevant to personnel managers, since they help determine the extent of an organization's personnel functions and activities and the criteria used to evaluate their effectiveness.

Individual Qualities

Certain qualities or aspects of individuals are critical for understanding the effects of personnel functions and activities—specifically, needs and values, expectations, perceptions, motivation, ability, performance and satisfaction, and individual stress.

Needs and Values.   The concept of **need** refers to the conditions required to sustain life and well-being.[4] The two major categories of needs are the physical or physiological needs, which are the body's requirements (for food, water, and the like), and the psychological needs, which are requirements of the mind. Needs are requirements whether the individual is aware of them or not.

Some of the needs that a personnel manager should be aware of:
- Achievement
- Feedback (knowledge of results)
- Self-control
- Autonomy
- Certainty and predictability
- Fairness or justice
- Interpersonal recognition, acceptance, and status
- Ethical conduct
- Responsibility and meaningfulness
- Stimulation (physical and mental)
- Self-esteem
- Physical and job security
- Food, shelter, and comfort[5]

To the extent that personnel managers have the potential to fulfill these needs, they can predict what an employee is likely to do or feel about the job.

An employee's behavior and attitudes are also affected by lack of need fulfillment. For example, a blue-collar worker who feels a lack of autonomy and loss of self-control due to close supervision and extensive rules and procedures may find other ways to fill his or her needs:

. . . smoking in the bathroom has evolved into something more than simply breaking a rule. The worker has found . . . a place that has not been designated by the company. Since a worker often feels that much if not all of what he does is done in places designated by the company, under company control, finding ways to express personal freedom from this institutional regimentation is important.[6]

Other behaviors employees often use in trying to regain some self-control are
- *Spreading rumors and gossip to cause trouble at work*
- *Doing work badly or incorrectly*
- *Stealing merchandise, supplies, or equipment*
- *Damaging the employer's property, equipment, or product accidentally, but not reporting it*
- *Damaging the employer's property, equipment, or product on purpose*[7]

Values—the importance a person places on objects, thoughts, and other people—are also of great significance in personnel management. Values exist only to the extent that the individual consciously or subconsciously evaluates an object, thought, or person. Both needs and values can help initiate an individual's behavior, but since values are more conscious than needs, they may better explain what an individual is likely to do. Needs, however, must be met for survival, so they partially determine actions and values. Personnel managers can better predict the effect of personnel functions and activities by understanding both. It pays to listen to workers, to try to understand their needs and values, and to provide outcomes that are satisfying to them.

Expectations. What individuals think they should receive from organizations has a significant influence on the personnel department's effectiveness. This factor has also contributed to the growth of personnel management. Younger workers, for example, are increasingly inclined to challenge management's judgments, to expect involvement in decision making, and generally to expect "the possibilities for satisfying higher level needs as well as lower level needs at the work place."[8] And as the general conditions of society improve, workers come to expect an increasing share in the good life, including adequate working conditions, challenge, advancement opportunities, and financial gain.

However, the workplace has in many cases not been keeping up with the changing expectations of the work force and the changing values of society. As a result, employee satisfaction is decreasing. A nationwide study by the University of Michigan Survey Research Center, conducted from 1969 to 1977, found that employee job satisfaction declined markedly and that over time employees had come to feel that their jobs were less useful, less relevant to future productivity, and in many cases not equal to their skills.

The decrease was about equally distributed among five areas—comfort, challenge, financial rewards, resource adequacy, and promotions—but was absent for the sixth, relations with coworkers. . . . Men reported greater declines in satisfaction between 1969 and 1977 than did women. . . . The decline was virtually identical for white and black workers. . . . Workers in the higher skilled occupations (professional, technical, and managerial jobs) exhibited a smaller decline than did those in lower skilled occupations (operatives and laborers).[9]

Perceptions. It is not the objective situation that is important in understanding employee attitudes and behaviors but the situation as it exists for the individual—his or her **perception**. This statement has two implications for the personnel manager: (1) What employees are likely to do in an organization is related to what's going on in the organization, and (2) what's going on in the organization has two components—what is actually (objectively) going on and what the employees perceive (subjectively) is going on. Just because an organization has an incentive system that pays employees does not mean that all employees will perceive that they are paid by the piece.[10] In fact, in many organizations employees perceive the truth to be something quite different from actuality.

Employees have many perceptions, but three critical ones related to employee behavior are

● The employee's perception of the likelihood that his or her behavior will result in satisfying first-level outcomes (called **expectancy two**)

● The employee's perception of the likelihood of the first-level outcomes resulting in satisfying second-level outcomes (called **instrumentality**)

● The employee's perception of the likelihood that he or she will be able to exhibit the behavior that results in satisfying first- and second-level outcomes (called **expectancy one**).[11]

Outcomes are the conditions or aspects of the organization that serve the employee's needs and values. **First-level outcomes** are those provided to the employee for exhibiting behavior (such as performance) that the organization wants to reward. **Second-level outcomes** are those that come from obtaining the first-level outcomes. A typical first-level outcome is pay. The employee can take the pay and buy a house, food, clothes, and entertainment—all second-level outcomes. Furthermore, the pay serves other needs and values. For example, pay can serve an employee's needs for status and recognition and for food, shelter, and comfort.

Other outcomes that organizations can provide employees are related to (1) qualities of the job, such as variety and freedom from the risk of physical harm; (2) interpersonal characteristics, such as pleasant and considerate supervisors and cohesive work groups; (3) organizational characteristics, such as its practices and climate; and (4) other personnel and human resource activities, such as career-development programs, stress management programs, and employee training and development.

Just providing an outcome does not ensure that it will be satisfying. To be satisfying, an outcome must be perceived by the individual, be related to needs and values that the individual really wants to fulfill, and be consistent with what the individual expects he or she should receive.

Individuals differ in the needs and values they really want to fulfill, and it is likely that even the needs and values that one individual most wants to fulfill will change over time. However, most employees go through a similar process in determining whether they are satisfied with a job. As Exhibit 2.4 shows, perceptions play a big part in satisfaction.

It should be noted that organizations generally offer many outcomes and that a different level of satisfaction is associated with each outcome. An employee may be highly satisfied with pay but be extremely dissatisfied with the supervisor. The model in Exhibit 2.4 can be used to determine the level of satisfaction for outcomes singly or together. But for purposes of analyzing and improving employee satisfaction, determining satisfaction for each outcome is more useful.

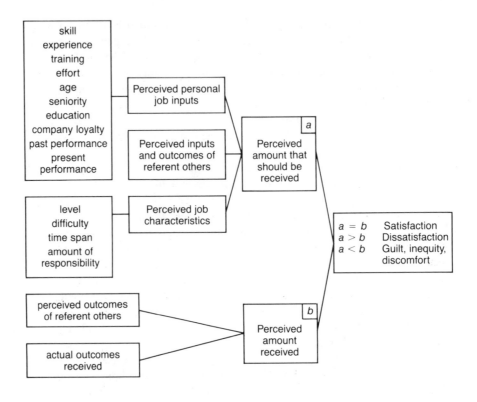

Exhibit 2.4   Determinants of Job Satisfaction

From *Motivation in Work Organizations*, by E. E. Lawler III. Copyright © 1973 by Wadsworth, Inc. Reprinted by permission of the publisher, Brooks/Cole Publishing Company, Monterey, California.

Motivation.   Everyone is motivated, but people differ in what motivates them and how strongly. In general, people are motivated to do things that provide them with satisfying outcomes. They are even more motivated to the extent that they perceive a reasonable chance of successfully exhibiting the behavior by trying (expectancy one), a high likelihood that the behavior will result in a satisfying outcome, and a good chance that increasing amounts of the behavior will bring increasing levels of outcomes (expectancy two). Thus an employee will be motivated to do what the organization wants only if it seems possible with moderate effort (expectancy one), if there is a good chance that performing the behavior will result in satisfying outcomes, and if there is a good chance that a better performance will bring greater rewards (expectancy two). This is the essence of the **expectancy theory** for explaining motivation.

The first step an organization needs to take in getting employees motivated is to specify the desired behaviors and to provide rewards for them. One of the behaviors that most organizations want from employees is participation, which involves joining the organization, remaining with the organization if they are good (low turnover), and attending the organization on a regular, consistent, and timely basis (low absenteeism). Another important behavior is performance, which means producing a lot, with high quality, in regular duties; producing a lot, with high quality, in innovative duties; and producing in a dependable and safe manner.[12] As an example, consider the performance behavior of producing a lot in regular duties. The organization can get its employees to perform that behavior only by ensuring that they perceive a moderately high expectancy one, a high expectancy two, and associated outcomes that will satisfy them. If pay would satisfy employees as an outcome, the organization could design a compensation plan to reward performance on a contingent basis. A high level of output would result in more pay, and a low level of output would result in less pay.

The second step an organization needs to take is to communicate the desired behaviors and rewards to employees. It must communicate these so that employees accurately perceive them.

An organization must also investigate role awareness and role conflict, two other perceptions that influence employee motivation. **Role awareness** is how well employees know what other employees expect, what their own levels of authority and responsibility are, and on what basis their performance will be evaluated. For example, although the organization may have an incentive pay plan, the employees may not know how performance is measured. **Role conflict** describes the extent to which employees perceive incompatibility and conflict among what others expect of them. For example, an employee may know how performance is measured and want to perform, but the supervisor may not provide enough time or materials to allow the employee to perform. Or an employee may have two supervisors, each wanting the employee to do something different at the same time. Low role awareness and high role conflict make employees more likely to perceive a lower expectancy one, to be less satisfied, and to perform less well than with high role awareness and low role conflict.

Ability.   Expectancy one may also be reduced by insufficient ability. Two aspects of employee ability are aptitude and skill. **Aptitude** refers to one's potential to master a situation or idea; **skill** refers to one's current level of mastery of a situation or idea. Skill level gives a good indication of how well someone will do in the present; aptitude gives a better indication of how well someone is likely to adapt to a new situation or to perform newer, more innovative duties. Thus these two features of ability can be seen as complementary. Knowing the extent to which a job applicant possesses both aptitude and skill is useful in selection decisions. For example, if the demands of a job are expected to remain the same over the next several years, aptitude is less important than skill. But if the demands of the job are expected to change, aptitude is likely to be at least as important as skill.

Skills can be divided into two categories. Cognitive skills are generally associated with intelligence. There are also at least eleven fairly independent types of motor skills (physical skills).[13]

Performance and Satisfaction.   There are many times when an employee can perform well and be satisfied, but those are usually when performing well results in satisfying outcomes. It is possible, however, that those same outcomes could be provided regardless of how well the employee performs. In many organizations, basic pay is generally given regardless of performance. These organizations miss the full motivational potential of their compensation systems. Other organizations make pay contingent on participation: Workers get paid only when they come to work and not when they are absent. But many organizations pay for absenteeism as well as for poor performance.

Pay is not the only satisfying outcome organizations can provide. But these other outcomes, like pay, can motivate employees when they are made contingent on performance. For instance, employees can be quite satisfied with the outcomes provided by their work group. If the work group is cohesive and attractive to its members, it can exert control over their behavior. Whatever the group decides is appropriate behavior is what the members will do. If the appropriate behavior is low production, employees are not likely to perform well, but they are likely to be satisfied.

On the other hand, employees can perform well and be dissatisfied. Supervisors who exert pressure on their employees can obtain higher production, at least in the short run and while the supervisors are around. But this kind of pressure is one of the main behaviors of supervisors that employees deeply resent. Thus production is obtained at the cost of satisfaction. The longer-run consequences are employee sabotage, absenteeism, and turnover.

To expect a production worker to work at his peak for a whole day is like asking a long-distance runner to sprint the whole race the way he does in the last 100 yards.[14]

Although there can be tradeoffs between performance and satisfaction, there can also be a positive relationship between them. It is possible for personnel managers to obtain both performance and satisfaction. This is not always an easy thing to do, especially when personnel managers accept the challenge of safeguarding employee health.

Individual Stress.   One aspect of employee health is stress. **Stress** is a dynamic condition giving individuals the opportunity to fulfill some of their important needs and values while preventing them from fulfillment.[15] People under stress want to resolve the conflict and obtain some favorable results, but they are faced with uncertainty about how to resolve it. The result is stress.

The greater the stress, the more severe the symptoms (see Chapter 18). Briefly, the symptoms of stress are short-term physiological conditions such as headaches, backaches, and rashes and short-term psychological conditions such as dissatisfaction, tunnel vision, insomnia, and forgetfulness. Longer-term symptoms are the physiological conditions of high blood pressure and coronary heart disease, the psychological conditions of apathy, boredom, and withdrawal, and the behavioral conditions of altered performance, accidents, absenteeism, and turnover.

Other aspects of employee health are accidents and diseases (which may also be related to stress). Because employee health is so important, strategies for dealing with stress, accidents, and diseases are presented in Chapters 17 and 18.

Job Qualities

Another element of the internal environment is related to the jobs themselves. Four qualities of jobs that personnel managers should be familiar with are job security, job load, task characteristics, and job conditions or setting.

Job Security. "Unemployment and the threat of job loss are exquisitely threatening to many, seriously disrupting to others."[16] And job loss is even more of a threat for blue-collar workers than for white collar workers, with good reason. In the last half of the 1970s, blue-collar employment grew only 6 percent; white-collar employment grew 17 percent.

The threat of job loss as well as actual job loss and the state of being unemployed are extremely stressful. The threat of job loss implies there is a chance of being unemployed, with the uncertainty of knowing exactly when and under what conditions. With actual job loss there is the uncertainty of when and how to get back to work.

Job Load. Although blue-collar workers may be more concerned with job security, some white-collar workers are more concerned with their work load, especially when it is too heavy. Heavy work loads come in the form of qualitative overload and quantitative overload.[17] *Qualitative overload* describes a situation in which job demands exceed the worker's abilities. Have you ever been in a course or on a job where you thought that you were really not bright enough? If so, you have experienced qualitative overload. *Quantitative overload* describes a situation in which there is just too much to do in the time provided, although the worker has the ability to do all the tasks. A common response to this situation for some is working late or taking work home.

We generally tend to think that individuals with a lot of work to do are under the most stress. But people with very little work to do are also under stress. Light work loads can be classified as qualitative underload and quantitative underload. *Qualitative underload* means the worker's abilities exceed the demands of the job. Too little work for the available time results in *quantitative underload*. Having too little to do prevents employees from satisfying many needs and values. When this situation is combined with lack of control over the pace of the work, such stress symptoms as ulcers, depression, high blood pressure, and severe headaches and backaches are likely to occur.

Work overload and underload are relative to the employee. Thus the same job may be an overload for one and an underload for another. Personnel managers can reduce the possibility of severe stress symptoms, and thus be more effective, by appropriately matching individuals to jobs on the basis of abilities. Personnel managers can be even more effective by also matching individuals and jobs on the basis of needs, which requires consideration of task characteristics.

Task Characteristics. Of the many task characteristics that are associated with an individual's needs, five have been examined extensively in relation to employee satisfaction and performance. Task skill variety, autonomy, significance, identity, and feedback influence employee satisfaction and performance through their effect on an employee's needs for responsibility, meaningfulness, and knowledge of results (see Chapter 18). To the extent a given task's variety, significance, and identity characteristics are high, the task can serve an employee's needs for meaningfulness. Task autonomy is associated with an employee's need for responsibility, and task feedback is associated with the need for knowledge of results.

Task Conditions.   The task conditions that most directly influence personnel and human resource management are those of the physical work environment and those of the sociopsychological environment. The physical work environment influences an employee's need for safety and physical health; the sociopsychological environment influences an employee's needs for achievement, certainty, support, and acceptance—essentially all the needs of the mind. The importance of both these aspects of the workplace is recognized in the Occupational Safety and Health Act of 1970, which covers "diseases" of the mind as well as the body.

Interpersonal Relationships

A third aspect of the internal environment is the quality of the interactions among the people in a particular workplace.

Groups.   If work groups are cohesive, they can influence the behavior of group members through their norms. Groups are cohesive to the extent that they can satisfy the needs of group members.[18] Members of a group are motivated to behave in accordance with group desires when the goals of the group are clear and valued by the members, when the paths to the goals are clear, and when the structure of the group (who does what) is clear.[19]

If group goals are consistent with those of the organization, the impact of the group on the individual is favorable for the organization. The group can increase an employee's expectancy one and expectancy two relationships to performance.[20] The employee is then motivated to perform (for the goals of the group directly and those of the organization indirectly). The result is employee performance and satisfaction. Therefore, personnel managers should consider the influence of groups on employees and seek to integrate group goals with those of the organization.

Another important aspect of groups for personnel managers to be aware of is their impact on employee health. Groups help clarify paths and goals and provide structured expectations, and through their social support, groups can offer a buffering effect. This support can come from groups within the organization or outside:

The idea here is that social support from persons outside the work setting as well as those within it can alter the relationship between occupational stress and health. Whereas in the absence of social support, physical, and/or mental disorders should increase as occupational stress increases, as levels of social support rise, this relationship should diminish in strength, even perhaps disappearing under maximal social support.[21]

A SLICE OF LIFE

The cohesiveness of a work group is a two-edged sword. If the goals of the group are congruent with those of the organization, cohesive work groups may be very productive. But what if the goals are not congruent?

Cohesive work groups are sympathetic to the needs and feelings of their members. Thus people who might ordinarily operate very effectively in an incentive system may opt in a cohesive group to avoid "making the others look bad." Or the group may "carry" low performers, "looking out" for their own. What do you think would happen if someone from a group like this required disciplinary action?

In a larger view, a labor union is a group of people who are most effective in attaining their goals if they are cohesive. It is something of an understatement to suggest that such cohesion can be dysfunctional, disruptive, and even destructive to an organization.

When was the last time you heard of a baseball team being fired for poor performance? The point is that managers are let go—not teams. The same may be said for work groups: Work groups aren't transferred, work groups aren't demoted, work groups aren't let go. Supervisors are. A highly cohesive work group can make you or break you.

By encouraging cohesive groups whose goals are congruent with those of the organization, personnel managers facilitate a favorable group impact on employee satisfaction, performance, and health.

Leadership. It may sound like there is little room left for the supervisor to have an impact on employees, but such is not the case. For example, two major sources of stress for blue-collar workers are supervisors who establish petty work rules and those who apply relentless pressure for more production.[22] Both of these behaviors contribute little to effective performance or worker satisfaction. There is always a chance that a cohesive group will not have goals congruent with those of the supervisor or the organization. Supervisors can improve their chances of meeting personnel effectiveness criteria in such a situation by behaving in supportive and instrumental ways.[23] Supportive behavior indicates that the leader is friendly, approachable, and considerate of employees' needs, both as individuals and as a group.[24] Instrumental behavior is task-oriented and directed at clarifying the roles and tasks of employees, as individuals and as a group. Supportive behavior encourages group drive to accomplish a task by enhancing individuals' feelings of self-worth and thus motivating them to engage in "cooperative behavior focused on achieving organizational goals."[25] Instrumental behavior helps clarify where the group is going and thus increases the group's expectancy one. The result is more successful task performance.

The group, too, can be seen as a place for obtaining task-related and socioemotional rewards. Supportive and instrumental behaviors result in social support, friendliness among group members, and consequently, increased cohesiveness and

> The term *supervisor* refers to the individual who manages others who are not managing other people. The term *manager* refers to someone who manages others who themselves manage people.

team effort.[26] To sum up, supportive and instrumental behavior can help a supervisor do well by increasing group performance and morale (individual satisfaction) and by increasing group cohesiveness, which is a prerequisite to the group being a source of social support and employee health.

Supervisors' interactions with individual employees also affect their performance. Supportive and instrumental behaviors are a factor, as well as participative behaviors.[27] The supportive behavior helps serve an employee's need for affiliation; instrumental and participative behaviors help clarify role expectations, increase expectancy one, and increase an employee's sense of ownership through having influence on decisions.

To summarize, supervisors and managers can exert leadership by
- Letting employees know what work they are expected to do, how performance is measured, the minimum standards of performance, and how their work fits in the total picture
- Establishing and maintaining high performance expectations
- Letting employees know where they stand
- Employing broad-based two-way communication
- Creating a supportive climate
- Learning how to delegate
- Establishing workable appraisal and coaching programs[28]

A major challenge in organizations today is "to give to the people who give us their energy a sense of personal worth in return," according to William M. Ellinghaus, president of AT&T. Furthermore, "our problem, after all, isn't the attitude of the workers. It is the leadership and responsiveness of our management."[29] However, because only the individual or the group can generate the energy for motivation, "what managers can do is create a work environment that doesn't put any barriers in the way of motivation. And we can make sure our organizations are worthy of our employees' commitment."[30] By engaging in supportive, instrumental, and participative behaviors, a supervisor can effectively respond to Ellinghaus's concerns.

Organizational Characteristics

Leader behaviors, group characteristics, and task qualities are just parts of the total organization. Of the many organizational characteristics that influence personnel and human resource management, the most significant are
- Top management
- Organizational policies and practices
- Size of the organization
- Type of industry, particularly whether it is public or private
- Organizational growth

- Diversity of structure
- Types of employee abilities needed

Top Management of the Organization.   The top management makes the strategic decisions for the organization, including those related to the management of human resources.[31] For example, it determines the relative importance of human resources, which helps establish the roles that the personnel department will play in the management of human resources as well as the climate of the personnel department (see Chapter 1). The roles played by the personnel department generally define the personnel functions and activities that will be implemented. If the personnel manager helps top management formulate personnel policy, more personnel functions and activities may be performed.

Organizational Policies and Practices.   The policies and practices of the organization, generally established by top management, spell out how personnel functions and activities will be administered. For example, policies about hiring employees and sick pay help determine how and where recruiting will be done and what fringe benefits the organizations will provide.

Size of Organization.   Personnel policies and practices vary with the size of the organization. Once personnel functions and activities were the exclusive domain of larger organizations, but

. . . as the federal government initiates increasingly comprehensive regulation regarding the selection, hiring and promotion of employees, even small business management finds itself spending more and more time with employee/labor relations. Small businesses, those employing from 100 to about 1,000 employees, are establishing or expanding a personnel function.[32]

In a small business there may be only one person or a small staff performing the personnel function, but the personnel administrator's job is still helping line managers by recruiting, selecting, and hiring employees, administering wages, guiding employee relations, and appraising performance—all within the guidelines of legal compliance. Small organizations less frequently conduct personnel research, training, and human resource planning. All of a small organization's personnel activities are often much more informal and nonstandardized than in larger organizations: "Recruitment, selection and hiring procedures in the small organization just seem to evolve."[33]

Type of Industry.   Just as the size of the organization influences the conduct of personnel functions and activities, so does the type of organization. For example, Exhibit 2.5 shows that the largest personnel budgets, as a percentage of total payroll, are in the insurance and the transportation and distribution industries, and in nonprofit organizations. The banking industry has the greatest percentage of personnel executives with complete responsibility for the personnel budget; the transportation and distribution industry and government agencies have the smallest percentage.

Exhibit 2.5 Personnel Department Budgets

Industry	Percentage of Firms Giving Personnel Executive Definite Budget	Percentage of Total Payroll Going to Personnel Budget (Average)	Percentage of Firms Giving Personnel Executive Complete Financial Responsibility
Manufacturing (under 500 employees)	31.9	4.2	86.8
Manufacturing (500–999)	63.2	3.9	79.5
Manufacturing (1,000–4,999)	77.4	3.9	80.3
Manufacturing (over 5,000)	80.0	1.6	66.7
Research and development	71.4	3.0	76.9
Public utilities	65.4	1.8	66.7
Hospitals	73.3	2.8	81.8
Retail stores	44.7	1.0	85.7
Banks	53.5	4.2	90.6
Insurance companies	63.3	5.6	82.1
Transportation and distribution	47.8	5.4	63.6
Government agencies	77.5	1.0	65.5
Education	73.5	1.2	76.0
Nonprofit organizations	46.2	5.6	84.6
Other firms	64.9	3.0	74.2

From *The Personnel Executive's Job* (Englewood Cliffs, N.J.: Prentice-Hall/ASPA, 1977).

Private and public organizations also have different requirements, although the comment that "business and government are alike in all unimportant respects"[34] may be overstating the case. To begin with, "it is almost true that the business executive's *enabling* resources—structure and people—are the public executive's *constraints*."[35] This is in part because of the pay system. Most large organizations have a serious problem in trying to administer rewards on the basis of performance. "Most public pay plans have opted in favor of merit-pay progression, geared to service," yet many private pay plans still try to reflect some pay for performance.[36] Furthermore, "many public employees enjoy one relatively priceless benefit, and the most envied of all: job security."[37] Although public employees have been subject to staff reductions in force (RIFs), the employment stability in public and private organizations is still quite different.

Another major difference between public and private organizations is the emphasis on training and development:

Somehow training, which is considered to be a virtual necessity in the private sector, is a blurred goal in the public sector. One does not sense the same degree of top-management commitment to training that exists in the leading corporations. The connection between training and productivity is rather obscure in public service. Because there is also a lack of strong economic incentives on the part of management, training is not fostered with the same degree of commitment and continuity that is evident in the private sector.[38]

Recruitment, selection, and career development also vary. Recruitment and selection in public organizations are based in large measure on competitive written entrance exams, and careers in government are more clearly defined by occupational categories than in the private sector. Promotion is limited by "insider" rules and by regulations within strong occupational specialization. As a result, career progression in a public organization is basically narrow and vertical (within one specialization), whereas it is broad, diagonal, and vertical in a private organization. Careers in government also tend to be longer-term, resulting in less turnover. Therefore, public managers (line and personnel) may need to be more concerned about the poor performer or dissatisfied employee than private managers. Taxpayer demands for increased productivity and employee job involvement intensify this concern.

American workers are increasingly demanding a voice in what goes on in the workplace. In fact, "the majority of American workers indicate that they consider it their *right* to participate in decisions that affect them directly on the job."[39] Yet public organizations show less interest in and are engaged in fewer projects involving increased participation and teamwork than private organizations are. Furthermore, the prospects for increased employee participation in public organizations are poor, since it is extremely difficult to make changes in government organizations.[40]

Despite these apparent disadvantages for public employees,

Human dignity in the public sector workplace is greatly enhanced by the protection afforded by legislation, published rules and regulations, and established custom and practice. Public personnel administration operates in a fishbowl, so employee rights and privileges, as well as pay and benefit systems, are public knowledge. This is a definite edge over the private sector.[41]

Organizational Growth. Organizational growth requires employees to change their attitudes and behaviors to fit new job demands and changing organizational needs. The biggest impediment to successful growth is the inability of employees to change.[42] Inability to change hurts employees too, by creating unmet career expectations when higher-level jobs are filled by competent people from outside the organization.

Perhaps the most obvious personnel problems faced by fast-growing organizations are recruiting and training. Slow-growing and stable organizations can often satisfy their hiring needs by waiting for the right person to walk through the door, but fast-growing organizations are forced to seek potential employees aggressively. Since aggressive recruiting takes time, other personnel activities remain unattended. The personnel manager of a fast-growing organization has described the problem thus:

I go through a hundred resumes a day. So do other people here, including some line managers. Our whole department is constantly involved in recruiting and hiring. And that's not necessarily good, because we neglect other duties like training and organizational development activities. But even though we are so focused on just recruiting, we still do not bring people in as quickly as many of our line managers want. To get the kind of engineers we need, for example, it usually takes us six months. In the company I worked for ten years ago, which wasn't growing very fast at all, six months for hiring was fine. Here it's not. Our engineering vice president says the strain we put on his department by hiring so slowly is enormous.[43]

With such aggressive recruiting, the organization always has a lot of new people. Socialization and accommodation efforts (such as orientation programs) are more vital, since there are fewer people who have been around long enough to "show the ropes" to all the new people.

Other aspects of fast-growing organizations that have implications for human resource management are the inevitability of change and the associated uncertainty, the need for important decisions to be made quickly, and the scarcity of human resources, since positions can never be filled as rapidly as they are created. The consequences of these and other aspects of fast-growing organizations can create severe human resource problems and equally severe employee symptoms, as shown in Exhibit 2.6. Thus the fast-growing organization is exciting but a real challenge for the personnel manager.

Diversity of Structure.   Chapter 1 describes how organizational structure is related to organization of the personnel department, particularly in relation to centralization

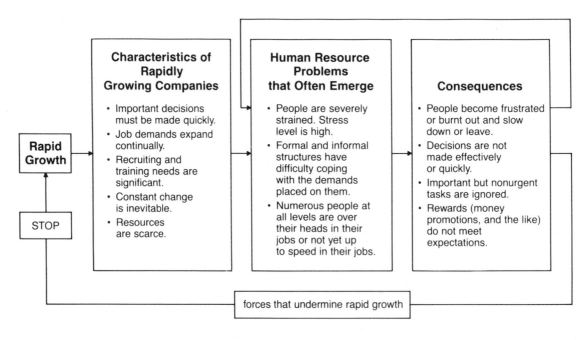

Exhibit 2.6   The Consequences of Rapid Growth for Personnel Management

From J. Kotter and V. Sathe, Problems of Human Resource Management in Rapidly Growing Companies. © 1978 by the Regents of the University of California. Reprinted from *California Management Review*, vol. XXI, no. 2, p. 33, Figure 1 by permission of the Regents.

and decentralization of personnel functions and activities. Decentralization is an important way for the personnel staff to stay in touch with what's going on and to serve the needs of the various parts of the organization.

As organizations expand and take on new products and activities, they often become more diverse in structure.[44] The different parts of the organization have different needs. Some parts may be small but growing fast; others may be large and growing slowly. There is little doubt that those parts would have different personnel problems and need to operate their personnel activities differently. Thus as organizations become more diverse, the ways in which their personnel functions and activities are performed must also become more diverse.

Even though decentralization of personnel functions and activities is often necessary for diverse organizations, there are still important advantages to some centralization. Greater diversity requires both decentralization and centralization. Balancing these needs can be a real challenge for personnel managers.

Employee Abilities Needed.   As organizations become more diverse, the types of employee abilities that are needed also increase. Some parts of the organization may require minimal employee abilities, but others may require professionals, engineers, and scientists—the knowledge workers. Since these types of employees have not only different abilities but also different values, expectations, and attitudes, they need to be managed differently. The personnel functions and activities necessary for knowledge workers, such as career development and extensive training and development opportunities, may not be necessary for other employees. Even the methods of determining the effectiveness of personnel activities may be different. Determining the productivity of an assembly worker is much different from measuring the output of a research chemist.[45]

THE EXTERNAL ENVIRONMENT

Rather than referring to the external *environment* of an organization, it is more accurate to refer to external *environments*. As shown in Exhibit 2.2, the external forces that affect organizations' personnel functions and activities are suppliers, regulators, competitors, and the labor force.[46] These all have a general impact on the total organization, but each also has a unique impact on the management of human resources. Personnel managers should be familiar with each of these components and should understand how they relate to personnel functions, activities, and techniques. In addition, they should be aware of relationships among the four external factors. For example, a change in the minimum-wage law may influence the supply of potential employees for an organization. Or an increase in the number of competitors could reduce the supply of potential employees.

Suppliers

For personnel management, suppliers are those who provide the human resources necessary for the operation of the organization. Suppliers can be classified into two groups—the organized and the unorganized. Organized suppliers include associations, professional organizations, and unions. Traditionally, organized suppliers have most frequently been found in heavy manufacturing, such as the steel, auto, and rubber industries. More recently, however, public employees have begun to organize. Unorganized suppliers are individuals who deal separately with the organization.

Organized suppliers of human resources directly influence the bargaining function of the personnel department by making its activities more formal and complex. In addition, the power of organized employees to strike or walk out may have serious consequences for the organization, as noted in a *Business Week* article on Teamster negotiations:

The union's strike leverage practically renders the industry powerless. Even a short walkout can bankrupt small, cash-weak operators almost immediately. This is why hundreds of carriers have broken ranks in the past and granted rich settlements at the mere threat of a strike.[47]

To be fair, organized labor suppliers are also helpful in providing a constant supply of employees. They frequently help determine job evaluation and performance appraisal techniques, although to some extent they may limit the flexibility of an organization in rewarding and punishing its employees. Organized suppliers also influence the staffing and compensating functions.

Regulators

The primary regulators of organizations are agencies of federal and state governments established to protect the rights and well-being of individuals, organizations,

---

Some terms used in government labor studies:
- *Civilian labor force*: All people classified as employed or unemployed
- *Employed*: All those who worked for pay at any time during the survey week; worked fifteen hours or more as unpaid workers in the family business; or had a job but were not working due to illness, bad weather, or the like
- *Unemployed:* All those who were not working during the survey week, but made specific efforts to find a job in the preceding four weeks; were laid off and waiting to be recalled; or were waiting to report to a new job within thirty days
- *Not in civilian labor force:* All people not classified as employed or unemployed
- *Labor force participation rate:* The labor force as a percentage of the population
- *Unemployment rate:* The unemployed as a percentage of the labor force
- *Fulltime workers:* Those who usually work thirty-five hours or more per week
- *Parttime workers:* Those who usually work one to thirty-four hours per week

and society. Although regulators have varying degrees of influence on the operations of organizations, their impact on the management of human resources is fairly uniform across all types of organizations, except those that are extremely small.

The number of regulatory agencies, as well as the rules, laws, and regulations they have established, has increased dramatically over the past two decades. Very few personnel activities escape regulation. The specific regulators and their impact are discussed in detail throughout the book.

Competitors

Competition plays a significant role in some of the personnel functions and activities. As the number of organizations competing for human resources increases, so does the importance of the staffing function and its appraisal and compensation activities. If several companies make job offers to one individual, the organization with more extensive and elaborate recruiting procedures may win. When employees with particular skills are hard to obtain, the organization may need to consider "growing its own" through well-managed human resource planning programs coordinated with employee training and development activities.

Labor Force

Several specific qualities of the human resource supply are discussed in Chapter 3, so only a few selected characteristics of the labor force are presented here.

Who's in the Labor Force? The federal government (through a variety of agencies) compiles data on who's in the labor force, participation rates, and rates of unemployment for twelve basic categories of people: white males and females, black males and females, and hispanic males and females, with each of these six groups further divided into adults and teenagers. Presently there are approximately 43 million female workers and 57 million male workers. About 50 percent of all females in the population now work; 78 percent of the male population work. Exhibit 2.7 describes what industries the civilian labor force is employed in.

Exhibit 2.7 Distribution of the Civilian Labor Force, Sixteen Years Old and Over

Industry	Number (in thousands)	Industry	Number (in thousands)
Public administration	5,142	Transportation and public utilities	6,274
Agriculture	2,836	Wholesale and retail trade	19,507
Mining	907	Finance, insurance, and real estate	5,811
Contract construction	5,765	Services	28,110
Manufacturing	21,911		

Adapted from U.S. Department of Labor, Bureau of Labor Statistics, *Employment and Earnings*, Vol. 27, no. 3 (Washington, D.C.: Government Printing Office, March 1980), p. 41.

Labor Force Characteristics.   A variety of government agencies collect data on the composition of the labor force, among them the U.S. Department of Commerce, Bureau of the Census; the U.S. Department of Health and Human Services, National Center for Social Statistics; and the U.S. Department of Labor, Bureau of Labor Statistics and Employment and Training Administration. Some of their findings:

• A majority of women work because of economic need. Nearly two-thirds of all women in the labor force in 1980 were single, widowed, divorced, or separated or had husbands whose earnings were less than $10,000.

• About 43 million women were in the labor force in 1980; they constituted more than two-fifths of all workers.

• Black women, 53 percent of whom were in the labor force in 1980 (4.9 million), accounted for nearly half of all black workers.

• Hispanic women, 45 percent of whom were in the labor force in 1980 (1.8 million), accounted for 39 percent of all hispanic workers.

• Women accounted for nearly three-fifths of the increase in the civilian labor force in the last decade—13 million women compared with 9 million men.

• More than one-fourth of all female workers held parttime jobs in 1980.

• The average work life expectancy of women increased by more than one-half over the two decades since 1950. In 1970 the average woman could expect to spend 22.9 years of her life in the work force.

• The average female worker is as well educated as the average male worker; both have completed a median of 12.6 years of schooling.

• The number of working mothers has increased more than tenfold since the period immediately preceding World War II, and the number of working women has more than tripled. About 53 percent of all mothers with children under eighteen years old (16.1 million) were in the labor force in 1978.

• Fully employed female high school graduates (with no college) had less income on the average than fully employed men who had not completed elementary school—$8,462 and $9,332 respectively in 1977. Women with four years of college also had less income than men with only an eighth-grade education—$11,134 and $11,931 respectively.

• Among all families, about one out of seven was headed by a woman in 1980 compared with about one out of ten in 1968; 39 percent of black families were headed by women. Of all women workers, about one out of eight was a family head; about one out of four black women workers was a family head.

• Among all poor families, nearly half (49 percent) were headed by women in 1980; more than two out of three poor black families were headed by women. In 1968 about one-third (35 percent) of all poor families were headed by women and 51 percent of poor minority families had female heads.[48]

Although they have not been discussed so far, handicapped workers also have a role in the labor force. Characteristics and problems unique to handicapped workers are discussed in Chapters 5, 6, and 7.

Who Does What?   In the *Dictionary of Occupational Titles*, the Bureau of Labor Statistics classifies 30,000 jobs representing about 100 million jobholders in nine general groups. The approximate percentage of the U.S. labor force in each of these groups in 1980 and the breakdown by gender is shown in Exhibit 2.8. The data indicate that women hold a disproportionate share of clerical and service jobs and are underrepresented in skilled craftwork and managerial and administrative jobs. In addition, women's earnings as a percentage of men's in all types of jobs were just slightly over half, as shown here:

Professional and technical	66%
Managerial and administrative	59
Clerical	60
Sales	41
Operatives	58
Service workers	60

Exhibit 2.8 Occupational Makeup of the Civilian Labor Force

Occupational Group	Percentage of Total Labor Force	Percentage of Male Workers	Percentage of Female Workers
Professional and technical	14	14	16
Managerial and administrative	11	14	7
Sales	6	6	7
Clerical	18	6	34
Craftworkers	14	21	2
Operatives	15	17	11
Laborers	6	9	1
Service workers	14	10	21
Farmworkers	2	3	1

Adapted from U.S. Department of Labor, Bureau of Labor Statistics, *Employment and Earnings,* vol. 27, no. 3 (Washington, D.C.: Government Printing Office, March 1980), p. 41.

SUMMARY

This chapter examines several components of the internal and external environments of personnel and human resource management. Although personnel managers are generally unable to influence the external environments, they can exert some influence over the components of the internal environment. Thus an understanding of these components is critical for personnel managers. They are also critical for line managers, who often are responsible for "breathing life" into personnel functions and activities.

Personnel management should not be regarded as a set of mechanistic functions and activities but rather as a set of functions and activities to be shared by personnel managers and their staffs and by line managers for the purpose of using the organization's human resources in the most effective and fair way possible. The effectiveness of their use is determined against criteria reflecting such concerns of the organization, individual employees, and society as performance, absenteeism, turnover, satisfaction, and employee health.

PERSONNEL PROBLEM
Expansion: Production, Yes; Personnel, ???

Dalton Manufacturing is opening a new production installation about 10 miles (within the same county) from an existing Dalton Manufacturing plant. The new plant will produce nearly as much as the older plant but with state-of-the-art technology. But there is absolutely no intention of shutting the old plant; it remains productive and profitable. Both plants will employ hundreds of workers. Their line management is separate, although both plant managers will report to the same regional manager.

There has been a dispute over whether the new plant should have its own personnel department. Not surprisingly, the new plant manager is in favor of establishing a separate personnel function. The personnel department that already exists doesn't really care one way or the other but would prefer not to have the extra work involved in taking over the personnel function of a new plant. Corporate headquarters favors expanding the existing personnel department and having it serve both locations.

1. What are the advantages, if any, of establishing a personnel department exclusively for the new plant?

2. What are the advantages, if any, of expanding the existing personnel department and having it serve both locations?

3. Which of these two suggestions would you recommend? Why?

KEY CONCEPTS

aptitude
expectancy one
expectancy theory
expectancy two
external environment
first-level outcomes

instrumentality
internal environment
need
perception
role awareness

role conflict
second-level outcomes
skill
stress
values

DISCUSSION QUESTIONS

1. Why is the environment so important for personnel and human resource management? How has its importance changed over the past few years?
2. What are the components of the internal environment? How do they relate to the effective management of human resources?
3. How can a personnel manager use knowledge of individual qualities to be more effective?
4. What are some individual perceptions that are important in personnel management? Describe the relationships of these perceptions to personnel functions and activities.
5. What is the relationship between employee performance and satisfaction?
6. What are the task load qualities? How do they relate to personnel management?
7. How do the interpersonal relationships in an organization influence the management of human resources?
8. Discuss the relationships between organizational qualities and personnel management.

ENDNOTES

1. E. J. Gibbin, "The Evolution of Personnel," *Human Resource Management*, Fall 1978, p. 27.

2. T. Mills, "Human Resources: Why the New Concern?" *Harvard Business Review*, March/April 1975, p. 128.

3. For example, compare the coverage of E. L. Loen's book on *Personnel Management Guides for Small Business* (Washington, D.C.: Small Business Administration, 1974) with this textbook.

4. E. A. Locke, "The Nature and Causes of Job Satisfaction," in M. D. Dunnette (ed.), *Handbook of Industrial and Organizational Psychology* (Chicago: Rand McNally, 1976), p. 1303.

5. This list incorporates the thoughts of many researchers and reflects the needs that appear to be most related to the work situation. For an extended discussion of the existence and importance of each of these needs, see
   J. S. Adams, "Inequity in Social Exchange, in L. Berkowitz (ed.), *Advances in Experimental Social Psychology*, vol. 2 (New York: Academic Press, 1965).
   C. Argyris, *Integrating the Individual and the Organization* (New York: Wiley, 1964).
   V. S. Cleland, "The Effect of Stress on Performance," *Nursing Research*, no. 14, (1965), pp. 292–298.
   S. A. Corson, "The Lack of Feedback in Today's Societies: A Psychosocial Stressor," in L. Levi (ed.), *Society, Stress and Disease*, vol. 1 (London: Oxford University Press, 1971).
   M. Frankenhaeuser and B. Gardell, "Underload and Overload in Working Life: Outline of a Multidisciplinary Approach," *Journal of Human Stress*, no. 2 (1976), pp. 35–45.
   F. Herzberg, "The Human Need for Work," *Industry Week*, July 24, 1978, pp. 49–52.
   F. Herzberg, B. Mausner, and B. Snyderman, *The Motivation to Work* (New York: Wiley, 1959).
   R. L. Kahn, D. M. Wolfe, R. P. Quinn, J. D. Snoek, and R. A. Rosenthal, *Organizational Stress: Studies in Role Conflict and Ambiguity* (New York: Wiley, 1964).
   D. C. McClelland, "N Achievement and Entrepreneurship: A Longitudinal Study," *Journal of Personality and Social Psychology*, no. 1 (1965), pp. 389–392.
   D. C. McClelland, J. W. Atkinson, R. A. Clark, and E. L. Lowell, *The Achievement Motive* (New York: Irvington, 1975).

   D. C. McClelland and D. H. Burnham, "Good Guys Make Bum Bosses," *Psychology Today*, December 1975, pp. 69–70.
   A. Zaleznik, M. F. R. Kets de Vries, and J. Howard, "Stress Reactions in Organizations: Syndromes, Causes and Consequences," *Behavioral Science*, no. 22 (1977), pp. 151–161.

6. Excerpt from *Life In and Outside an American Factory* by Richard Balzer, p. 142. Copyright © 1976 by Richard Balzer. Reprinted by permission of Doubleday & Company, Inc.

7. A. B. Shostak, *Blue-Collar Stress*, © 1980, Addison-Wesley Publishing Company, Inc., p. 50. Reprinted with permission.

8. F. E. Schuster, "Human Resources Management: Key to the Future," *Personnel Administrator*, December 1978, pp. 22–25, 66–68.

9. G. L. Staines and R. P. Quinn, *The 1977 Quality of Employment Survey* (Ann Arbor, Mich.: Survey Research Center, University of Michigan, 1977). Cited in "American Workers Evaluate the Quality of Their Jobs," *Monthly Labor Review*, January 1979, p. 4.

10. E. E. Lawler III, *Pay and Organizational Effectiveness: A Psychological View* (New York: McGraw-Hill, 1971), p. 159.

11. D. A. Nadler and E. E. Lawler, "Motivation: A Diagnostic Approach," in J. R. Hackman, E. E. Lawler, and L. Porter (eds.), *Perspectives on Behaviors in Organizations* (New York: McGraw-Hill, 1977), pp. 26–38.

12. For fuller discussion and extension of desired behaviors in organizations, see
    J. R. Galbraith, *Organization Design* (Reading, Mass.: Addison-Wesley, 1977).
    D. Katz and R. L. Kahn, *The Social Psychology of Organizations*, 2nd ed. (New York: Wiley, 1978).

13. E. A. Fleishman, "The Description and Prediction of Perceptual-Motor Skill Learnings," in R. Glaser (ed.), *Training Research and Education* (Pittsburgh: University of Pittsburgh Press, 1962), pp. 140–144.

14. Shostak, p. 31.

15. T. A. Beehr and J. E. Newman, "Job Stress, Employee Health, and Organizational Effectiveness: A Facet Analysis, Model and Literature Review," *Personnel Psychology*, Winter 1978, pp. 665–699.
    R. S. Schuler, "Definition and Conceptualization

of Stress in Organizations, *Organizational Behavior and Human Performance*, no. 25 (1980), pp. 184–215.

16. J. Miller and L. L. Fry, "Work-Related Consequences of Influence, Respect and Solidarity in Two Law Enforcement Agencies," *Sociology of Work and Occupation*, November 1977, p. 472.

17. C. L. Cooper and J. Marshall, "Occupational Sources of Stress: A Review of the Literature Relating to Coronary Disease and Mental Health," *Journal of Occupational Psychology*, no. 49 (1976), pp. 11–28.

18. A. P. Hare, *Handbook of Small Group Research*, 2nd ed. (New York: Free Press, 1976).
D. Cartwright and A. Zander (eds.), *Group Dynamics: Theory and Research* (New York: Harper & Row, 1968).
R. Likert, *The Human Organization* (New York: McGraw-Hill, 1967).

19. B. H. Raven and J. Rietsema, "Effects of Varied Clarity of Group Goal and Group Path upon the Individual and His Relation to His Group," *Human Relations*, no. 10 (1957), pp. 29–45.
E. E. Smith, "The Effects of Clear and Unclear Role Expectations on Group Productivity and Defensiveness," *Journal of Abnormal and Social Psychology*, no. 55 (1957), pp. 213–217.

20. J. R. Hackman, "Group Influences on Individuals," in M. D. Dunnette (ed.), *Handbook of Industrial and Organizational Psychology* (Chicago, Rand McNally, 1976), p. 1461.

21. J. S. House, *Work Stress and Social Support*, p. 41, © 1981, Addison-Wesley Publishing Company, Inc., to be published in 1981. Reprinted with permission.

22. Shostak, p. 49.

23. See C. N. Greene and C. A. Schriesheim, "Leader-Group Interactions: A Longitudinal Field Investigation," *Journal of Applied Psychology*, no. 1 (1980), pp. 50–59.

24. R. J. House and T. R. Mitchell, "Path-Goal Theory of Leadership," *Journal of Contemporary Business*, Autumn 1974, pp. 81–98.

25. House and Mitchell, p. 90.

26. R. J. House and M. L. Baetz, "Leadership: Some Empirical Generalizations and New Research Directions," in B. Staw (ed.), *Research in Organizational Behavior*, vol. 2 (Greenwich, Conn.: JAI Press, 1980).

27. V. H. Vroom and E. W. Yetton, *Leadership and Decision Making* (Pittsburgh: University of Pittsburgh Press, 1973).
For a description of additional behaviors a leader can engage in, see
G. Graen, "Role Making Processes within Complex Organizations," in M. D. Dunnette (ed.), *Handbook of Industrial and Organizational Psychology* (Chicago: Rand McNally, 1976), Chapter 28.
G. R. Oldham, "The Motivational Strategies Used by Supervisors: Relationships to Effectiveness Indicators," *Organizational Behavior and Human Performance*, no. 15 (1976), pp. 66–86.
See also House and Baetz for a complete review of this literature.

28. B. K. Scanlan, "Managerial Leadership in Perspective: Getting Back to Basics," *Personnel Journal*, March 1979, pp. 168–171, 183–184.

29. D. D. Steinbrecher, "Prescription for Leadership," *Personnel*, November/December 1979, pp. 58–59.

30. Steinbrecher, p. 58.

31. F. K. Foulkes and H. M. Morgan, "Organizing and Staffing the Personnel Function," *Harvard Business Review*, May/June 1977, pp. 142–154.

32. R. C. Griever, "Personnel Management in the Small Organization," p. 38. Reprinted with permission from the March 1978 issue of the *Personnel Administrator* copyright, 1978, The American Society for Personnel Administration, 30 Park Drive, Berea, OH 44017.

33. Griever, p. 38.

34. J. L. Bower, "Effective Public Management," *Harvard Business Review*, March/April 1977, p. 132.

35. J. M. Rosow, "Human Dignity in the Public-Sector Workplace," *Public Personnel Management*, February 1979, p. 11.

36. Bower, p. 134.

37. Rosow, p. 12.

38. J. M. Rosow, "Human Dignity in the Public-Sector Workplace," p. 13. Reprinted with permission from the February 1979 issue of *Public Personnel Management* copyright, 1979, International Personnel Management Association, Suite 870, 1850 K. Street N.W., Washington, D.C. 20006.

39. Rosow, p. 13.

40. Rosow, p. 13.

41. J. M. Rosow, "Human Dignity in the Public-Sector Workplace," p. 13. Reprinted with permission from the February 1979 issue of *Public Personnel Management* copyright, 1979, International Personnel Management Association, Suite 870, 1850 K. Street N.W., Washington, D.C. 20006.

42. P. Drucker, *Managing for Results* (New York: Harper & Row, 1964).

43. J. Kotter and V. Sathe, "Problems of Human Resource Management in Rapidly Growing Companies," © 1978 by the Regents of the University of California. Reprinted from *California Management Review*, vol. XXI, no. 2, pp. 31–32, by permission of the Regents.

44. T. Burns and G. M. Stalker, *The Management of Innovation*. (London: Tavistock, 1961).
     J. D. Thompson, *Organization in Action* (New York: McGraw-Hill, 1977).
     Woodward, J. *Industrial Organization: Theory and Practice* (London: Oxford University Press, 1965).
     For reviews of the technology/structure literature, see
     J. Kimberly and M. Evanisko, "Organizational Technology, Structure, and Size," in S. Kerr (ed.), *Organizational Behavior* (Columbus,

Ohio: Grid, 1979), pp. 263–88.
     For a nice conceptualization of the impact of contextual influences on personnel management, see
     V. V. Murray and D. E. Dimick, "Contextual Influences on Personnel Policies and Programs: An Exploratory Model," *The Academy of Management Review,* October 1978, pp. 750–761.

45. E. Mandt, "Managing the Knowledge Worker of the Future," *Personnel Journal*, March 1978, pp. 138–143, 162.

46. For a more complete description of these environments, see
     J. D. Thompson, *Organization in Action* (New York: McGraw-Hill, 1967).
     J. Galbraith, *Organizational Design* (Reading, Mass.: Addison-Wesley, 1977).

47. "The Teamsters Aim at the Guidelines," p. 62. Reprinted from the April 2, 1979 issue of *Business Week* © 1979 by McGraw-Hill, Inc., 1221 Avenue of the Americas, New York, N.Y. 10020. All rights reserved.

48. U.S. Department of Labor, Office of the Secretary, Women's Bureau, *20 Facts on Women Workers* (Washington, D.C.: Government Printing Office, August 1977), pp. 1–3.

SECTION TWO

Planning for Human Resource Needs

CHAPTER THREE
Human Resource Planning and Programming
CHAPTER FOUR
Job Analysis

OBJECTIVES

● To discuss reasons for human resource planning and programming

● To describe the growing necessity for human resource planning

● To describe the four phases of human resource planning and programming

● To explain the relationship between human resource planning and programming and the other personnel functions and activities

THOUGHT STARTERS

● What are the phases of human resource planning?

● Why is human resource planning becoming more important?

● What is a human resource information system?

● How can an organization tell if its human resource planning and programming activities are effective?

CHAPTER THREE
Human Resource Planning and Programming

At United California Bank, we are committed to achieving a staff and management population within the next nine years that reflects the relative numbers of females and minorities in the labor markets of California. On the basis of current estimates of our 1983 work force, we are going to make every reasonable effort to have 1,200 blacks and 2,000 Spanish-surnamed Americans in the bank by 1983. We anticipate that there will be over 1,000 women in management by then and approximately 300 blacks and 500 Spanish-surnamed Americans.—Norman Barker, Jr., Chairman, United California Bank

For many years it has been said that capital is the bottleneck for a developing industry. I don't think this any longer holds true. I think it's the work force and the company's inability to recruit and maintain a good work force that does constitute the bottleneck for production. I don't know of any major project backed by good ideas, vigor, and enthusiasm that has been stopped by a shortage of cash. I do know of industries whose growth has been partly stopped or hampered because they can't maintain an efficient and enthusiastic labor force, and I think this will hold true even more in the future.—Pehr Gyllenhammar, President, AB Volvo

The satisfactions that come from the job have disappeared. The professional is working in an environment that is more and more dehumanized. He's working in greater and greater masses. You can go to the aerospace industry and see the way an engineer works, in row on row of engineers. He's just one of hundreds of thousands. And in the universities there's less of a one-to-one relationship with the policymakers, so the faculty member feels less and less important. It's no different from what happened to the blue-collar worker who once was a craftsman with dignity, an individual.—Jack Golodner, Executive Secretary, Council of AFL-CIO Unions for Professional Employees

Reprinted by permission of the Harvard Business Review. *Excerpt from "Expanding the Role of the Personnel Function" by F. K. Foulkes (March/April 1975), pp. 71–72. Copyright © 1975 by the President and Fellows of Harvard College; all rights reserved.*

Whenever labor was in short supply, organizations concerned themselves with what they would do to "staff up," but only recently have they turned to manpower planning as a preventive measure and sensible basis for administrative action.

Although manpower planning involves both present and potential employees, it should be especially concerned with workers who are already on the payroll. . . . An increase in the efficiency of present employees may be a better solution to manpower needs than hiring additional workers. Frequently, some combination of the two may be best. . . . A manpower planning program should be set up to cause change. It should start out with clear goals (Here's what we want) and plan the means for reaching them. Frequently, micro manpower planning is a sterile exercise: that is, it results in manpower forecasts without plans for

action. . . . It is generally better to integrate plans for internal employee development with plans for external recruiting than to develop a recruiting schedule that gives projected needs to 20 decimal places.

Reprinted by permission of the author, E. W. Vetler, Manpower Planning for High Talent Personnel *(Ann Arbor, Mich.: Bureau of Industrial Relations, Graduate School of Business, The University of Michigan, 1967), p. 15.*

ll of these quotes relate to important aspects of human resource planning and programming in organizations—minority involvement, motivation of employees, job satisfaction—although they provide only a limited view. Other aspects of human resource planning and programming include

• Management development, with emphasis on making sure managers are skilled in their functions and reasonably qualified for promotions.

• Forecasting and estimating future human resource needs in quantitative terms, ignoring skill and knowledge requirements since they result from "natural" developmental processes anyway.

• Organizational planning, which views the current and future structure of the organization and identifies the location of current employees, especially top-level management, and the location of employees needed for the future structure. This aspect considers the events, trends, and changes inside and outside the organization that may influence its human resource needs in the future but fails to specify action plans for assuring that the needs of the organization are met.

• Macro, or societal-level, human resource planning, which is concerned with the national labor force and includes projections of labor supply and forecasts of occupational, industrial, and total labor force requirements.

• Micro, or organizational-level, human resource planning, which includes the aspects already listed as well as the full range of traditional personnel functions.[1]

This chapter addresses these issues, showing how personnel and human resource departments become involved in planning for the future of an organization. After an overview of the planning and programming function, the chapter provides a detailed description of the steps that are involved in drawing a picture of human resource needs. Implementation of a human resource plan, the final step, demands attention to several factors that are discussed in the last part of the chapter.

HUMAN RESOURCE PLANNING AND PROGRAMMING

In general terms, **human resource planning and programming (HRPP)** is

. . . the process by which management determines how the organization should move from its current human resource position. Through planning, management strives to have the right number (quantitative) and the kinds (qualitative) of people, at the right places, at the right time, doing things which result in both the organization and the individual receiving maximum long-run benefit.[2]

In other words, a major purpose of HRPP is to help the organization use human talent effectively and in the interests of the individual employee and the organization.[3] HRPP can also reduce expenses associated with excessive turnover and absenteeism, low productivity, inefficient internal labor markets, and an unproductive training program.

Specific purposes of human resource planning and programming are to

• Reduce personnel costs by helping management to anticipate shortages or surpluses of human resources and to correct these imbalances before they become unmanageable and expensive

• Provide a better basis for planning employee development that makes optimum use of workers' attitudes
• Improve the overall business planning process
• Provide more opportunities for women and minority groups in future growth plans and to identify the specific development or training programs that will make specific skills available
• Promote greater awareness of the importance of sound human resource management throughout all levels of the organization
• Provide a tool for evaluating the effect of alternative human resource actions and policies[4]

The Elements of HRPP

The specific needs of an organization determine how it applies human resource planning and programming. Yet all organizations must consider having nine common elements of HRPP:
• Human resource policy formulated within the broader framework of corporate policy
• Human resource goals and objectives spanning entry, individual development, and separation
• Multiple time perspectives in keeping with company stability, objectives of particular analyses, and variables in the institution's environment
• Programs or designs for undertaking a systematic approach in the future
• Programming that encompasses all the critical processes of human resource planning, from recruitment through development
• Suitable controls that provide for securing goals and that permit redirection as necessary
• Organization that permits a timely integration of all necessary functions and programming elements and that is lodged high enough in the hierarchy for necessary authority and status
• An information base, frequently supported by computers, that provides necessary support for farflung activities, including information for both data processing and decision making
• Cognizance of the human dimensions of the human resource plan—behavioral approaches that support the dignity of individuals and that assist them in realizing important personal goals while achieving performance objectives of the organization

The Importance of HRPP

The recent emphasis on human resource planning and programming reflects a number of changes in the environment and in organizations. These changes are pushing personnel management into a future-oriented, comprehensive, and integrative perspective. This perspective has a number of fundamental attributes: (1) It considers human resource costs an investment rather than an uncontrollable expense; (2) it is proactive rather than passive or reactive in its approach to developing human resource policies and resolving human resource problems; (3) it is characterized by a change in role perspective from an emphasis on the completion of personnel transactions toward a future-oriented approach in which the personnel department acts as a controller of the organization's human resources; (4) it recognizes that there must be an explicit link between human resource planning and other organizational functions, such as strategic planning, economic and market forecasting, and investment and facilities planning; (5) it recognizes that such personnel activities as recruitment, selection, labor relations, compensation and benefits, training, organizational planning, and career management must be visualized as dynamic interconnecting activities rather than a series of separate and nonintegrated functions; and (6) it focuses on approaches that further both organizational and individual goals.[5]

One of the changes that is making HRPP more important is the growing recognition of the extensive set of relationships that HRPP has with other personnel and human resource activities. HRPP helps establish the organization's staffing needs and provides the basis for meeting those needs.

Another change is the growing shortage of human resources to fill jobs in industry, government, education, and other segments of our society—and it promises to continue into the future.[6] The shortage of human resources is usually related to specific skills or occupations and age groupings. For example,

A dwindling young work force will make it more difficult to fill entry-level positions. Already there are predictions about shortages in blue-collar occupations by the mid-1980's. It is not too soon for managers to start investigating their company demographics.

In the Pacific Northwest, tool and die makers are in such short supply that one company asked the Washington State Employment Service for permission to import a worker from Norway. Another firm requested 12 bricklayers from Canada.

Shipbuilders, legal secretaries, engineers, aerospace workers, nurses, machinists, mechanics, bricklayers, even "poultry eviscerators"; somewhere in the country there is an acute shortage of these and other workers.

The shortage of skilled workers has become so critical in some areas that state officials are curtailing efforts to lure industries to relocate in their area.

"Anybody who wanted to locate a manufacturing establishment here now should have his head examined," said James J. Archey of the Southern New Hampshire Association of Commerce and Industry.

Seymour Colman of Beech Aircraft in Wichita said Kansas aircraft companies will need 14,000 new employees within five years. But he, too, suggested his state stop trying to attract new industry.

"It is almost un-American to say to outside industry that we don't want them in our state," he told a meeting of Kansas economists. "But all we're saying is we ought to take care of the industries we already have rather than dilute the already minuscule labor force."[7]

Despite shortages of young people for entry-level positions in the 1980s and 1990s, the young people who do enter the labor force will have a hard time being promoted.

*As a consequence of the 43 million babies born in the years immediately
following World War II, a middle-aged bulge is forming and eventually the 35- to
45-year-old group will increase by 80%.*[8]

It is only by the year 2030 that this group will cross the bridge to sixty-five. "Young
people can probably look forward to relatively static income and rivalry with older
workers for some period of time."[9]

Combined with the shortage of human resources is the increasing demand for
certain types of jobs and the mismatch between the available work force and the
jobs that do exist. This change has been most apparent at the professional, managerial, and technical levels:

*Centronics Data Computer Corp. in Hudson, N.H., employs 2,000 people and
has 125 vacant jobs in another field where job shortages abound—computer
technicians and programmers. It decided to build a plant employing 1,000 people
in Ireland because it couldn't find enough workers in New Hampshire.*

*"New Hampshire is just about pumped dry for people, especially in the
southern part of the state," said Richard Leven, Centronics industrial relations
director.*[10]

The issue of managerial obsolescence also reflects change. Rapid changes in
knowledge make it difficult for professionals, engineers, and managers to remain
adept at their jobs. They must be provided with the opportunity for continued
training. However, organizations are not sure what to do, nor do they always recognize the potential for obsolescence. But "the unsolved problem of professional
obsolescence posed by the production of knowledge is a threat to the growth potential of organizations and society as a whole."[11]

Another major reason for organizational concern with human resource planning
and programming is the relatively poor quality of available human resources and
the need to increase worker and managerial productivity and efficiency. The seriousness and pervasiveness of these concerns are reflected in this story:

*The problem is so bad that companies import employees with particular skills
from overseas. And at least one company decided to locate a plant overseas
because it could not find enough trained employees in the United States.*

*Take the case of Halter Marine Services, Inc., which runs the television
commercial seeking shipbuilders. The commercial touts Halter's high pay and
benefits and offers a toll-free number for potential employees to call.*

*Halter began running the commercial, and others, after it couldn't find enough
workers to keep its shipyard in Pierre Part, La., going.*

*"Everybody says there's 6 percent, 7 percent unemployment. But those people
don't have the skills to fill the jobs," said Leonard Morgan, Halter personnel
director.*

*"It's a 'Catch 22.' They're unemployed, we have jobs and we should be able to
fill those jobs with those people. I wish it was that simple," Morgan said. "The
problem is those people aren't qualified. They need training."*[12]

The general expansion and diversification of organizations also makes HRPP more important. Trends toward multinational operations are attended by difficulties in transferring workers and in operations and staffing in foreign cultures.

Another set of changes that makes HRPP more important is recent legislation in support of affirmative action and other employment matters. Equal Employment Opportunity, the Employee Retirement Income Security Act, and the Occupational Safety and Health Act were established in response to directives from the Labor Department, Justice Department, Equal Employment Opportunity Commission, and Civil Service Commission (now the Office of Personnel Management).

"The presence of a strong personality, typically a senior officer or the president, who is committed to the concept of human resource planning" is another reason for the development of HRPP.[13] But although the senior person may initiate the movement, the line and staff managers must perpetuate the programs by participating once they have been developed.

The new retirement options available to workers are also causing a shift in concern for staffing positions. Workers now have options ranging from early retirement in their mid-fifties to retirement in their seventies.

Another compelling reason for human resource planning is the investment an organization makes in its human resources. Human assets, as opposed to other assets, can increase in value. An employee who is forced to develop skills and abilities becomes a more valuable resource. Because an organization makes investments in its personnel either through direct training or job assignments, it is important that employees are used effectively throughout their careers. The dollar value of a trained, flexible, motivated, and productive work force is difficult to determine, although attempts are being made to do so, as in human resource accounting (HRA).[14] An increasing number of organization leaders are acknowledging that the quality of the work force can be responsible for significant differences in short- and long-run performances.

Many corporate executives are concluding that insufficient or unqualified manpower is at least as serious a production bottleneck as a scarcity of capital and that manpower investments are as important a factor in company planning as the acquisition of plants, equipment or materials.[15]

The final reason for the increased emphasis on human resource planning and programming is the growing resistance of employees to change and to moving. There is also a growing emphasis on self-evaluation and on evaluation of loyalty and dedication to the organization. All these changes are making it more difficult for the organization to assume it can move its employees around anywhere and anytime it wants, thus increasing the importance and necessity of planning ahead.

HRRP in Relation to Other Personnel Functions

HRPP has an extensive set of relationships with other personnel and human resource activities and functions. All these relationships are important, but this section concentrates on two.

A SLICE OF LIFE

Human resource planning is an important factor in organizational policy and in a societal context. Consider the following.

A very large manufacturing company produces a variety of consumer goods. Market demand for its products now exceeds the capability of all three of its plants. A fourth plant is on the drawing boards, but it will not be completed for nearly three years. However, state-of-the-art manufacturing methods at this new plant will ensure that the demand for the company's products is met.

But what happens during the three years the plant is being built? Inability to supply the market with the products for that length of time invites competition. Naturally, the company prefers that this does not happen. It has been suggested that a vacant existing plant be purchased and modified to meet current demand. Certainly, the temporary plant will not be so efficient as the existing three plants or the new plant, but it will meet manufacturing requirements and take only six months to refit.

The modified plant is located in a rural area that does not have enough workers to meet the 1,100-person staff requirement. In order to operate this stopgap plant, literally hundreds of people will have to be recruited into this area. This infusion of people will cause substantial pressure on the community, and new housing and schools will have to be built. Herein lies your problem. You know for a fact that in approximately 2½ years this temporary plant will permanently be shut down.

Consider the impact of human resource decisions for this plant on overall corporate policy and the societal implications of such decisions. A community will probably spring up around your temporary plant, with new restaurants, theaters, and the like to serve the employees. Do you tell the employees that their job is only temporary? Do you think they would move their families for a 2½-year job? Would you? Suppose you give them first chance to transfer to the new plant, which will be only 300 to 500 miles away? Do you think they would like moving their children out of school, selling their homes, and leaving their friends again? Clearly, some human resource decisions are very important.

Staffing.   HRPP helps determine the human resource needs of an organization. In conjunction with job analysis, it indicates how many and what types of people need to be recruited. Recruitment influences the pool of available job applicants, which in turn influences the need for socialization and accommodation. Thus HRPP can be viewed as a major input into an organization's staffing function.

Without HRPP, recruitment and selection are more frequently concerned with an organization's immediate, short-term needs. One consequence is that recruiting and selection may be done inefficiently. For example, a recruiter may overlook job applicants who are not qualified for a *current* job opening only to find two months later that those applicants would have been ideal for another position. Had an HRPP existed, the recruiter could have used the first recruiting effort more efficiently.

Career Management. Career-management programs aid an organization in retaining valued employees and keeping them from becoming obsolete. Thus career-management programs play an important role in determining an organization's supply of human resources and ultimately its needs. For example, if career-management programs and career planning by employees help reduce employee turnover and absenteeism, the organization can plan on a larger qualified supply of human resources and therefore a smaller need for additional human resources.

Because managing careers is becoming so important for organizations and individuals, Chapter 14 examines career-management programs and career planning in detail. Chapter 14 is also designed to help you with your own career planning.

Who's Responsible for HRPP?

The responsibility for HRPP rests with top management, the personnel manager, and the line managers. Together they determine the success and effectiveness of HRPP, but each plays a different role. Top management is responsible for encouraging HRPP, aiding in its implementation, and ensuring its use. The personnel manager is responsible for developing HRPP, gathering the necessary information, creating a human-resource information system, making it usable and available, coordinating HRPP with the other personnel activities, and evaluating the effectiveness of HRPP. Line managers and supervisors are responsible for providing the necessary information for HRPP and for working with the personnel manager to ensure that the organization's human resources are used as effectively as possible and that its human resource needs are provided for.

The Phases and Processes of HRPP

Human resource planning is generally accomplished in four phases:
1. Gathering and analyzing data through human resource inventories and forecasts
2. Establishing human resource objectives and policies and gaining approval for them from top management
3. Designing and implementing plans and action programs in such areas as recruitment, training, and promotion that will enable the organization to achieve its human resource objectives
4. Controlling and evaluating human resource plans and programs to facilitate progress toward human resource objectives[16]

Exhibit 3.1 shows the relationships among these phases as well as their relationships with corporate objectives, policies, and plans and with environmental components.

HUMAN RESOURCE INVENTORY AND FORECAST

The first phase of HRPP involves developing data that can be used in determining corporate objectives, policies, and plans as well as human resource objectives and policies. As shown in Exhibit 3.1, the human resource inventory and forecast are both influenced in turn by corporate objectives, policies, and plans and by human resource objectives and policies. The interaction of these aspects of human resource

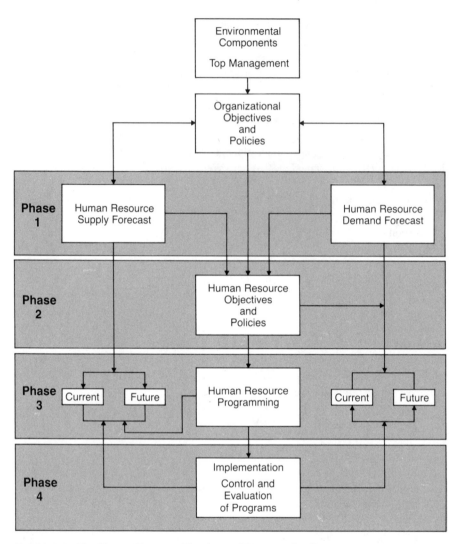

Exhibit 3.1 The Human Resource Planning and Programming Process
Adapted from E. W. Vetter, *Manpower Planning for High Talent Personnel* (Ann Arbor, Mich.: Bureau of
Industrial Relations, Graduate School of Business, The University of Michigan, 1967), p. 29.

planning help determine the current human resource situation and future human
resource needs.

The data developed in phase 1 represent information retrieved from the past,
observed in the present, and forecasted for the future. Obtaining data from the past
may be difficult because of inadequate or nonexistent records, and forecasting data
with reliability and accuracy may be difficult because of uncertainties. Nevertheless,
they need to be provided, however tentatively. The more tentative the data, the more
flexible and subject to revision they should be. Contingencies causing uncertainties
in the forecasts should be incorporated into the forecasts, perhaps in the form of

estimated ranges. Organizations in more unstable and complex environments are faced with many more contingencies than organizations in more stable and simple environments.

As shown in Exhibit 3.2, there are five steps in phase 1. Each is important for the success of human resource planning and programming.

Analyzing the Internal Supply of Labor

Step 1 consists of an analysis of the human resource situation in an organization. As Exhibit 3.2 indicates, this step consists of four aspects.

Inventory. One aspect of a human resource analysis is an inventory of the current work force in the organization and the current jobs in the organization. Both elements are necessary if the organization is to determine its capability to meet current and future human resource needs. Knowing the skills, abilities, interests, and needs

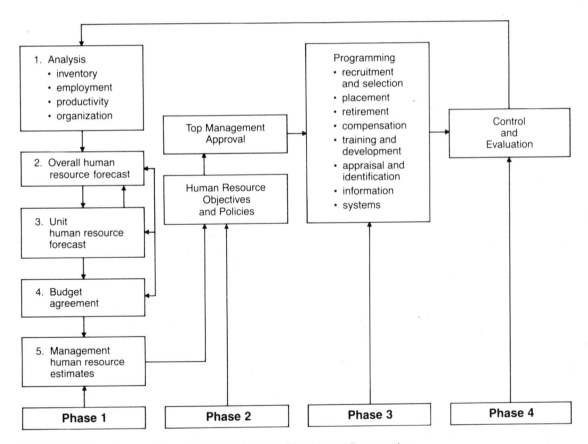

Exhibit 3.2 Procedures and Steps for Human Resource Planning and Programming
Adapted from E. W. Vetter, *Manpower Planning for High Talent Personnel* (Ann Arbor, Mich.: Bureau of Industrial Relations, Graduate School of Business, University of Michigan, 1967), p. 34.

of the current work force is only half of the inventory. The other half consists of knowing the characteristics of current jobs and the skills required to perform them. An updated job analysis program facilitates this half of the inventory and the matching of employees and jobs.

Manual inventories have been used successfully for years in matching employees with jobs.[17] Use of computers is making the compilation of inventories much more efficient and is allowing for a more dynamic, integrative human resource program. Through computers, employees in separate divisions and different areas of the country are finding it easier to participate in the organization's network for matching jobs and employees.

A common computer-oriented information system used in the management of human resources is often referred to as a **human resource information system (HRIS)**:

Any human resource information system is logically an inventory of the positions and skills extant in a given organization. However, HRIS is more than a simple aggregation mechanism for inventory control and accounting; it is the foundation for a set of management tools enabling managers to establish objectives for the use of their organization's human resources and to measure the extent to which those objectives have been achieved.[18]

Many larger organizations have an HRIS, including Nationwide Life Insurance Co., Frito-Lay, IBM, XEROX, AMAX, and the U.S. State Department.

The data base of the HRIS at the U.S. State Department has two major components: position data and personnel data. The *position* data include descriptions of
● The location and level of each position. For the State Department, these would necessarily include measures of the optimal time for someone to be in a particular position.
● The optimal requirements for performing a given job adequately. At a minimum these requirements should include education, experience, training, language proficiency, supervisory experience, and any special professional licenses.
● The basic tasks of each job, weighted in terms of time and relative importance. One of the advantages of providing this information is that it can replace traditionally destructive labels for positions. Component descriptions more accurately illustrate the specific duties that are actually performed.[19]
The *personnel* data gathered by the U.S. State Department include employees' personal preferences, education and training, and experience and skill. The position and personnel data in the HRIS are useful for many other personnel functions and activities besides HRPP.

The principal goals to be achieved with an HRIS are
● Determination of the needs for personnel information in each functional area
● Design of a comprehensive data base to support these needs
● Development of complete functional specifications for the HRIS
● Design of necessary transaction processing and update forms
● Identification of information retrieval and reporting needs
● Development of relevant supporting documentation[20]
Only if all these goals are attained can the HRIS be useful for and used by those in human resource planning and programming.

Employment.   A second aspect of human resource analysis is an analysis of the probable future composition of the society's work force. Often this analysis is based on wage, occupational, and industrial groups. Historical data on work force composition, along with current demographic and economic data, are used to make human resource projections. These employment projections are not specific to any single organization, but they can often provide an organization with useful information for its human resource plans, particularly for long-run needs.

Productivity.   Another aspect of human resource analysis is the determination of labor productivity and its probable productivity in the future. The State Department can use its HRIS to measure performance for evaluating the productivity of specific programs, offices, or positions.

   Related measures are projections of employee turnover and absenteeism. These influence the productivity of an organization's work force at any one time and thus its future human resource needs. Projections of turnover and absenteeism might also suggest a need to analyze the reasons for turnover and absenteeism and then form the basis for strategies to deal with them. It should be noted, however, that in some times and for some employees increased turnover is desirable. For example, if an organization suddenly finds itself with too many employees, increased turnover, especially among poor performers, might be welcomed.

Organization.   The final aspect of the first step in HRPP is the examination and projection of organizational structure. This helps determine the probable size of the top, middle, and lower levels of the organization, for both managers and nonmanagers. In addition, it provides information about changes in the organization's human resource needs and about specific activities or functional areas that can be expected to experience particularly severe growth or contraction.

   The type of organization is a major factor determining both structure (as discussed in Chapter 2) and the amount and intensity of changes. As organizations become more technologically complex and face more complex and dynamic environments, they will possess more complex structures—with more departments and a greater variety of occupations—and face more changes in the environment. Thus the type of organization and its environment play an important role not only in determination of the organization's structure but also in providing information useful for forecasting its human resource needs.

Forecasting Human Resource Needs

Step 2 in the human resource inventory and forecast determining the organization's overall human resource needs; step 3 involves forecasting human resource needs only in certain units or functional areas of the organization. These two steps provide information related to the demand for human resources, whereas step 1 covered considerations related to the supply of human resources.

   An organization's demand for human resources can be determined by a variety of forecasting methods, some simple and some complex. The type of forecast that is used depends on the time frame and the type of organization, its size and dispersion, and the accuracy and certainty of information that is available. The time frame used in forecasting the organization's demand for human resources frequently parallels that used in forecasting the potential supply of human resources for the organization. Comparison of the demand and supply forecasts then determines the organization's short-term, intermediate-term, and long-term needs. These needs form the basis for human resource programming.

Forecasting results in approximations—not absolutes or certainties. The quality of the forecast depends on the accuracy of information and the predictability of events. The shorter the time horizon, the more predictable events are and the more accurate the information. For example, organizations are generally able to predict how many MBAs they may need for the coming year but are less able to predict their needs for the next five years.

Three classes of forecasting techniques are frequently used to determine the organization's projected demand for human resources. In order of increasing complexity, these are expert forecasts, conventional statistical projections, and computer simulations and modeling. These three techniques parallel the four stages of forecasting, as shown in Exhibit 3.3. In addition, forecasting for specific units in an organization (step 3) often entails a fourth technique.

Expert Forecasts.   The most common method of the expert forecast is the **Delphi technique**, which tends to be less quantitative and perhaps more subjective than other methods. At a Delphi meeting, a large number of experts take turns at presenting a forecast statement and assumptions. An intermediary passes each expert's forecast and assumptions to the others, who then make revisions in their forecasts. This process continues until a viable composite forecast emerges. The composite

Expert Forecasts	Conventional Statistical Projections		Computer Simulations
Stage 1	**Stage 2**	**Stage 3**	**Stage 4**
Managers discuss goals, plans, and thus types and numbers of people needed in the short term. This stage is highly informal and subjective.	Annual planning and budgeting process includes human resource needs. Quantity and quality of talent needs are specified as far out in time as possible. Problems requiring action, individual or general, are identified. Management succession and readiness of successors are analyzed.	Using computer-generated analyses, causes of problems and future trends in supply and demand (the flow of talent) are examined. Computer is used to relieve managers of routine forecasting tasks (such as vacancies or turnover). Career paths and career progress are analyzed, using computer data files.	On-line modeling and simulation of talent needs, flows, and costs aid in a continuing process of updating and projecting needs, staffing plans, career opportunities, and thus program plans. Best possible current information for managerial decisions is provided. Data (such as economic, employment, and social data) are exchanged with other companies and with government.

Exhibit 3.3   Forecasting Stages and Techniques
Adapted from J. Walker, "Evaluating the Practical Effectiveness of Human Resource Planning Applications," *Human Resource Management*, Spring 1974, p. 21. Used with permission.

may represent specific projections or a range of projections, depending on the positions of the experts.

The Delphi technique has been shown to produce better one-year forecasts in comparison with linear regression analysis.[21] But it does have some limitations. There may be difficulties, for example, in integrating the opinions of the experts. However, this technique appears to be particularly useful for generating insights into highly unstructured or undeveloped subject areas, such as human resource planning.[22]

A related method is the **nominal grouping technique**. Several people sit around a conference table and independently list their ideas on a sheet of paper. After ten to twenty minutes, they take turns expressing their ideas to the group. As these ideas are presented. they are recorded on larger sheets of paper so that everyone can see all the ideas and refer to them in later parts of the session.

Although the two techniques are similar in process, the Delphi technique is more frequently used to generate predictions, and the nominal grouping technique is used more for identifying current organizational problems and solutions to those problems.[23]

Statistical Projections. The most common statistical procedures are simple linear regression analysis and multiple linear regression analysis. In **simple linear regression analysis** a projection of future demand is based on a past relationship between the organization's employment level and a variable related to employment, such as sales. If a relationship can be established between the level of sales and the level of employment, predictions of future sales can be used to make predictions of future employment. However, although there may be a relationship between sales and employment, the relationship is often influenced by an organizational learning phenomenon. For example, the level of sales may double, but the level of employment necessary to meet this increase may be less than double. And if sales double again, the amount of employment necessary to meet this new doubling may be even less than that necessary to meet the first doubling of sales. An organizational learning curve can usually be determined by logarithmic calculations. Once the learning curve has been determined, more accurate projections of future employment levels can be established.

Multiple linear regression analysis is an extension of simple linear regression analysis. Instead of relating employment to one other variable related to employment, several variables are used. For example, instead of using only sales to predict employment demand, productivity data and equipment-use data may also be used. Because it incorporates several variables related to employment, multiple regression analysis may produce more accurate demand forecasts than linear regression analysis. It appears, however, that only relatively large organizations use multiple regression analysis.[24]

Computer Simulations. Computer simulations and modeling techniques are even less frequently used by organizations. However, they offer the advantage of being able to quickly revise forecasts based on changes in the determinants or assumptions. For example, the General Electric Company has developed a computer simulation called MANPLAN to determine labor forecasts.[25] These forecasts may be used on a number of different product lines, the forecasted sales for each product line for the next year, the existing plant capacity, and the possibility of working the current work force overtime. Since each of these determinants of the labor forecast has its own relationship with the level of employment, the projected level of employment can be altered by changing estimates of the determinants or the assumed relationships between them and the level of employment. As with multiple linear regression analysis, the use of simulation and modeling is found only in extremely large organizations, such as General Electric, IBM, and the U.S. State Department.

Unit Demand Forecasting. The previous three techniques are used for forecasting the organization's total human resource demand, but there is an additional technique to be used by parts of the organization. The **unit demand forecasting** technique relies on labor estimates provided by the unit or functional area managers. This technique may produce forecasts of demand that, when added up for all unit managers, are discrepant with the total organization's forecasted demand. However, it encourages unit managers to be more aware of the skills, abilities, and desires of their employees. Such an awareness may also produce a higher-quality forecast. Of course, each unit may also use the same statistical techniques that are used for the total organization.

Since the use of unit demand forecasting often produces discrepant forecasts, reconciliation of the difference is necessary before planning can be undertaken. But the discrepancies can often provide a useful basis for questioning and examining the contributions of each unit in the organization as compared to what it demands.

A method related to unit demand forecasting is the development of **replacement charts,** which show the names of the current occupants of positions in the organization and the names of likely replacements (see Exhibit 3.4). Replacement charts make it readily apparent where potential vacancies are and what types of positions most urgently need to be filled.

Reconciling the Budget

Step 4 in the first phase of human resource planning and programming puts the whole activity into economic perspective. The human resource forecast must be expressed in terms of dollars, and this figure must be compatible with the organization's profit objectives and budget limitations.[26] Of course, the budget reconciliation process may also point up the importance of adjusting the budget to accommodate the human resource plan. This reconciliation stage also provides an opportunity to align the objectives and policies of the organization with those of the personnel department.

Forecasting Human Resource Supplies

As stated earlier, there are five steps in the first phase of HRPP (see Exhibit 3.2). Step 5, estimating short-term and long-term human resource needs, is based on data gathered in steps 1, 2, and 3. Estimating human resource needs is really a match of forecasted supply with forecasted demand.

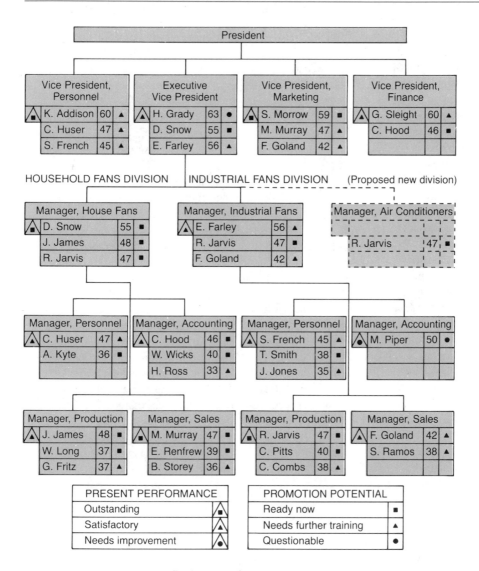

Exhibit 3.4   Sample Employee Replacement Chart*
From *The Expanded Personnel Function*, Studies in Personnel Policy 203 (New York: National Industrial Conference Board, 1966).
*The ages of potential replacements appear next to their names.

Although forecasted supply can be derived from both internal and external sources of information, the internal source of information is generally most crucial and most available. There are basically two techniques to help forecast internal labor supply—replacement charts and Markov models. A forecast of the internal labor supply can be compared with projected trends in the external labor pool to paint a picture of the organization's overall human resource supply. This supply forecast can then be compared with the human resource demand forecast to help determine, among other things, action programming for identifying human resource talent and balancing supply and demand forecasts. However, most current forecasting of labor supply and demand is short-range and for the purposes of budgeting and controlling costs. Forecasts for over a five-year period, when done, are used in planning corporate strategy, planning, facilities, and identifying managerial replacements.[27]

Replacement Charts.   Data in the skills inventory can often be used in drawing up replacement charts, which generally are used to forecast the human resource supply. In the process of forecasting unit demand, managers also determine a supply forecast.

Managers often determine the productivity of their employees in relation to other employees in the unit as well as those in other units. On the basis of productivity data and adjustments for absenteeism and turnover, managers can begin to establish forecasts for the supply of labor. However, evaluation of employees' promotion potential and dismissal potential is more directly related to the forecast. Although replacement charts have traditionally been devised only for managers, nonmanagerial employees are now being included as well.

Markov Models.   The model used in human resource planning to depict the probabilities of organization members moving from one position to another over time is the **Markov model**. Probabilities of movement are based on historical data, and they are established for job clusters or classes (for example, all the supervisory jobs or all the first-level management jobs). For each class, probabilities of promotion, attrition, and replacement are developed. Using these probabilities, the supply of labor can be forecasted for any given time in the future.

Both Markov models and replacement charts are useful for forecasting labor supply. The Markov model tends to be more organizationally and quantitatively oriented, although it can isolate trends in specific occupational classes or in functional areas; replacement charts are more unit and qualitatively oriented. These two techniques are complementary, but use of Markov models is relatively rare.[28]

OBJECTIVES AND POLICIES IN HRPP

As shown in Exhibit 3.1, phase 2 in the human resource planning and programming process is setting human resource objectives and policies. These objectives and policies are directly related to corporate objectives and policies. The impact of the organization's objectives, policies, and plans on human resource planning would seem difficult to deny, but

only one-quarter of the organizations in the sample had achieved a substantial link between their general institutional planning and their manpower planning. An additional 45 percent reported some link, 20 percent had none.[29]

Thus there appears to be some discrepancy between the ideal link of corporate and human resource objectives and policies and what is actually practiced in many organizations. One study found that 85 percent of the organizations surveyed were using a human resource information system (HRIS), but that about one-third were operating at the departmental or division level rather than organizationwide. In addition, most HRISs were used for payroll processing, personnel listings, and placement and, less often, for forecasting and human resource development planning.[30]

It may seem to you that HRPP activity is divorced from mainstream operations of the organization, but the quotes at the beginning of this chapter should indicate the growing importance of HRPP in determination of an organization's goals, plans, and objectives. The relationship runs both ways. Ideally, organizational policies, plans, and objectives influence the personnel inventory and forecasting analysis, and these in turn influence organizational policies, plans, and objectives by permitting the effective use of human resources in attaining the organization's goals.

HUMAN RESOURCE PROGRAMMING

The third phase in HRPP, human resource programming, is an extremely important extension of human resource planning. After the assessment of an organization's human resource needs, action programming must be developed to serve those needs. Action programs may deal with recruitment policies and procedures, especially if more people need to be hired, training and development, policies and procedures, and dismissal of employees.

Planning is an important element in the design of action programs for three reasons: (1) It helps coordinate the activities of the programs and reduces duplication and inefficiencies; (2) it applies pressure for developing programs that might otherwise be neglected; and (3) it stimulates the development and use of individualized programs rather than programs that may be used because they are available or everyone else is using them.[31]

In developing action programs, care must be taken to specify in detail what each program contains and how it is to be done. Furthermore, each program should reflect an awareness of current problems and issues pertaining to human resource management. The range of action programs is too broad to cover them all here. Recruitment, selection, and training and development are discussed in separate chapters. Legal awareness and compliance, career planning and obsolescence, and program control and evaluation are discussed in the remaining pages of this chapter as well as in other chapters. Only one of those issues—career planning and obsolescence—will be presented here as an example.

As the pace of technological change continues to accelerate, the potential for obsolescence increases among both managers and nonmanagers. Obsolescence, of course, has severe implications for human resource planning and programming. The organization may have the appropriate numbers of employees for the future, but by the time the future arrives, those employees may not have the skills to do the jobs. Similarly, the organization may forecast an adequate internal supply of human resources, but employees may leave the organization in numbers larger than assumed. In either of these situations, the organization will find itself fighting "personnel fires" and spending less time with long-term planning and programming activities. Because career planning and obsolescence is so important for the future of human resource management, Chapter 14 is devoted to it.

PROGRAM CONTROL AND EVALUATION

Control and evaluation of human resource plans and programs are essential to the effective management of human resources, and therefore Exhibit 3.1 shows program control and evaluation as the last phase of HRPP. Efforts in this area are clearly aimed at quantifying the value of human resources. These efforts recognize human resources as an asset to the organization. Of course, the quality of work activities must also be evaluated.

An HRIS facilitates program control and evaluation by allowing for more rapid and frequent collection of data to back up the forecast. This data collection is important not only as a means of control but also as a method for evaluating plans and programs and making adjustments.

The collection of data should be formalized to occur at the end of each year and at fixed intervals during the year. The evaluation should occur at the same time in order to hasten revisions of existing forecasts and programs. It is likely that revisions will influence short-run, intermediate, and long-run forecasts. The degree of formality present in the data-collection process varies with the activity or program:

A written progress report by the college recruiter might be an adequate control device for that activity. In salary administration, however, statistical evaluation of the distribution of wages by salary grade, departments, and job classifications may be desired.[32]

Evaluation Criteria

Evaluation of human resource plans and programs is an important process not only for determining effectiveness of HRPP but also for demonstrating the significance of HRPP and the personnel department in the organization as a whole. Measurement of the use and effectiveness of human resources is often lacking, yet numbers are the name of the game.

Possible criteria or standards for evaluating some aspects of personnel activities are listed in Exhibit 3.5. These activities can also be evaluated in terms of how many employees have been laid off during a year. The more who have been laid off, the less adequate the balancing of human resource supply and demand—and the greater the cost to the organization in contributions to state unemployment compensation funds.

Cause-and-Effect Relationships

Another important aspect related to evaluation, revisions, and adjustments is the issue of cause and effect. The life cycle model of personnel management is based on the notion of integrated activities. Thus if the recruiting program is not working well, it is not valid to conclude that the recruitment program needs revision. Perhaps the salaries offered to recruits were too low and not competitive with other organizations. It is also possible that, despite the best recruiting efforts, few acceptable applicants applied.

Exhibit 3.5 Some Possible Criteria for Evaluating Personnel Activities

Activity	Goals and Standards
Recruitment	Recruit college graduates to fill annual quotas based on forecasts
Selection	Hire college graduates from top half of class
Placement	Assign highest-rated managers to most critical jobs
Managerial appraisal	Identify strongest and weakest managers to determine supply of human resources
Development	Target below-average managers for improvement in performance appraisals
Retirement	Plan pattern for volume of annual retirements by levels and units
Information systems	Make up-to-date information on total work force and individual managers easily available
Compensation	Maintain total wage bill within forecasted limits
Organizational planning	Identify potential new positions and employees capable of filling them

Adapted from E. W. Vetter, "Manpower Planning for High Talent Personnel," (Ann Arbor, Mich.: Bureau of Industrial Relations, Graduate School of Business, The University of Michigan, 1967), p. 181.

The integrated approach not only makes the evaluation of any single program complex. Indeed, evaluation of planning and programming activities may need to consider only the "bottom line"—the composite results of a set of activities rather than separate results for each activity. But because many of the program activities for implementing human resource plans are developed by separate units or individuals, it is still necessary to develop standards and controls for separate activities, while recognizing the interdependence among units. The personnel department can then use the "bottom-line" evaluation to evaluate the performance of the total HRPP activity.

> Throughout this book, the term *bottom line* generally refers to a common index of how well the total organization is doing. Profitability is one example of such an index. When used in reference to equal employment practices, *bottom line* refers to how well the organization is doing at providing employment and advancement for all groups of employees. In essence, the bottom line in this case would indicate the quality of the organization's affirmative action and equal employment opportunity programs.

Behavioral Concerns

Behavioral problems frequently arise in an organization, sometimes because managers perceive the control devices as limits to their freedom to manage or as threats to their ability to perform. It is important, therefore, that devices and standards be developed with input from as many affected managers as possible. Furthermore, programs must be implemented and administered fairly, which can also be facilitated by managerial involvement in these processes.

Other behavioral problems arise because people tend to do what is rewarded and tend to avoid doing what is not rewarded. If evaluation procedures fail to cover all the necessary activities, then reward systems for some activities may not be developed. A closely related matter is the establishment of standards and goals that have a fair relationship to a task's level of difficulty.

Behavioral problems are not unique to HRPP activities; they are common to all personnel and human resource activities. The problems occur whenever evaluation and control procedures are established.

Legal Compliance

A final issue related to program control and evaluation is legal compliance. This issue continues to have a pervasive influence on organizations, and personnel departments can play a vital role in guiding legal compliance.

The most important legal regulations affecting human resource management are discussed in the chapters where they are most relevant, and Appendix B provides a skeletal outline of them. One of the most demanding aspects of legal regulation in HRPP is affirmative action. Because affirmative action also has a major impact on the selection process, it is discussed in detail in Chapter 7. In addition, an example of an affirmative action plan for a large organization is shown in Appendix C.

SUMMARY

"There is nothing we can do about the performance of past management or the qualifications of today's management. But tomorrow's management can be as good as today's managers are to make it."[33] This quote sums up the need for human resource planning and programming, at least for managerial employees. Of course, HRPP must also be implemented for entry-level and nonmanagerial employees, technical and professional employees.

The potential benefits from an effective planning and programming system include reduced personnel costs, better employee development, improved overall organizational planning, more opportunities for a better-balanced and more integrated work force, greater awareness of the importance of human resource management in the total organization, and tools to evaluate the effectiveness of alternative human resource actions and policies.

Careful attention to the four phases of HRPP will help ensure its effectiveness. The first phase is a determination of what the organization has and what it will be like in the future that can be used to develop a forecast of human resource needs. In the second phase, objectives and policies are developed for meeting these needs, but these objectives and policies must be compatible with the objectives of the organization. Then action programs must be developed and implemented in the third phase. To help ensure effectiveness of these programs, the fourth phase stipulates an evaluation of the implementation and administration of each program. On the basis of the results of the evaluation, the programs can then be modified or revised as necessary. There are several potential problems in each phase of the planning and programming activity, but they can be minimized by an alert personnel department.

The personnel functions and activities described in this chapter are dynamic and highly interdependent. In fact, it is somewhat artificial to treat each one separately.

PERSONNEL PROBLEM
Somebody's Got to Go

The Evermatic Company faces a dilemma not unlike the dilemma faced by many other organizations. Federal and state legislation is exerting pressure to extend compulsory retirement ages to seventy and beyond. There has been pressure in some areas to discard compulsory retirement altogether.

The problem is that Evermatic has a young work force with no place to go. There are precious few opportunities for advancement within the company as it is, because there are already so many senior employees. Furthermore, the company, although successful, is not rapidly expanding. As a result, Evermatic is losing more and more of their capable people to other organizations that have relatively more room for promotion.

The large picture, naturally, transcends Evermatic's immediate concerns. You may want to view this as a potential problem of national concern to personnel departments and governments alike.

1. What are the positive and negative implications of extending retirement ages in industry?

2. Is this a legitimate area of concern for the federal government?

3. On the local level, what would be best for Evermatic?

4. Who has the greater right—the younger worker who wants to advance or the older worker who wants to keep working?

KEY CONCEPTS

Delphi technique
human resource information
   system (HRIS)
human resource planning
   and programming (HRPP)

Markov model
multiple linear regression
   analysis
nominal grouping technique

replacement charts
simple linear regression
   analysis
unit demand forecasting

DISCUSSION QUESTIONS

1. Why should organizations have an effective human resource planning and programming (HRPP) activity?
2. Why have some organizations failed to implement an extensive HRPP activity?
3. What are the four phases of HRPP?
4. Discuss the relationships among human resource programming and other personnel functions and activities.
5. What are the techniques used to forecast the demand for human resources? Which are used most?
6. Why is it important that organizations forecast their human resource supply and needs?
7. Why has HRPP become so important recently?
8. What are the issues in the measurement of HRPP and other personnel functions and activities?

ENDNOTES

1. E. H. Burack and J. W. Walker (eds.),
    Manpower Planning and Programming (Boston:
    Allyn & Bacon, 1972), p. 55.

2. E. W. Vetter, *Manpower Planning for High
    Talent Personnel* (Ann Arbor, Mich.: Bureau of
    Industrial Relations, Graduate School of
    Business, The University of Michigan, 1967),
    p. 15.

3. Vetter, p. 15

4. Vetter, pp. 11–25.

5. E. H. Burack and T. J. McNichols, *Human
    Resources Planning, Technology, Policy Change*
    (Kent, Ohio: Comparative Administration
    Research Institute, 1973), p. 128.

6. E. H. Burack and T. G. Gutteridge,
    "Institutional Manpower Planning: Rhetoric
    Versus Reality," *California Management Review*,
    Spring 1978, pp. 13–22.

7. P. Zollman, "There's Jobs in Abundance for
    Americans with Skills," *Columbus Dispatch*, 20
    May 1979, UPI Business Writer, sec. C, pp. 1,
    8. Reprinted by permission of United Press
    International.

8. Zollman, sec. C, p. 8.

9. Zollman, sec. C, p. 8.

10. Zollman, sec. C, p. 8

11. Vetter, p. 118.

12. Zollman, sec. C, p. 8.

13. Burack and Gutteridge, p. 17.

14. J. B. Paperman and D. D. Martin, "Human
    Resource Accounting: A Managerial Tool?"
    Personnel, March/April 1977, pp. 41–50.

15. E. H. Burack and T. G. Gutteridge,
    "Institutional Manpower Planning: Rhetoric
    Versus Reality," © 1978 by the Regents of the
    University of California. Reprinted from
    California Management Review, Vol. XX, no. 3,
    p. 14 by permission of the Regents.

16. Vetter, p. 15.

17. P. S. Greenlaw and W. D. Biggs, *Modern
    Personnel Management* (Philadelphia: Saunders,
    1979), p. 83.

18. A. C. Hyde and J. M. Shafritz, "HRIS:
    Introduction to Tomorrow's System for Managing
    Human Resources," p. 70. Reprinted with
    permission from the March/April 1977 issue of
    Public Personnel Management copyright 1977,
    International Personnel Management Association,
    1850 K. Street, N. W., Washington, D. C.
    20006.

19. Hyde and Shafritz, pp. 71–72.

20. "A Guide for Building a Human Resource Data
    System," by V. R. Ceriello, p. 497. Reprinted
    with permission *Personnel Journal*, Costa Mesa,
    CA, copyright September 1978.

21. M. J. Gannon, *Organizational Behavior* (Boston:
    Little, Brown, 1979), p. 97.

22. "Forecasters Turn to Group Guesswork,"
    Business Week, March 14, 1970, p. 130.

23. Greenlaw and Biggs, p. 87.

24. G. Milkovich and T. Mahoney, "Human
    Resources Planning and PAIR Policy," in Dale
    Yoder and Herbert Heneman (eds.), *PAIR
    Handbook*, Vol. 4 (Berea, Ohio: American
    Society of Personnel Administrators, 1976).

25. Greenlaw and Biggs, p. 85.

26. Vetter, p. 35.

27. Burack and Gutteridge, p. 20.

28. Burack and Gutteridge, p.20.

29. Burack and Gutteridge, p. 18.

30. Burack and Gutteridge cite a 1971 survey,
    Corporate Manpower Planning, conducted by
    Towers, Perrin, Foster, and Crosby (TPF&C).

31. Vetter, pp. 30–32.

32. Vetter, p. 67.

33. R. M. Besse, Tomorrow's Managers, address
    before the Edison Electric Institute, New York
    City, 7 June 1967.

CHAPTER OUTLINE

OBJECTIVES

- To discuss the relationships among organizational technology, goals, job design, and job analysis

- To identify the purposes of job analysis

- To discuss the problems in collecting job information

- To explain how job descriptions are written

THOUGHT STARTERS

- What is a job description?

- What are job specifications?

- What is job design?

- Why is job analysis so important?

CHAPTER FOUR
Job Analysis

The Dashman Company was a large concern making many types of equipment for the armed forces of the United States. It had over twenty plants, located in the central part of the country, whose purchasing procedures had never been completely co-ordinated. In fact, the head office of the company had encouraged the plant managers to operate with their staffs as separate, independent units in most matters. Late in 1940, when it began to appear that the company would face increasing difficulty in securing certain essential raw materials, Mr. Manson, the company's president, appointed an experienced purchasing executive, Mr. Post, as vice president in charge of purchasing, a position especially created for him. Manson gave Post wide latitude in organizing his job, and he assigned Mr. Larson as Post's assistant. Larson had served the company in a variety of capacities for many years and knew most of the plant executives personally. Post's appointment was announced through the formal channels usual in the company, including a notice in the house organ which was published monthly by the Dashman Company.

One of Post's first decisions was to begin immediately to centralize the company's purchasing procedure. As a first step, he decided that he would require each of the executives who handled purchasing in the individual plants to clear with the head office all purchase contracts which they made in excess of $10,000. He felt that if the head office was to do any co-ordinating in a way that would be helpful to each plant and to the company as a whole, he must be notified that the contracts were being prepared at least a week before they were to be signed. He talked his proposal over with Manson, who presented it to the board of directors. They approved the plan.

Although the company made purchases throughout the year, the beginning of its peak buying season was only three weeks away at the time this new plan was adopted. Post prepared a letter to be sent to the twenty purchasing executives of the company. The letter follows:

Dear ―――――――

The board of directors of our company has recently authorized a change in our purchasing procedures. Hereafter, each of the purchasing executives in the several plants of the company will notify the vice president in charge of purchasing of all contracts in excess of $10,000 which they are negotiating, at least a week in advance of the date on which they are to be signed.

I am sure you will understand that this step is necessary to co-ordinate the purchasing requirements of the company in these times when we are facing increasing difficulty in securing essential supplies. This procedure should give us in the central office the information we need to see that each plant secures the optimum supply of materials. In this way the interests of each plant and of the company as a whole will best be served.

Yours very truly,

Post showed the letter to Larson and invited his comments. Larson thought the letter an excellent one, but suggested that since Post had not met more than a few of the purchasing executives, he might like to visit all of them and take the matter up with them personally. Post dismissed the idea at once because, as he said, he had so many things to do at the head office that he could not get away for a trip. Consequently, he had the letters sent out over his signature

During the two following weeks, replies came in from all except a few plants. Although a few executives wrote at greater length, the following reply was typical:

Dear Mr. Post:

Your recent communication in regard to notifying the head office a week in advance of our intention to sign contracts has been received. This suggestion seems a most practical one. We want to assure you that you can count on our co-operation.

Yours very truly,

During the next six weeks, the head office received no notices from any plant that contracts were being negotiated. Executives in other departments, who made frequent trips to the plants, reported that the plants were busy, and the usual routines for that time of year were being followed. It appeared, however, as if Mr. Post's wishes were not being followed. Can you explain why?

Dashman Company, case 9-642-001. Copyright © 1947 by the President and Fellows of Harvard College. Reproduced by permission. The case was prepared by George F. F. Lombard.

T his scenario illustrates nicely what can happen when a new activity requested of employees is not clearly spelled out or is not formally made a part of their job description. Although the plant purchasing managers' failure to comply with Mr. Post's new directive may just be an example of resistance to change, a careful analysis of the scenario suggests that they were really unaware of what was expected of them and why they had to do it, how they could comply, what performance standards existed, and what were the rewards for compliance. All of these concepts are a part of job and organizational analysis. However, the managers also probably saw the one major disadvantage of complying, and that was the loss of power and control to Mr. Post at central headquarters. Perhaps Post failed to consider that his request really involved a change in organizational structure—from fairly decentralized to fairly centralized. You might have guessed that compliance with Post's new directive was unlikely because of the lack of information and because the managers would have been unable to fulfill their needs for self-control and responsibility.

The reality of organizational operations is that for anything to get done, it must get done through people. And those people are generally as interested in satisfying their own needs and goals as they are interested in satisfying those of the organization. Furthermore, a task that appears simple is frequently embedded in vague and ambiguous expectations and performance standards and hampered by conflicting rewards and punishments for performing the task. Therefore, in describing what tasks employees must perform and what qualifications they must have to do it (job analysis, in essence), it is necessary to discuss the impact of the organization (organizational analysis). Reflecting the importance of job and organizational analysis in understanding what employees actually do, the plan of this chapter is to examine job analysis, including its purposes, methods, and techniques, and then to examine the organizational context in which job analysis takes place. Examination of the organizational context includes a discussion of job design and worker rewards as well as organization design and organization goals.

ANALYZING JOBS

In large part, many of the functions and activities of personnel management and the behaviors and attitudes of employees have their roots at the interface of employees and their jobs. As indicated in Exhibit 4.1, job analysis influences staffing, compensation, training and development, quality of work life, and labor-management relations.

It has been proposed that about half the behavior in organizations is due to individual differences and the other half to situational variables, some of which pertain to the nature of the job and some of which pertain to aspects of the organization. Therefore, many of the personnel "problems" in organizations, such as turnover, absenteeism, and low performance, can only be solved with consideration for the nature of the tasks. But in order to seriously consider the nature of the tasks, the personnel department must know what the tasks are all about. In other words, the jobs must be analyzed.

Job analysis is "the process of determining by observation and study . . . the tasks that comprise the job and the skills, knowledge, abilities, and responsibilities

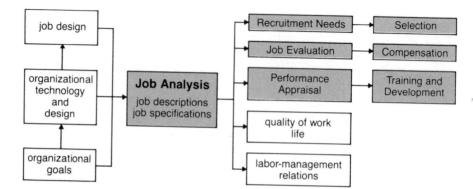

Exhibit 4.1   The Relationship of Job Analysis to Other Personnel Activities

required of the worker for successful performance."[1] A comprehensive list of the type of information that can be elicited by job analysis procedures is shown in Exhibit 4.2.

Often job analysis results in written job descriptions and specifications. A **job description** is a written statement about the tasks, duties, activities, and results associated with a given job. The **job specifications** describe the skills, abilities, traits, or attributes an individual should have to perform the tasks, duties, and activities in order to attain at a satisfactory level the results desired by the organization.

The Purposes of Job Analysis

As shown in Exhibit 4.1, the job-related information obtained through job analysis can be used to influence several personnel functions and activities. A more specific enumeration of the functions and activities partially influenced by job analysis is presented in Exhibit 4.3. An organization rarely uses job analysis for all these purposes, but the expanse of the list suggests the importance of job analysis in an organization.

The importance of the job description document lies in the fact that it is a key element in the personnel subsystem. The rationale for its existence is that the personnel activities cannot be implemented effectively without it. Similarly, the ineffective operation of the personnel area will have repercussions throughout the entire organization.[2]

The particular purposes of job analysis an organization wishes to attain help determine the information to be gathered. For example, information on personnel requirements can be used to help determine the organization's training needs. In addition, the level of detail in the job analysis may reflect characteristics of the organization as well as the job. Managerial positions may be described in more general terms than nonmanagerial positions. Relatively stable positions can be described in more detail than positions that are changing rapidly. The purposes of job analysis also help determine the methods for collecting information.

Exhibit 4.2 Types of Information Obtained through Job Analysis

Work Activities
Job-oriented activities (usually expressed in terms of what is accomplished; sometimes indicating how, why, and when a worker performs the activity)
    work activities/processes
    procedures used
    activity records (films, etc.)
    personal accountability/responsibility
Worker-oriented activities
    human behaviors performed in work (sensing, decision making, performing physical actions, communicating, etc.)
    elemental motions (such as those used in methods analysis)
    personal job demands (energy expenditure, etc.)

Machines, Tools, Equipment, and Work Aids Used

Job-Related Tangibles and Intangibles
Materials processed
Products made
Knowledge dealt with or applied (such as law or chemistry)
Services rendered (such as laundering or repairing)

Work Performance
Work measurement (time taken)
Work standards
Error analysis
Other aspects

Job Context
Physical working conditions
Work schedule
Organizational context
Social context
Incentives (financial and nonfinancial)

Personnel Requirements
Job-related knowledge/skills (education, training, work experience, etc.)
Personal attributes (aptitudes, physical characteristics, personality, interests, etc.)

Adapted from E. J. McCormick, "Job and Task Analysis," in M. D. Dunnette (ed.), *Handbook of Industrial and Organizational Psychology*, copyright © 1976 by Rand McNally College Publishing Company, p. 653.

Job Analysis and Other Personnel Functions

Because job analysis serves so many purposes, it has extensive relationships with several other personnel and human resource management activities. For example, on the basis of job analysis and in conjunction with HRPP, the organization knows who to recruit. Only with job analysis information can an organization show that its selection procedures are job-related. To effectively evaluate employee performance, the appraisal method that is used must reflect the duties of the job. (This relationship is discussed again in Chapter 9.) And only by examining the skills required for a job (as defined in the job specifications) can the organization train and promote employees.

Job analysis also plays a vital role in one of the most important concerns of individuals in organizations—pay. It is on the basis of the job analysis that jobs are

Exhibit 4.3   Purposes of Job Analysis

Individual
Vocational guidance
Vocational preparation

Organization
Human resource planning
Job design
Job evaluation
Recruiting
Selection and placement
Training
Personnel appraisal

Labor Relations
Management-union relations

Public Policy and Administration
Legal aspects (standards, licensing, certification, etc.)
Public employment services
Public training and education programs
Social security administration
Safety programs

Research
Population analysis (economic, social, etc.)
Behavioral research related to job or occupational characteristics
Validation of selection test and performance appraisal form

Adapted from E. J. McCormick, "Job and Task Analysis," in M. D. Dunnette (ed.), *Handbook of Industrial and Organizational Psychology*, copyright © 1976 by Rand McNally College Publishing Company, p. 683.

evaluated. Since job evaluation determines the worth or value of a job to the organization, it often determines how much an employee gets paid for doing that job. Job analysis is also important in ensuring that the level of pay for a job is fair in relationship to other jobs. That is, job analysis helps ensure that employees in jobs of equal worth receive the same pay.

Who's Responsible for Job Analysis?

The responsibility for job analysis lies with top management, the line managers, and the personnel manager. More recently, employees have been assuming some responsibility through writing their own job descriptions.

As in HRPP, top management plays a critical role. Without support from top management (meaning authority), the personnel manager can have a difficult time getting the cooperation from line managers that is necessary to make job analysis effective. Cooperation can be difficult, however, because job analysis is so important in determining the value of jobs and thus how much people will be paid for doing them. Line managers often try to get the jobs of their employees evaluated higher so that they can get more money to give the employees.

In addition to providing information for job analysis, line managers may also play a role in initiating job analysis. Generally, when line managers want a job analysis done, they ask the personnel manager to come and do it. The personnel manager gathers the necessary information, writes the job descriptions and specifications, and then gives them back to the line manager.

An important part of this personnel role is that it be done within the constraints of the organization. That is, the job analysis must be done with the same standards and methods for all managers in order to ensure fairness.

COLLECTING JOB INFORMATION

Exhibit 4.4 lists eleven methods for collecting job information. The people who have traditionally gathered this information are job analysts, supervisors, or both.

Job information is usually gathered for at least four major categories of positions:

- *Nonsupervisory, not office workers:* Hourly rated, **nonexempt** (the employer pays for any overtime work)
- *Nonsupervisory office workers:* Salaried, nonexempt
- *Supervisory, technical, and office employees:* Salaried, **exempt** (the employer does not pay for overtime work)
- *Managerial, executive, and professional employees:* Salaried, exempt

However, not all organizations have job descriptions for all four groups of employees. Job descriptions have traditionally been used only for hourly rated employees. But as it becomes necessary for organizations to demonstrate that their selection procedures (measures to predict performance) are related to the skills required to perform the job, more are writing job descriptions for all four groups of employees. It is also becoming more common for the job incumbent (the person presently in the position) to describe the job.

Exhibit 4.4   Methods for Collecting Job Information

Observation

Interview with job incumbent

Interview with several job incumbents as a group

Technical conference with experienced personnel

Structured questionnaire

Open-ended questionnaire

Diary

Critical incidents (records of worker behaviors that are "critical" for very good or very poor job performance)

Equipment design information (blueprints and other design data of equipment being developed)

Recordings of job activities (films, mechanical recordings of certain job activities, etc.)

Available records (maintenance records, etc.)

Adapted from E. J. McCormick, "Job and Task Analysis," in M. D. Dunnette (ed.), *Handbook of Industrial and Organizational Psychology,* copyright © 1976 by Rand McNally College Publishing Company, p. 683.

Observing Behaviors

Perhaps "the central role or purpose of job analysis information is to provide the basic clues for choosing potentially useful predictor measures and for developing the measures of job behavior we desire to predict."[3] Therefore, it is mandatory to gather job information that is behavior-oriented. It is easier to make behavior-centered statements if jobs are defined in terms of work tasks rather than job titles. For example, the behavioral requirements for a sales job include the ability to present ideas forcefully, operate comfortably under time pressure, originate new approaches to selling, ask for an order without reluctance, and discern accurately the reactions and feelings of customers and prospects.[4]

Without awareness of the behaviors required for a particular job and the changes occurring on the job, it is difficult to accurately predict who will be successful in it. There are several methods for ensuring that the important behaviors get observed and for determining their relative frequencies—including extensive sampling, interviewing employees and supervisors, and recording the critical incidents (the behaviors that are especially important to the position).

Sources of Error

There are several sources of potential error in behavioral observation. Being aware of them is a first step to reducing or eliminating them. One of these errors is inadequate sampling. Too few observations may result in a deficient description. Too many behavioral observations, some of which really do not belong to the job, result in a set of observations that are contaminated.

Other errors result from the observer's lack of knowledge, understanding, or rapport or from plain resistance. For example, if a supervisor is asked to observe the behaviors of employees and really does not want to cooperate or has only a limited chance to observe the employees, he or she may make a number of errors.[5] Specific types of errors are described more fully in Chapter 9.

JOB ANALYSIS TECHNIQUES

The conventional job analysis programs used in many organizations typically involve the collection of job-related information by observation of and/or interview with job incumbents, and the preparation of job descriptions that usually are written in essay form.[6]

The major components of these job descriptions are
- Job or payroll title
- Job number and job group the job belongs to (as a result of job evaluation and for compensation purposes)
- Department and/or division where the job is located
- Name of the incumbent (optional) and name of the job analyst
- Primary function or summary of the job
- Description of the major duties and responsibilities of the job, sometimes with a percentage of time for each duty

A conventional job analysis may also include a list of worker traits or abilities required for the job and a description of the physical demands and the environmental conditions that the job has to be performed in. Exhibit 4.5 is a conventional job description for a secretary to the manager of marketing research in a fictitious company.

Another aspect of most conventional job descriptions is a common writing style, which is described in the *Handbook for Analyzing Jobs* as follows:

● *A terse, direct style should be used.*

● *The present tense should be used throughout.*

● *Each sentence should begin with an active verb.*

● *Each sentence must reflect an objective, either specifically stated or implied in such manner as to be obvious to the reader. A single verb may sometimes reflect both objective and worker action.*

● *All words should impart necessary information; others should be omitted. Every precaution should be taken to use words that have only one possible connotation and that specifically describe the manner in which the work is accomplished.*

● *The description of tasks should reflect the assigned work performed and worker traits ratings.*[7]

Even though this straightforward, simplistic writing style pervades most conventional job descriptions, there is still some problem in conveying the meaning that is intended. Nevertheless, because the conventional technique is relatively easy to use, you are likely to find it in many organizations today. But there have been several more structured and systematic techniques developed to prevent reader misunderstanding of job descriptions.

Structured Job Analysis

The study of human work probably has not generally benefitted from the systematic, scientific approaches that have been characteristic of other domains of inquiry, such as the study of physical phenomena, biological phenomena, or of the behavior of man himself (as through psychological and sociological research). The study of human work during the bygone years, however, has not been entirely unsystematic and lacking in the scientific approach.[8]

Structured job analysis is the use of a standard format for job descriptions so that all organizations can use the same job categories. The most common approaches for structured job analysis are functional job analysis, the position analysis questionnaire, the management position description questionnaire, and the Hay plan. Once organizations start using similar methods to analyze jobs, they can (among other things) exchange compensation information and develop more valid methods of recruitment, selection, and performance appraisal.

Functional Job Analysis (FJA).   The United States Training and Employment Service (USTES) developed **functional job analysis** to describe the nature of jobs and to develop job summaries, job descriptions, and employee specifications. FJA, originally meant to improve job placement and counseling for workers registering for employment at local employment offices, was part of an intensive research

JOB DESCRIPTION FOR SALARIED POSITIONS		Job Group V	Job Number DO501

Secretary			
PAYROLL TITLE	NAME		
Mgr., Marketing Research			
SUPERVISOR'S TITLE	NAME		
Corporate	Marketing		October 18, 1977
DIVISION	DEPARTMENT		DATE

DUTIES OF JOB (list in order of importance)	Percentage of time

PRIMARY FUNCTION

Provide secretarial assistance to the Manager of Marketing Research by maintaining files and library data, typing, and recording expense information

MAJOR DUTIES AND RESPONSIBILITIES

1. Typing   40
   a. Type letters, memos, marketing research reports, statistical data, etc.
   b. Take and transcribe dication; type from machine dictation

2. Files   20
   a. Maintain departmental filing system for marketing reports, correspondence, customer and sales report data, etc.
   b. Maintain index source file to record file locations of material

3. Library   20
   a. Maintain departmental library of all reference material, such as D & B reports, annual reports, research agencies and data, conference board publications, directories, periodicals, etc.
   b. Maintain library loan bank to record who has material outside of department
   c. Get material from library and return information to proper location as necessary

4. Expenses   5
   a. Process departmental travel expense reports
   b. Forward invoices for payment and record expenses onto departmental expense sheets; maintain monthly total for each subaccount

5. Miscellaneous   15
   a. Open, sort, and distribute departmental mail
   b. Answer telephone, respond to questions about library information
   c. Order office supplies
   d. Perform related duties as required

THE ABOVE STATEMENT REFLECTS THE GENERAL DETAILS CONSIDERED NECESSARY TO DESCRIBE THE PRINCIPAL FUNCTION OF THE JOB IDENTIFIED AND SHALL NOT BE CONSTRUED AS A DETAILED DESCRIPTION OF ALL THE WORK REQUIREMENTS THAT MAY BE INHERENT IN THE JOB.

Exhibit 4.5   Sample of a Conventional Job Description

program directed toward producing the 1965 edition of the ***Dictionary of Occupational Titles (DOT).*** Today, many aspects of FJA are used by a number of private and public organizations.[9]

FJA is both a conceptual system for defining the dimensions of worker activity and a method of measuring levels of worker activity.[10] The fundamental premises of FJA:

- A fundamental distinction must be made between what gets done and what workers do to get things done. Bus drivers do not carry passengers; they drive vehicles and collect fares.
- Jobs are concerned with data, people, and things.
- In relation to things, workers draw on physical resources; in relation to data, on mental resources; and in relation to people, on interpersonal resources.
- All jobs require the worker to relate to data, people, and things to some degree.
- Although the behavior of workers or the tasks they perform can apparently be described in an infinite number of ways, there are only a few definitive functions involved. Thus, in interacting with machines, workers feed, tend, operate, and set up; in the case of vehicles or related machines, they drive or control them. Although these functions vary in difficulty and content, each draws on a relatively narrow and specific range of worker characteristics and qualifications for effective performance.
- The functions appropriate to dealing with data, people, or things are hierarchical and ordinal, proceeding from the simple to the complex. Thus to indicate that a particular function, say compiling (data), reflects the requirements of a job is to say that it also includes the requirements of lower functions, such as comparing, and that it excludes the requirements of higher functions, such as analyzing.[11]

The worker functions associated with data, people, and things are listed in Exhibit 4.6. The USTES has used these worker functions as a basis for describing over 30,000 job titles in the *Dictionary of Occupational Titles.*

The USTES has also used worker trait ratings and job summaries to develop job analysis schedules for each job title. An example, for a dough mixer, appears in Exhibit 4.7. A brief explanation of item 5 can illustrate the use of job analysis schedules, In item 5, worker functions in relation to data, people, and things are

Exhibit 4.6   Functions Associated with Data, People, and Things

Data	People	Things
0 synthesizing	0 mentoring	0 setting up
1 coordinating	1 negotiating	1 precision working
2 analyzing	2 instructing	2 operating-controlling
3 compiling	3 supervising	3 driving-operating
4 computing	4 diverting	4 manipulating
5 copying	5 persuading	5 tending
6 comparing	6 speaking-signaling	6 feeding-offbearing
	7 serving	7 handling
	8 taking instructions-helping	

Adapted from U.S. Department of Labor, Employment Service, Training and Development Administration, *Handbook for Analyzing Jobs* (Washington, D.C.: Government Printing Office, 1972), p. 73.

U.S. Department of Labor   OMB 11-RO722
(USTES)   Estab. & Sched. No. 522-146-3-10

JOB ANALYSIS SCHEDULE

1. Estab. Job Title _____ DOUGH MIXER _____

2. Ind. Assn. _____ (bake prod.) _____

3. SIC Code(s) and Title(s) _____ 2051 Bread and other bakery products _____

4. JOB SUMMARY:

Operates mixing machine to mix ingredients for
straight and sponge (yeast) doughs according to
established formulas, directs other workers in
fermentation of dough, and cuts dough into pieces
with hand cutter

5. WORK PERFORMED RATINGS:

	D	P	(T)
Worker Functions	Data	People	Things
Work Field	5	6	2

M.P.S.M.S. _____

6. WORKER TRAIT RATINGS:

GED   1 (2) 3 4 5 6

SVP   1 2 3 (4) 5 6 7 8 9

Aptitudes $G\underline{3}$ $V\underline{3}$ $N\underline{3}$ $S\underline{3}$ $P\underline{3}$ $Q\underline{4}$ $K\underline{3}$ $F\underline{3}$ $M\underline{3}$ $E\underline{4}$ $C\underline{4}$

Temperaments D F I J (M) P R S (T) V

Interests (1a) 1b 2a 2b 3a 3b 4a (4b) 5a (5b)

Phys. Demands S L M (H) V 2 (3) (4) 5 (6)

Environ. Cond. (1) 0 B 2 3 4 (5) 6 7

MA-7-36

Exhibit 4.7 Sample Job Analysis Schedule

Exhibit 4.8 Sample Work Field*

Cooking—Food Preparing

Preparing foods for human or animal consumption by any combination of methods, which may include methods specific to other work fields, such as *Baking-Drying, Mixing, Shearing-Shaving, Stock Checking,* and *Weighing.*

Methods Verbs

Basting	Curing	Measuring	Roasting
Boiling	Flavoring	Pasteurizing	Rolling
Brewing	Frying	Pickling	Seasoning
Churning	Heating	Rendering	Spreading
		Kneading	

Machines	**Tools**	**Equipment**	**Work Aids**
Continuous churn	Cutters	Cleaver Broilers	Charts
Pasteurizer	Forks	Grills	Dishes
Vane churn	Ice Picks	Ovens Hoppers	Mixing bowls
	Knives	Ranges Kettles	Pans
	Paddles	Roasters	Pots
	Sifters	Smoke chambers	Recipes
	Spatulas	Steam digesters	Storage bin
	Spoons	Storage tank	

Controls battery of smoke chambers in which such meat products as bacon, hams, meat loaf, sausage, shoulders, and weiners are cooked and cured.

Mixes and bakes ingredients, according to recipes, to produce breads, pastries, and other baked goods.

Mixes, cooks, and freezes ingredients to prepare frozen desserts such as sherbets, ice cream, and custards.

Operates ovens to roast dry breakfast cereals made from corn, rice, bran, and oats.

Plans menus and cooks meals in private home, according to recipes or tastes of employer.

Adapted from U.S. Department of Labor, Employment Service, Training and Development Administration, *Handbook for Analyzing Jobs* (Washington, D.C.: Government Printing Office, 1972), pp. 121–122.
*The work field for any given job is entered in the job analysis schedule (see Exhibit 4.7) in space 5, Work Performed Ratings.

coded in the terms shown in Exhibit 4.6. For instance, a dough mixer must be able to copy data. In the space for listing the work field, the job analyst indicates what a dough mixer may have to do. There are several work fields for any specific job. An appropriate work field for a dough mixer is shown in Exhibit 4.8. Finally, the M.P.S.M.S. section (item 5 in Exhibit 4.7) refers to the materials, products, subject matter, and services related to a job. Entries are taken from a list similar to that for work fields.

Item 6 in Exhibit 4.7 refers to worker trait ratings. The codes are too complex to explain here, but they indicate the qualities a worker should have for the job. These include

- Experience (job knowledge)
- Training and education (level, type, time)

- Physical characteristics (strength, coordination, senses)
- Manual and manipulative skills (dexterity, accuracy)
- Mental skills (adaptability, judgment, initiative, creativity, technical)
- Aptitudes (type, level)
- Interests and motivation (activity preferences)
- Personality (adjustment to job situations)
- Social skills (human interactions)

For each of these worker traits there is a specific rating scale, all of which appear in the *Handbook for Analyzing Jobs*.

A personnel manager who has to prepare job descriptions and job specifications may start with the *Dictionary of Occupational Titles* to determine the general job analysis information and use the *Handbook for Analyzing Jobs* for more specific information. A job analysis based on these two books can be used for human resource planning, recruitment, selection, placement, performance evaluation, training, and job design.

McCormick's Position Analysis Questionnaire (PAQ).   Although the FJA approach is complete, it requires considerable training to use well and is quite narrative in nature.[12] The narrative portions tend to be less reliable than more quantitative approaches, such as the **position analysis questionnaire**, which describes jobs in terms of worker activities. The six activities analyzed in the PAQ are

- *Information input:* Where and how does the worker get the information used in performing the job? Examples are the use of written materials and near-visual differentiation.
- *Mental processes:* What reasoning, decision-making, planning, and information-processing activities are involved in performing the job? Examples are the level of reasoning in problem solving and coding/decoding.
- *Work output:* What physical activities does the worker perform, and what tools or devices are used? Examples are the use of keyboard devices and assembling/disassembling.
- *Relationships with other people:* What relationships with other people are required in performing the job? Examples are instructing and contacts with the public or customers.
- *Job context:* In what physical or social contexts is the work performed? Examples are high temperature and interpersonal conflict situations.
- *Other job characteristics:* What other activities, conditions, or characteristics are relevant to the job?[13]

The PAQ rates each job on the basis of 194 descriptors related to these six activities.

In FJA the nature of jobs is essentially determined in terms of data, people, and things. In the PAQ the nature of jobs is essentially determined in terms of communication/decision making/social responsibilities; performance of skilled activities; physical activity and related environmental conditions; operation of vehicles and equipment; and processing of information. Using these five dimensions, jobs can be compared and clustered. The job clusters can then be used for, among other things, staffing decisions and the development of job descriptions and specifications.

The PAQ's reliance on person-oriented traits allows it to be applied across a variety of jobs and organizations without modification. This, of course, allows organizations to more easily compare their job analyses with those of other organizations.

The major drawback in adopting the PAQ is its sheer length, even though its checklist format helps speed up the analysis process.

Management Position Description Questionnaire (MPDQ). The MPDQ is another method of job analysis that relies upon the checklist method to analyze jobs. It contains 208 items related to the concerns and responsibilities of managers, their demands and restrictions, and miscellaneous characteristics.[14] These 208 items have been condensed into thirteen job factors:
- Product, market, and financial planning
- Coordination of other organizational units and personnel
- Internal business control
- Products and services responsibility
- Public and customer relations
- Advanced consulting
- Autonomy of action
- Approval of financial commitments
- Staff service
- Supervision
- Complexity and stress
- Advanced financial responsibility
- Broad personnel responsibility

The MPDQ is designed for managerial positions, but responses to the items vary by managerial level in any organization and also in different organizations. The MPDQ is appropriate for determining the training needs of employees moving into managerial jobs; evaluating managerial jobs; creating job families and placing new managerial jobs into the right job family; and compensating managerial jobs.

The Hay Plan. Another method of analyzing managerial jobs is the **Hay plan**, which is used in a large number of organizations. Although much less structured than the MPDQ and PAQ, it is systematically tied into a job evaluation and compensation system. Thus use of the Hay plan allows an organization to maintain consistency not only in how it describes managerial jobs but also in how it rewards them. The purposes of the Hay plan are management development, placement, and recruitment; job evaluation; measurement of the execution of a job against specific standards of accountability; and organization analysis.

The Hay plan is based on an interview between the job analyst and the job incumbent. The information that is gathered relates to four aspects of the incumbent's job: the objectives, the dimensions, the nature and scope of the position, and the accountability objectives. Information about the objectives allows the reader of the job description to know why the job exists in the organization and for what reason it is paid. Information about dimensions conveys to the reader how big a "show" the incumbent runs and the magnitude of the end results affected by his or her actions.

The real heart of the Hay job description is the information about the nature and scope of the position, which covers five crucial aspects:
- How the position fits into the organization, including reference to significant organizational and outside relationships.

● The general composition of supporting staff. This includes a thumbnail sketch of each major function of any staff under the incumbent's position—size, type, and the reason for its existence.

● The general nature of the technical, managerial, and human relations know-how required.

● The nature of the problem solving required: What are the key problems that must be solved by this job, and how variable are they?

● The nature and source of control on the freedom to solve problems and act, whether supervisory, procedural, or vocational or professional.

Information related to the accountability objectives tells what end results the job exists to achieve and the incumbent is held accountable for. There are four areas of accountability: organization (including staffing, developing, and maintaining the organization); strategic planning; tactical planning, execution, and directing the attainment of objectives; and review and control.

Because the Hay plan is based on information gathered in an interview (as opposed to the checklist method in the MPDQ), the success of the plan depends upon the skills of the interviewer. Interviewers can be trained, however, and the Hay plan grows in popularity.

Methods Analysis

Conventional job analysis procedures and structured procedures generally focus on describing the job and its general duties, the conditions under which the duties are performed, and the levels of authority, accountability, and know-how required. Equally important, however, is a description of how to do the job as efficiently and effectively as possible. This is the purpose of methods analyses. Although methods analysis could be used for many jobs, it is more frequently applied to nonmanagerial jobs. In these jobs, individual activity units can often be identified more readily.

Methods analysis, or motion study, had its origins in industrial engineering. Some of the principles it is based on:

● *The movements of the two hands should be balanced and the two hands should begin and end their motions simultaneously.*

● *The hands should be doing productive work and should not be idle at the same time except during rest periods.*

● *Motions of the hands should be made in opposite and symmetrical directions and at the same time.*

● *The work should be arranged to permit it to be performed with an easy and natural rhythm.*

● *Momentum and ballistic-type movements should be employed wherever possible to reduce muscular effort.*

● *There should be a definite location for all tools and materials, and they should be located in front of and close to the worker.*

● *Bins or other devices should be used to deliver the materials close to the point of use.*

● *The workplace should be designed to insure adequate illumination, proper work-place height, and provision for alternated standing and sitting by the operator.*

A SLICE OF LIFE

In the analysis of methods and tasks, it is one thing to describe the duties of a particular job and the means for efficiently and effectively accomplishing that job and another thing to impose these as guidelines on employees. Such descriptions often lead to constraints on employee behavior. How often have you heard someone say, "That's not in my (your) job description"?

Similarly, describing how a job might be done efficiently and effectively is quite different from insisting that the job be done only that way. Formalization is the description of appropriate behavior in writing; standardization prescribes or limits behavior and procedures for employees on a particular job. Formalization in this sense may take the form of a job description outlining activities in a job classification. For example, "the assistant personnel managers will be responsible for testing prospective employees." Notice that although this written statement describes a certain behavior expected of any person in the classification, it does not limit or prescribe the procedures for fulfilling the responsibility. Standardization would specifically outline the procedures for testing prospective employees. Formalization, then, is what one is asked to do; standardization is how one is to do it.

Ordinarily, employees have no problem with formalization. In fact, without a minimum level of formalization, employees may not know what to do (role ambiguity), and this may affect their attitudes and performance. On the other hand, excessive formalization and standardization may limit job scope, resulting in boredom, alienation, job dissatisfaction, absenteeism, turnover, and low output. Task and methods analysis must be done carefully, especially when it is used to direct, rather than describe, employee behavior. The optimal level of formalization and standardization reduces role ambiguity yet maintains reasonable levels of job interest.

In the classroom environment, for example, the assignment to write a paper or to read several chapters is appropriate. But how would you feel if you were told exactly how many pages you had to read, exactly how many footnotes you had to write, exactly how much time you had to spend in the library, and exactly how the paper had to be typed? What if the instructor was prepared to carefully check all these demands? You would probably be quite upset. Do you think the instructor who issued these guidelines would get better papers from the class?

● *Wherever possible, jigs, fixtures, or other mechanical devices should be used to relieve the hands of unnecessary work.*

● *Tools should be pre-positioned wherever possible in order to facilitate grasping them.*[15]

Proper application of these principles results, according to the industrial engineers, in greater motion economy and working efficiency.

Work Measurement.   One form of methods analysis is **work measurement** or **time study**. In essence, work measurement determines standard times for all units of work activity in a given task or job. Combining these times gives a standard time for the entire job. These standard times can be used as a basis for wage-incentive plans (incentives generally are given for work performance that takes less than the standard time), cost determination, cost estimates for new products, and balancing production lines and work crews.[16] Establishing standard times is a challenge of some consequence, since the time it takes to do a job can be influenced as much by the individual doing the job as by the nature of the job itself. Consequently, determining standard times often requires measurement of the "actual effort" the individual is exerting and the "real effort" required. This process, as you can imagine, often means trying to outguess someone.

Common methods of collecting time data and determining standard times include the stopwatch time studies, standard data, predetermined time systems, and work sampling for determining standard time.

Work Sampling.   **Work sampling** is not only a technique for determining standard times but also another form of methods analysis. "Work sampling is the process of taking instantaneous samples of the work activities of individuals or groups of individuals."[17] The activities from these observations are timed and classified into predetermined categories. The result is a description of the activities by classification of a job and the percentage of time for each activity.

Work sampling can be done in several ways: The job analyst can observe the incumbent at predetermined times; a camera can be set to take photographs at predetermined times; or at a given signal, all incumbents can record their activity at that moment.

Work sampling lends itself to use in many types of jobs. Exhibit 4.9 shows its use with two different types of managerial jobs.

Improving Conventional Job Analysis

Despite the availability of all these alternative methods of job analaysis, conventional job analysis and job descriptions like the one in Exhibit 4.5 remain the most popular. They are quick and easy to prepare. They are, however, far from perfect.

This job description is deficient in two respects: It does not specify the performance expected of the employee, and it does not specify the linking or enabling relationship between standards, skills and minimum qualifications. It lists only the general duties performed by any number of incumbents because it applies to a range of positions. Second, there are no clues provided concerning the conditions under which the job is to be performed. For example, is an electric typewriter available or not? Most critically, there are no standards set for minimally acceptable employee performance of each of the duties of a position.

Moreover, conventional job descriptions specify a general set of minimum qualifications for each position. If jobs have been classified according to the type of skill required, these minimum qualifications may be based on skills required to

Exhibit 4.9   Results of a Work Sampling Study

Activity	Percentage of Time in Activity	
	Top managers*	Operating managers†
Talking (oral communication)		
Consulting with colleagues	10.5	3.6
Deciding on course of action	9.4	6.3
Discussing with colleagues	6.2	4.0
Interviewing visitors	3.0	3.5
Telephoning	8.8	8.2
Dictating	3.7	1.9
Meeting	3.7	1.9
Regularly scheduled	1.4	4.0
Special	8.0	6.0
Discussing at lunch	14.3	11.0
Visiting other offices	14.7	36.1
Writing	4.1	3.8
Reading	13.2	9.2
Miscellaneous	2.7	2.4

Adapted from C. L. Brisley, "Tips to Help You Save Time," *Factory Management and Maintenance* (December, 1958), p. 60

*General manager, plant manager, director of industrial and public relations, and so on.

†Managers of operations, quality control, industrial engineering, and so on.

perform duties. In general, however, conventional methods blur the logical sequence of relationships between task, standards, skills and qualifications.[18]

Another important difficulty with the conventional way of describing jobs is that it omits reference to either that portion of a job that is personally meaningful to the employee or to those aspects of a job which contribute to the enlargement of an employee's skills.[19]

Thus, if an organization is going to continue to use conventional job analysis, the relevant question for the personnel manager is, How can it be improved? There are two suggested revisions in conventional job descriptions aimed at removing the deficiencies described above.

Results Oriented Description.   The first revision is the **results-oriented description (ROD)**, which contains the following information:

● *Tasks:* What behaviors, duties, or functions are important to the employee's job?

● *Conditions:* How often is a task done? What conditions make the task easier or harder to complete? What written or supervisory instructions are available to aid the employee in performing a task?

● *Standards:* What objective performance expectations are attached to each task? These standards of quantity, quality, and timeliness should relate meaningfully to organizational objectives.

● *SKAs:* What skills, knowledge, and abilities are required to perform each task at the minimally acceptable standard?

- *Qualifications:* What education and/or experience (length, level, and type) are needed to ensure that employees will have the necessary SKAs for task performance? The ROD thus contains information on the links among tasks, standards, skills, and minimum qualifications.

The information for writing RODs can be obtained in part from the traditional sources—observation, interview, critical incidents, job skills inventories, the PAQ, the DOT, and the *Handbook for Analyzing Jobs.* The ROD combines aspects of behavioral job objectives or standards with specifications of the skills, knowledge, and abilities (SKAs) tied to these standards and with minimum qualifications (specifications) related to them. The job-related SKAs become the basis for selecting employees. Thus the ROD format meets equal employment guidelines.

Examples of job descriptions written by the conventional method and the results-oriented method are shown in Exhibit 4.10.

Skills Categories.   The second suggested revision lists the skills that an employee would acquire by being in a given position. It can facilitate the career-planning efforts of individuals and the organization and reduce job placements that have a high potential for being unsuccessful. The skills that could be acquired on a job might include

- *Analytical:* Needs assessment, evaluation, value analysis, problem solving, decision making
- *Personal development:* Career development, group participation, leadership development, motivation, self-concept development
- *Social skills:* Change agent, communication, conflict analysis and reduction, innovation, facilitation[20]

Many of these aspects of skill acquisition are not an explicit part of most job descriptions now, but their inclusion would make many jobs more attractive and would help the organization retain and develop its valued employees. Correctly specifying the skills (SKAs) required to effectively perform a job can also help the organization attract new employees in a fair and nondiscriminatory manner.

Establishing Job Specifications

Correctly specifying the necessary skills, knowledge, and abilities to do a job is important for fair and effective use of human resources, but it is not always easy to do. Nevertheless, as an essential basis for many personnel activities, job specifications must be determined.

Job specifications are often a part of the job description. For example, the job description of the dough mixer (see Exhibit 4.7) indicated the required worker qualities, including skills, knowledge, aptitude, interests, temperament, and physical requirements.[21] Of course, not all job descriptions have such an extensive list of required worker qualities. But the more extensive the list of qualities required, the more job information that can be conveyed to the potential job applicant. The more information the applicant has, the more informed his or her job choice can be. The more information the organization has, the better it can determine its selection and training needs.

How are job specifications determined? Often by the judgment of the job analyst.

Exhibit 4.10   A Comparison of Conventional and Results-Oriented Job Descriptions

Conventional Job Description

Administrative Assistant

Responsibilities: works under the direction of the supervisor, operations control
section

Duties:

types correspondence and reports
compiles reports
maintains inventory of supplies
arranges meetings and conferences for supervisor
handles routine correspondence
other duties as assigned

Qualifications:

high school degree or equivalent
type 40 wpm
two years' experience in a secretarial position or equivalent education

Results-Oriented Description (RODs)

Typist/Receptionist

Tasks	Conditions	Standards
Type letters	When asked to by supervisor; using an IBM Selectric typewriter; according to office style manual	All letters error-free; completed by 5 p.m. if assigned before 3 p.m.
Greet visitors	As they arrive, referring them to five executives with whom they have scheduled appointments	No complaints from visitors referred to wrong office or waiting before being referred

Skills, knowledge, and abilities required:

ability to type 40 wpm
ability to use Selectric typewritier
knowledge of office style manual
courtesy

Minimum qualifications:

high school degree or equivalent
six months' experience as a typist or an equivalent performance test

Adapted from "When the Traditional Job Description Is Not Enough" by D. E. Klingner.
Reprinted with permission *Personnel Journal,* Costa Mesa, CA, copyright April 1979,
pp. 244, 246.

(Many organizations are also asking job incumbents to provide job specifications, as well as job descriptions.) The job analyst who becomes familiar with jobs can infer what qualities a worker needs to perform the job, by looking at the dimensions of the job shown in the job description. The more systematically jobs are described, the better the chance that the analyst can infer qualities that will be related to job performance.[22] In other words, the more the analyst knows the jobs, the more likely it is that valid job descriptions will be established.

For the purpose of fairly selecting employees, the organization can only use measures on those qualities that are related to job performance. To select potential employees by any other method is not only illegal but also may result in selection of an unqualified person. Establishing valid job specifications becomes particularly important to an organization when it has to defend its selection policies against charges of bias or discrimination. If an organization requires, say, a high school diploma, it must be able to show that the skills associated with a high school diploma are related to the dimensions shown in the job description. This correspondence between job requirements and candidate qualifications is called **job content validity.** Other types of validity that an organization can use for its selection methods are discussed in Chapter 7.

JOB DESIGN

Traditionally, job analysis has been used to describe the dimensions of the job to be performed and the required worker specifications. And as illustrated in Exhibit 4.1, the dimensions of the job described in the analysis are largely determined by **job design.** Under the scientific approach, job analysts took special pains to design jobs so that the tasks performed by employees did not exceed their abilities.[23] In fact, the jobs designed by scientific management often resulted in work being partitioned into small, simple segments. These tasks lent themselves well to motion and time studies and to incentive pay systems, both for the purpose of obtaining high productivity.

It turned out, however, that many workers did not like jobs designed according to the dictates of scientific management. In effect, the person-job relationship had been arranged so that achieving the goals of the organization (high productivity) often meant sacrificing important personal goals (the opportunity for interesting, personally challenging work).[24]

Worker Rewards

The only reward that employees received under scientific job design was monetary. Yet many employees had needs not served by monetary rewards, such as the need for responsibility and autonomy. Yet organizations continued to treat the design of the job as inviolate, something not to be changed. Methods were developed to select people who would be satisfied with economic rewards and jobs with simple segments.

It is not hard to understand why the success of this strategy has been limited. Many employees want jobs that give them responsibility and autonomy, as well as good pay. Organizations have responded by redesigning jobs. Popular programs to redesign jobs include job enlargement and job redesign. Since job redesign is now such an important force in the management of human resources, it is discussed more thoroughly in Chapter 18.

Organizational Context

Just as job analysis is influenced by job design, so is job design influenced by organizational design, technology, and organizational goals. Thus there are limits on the extent of job redesign.

Organizational Design and Technology. Technology is the complex of physical objects and technical operations (both manual and machine) regularly employed in turning out the goods and services of the organization.[25] Technology is critical because it determines what types of job designs are possible and what types of jobs are appropriate for various organizational designs.[26] For example, U.S. automobile manufacturers, with huge investments in plants and machinery to make cars on assembly lines, find it almost impossible to convert their car-making technology so that groups of workers make the cars. The result is that most assembly jobs are fairly segmented and repetitive and remain that way. Furthermore, assembly line technology helps determine the structure or design of the organization and in turn the most appropriate types of job designs.[27]

Organizational Goals. The design of jobs not only reflects the design of the organization but also its goals. "Because organizations create them, jobs are in fact very explicit statements by organizations of what they have determined to be the most appropriate means for accomplishing their goals."[28] Furthermore, if the concepts that workers have of their organization help determine their behavior, then the stated goals and the subsequent standards of excellence that an organization establishes gives very clear cues to employees about what is important and where their efforts are required.[29] In addition, since goals also help determine the products and environments of organizations, they help determine the criteria against which workers will be evaluated—hence their behaviors. The criteria and goals, in turn, also determine the kinds of individuals who will be attracted to the organization, evaluated highly, and promoted.

Thus organizational goals can help establish the reasons for jobs, the nature of the organization's expectations from the workers performing the jobs, and even the legitimacy of the job demands. Goals have several other consequences through their relationship with the structure of the organization, which is in turn related to the design of jobs. Finally, job design is associated with
- Employees' job satisfaction
- The styles of leadership that are most effective in supervising employees
- The effectiveness of the organization
- Employee motivation[30]

SUMMARY

The point at which employees and the organization meet is the job. Such organizational problems as absenteeism, turnover, low performance, and dissatisfaction are related in varying degrees to the nature of the jobs. The conventional functions and activities of personnel management—such as attracting, motivating, retaining, recruiting, selecting, and training—are also closely related to the nature of the jobs in the organization. Thus to deal with personnel problems and to perform other personnel activities, jobs must be analyzed and described.

This chapter examines some issues related to analyzing and describing a job with a given design—such issues as how to gather what type of information, the problems in gathering the information, and presenting the information in a form that can be used to perform such personnel functions as human resource planning, recruitment, and selection. As the chapter notes, there are several standard procedures used to gather job-related information for analyzing and describing jobs, some of which are a combination of others. Regardless of which procedure is used, information must be collected about job behaviors, the conditions in which the job is performed, the standards of performance, and the skills, knowledge, and abilities needed to achieve the minimum standards of performance. When all this information has been obtained, it can be used in writing job descriptions and specifications.

Many organizations still use conventional job descriptions, which do not present detailed job information. However, conventional job descriptions may not be useful either for obtaining the most appropriate employees or for helping an employee select an organization to work for. Furthermore, because traditional job descriptions usually make vague connections among job demands, worker qualifications, and worker skills and abilities, they often run counter to equal employment guidelines.

PERSONNEL PROBLEM
Qualified for the Job?

"Miriam Webster was in this morning and is very upset about not receiving the transfer to job level 4. What exactly happened there?" asked P. J. Ramsey, plant manager.

"Simple matter, P. J.," replied Beth Pelley, personnel assistant. "She does not have the stated qualifications for that position."

"For instance?"

"As you know, there are a variety of attributes we insist on for that position. Miriam is OK on most of them, but she doesn't meet the general education requirement. It turns out that she didn't finish high school. I told her I was sorry but that the transfer couldn't go through under those circumstances. I did tell her of our tuition aid policy. I explained that the company would defray all her expenses if she would complete her education at night school or get some type of GED equivalent."

"What is this equal employment opportunity or whatever business Ms. Webster was talking about this morning?" Mr. Ramsey asked.

"No problem there. I explained to Ms. Webster—who is, as you know, black—that the education requirement for that job level is applied to everyone who wants to enter that job classification. We make absolutely no exceptions."

1. Do you think that a high school education may be a reasonable minimum qualification for a job? Why?

2. If a qualification is required of every applicant, are there equal employment implications?

3. Does the fact that the company is willing to pay for the employee to attain the required qualification make any difference in this case?

4. Do you think that Ms. Webster can properly be denied the transfer based on the information in this case?

KEY CONCEPTS

Dictionary of Occupational Titles (DOT)
exempt
functional job analysis
Hay plan
job analysis
job content validity

job description
job design
job specifications
nonexempt
position analysis questionnaire (PAQ)

results-oriented description (ROD)
structured job analysis
time study
work measurement
work sampling

DISCUSSION QUESTIONS

1. What is job analysis, and what are its purposes? How important is job analysis in personnel management?

2. What part does job analysis play in selecting employees in a fair and effective manner?

3. What are the major difficulties in collecting job information, and how can they be overcome?

4. What is the conventional job description? What revisions to the conventional job description have been suggested?

5. What are the components of FJA? What roles does the DOT play in FJA?

6. What is McCormick's PAQ? Compare and contrast the PAQ and FJA.

7. Describe conventional and structured approaches to job analysis.

8. How are organizational design and technology related to job design? How are job design and organizational goals related?

ENDNOTES

1. U.S. Department of Labor, Employment Service, Occupational Analysis and Industrial Services Decisions, *Training and Reference Manual for Job Analysis* (Washington, D.C.: Government Printing Office, June 1944), p. 1.

2. "Job Descriptions: Key Element in the Personnel Subsystem" by J. S. Rakich. Reprinted with permission *Personnel Journal*, Costa Mesa, CA, Copyright January 1972, p. 46.

3. *Personnel Selection and Placement* by M. D. Dunnette. Copyright © 1966 by Wadsworth, Inc. Reprinted by permission of the publisher, Brooks/Cole Publishing Company, Monterey, CA, p. 69.

4. Dunnette pp. 69–70.

5. Dunnette, pp. 89–90.

6. E. J. McCormick *Job Analysis: Methods and Applications* (New York: AMACOM, a division of American Management Association, 1979), p. 48.

7. McCormick, p. 64.
    For an extensive discussion, see
    U.S. Department of Labor, Manpower Administration, *Handbook for Analyzing Jobs* (Washington, D.C.: Government Printing Office, 1972).

8. E. J. McCormick, "Job and Task Analysis," in M. D. Dunnette (ed.), *Handbook of Industrial and Organizational Psychology*, copyright © 1976 by Rand McNally College Publishing Company, p. 655.

9. McCormick, 1979, p. 111.

10. S. A. Fine, "Functional Job Analysis: An Approach to a Technology for Manpower Planning," *Personnel Journal*, November 1974, pp. 813–818.

11. McCormick, 1979, p. 111.

12. B. Schneider, *Staffing Organizations* (Santa Monica, Calif.: Goodyear, 1976), p.23.

13. E. J. McCormick and J. Tiffin, *Industrial Psychology*, 6th ed. © 1974, p. 53, Reprinted by permission of Prentice-Hall, Inc., Englewood Cliffs, New Jersey.
    The Position Analysis Questionnaire (PAQ) is copyrighted by the Purdue Research Foundation. The PAQ and related materials are available through the University Book Store, 360 West State Street, West Lafayette, Indiana 47906. Further information regarding the PAQ is available through PAQ Services, Inc., P.O.

    Box 3337 Logan, Utah, 84321. Computer processing of PAQ data is available through the PAQ Data Processing Division at that address.

14. W. W. Tornow and P. R. Pinto, "The Development of a Managerial Job Taxonomy: A System for Describing, Classifying and Evaluating Executive Postions," *Journal of Applied Psychology*, No. 11 (1976), pp. 410–418.

15. H. T. Amrine, J. Ritchey, and D. S. Hulley, *Manufacturing Organization and Management* 3rd ed. © 1975, p. 130. Reprinted by permission of Prentice-Hall, Inc., Englewood Cliffs, New Jersey.

16. McCormick, 1979, pp. 77, 79.

17. McCormick, 1979, p. 83.

18. "When the Traditional Job Description Is Not Enough," by D. E. Klingher. Reprinted with permission *Personnel Journal*, Costa Mesa, CA, copyright April 1979, pp. 243–248.

19. McCormick, 1976, pp. 663–670.

20. "A New Approach to Position Descriptions," by D. L. Austin. Reprinted with permission *Personnel Journal*, Costa Mesa, CA, copyright July 1977, pp. 354–366.

21. For an excellent discussion of the issues related to providing complete job information to job applicants, often referred to as realistic job previews, see
    J. P. Wanous, *Organizational Entry* (Reading, MA.: Addison-Wesley, 1980).
    T. D. Jick and L. Greenhalgh, "Realistic Job Previews: A Reconceptualization," paper presented at the National Academy of Management, Detroit, August 1980.

22. McCormick, 1979, pp. 240–271.

23. F. W. Taylor, *The Principles of Scientific Management* (New York: Harper & Row, 1911).

24. J. R. Hackman, "Work Design," in J. R. Hackman and J. L. Suttle (eds.), *Improving Life and Work*, p. 101, copyright 1977. Reprinted by permission of Goodyear Publishing Company, Inc., Santa Monica, CA.

25. R. Blauner, *Alienation and Freedom* (Chicago: University of Chicago Press, 1964).

26. Hackman and Suttle, p. 126.

27. For a detailed discussion of the relationships among the environment, technology, structure and job design, see

T. Burns and G. M. Stalker, *Management of Innovation* (London: Tavistock, 1961).

J. Woodward, *Management and Technology* (London: H. M. Stationary Office, 1958).

28. B. Schneider, Staffing Organizations, p. 23, copyright 1976. Reprinted by permission of Goodyear Publishing Company, Inc. Santa Monica, CA.

29. Schneider, p. 47.

30. Schneider, p. 23.

SECTION THREE

Staffing the Organization

CHAPTER OUTLINE

THE RECRUITMENT FUNCTION
Purposes of Recruitment
Recruitment in Human Resource Management
    Human Resource Planning
    Job Analysis
    Employee Training
Human Resource Information Systems (HRIS)

OBTAINING A POOL OF APPLICANTS
Recruitment: A Two-Way Street
    The Personnel Department-Line Manager
    Relationship
    The Organization-Job Applicant
    Relationship
Sources of Job Applicants
    Internal Sources
    External Sources
Organizational Enticements
    Organizational and Occupational Rewards
    Career Opportunities
The Recruitment Interview

LEGAL ISSUES IN RECRUITMENT
Regulations and Progress
Equal Employment Opportunity

EVALUATION OF RECRUITMENT

PERSONNEL PROBLEM   **Transfer or New Hire?**

OBJECTIVES

● To discuss the purposes of recruitment in organizations

● To describe the organizational issues in recruitment

● To explain the impact of equal employment on recruitment

THOUGHT STARTERS

● What enticements can an organization use to attract job applicants?

● What is the relationship between job analysis and recruiting?

● What are the characteristics of a good interview?

● What is job matching?

● Can television be used to recruit job applicants?

CHAPTER FIVE
Recruitment

The hunt is on. And there's a new prey in the jungles of corporate America. A different need that companies are fighting tooth and nail to fill. The headhunters are now stalking the young lions.

No longer are executive search firms—so-called headhunters—concentrating primarily on filling top corporate positions. The new targets are young middle-management executives, men and women with MBAs and three to five years of managerial experience who can do the work in the trenches today and lead the troops tomorrow. Skyrocketing demand has pushed salaries from the $22,000 to $27,000 bracket up to $30,000, $35,000 and higher.

"A high-potential individual can virtually write his own ticket," says Robert Staub of Staub Warmbold Associates, a management consultant firm. "I have never seen the market this strong for young executives to fill slots on the lower rung of middle-management, those who have the first line of responsibility."

The statistics prove it. One survey showed that 47 per cent of all executive searches last year were in the $25,000 to $45,000 salary range. "It's evident that searches to fill middle-management slots are on the rise in all management-consultant firms, big and small," states John F. Schlueter, executive director of the Association of Executive Recruiting Companies, which conducted the survey. "In the past couple of years," he adds, "searches in the area of relatively smaller industries—like hotels, fast food, hospitals, construction, publishing—have grown from three per cent of the total to 12 per cent."

"In the current heated-up recruiting atmosphere," says William Swanson, a headhunter for William H. Willis in New York, "we are even beginning to see middle-management people being pirated away from competing organizations. Not just anybody, of course, but quality people, those with a wide variety of skills applicable to today's volatile marketplace. We are seeing executives seduced by salary raises of as much as 25 to 40 per cent. Recruiters are even raiding each other for talent."

Nor are the headhunters just after promising young men. "The technically oriented woman, with a background in research, engineering, electronics and so on, is the hottest item in recruiting today," notes Roger Kenny of Spencer, Stuart & Associates. "It used to be said that women didn't have the background we were looking for. That is no longer true. There are qualified women in every field—law, accounting, sales, marketing, whatever—and they are getting hired when they fill the bill."

From A. D. Haas, "Hunting the Young Lions," pp. 59–60, 89. Reprinted from TWA Ambassador *Magazine, May 1979, with permission of the author and publisher; copyrighted 1979 by Trans World Airlines, Inc.*

Not all recruiting activities have th. ; level of excitement. However, recruiting is a crucial part of effective human resource management in all organizations, fulfilling the human resource needs of the organization for both the present and the future.

Because recruitment is important in the management of human resources, this chapter thoroughly discusses the purposes or objectives of recruitment, the relationship of the recruitment activity to other personnel activities and functions, internal and external sources of job applicants, legal issues related to recruitment, and evaluation of the recruitment activity.

THE RECRUITMENT FUNCTION

Recruitment is generally defined as searching for and obtaining potential job candidates in sufficient numbers and quality so that the organization can select the most appropriate people to fill its job needs.[1] In addition to filling job needs, the recruitment activity should also be concerned with filling the needs of job candidates.[2] Consequently, recruitment not only attracts individuals to the organization but also increases the chance of retaining the individuals once they are hired. Of course, the recruitment activity must be done in compliance with an extensive set of rules and legal regulations. Thus **recruitment** is specifically the set of activities and processes used to legally obtain a sufficient number of the right people at the right place and time so that the people and the organization can select each other in their own best short-run and long-run interests. This definition reflects the relationship between recruitment and several other personnel activities.

Purposes of Recruitment

The general purpose of recruitment is to provide a pool of potential job candidates to select from. More specifically, the purposes of recruitment are to
● Determine the present and future recruitment needs of the organization in conjunction with the human resource planning and programming (HRPP) activity and the job analysis activity
● Increase the pool of job applicants with minimum cost
● Help increase the success rate of the selection process by reducing the number of obviously underqualified or overqualified job applicants
● Help reduce the probability that job applicants, once recruited and selected, will leave the organization after only a short period of time
● Meet the organization's responsibility for affirmative action programs and other legal and social obligations regarding the composition of its work force
● Start identifying and preparing potential job applicants who will be appropriate candidates
● Increase organizational and individual effectiveness in the short and long term
● Evaluate the effectiveness of various techniques and locations of recruiting for all types of job applicants.[3]

Several important activities are part of recruitment, including determining the organization's long- and short-range needs by job title and level in the organization, staying informed of job market conditions, developing effective recruiting materials, developing a systematic and integrated program of recruitment in conjunction with other personnel activities and with the cooperation of the line managers, obtaining a pool of qualified job applicants, recording the number and quality of job applicants produced by the various sources and methods of recruiting, and following up on applicants, those hired and not hired, in order to evaluate the effectiveness of the recruiting effort.

Recruitment in Human Resource Management

Recognizing the relationships that recruitment has with other personnel activities is necessary for the effective management of human resources. Three critical relationships are those with human resource planning, job analysis, and training (see Exhibit 5.1). In essence, they determine who are appropriate job candidates. An organization's human resource information system (HRIS) helps to tie these activities together.

Human Resource Planning.   Recruiting programs are developed around three components of planning: strategic business planning, job role planning, and human resource planning.[4] Strategic business planning determines the organization's goals, future products and services, growth rate, location, legal environment, and structure. **Job/role planning,** which follows strategic business planning, specifies what needs to be done at all levels in order to meet the strategic business plans.

This activity can be thought of as a dynamic kind of job analysis where a continual review is made of skills, knowledge, values, etc. which are presently needed and will be needed in the future.[5]

Human resource planning assesses the skills and abilities of the current work force in order to spot employees who meet the requirements developed through job/role planning. Recruitment programs are then developed to improve the match between existing skills and needed skills.

Job Analysis.   Once planning has established the overall goals and needs of the organization, it must acquire the appropriate human resources to fulfill these goals. The exact number, types, and critical dimensions of jobs that need to be filled must

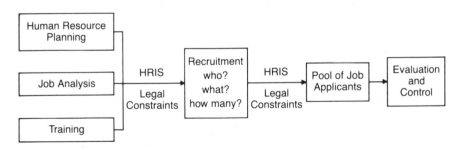

Exhibit 5.1   Components of the Recruitment Activity

be determined, as well as the skills and abilities that job applicants need. This information is provided by job analysis (see Chapter 4).

However, recruitment based on job analysis only helps ensure that the people who are hired have the ability to do the job. Recruitment must also match the needs of the applicants with the rewards of the job if it is to serve the long-run interests of the organization and the individual. These rewards can include monetary compensation, hours of work, training programs, and career opportunities in the organization. The design of the job can also be an important reward. Since all of these are important components of other personnel activities, they are discussed in later chapters. But it is important to note here that all these rewards are capable of satisfying many needs of potential employees (such as those discussed in Chapter 2) and that job applicants often have different needs. Although the matching process is complex and difficult, appropriately matching job rewards with applicant's needs can result in satisfied employees who are less likely to quit their jobs.

A SLICE OF LIFE

Matching individual abilities with particular job requirements often presents an organization with a dilemma. In professional athletics, for example, a football team may have a pressing need for a running back, but when it is the team's turn to draft players, there may be no exceptional running backs left. However, several outstanding athletes who ordinarily play other positions may remain. The question, then, is whether to choose a person who fits the team's particular need even though he may not be outstanding or to choose the best available athlete.

Similar situations occur in business. Suppose you are recruiting for an accountant at a college and you encounter an outstanding young economist. You are constrained, however, because you have only one approved position to fill for your firm. There are several adequate, even good, accounting prospects, but the economist is truly outstanding. Who would benefit the organization most, an accountant or the economist? Do you hire the best person available for the position or the best person available? There is no set answer to such questions, but the issue is one that responsible recruiting personnel should address.

Suppose your school of business has a need for a finance professor. There are several available, but only one truly outstanding professor and researcher has expressed an interest in the job, and his area of expertise is marketing. Which person is best for the school? As a student, which person would you prefer that the school hire?

Employee Training.   If recruiting activities produce a large pool of qualified job applicants, the need for employee training may be minimal. But if recruiting activities produce a large but unqualified pool of job applicants, the organization and its training budget may really suffer. Consider the U.S. Army's recruiting situation:

*Alleged widespread U.S. Army recruiting malpractices appear to be a
contributing factor to the $1 billion a year cost of training military recruits who
drop out before finishing their enlistments.*

*Dr. Albert Martin, a Defense Department manpower planning expert, told a
House veterans' affairs subcommittee yesterday that recruiting malpractices can
be expected to increase the service's dropout ratio because unqualified people are
being enlisted.*

*Allegations of widespread cheating by Army recruiters to meet quotas are
under investigation in several parts of the nation. . . .*

*Initially, the allegations were not given a high investigation priority until it
was discovered that the Army is facing ever-increasing costs for training enlistees
who drop out of the military before completing their enlistments.*

*Rep. Donald M. Mottl, D-23, chairman of the subcommittee, said the
government spent about $1.2 billion last year to train recruits who dropped out.*

*"Many of these individuals then become eligible for veterans' benefits such as
medical care and disability compensation, further increasing the tab," Mottl
said. Most dropouts are not given dishonorable discharges.*

*In 1978 about 122,000 recruits dropped out for failing to meet minimum
standards of performance or behavior.*

*The subcommittee is investigating whether legislation is necessary to deny
veterans' benefits to military dropouts. It is also exploring ways to combat the
dropout rate.*

*I. M. Greenberg, deputy defense secretary for program management, said
such legislation would probably have no effects on Army recruiting.*

*"It is rational to assume that the loss of benefits could have a deterrent effect
on the conduct of some people," he said. "Unfortunately, the group who fail to
succeed in military service are not noted for planning ahead in a rational way."*

*The latter comment indicated that most enlistees do not conspire to join the
military and then drop out before completing their enlistment period—knowing
they can be eligible for low veteran's interest, generous housing loans, medical
care and other benefits.*[6]

Human Resource Information Systems (HRIS)

It should be apparent that the recruitment process, to be done effectively, requires
a great deal of information. This information must also be centralized so that all
the personnel activities related to recruitment can be coordinated. For example, the
State Department's HRIS, described in Chapter 3, provides a vehicle for collecting
a great deal of information, integrating it, and making it readily available. An HRIS
also provides information for many other personnel activities. The HRIS at the State
Department maintains extensive information on position classifications, skills and
qualifications of existing employees, promotions, employee race and sex by job
level, and career planning. An HRIS can also be useful for recruitment, since it can
rapidly simulate organizational changes and conditions and thereby determine future
personnel needs. An HRIS is also important in implementing job matching systems,
which are described in the next section.

OBTAINING A POOL OF JOB APPLICANTS

Whether in response to a present or future need, all organizations should strive to maintain a pool of potential employees. Then when line managers ask for someone to fill a specific position, the personnel department can quickly and efficiently find the right person. There are four important concerns in obtaining a pool of applicants: the mutuality of recruitment, the sources of potential applicants, the enticements the organization can offer them, and the recruitment interview.

Recruitment: A Two-Way Street

Mutuality in recruitment refers to the reciprocal relationships among parties to the recruitment process. Two particular relationships have been identified: the relationship between the personnel staff and the line managers and the relationship between the organization and the job applicant.[7]

The Personnel Department–Line Manager Relationship. The personnel department and the line managers can often work together to get the right person on the right job. Line managers often initiate a personnel requisition for additional employees. They can help by specifying the nature of the job and necessary employee qualifications (particularly if it's a new job or one that has changed since the last job analysis). They often play an important role in interviewing and decision making, and they can help evaluate the effectiveness of the recruitment process.

The Organization–Job Applicant Relationship. The traditional approach to recruiting is concerned with matching the abilities of the job applicant with the skills required by the job. The more recent approach to recruiting, although still concerned with matching skills and abilities, is also concerned with matching the needs of the job applicant and the rewards supplied by the job.[8] Getting job applicants to stay is as important as recruiting job applicants who can do the job.

Two components of the newer approach to recruiting are job matching programs and the realistic job interview. The realistic interview is discussed in a separate section near the end of this chapter. **Job matching** is essentially fitting the needs of people to the job requirements. Increasing pressure on organizations to maintain effective recruitment, selection, and placement of new and current employees may make an automated job matching system worthwhile.[9] For example, Citibank's job matching system for nonprofessional employees evolved from an automated system designed to monitor job requisition and internal placement processes. The system is currently used to identify suitable positions for staff members who wish to transfer or who are seeking another job due to technological displacement or reorganization and to ensure that suitable internal candidates haven't been overlooked before recruiting begins outside the organization. Thus the system appears not only to help recruit people and ensure that they stay but also to provide a firm basis for job-related recruitment and selection procedures (job-relatedness is an important part of legal compliance).

IBM has a job matching system called IRIS for recruiting experienced professionals. The system was developed as follows:

Coupon ads were placed in newspapers and magazines. Response to an ad was considered an expression of interest on the part of the individual and a "Data-Pak" was forwarded to the respondent for completion and return. Information on an applicant was kept in the active file on the system for a two-year period; when a match was made, the applicant was notified. While statistics of performance have not been provided, IRIS has been considered a success by IBM officials.[10]

There are two major components in a job matching system—job profiles and candidate profiles. The job profiles at Citibank were developed from prior job-family studies conducted at Citibank, the U.S. Department of Labor's *Handbook for Analyzing Jobs,* and such job analysis instruments as the PAQ. The candidate profiles contain information regarding the candidate's experience or skills related to specific jobs. It also lists their job preferences, reflecting their needs. These jobs are the same ones described in the job profiles. Thus with these profiles, the organization can identify many more job applicants for specific jobs than ever before.

Sources of Job Applicants

There are two major sources of job applicants, each with advantages and disadvantages (see Exhibit 5.2). **Internal sources** include present employees, friends of employees, former employees, and former applicants. Promotions, demotions, and transfers can also provide applicants for departments or divisions within the orga-

Exhibit 5.2 Sources of Job Applicants

Internal	
Advantages	Disadvantages
Morale of promotee	Inbreeding
Better assessment of abilities	Possible morale problems of those not promoted
Lower cost for some jobs	"Political" infighting for promotions
Motivator for good performance	Need strong management development program
Causes a succession of promotions	
Have to hire only at entry level	

External	
Advantages	Disadvantages
"New blood," new perspectives	May not select someone who will "fit"
Cheaper than training a professional	May cause morale problems for those internal candidates
No group of political supporters in organization already	Longer "adjustment" or orientation time
May bring competitors' secrets, new insights	

nization. **External sources** include unions, professional associations, walk-ins, schools and colleges, employment agencies (public and private), and various advertising media.

Internal Sources. Current employees are a source of job applicants in two respects: They can refer friends to the organization, and they can also become applicants themselves by potential promotion or transfer.

Promotion from within may occur in several ways. One is to move an employee up a level within the same department. When the major qualifications of a vacant position involve general managerial skills, the search for qualified candidates can be organization wide. An individual in one department may be promoted to the next organization level in another department. A vacancy can be filled by an employee at the same level who is willing to make a lateral transfer for a raise in pay, increase in status or a more interesting job. This could be viewed as a promotion within the same job level. Another type of "promotion" occurs when a valued employee receives a change in job responsibilities. [11]

The case for promotion from within rests on several good arguments. One is that internal employees are better qualified. "Even jobs that do not seem unique require familiarity with the people, procedures, policies and special characteristics of the organization in which they are performed." [12] Another is that employees are likely to feel more secure and to identify their long-term interests with the organization that provides them the first choice of job opportunities. [13] Availability of promotions within an organization can also motivate employees to perform. Internal promotion can also be much less expensive to the organization in terms of both time and money.

Disadvantages of a promotion-from-within policy may include an inability to find the best qualified person. Also, infighting, inbreeding, and lack of varied perspectives and interests may result.

It is not surprising to find organizations doing some internal promoting and obtaining some applicants from external sources. Organizations tend to obtain particular types of employees from particular sources. For example, many organizations are more likely to hire highly trained professionals and high-level managers from the outside than to promote from within. [14]

If an organization has a policy of promotion from within, it must identify and select candidates for the promotion. The initial step in the process is determining whether affirmative action dictates selections. [15] Like other personnel practices, including transfers and layoffs, promotion decisions are subject to government guidelines and regulations. Barring women and minorities from higher-level jobs is illegal.

The next step is the identification of candidates. As Exhibit 5.3 indicates, there are many methods for internally advertising job vacancies. Candidates can also be identified by word of mouth, company personnel records, promotion lists based on performance, potential ratings obtained from assessment activities, seniority lists, and lists generated by the skills inventory in an organization's HRIS.

One of the major issues in promoting candidates from within is seniority versus performance or merit. Unions seem to prefer promotion based on seniority, and some organizations prefer promotion based on ability. Many organizations strike a

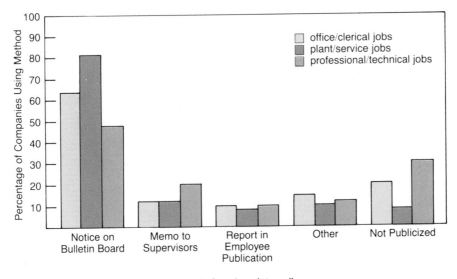

Exhibit 5.3 Methods for Advertising Job Openings Internally
Adapted from "Employee Promotion & Transfer Policies," *PPF Survey No. 120* (Washington, D.C.: The Bureau of National Affairs, Inc., January 1978), p. 2.

balance between the two. However, promotion decisions based on seniority appear to be coming under attack from affirmative action proponents and the courts. Seniority is discussed again in Chapter 16.

Occasionally the criterion for promotion is personal judgment. This is particularly true for middle- and upper-level managerial positions. Again, this criterion is difficult to defend under legal guidelines, so many organizations have had to reconsider their methods for promotion. The use of test results from managerial assessment centers appears to be one alternative to personal judgments and impressions. Since assessments centers are used more frequently as a selection device than as a recruiting device, they are discussed more extensively in Chapter 7.

External Sources. Recruiting internally does not always produce enough qualified job applicants. This is especially true for organizations that are growing rapidly or that have a large demand for high-talent professional, skilled, and managerial employees. These organizations need to recruit from external sources. Recruiting from the outside has a number of advantages, including bringing in people with new ideas. It is often cheaper and easier to train a professional or skilled employee, particularly when the organization has an immediate demand for scarce labor skills and talents. External sources can also supply temporary employees, who provide the organization with much more flexibility than permanent employees. Some uses for temporary employees are shown in Exhibit 5.4.

Employment agencies are a good source of temporary employees—and an excellent source for permanent employees. Employment agencies may be public or private. The **public employment agencies** in the United States are under the umbrella of the U.S. Training and Employment Service (USTES). The USTES sets

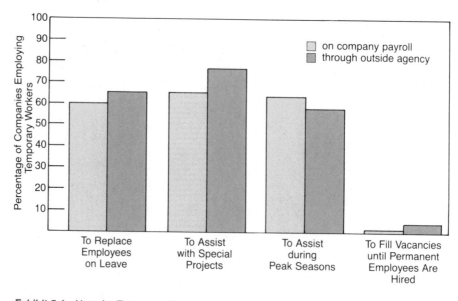

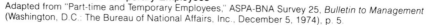

Exhibit 5.4   Uses for Temporary Employees
Adapted from "Part-time and Temporary Employees," ASPA-BNA Survey 25, *Bulletin to Management* (Washington, D.C.: The Bureau of National Affairs, Inc., December 5, 1974), p. 5.

national policies and oversees the operations of state employment services, which have branch offices in many cities. The Social Security Act provides that laid-off workers need to register with the state agencies to be eligible for unemployment benefits. The agencies then have a roster of potential applicants to assist organizations looking for job applicants.

State agencies provide a wide range of services. Most of the services are supported by employer contributions to the state unemployment funds. The agencies offer counseling, testing, and placement services to everyone. They provide special services to individuals, military veterans, minority groups, and college, technical, and professional people. The state agencies also make up a nationwide network of job information and applicant information in the form of job banks. These job banks have one drawback, however: USTES and its state agencies do not actually recruit people but passively assist those who come to them.[16]

Private employment agencies tend to serve two groups of job applicants—professional and managerial workers and unskilled workers. The agencies dealing with the unskilled group often provide job applicants that employers would have a difficult time finding otherwise. Many of the employers looking for unskilled workers do not have the resources to do their own recruiting or have only temporary or seasonal demands for unskilled labor.

Private agencies play a major role in recruiting professional and managerial applicants. These agencies supply services for all ages of job applicants, although most have had some work experience beyond college. During the past ten years, the executive recruiting industry has grown phenomenally. Some estimates suggest that the industry now generates more than $150 million in fee billings. There are over

150 search firms listed in New York City alone, but approximately 10 firms are most visible.[17]

The importance of these private employment agencies is growing. It is likely that you will have occasion to use one or several in your lifetime. Because there are so many agencies, selecting one may be difficult. Before you choose, consider the extent of the services they provide and their track record in matching applicants and companies.

In some industries, such as the building trades and the maritime, unions often assume responsibility for supplying employers with skilled workers. This practice removes the company from many labor decisions, including layoffs, recalls, and even job assignment. However, the Taft-Hartley Act restricts these "hiring hall" practices to a limited number of industries.

Trade and professional associations are also important sources for recruiting. They often have newsletters and annual meetings, which can be used to provide notice of employment opportunities. Annual meetings can also provide employers and potential job applicants an opportunity to meet. Some communities and schools have picked up on this idea and now bring together large numbers of employers and job seekers for "job fairs." Of course, these fairs provide only a limited time for interviews and thus serve only as an initial step in the recruitment process, but they do provide an efficient way of recruiting for both employers and individuals.

Schools can be categorized into three types—high schools, vocational and technical schools, and colleges and universities. All are important sources of recruits for most organizations, although their importance varies depending on the type of applicant sought. For example, if an organization is recruiting for managerial, technical, or professional applicants, then colleges and universities are the most important source. But they become less important when an organization is seeking blue-collar and clerical employees.

Recruiting at colleges and universities is often an expensive process, even if the recruiting visit eventually produces job offers and acceptance. Approximately 30 percent of the applicants hired from college leave the organization within the first five years after initial employment. This rate of turnover is even higher for graduate management students (MBAs).[18] Some people attribute this high rate of turnover to the lack of job challenge provided by organizations. Organizations claim, however, that people just out of college have unreasonable expectations.[19] Partly because of the expense, organizations are questioning the necessity of hiring college graduates for some of their jobs. Another reason for reevaluation of college graduates is legal guidelines requiring the employer to show that a college degree is related to performance of the job. If it cannot, it may want to question the policy of recruiting and hiring only college graduates.

Many organizations looking for applicants engage in extensive advertising in the local paper, in the *Wall Street Journal* or *New York Times*, and on radio and television. When it becomes difficult to recruit job applicants, advertising can become very innovative:

A beefy, leathered man in a white hardhat stands next to a welder, stares into the television camera and shouts: "If you're a shipbuilder who's good at your job and proud of it, I'd like to talk to you!"

*Just like the Marines, who always are looking for "a few good men,"
Louisiana shipbuilders and dozens of other companies around the country in a
wide range of businesses have thousands of jobs begging to be filled.*

*Halter Marine's toll-free number and television commercials are backed by
large display ads in newspaper sports sections, listing the types of jobs available
and the pay.*

*Perhaps the most bizarre recruiting effort came in Wichita, where the Chamber
of Commerce estimates 1,500 openings are available for skilled workers.*

*KLEO Radio disc jockey Ken Clifford sat in a Beech Bonanza A-36 parked
downtown for more than 80 hours last November, urging listeners to call the
station or the chamber with names of skilled people who might want to relocate.*

*More than 500 names were collected. Each person was sent an information
packet by the chamber and a letter from Mayor Connie Peters advising them of
current job openings.*

"Local employers expect 10,000 new jobs by year-end 1980," she wrote.

*Sometimes recruiters work against their own company—such as the Boeing
Co., which needs machinists and engineers at its Wichita plant. It also needs
them in Seattle, along with computer specialists, design engineers and tool and
die makers.*

Wichita runs one recruiting campaign, Seattle, another.

*Raids on other companies for skilled employees are common, though few firms
admit them.*

*Hughes Aircraft Co. in Los Angeles hired an airplane to fly over crowded
beaches last Memorial Day towing a banner that said: "Hughes Needs
Engineers." Company officials said later the idea failed to help recruitment.*

*But another aerospace manufacturer, Northrop Corp., had success running TV
commercials and radio spots for engineers during the World Series.*[20]

Organizational Enticements

Although organizations have many sources of recruitment, they may not always
obtain the applicants they want. This is especially true in highly competitive markets
and for highly skilled individuals. But the organization can enhance recruitment
through the enticements it offers or possesses. The term **enticements** is used to
convey all the positive characteristics a potential job applicant sees in or is offered
by an organization, whether prior to or during the recruitment process. These characteristics are part of the package of job rewards that can be matched with individual
needs.

Organizational and Occupational Rewards.   Organizations can offer potential job
applicants such rewards as prestige, social acceptance, pride in work, and a large
number of work culture ideals. They can also offer money, fringe benefits, security,
promotion opportunities, choice of alternative work arrangements, and even bonuses.

*Companies occasionally offer bonuses, either to the new employee directly or as
finder's fees for the person who recommends a new employee. Other times,
companies offer whopping relocation payments to lure new workers.*

Solar Turbines International, a turbine engine manufacturer in San Diego, offered $500 to any of its employees who recommended a new machine operator. Only two people responded.

Northrop Corp. in Los Angeles has a similar program, with bonuses ranging from $100 to $1,000.

Warm climates, fringe benefits and other intangibles play a big part in some recruiting drives.

Judy Flachsbart, a nursing recruiter for Huntington Memorial Hospital in Pasadena, Calif., flew to Chicago in the middle of a bitter cold winter. She interviewed 70 job prospects after her hospital took out an advertisement in a Chicago newspaper. The ad showed a rose and said simply: "In Pasadena, roses bloom year-round." [21]

Organizations sometimes have prestige or an image because of their unique qualities and association with a particular industry.

Rockwell International tried . . . to appeal to the pride and imagination of job prospects.

"What aerospace work could be more prestigious than design and development of spaceships for the world's first reusable space transportation system?" one Rockwell ad said. "Rockwell's space systems group is making a name for itself. We invite you to do likewise." [22]

Other organizational qualities that can influence prestige include reputation of the company's product, quality, service, social responsibility, and fair employment practices. An organization may not actually need to have favorable characteristics for prestige but may possess just the image of having them. It has been shown, however, that if organizations "tell it like it is" in the initial recruiting interview, the chances of an individual remaining with the organization, or of accepting the job, are greater than without the realistic job preview.

Both the overall prestige of the organization and the prestige of the jobs it offers contribute to its ability to recruit the best applicants. It is much easier to recruit applicants for high-prestige jobs than it is to fill lower-prestige positions. The prestige of jobs is based only in part on the salary the job commands. Organizational prestige can also have important off-the-job influences. For example, it might be much easier to join social clubs if you work for IBM than for some other company.

Career Opportunities. The decision to provide career opportunities involves several choices for the organization. First, should the organization have an active policy of promotion from within? Second, should the organization be committed to a training and development program to provide sufficient candidates for internal promotion? If answers to these questions are yes, then the organization must identify career ladders consistent with organizational and job requirements and employee skills and preferences.

An organization may identify several career paths for different groups or types of employees. This notion is based on the premise that an organization cannot afford to recruit applicants for jobs at the lower rungs of the ladder who already possess those skills necessary for jobs at the top rungs of the ladder. This is what happens, however, with many people recruited from college. Although they are essentially overqualified for their first jobs, the organization hires them for more difficult "future" jobs. This policy is partially to blame for the high turnover rate of new college graduates. It is also cause for concern regarding legal compliance. Employers may claim that a college degree is necessary for an entry-level managerial job when they actually consider it necessary for the second or third job. Such a policy can lead to discriminatory barriers for recruitment and promotion.

One way to reduce this possibility is for an organization to establish career ladders and career paths.

If job progression structures and seniority provisions are so established that new employees will probably, within a reasonable period of time and in a great majority of cases, progress to a higher level, it may be considered that candidates are being evaluated for jobs at that higher level. However, where job progression is not so neatly automatic, or the time span is such that higher level jobs or employee's potential may be expected to change in significant ways, it shall be considered that candidates are being evaluated for a job at or near the entry level. This point is made to underscore the principle that attainment of or performance at a higher level job is a relevant criterion in validating employment tests only when there is a high probability that persons employed will in fact attain that higher level job within a reasonable period of time.[23]

When organizations have career ladders and paths with clearly specified requirements, the organization can present a better defense for its recruitment policy. Organizations with clearly defined career ladders also have an easier time recruiting qualified job applicants and a better chance of keeping the employee.

The Recruitment Interview

A vital aspect of the recruitment process is the interview. A good interview can definitely be an enticement for an applicant to join an organization, just as a bad one can turn away many applicants.[24]

The quality of the interview is just one aspect of the recruitment process. Other things being equal, the chances of a person's accepting a job offer increase when interviewers show interest and concern for the applicant. In addition, it has been found the college students feel most positive toward the recruitment interview when they can take at least half of the interview time to ask questions of the interviewer and they are not embarrassed or put on the spot by the interviewer.[25]

The content of the recruitment interview is also important. Organizations often assume that it is in their best interests to tell a job applicant only the positive aspects of the organization. But it has been reported in studies of the life insurance industry that providing realistic (positive and negative) information increases the number of eventual recruits. In the long run, those who received realistic information stayed on the job much longer.[26]

Assuming that job applicants pass an initial screening, they should be given the opportunity to interview with a potential supervisor and even co-workers. The interview with the potential supervisor is crucial, for this is the person who often makes the final decision.[27]

LEGAL ISSUES IN RECRUITMENT

So far, the discussion of recruitment has focused on the concerns of the individual and the organization. But there is another important aspect—the legal aspect. The major issue is what questions can be asked or discussed in an interview. Legal constraints, however, influence the entire recruiting activity.

Regulation and Progress

One of the most complex and significant constraints on an organization's recruitment and selection processes is government regulation and guidelines in such matters as equal employment, privacy, and affirmative action. Currently, federal and state laws protect most employees and potential employees from two types of discrimination. **Overt discrimination** refers to a "specific act of discrimination against one individual." **Systemic discrimination** results from personnel practices that "over the years, have unintentionally led to the different treatment" of minority (or female) employees.[28]

Title VII, Section 303 of the Civil Rights Act of 1964 makes it unlawful for an employer to fail to hire, refuse to hire, discharge, or discriminate in employment against an individual because of race, color, religion, sex, or national origin. The act further prohibits employers from uniting, classifying, or segregating employees in any way that would tend to deprive them of employment opportunities when the basis is race, color, religion, sex, or national origin. Federal law now also prohibits discrimination on the basis of age and has special provisions for the recruitment and selection of Vietnam veterans, individuals with criminal records, and physically handicapped people.

There are exceptions to the broad protection provided by federal and state equal employment provisions. It is not unlawful to recruit, hire, and employ people "where *religion*, *sex* or *national origin* is a bona fide occupational qualification (BFOQ) necessary to the normal operation of that particular business or operations."[29] An example of this is when a play or movie requires a woman or man for a particular role. The number of examples in this category are few.

Although compliance with federal and state regulations is sometimes difficult, the impact of these regulations has been significant. As organizations find themselves committed to fulfilling employment goals and quotas, they are actively recruiting minorities and women. More organizations than ever before are using the state employment services to do this. They are also recruiting in many more geographical areas than ever before.

Equal Employment Opportunity.   It is difficult to name all the recruitment questions that can give rise to legal problems. However, government attorneys and others close to the field have identified several topical areas that should be avoided in the recruitment interview:

● *Marital status* (including spouse's name): Status could be used to discriminate against women.
● *Height and weight*: This information may be used to discriminate, because protected groups—for example, women and orientals—tend to be smaller than men of other races.

- *Hair and eye color*: These may suggest race and nationality.
- *Child care and demographics*: These have been used to discriminate against women.
- *Availability for Saturday or Sunday work*: This may tend to discriminate against applicants whose religion prohibits their working Saturday or Sunday.
- *Credits, garnishments, or home ownership*: This information may favor continued representation of employees not currently underrepresented.
- *Age*: Although the Age Discrimination Act only protects those between the ages of forty and sixty-five, it is best not to ask anyone.
- *Education*: Formal education is not always related to job performance, nor is it the only way to acquire job skills. This area may discriminate against minority groups.[30]

Not all questions related to these areas are necessarily discriminatory, but they may lessen **equal employment opportunity** by revealing information about an applicant that is not pertinent to the job. Thus questions to be used in recruitment interviews should carefully be evaluated for relevance to job performance, subjective interpretation in responses, and influence of stereotypical images. Interviewers should also avoid questions that tend to identify or disqualify minorities or women. All of the do's and don'ts regarding recruitment interviews also apply to selection interviews (see Chapter 6).

EVALUATION OF RECRUITMENT

The recruitment activity is supposed to attract the right people at the right time within legal limits so that people and organizations can select each other in their best short-run and long-run interests. Since this is what recruitment is supposed to do, this is how it should be evaluated. More specific criteria for evaluating recruitment are shown in Exhibit 5.5. The criteria in Exhibit 5.5 are grouped by the stage of the recruitment process in which they are most applicable.

Recruitment is not just concerned with attracting people but rather with attracting those whose needs will most likely be served by the organization and who have the

Exhibit 5.5 Some Criteria for Evaluating Recruitment

Stage of Entry	Type of Criteria
Preentry	Ability of the organization to recruit newcomers
Entry	Initial expectations of newcomers
	Choice of organization by the individual (needs being matched with climate)
Postentry	Initial job attitudes, such as
	• satisfaction with one's job
	• commitment to the organization
	• descriptive statements about the job (to be compared with the expectations held as an outsider)
	• thoughts about quitting
	Job performance
	Job survival and voluntary turnover rates

From J. P. Wanous, *Organizational Entry*, © 1980, Addison-Wesley Publishing Company, Inc., p. 62. Reprinted with permission.

abilities to perform adequately. It is only by matching needs and abilities that the recruitment activity will result in productive, satisfied, and committed employees. Furthermore, these employees will be less likely to leave the organization.

As indicated in Exhibit 5.5, an organization's recruitment activity at the preentry and entry stages can be evaluated by the number of qualified job applicants it attracts and by whether the applicants have a realistic picture of what the organization is like and whether it fits their needs. Postentry criteria measure how well the long-run interests of the individual and the organization are being served. Organizations prefer employees that perform well and prefer that good performers stay. Individuals prefer to be satisfied, to have a job that fits their needs and abilities, and to work in an organization they like. In essence, the longer the better-performing employees stay and the more satisfied they are, the more effective the recruitment activity is.

One criterion of recruiting effectiveness that covers all stages is legal compliance. Job applicants must be recruited fairly and without discrimination. During the entry and postentry stages, they must also receive fair and affirmative opportunities to be matched to appropriate jobs and to perform to their maximum abilities. (Legal compliance is also discussed in Chapters 6 and 7.)

SUMMARY

Recruitment is a major activity in an organization's program to manage its human resources. After human resource needs have been established and job requirements have been identified through job analysis, a program of recruitment can be established to produce a pool of job applicants. These applicants can be obtained from internal or external sources.

For recruitment to be effective, it must not only consider the needs of the organization but those of society and the individual as well. Society's needs are most explicitly defined by various federal and state regulations in the name of equal opportunity. The needs of individuals figure prominently in two aspects of recruiting—attracting candidates and retaining desirable employees.

PERSONNEL PROBLEM
Transfer or New Hire?

"Our transfer policy is killing us," said J. T. Tomlin, general manager, "I think we should seriously consider changing it."

"What's the problem? I'm not aware of any particular difficulties," said Tom Wilcox, vice president of personnel.

"As you know, turnover is very expensive, and every time someone leaves, the company incurs recruiting, replacement, and training costs. Even though the personnel department and the administrative staff have established a new transfer policy so employees can transfer into an available job before someone new is hired, this policy is nearly twice as expensive as hiring someone new."

1. What is Tomlin talking about? Why might transfer be more expensive than turnover?

2. Turnover is ordinarily thought of as dysfunctional to the organization, and internal transfer programs are ordinarily thought of as positive for the organization. Comment on these traditional beliefs given your answers to question 1.

3. Is the transfer policy described here a good one?

4. How might the transfer policy be modified tc reduce its expense?

KEY CONCEPTS

enticement	job matching	public employment agency
equal employment opportunity	job/role planning	recruitment
external source	overt discrimination	systemic discrimination
internal source	private employment agency	

DISCUSSION QUESTIONS

1. What relationships does recruitment have with other personnel activities, especially human resource planning and job analysis?
2. What are the internal and external sources of recruitment?
3. What are organizational and occupational rewards? What is their role in recruitment?
4. What are the advantages and disadvantages of promotion systems?
5. How has equal opportunity affected recruitment?
6. What is job matching? How does it help or hinder an organization's recruitment activity?
7. What are some do's and don'ts in recruitment interviewing?
8. What is meant by matching on individual skills and job demands and on individual needs and job rewards?

ENDNOTES

1. C. J. Coleman, *Personnel: An Open System Approach* (Cambridge, Mass.: Winthrop, 1979). P. G. Greenlaw and W. D. Briggs, *Modern Personnel Management* (Philadelphia: Saunders, 1979).

2. B. Schneider, *Staffing Organizations* (Santa Monica, Calif.: Goodyear, 1976).

3. R. H. Hawk, *The Recruitment Function* (New York: AMACOM, a division of American Management Associations, 1967).

4. E. H. Schein, "Increasing Organizational Effectiveness through Better Human Resource Planning and Development," *Sloan Management Review*, Fall 1977, pp. 1–20.

5. Schein, p. 5.

6. G. P. Rasanen, "Recruiting Misconduct Blamed for Drop Out Rate," *Cleveland Plain Dealer*, 20 October 1979, p. A12. Reprinted with permission.

7. R. M. Coffina, "Management Recruitment Is a Two-Way Street," *Personnel Journal*, February 1979, pp. 86–89.

8. J. P. Wanous, *Organizational Entry* (Reading, Mass.: Addison-Wesley, 1980).

9. P. Sheibar, "A Simple Selection System Called Jobmatch," *Personnel Journal*, January 1979, pp. 26–29, 53.

10. E. Burack, *Strategies for Manpower Planning and Programming* (Belmont, Calif.: General Learning Press, 1972), pp. 99–100.

11. "What Every Personnel Director Should Know About Management Promotion Decisions," by M. London. Reprinted by permission *Personnel Journal*, Costa Mesa, Calif., copyright October 1978, p. 550.

12. L. R. Sayles and G. Strauss, *Managing Human Resources* (Englewood Cliffs, N. J.: Prentice-Hall, 1977), p. 147.

13. J. P. Campbell, M. D. Dunnette, E. E. Lawler III, and K. E. Weick Jr., *Managerial Behavior, Performance and Effectiveness* (New York: McGraw-Hill, 1970).

14. Campbell et al.

15. London, p. 555.

16. G. K. Davies, "Needed: A National Job-Matching Network," *Harvard Business Review*, September/October 1969, pp. 63–72.

17. R. M. Kenney, "Executive Search Today," *California Management Review*, Summer 1978, pp. 79–83.

18. L. Stessin, "Developing Young Managers: Immediacy Sets the Tone," *Personnel*, November/December, 1971, pp. 31–37.

19. Wanous.

20. P. Zollman, "There's Jobs in Abundance for Americans with Skills," *Columbus Dispatch*, May 20, 1979, UPI Business Writer, p. C1, 8. Reprinted by permission of United Press International

21. Zollman, p. C1.

22. Zollman, p. C1.

23. Equal Employment Opportunity Commission, "Guidelines on Employee Selection Procedures," *Federal Register* 35, no. 149, 1 August 1970. This section is also consistent with "Uniform Guidelines on Employee Selection Procedures," *Federal Register* 42, no. 251, 25 August 1978.

24. T. M. Higham, "Graduate Selection: A New Approach," *Occupational Psychology*, 45 (1971), pp. 209–216.

25. G. S. Odiorne and A. S. Hann, *Effective College Recruiting* (Ann Arbor, Mich.: Bureau of Industrial Relations, Graduate School of Business, University of Michigan, 1961).

26. Schneider, p. 102.

27. Coffina, p. 88.

28. O. A. Ornati and E. Giblin, "The High Cost of Discrimination," *Business Horizons*, February 1975, p. 35.

29. R. L. Greenman and E. J. Schmertz, *Personnel Administration and the Law*, 2nd ed. (Washington, D.C.: Bureau of National Affairs, 1979), p. 64.

30. J. Ledvinka and R. D. Gatewood, "EEO Issues with Pre-employment Inquiries," *Personnel Administrator*, February 1977, pp. 22–26.

CHAPTER OUTLINE

SELECTION AND PLACEMENT
Purposes of Selection and Placement
Selection and Placement in Context
    Job Analysis
    Recruitment
    Performance Appraisal
Who's Responsible for Selection and Placement?
    The Individual
    Personnel and Line Managers

JOB APPLICANTS FOR SELECTION AND PLACEMENT
Promotion and Transfer
    Types of Promotion and Transfer
    Making Promotion and Transfer Decisions
    Identifying Candidates for Promotion and Transfer
    Comparing Candidates
    Making the Final Choice
    Why Not the Best?
Organizational and Job Previews

SELECTION AND PLACEMENT INFORMATION
The Organizational Context
Job Qualities
The Job Context

OBTAINING JOB APPLICANT INFORMATION
The Selection and Placement Interview
    Common Interview Problems
    Overcoming Potential Interview Problems
    Nonverbal Cues in Interviews
    What to Ask
    What Not To Ask
Employment Tests
    Aptitude Tests
    Achievement Tests
    Motivation Tests
The Application Blank

PERSONNEL PROBLEM   I'm Sorry I Asked

LEARNING OBJECTIVES

- To identify the information needed for selection and placement

- To explain why the best are not always promoted

- To describe the problems with interviews

- To explain why organizations are reluctant to provide reference data

THOUGHT STARTERS

- What's a confirmation strategy?

- Why are selection and placement so important?

- What's a realistic organizational preview?

- What's a motivation test?

CHAPTER SIX
Selection and Placement: Information and Procedures

We have only to listen to a pianist, examine the work of an artist, or observe an actress on the stage to determine whether or not they are of outstanding rank. In other fields, there are recognized standards to aid judgment. A lawyer must pass a bar examination, a surgeon can refer you to his diploma from the American College, a ball player's batting average is published in the newspapers daily. Among executives, we can recognize competence only after long periods of observation and, even then, there are sometimes large differences of opinion. How much more difficult it is to appraise potential in advance! In this area I am sure we have all made bad guesses, even with candidates who appeared highly promising.

Achievement in the executive field is much less spectacular than comparable success in many of the professions—the scientist, for example, who wins the Nobel Prize, the headline name who is elected governor, the skillful politician, the articulate college president. In fact, the more effective executives are, the more their identities and personalities blend into the background of their organizations. Here is a queer paradox— the more able executives are, the more they stand out, and the greater their relative anonymity outside their own immediate circles.

So, as we pass more and more away from special, measurable skills into the less definable, intangible talents, it becomes clear that the selection of executives becomes more of an art and less of a science. We must rely in large measure on intuition and hope and pray that our candidate's performance will reflect our wisdom rather than our incompetence.

I am sure that all organizations have made mistakes in judgment of personnel and that the equities are sometimes compromised if not outraged by such errors. On the other side, however, I can't remember more than a very small handful of people whom I would say had not gotten their just desserts in terms of their abilities. I have worked at all levels of the Du Pont Company in 36-odd years, and I know a great many people, from wage-roll workers up. The cases in which someone suffered an injustice are nearly negligible.

It may take time—I've often seen instances in which a person who was ready for a promotion had to wait two or three years, or perhaps four or five years, before it came. The realities of the situation were such that it couldn't be given at the instant in which that person was ready for it. But given time he got there.

How much more difficult it is to appraise potential in advance!" And yet, appraising an individual's potential for future performance is a major purpose of the selection and placement activity. As the author of this scenario indicates, the selection of executives is particularly difficult because of their "less definable, intangible talents." Does the selection of executives, and all other employees, have to be left in large measure to intuition, hope, and prayer? Definitely not. With pressures from increasing international competition and government rules and regulations, perhaps the crucial question is, Can organizations survive if they leave their selection and placement decisions to intuition, hope, and prayer? Probably not.

The specific purposes of this chapter are to look at the external and internal sources of job applicants; to describe the methods used to gather information needed in selection and placement; to analyze the techniques for making selection and placement decisions; to examine the validity and utility of selection and placement; and to familiarize you with several organizational, individual, and legal issues in selection and placement. First, however, it is necessary to present an overview of selection and placement—their purposes and importance, their relationships with the other personnel functions and activities, and the people responsible for selection and placement.

SELECTION AND PLACEMENT

Selection is the process of gathering information for the purposes of evaluating and deciding who should be hired, under legal guidelines, for the short- and long-term interests of the individual and the organization. **Placement** is concerned with ensuring that job demands are filled and that individual needs and preferences are met.[1] Traditionally, selection and placement have primarily been concerned with matching employee skills and abilities with the demands of the job. Now, however, there is an additional emphasis on matching employee needs and preferences with job rewards.

The concern for two-way matching in selection and placement is consistent with the recent emphasis in recruitment. In fact, although these two activities are treated separately in this book, they share many qualities. For example, both use information on the characteristics and qualities of the organization, the job, and the individual. Both seek to serve the short- and long-term interests of the organization and the individual. They also share many of the same purposes and goals.

Purposes of Selection and Placement

Selection and placement activities provide the very essence of organizations—their human resources. Above all, "business is a human organization, made or broken by its people."[2] Without the human resources, organizations would not exist. People may not be any more important today than they were fifty years ago, but today organizations recognize their importance. As the importance of selection and placement activities has increased, so have the complexity and challenge in doing them as effectively as possible.

Specifically, the purposes of selection and placement are
- To fairly, legally, and in a nondiscriminatory manner evaluate and hire the appropriate job applicants
- To evaluate, hire, and place job applicants in the best interests of the organization and the individual
- To engage in selection and placement activities that are useful for initial hiring as well as future selection and placement decisions for the individual (for example, in promotions or transfers)
- To gather information about the individual, the organization, the job, and the environment in an efficient, legal, and effective manner
- To make selection and placement decisions with consideration for the uniqueness of the individual, the job, the organization, and the environment, even to the extent of adapting the job or organization to the individual or the environment

The discussion of selection and placement in this chapter is designed to help you attain these purposes if and when you are involved in these activities, whether as a personnel specialist or not.

Selection and Placement in Context

The success of an organization's selection and placement activities depends on their relationships to several other personnel and human resource activities. As Exhibit 6.1 illustrates, selection and placement decisions begin with a pool of job applicants, an analysis of the qualities of the jobs that are open, and a description of the organizational context. The first two of these are directly related to recruitment and job analysis activities.

Job Analysis.   Selection and placement decisions should be made to benefit the individual and the organization. In order to do this, the qualities of the jobs to be filled must clearly be identified. When the essential job dimensions and worker qualifications are known, selection devices can be developed. Selection devices

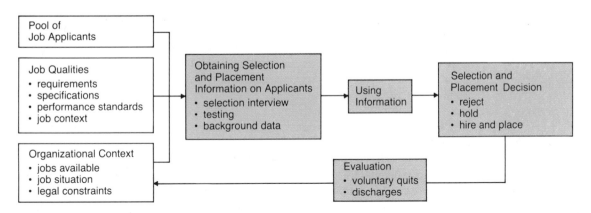

Exhibit 6.1   Selection and Placement Procedures

developed on the basis of a job analysis are more likely to be job-related—thus more effective.

However, selection devices based on job analysis tend to focus on the worker's ability to do the job. It is also necessary to use information about job rewards so that job applicants can be placed in jobs that match their needs. As noted in Chapter 5, this two-way match helps ensure that the short-run and long-run interests of both individuals and organizations are served.

Recruitment.   The success of selection and placement activities often depends on the effectiveness of the recruiting activity. If recruiting does not provide a pool of qualified, ready job applicants, it is impossible for the organization to select and place individuals who will perform well and not quit. Furthermore, a smaller pool may reduce the effectiveness of the selection and placement activities.

Performance Appraisal.   Selection and placement also depend on performance appraisals to show that the selection devices do indeed predict performance. If performance appraisal is done poorly, it is difficult for the organization to develop and use selection devices to predict meaningful employee performance. As a result, selection and placement are unable to serve their purposes.

Who's Responsible for Selection and Placement?

The Individual.   As shown in Exhibit 6.1, one aspect of selection and placement is the individual—either as a job applicant looking for the first job with the organization or as a current employee being considered for a transfer, promotion, or demotion. The individual is important in the initial phase of gathering information about aptitudes, experiences, needs, and preferences; in the second phase of accepting a job offer; and in the third phase of staying with the organization.

It is interesting to note that 10 to 15 percent of the individuals who are offered a management job back out. Those who back out apparently do so because the organization fails to recognize that selection and placement are a two-way street. The organization fails to follow up on the job offer with phone calls or letters and just waits until the individual replies.[3]

The Life Insurance Marketing and Research Association recommends that individuals assume responsibility in the selection and placement process by providing as much information about needs, preferences, skills, and experience as possible. They should also seek out as much information about the organization and the job as possible—if they want an opportunity to choose from several alternative organizations and jobs.

Personnel and Line Managers.   Line managers may help identify the need for staffing through the human resource planning activity of the organization. They may help with job analysis and evaluate the performance of employees. However, they most likely lack the time to do an effective and efficient job of selection and placement. Therefore, the personnel department should be responsible for gathering information and should arrange interviews between the job applicant and the managers. It should coordinate the information necessary to make a decision to hire, reject, or hold.

There are several advantages to letting the personnel department coordinate selection and placement activities:

● The applicant has only one place to go to apply for a job.

● Outside sources of applicants can clear issues pertaining to employment through one central location.

● Operating managers can concentrate on their operating responsibilities, which is especially helpful during peak hiring periods.

● Hiring is done by specialists trained in staffing techniques, and so selection is often better.

● The applicant has a better chance of being considered for a greater variety of jobs.

● Hiring costs may be cut because duplication of effort is avoided.

● With increased government regulations of selection, it is important that people who know about these rules handle a major part of the hiring process.[4]

JOB APPLICANTS FOR SELECTION AND PLACEMENT

Selection and placement seek to put the right person in the right job. The right person may be found outside or inside the organization. Whether a person is "right" depends on the match between the person's abilities and job skill demands and between the person's needs and job rewards. An organization may want job applicants to fill newly created jobs or jobs that have become vacant as a result of retirement, transfer, or voluntary quitting (turnover). Vacancies may also be created by demotions and discharges. Because demotions and discharges are an important part of human resource management, they are discussed in Chapter 9. Job transfer is discussed later in this chapter and, along with retirement and voluntary quitting, in Chapter 14.

As indicated in Chapter 5, an organization can seek job applicants from inside or outside the organization. Each source has advantages and disadvantages. The legal constraints on selection and placement are essentially identical, but some of the procedures are different. Many of these differences exist mainly because the organization already has some information on job applicants who are current employees; others exist because current employees have more information about the organization than outsiders and are often given first priority in being considered for a job opening.

Promotion and Transfer

"Going outside is the exception rather than the rule, and promotion from within is a standard practice in most organizations."[5] Some job vacancies, however, are filled by outside sources, particularly for highly skilled jobs or when the organization has been caught by surprise and has no one ready internally to take the job. To help prevent surprises, organizations like BancOhio, XEROX, IBM, Nationwide Insurance Company, and AMAX have managerial succession programs. In these programs, which are really part of the organization's human resource planning and programming, current managers identify employees who may one day be able to take over their jobs.

Types of Promotion and Transfer.   Promotions can occur within a department, a division, or an entire organization.[6] They also can occur between two nonmanagerial positions (for example, from Typist I to Typist II), between two managerial positions, and between a nonmanagerial and a managerial (or supervisory) position.

Although promotions generally refer to vertical moves in the organization, promotions may occur when an employee moves to another job at the same level but with more pay or status. However, this type of promotion may violate federal wage guidelines and equal pay regulations, and so it should be made advisedly. Although such a move could be regarded as a transfer, a transfer generally refers to a move at the same level and at the same pay.

Making Promotion and Transfer Decisions.   Immediate supervisors have a major role in deciding who to promote or transfer.

In many cases, the immediate supervisor must search for qualified candidates and make a choice when a vacancy arises. This process may be carried out in close consultation with one or more higher level supervisors who ultimately have to approve the choice. On the other hand, the immediate supervisor may have almost total control over the decisions.[7]

Immediate supervisors may have most control when a new job is being created. They may be able to determine exactly who will be promoted by writing the job description to fit only one person. This is not necessarily a fair practice, but it's a common one.

Identifying Candidates for Promotion and Transfer.   Candidates may be identified by word of mouth, inspection of the organization's personnel records (this is easy if the organization has a computerized HRIS), promotion lists based on performance or managerial ratings, and formal programs for identifying potential candidates for promotion such as assessment centers.

Comparing Candidates.   Methods for identifying candidates can also be used to evaluate and compare candidates. Although many companies administer a battery of tests to assess mental ability, personality, and interests, one study concluded that "tests are ignored more often than not as decision making aids for internal promotions."[8] Behavioral tests are used extensively by Standard Oil of Ohio, General Electric, Sears, Wickes, and J. C. Penney.

Job experience and performance history are also used to evaluate candidates. Interviews are used as well, although they are used more widely for candidates from external sources. A powerful sponsor (often a manager at a higher level in the organization who "adopts" and looks out for an employee at a lower level) can help ensure that an individual's strengths are noted by others. A final basis for comparing candidates is seniority.

Making the Final Choice.   Making a decision is difficult if different types of information are available for competing job applicants. Even if this is the case, however, all of the candidates can be screened quickly, and only those with an obvious potential to do well are retained. Those remaining can be sequentially evaluated. Although this may not result in selection of the best candidate, at least the one who is chosen should perform adequately.

A strategy used by managers who favor a particular candidate, the inside candidate, is the **confirmation approach**. To make the selection process appear legitimate, a manager may select several candidates, in addition to the favorite, for others to evaluate. The catch is that the other candidates are far less qualified than the favorite. Although there is a choice, it is more apparent than real.

Why Not the Best?   All too often, the best people are not the ones who are promoted or transferred.[9] There are several reasons for this.

First, staff people are often not considered for line jobs. Many organizations promote only line managers to upper management. Exceptions to this tradition are occurring, however, as shown in the scenario at the beginning of Chapter 1. IBM has a company policy of promoting managers in and out of line and staff jobs.

Second, decentralized departments and divisions operate like independent organizations. Thus when vacancies occur, that department or division tends to select only from its own employees and not from the total organization. Decentralization can also result in a separate performance appraisal system for each division; even if divisions did obtain candidates from other divisions, they could be hard to evaluate. This issue is discussed again in Chapter 9.

A third reason that the most qualified person may be overlooked is related to sex discrimination.

Probably one of the more overlooked banks of promotable talent is the huge reservoir of women in the work force. Except in service industries such as banks, insurance companies, and advertising firms, women have been largely ignored in management promotions.[10]

Ignoring women (and minorities) means selecting managers (often illegally) from a small percentage of the employees.

Fourth, the best person may not be promoted because subjective, personal criteria are used in selection rather than objective criteria. Subjective criteria include how well they are liked by the manager, how they dress, and how popular they are.

Finally, many competent managers are refusing promotion because it often means moving to another location. Increasingly members of dual-career families are refusing promotions involving a geographic change because the change may require a career sacrifice on the part of the other person. In addition, some managers refuse promotions because they are more interested in pursuing leisure rather than work.

Organizational and Job Previews

External sources are especially critical for an organization selecting job applicants for entry-level positions. For these positions, there is basically no other choice, except transfer. External sources are also important for upper-level management positions and for those that require unique skills and abilities. Since external sources of job applicants are identified in Chapter 5, it is most useful here to highlight one

A SLICE OF LIFE

The best people are not always promoted. There are a variety of reasons for this, but usually the ability of those who deserve to be promoted is not recognized. However, sometimes even when their abilities are recognized, they are not promoted.

Suppose that you were a manager with an especially competent person working for you and that this person was the source of many innovative ideas leading to increased performance in your area of responsibility. In fact, you have been complimented on the operation of your division. Now, be honest. Wouldn't you hesitate to recommend this person for a promotion that might lead to a transfer into another division? The promotion might be in the best interests of the organization, but it would certainly be your loss. You would lose you very best person, a person without whom your division will surely suffer, and if your division suffers, you suffer. Wouldn't you consider holding this person back maybe for "just a little more seasoning," "just a little more experience?" It wouldn't be the first time that a deserving person has not been promoted.

aspect of selection and placement unique to external sources—the realistic preview.[11] The **realistic job preview** is important because it increases an awareness of what a potential job is like; the **realistic organizational preview** creates an awareness of what the organization is like and what some job rewards are. The organizational preview describes such things as the reward policies of the organization, the philosophy of management, the quality of supervision, and the opportunities for career development and continuing education. A current employee knows at least what the organization is like and so needs only a realistic job preview. But the external job applicant needs both in order to be matched to a job on the basis of ability and need.

SELECTION AND PLACEMENT INFORMATION

The job preview and organizational preview are primarily means for conveying information about the job and organization to the job applicant. To complete the two-way process, the organization needs to obtain information about the job applicant. Then the organization can try to match the applicant with the appropriate job. As shown in Exhibit 6.1, there are three major sets of information needed for selection and placement: organizational context; job qualities; and job applicants.

The Organizational Context

Information about the organizational context necessary for effective selection and placement identifies the jobs available, job situations, and legal constraints. To determine who to select and place, job vacancies first need to be identified. This identification can be initiated through the organization's human resource planning and programming or through direct requisitions from supervisors. Because many organizations do not effectively plan human resource needs, supervisor requisitions often become the major source of information about job openings. However, with some forecasts of managerial shortages by the mid-1980s, more organizations are beginning to systematically program for their human resource needs. Managerial succession programs are evidence of this systematic effort. Organizations such as Nationwide Insurance Company, Detroit Edison, and Owens-Illinois also have department and division managers forecast job openings and human resource needs for one- and five-year periods. Without effective human resource planning, job availability is often not determined until there are job vacancies. Consequently, recruitment, selection, and placement may be undertaken without awareness of the jobs that are open or be done so quickly that a thorough recruitment and selection process is not possible.

Job performance may be determined only in part by the individual. Such characteristics of the organization as compensation policies, group pressures, philosophy of management, and quality of supervision also determine an individual's level of performance. In fact, there are many job situations in which employee performance is really determined by the pace of the machines more than any qualities of the employee. Because these aspects of the organization and job situation are so important, they must be accounted for in selection and placement procedures. For example, two jobs may require the same technical skills. But if one is isolated and the other is part of a larger group, the selection process for the job in the larger group may need to include a measure of interpersonel competence or need for affiliation; selection for the isolated job would not. The job situation not only influences employee performance but also determines job rewards. These can be conveyed in the organizational preview.

An organization's selection and placement activities are constrained by state and federal laws, executive orders, and court decisions. Because these are such important and extensive aspects of selection and placement, a major section of Chapter 7 examines them.

Job Qualities

Information about job requirements or demands and specifications is obtained from conventional job analysis. This information is needed to match individual ability with job demands. It is essential for a realistic job preview.

Part of the realistic job preview conveys to the job applicant the standards of performance. This information is contained on a results-oriented job description (see Chapter 4). Frequently, however, performance standards are not provided; only the information on the conventional job description and specification is provided.

The Job Context

In order to choose a job realistically, job applicants must know the conditions in which the job is performed. For example, it is important for both the applicant and the organization to know the physical conditions that the applicant may confront on the job. This is particularly true since the *Whirlpool Corporation v. Ray Marshall, Secretary of Labor* decision, which allows employees to decline a job assignment if they believe danger to life or limb is imminent. Other aspects of the job context are time pressures, the hours of work, and the design characteristics of the job.[12] These aspects are an integral part of the realistic job preview.

OBTAINING JOB APPLICANT INFORMATION

Information about the organizational context, job qualities, and job context are only about half of the information needed to match ability to demand and need to reward. The remaining half comes from the job applicant. The specific types of information obtained on an individual are aptitude, achievement or experience, and motivation (particularly personality, interest, and preferences). This information then becomes the basis for predicting how well a job applicant will perform. Procedures used to gather this information thus often are called predictors. The major information-gathering procedures for selection and placement decisions are interviews, tests, and background information, supplied by the applicant. Of course, all these procedures are subject to legal constraints (see Chapter 7).

It is important to note that using information on the individual to predict performance represents concern for only one match—the match between ability and job demands. This is the match that is subject to legal constraints and traditionally of major interest to organizations. However, individual information should also be gathered to predict employee satisfaction, absenteeism, and voluntary turnover. These predictions reflect a concern for the match between needs and rewards. Many organizations have not focused on needs and rewards, but with the high cost of absenteeism, turnover, and dissatisfaction, they may begin to find that it pays to do so.

Since all the selection and placement information can be used for both matches, both will be discussed. But the ability-demand match is the primary concern for many organizations and is subject to legal constraints, so it is highlighted in this chapter and the next. The need-reward match is the focus of Section Seven.

The Selection and Placement Interview

Although aptitude, achievement, personality interests, and preferences are more reliably assessed by paper-and-pencil or carefully developed situational tests, the interview remains the most important method of obtaining information (see Exhibit 6.2). It is a good procedure for gathering factual background information, although it is not a particularly good procedure for making assessments, because it is too subjective.[13]

Paradoxically, the use of interviews as the means of gathering and assessing information has increased, not decreased, with pressure for more objective methods of selection. This is partially due to the rules and regulations of several equal opportunity agencies:

As a consequence of this legal complexity and confusion, many companies abandoned employment testing altogether in favor of more subjective selection procedures designed to avert challenges and to hire enough minority candidates to avoid enforcement agency intervention. The more objective procedures were

"Our most important source is . . ."

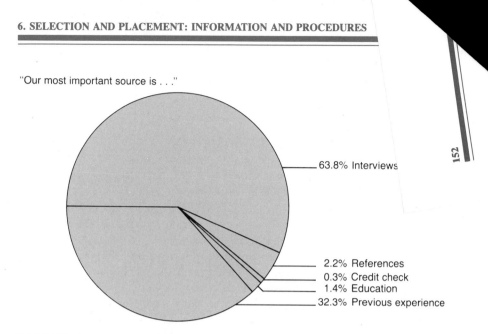

63.8% Interviews

2.2% References
0.3% Credit check
1.4% Education
32.3% Previous experience

Exhibit 6.2 Sources of Information about Job Applicants
Adapted from *Personnel Management: Policies and Practices,* Report No. 22 (Englewood Cliffs, N.J.:
Prentice-Hall, April 2, 1975).

*abandoned because few employers were able to prove the validity of their
selection procedures under the 1970 guidelines, and most didn't wish to risk
charges of noncompliance.*[14]

Thus the interview continues to be a much-used procedure for gathering selection
and placement information.

As shown in Exhibit 6.3, the interview process is important at two points—at the
beginning and end of the selection procedure. The way the interview is conducted
depends on the type of job being filled. In the case of middle- and upper-level
managerial and executive jobs, individuals often submit resumes (by mail or through
a placement or job search firm) to organizations. An initial interview is made over
the phone if the organization wants to gather more information from the applicant.
For lower-level management and nonmanagement jobs, an individual may see a job
advertised in the newspaper or posted on the organization's bulletin board and fill
out an application. Then the initial interview may follow. Because of the increased
legal necessity for organizations to keep records of the people who have applied for
jobs and have been hired, it makes good sense for an organization to document that
information before beginning the interview.

> Laws and regulations concerning employment practices are meant to ensure
> that employment decisions are made on the basis of performance and no
> other factors. Decisions made on the basis of how well a job applicant will
> perform are valid or job-related decisions. Measures or tests that provide
> information to make valid decisions are valid predictors. To the extent that
> these predictors generally lead to the same decision, they are reliable.
> Chapter 7 includes a more complete discussion of reliability and validity.

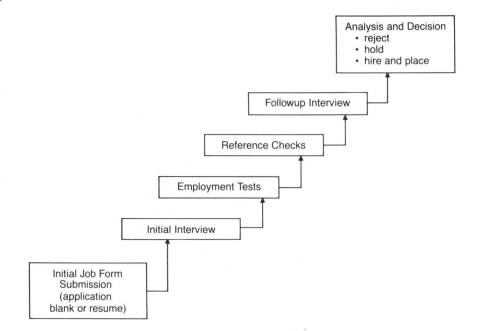

Exhibit 6.3   Steps in Selection

Frequently several individuals interview the applicant, especially if the job is a middle-level or upper-level managerial or executive one. Often these interviews ask for in-depth information about motivation, attitudes, and experience. These interviews are for the purpose of making assessments, not just gathering information. However, even the initial interview has an assessment aspect, because a reject/pass decision could be made at that stage. Therefore, both interview stages are crucial.

Common Interview Problems.   There are several problems that interviewers often encounter.[15] They relate to the interview as a procedure for gathering information as well as for assessing that information.

● Managers (as interviewers) do not seek applicant information on all the important dimensions needed for successful job performance.

Often the interviewers do not have a complete description of the job being filled or an accurate appraisal of its critical requirements. In addition, the interviewer often does not know the conditions under which the job is performed. Legally, it is important that all the information obtained be job-related.

● Especially with several interviews, managers overlap in their coverage of some job-related questions and miss others entirely.

It may happen that an applicant has not four interviews but one interview four times. All managers ask the same questions and are provided the same information.

● Managers permit one trait or job-related attribute to influence their evaluation of the remaining qualities of an applicant.

This process, called the **halo effect**, occurs when an interviewer judges an applicant's entire potential for job performance on the basis of one characteristic, such as how well the applicant dresses or talks. The halo effect may lead to poor and discriminatory choices by the interviewer; it may also affect the choices made by the job applicant:

The interviewer becomes the symbol for the company, and yet he represents a sample size of only one. Nevertheless, the applicant often places more importance on his estimate of the representative of the company than on his judgments based on the company literature.[16]

• Managers have not organized the various selection elements into a system. Exhibit 6.3 depicts an order in the selection activities, but often these activities are really not done so orderly. Key references may not be checked before the intensive interviews, resulting in interviews with unqualified applicants. Occasionally, applicants are treated differently, some given certain tests and others not. This may be a result of forgetfulness of lack of clarity on who was to do what. Regardless, the result is unfair and discriminatory selection practices.

• Information from interviews with an applicant is not integrated and discussed in a systematic manner.
If several interviewers share information on an applicant, they may do so in a very haphazard manner. They may not identify job-related information or seek to examine any conflicting information. This casual approach to decision making may save time and confrontation—but only in the short run. In the long run, everyone in the organization will pay for poor hiring decisions.

• Managers' judgments are often affected by the pressure (or price) to fill the position.
With pressure to fill a position, managers lower their standards. If this leads to a bad decision, the manager who made the decision can always claim an excuse. Managers may also hire an applicant because of the price (salary demands). Personnel managers can reduce this possibility by not revealing salary demands to the line managers responsible for hiring. The best philosophy is first to select the best person for the job and then to be concerned with the cost.

• Managers' judgments regarding an applicant are often affected by the available applicants.
Two important concepts—contrast and order effects—are important here. First, a good person looks better in contrast to a group of average or below-average people. An average person looks below-average or poor in contrast to a group of good or excellent people. Second, there are two important **order effects**—first impression and last impression. At times a first impression is important and lasting; the first person may become the standard used to evaluate the quality of all the other people. But an interviewer, especially at the end of a long day of interviewing, may be more likely to remember the last person better than many of the other people. As an applicant, you should be aware of these effects. Try to get an interview in the middle of an interviewer's schedule and try to be interviewed around the time that applicants less qualified than you are being interviewed.

Overcoming Potential Interview Problems. There are several ways to overcome the above problems. The methods suggested below are essentially ways to increase the validity and reliability of the interview (increase its job-relatedness, the scope of qualifications measured, and the consistency and objectivity of the information gathered).

• *Gather only job-related information*: That is, be sure to use only information from job-related questions as predictors of future performance. This requires that a job analysis be done on the jobs to be filled and, if possible, validation results be obtained for the predictors being used. (These issues are examined in more detail in Chapter 7.)

Although it is not always easy to know what is job-related or what will predict future performance, a job analysis will make it easier. Exhibit 6.4 lists some factors (predictors) that often are determined in interviews. Whether these are job-related or not depends in part on the results of the analysis and validation studies.

• *Use past behavior to predict future behavior*: Essentially, concentrate on getting information about the applicant's job-related behavior. This background information can be obtained conveniently in the initial interview.

It is best to get specific examples of performance-related experiences and the events surrounding those examples. Although Exhibit 6.4 shows that work experience is the third most important factor in hiring interviews, specific examples of work experience may not be a sufficient justification for legally using this information in a selection decision. A judge in an Ohio court ruled that the use of past experience is not a predictor of what an individual will do on the next job and therefore cannot be used in selection. The reasons for this decision are explained in the discussion of the application blank at the end of this chapter.

• *Coordinate the initial interview and succeeding interviews with each other and with the other information-gathering procedures*: The information should be combined in an objective, systematic, job-related manner.

The coordination and combination of information can aid in reducing quick decisions, bias, and the use of sterotypes in selection. Also assisting in this reduction is the final step.

• *Getting several managers involved in interviewing and in the final decision*: This can be done as a group or individually.

Although the final decision may be made by only one person, several should be involved in gathering the information and assessing its merits.

Exhibit 6.4 Predictors of Job Success Elicited in Interviews

Characteristics	Rank	Characteristics	Rank
Communications skills	1	Location preference	6
Grade-point average	2	Academic accomplishments	7
Work experience	3	Draft status	8
Appearance	4	Percentage of college expenses earned	9
Extracurricular activities	5	References	10

Adapted from Conely, J. H., Hueghi, J. M. and Minter, R. L. *Perspectives on Administrative Communication* (Dubuque, Iowa: Kendall/Hunt, 1976), p. 172.

Nonverbal Cues in Interviews.   Another important aspect of the interview is the nonverbal component, the part not said with words. Things like body movements, gestures, firmness of handshake, eye contact, and physical appearance are all **nonverbal cues**. Often interviewers put more importance on the nonverbal than on the verbal.

It has been estimated that, at most, only 30 to 35 percent of the meaning
*conveyed in a message is verbal; the remainder is nonverbal. Similarly, in terms
of attitudes or feelings, one estimate is that merely seven percent of what is
communicated is verbal, while nonverbal factors account for the remaining 93
percent.*[17]

Therefore, it is important to be aware of nonverbal cues. "In fact, one of the reasons that nonverbal cues are so powerful is that, in most cases interviewers are not aware of them as possible causal agents of impression formation."[18]

What to Ask.   Interviewers may ask anything that, when combined with other information about the job applicant, can be a useful predictor of how well the applicant will perform once hired. Useful questions include:
● Has the applicant performed in a similar capacity before?
● How does the applicant feel about present job qualities and organizational context?
● If the applicant is changing jobs, why is a change being made?
● Is the applicant likeable?
● What are the applicant's career objectives?
● Does the applicant like working closely with other people?
● How has the applicant performed considering the environment of that performance?[19]
The last question is an important one because it goes to the heart of a newer kind of exam—the **bio-data test**:

*To cope with the new regulations on formal tests, some employers have turned to
the so-called bio-data test—a kind of exam on which blacks and whites score
about the same and which shows encouraging signs of being a reliable predictor
of performance. A bio-data test evaluates a candidate in terms of how well he has
performed in his milieu, rather than according to an absolute standard. The
underlying principle is a familiar one. For example, many employers recognize
that while the top student in a ghetto high school may score lower than a middle-
ranking student at a suburban high school on a general information test, the fact
he made it to the top indicates ambition, pride, and discipline—qualities that are
strong indicators of how well a person will perform in a job.*

*In a formal bio-data exam, a candidate might be asked to rank himself on such
questions as, "How fast do you work compared to other people?" and "How old
were you when you first earned money?" Some employers have also found bio-
data tests helpful in coping with another development that has complicated the
hiring process in this litigious era—the reluctance of former employers, fearful of
lawsuits, to supply prospective employers with anything more than a terse*

confirmation that so-and-so did indeed work for the company during such-and-such a period. In a bio-data exam the prospective employer can ask the candidate, "If we were to ask your former employer to rate your performance, how do you think he would rate you?" The candidate then checks off one of five blocks on a scale of from "very good" to "very poor." Fran W. Erwin, a Washington, D.C., personnel consultant who, among other things, helps design such tests, says applicants answer that question with surprising frankness.

So far, bio-data tests have not been widely used, and they have not yet been refined to the point where they predict performance with precision. The Life Insurance Marketing Research Association in Hartford, Connecticut, which has used them for forty years in hiring salesmen, says they are extremely accurate in predicting which applicants will do very poorly, but not as accurate in anticipating which ones will do very well.[20]

What Not to Ask.   A list of inappropriate (but not illegal) questions to ask in the selection interview is shown in Exhibit 6.5, along with recommended substitutes. Chapter 5 mentions questions and topics that are illegal.

Employment Tests

Testing is another important procedure for gathering, transmitting, and assessing information about an applicant's aptitudes, experiences, and motivations. Employment tests include any paper-and-pencil or performance measures used as a basis for an employment decision. The three most common types of tests measure aptitude, achievement, and motivation.

The validity and reliability of these approaches are of utmost importance for both the organization and the job applicant. Validity and reliability help ensure that an applicant will perform at a certain level. They also help provide the job applicant with a sense of fairness and legality in the selection procecure.

It is recommended that organizations inform job applicants of the procedures used in gathering information, particularly from paper-and-pencil tests. The Life Insurance Marketing and Research Association also recommends that organizations using tests inform those taking tests
- That the test is only one step in the hiring process
- What the test measures and that it does so with validity and reliability
- Why it is being used
- What passing or failing means to them and about them[21]

Aptitude Tests.   **Aptitude tests** measure the potential of individuals to perform. Measures of general aptitude, often referred to as general intelligence tests, include the Wechsler Adult Intelligence Scale and the Stanford-Binet test. These tests are primarily used to predict academic success in a traditional setting. Thus several multidimensional job-related aptitude tests were developed, including: Differential Aptitude Tests, the Flanagan Aptitude Classification Test, the General Aptitude Test Battery, and the Employee Aptitude Survey. Exhibit 6.6 shows what these tests measure. Because they are standardized, they are not specific to any particular job.

Exhibit 6.5   What Not to Ask in a Selection Interview

Inappropriate Question	More Appropriate Questions
Do you have any physical defects?	Do you have any physical defects or impediments that might hinder your ability to perform the job you have applied for?
Have you had any recent or past illness or operations?	Have you had any recent or past illness or operations that might hinder your ability to perform the job you have applied for?
What was the date of your last physical exam?	Are you willing to take a physical exam at our expense if the nature of the job requires one?
Are you a U.S. citizen?	Do you have the legal right to live and work in the U.S.?
What is your date of birth?	Are you over eighteen and less than seventy?
What is your age?	Are you over eighteen and less than seventy?
Who should we contact in an emergency? What is the relationship?	Who should we contact in an emergency?
Do you possess a legal driver's license?	Do you possess a legal and current driver's license? (only for applicants who want a job driving a company vehicle)
What are your hobbies? Interests?	Do you have any hobbies or interests that have a direct bearing on the job you are seeking?
Have you ever been convicted of a misdemeanor or felony?	Have you, since the age of eighteen, ever been convicted of a misdemeanor or felony? (Note: A conviction will not necessarily bar you from employment. Each conviction will be judged on its own merits with respect to time, circumstances, and seriousness.)
When did you attend high school? Grammar school?	Did you complete grammar school? High school?
When did you graduate or last attend high school? Grammar school?	Did you complete grammar school? High school?
In what extracurricular activities did you participate? Clubs?	While in school, did you participate in any activities or belong to any clubs that have a direct bearing on the job you are applying for?
What subjects interested you in college?	While in college, did you take any courses that directly relate to the job you are applying for?
What salary or earnings do you expect?	If you are employed, are you willing to accept the prevailing wage for the job you are seeking?
What organizations do you belong to? (with or without EEO disclaimer)	Have you ever belonged to a club, organization, society, or professional group that has a direct bearing on your qualification for the job you are seeking?

From E. C. Miller, "An EEO Examination of Employment Applications," p. 68. Reprinted with permission from the March 1980 issue of the *Personnel Administrator*, copyright 1980, The American Society for Personnel Administration, 30 Park Drive, Berea, OH 44017.

But they are reliable and general enough to be used in job situations, especially for indicating the contribution that more specific tests can make.[22]

The U.S. Training and Employment Service uses the General Aptitude Test Battery (GATB) to evaluate individuals seeking employment. Most job analyses estimate the aptitudes measured by the GATB. (In the job description of the dough mixer in Chapter 4, the aptitude scores listed at the bottom of Exhibit 4.7, under Worker Trait Ratings, are GATB scores.) In addition, the GATB measures two eye-hand abilities.

These eye-hand measures are only two of the physical job-related aptitudes that can be measured. Others include dynamic strength, trunk strength, static strength, explosive strength, extent flexibility, gross body coordination, balance, and stamina.[23] Of course, intellectual as well as physical aptitudes are important. Job-matching and redesign programs can be devised around both.[24]

Differential Aptitude Tests (DAT)	Flanagan Aptitude Classification Test (FACT)	General Aptitude Test Battery (GATB)*	Employee Aptitude Survey (EAS)†
Verbal reasoning Numerical ability Abstract reasoning Space relations Mechanical reasoning Clerical speed and accuracy Language usage (spelling) Language usage (sentences)	Inspection Coding Memory Precision Assembly Scales Coordination Judgment and comprehension Arithmetic Patterns Components Tables Mechanics Expression	Verbal Numerical Spatial Form perception Clerical perception Motor coordination Finger dexterity Manual dexterity General intelligence	Verbal comprehension Numerical ability Visual pursuit Visual speed and accuracy Space visualization Numerical reasoning Verbal reasoning Word fluency Manual speed and accuracy Symbolic reasoning

Exhibit 6.6   Some Multidimensional Aptitude Tests for Use in Selection
From *Staffing Organizations* by B. Schneider, p. 153. Copyright © 1976 by Goodyear Publishing Co. Reprinted by permission.
*General intelligence is a combination of spatial, verbal, and numerical scores.
†Designed specifically for industrial situations.

Another group of aptitude tests, called **psychomotor tests**, combine the mental and the physical. Two of the more widely used psychomotor tests are the MacQuarrie Test for Mechanical Ability and the O'Connor Finger and Tweezer Dexterity Tests. The MacQuarrie test measures skills in tracing, tapping, dotting, copying, locating, arranging blocks, and pursuing. This test seems to be a valid predictor for such occupations as aviation mechanic and stenographer. The O'Connor test is a valid predictor for power sewing machine operators, dental students, and other workers requiring manipulative skills.[25]

A final group of aptitude tests relates to personal and interpersonal competence. One test of **personal competence**, called the Career Maturity Inventory, measures whether individuals know how to make appropriate and timely decisions for themselves and whether they really put forth the effort to do so. It includes five competence tests related to problems, planning, occupational information, self-knowledge, and goal selection. The better the score on these five competency tests, the more likely an individual is to make career decisions resulting in higher satisfaction and performance.

Interpersonal competence tests have been designed to measure social intelligence. These include aspects of intelligence related to

information, non-verbal, which is involved in human interactions where awareness of attention, perceptions, thoughts, desires, feelings, moods, emotions, intentions and actions of other persons and of ourselves is important.[26]

Achievement Tests.   **Achievement tests** predict an individual's performance on the basis of what he or she knows. Validation is required of any test used by an organization, but validating achievement tests is a rather straightforward process.[27] The achievement tests almost become samples of the job to be performed. However, hiring on the basis of achievement tests may exclude applicants who have not had equal access to the opportunities to acquire the skills. It should also be noted that not all achievement tests are samples of the job, some are less job-related than others.

Paper-and-pencil achievement tests tend to be less job-related because they measure facts and principles—not the actual use of them. For example, you could take a paper-and-pencil test measuring your knowledge of tennis and pass with flying colors and yet play very poorly. Although this is a serious deficiency, paper-and-pencil achievement tests continue to be used in many areas. For example, admission to the legal profession is through the bar exam, and the medical profession is entered through medical boards.

The **recognition test** is often used in advertising and modeling to select applicants. The applicants bring to the job interview portfolios of their work, samples of the work they have done. However, portfolios contain no clues to the conditions or circumstances under which they were done. Some organizations may insist on seeing written samples from school work for jobs where written expression may be important.

Recognition tests are really examples of past behavior; **simulation tests** are used to see how applicants perform now. Only the task itself—not the situation in which the task is performed—is recreated. Even so, simulation can be extremely useful as a training and practice device. You may recall from good crime movies, that the crime is rehearsed many times before actually being committed. Simulations are especially good preparation for events that happen only once, like the first moon landing.

Some achievement tests overcome the artificiality of simulations by using the actual task and working conditions. These are called **work sample tests**. Work sample tests are frequently given to applicants for secretarial jobs. Applicants may be asked to type a letter in the office where they would be working. There still tends to be some artificiality in work sample tests, however, because the selection process itself tends to promote some anxiety and tension.

Anxiety and tension may not be artifical for some jobs, such as a managerial job under time pressure. In fact, a work sample test referred to as the **in-basket exercise** has been created for that type of job. Its objective is to create a realistic situation that will elicit typical on-the-job behaviors. Situations and problems encountered in the job are written on individual sheets of paper and set in the in-basket. The applicant is asked to arrange the papers by priority. Occasionally the applicant may need to write an action response on the piece of paper. The problems or situations described to the applicant involve different groups of people—peers, subordinates, and those outside the organization. The applicant is usually given a set time limit to take the test but is often interrupted by phone calls meant to create more tension and pressure.

Motivation Tests. Designed to measure an individual's motivation to perform, **motivation tests** may focus on personality, interests, or preferences for certain types of jobs. Tests of the individual's traits or characteristics are sometimes referred to as **personality inventories**. Several common multidimensional tests of personality are the Edwards Personal Preference Schedule: the California Psychological Inventory; the Gordon Personal Profile; the Thurstone Temperament Survey; the Guilford-Zimmerman Temperament Survey; and the Minnesota Multiphasic Personality Inventory. These personality inventories have limited validity for organizations but may be useful for predicting the performance of salesclerks, clerical workers, and the like.[28] At present, the utility of personality tests for selection appears limited. Once a selection decision is made, however, they may be useful for placement and career counseling.

Placement and career counseling decisions can also be facilitated by **interest tests**. Two major interest tests are the Strong Vocational Interest Blank and the Kuder Preference Records. Both are essentially inventories of interests. Although generally not predictive of performance on the job, they can predict which occupation will be more in tune with an individual's interests. Many people take the Kuder Preference Records in high school to find out what jobs or occupations might match their interests. Records are grouped into ten vocational categories—outdoor, musical, computational, scientific, persuasive, artistic, literary, musical, social service, and clerical. Specific jobs can be identified within each of the ten groupings. Both of these interest tests should be used with caution. It is unlikely that either could predict performance in a job, nor are they always valid for predicting the specific type of job one will choose within a vocational or occupational grouping.

Preference tests are especially useful in matching employee needs with rewards of the job. One scale that may be used to infer an individual's preferences for a specific job design is the Job Diagnostic Survey, a sample of which appears in Exhibit 6.7.

Listed below are a number of characteristics that could be present on any job. People differ about how much they would like to have each one present in their own jobs. We are interested in learning *how much you personally would like* to have each one present in your job.

Using the scale below, please indicate the *degree* to which you would like to have each characteristic present in your job.

Would mildly like having this			Would strongly like having this			Would very strongly like having this
4	5	6	7	8	9	10

_____ 1. High respect and fair treatment from my supervisor
_____ 2. Stimulating and challenging work
_____ 3. Chances to exercise independent thought and action in my job
_____ 4. Great job security
_____ 5. Very friendly co-workers
_____ 6. Opportunities to learn new things from my work
_____ 7. High salary and good fringe benefits
_____ 8. Opportunities to be creative and imaginative in my work
_____ 9. Quick promotions
_____10. Opportunities for personal growth and development in my job
_____11. A sense of worthwhile accomplishment in my work

Exhibit 6.7 Sample from the Job Diagnostic Survey
From J. R. Hackman and G. R. Oldham, *Task Design* (Reading, Mass.: Addison-Wesley, 1980), p. 136. Reprinted by permission of the authors.

The Application Blank

Many of the interviewing and testing procedures used in the selection process are only moderately valid or not valid at all. Therefore, organizations typically gather additional information a third way—directly from the applicant through an application blank. The **application blank** is a form seeking information about the job applicant's background and present conditions (including current address and telephone number). Although application blanks used to request a great deal of information, often including a photograph, legal constraints have reduced the requests substantially. As mentioned earlier, there are many topics the organization may not and should not inquire about. This is true whether the organization tries to obtain the information through the selection interview or the application blank.

What is asked on the application blank should help predict how well a job applicant will perform once on the job. Because the job situation can influence an employee's performance, information about an employee's past performance record is especially helpful in predicting future performance when job situations are similar. When they are not similar, accurate prediction is more difficult, and incorrect decisions may be made. You might be saying to yourself, "To prevent that from happening, all you need to do is call the previous employer and find out what happened." Easier said than done. Today, many organizations are reluctant to provide more data than the fact that the person in question did work there at one time for a certain number of years.

The reluctance to provide additional data is explained by recent events surrounding **reference verification,** which is a method of measuring individual differences among job applicants by acquiring personal information about them. The more common approaches include checking an applicant's record with a previous employer, creditor, high school or college office, and teachers. Physical and mental health examinations and even polygraph tests are sometimes administered.

However, reference verification involves conflicting values—liberty and privacy. On the one hand, employers should be free (have the liberty) to discriminate among job applicants, especially when seeking performance-related information about them. On the other hand, liberty for the organization often leads to infringement of an individual's privacy.[29] Currently, this conflict has led to several lawsuits. The result has been several state and federal laws regarding the use of personal information for employee decisions. (See Appendix F for a description of the laws pertaining to the use of personal information and an illustration of one company's policy on it.) The conflict between liberty and privacy promises to remain a central issue in personnel management for the next several years.

SUMMARY

This chapter examines what selection and placement activities are and how they relate to other personnel activities. Organizations want to ensure that they hire job applicants with the abilities to meet job demands. Increasingly, they also want to ensure that job applicants will not only perform well but also stay. Thus organizations want to attain a match between the needs of the job applicants and the rewards offered by the job qualities and organizational context.

In order to match individual ability to job demands and individual needs to job rewards, organizations need to gather information about job applicants. The three most common methods for doing so—interviewing, testing, and application blanks—must operate within legal regulations. These legal regulations are not intended to discourage the use of these methods but rather to ensure that information is collected, retained, and used with recognition of an individual's right to privacy and an organization's right to select individuals on the basis of bona fide occupational qualifications.

PERSONNEL PROBLEM
I'm Sorry I Asked

Of these questions that might be asked of a job applicant, which do you think are discriminatory? Why do you think so?

1. Have you ever been arrested?

2. Have you ever been convicted of a felony?

3. Were you fired from your last job?

4. What does your spouse do for a living?

5. How many children do you have?

6. Have your wages ever been attached?

7. What was your salary at your last job?

8. How did you hear of this job?

9. Are you a homosexual?

10. Are you bondable?

KEY CONCEPTS

achievement test
application blank
aptitude test
bio-data test
confirmation approach
halo effect
in-basket exercise
interest test
interpersonal competence

motivation test
nonverbal cue
order effect
paper-and-pencil
   achievement test
personal competence
personality inventory
placement
preference

psychomotor test
realistic job preview
realistic organizational preview
recognition test
reference verification
selection
simulation
work sample test

DISCUSSIONS

1. What are the purposes of selection and placement?

2. What is meant by the description of selection and placement as a two-way street?

3. How can organizations get a match between ability and demands and between needs and rewards?

4. What are the advantages of filling positions by promotion rather than be hiring from outside?

5. Why aren't the best people always promoted?

6. What are the best ways to collect selection and placement information?

7. What are some common interview problems, and how can they be overcome?

8. In what topical areas can an organization obtain information for selection and placement? What areas are forbidden?

ENDNOTES

1. For a similar definition and concern for selection and placement, see
   R. E. Arvey, *Fairness in Selecting Employees* (Reading, Mass.: Addison-Wesley, 1979).
   J. P. Wanous, *Organizational Entry* (Reading, Mass.: Addison-Wesley, 1980).

2. T. F. Cawsey, "Why Line Managers Don't Listen to Their Personnel Department," *Personnel*, January/February 1980, pp. 11–20.

3. W. F. Glueck, *Personnel: A Diagnostic Approach*, 2nd ed. (Dallas, Texas: Business Publications, Inc., 1978).

4. J. B. Miner and M. G. Miner, *Personnel and Industrial Relations*, 3rd ed. (New York: Macmillan, 1977), pp. 88–123.

5. H. J. Sweeney and K. S. Teel, "A New Look at Promotion from Within," *Personnel Journal*, August 1979, p. 532.

6. M. London, "What Every Personnel Director Should Know About Management Promotion Decisions," *Personnel Journal*, October 1978, p. 550.
Sweeney and Teel, pp. 532–533.

7. "What Every Personnel Director Should Know About Management Promotion Decisions" by M. London, p. 551. Reprinted with permission *Personnel Journal*, Costa Mesa, CA, copyright October 1978.

8. J. P. Campbell, M. D. Dunnette, E. E. Lawler III., and K. E. Weick, *Managerial Behavior, Performance and Effectiveness* (New York: McGraw-Hill, 1970), p. 28.

9. D. D. McConkey, "Why the Best Managers Don't Get Promoted," *The Business Quarterly*, Summer 1979, pp. 39–43.

10. "Why the Best Managers Don't Get Promoted," by D. D. McConkey, p. 40. *Business Quarterly*, Summer 1979 published by School of Business, the University of Western Ontario, Canada.

11. D. R. Ilgen and W. Seeley, "Realistic Expectations as an Aid in Reducing Voluntary Resignations," *Journal of Applied Psychology*, 54 (1974), pp. 452–455.
T. D. Jick and L. Greenhalgh, "Realistic Job Previews: A Reconceptualization," paper presented at the National Academy of Management, Detroit, Mich., August 1980.

12. *Whirlpool Corporation v. Ray Marshall, Secretary of Labor*, U. S. Supreme Court, February 26, 1980, 8OSHC 1001.

13. B. Schneider, *Staffing Organizations* (Santa Monica, Calif.: Goodyear, 1976).

14. "New Directions in EEO Guidelines" by D. E. Robertson, p. 360. Reprinted with permission *Personnel Journal*, Costa Mesa, CA, copyright July 1978.

15. W. C. Byham, "Common Selection Problems Can Be Overcome," *Personnel Administrator*, August 1978, pp. 42–47.

16. C. W. Downs, "What Does the Selection Interview Accomplish?" *Personnel Administration*, 31 (1968), p. 100.

17. J. D. Hatfield and R. D. Gatewood, "Nonverbal Cues in the Selection Interview," p. 35. Reprinted with permission from the January 1978 issue of the *Personnel Administrator*, copyright, 1978, The American Society for Personnel Administration, 30 Park Drive, Berea, OH 44017.

18. Hatfield and Gatewood, p. 37.

19. D. T. Michaels, "Seven Questions That Will Improve Your Managerial Hiring Decisions," *Personnel Journal*, March 1980, pp. 199–200, 224.

20. L. Smith, " 'Equal Opportunity' Rules Are Getting Together," *Fortune*, June 19, 1978, p. 156. Courtesy of *Fortune* Magazine; © 1978 Time, Inc.

21. Life Insurance Marketing and Research Association, *Recruitment, Selection, Training and Supervision in Life Insurance* (Hartford, Conn.: Life Insurance Marketing and Research Association, 1966).

22. Schneider.

23. E. A. Fleishman, "Evaluating Physical Abilities Required by Jobs," *Personnel Administrator*, June 1979, pp. 82–90.

24. M. A. Jones, and E. P. Prien, "A Valid Procedure for Testing the Physical Abilities of Job Applicants," *Personnel Administrator*, September 1978, pp. 33–40.

25. Miner and Miner, p. 315.

26. J. P. Guilford, *The Nature of Human Intelligence* (New York: McGraw Hill, 1967), p. 77.

27. Schneider.

28. E. E. Ghiselli, *The Validity of Occupational Aptitude Tests*. (New York: Wiley, 1966).

29. E. L. Levine, "Legal Aspects of Reference Checking for Personnel Selection," *Personnel Administrator*, November 1977, pp. 14–16, 28.

OBJECTIVES

- To describe how an assessment center is operated

- To explain the multiple hurdles approach to combining information

- To explain the differences between empirical and content validity

- To describe false positive and false negative decisions

THOUGHT STARTERS

- What is the 80-percent rule?

- What is meant by the term *cosmic search*?

- Why are AAPs used?

- Do you support reverse discrimination?

CHAPTER SEVEN
Selection and Placement: Decisions and Constraints

What Congress has commanded is that any tests used must measure the person for the job and not the person in the abstract. . . . The touchstone is business necessity. If an employment practice which operates to exclude Negroes cannot be shown to be related to job performance, the practice is prohibited.

From Griggs v. Duke Power Co., *401 U.S. 424, 3 FEP 175, 1971, p. 4.*

Congress has not commanded that the less qualified be preferred over the better qualified simply because of minority origins. Far from disparaging job qualifications as such, Congress has made such qualifications the controlling factor, so that race, religion, nationality, and sex become irrelevant.

From Griggs v. Duke Power Co., *401 U.S. 424, 3 FEP 175, 1971, p. 42.*

Section 703(a), 42 USC Section 2000e-2(a) (42 USCS Section 2000e-2(a)), provides: "(a) It shall be an unlawful employment practice for an employer—(1) to fail or refuse to hire or to discharge any individual, or otherwise to discriminate against any individual with respect to his compensation, terms, conditions, or privileges of employment, because of such individual's race, color, religion, sex, or national origin; or (2) to limit or classify his employees or applicants for employment in any way which would deprive or tend to deprive any individual of employment opportunities or otherwise adversely affect his status as an employee, because of such individual's race, color, religion, sex, or national origin."

Section 703(d), 42 USC Section 20003-2(d) (42 USCS Section 2000e-2(d)), provides: "It shall be unlawful employment practice for any employer, labor organization or joint labor-management committee controlling apprenticeship or other training or retraining, including on-the-job training programs, to discriminate against any individual because of his race, color, religion, sex, or national origin in admission to, or employment in, any program established to provide apprenticeship or other training."

From Title VII, Civil Rights Act of 1964, used by the defense in United Steelworkers of America, AFL-CIO v. Brian F. Weber, *61 L. Ed. 2d 480 (1979).*

ongress chose not to forbid all voluntary race-conscious affirmative action. . . . We therefore hold that Title VII's prohibition in Sections 703(a) and (d) against racial discrimination does not condemn all private, voluntary, race-conscious affirmative action plans.

The purposes of the plan mirror those of the statute. Both were designed to break down old patterns of racial segregation and hierarchy. Both were structured to "open employment opportunities for Negroes in occupations which have been traditionally closed to them."

At the same time the plan does not unnecessarily trammel the interests of white employees. The plan does not require the discharge of white workers and their replacement with new black hires. . . . Nor does the plan create an absolute bar to the advancement of white employees; half of those trained in the program will be white. Moreover, the plan is a temporary measure; it is not intended to maintain racial balance, but simply to eliminate a manifest racial imbalance.

From United Steelworkers of America, AFL-CIO *v.* Brian F. Weber, *61 L. Ed. 2d 480 (1979).*

ll of these quotes illustrate the growing complexity of the laws and regulations governing an organization's selection and placement activities. These quotes also reveal the uncertainty an organization confronts when attempting to comply with equal employment obligations. Nevertheless, it is in the organization's best interests to comply with these guidelines, because the costs of noncompliance can be imposing. AT&T paid in excess of $75 million as a result of its settlement with the Equal Employment Opportunity Commission. But it is difficult to tell whether an organization is in compliance—especially for the organization. According to Virgil B. Day, attorney for the Ad Hoc Group on Employee Selection Procedures, "Anyone who thinks he understands these guidelines [the 1978 Uniform Guidelines on Employee Selection Procedures] is likely to be standing on quicksand."[1]

Of course, compliance with legal constraints is also good business. Only by using valid predictors can the organization hire and promote the most qualified individuals. Thus an organization may view compliance as an opportunity to use its work force fully. Remember, however, that legal regulations deal only with the match between abilities and demands. An organization should be concerned on its own with all the issues related to effective selection and placement.

This chapter first addresses the issues related to effective selection and placement decisions and then examines the legal constraints on them. Because the majority of discrimination cases (except for terminations) relate to either hiring or promotion, this chapter focuses on hiring and promotion decisions. Demotion, transfer, and termination decisions are discussed in Chapter 9.

SELECTION AND PLACEMENT DECISIONS

The methods for collecting selection and placement information—interviews, tests, application blanks, and the like—are outlined in Chapter 6. The question now becomes, How can they be used in making selection and placement decisions? Generally, one method can be used alone in making the decision (the single predictor approach) or several methods can be combined (the multiple predictor approach).

The Single Predictor Approach

When personnel managers use only one piece of information or one method for selecting an applicant, they are taking the **single predictor approach**.

Typical is the personnel director of one farm- and earth-moving-equipment manufacturer in the Midwest, who says he uses a seat-of-the-pants approach in hiring assembly-line workers. If the applicant looks big enough to lift the heavy parts on the assembly line, he or she gets the job; if the personnel man has any doubts, the foreman is consulted.[2]

In this example, the personnel manager assumes that physical size alone predicts how well the individual will perform. "That may be an evenhanded approach, but it is not very scientific and could be challenged in court by a rejected applicant."[3]

Nevertheless, single predictors are used by many organizations to select employees, especially when they can readily be validated. This occurs most frequently when a single predictor, such as an actual sample of the job, represents the main dimension of the job:

A few hiring tests are easy enough to validate, especially those in which the candidate actually performs a task he will have to perform on the job. It makes obvious good sense, for example, to require a candidate for a secretarial job to pass a typing test, and generally the equal-opportunity establishment accepts such tests.[4]

But for many jobs, a job sample test cannot be used, nor can a single dimension, such as typing, really be used to explain the essence of the job. Many jobs can be explained only with several job dimensions, as illustrated in the job descriptions shown in Chapter 4. Thus several predictors are used in making the selection and placement decisions.

The Multiple Predictor Approach

When information from several sources or methods is combined, selection and placement decisions are made with a **multiple predictor approach**. As you might guess, there are several ways to combine information.

Assessment Centers.   In the assessment center approach, job applicants or current employees are evaluated as to how well they might perform in a managerial or higher-level position.[5] Over 2,000 companies now use this method, and its use grows each year because of its validity.[6] (The assessment center is mentioned as an aspect of recruiting in Chapter 5. It is also discussed in Chapter 14 as a method for helping an individual in career planning.)

An **assessment center** is usually composed of a half dozen to a dozen people who have been chosen or have chosen to attend the center. The center is usually run by the organization, for one to three days, but off the premises. The performance of attendees is usually determined by managers in the organization who are trained assessors. Each attendee is rated on twenty to twenty-five characteristics. For example, the twenty-five variables used in the AT&T Management Progress Study were

- Organization and planning
- Decision making
- Creativity
- Human relations skills
- Behavior flexibility
- Personal impact
- Tolerance of uncertainty
- Resistance to stress
- Scholastic aptitude
- Range of interests
- Inner work standards

- Primacy of work
- Oral communications skills
- Perception of social cues
- Self-objectivity
- Energy
- Realism of expectations
- Bell System value orientation
- Social objectivity
- Need for achievement
- Ability
- Need for superior approval
- Need for peer approval
- Goal flexibility
- Need for security[7]

The composite performance in the exercises and tests is often used to determine an attendee's future promotability and the organization's human resource planning requirements and training needs, as well as to make current selection and placement decisions. The schedule of a typical assessement center is shown in Exhibit 7.1.

Multiple Hurdles.   This method of combining information is based on the idea that every job to be performed has several dimensions and thus several predictors (hurdles). A job applicant must be able to get over every selection hurdle in order to perform adequately on the job. Failing on one predictor cannot be compensated for by doing extremely well on another one. For example, an applicant for an air traffic controller job cannot compensate for failure on a visual recognition test.

The use of multiple hurdles excludes many job applicants—who may fail only one hurdle. Unless the organization has a large number of applicants, it may not fill all job openings. But even if it does, this approach may unnecessarily exclude people who, except for one deficiency, could do well. In an effort to accommodate applicants, some organizations are making multiple hurdles unnecessary through physical

Day 1	Orientation (12–25 participants and 6 observers)	Management game (participants divided into groups)	Psychological tests Interviews with participants Case discussion
Day 2	Decision-making exercise (such as case problem to solve alone)	In-basket exercise Role-playing exercise	Group problem-solving exercise (such as management game, case, or simulation)
Day 3 (half day)	Written case analysis and oral presentations Peer evaluations		

Exhibit 7.1   Activities in a Typical Assessment Center
Adapted from J. L. Gibson, J. M. Ivancevich, and J. H. Donnelly, Jr., *Organizations: Behavior, Structure, Processes*, 3rd ed. (Dallas, Texas: Business Publications, Inc., 1979), p. 369.

changes in buildings and floor arrangements, more alternative work arrangements, and job design changes.

Compensatory Approach to Multiple Predictors. You know from your own experience that what people lack in ability they can make up for in drive and motivation. In classes, there are always students who do well by working harder than other students. The same in organizations. If a job applicant scores low on motivation, he or she can make up for it by scoring well on the ability test.

The compensatory approach is applied when one quality can compensate for another quality. It is also applied when not doing well on one dimension of a job can be compensated for by doing well on all the other dimensions.

Combined Approach to Multiple Predictors. Many organizations use the combined approach, often beginning with recruitment. The combined approach uses aspects of both the multiple hurdles and compensatory approaches. Generally, the multiple hurdle component is used first: "You have to get through the door before we'll consider you." Once in, the compensatory approach applies. For example, an organization may establish minimum requirements—an undergraduate major in accounting or a high grade-point average—for students who want an interview. After that requirement has been met, strong areas can offset weak areas.

THE UTILITY OF SELECTION AND PLACEMENT ACTIVITIES

Organizations use selection and placement activities to make hiring job applicants more efficient and effective. If anyone could do a particular job, it would be completely unnecessary to administer any test of ability to select job applicants. The use of some predictor would not increase the chance of hiring people who would do well. Furthermore, a predictor that is unrelated to job performance has no validity and could result in discriminatory hiring practices. In cases like this, there is little utility in using a test to make selection and placement decisions.

There are several aspects of utility in selection and placement activities, including the validity and reliability of predictors, the base rate, the selection ratio, the availability of job applicants, and the costs and benefits of decisions. All these aspects are important, particularly validity.

Validity

When a test is said to exhibit **validity** or to be a valid predictor, it statistically predicts what it is supposed to predict. A job applicant who passes a welding test, for example, should be able to perform well as a welder if the test is valid.

It is important to note that there is a **range of validity**. The degree of validity for a particular test is indicated by the magnitude of the correlation coefficient, which ranges from -1 or $+1$ (most valid) to 0 (least valid). In fact, -1 and $+1$ show perfect validity (perfectly correlated), and 0 shows the absence of validity (perfectly uncorrelated). Perfect validity comes in two forms: Perfectly positive validity ($+1$)

means the two variables move in the same direction at the same rate; perfectly negative validity (-1) means they move in the opposite direction at the same rate. Chapter 19 includes an example of computing a correlation coefficient to determine the validity of an organization's performance appraisal form.

But what do these values of validity mean in the real world? Perfect validity means that a job applicant who scores high on a test will score exactly that high on what the test predicts. An applicant who scores twice as well on the test as another applicant will perform twice as well on the job. If the test lacked validity, it would be impossible to predict on the basis of test scores whether one job applicant would be a better performer than the other. More commonly, however, tests have less than perfect validity, (say, $+.50$) but are not without validity. Then an applicant who scores twice as well on the test as another applicant would be likely to perform better on the job but not by twice as much.

The term *validity* is extremely important for you to know. It is the heart of many personnel decisions. In fact, the more valid the test, the more efficient selection and placement decisions can be. And the more efficient these decisions, the better the hired workers will likely perform—thus the more efficient the organization.

The techniques applied to determining the validity of a performance appraisal form are identical to those applied to validating a hiring test, such as the welding test. After all, both are tests (or predictors). A **test** is

any paper-and-pencil or performance measure used as a basis for any employment decision. . . . For example, . . . ability tests which are designed to measure eligibility for hire, transfer, promotion, membership, training, referral or retention. This definition includes, but is not restricted to, measures of general intelligence, mental ability and learning ability; specific intellectual abilities; mechanical, clerical and other aptitudes; dexterity and coordination; knowledge and proficiency; occupational and other interests; and attitudes, personality or temperament. The term "test" includes all formal, scored, quantified or standardized techniques of assessing job suitability including, in addition to the above, specific qualifying or disqualifying personal history or background requirements, specific educational or work history requirements, scored interviews, biographical information blanks, interviewers' rating scales, scored application forms, etc.[8]

Thus the term *test* applies to many methods of gathering data in organizations. Tests become subject to validation (and legal constraints) when used to make employment decisions.

There are several types of validity, three of which are particularly relevant in selection and placement decisions: empirical, content, and differential validity. Although all are determined to be critical, the strategies used to collect the information to correlate them are substantially different.

Empirical Validation. **Empirical validity** is a measure of how well a test predicts performance. There are two types of empirical validation strategies—concurrent and predictive—shown in Exhibit 7.2.

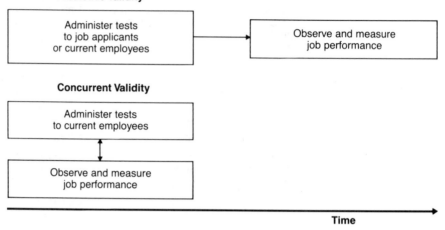

Exhibit 7.2 Empirical Validation Strategies
Adapted from M. D. Dunnette, *Personnel Selection and Placement* (Monterey, Calif.: Brooks/Cole, 1966), pp. 115–116.

Concurrent validation determines the relationship between a predictor and a performance score for all employees in the study at the same time. For example, to determine the concurrent validity of the correlation between years of experience and job performance, personnel would collect from each person in the study (by the way, they all would have to be working in similar jobs) information about years of experience and performance scores. Then a correlation would be computed.

The steps in determining predictive validity are similar, except that the predictor is measured some time before performance is measured, as shown in Exhibit 7.2. Thus the predictive validity of a predictor could be determined by measuring an existing group of employees on a predictor and waiting to gather their performance measures later or by hiring a group of job applicants regardless of their scores on the predictor measuring them on their performance later.

Although it may sound easy to determine concurrent or predictive validity, many organizations are not able to do it.

Only a large work force with a substantial stream of new workers can supply enough data to make a convincing case that there is a relationship between hiring tests and job performance. Many employers don't have a big enough job pool to permit such measurements—and for that matter even large corporations do not necessarily have armies of people doing identical work. [However,] companies with similar job classifications can form consortiums and devise tests to be used throughout the industry or even extended to other industries. For example, Reynolds Metals, United Parcel Service, PPG Industries, Owens-Illinois, and Clark Oil & Refining, as well as the city of Tulsa, banded together not long ago to design a test that would measure the ability of candidates for jobs as foremen.[9]

Furthermore, conducting empirical validity studies is extremely expensive. For example, it may cost over $25,000 to validate a single predictor with as few as 200 employees. Faced with these circumstances, employers "are more and more turning to content validity in search of solutions."[10]

Content Validity.   **Content validity** differs from empirical validity in that it estimates or judges the relevance of a predictor for a specific performance criterion without actually collecting the performance information. "The administration of a typing test as a selection device for hiring typists is a classic example of a predictor *judged* to have content validity."[11] Notice that in this case the predictor is a skill related to a task that is actually part of the job. Content validity thus refers to predictors that measure skills, knowledge, or behaviors related to those required of the actual job.[12] Thus to demonstrate content validity, it is useful to know the dimensions of the actual job, the individual qualities needed to perform the job, and even the performance criteria. Predictors that measure such traits as intelligence or personality are generally unacceptable for content validity studies. Validity studies using personality-type predictors determine **construct validity**.

As discussed in Chapter 4, information about job tasks and responsibilities can be obtained using several standardized forms, and then it can be used to develop job descriptions. These descriptions can be used in turn to determine the individual qualities assumed necessary to perform the tasks and to determine the criteria for job success.

Although job analysis is discussed here as a critical element in content validation, it should be regarded as the starting point and the thread that ties together any basic validation study (see Exhibit 7.3). But even on the basis of job analysis and well-established performance criteria, predictors still should not be used without further evidence regarding their reliability and differential validity.

Differential Validity.   So far, validity has been discussed as the extent to which a predictor really predicts. That is, if an individual scores well on a valid predictor, that person is likely to do well in the future. But there may be situations in which the predictor is valid for some people and not valid or less valid for others. For example, a person with high ability may perform well regardless of the score on a manual dexterity test. But for a person with low ability, only high scores on the manual dexterity test may mean high actual performance. This difference in individual ability is generally the basis for **differential validity**.

It is also possible that a predictor may be valid for only certain individuals and groups in the organization because of different conditions in different parts of the organization. In certain sections there may be group pressure to keep everyone's performance at some easily attained level, whereas in other sections performance may vary a great deal. A validation study in sections with group pressure may indicate no validity for the predictor, but a validation study in sections without group pressure may indicate validity for the predictor. An example in Chapter 19 further demonstrates differential validity.

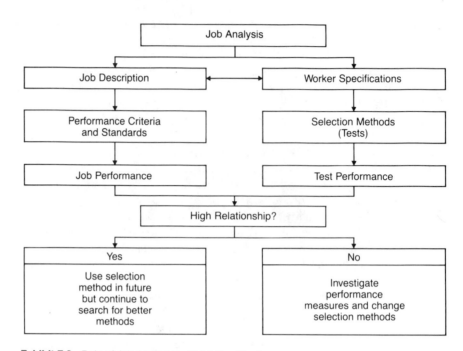

Exhibit 7.3   Role of Job Analysis in Validation Studies
Adapted from M. L. Blum and J. C. Naylor, *Industrial Psychology: Its Theoretical and Social Foundations* (New York: Harper & Row, 1968), p. 27.

Reliability

An important aspect of any hiring system is the quality of the predictors used and the performance information collected. The relationship between predictors and performance information indicates the predictor's validity. **Reliability** indicates whether a test measures the same thing consistently. There may be times when the validity of a predictor is low because of low reliability.

Reliability is an important concept in the use of predictors because it determines the limits on how valid a predictor can be and because it helps determine whether the results of one validation study will be consistent with the results from the same study done at a later point in time or using another group of individuals.

Base Rate and Selection Ratio

The importance of the base rate and selection ratio in determining the utility of selection and placement decisions can best be illustrated with an example. The following example also shows the importance of the magnitude of validity.

Suppose a personnel manager was able to collect test-score data on 100 employees who were eventually hired and that at a later date, he or she was able

---

A SLICE OF LIFE

The concepts of reliability and validity are critical when collecting data. If, for example, a desk ruler is used to determine the distance from one point to another, it is expected that several measurements using the same ruler would be consistent. The same assumption could be made for any method that measures absenteeism; the measurements should be consistent. This sounds like a fundamental truth, but it is often disregarded. The traditional measurements of absenteeism are relatively inconsistent. It has been reported that the reliability of absenteeism measures ranges from 0 (absolutely no reliability) to .74 (reasonable reliability), with a mean of .36 (very poor reliability).

For an example of the practical meaning of the reliability coefficient, return to the desk ruler. If the distance between the two points on the table were measured several times by the same ruler and exactly the same measurements were obtained, the reliability coefficient would be $+1$. In other words, the measurement would be totally consistent. If the measurements were very close to the same, the reliability coefficient would be high (near $+1$); if the measurements varied considerably, the coefficient would be low (near 0). Therefore, the reported mean value (.36) for absenteeism information is very poor and strongly suggests that most measurements of absenteeism are not consistent.

Validity is a more complex notion that involves several distinct concepts. Note that just because a measurement is consistent does not mean it is valid. If the ruler is not actually 12 inches long, the results will never be accurate—no matter how often the distance is measured or how consistent the measurements are. Obviously, this is an important concept, not only for the measurement of desks but also for the measurement of any attitude or behavior, such as absenteeism. By the way, no study has ever directly addressed the validity of absenteeism measures.

---

to collect job-performance data on all of these individuals using a 1–5 rating scale. Assume that the correlation between the test scores and job-performance ratings was calculated to be .70. [Exhibit 7.4] depicts this relationship graphically using an ellipse diagram. Assume that the heavy horizontal line in the diagram represents a dividing line: Those individuals rated at or above this line were considered successful in the job as rated by their supervisor; those rated below the line were considered not successful.

The heavy vertical line represents the cutting point (C) on the test when individuals scoring above this point would be selected (in the future) and those scoring below the point would be rejected. These two lines allow the division of the diagram into four quadrants.

1. Quadrant I (true positive) represents those individuals for whom success was predicted, and who were indeed successful.

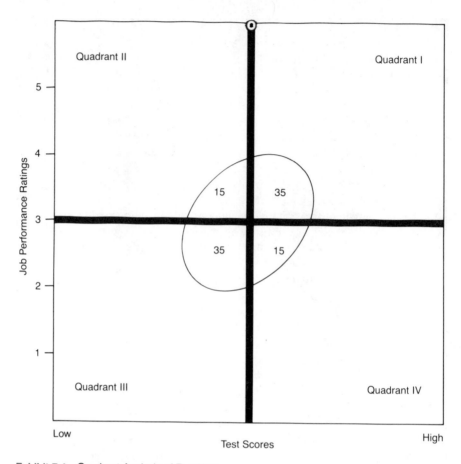

Exhibit 7.4 Quadrant Analysis of Test Utility
From R. D. Arvey, *Fairness in Selecting Employees,* © 1979 Addison-Wesley Publishing Company,
Inc., p. 35. Reprinted with permission.

*2. Quadrant II (false negative) represents those individuals for whom success
was not predicted, but who actually would succeed if hired.*
*3. Quadrant III (true negative) represents those individuals for whom success
was not predicted, and who actually did not succeed in the job.*
*4. Quadrant IV (false positive) represents those individuals for whom success
was predicted, but who did not succeed in the job.*
  *In [Exhibit 7.4] the number of individuals who fell into the different quadrants
is given. For example, the number of individuals for whom job success was
predicted and who actually were successful (Quadrant I) is 35.*
  *The first question we might ask is "How accurate were the predictions made by
the test? This could be calculated by applying the following formula:*

$$\frac{I + III}{I + II + III + IV} \; = \; \frac{70}{100} \; = \; .70$$

That is, 70 percent of the predictions made using the test were correct. This seems to be fairly impressive evidence in favor of the test. However, a second question which must be asked in evaluating a prediction is "How accurate would I have been if no predictor was used?" This figure may be calculated by using the following formula:

$$\frac{I + II}{I + II + III + IV} = \frac{35 + 15}{35 + 15 + 35 + 15} = .50$$

*This is referred to as the **base rate**—the proportion of applicants who would succeed on the job if tests were not used to select them. In the example given, the accuracy of the predictions made using the test was .70 compared to a base rate of .50. Thus, the use of the selection system represents a gain in the accuracy of predictions made compared with using no selection test.*

It should be noted that, as the base rate increases, it becomes relatively more difficult for a selection system to show improvement. For example, if 95 percent of employees selected are successful, it becomes difficult to improve on the current system.

*A further concept which is important in evaluating a selection device is the notion of the **selection ratio**. The selection ratio is defined as the proportion of individuals actually hired to those who applied. For example, there may be 200 applicants and only 10 individuals are hired. This would represent a selection ratio of 10/200 or .05 percent. Generally speaking, a selection system has greater value when the selection ratio is small—that is, when there are many more applicants than jobs.*

To summarize, the value of a prediction system varies as a function of three basic variables:

1. The magnitude of the validity coefficient—As validity increases, so does the value of the system.

2. The base rate—As the base rate approaches 50 percent, the selection system demonstrates greater value.

3. The selection ratio—As selection ratios become smaller, the value of a selection system increases. [13]

Availability of Applicants

The fewer applicants an organization has, the less assured it is that it has the best possible applicants. With few applicants, it must be more careful in matching them to the jobs available. If an organization must hire all the applicants because there are so few, the validity of the selection and placement devices becomes irrelevant. This is especially true when there is only one type of job available.

When everyone who applies is hired, the chance that all will turn out to be good is low. Consequently, the organization may need to establish extensive training programs, but even this doesn't always work. It can also try to attract more job applicants by raising wages, but that may only lead to more trouble. These two problems were particularly apparent at Cessna Aircraft Company, Beach Aircraft Corporation, and General Dynamics as illustrated here:

"You can outbid someone else—but this is not a good way because it's liable to come back and bite you," said Dave Franson of Cessna Aircraft Co. in Wichita, which is the No. 1 employer in Kansas with a payroll of more than 14,000.

"The other [way to recruit] is to hire people who want to work and train them for the skills you need," Franson said. "That's what we've been doing."

Other companies echoed Franson's remarks. Bidding wars are clearly unpopular.

"Even if you raise wages, the shortage is still there," said Louis M. Whitney, a personnel official with the General Dynamics Convair division in San Diego.

Business also hesitates to operate expensive training programs.

One reason is turnover particularly in fields where openings are plentiful.

Beech Aircraft Corp. in Wichita hired 2,800 new employees last year and trained 4,000 in its own education programs, but finished with a net gain of only 800 employees.

Reducing standards in hiring new employees is one way companies cope with the shortages.[14]

But reducing standards also reduces the chance that the applicant will be satisfied with the job. After all, abilities and needs are not carefully matched with job demands and rewards.

It is in the best interests of organizations and individuals to have a choice—of applicants and of jobs. Without choice, the utility of selection devices is minimal; with choice, their utility is high. The more choice, the greater the chances the applicant chosen will do well and be satisfied.

Costs and Benefits

Another condition influencing the utility of selection and placement procedures is the cost of the increase in actual job performance versus the cost of getting the same increase using other techniques, such as job design or supervisory training programs. There are two major types of costs in selection and placement:

1. Actual costs *(costs actually incurred in hiring applicants).*
    a. *Recruiting and assessment costs—salaries of personnel staff, advertising expenses, travel expenses, and testing personnel evaluation costs.*
    b. *Induction and orientation costs—administrative costs of adding the employee to the payroll, and salaries of the new employee and of those responsible for orienting him to his new job.*
    c. *Training costs—salaries of training and development staff, salary of the new employee during training, and costs of any special materials, instruments, or facilities for training.*
2. Potential costs *(costs that might be incurred if a wrong selection decision is made).*
    a. *Costs associated with hiring a person who subsequently fails— recordkeeping costs, termination costs, costs of undesirable job behavior*

such as materials or equipment damaged; loss of customers, clients, or patients; loss of good will, etc.; and costs incurred in replacing a failing employee.

b. *Costs associated with rejecting a person who would have been successful on the job—competitive disadvantage if he is hired by another firm (for example, loss of a top sports star to a competing team), and costs of recruiting and assessing an additional applicant to replace the rejectee.*[15]

The two types of potential costs are associated with false positive decisions (type a) and false negative decisions (type b).

LEGAL CONSTRAINTS

The legal environment for most organizations is growing so complex that equal employment legislation is of first consideration:

The effects of EEO [equal employment opportunity] on promotion decisions deserve special comment. Assuring equal employment opportunity is a major consideration in most organizations today. Like other personnel practices, such as hiring, transfers and layoffs, management promotion decisions are subject to EEO regulations. Discrimination barring women and minorities from higher level jobs is illegal, and the courts have not been lax in imposing remedies or obtaining stringent settlements. Often, the first step in a promotion process is to determine whether affirmative action obligations will influence the choice of candidates.[16]

But determining exactly what an organization's equal employment obligations are is complicated by the numerous federal laws, court decisions, executive orders, and guidelines. Before the 1960s, there were few federal laws that required equal opportunity in the field of employment; Appendix B reviews the large number of equal employment laws enacted since 1960.

The most significant federal laws related to selection and placement decisions are the Fifth and Fourteenth Amendments, the Civil Rights Act of 1964 (particularly Title VII), the Age Discrimination Act of 1967, the Equal Employment Act of 1972 (amendment to the 1964 Civil Rights Act), and the Rehabilitation Act of 1973.[17] Three important executive orders (EOs) in this area are EO 10925 signed by President Kennedy in 1961, EO 11246 signed by President Johnson in 1965, and EO 11375 signed by President Ford in 1975.

In addition to these laws, executive orders, and related court decisions, two sets of guidelines on equal employment procedures have had a major impact. The first set was issued in 1970 by the Equal Employment Opportunity Commission (EEOC); the second set was promulgated in 1976 by three other agencies charged with equal employment responsibility: the Office of Federal Contract Compliance, the Department of Labor, and the Justice Department. In 1978 the EEOC joined these three agencies to adopt what is known as the Uniform Guidelines on Employee Selection Procedures, a 14,000 word catalog of do's and don'ts for hiring and promotion. Today these Uniform Guidelines and several court decisions constitute the legal constraints on selection and placement activities.[18] They can be divided into four basic categories: adverse impact, job relatedness, alternative procedures, and affirmative action programs.

Adverse Impact

Shortly after the EEOC established the 1970 guidelines, the Supreme Court established in *Griggs* v. *Duke Power* (1970) the legal framework for employment testing and approved the procedures in the EEOC guidelines. These procedures also became the essence of EO 11246 and EO 11375. One provision of the guidelines was that tests used for selection be job-related. The only way job-relatedness could be proven was by validation procedures, a comparison of test scores with job performance.

However, according to the 1978 guidelines, validation is no longer required in all cases.

It is essential only in instances where the test or other selection device produces an adverse impact on a minority group. Under the new guidelines, adverse impact has been defined in terms of selection rates, the selection rate being the number of applicants hired or promoted, divided by the total number of applicants.[19]

A selection rate for any minority group of less than 80 percent of the rate for the group with the highest rate is generally regarded as evidence of adverse impact.[20] Thus this aspect of the 1978 guidelines is called the **80 percent rule** or the **bottom-line criterion**. If, for example, a company hires 50 percent of all white male applicants who apply in a particular job category, then it must hire at least 40 percent (80 percent × 50 percent) of all blacks who apply and 40 percent of all women and other protected groups. It need not meet the 80 percent rule, however, if it can show that the selection procedures being used are job-related.

Once adverse impact has been demonstrated, the burden of proof to show job relatedness shifts to the defendant (see *Griggs* v. *Duke Power* and *Albermarle Paper Co.* v. *Moody*). In addition, to show no adverse impact, the organization has to keep records of the number of applicants and those hired by sex and by racial and ethnic group, including separate figures for black, Indian, hispanic, and white people.

Job Relatedness

Job relatedness means that the company must show that its selection and placement procedures are related to being successful on the job. That is, the predictors must be validated by empirical, content, or construct strategies. The 1970 Uniform Guidelines gave the most importance to empirical validity. The 1978 Uniform Guidelines give equal importance to the three types of validity, even though content and construct validity are less structured and may result in extensive elaboration of special conditions and requirements in cases yet to be brought before the courts.

The essence of job relatedness is that if a predictor is used as a basis for selection and placement decisions and if those decisions result in adverse impact, then the predictors must be shown to be related to doing the job successfully. Job relatedness encompasses the concept of bona fide occupational qualification (BFOQ), which generally refers to the idea that if selection is made on the basis of sex or race, it must be job-related. For example, it is legitimate to audition only men for the part of a man in a play.

To ensure fairness, tests must also be differentially validated. The 1970 guidelines contained a provision for the differential validation of tests. It was thought that a test may be a valid predictor of performance for one group but not another. Therefore, separate validation was required for each group. Many psychologists and much research suggest, however, that differential validity is a specious concept and that carefully constructed tests are equally valid for all groups. But the new guidelines not only continue to suggest differential validity but also describe the procedures for making such studies in substantial detail in the name of special studies of fairness.

Job relatedness is not the only basis for tolerating adverse impact:

For example, in Diaz *vs.* Pan American World Airways, Inc., *Pan Am had demonstrated that selection of female flight attendants and exclusion of male flight attendants was based on evidence that females were better at attending to the unique "psychological needs of its passengers." Further, while the company did not make the case that males could never perform this task successfully, it did demonstrate that very few males had the requisite abilities and that it was too costly to search for those few males. Hence, the company relied on sex as a hiring criterion for flight attendants. The court struck down this criterion on the grounds that "the primary function of an airline is to transport passengers safely from one point to another. . . . No one has suggested that having male stewards will so seriously affect the operation of an airline as to jeopardize or even minimize its ability to provide safe transportation from one place to another."*

The court went on to note that "discrimination based on sex is valid only when the 'essence' of the business operation would be undermined by not hiring members of one sex exclusively." In short, while the job relatedness of sex was demonstrated, the job in question was not the heart of the business, and therefore the criterion of sex could not be used. What the Diaz case seems to suggest is that job relatedness and business necessity are not identical concepts. It also plainly suggests that job relatedness may be necessary evidence for defending oneself against adverse impact, but it is clearly not sufficient, at least not in this case.[21]

Thus in many cases business necessity can modify adverse impact. In fact, in cases where business necessity clearly is high, it is not even necessary to demonstrate that the selection device is job-related (see *Spurlock* v. *United Airlines* and *Hodgson* v. *Greyhound Lines, Inc.*). For example, Greyhound had a hiring rule (the predictor) that ruled out all applicants over forty years old from being considered for bus drivers. Thus the discrimination suit filed by Mr. Hodgson (who was over forty) was filed under the Age Discrimination in Employment Act of 1967. The court ruling in favor of Greyhound:

In our view, Greyhound's position as to the potential increase of risk or harm which would be incurred is well founded and grounded on an adequate factual basis. . . . Greyhound need not establish its belief . . . to go so far as to experiment with the lives of passengers in order to produce the statistical evidence. . . . Greyhound has amply demonstrated that its maximum hiring age policy is founded upon a good faith judgment that its hiring policy is not the result of an arbitrary belief lacking in objective reason or rationale.[22]

Alternative Procedures

Even when business necessity or job relatedness can be shown to exist, a company could be required to show that there are no other procedures that would have been as effective in screening out unsuitable candidates and yet not have as much adverse impact. This is called the alternative procedures requirement.

There are two important aspects to alternative procedures. The first is the necessity of searching for an alternative selection device that predicts at least as well as the present predictor but has less adverse impact. This requirement was contained in the 1970 guidelines, but in the 1978 guidelines the burden of meeting these requirements shifted from the individual to the organization. Because finding a "better" predictor could almost be a never-ending process, it has been referred to as a **cosmic search**.

The second aspect of alternative procedures involves a provision that may be contrary to the intent of Congress. Congress has not commanded that the less-qualified be preferred over the better-qualified simply because of minority origins.[23] The 1978 guidelines, however, suggest that employers may choose alternative selection procedures (not necessarily validated) to eliminate adverse impact. These procedures include affirmative action programs;

measures of superior scholarship; culture, language or experience factors; selected use of established registers, selection from a pool of disadvantaged persons who have demonstrated their general competency; [or] use of registers limited to qualified persons who are economically disadvantaged.[24]

However, some of these procedures can easily amount to reverse discrimination, for which a company can be sued. Thus "the employer who chooses to use these preferential hiring procedures runs the risk of violating both the Civil Rights Act and the Constitution,"[25] although this has not been found to be true in the two most recent Supreme Court decisions regarding selection and placement practices—the Bakke decision and the Weber decision.

Affirmative Action Programs (AAPs)

Although it is important for an organization to make certain that its present employment practices do not discriminate on the basis of race, color, religion, or sex, many organizations must do more. The organization must also demonstrate that it employs these groups in proportions that are representative of their availability in the area of recruitment. Programs designed to ensure proportional representation are referred to as **affirmative action programs (AAPs)**. An example of an AAP appears in Appendix C.

AAPs arise from three different conditions:

● If a company has a federal contract greater than $50,000, it is required to file with the Office of Federal Contract Compliance an affirmative action plan outlining steps to be taken for correcting "underutilization" in places where it has been identified.

● A federal court may require an AAP if a discrimination suit brought against the organization through the EEOC has found past discrimination. An AAP under these conditions is generally part of a **consent decree**, a statement indicating the specific affirmative action steps an organization will take.

● The organization may voluntarily decide to establish certain goals for hiring and promoting women and members of minority groups.

The exact content of AAPs depends on the organization, the area it is located in, and the extent to which various minorities are underrepresented.

Goals and Quotas. The specific components of AAPs are specified by the Department of Labor. One important component is goal setting. AAPs attack employment discrimination by relying on goals to provide relief:

An acceptable affirmative action program must include an analysis of areas within which the contractor is deficient in the utilization of minority groups and women, and further, goals and timetables to which the contractor's good faith efforts must be directed to correct the deficiencies.[26]

The AAPs are currently enforced by the OFCC and EEOC through EO 11246.

The other component of AAPs is the establishment of quotas as a form of relief. Use of quotas was imposed by the courts under Title VII of the Civil Rights Act of 1964 and has been upheld by the U.S. Constitution, the post–Civil War Civil Rights Act, and EO 11246. Three consistent prerequisites used by the courts to establish quotas are

1. That quotas be used only to remedy the effects of past discrimination.
2. That quotas provide the only adequate remedy.
3. [That] there must first be a "clear-cut pattern of long-continued and egregious racial discrimination." Second, the effects of reverse discrimination must not be identifiable, that is to say, concentrated upon a relatively small, ascertainable group of nonminority persons.[27]

This third prerequisite was used to reject a quota for promotion:

A hiring quota deals with the public at large, none of whose members can be identified individually in advance. A quota placed upon a small number of readily identifiable candidates for promotion *is an entirely different matter.*[28]

At this time, quotas are more likely to be upheld or imposed by courts for hiring than for promotion. Such is not necessarily the case with goals established as part of an AAP. The Department of Labor regulations call for goals in all areas in which the contractor is deficient in using minority groups and women.

Thus, goals are required wherever there is a statistical imbalance, without a finding of past discrimination, without considering the adequacy of alternative remedies and without considering the effects of reverse discrimination.[29]

How are goals and quotas established for an organization? First, the exact numbers of minorities and women available are calculated and then related to these factors:
● The minority population of the labor area surrounding the organization
● The proportion of minority and female workers in the total work force in the immediate labor area
● The availability of promotable and transferable minorities and women within the operating location
● The availability of minorities and women with the requisite skills in the immediate area
● The existence of training institutions capable of training them in the requisite skills
● The degree of training that the operating location is reasonably able to undertake as a means of making all job classes available
● The availability of women seeking employment in the labor recruitment area of the operating location
● The availability of minorities and women with the requisite skills in an area in which the operating location can reasonably recruit (this refers primarily to nation-wide recruitment of managers, professionals, and salespeople)[30]

The establishment of goals and quotas has a significant impact on the organization's selection and placement activities: It determines the types of individuals who will be hired. However, goals and quotas relate only to future hiring decisions. That is, current employees cannot be laid off in order to hire minorities or women to accommodate goals and quotas.

Consent Decrees.   One of the most famous AAPs resulting from a consent decree involved AT&T, which the EEOC found to be discriminating against women. Although AT&T did not admit nor was it required to admit any act of discrimination, it entered into a consent decree after the EEOC opposed its application for a rate increase. The first five-year cost of this settlement (1973 to 1978) is estimated to have been more than $75 million. However,

The real impact came from a drastic overhaul of employment procedures that the Bell companies were required to make. The companies became obliged to desegregate jobs (in terms of both race and sex), to set up procedures by which the transfer of women and minority men into higher-paying jobs could be eased and encouraged, and to establish certain "goals and timetables" for getting those employees into those jobs and for getting males into "female" jobs. Little about those obligations is noteworthy per se; they are the standard stuff of affirmative-action plans. The cutting edge, however, was the means by which these obligations were met and the seriousness with which they ultimately were taken.

The means are complicated, but started with fifteen broad job classifications created by A.T.&T., ranging upward in pay from "service worker," designated Job Class 15, to "third-level management and above," designated Job Class 1. In A.T.&T.'s traditional bureaucratic stratifications, "third level" includes a variety of managers earning $25,000 to $40,000 a year, and "above" reaches to deButts, who, as the lone tenth-level manager, earned $600,000 in 1978.

In most of these job classes, A.T.&T. has an "ultimate goal" for one sex—i.e., the "underutilized" one—and within each sex, it has a goal for each minority group. The ultimate goals are among those key understandings no one bothered to include in the decree. However, in most jobs for which the diagnosed problem was too few women, the ultimate goal for women is 38 percent, a proportion reflecting their representation in the civilian labor force in the 1970 census. An exception is made for "outside" craft jobs (i.e., outside A.T.&T.'s premises), two classes in which A.T.&T. argued for very low goals, contending that it would have great difficulty finding women who could handle the physical demands of these jobs—pole climbing, for example—and who would be attracted to the work. The government, unpersuaded, maintained A.T.&T. could find the women if it tried hard enough. In the end, the compromise was 19 percent, half the standard goal.[31]

In essence, AT&T's affirmative action program was the establishment of ultimate goals for bringing women into management positions and for putting more men into telephone operator positions.

Since AT&T's consent decree, many other organizations have entered into agreements. Anaconda Aluminum, Virginia Electric Power, Lorillard, Wheaton Glass, Braniff Airways, and Libbey-Owens-Ford are just a few examples.

Voluntary AAPs.   Organizations may establish their own affirmative action programs without pressure from the EEOC or OFCC. By doing so, however, they may run the risk of being charged with reverse discrimination, although the risk seems to have lessened since the Bakke and Weber cases. In both cases, the courts supported the qualified use of quotas.

The Weber case is clearer in its support of voluntary AAPs and illustrates the issues involved when unions and seniority concerns are at stake. In brief, the United Steelworkers and Kaiser Aluminum set up a training program that reserved 50 percent of its openings for blacks. A white worker, Brian Weber, charged that the program was discriminatory.

Upholding Weber's challenge, the U.S. Court of Appeals at New Orleans ruled that all racially based employment preferences, including those arising under "bona fide" affirmative action programs, were unlawful in the absence of a court or agency finding of discrimination.

. . . The Supreme Court, however, stresses that Title VII's ban on racial discrimination in hiring practices and apprenticeship selections for training does not "condemn all private, voluntary, race-conscious affirmative action plans." To interpret Title VII's prohibition against racial discrimination as forbidding all race-conscious affirmative action steps, the Court maintains, "would bring about an end completely at variance with the purpose of the statute." Noting that Kaiser's training program voluntarily was "adopted by private parties to eliminate traditional patterns of racial segregation," the Court did not intend "to prohibit the private sector from taking effective steps to accomplish the goal that Congress designed Title VII to achieve." The Court points out that it is not defining "in detail the line of demarcation between permissible and impermissible affirmative action plans," saying only that the Kaiser plan "falls on the permissible side of the line." Underscoring the fact that "the plan does not unnecessarily trammel the interests of the white employees" because it does not require the discharge of white workers or create any absolute bar to their advancement, the Court also stresses that "the plan is a temporary measure; it is not intended to maintain racial balance, but simply to eliminate a manifest racial imbalance."

AAPs and the Handicapped Worker. The Vocational Rehabilitation Act of 1973 prohibits discrimination against handicapped individuals in hiring and promotion, but it applies primarily to affirmative action programs of federal contractors.[32] Thus organizations that must submit AAPs to the OFCC must also submit AAPs for the handicapped to the Department of Health and Welfare. As an example, here is the AAP policy statement regarding handicapped employees of the Tennessee Valley Authority (TVA):

TVA conducts a program for the hiring, placement, and advancement of handicapped employees, former employees, applicants, and disabled veterans. Activities to promote, expand, and enhance employment opportunities are encouraged with special emphasis on returning injured employees to their original or alternate positions. Work environments are modified where possible to provide employment opportunities for handicapped persons. Handicapped employees are encouraged to increase their knowledge, skills, and abilities to facilitate their placement and upward mobility opportunities. Recruitment efforts to attract handicapped persons are enhanced by collaborative efforts with educational institutions, State Veterans' Administration, and other vocational rehabilitation programs.[33]

A Matter of Commitment. Although equal employment guidelines, goals, and quotas are usually established for the organization by the EEOC, the OFCC, or the courts, the actual implementation of these efforts is in the hands of the managers in organizations. As with many other personnel techniques, having them is one thing and using or abiding by them is another. If organizations are really to fulfill the spirit as well as the letter of the law, managers must be committed to implementing goals and quotas. Six important characteristics of EEO efforts that increase managerial commitment are

1. *Government influence on goals, policies and practices*
2. *The clarity of goals*
3. *Top management support for implementing goals*
4. *Managerial accountability for implementing goals*
5. *Managerial participation in setting goals and policies*
6. *The amount of training managers receive for implementing goals*[34]

The government not only establishes goals, policies, and practices for EEO but also furnishes technical assistance to organizations trying to comply. Several manuals have been developed for this purpose.[35]

Knowledge of these laws and regulations is an important first step in developing an effective EEO program and an AAP. Seven other steps are shown in Exhibit 7.5.

The Personnel Manager and EEO

The EEO issue for personnel managers is to stay aware of and on top of the most recent court decisions about hiring practices. But as you have seen, even personnel managers who do so cannot be guaranteed an easy job or be certain of legal compliance. The lack of certainty and the apparent conflict between legislation and the Constitution may be tempting reasons for the personnel department to address the issue less than enthusiastically, but as one personnel specialist suggests,

---

Exhibit 7.5 Steps for Developing an Affirmative Action Program

1. Issue written EEO policy and Affirmative Action Commmitment.
2. Appoint a top official with responsibility and authority to direct and implement the program.
3. Publicize the policy internally and externally.
4. Survey present minority and female employment by department and job classification.
5. Develop *goals* and *timetables* to improve utilization of minorities, males, and females in each area where underutilization has been identified.
6. Develop and implement specific programs to achieve goals.
7. Establish internal audit and reporting systems to monitor progress.
8. Develop supportive in-house and community programs.

From R. L. Mathis and J. H. Jackson, *Personnel*, 2nd ed (St. Paul: West, 1979), p. 103.

EEO is a concept that will invariably step on someone's toes. The EEO professional must continually say to him or herself "ever so gently." The efforts of these people must be deliberate, well thought-out approaches toward meeting an established goal or objective. It takes guts, savvy, communication and, most of all, understanding—understanding not only of the many and different individuals involved but of the subject matter itself.[36]

The personnel department is in the best position in the organization to address this issue, and it must.

EVALUATION OF SELECTION AND PLACEMENT

Selection and placement activities are meant to determine which job applicants should be selected and what jobs they should be placed in. As with the recruitment activity, selection and placement must serve the interests of both the individual and the organization. In addition, these activities must take place within a specified set of legal constraints.

Selection and placement activities can be evaluated by measuring employees' satisfaction with work, the extent to which they feel their skills and abilities are being used and their needs satisfied, and their level of involvement with the job and the organization. Since employee satisfaction, involvement, and skill levels can change, personnel managers must continually monitor these activities. Regular, periodic organizational surveys are one method (see Chapter 19).

The organization's interests are often closely related to the individual's. If the best person is selected and placed in a job, the organization will gain from having a productive employee who is satisfied, who attends work regularly, and who stays with the organization. Thus selection and placement activities can be measured from the organization's viewpoint by employee satisfaction, performance, absenteeism, and turnover. These, too, can be monitored.

An important aspect of the evaluation of selection and placement activities is the calculation of percentages: How many employees of each race, sex, religion, national origin, and age are at various levels in the organization? What proportion do they bear to protected groups in the community? This aspect of evaluation not only complies with legal constraints but also helps put the right person in the right job. As a way of monitoring progress in meeting legal constraints, the personnel department can gather figures on the rates of promotion for various groups, the numbers of minorities hired from the number recruited, and even the number of actionable charges filed by employees for violation of equal employment opportunity guidelines.

SUMMARY

This second chapter on selection and placement activities examines approaches to making selection and placement decisions and the legal constraints under which those decisions are made. Making decisions without consideration for legalities not only risks violation of equal employment opportunity laws but also ineffective decisions. Although much of the discussion in this chapter is concerned with hiring and promotion decisions, many of the procedures and legal constraints also apply to demotion, layoff, and termination decisions.

The last two chapters have assumed that an essential goal of selection and placement is to get the right person for the right job in order to serve the short- and long-run interests of both the organization and the individual. This means that organizations should make selection and placement decisions based on information about an individual's needs and the rewards of the job as well as about an individual's abilities and the demands of the job. Only by considering both matches can the major purposes of selection and placement be attained.

PERSONNEL PROBLEM
You Be the Judge

"Business necessity" is an interesting notion. In theory, a company could refuse to employ someone for a particular position if it could prove that doing so would undermine business operations.

Suppose, for example, that a controlled experiment were conducted in which one airline used only women as cabin attendants, another airline operated the same route using only male attendants, and a third airline operated the same route using a combination of male and female attendants. Assume it was conclusively shown that the airline using only women had more passengers. Assume also that a survey administered to all passengers showed that passengers preferred female cabin attendants. Furthermore, assume that they claimed to prefer traveling on an airline that adhered to this policy.

Based on this information, a case has been taken to court. A man who has been denied employment by an airline has brought suit charging sex discrimination. The airline argues that hiring only women as cabin attendants is a "business necessity" and that to do otherwise would seriously undermine business profitability.

1. As court judge, how do you rule?

2. Review *Diaz* v. *Pan American World Airways, Inc.* Is the essence of Pan American's operation to "transport passengers safely from one point to another" or to make a profit?

3. Suppose the same argument could be established about hiring black or white employees. Would this argument justify discrimination in employment practices?

4. Do you think business necessity justifies discriminatory employment practices?

KEY CONCEPTS

affirmative action
    program (AAP)
assessment center
base rate
bottom-line criterion
consent decree
construct validity

content validity
cosmic search
differential validity
80-percent rule
empirical validity
multiple predictor approach

range of validity
reliability
selection ratio
single predictor approach
test
validity

DISCUSSION QUESTIONS

1. What are the differences between single and multiple predictor approaches?
2. What are the major components of the utility of an organization's selection and placement procedures?
3. What are the differences among empirical, content, construct and differential validity?
4. What is meant by the term *job relatedness?* The term *business necessity?*

5. What are the three types of AAPs?
6. What is meant by adverse impact? How is it demonstrated?
7. What are some important legal constraints on an organization's selection and placement activities? Are these constraints useful?
8. Do you think goals and quotas are necessary for organizations? Would they attain EEO obligations without legal sanctions?

ENDNOTES

1. L. Smith, " 'Equal Opportunity' Rules Are Getting Tougher," *Fortune*, June 19, 1978, p. 152. Courtesy of *Fortune* Magazine, © 1978 Time, Inc.

2. Smith, p. 154.

3. Smith, p. 154.

4. Smith, p. 154.

5. B. Schneider, *Staffing Organizations* (Santa Monica, Calif.: Goodyear, 1976).

6. L. A. Digman, "How Well-Managed Organizations Develop Their Executives," *Organizational Dynamics*, Autumn 1978, pp. 65–66.
   See also the entire February 1980 issue of *The Personnel Administrator*—which is devoted to an analysis of assessment centers—for selection, training, development, and career management.

7. D. W. Bray, R. J. Campbell, and D. L. Grant, *Formative Years in Business* (New York: Wiley, 1974), pp. 18–20. © 1974 Wiley Publishing Company. Reprinted with permission.

8. Equal Employment Opportunity Commission, Civil Service Commission, Department of Labor and Department of Justice, "Guidelines on Employee Selection Procedures." *Federal Register* 35, no. 149, 1 August 1970, p. 12333. This definition is essentially maintained in "Uniform Guidelines on Employee Selection Procedures," *Federal Register* 43, no. 156, 25 August 1978, pp. 38295–38309.

9. Smith, p. 154.

10. Smith, p. 154.

11. Smith, p. 154.

12. S. Wollack, "Content Validity: Its Legal and Psychometric Basis," *Public Personnel Management*, November/December 1976, pp. 397–408.
    E. P. Prien, "The Function of Job Analysis in Content Validation," *Personnel Psychology*, 30 (1977), pp. 167–174.
    L. S. Kleiman and R. H. Faley, "Assessing Content Validity: Standards Set by the Court," *Personnel Psychology*, 31 (1978), pp. 701–713.

13. R. D. Arvey, *Fairness in Selecting Employees*, © 1979 Addison-Wesley Publishing Company, Inc., pp. 35–37. Reprinted with permission. Arvey provides an excellent in-depth discussion of these issues.

14. P. M. Zollman, "There's Jobs in Abundance for Americans with Skills," *Columbus Dispatch*, 20 May 1979, UPI Business Writer, p. c.1. Reprinted by permission of United Press International.

15. *Personnel Selection and Placement* by M. D. Dunnette. Copyright © 1966 by Wadsworth, Inc. Reprinted by permission of the publisher, Brooks/Cole Publishing Company, Monterey, CA, pp. 174–175.

16. "What Every Personnel Director Should Know About Management Promotion Decisions," by M. London, p. 555. Reprinted with permission *Personnel Journal*, Costa Mesa, CA, copyright October 1978.

17. For a review of related court decisions and rulings, see
    Arvey, *Fairness in Selecting Employees*.
    F. S. Hills, "Job Relatedness vs. Adverse Impact in Personnel Decision Making," *Personnel Journal*, March 1980, pp. 211–215, 229.

18. Since new rulings and decisions are frequent, a good way to stay current is to consult the Bureau of National Affairs, Inc., 1231 25th St. NW, Washington D.C. and *Employment Practices Decisions*, Commerce Clearing House Publications, 4025 W. Petersen Ave., Chicago, Ill.

19. "New Directions in EEO Guidelines," by D. E. Robertson, p. 361. Reprinted with permission *Personnel Journal*, Costa Mesa, CA, copyright July 1978.

20. Robertson, "New Directions in EEO Guidelines."

21. "Job Relatedness vs. Adverse Impact in Personnel Decision Making," by F. S. Hills, p. 212. Reprinted with permission *Personnel Journal*, Costa Mesa, CA, copyright March 1980. See also
    Diaz v. *Pan American World Airways Inc.*, 442 F 2d 385, 3 FEP 337 (1971).

22. Hills, p. 212.

23. Robertson, p. 362.

24. Equal Employment Opportunity Commission, "Uniform Guidelines on Employee Selection." *Federal Register* 42, no. 251, 30 December 1977, p. 65544.

25. Robertson, p. 362.

26. D. A. Brookmire, and A. A. Burton, "A Format for Packaging Your Affirmative Action Program," *Personnel Journal*, June 1978, p. 295.
    Also for an excellent discussion of AAPs and how to make one for your organization, see

H. J. Anderson, *Primer of Equal Employment Opportunity* (Washington D.C.: Bureau of National Affairs, 1978).

B. W. Fragner, "Affirmative Action Through Hiring and Promotion: How Fast a Rate?" *Personnel*, November/December 1979, pp. 67–71.

D. Gaymon, "Underutilization in Affirmative Action Programs: What Is It and What Can We Do About It?" *Personnel Journal*, July 1979, pp. 457–459.

C. F. Goodman, "Equal Employment Opportunity: Preferential Quotas and Unrepresented Third Parties," *Public Personnel Management*, November/December 1977, pp. 371–396.

D. H. Rosenbloom, "*Kaiser* vs. *Weber*: Perspective from the Public Sector," *Public Personnel Management*, November/December 1979, pp. 392–396.

27. S. C. Swanson, "Quotas for Equal Opportunity in Employment," *Personnel Administrator*, April 1978, pp. 51–54.

28. Swanson, p. 52. Reprinted with permission from the April 1978 issue of the *Personnel Administrator* copyright 1978, The American Society for Personnel Administration, 30 Park Drive, Berea, OH 44017

29. Swanson, p. 53.

30. Office of Federal Contract Compliance, "Revised Order No. 4," 36 *Federal Register* 23, no. 152, 1971, as amended at 39 *Federal Register* 5, no. 360 1974. See 41 C.F.R., sec. 60-2.11.

31. C. J. Loomis, "A.T.&T. in the Throes of 'Equal Employment,' " *Fortune*, January 15, 1979, p. 47. Courtesy of *Fortune* Magazine, © 1979 Time, Inc.

32. T. Bronsman, "There's More to Affirmative Action Than Just Hiring 'The Handicapped,' " *Personnel Administrator*, January 1978, pp. 18–21.

C. Grazulis, "Understanding Section 503: What Does It Really Say?" *Personnel Administrator*, January 1978, pp. 22–23.
For more information regarding compliance efforts for the handicapped, contact Mainstream Inc., 1200 15th St. NW, Suite 403, Washington D.C. 20005.

33. "A Comprehensive Model for a Handicapped Affirmative Action Program," by G. C. Pati and E. F. Hilton, Jr., pp. 100. Reprinted with permission *Personnel Journal*, Costa Mesa, CA, copyright February 1980.

34. F. S. Hall and S. A. Meier, "Developing Managerial Commitment to EEO," pp. 36–39. Reprinted with permission from the May 1977 issue of the *Personnal Administrator* copyright 1977, The American Society for Personnel Administration, 30 Park Drive, Berea, OH 44017.

35. Government manuals designed to assist organizations in complying with EEO policies and guidelines include
Office of Federal Contract Compliance, "Revised Order No. 4," 36 *Federal Register* 23, no. 152 (1971). See 41 C.F.R. § 60-2.11 for guidelines regarding race and sex.

Office of Federal Contract Compliance, "Revised Order No. 4," 36 *Federal Register* 23, no. 152 (1971). See 41 C.F.R. § 60.50 for religious discrimination guidelines and 41 C.F.R. § 60-250 for guidelines on discrimination based on national origin.

U.S. Department of Labor, Employment Standards Administration, *Discrimination in Employment Act of 1967: A Report Covering Activities under the Act in 1974*, January 31, 1975.

36. S. A. McCollister, "EEO: An Approach for the 70s," p. 39. Reprinted with permission from the January 1978 issue of the *Personnel Administrator* copyright 1978, The American Society for Personnel Administration, 30 Park Drive, Berea, OH 44017.

OBJECTIVES

- To discuss the purposes of socialization

- To distinguish between socialization and accommodation

- To describe how organizations can accommodate employees by offering alternative work schedules

- To explain the uses and effects of flextime

THOUGHT STARTERS

- What is socialization?

- What is accommodation?

- What are nonstandard schedules?

- Do your values, norms, attitudes, and behaviors seem appropriate for a traditional organization?

CHAPTER EIGHT
Socialization and Accommodation

One more thing, Stanley," said Ben Franklyn. "I've put your name on the list. Just tell the guard who you are." Stanley hesitated a moment and thought . . . list? The list? Sure, the loading gate list and the guard. He'd almost forgotten. And it was just like Ben to assume that everyone knew about the list and the guard, though no one ever talked about it.

"Yes, sir," said Stanley, beaming. He bounced down the stairs back to his office, and in spite of himself spent the rest of the day looking forward to going home through the back door. At quitting time he strode to the door, gave his name in a confident tone and was standing in the parking lot in a second. The rainy season was over, and the sun shone warmly down on Stanley as he walked the twenty-five feet to his car. All the way home he thought what a good day it had been.

Now, Stanley isn't the kind of person who likes to play The Company's game, and he's likely to tell anyone where to get off if they play "Mickey Mouse" with him, so to this day he still can't figure out why he didn't tell Franklyn to take the loading gate and shove it, that it was none of his damn business who went where. Because, really, it wasn't.

But Stanley still remembers that his feelings that day had been quite the opposite—not irritated, or even indifferent, but genuinely pleased and grateful. That day he was part of the mill management. That day he knew he was one of Ben Franklyn's boys.

When you worked for Ben Franklyn, you did more than work; you became part of his family. By contrast, when you worked for Ted Shelby you became part of his "team," were "welcomed aboard," and were entered onto the payroll through the data terminal.

But family or team, you were incorporated into the group through certain events which marked the fact—nor did these events happen right away, because it takes a little time for true acceptance to happen. Everybody, for a while, is a provisional member of the men's hut.

Different men have different styles, and Franklyn bull o' the woods had grown up in the traditional kind of organization, based not so much on paperwork as on personal relationships and loyalty. He will never trust "the new approach," and instead find ways of extending his own authority into areas not covered by the formal rules. By his control of favors and sanctions he maintains the personal loyalty of His Boys and broadens the range of his influence.

Franklyn, in his way of handling his territory, is not too different from the medieval church. It granted indulgences to parishioners, who, in accepting the benefit, implicitly recognized the right of the church to bestow it. Thus they bound themselves even more completely in the system.

Reprinted with permission from The Ropes to Skip and the Ropes to Know, *by Ritti and Funkhouser.* © *1977, Grid, Inc., Columbus, Ohio, pp. 7–8.*

This passage illustrates the existence and importance of values, norms, and behavior patterns in an organization. Every person joining the organization must learn the appropriate ones, because they provide an employee with information about the organization's basic goals, the preferred means for attaining these goals, the employee's basic role responsibilities, the behavior patterns required for effective performance in that role, and a set of rules or principles for maintaining the organization's identity and integrity.[1]

It is unlikely that recruitment and selection processes will produce new employees who know the "ropes" (the values, norms, and behavior patterns) of the organization. Therefore, the organization must "socialize" new employees. Socialization can be difficult, especially when organizational values differ from a new employee's existing values. If the organization is not successful in socializing new employees, they may soon leave the organization.

The organization can prevent premature exits by accommodating itself to employees' values, norms, and behavior patterns. Since the drive for equal employment opportunity, organizations have had to make many accommodations to minorities and women. The values of the younger generation have also forced organizations to consider alternative values, norms, and behavior patterns.

Socialization and accommodation activities do not always go smoothly. Often they are not consciously managed by the personnel department or anyone else. The results can be employee dissatisfaction, poor performance, absenteeism, and low morale. In addition, an organization's work force is often disrupted by new employees who have not properly been socialized. The result may be low morale and a feeling of unfairness or injustice that causes conflict between current employees and new employees.

If socialization and accommodation activities are managed well, however, the results will be a more satisfied and productive work force, less conflict among employees, and an easier transition to the goals of equal employment. Since socialization and accommodation play such an important role in the management of human resources, they should be under the direction of the personnel department. But they must be implemented with the cooperation of the line managers and supervisors.[2]

Socialization and accommodation are important in personnel and human resource management. They are also related to several other personnel activities. The specific goals of this chapter are to examine the socialization activities of organizations, particularly employee orientation and accommodation.

SOCIALIZATION

Socialization has been defined as the process by which people acquire the knowledge, skills, and dispositions that make them more or less able members of their organizations,[3] as the processes of situational adjustment and commitment,[4] as a continuing interaction between individuals and those who seek to influence them,[5] and as the development of new attitudes, values, and competencies leading to a new self-image and new behaviors that are needed to meet new role demands. Socialization continues throughout the relationship between the organization and the employee. It involves teaching new employees, and even current ones, the appropriate values, norms, attitudes, and behaviors for the roles they play in the organization. It is primarily accomplished through the employee's interaction with others. In short, **socialization** is the process by which employees learn the norms, values, attitudes, and behaviors appropriate for their roles in the organization.

An important aspect of this definition is that socialization is concerned with the roles played rather than with the jobs occupied by employees. Although employees need specific skills to perform their jobs and are trained to perform them, they also need an awareness of the basic goals of the organization, the means to attain those goals, their responsibilities, and the acceptable behavior patterns for the roles they are expected to play. Employees acquire all this awareness by being socialized, formally and informally, through continuing contacts and experiences with others. Of course, employees must also be aware of what their jobs are about and what skills are required. But this awareness is generally acquired through job descriptions and job previews, which are predominantly preemployment activities.

Purposes of Socialization

Ensuring Predictability.   Socialization is important because it increases the predictability of employee behavior—predictability that employees will act in the interests of the organization, be loyal, be productive, and remain with the organization. When an organization asks how it can get people it can depend on and who will be loyal to it, it often means how can it get people who will help perpetuate the organization, who will improve it, and who will always consider the organization first when making decisions?

Many organizations use, intentionally or unintentionally, their recruitment and selection activities to answer those questions. Organizations usually recruit from familiar sources that have in the past supplied good applicants. Organizations may also recruit individuals who are already socialized. For example, business organizations tend to recruit and hire students from colleges of business rather than those from colleges of social science. But recruitment and selection from the old familiar sources may not always be feasible or legal. If so, new employees' norms, values, and behaviors may be unpredictable.

Although socialization must take place, even for people recruited from the familiar sources, the socialization of those from less-familiar sources may involve an additional stage:

If the novice comes to the organization with values and behavior patterns which are in varying degrees out of line with those expected by the organization, the socialization process first involves a destructive or unfreezing phase. This phase serves the function of detaching the person from his former values, of proving to him that his present self is worthless from the point of view of the organization and that he must redefine himself in terms of the new roles which he is to be granted.[6]

Substituting for Rules to Guide Behavior.   Socialization tends to be extremely useful as a substitute for rules and regulations or direct supervision when employees

A SLICE OF LIFE

The notion of presocialization is interesting. Presumably, recruiting people who are already acquainted with many of the norms and expectations that accompany a particular job or profession shortcuts the socialization process. But it may be that a very positive process—the importation of new ideas and new sensitivities—is truncated as well.

Cultural anthropologists have noted a fascinating phenomenon in the development of peoples and cultures. Apparently, many cultures that are undeveloped by Western standards have an interesting prejudice in common: They tend to restrict immigration. More developed cultures are more likely to allow the influence and relatively free access of strangers.

Is it possible that strangers bring innovation and new curiosity that is unconstrained by "the way it has always been"? With a static culture, the members must rely on the development and innovations of those already immersed in the culture. Imagine Japan if it had pursued its policy of denying foreigners access to its shores. Can this anthropological phenomenon be applied to business? Do excessive socialization and presocialization bring stodginess, a reliance on "what was"?

are working in remote conditions. It is also useful for sensitive jobs involving company secrets and research activities and in jobs that are continuously changing (where appropriate rules and regulations cannot be kept up-to-date).

St. Augustine once gave as the only rule for Christian conduct, "Love God and do what you like." The implication is, of course, that if you truly love God, then you will only ever want to do things which are acceptable to Him. Equally, Jesuit priests are not constantly being rung up, or sent memos, by the head office of the Society. The long, intensive training over many years in Rome is a guarantee that wherever they go afterwards, and however long it may be before they even see another Jesuit, they will be able to do their work in accordance with the standards of the Society.

Like the Romans and the Jesuits, the British Army takes great pains to make sure that field commanders are really deeply ingrained with the thinking of the army as a whole: tours of duty abroad, spells at home, staff college, all to ensure that when they take decisions on their own, they take the right ones, or at least the best the army knows.[7]

Increasing Performance and Satisfaction.   Socialization conveys others' expectations for new employees. If socialization activities can minimize employees' uncertainty and conflict, they are more likely to be satisfied with their roles. It must be noted that increased satisfaction results only if the employees accept socialization. If it is unacceptable, they are more likely to be less satisfied. Effective socialization may also help them learn the "desired" behaviors, values, norms, and policies of the organization more quickly. As a result, the organization can help reduce the start-up costs for new employees. Such costs can range between $2,000 for a top-level manager to $400 for a secretary.[8]

Reducing Anxiety. Effective socialization activities should reduce the anxiety of new employees. At Texas Instruments it was discovered through interviews that new employees suffered a great deal of anxiety. The interviews revealed that

- *Their first days on the job were anxious and disturbing ones.*
- *"New employee initiation" practices by peers intensified anxiety.*
- *Anxiety interfered with the training process.*
- *Turnover of newly hired employees was caused primarily by anxiety.*
- *The new operators were reluctant to discuss problems with their supervisors.*
- *Their supervisors had been unsuccessful in translating motivation theory into practice.*[9]

Anxiety was reduced after the initial socialization activity (often referred to as orientation) was extended to include more information about the new job situation and supervisors. In addition, questionnaire analysis indicated that supervisors felt they lacked the skills to socialize new employees. Also, they often provided very little feedback to new employees about their performance.

As a consequence, Texas Instruments initiated a three-day supervisory training program to establish procedures for bringing new employees on board. In addition, a one-day workshop for supervisors, their new employees, and a facilitator was designed to increase communication and resolve any discrepancies. The results of these training programs and increased information for new employees were a 50-percent reduction in tardiness and absenteeism, an 80-percent reduction in waste, a 50-percent reduction in training time, and a 66-percent cut in training costs.[10]

Socialization and Other Personnel Activities

Socialization activities have extensive relationships with the other personnel activities. In fact, many of the other personnel activities are in part vehicles for socialization. For example, in the recruiting and selection interviews, a realistic portrait of the organization can be presented to job applicants. The relationship works the other way, too: As reported in the Texas Instruments study, more effective socialization reduces absenteeism and tardiness and therefore the need to replace, transfer, or terminate employees. The more realistic the job interview, the less the turnover and the less the need for hiring. The effectiveness of the organization's socialization activities also has an impact on human resource planning and programming, particularly through its impact on turnover.

Training activities are also closely tied to socialization. With less need to hire new employees due to reduced turnover, there is less need and expense for training programs. Effective socialization, however, may require training programs for supervisors and managers like those established at Texas Instruments. The extent and content of these programs vary according to the values, norms, and behaviors of the employees who have been recruited. This has been one result of the increased hiring of minorities and women.[11]

Another vehicle by which socialization works is the design of the employee's task. New employees are most impressionable. Thus the first messages or cues that the organization conveys are long-lasting ones. It is important that the organization communicates a high level of value for new employees in their first job assignments.[12] The quality or challenge of the first job often becomes an important determinant of how well new employees will do in their careers with the organization. The more challenge in the design of the job, the more chance the employee has for doing well in the organization.

Methods of Socialization

Orientation Programs.   Orientation programs are frequently used to brief new employees on benefit programs and options, to advise them of rules and regulations, and to provide them with a folder or handbook of the policies and practices of the organization.[13] The table of contents from a large organization's orientation handbook is shown in Exhibit 8.1.

Orientation programs also usually contain information about EEO practices, safety regulations, work times, coffee breaks, the structure and history of the organization, and perhaps the products or services of the organization. Typically, however, the orientation program does not tell employees about the real politics of the organization—for example, the fact that the organization may soon be going out of business or be merging with another company or even that there may soon be an extensive layoff.[14]

The orientation program conveys some information about the norms, values, attitudes, and behaviors appropriate for new employees, but much of the socialization is left to informal day-to-day interactions among employees. Nevertheless, orientation programs are useful for factual information, and the handbook can be used to tell employees where to get additional information after orientation is over.

Orientation programs are almost always coordinated by the personnel director of the organization. The program is often run by a staff member of the personnel department, with some participation by line managers or representatives from other departments or divisions in the organization.

When organizations are large, orientation programs are often conducted every week. Some organizations even have two orientation sessions one week apart. Typically these programs are run for groups of new employees. Although this is an efficient method, it tends to negate each employee's sense of identity and consequence.[15] Therefore, each employee is often assigned to a trainer or buddy (sometimes the immediate supervisor) who can answer further questions and introduce him or her to the other employees in the work unit or department.

Orientation programs are usually conducted within a week of an employee's initial employment date. For maximum effectiveness, the earlier the better. Organizations that put off orientation programs run the risk of letting the new employees gain critical information about the company from current employees. This may not be in the best interests of the organization or the new employees.[16]

Orientation programs are effective if they transmit appropriate and timely information to new employees regarding values, norms, attitudes, and behaviors and if they benefit the organization as well as the employee. Reduced turnover and in-

CONTENTS

Exhibit 8.1   Sample Orientation Handbook

creased employee motivation and commitment to the organization have all been shown to be related to effective, realistic orientation activities.

Although orientation programs are an important part of the "joining-up process," they are only one part. Most orientation programs last for only a few hours and are done within the first week or two of employment. Occasionally there is an orientation followup a year or so later. But most employees take longer to acquire all the information contained in the orientation program than just one or two weeks. In addition, orientation programs do only part of the job of socialization. Therefore, other methods are also used.

Job Assignments. The important socializing aspects of job assignments are the characteristics of the initial job, the nature of early experiences on the job, and the first supervisor. As indicated above, the initial job often determines the new employee's future success. The more challenge and responsibility the job offers, the more likely it is that an employee will be successful with the organization.[17] A challenging (but not overwhelming) job assignment implies that the organization believes the employee can do well and that the organization values him or her. Many times organizations give new employees simple jobs or rotate them through departments to get a feel for different jobs. But employees may interpret these practices to mean that the organization does not yet trust their abilities or loyalties.[18]

Closely related to the first job are employees' initial experiences, which are often provided by supervisors. Here's an example of how a supervisor can socialize an employee into playing a more humble role,

> . . . *from an engineering company where a supervisor had a conscious and deliberate strategy for dealing with what he considered to be unwarranted arrogance on the part of engineers whom they hired. He asked each new man to examine and diagnose a particular complex circuit, which happened to violate a number of textbook principles, but actually worked very well. The new man would usually announce with confidence, even after an invitation to double-check, that the circuit could not possibly work. At this point the manager would demonstrate the circuit, tell the new man that they had been selling it for several years without customer complaint and demand that the new man figure out why it did work. None of the men so far tested were able to do it, but all of them were thoroughly chastened and came to the manager anxious to learn where their knowledge was inadequate and needed supplementing. According to this manager, it was much easier from this point on to establish a good give-and-take relationship with his new man.[19]*

These types of experiences help prepare new employees for the acquisition of the appropriate values, norms, attitudes, and behaviors.

Supervisors of new employees can also serve as role models and set expectations. The positive influence that the supervisor's expectations can have on the new employee is referred to as the **Pygmalion effect**. If the supervisor believes that the new employee will do well, this belief will be conveyed to the employee, who will be apt to live up to those expectations.[20]

ACCOMMODATION

Viewing the joining-up process and all that follows through the eyes of the organization is called socialization. Socialization is concerned with employees changing to fit the expectations of the organization and adapting to its norms, values, attitudes, and behaviors. Viewing the joining-up process and all that follows through the eyes of employees and adapting the organization to employees' needs, values, attitudes, and behaviors is called accommodation. The organization accommodates to employees when it recognizes that individuals may have values and behaviors that are different from those of the organization and then accepts and adapts to them.

Recently, accommodation has been a result of compliance with federal and state regulations. This accommodation, however, is not always complete. Although organizations may hire more minorities and women, their expectations of the "appropriate" norms, values, attitudes, and behaviors may change only minimally. As a result, minorities and women may find themselves in a dilemma:

To succeed women are told they must enjoy responsibility, authority and money; if they don't, it's assumed they haven't the necessary drive and ambition. But if they blatantly display such an enjoyment, they risk being labeled "pushy"—or worse, thus becoming an even greater threat to male bastions.

Women are cautioned not to be "catty" or political. By some, that is. Others depict business in military or athletic terms, and first explain the rules, and then what it takes to win, i.e. how to beat 'em at their own game.

Aspiring women are told not to "change direction," lest they jostle memories of earlier "career girls" abruptly leaving jobs to start a family or follow a transferred husband. Hence, women are, statistics claim, more loyal, and less likely to jump ship for a bigger and better offer. Yet others maintain that a woman's star will rise faster when she does become more flexible and mobile. "They'll appear more desirable to their employers" one suggests.[21]

Accommodation moves the joining-up process beyond this seemingly one-way relationship in which the organization requires employees to adapt or else. Complete accommodation is similar to true two-way communication, where both parties are willing to be influenced and changed by the other. Thus **accommodation** is defined here as being the organization's recognition of and adaptation to the norms, values, attitudes, and behaviors of employees so as to redefine its own norms, values, attitudes, and behaviors. Accommodation and socialization together emphasize the mutuality of the joining-up process and the continuing relationship between the individual and the organization.

ALTERNATIVE WORK ARRANGEMENTS

Although work continues to be an important part of many people's lives, it has declined in importance.

Many people . . . desire an organization of work which acknowledges and facilitates what they must do (and want to do) in the rest of their life. Work is no longer to be the inflexible core around which the other parts of life must bend.[22]

There has been a growing preference for alternative lifestyles, more self-control, and more interesting work. This has come about because of the influx of women and teenagers into the work force, a reduction in the number of older workers, the increasing educational level of employees, rising levels of affluence, and the promise in industrialized countries of some minimum level of economic security, which allows people to be more selective.[23]

Two major ways organizations have accommodated to these trends are by improving the quality of work life and by giving workers more alternative work arrangements. Both help maintain good work relationships, but only alternative work arrangements are examined in this chapter. Programs to improve the quality of work life are examined in Chapters 17 and 18.

Although the majority (about 70 percent) of the work force is on standard work schedules of thirty-five to forty-two hours a week, an ever-growing segment of the work force is on nonstandard work schedules.[24] These nonstandard schedules can be described along three dimensions:

- *The degree to which nonwork time is taken or aggregated in longer periods*
- *The degree to which work is less than what is currently considered "full time" (forty to forty-four hours per week)*
- *The degree to which the individual controls the selection of the work schedules and uses of time*[25]

Thus **alternative work arrangements** include an organization's provisions for nonstandard work schedules and nonstandard uses of work time, as well as standard work schedules, from among which employees may choose in determining their hours of work within the constraints of the organization and the environment.

The primary purposes of alternative work arrangements are to allow the organization to use human resources more effectively and to enhance employee productivity, satisfaction, and health. These purposes can be attained by allowing employees to match their work arrangements with their desires for work and nonwork activities. But to maintain productivity, the organization's needs must also be considered. That is, employees who prefer night work would not be very productive working for an organization that depended on other organizations open solely during the daytime.

Another constraint on alternative work arrangements are federal and state laws and regulations. These laws and regulations define maximum work hours and overtime pay and make special provisions and exemptions. The laws having this impact, including the Davis-Bacon Act of 1935, the Walsh-Healey Public Contract Act of 1936, and the Fair Labor Standards Act of 1938, are examined in more detail in Chapter 10.

Types of Alternative Work Arrangements

Of course, organizations may always choose standard work schedules. But nonstandard work schedules include flextime, compressed work weeks, permanent part-time work, and job sharing. Other nonstandard uses of work time are earned time and differentiated staffing.

Standard Work Schedules. These included the standard daytime, evening, and night work sessions and forty-hour-per-week work schedules. (In the 1860s the average work week was seventy-two hours—twelve hours a day, six days a week. It was fifty-eight hours in 1900.) Standard work schedules also include overtime work, parttime work, and shift work over a forty-hour week.

Someone who does shift work might work from 7 a.m. to 4 p.m. one week and from 4 p.m. to midnight the next. Since the end of World War I, shift work systems have become more prevalent in industrialized countries. Currently about 20 percent of all industrial workers in Europe and the United States are on shift work schedules.[26]

The percentage of employees on parttime schedules has also increased steadily—from approximately 15 percent in 1954 to 23 percent today.

All of these standard work schedules have advantages and disadvantages, as shown in Exhibit 8.2, but traditionally they provide little choice to employees. Initially employees may have some choice in the schedules they choose, but after that the days of the week (generally five) and the hours of the day (generally eight) are fixed. Because employee needs and values change, what may have been at one time an appropriate work schedule becomes inappropriate. If alternative arrangements are not provided, the employee may leave the organization. Furthermore, the organization may have a difficult time attracting similar types of employees. Thus provisions for nonstandard work schedules become more necessary.[27] Employees are often given a choice between a nonstandard schedule and a standard schedule, as well as a choice of hours, days, and total number of hours to work per week.

Flextime Schedules. Since 1970, approximately 13 percent of private organizations have adopted flextime schedules, representing about 3 million workers.[28] This makes it the most popular nonstandard work schedule. It is popular with organizations because it decreases absenteeism, increases employee morale, induces better labor-management relations, and encourages a high level of employee participation

Exhibit 8.2 Advantages and Disadvantages of Standard Work Schedules

Type of Schedule	Advantages	Disadvantages
Regular	Allows for standardization, predictability, and ease of administration; consistent application for all employees	Does fit needs of all employees; not always consistent with preferences of customers
Shift	More effective use of plant and equipment; allows continuous operation and weekend work	Can be stressful, especially if rotating shifts; lower satisfaction and performance
Overtime	Permits more efficient utilization of existing work force; cheaper than alternatives; allows flexibility	Job performance may decline; may not be satisfying and may contribute to employee fatigue
Parttime	Allows scheduling flexibility to the organization, enabling it to staff at peak and unusual times; cheaper than fulltime employees	Applicable to only a limited number of jobs; increased costs of training; no promotion opportunities

in decision making, self-control, and discretion.[29] Commuting problems sometimes necessitate flextime. It is also popular with supervisors and employees. Smith Kline Corporation instituted flextime and then conducted an attitude study of the program, which found that

- Single-day sick leave decreased.
- Overtime costs went down more than 20 percent.
- 83 percent of nonsupervisory personnel opposed a return to standard work schedules.
- 93 percent of nonsupervisory personnel felt productivity had improved.
- 81 percent of supervisors opposed a return to standard work schedules.
- 85 percent of supervisors noticed improved employee morale.
- 32 percent of supervisors thought flextime enhanced productivity.
- 12 percent of supervisors thought the flexibility of their schedule was reduced somewhat.
- 17 percent of supervisors noticed a reduction in employee coverage of work stations.
- 18 percent of supervisors had to spend more time accounting for employees' time.[30]

Organizations may also provide flextime because it fits their philosophy of management:

We use flexible working hours because it is consistent with our philosophy of giving employees the maximum amount of choice. They choose their hours just as they can choose their vacation time or the color to paint their machine—within constraints, with as much individual choice as possible.[31]

Simply stated, **flextime** is a work schedule that gives employees daily choice in the timing of work and nonwork activities. Consideration is given to band width, or maximum length of the work day. This band (often ranging between ten and sixteen hours) is divided into core time and flexible time. **Core time** is when the employee has to work; **flexible time** allows employees the freedom to choose. Exhibit 8.3 shows how an eleven-hour band width can be divided into two eight-hour workdays.

Among the advantages of flextime are its ability to increase employee productivity, although it does not do so on all occasions.[32] The disadvantages are that it forces the supervisor to do more planning, sometimes makes communications between employees (especially with different schedules) difficult, and requires more records of employees' hours. Furthermore, most flextime schedules still require employees to work five days per week.

Compressed Work Weeks.   Provisions for employees who want to work fewer than five days per week have led to **compressed work weeks**. By extending the workday beyond the standard eight hours, employees generally need to work only three to four days per week for a standard forty-hour work week. In a few cases, employees may even work fewer hours per week yet be paid for a full week. At two General Tire & Rubber plants, some employees work only two twelve-hour shifts each weekend and yet are considered fulltime employees.[33] During the regular work

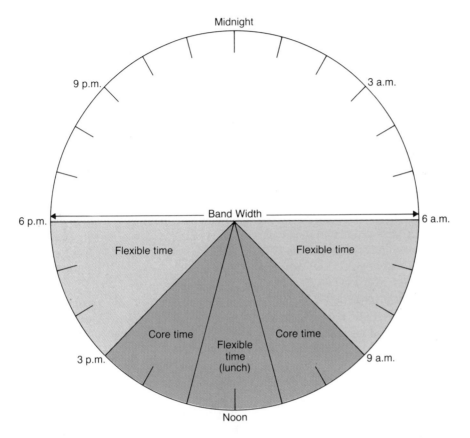

Exhibit 8.3 Sample of Flextime Scheduling
Adapted from A. Cohen and H. Gadon, *Alternative Work Schedules: Integrating Individual and
Organizational Needs* (Reading, Mass.: Addison-Wesley, 1978), p. 35.

week, other employees work standard schedules. The reasons for adopting this
compressed work schedule were several:

*General Tire's decision to adopt a two day weekend shift was sparked by the
growing capital costs of tiremaking. Traditionally, the tire industry has been
prevented from running its plants seven days a week because of union work rules
and overtime costs. But new plants and machinery to make tires have grown
much more expensive as the industry has converted to the radial tire, boosting
the incentive for companies to use their capacity more fully. Finally, General
decided against adopting rotating shifts, fearing that worker dissatisfaction
would result in high turnover and a drop in production.*[34]

Although the compressed work weeks gives employees more free time, it is easier
working five days for eight hours each day. The company, however, can make better

use of its equipment and can decrease turnover and absenteeism.[35] Scheduling and legal problems also accompany compressed work week arrangements, but legal exceptions can be made, and scheduling can become a joint process between supervisor and employees.

Permanent Parttime Work and Job Sharing.   Sometimes productive employees cannot maintain a fulltime commitment to the organization.

We realized several years ago it was stupid to cut off relations with good employees. Full-time Equitable employees can switch to parttime work after five years and enjoy a full range of fringe benefits. . . . Most so far have been women, mostly in the child-rearing years. (E. James Young, Vice-President, Equitable Life Insurance); I think that job sharing is fantastic. If I had to work full time I just couldn't give enough time to my year-old baby. This way I am a real part of the organization and have a chance for a full-time job when I'm ready. (Receptionist, Alza Corporation).[36]

Traditionally, parttime work has meant filling positions that only lasted for a short time, such as those in retail stores during holiday periods. Now some organizations have designated **permanent parttime** (PPT) positions. A PPT work schedule may be a shortened daily schedule (say, from 1 to 5 p.m.) or an odd-hour shift (say, between 5 and 9 p.m.). Organizations can also use PPT schedules to fill in the remainder of a day composed of two ten-hour shifts (representing a compressed work week).[37]

Job sharing is a particular type of parttime work. In job sharing, two people divide the responsibility for a regular fulltime job. Both may work half the job, or one could work more hours than the other.

Parttime workers generally receive little or no indirect compensation, but workers on PPT and job-sharing schedules often do. The benefits to these workers are not equal to those of fulltime workers but are prorated on the amount of time they work.

Both PPT and job sharing provide the organization and individuals with opportunities that might not otherwise be available. They provide organizations the flexibility in staffing to meet actual demands and do so with employees who are at least as productive, if not more so, than regular fulltime employees. Individuals benefit from being able to enjoy permanent work with less than a fulltime commitment to the organization.

Nonstandard Uses of Work Time

In addition to nonstandard work schedules, an organization can also provide nonstandard uses of work time. Two examples of this are earned time and idle time. Mt. Auburn Hospital in Cambridge, Massachusetts, in response to employee dissatisfaction with inequities in sick-leave practices, instituted a policy of **earned time**. Before this policy, some employees used up all their sick days because they were sick, whereas others "got sick" the exact number of days they were allowed.[38] The employees who were neither sick nor "got sick" became dissatisfied. The policy of earned time reduced this dissatisfaction by allowing employees who did not use their sick days to count them as earned days. The employees could then use these earned days at their discretion.

Similarly, employees can earn **idle time** by completing their eight hours' worth of work in fewer than eight hours. In contrast with earned time, employees earning idle time may be more restricted in how they can use it. For example, the organization may allow the employee to use idle time only to attend educational classes.

Another example of nonstandard use of work time is **differentiated staffing**, which may take many forms. One example is McDonald's Corporation, which may use permanent fulltime workers for skeletal coverage and supplement them with either parttime or permanent parttime employees.

Selection of Alternative Work Arrangements

Until the past several years, employees had little choice in their work arrangements. Now, with so many alternative schedules available, personnel managers can select those the organization finds most appropriate for its employees. But how can personnel managers select the schedules employees will prefer? Personnel managers can survey employees, of course, or can predict schedule preferences on selected demographic characteristics of employees, such as the stage in their career and life cycle. Using information like that in Exhibit 8.4, personnel managers can develop a profile of schedules the organization may need to offer and of who will be most attracted to particular schedules. Then, within the constraints of the organization and its environment, an alternative set of work arrangements can be offered that will help both the organization and its employees achieve their goals.

Career Stage	Exploration	Establishment	Tenure	Maintenance		Decline
Life Stage	**Ages 16–22** Experimentation with adulthood	**Ages 22–28** Establishment of working and family life	**Ages 28–33** Occupational change and divorce Increased financial needs	**Ages 33–40** Deepening commitments to work and family Youngest child leaves home to attend school	**Ages 40–55** Reevaluation and commitment to lifestyle Reordered priorities No children at home Renewal of important relationships	**Ages 55–65** Anticipation of retirement
Schedule Preferences	Parttime work Odd jobs Odd hours (after school, vacations)	Long hours, overtime, but not weekends or evenings Compressed work week (if single or without children)	Long hours, take work home (men) No job or parttime work (women)	Long hours, community work, flexibility (upwardly mobile men) Regular hours, second job (men at plateau in work) Parttime or fulltime job, shared jobs, flexible hours (women)	Steady but shorter hours, longer vacations and weekends, education for renewal in evenings or on sabbatical (men) Longer hours, perhaps flexible schedules (women) Reduced hours due to health problems	Parttime work

Exhibit 8.4 Career Stage, Life Stage, and Employee Schedule Preferences

Adapted from A. Cohen and H. Gadon, *Alternative Work Schedules: Integrating Individual and Organizational Needs* (Reading, Mass.: Addison-Wesley, 1978), p. 30.

SUMMARY

In the process of bringing an individual into an organization—in recruitment, selection, and placement and even in the process of keeping an individual on board—an organization must engage in socialization and accommodation. Most individuals do not know about the values, norms, attitudes, and behaviors that an organization expects of its members, so they must be taught (socialized). Thus socialization attempts to change the individual to fit the organization. Most organizations use many methods in their efforts to socialize new employees (and even old employees), including the initial job assignment, the manner of recruitment and selection, and the formal orientation program. However, many organizations use the orientation program as the key component of socialization. Much of the socialization takes place on the informal level, within the work group. Unless the group is socialized adequately, new employees may encounter conflicts or a lack of clarity. In either case, the employees may not perform effectively or may become dissatisfied and voluntarily quit. It is also possible that employees will quit because they don't like the values, norms, attitudes, and behaviors of the organization or group—which represents the organization's failure to accommodate employees. Failure to accommodate may also prevent individuals from even becoming job applicants.

Accommodation refers to the organization's consideration for the values, norms, attitudes, and behaviors of potential or current employees and implies an actual change in practices in order to attract and retain individuals. One major change that the organization can provide is work scheduling: The organization can provide more varied schedules and allow the individual a choice.

PERSONNEL PROBLEM
A Socialization Failure?

"I hate to drop in on you like this, but if you have a minute, there's a problem I'd like to discuss with you," James Whitman, regional sales manager, said to Jason Bovar, vice president of sales for Dalton Manufacturing.

"I have a few minutes. What's on your mind?"

"I'm having some problems with one of our new salespeople, Jane Elliott. She's having trouble fitting into our system. Her sales are quite good—in fact, she's number two in total sales for the last quarter and soon to be number one—but she's causing a lot of trouble with the other salespeople. They're somewhat jealous of her, but it's much more than that. They think she gets special treatment because she is allowed to disregard nearly all our rules."

"For instance?"

"She never attends the sales meetings. She uses her own car almost exclusively for her contacts, which is expressly against our policy. She refuses to carry our entire line of products. She tells me in confidence that some of our products are second-rate and that she would have trouble servicing the account if she sold them. So she won't carry them in her case. Rumor has it that her sales pitch is decidedly different from the one we encourage in our training sessions, and she has, on occasion, given credit for items that are out of warranty. She is definitely doing her own thing, and the other salespeople are complaining because I haven't taken any action. I have spoken to her about these problems, and she promises to stay in line, but she doesn't change. This is getting out of hand. What should I do?"

1. As vice president of sales, how would you counsel your sales manager?

2. Has the organization failed to socialize Jane Elliott properly?

3. Do you interpret Jane's behavior as arrogance or as lack of commitment to the organization? Is she insensitive to the problems of the organization and, more particularly, the sales manager?

4. What should be done with high performers who are not team players?

KEY CONCEPTS

accommodation
alternative work arrangements
compressed work week
core time
differentiated staffing

earned time
flexible time
flextime
idle time

job sharing
permanent parttime
Pygmalion effect
socialization

DISCUSSION QUESTIONS

1. What is socialization? Why do organizations socialize employees?
2. Do you regard socialization as an invasion of an employee's privacy? How should an organization be able to socialize an employee?
3. What are the alternatives to socialization?
4. How can an individual respond to the socialization of an organization? What are some qualities of socialization that might determine how an individual will respond?
5. How do orientation programs fit into the socialization process?
6. What is accommodation? What are the consequences of a lack of accommodation?
7. What are the two major types of alternative work schedules? Discuss the subtypes within each of them.
8. What are the work schedule preferences of employees? How do these preferences relate to employee career stages and life stages?

ENDNOTES

1. E. H. Schein, "Organizational Socialization and the Profession of Management," *Sloan Management Review*, Winter 1968, vol. 9, no. 2, p. 5.

2. H. Mintzberg, *The Structuring of Organizations* (Englewood Cliffs, N.J.: Prentice-Hall, 1979).

3. O. G. Brim and S. Wheeler, *Socialization After Childhood* (New York: Wiley, 1966).

4. H. S. Becker, "Personal Stages in Adult Life," *Sociometry*, 27 (1954), pp. 40–53.

5. J. A. Clausen (ed.), *Socialization and Society* (Boston: Little, Brown, 1968).

6. Reprinted from "Organizational Socialization and the Profession of Management," by E. H. Schein, *Sloan Management Review*, vol. 9, no. 2, p. 5, by permission of the publisher. Copyright © 1968 by the Sloan Management Review Association. All rights reserved.

7. A. Jay, *Management and Machiavelli* (Kent, England: Hodder & Stoughton Limited, 1967), pp. 70–71. Reprinted by permission of Hodder & Stoughton Limited.

8. R. Sibson, "The High Cost of Hiring," *Nation's Business*, February 1975, pp. 85–86.

9. Reprinted by permission of the *Harvard Business Review*. Excerpt from "Breakthrough in On-the-Job Training," by E. R. Gomersall and M. S. Myers (July/August 1966), p. 64. Copyright © 1966 by the President and Fellows of Harvard College; all rights reserved.

10. Gomersall and Myers.

11. G. Cavanagh, "Humanizing Influences of Blacks and Women in the Organization," in H. Meltzer and F. R. Wickert (eds.), *Humanizing Organizational Behavior* (Springfield, Ill.: Charles C Thomas, 1976).

12. D. Berlew and D. T. Hall, "The Socialization of Managers: Effects of Expectations on Performance," *Administrative Science Quarterly*, September 1966, pp. 207–223.

13. T. W. Johnson and G. Graen, "Organizational Assimilation and Role Rejection," *Organizational Behavior and Human Performance*, 8 (1973), pp. 72–87.
    M. Lubliner, "Employee Orientation," *Personnel Journal*, April 1978, pp. 207–208.

14. Lubliner.
    J. P. Wanous, *Organizational Entry* (Reading, Mass.: Addison-Wesley, 1980), pp. 167–197.

15. Lubliner, pp. 207–208.

16. Lubliner, pp. 207–208.
    Schein, pp. 1–19.

17. Berlew and Hall.

18. Schein.

19. Schein, p. 3.

20. J. S. Livingston, "Pygmalion in Management," *Harvard Business Review*, July/August 1969, pp. 81–89.

21. G. Cavanagh, "Humanizing Influences of Blacks and Women in the Organization," in H. Meltzer and F. R. Wickert (eds.), *Humanizing Organizational Behavior*, 1976, p. 68. Courtesy of Charles C Thomas, Publisher, Springfield, Ill.

22. R. M. Kanter, "Work in a New America," p. 59. Permission granted by *Daedalus*, Winter 1978, *A New America?*

23. D. Yankelovich, "The Meaning of Work," in J. M. Rosow (ed.), *The Worker and the Job: Coping with Change* (Englewood Cliffs, N.J.: Prentice-Hall, 1974), pp. 19–48.

24. T. A. Mahoney, "The Rearranged Workweek: Evaluations of Different Work Schedules," *California Management Review*, Summer 1978, pp. 31–39.

25. A. R. Cohen and H. Gadon, *Alternative Work Schedules: Integrating Individual and Organizational Needs*, © 1978, Addison-Wesley Publishing Company, Inc., p. 33. Reprinted with permission.

26. M. Maurice, *Shift Work* (Geneva, Switzerland: International Labor Office, 1975).
    D. L. Tasto and M. J. Collegan, *Shift Work Practices in the United States* (Washington, D.C.: National Institute for Occupational Safety and Health, 1977).

27. Cohen and Gadon.
    R. T. Golembiewski and R. J. Hills, "Drug Company Workers Like New Schedules," *Monthly Labor Review*, 100 (1977), pp. 65–69.
    R. T. Golembiewski, R. Hills, and M. S. Kagno, "A Longitudinal Study of Flextime Effects: Some Consequences of an O D Structural Intervention," *Journal of Applied Behavioral Sciences*, 4 (1974), pp. 503–532.

28. S. D. Nollen and V. H. Martin, *Alternative Work Schedules*, Part I: *Flextime* (New York: AMACOM, 1978).

29. S. D. Nollen, "Does Flextime Improve Productivity?" *Harvard Business Review*, 57 (1979), pp. 16–18, 76, 80.

30. D. J. Peterson, "Flexitime in the United States: The Lessons of Experience," *Personnel*, January/February 1980 (New York: AMACOM, a

division of American Management Associations, 1980), p. 27.

31. Cohen and Gadon, p. 33.

32. Cohen and Gadon.

R. B. Dunham and D. L. Hawk, "The Four-Day/Forty-Hour Week: Who Wants It?" *Academy of Management Journal*, 20 (1977), pp. 644–655.

M. D. Fottler, "Employee Acceptance of the Four-Day Workweek," *Academy of Management Journal*, 20 (1977), pp. 656–668.

J. S. Kim and A. F. Campagna, "Effects of Flexitime on Productivity: A Field Experiment in a Public Sector Setting," paper presented at the *National Academy of Management*, Detroit, Mich., 1980.

V. Schein, E. Maurer, and J. Novak, "Impact of Flexible Working Hours on Productivity,"

Journal of Applied Psychology, 62 (1977), pp. 463–465.

33. "A Full-Time Job—Weekends Only," *Business Week*, October 15, 1979, pp. 151–152.

34. "A Full-Time Job—Weekends Only," p. 151. Reprinted from the October 1979 issue of *Business Week*. © 1979 McGraw-Hill, Inc. 1221 Avenue of the Americas, New York, N.Y. 10020. All rights reserved.

35. "A Full-Time Job—Weekends Only." Cohen and Gadon.

36. Cohen and Gadon, p. 66.

37. Cohen and Gadon.

38. For a nice discussion of the reasons employees use sick leave, see D. Dalton, "Absenteeism and the Collective Bargaining Agreement: An Empirical Test," *Academy of Management Journal* (in press).

SECTION FOUR

Appraising and Compensating Employees

OBJECTIVES

- To discuss the purposes of performance appraisal

- To identify and explain the components of the performance appraisal system

- To match appraisal purposes with appraisal forms

- To explain some of the common problems in performance appraisal

THOUGHT STARTERS

- What is the difference between criticism and negative feedback?

- Why do supervisors resist giving negative feedback?

- Why evaluate employee performance?

- What is the most common way for organizations to appraise employee performance?

CHAPTER NINE
Appraising Employee Performance

You know, Jimmy, these damn appraisals are a pain in the neck. Doing the damn things not only takes time away from the job but at least half of my people resent my talking with them about how they are doing. Take those gals working on the capsule machines. Most of them are over forty, married, and have been with the company for at least a dozen years. They want a steady job and friendly people to work with. They're not after promotions, status, development, and all that crap. They know damn well that the only reason for appraisal is to bug the gals who are not carrying their share of the load. Once in awhile I can get a little bigger pay increase for one but I have to really build a big case for the old man."

"Jerry, you miss the point of why personnel wants us to do these appraisals every year. The aim is to discover who has the track record and the capability of handling a bigger job. Without this appraisal process, some of our best people would be overlooked and forgotten when bigger, better jobs are open in the company. Besides, it's important to emphasize to our people that their development on the job is an important thing around here. Without that, a helluva lot of people wouldn't find this place very attractive. What's

more, with the company's promotion-from-within policy, it's part of our job to be on the lookout for comers. When we do that, people react favorably to opportunities for feedback and suggestions for improvement."

Excerpt from L. L. Cummings and D. P. Schwab, "Designing Appraisal Systems for Information Yield," © 1978 by the Regents of the University of California. Reprinted from California Management Review, *vol. XX, no. 4, pp. 18–19 by permission of the Regents.*

John, this is our fourth little session like this, and I guess we can skip the details. You're late with the report on the Miller acquisition, which I'm well aware you oppose, and I still haven't seen the performance appraisals for your top men that our new development program calls for. I'm really disturbed at your refusal to cooperate fully on the computer services study. You seem to feel merchandising is exempt, and I've tried to explain this has to be a total approach if we're going to justify our data-processing investment.

I'm sorry to bring it up again so soon, but I guess what I'd really like to hear at this point, John, is how much thought you've given to the possibility of early retirement. You've given us twenty-seven years of loyal service, and you know you're highly regarded, personally, in the company and the industry. I've spoken to one or two key directors, in confidencce, of course, and I'm sure we can clear a special arrangement so you won't be hurt financially. Let me know your reaction, will you—say, by the end of this month?

It's shameful and inhuman—and it's unfair to the stockholders. We permit a person to vegetate because we haven't the courage to find something he can do, inside or outside the corporation. Sometimes complete honesty would be brutal.

But what bothers me is the number of situations I've seen in which one refrains from honesty because one lacks the courage to tell a person he's worked with for many years that time has passed him by. The more experienced I get, the more persuaded I am that we make more mistakes by trying to avoid hurting other people's feelings than we would be being more honest.

Excerpt from Robert C. Albrook, "Those Boxed-In, Left-Out Vice Presidents," Fortune, *May 1, 1969, p. 106. Courtesy of* Fortune Magazine; © *1969 Time, Inc.*

These quotes illustrate several important points about formal performance appraisals in organizations: (1) They can serve several purposes; (2) they are extremely important in organizations; and (3)

. . . however necessary some formal appraisal system appears to be, current systems are still widely regarded as a nuisance at best and a dangerous evil at worst. Many managers resent the time it takes to do the job well and, where the system requires that their appraisal be discussed with the subject, some managers are known to ignore the whole procedure when they can—or else fudge their comments to avoid the embarrassment inherent in criticizing a subordinate's performance on what they consider to be shaky grounds.[1]

Nevertheless, most organizations maintain their formal evaluation systems because they feel that performance evaluation is fundamental to organizational effectiveness; that if there were no formal appraisal program there would have to be an informal one; and that it is better to maintain the visibility of a formal program because it may help to improve systematically the fairness, validity, usefulness, and reliability of the appraisal process. In addition:

Evaluation is an inevitable consequence of the way organizations are structured and jobs are designed. The assignment of responsibility to particular individuals for the performance of certain tasks makes the assessment of how an individual performs both possible and necessary. It makes it possible because it identifies the results for which the person is responsible. It makes it necessary because in order to operate [effectively], complex, differentiated organizations need information on how well jobs are being performed.[2]

As a result, most organizations have some type of formal employee performance appraisal. Thus the question that faces personnel and human resource managers is not, Should we have formal performance appraisal? but rather, What type of performance appraisal should we have? Helping you to answer that question is a primary purpose of this chapter. To serve that purpose, it begins by defining what performance appraisal is, describes its purposes and importance, and illustrates its relationships with other personnel activities. Then it looks at performance appraisal as a system and examines the application of performance appraisals in organizations.

APPRAISING THE PERFORMANCE OF EMPLOYEES

Performance appraisal is a formal, structured system of measuring and evaluating an employee's job-related behaviors and outcomes to discover how and why the employee is presently performing on the job and how the employee can perform more effectively in the future so that the employee, the organization, and society all benefit. Note that this definition identifies employee **performance** in terms of the results or outcomes that people accomplish on the job and what they do (their job-related behaviors) that affects those results. There are four critical aspects of performance:

● Performance is always tied to results—the on-the-job outcome of what people do.

- Performance is also tied to behavior—the things people do that produce the results.
- Behavior can be either active or passive—do-something or do-nothing. Either way, it can affect job results.
- Most of the behavior discussed in performance appraisals is on-the-job behavior. But not necessarily all. Off-the-job behavior belongs in the appraisal if—and only if—it affects the results obtained on the job.

What's not performance? Anything a person does on the job that makes no difference in results. Performance appraisal should always be restricted to behavior that matters. "Trivial, inconsequential behavior—chewing gum while working on balance sheets, wearing a bow tie to work each day, whistling in the halls, etcetera—doesn't belong in a performance appraisal."[3] A good rule of thumb to use in deciding whether or not to evaluate a behavior is to ask the question, What difference does it make? If the answer is "none," don't evaluate it.

In this chapter, the terms *supervisor* and *manager* are generally discarded, because both the appraiser and the appraisee may be managers or supervisors. Thus the term *superior* is used to denote the person doing the appraising, and the term *subordinate* is used to refer to the person whose performance is being appraised. The terms *superior* and *subordinate* are used in this chapter only for clarity; they do not imply that the person doing the appraising is "better" than the appraisee or that the subordinate is "inferior" to the superior.

The Importance of Performance Appraisal

Appraising employee performance is important because it provides information about how well jobs are being performed. It also identifies who is responsible for doing those jobs and how well they are performing them.

Performance appraisal serves many specific purposes in addition to identifying how well an employee is doing. The most frequent uses of appraisal are

- *Management development:* Provides a framework for future employee development by identifying and preparing individuals for increased responsibilities
- *Performance measurement:* Establishes the relative value of an individual's contribution to the company and helps evaluate individual accomplishments
- *Performance improvement:* Encourages continued successful performance and strengthens individual weaknesses to make employees more effective and productive
- *Compensation:* Helps determine appropriate pay for performance and equitable salary and bonus incentives based on merit or results
- *Identification of potential:* Identifies candidates for promotion
- *Feedback:* Outlines what is expected from employees against actual performance level
- *Human resource planning:* Audits management talent to evaluate present supply of human resources for replacement planning

● *Communications:* Provides a format for dialogue between superior and subordinate and improves understanding of personal goals and concerns

Other purposes of performance appraisal are demotions, terminations, internal recruitment, and research.[4]

Performance Appraisal in Personnel Management

All these uses of performance appraisal indicate not only how important the activity is but also how extensive its relationships are with other personnel and human resource activities. The four critical relationships are with job analysis, selection, compensation, and training and development. All the purposes of performance appraisal affect the "terms and conditions of employment" for employees. Therefore, it is viewed as an "employee selection procedure" and must follow the same validation procedures as those used for selection tests (described in Chapter 7).

One way an organization can help ensure that the performance criteria are valid is by job analysis. Job analysis clarifies the critical elements of the job that are related to the needs and purposes of the organization. Developing performance appraisals that reflect those critical elements is necessary if the appraisals are to be considered valid. The U.S. Circuit Court in *Brito* v. *Zia Company* (1973) found that Zia Company was in violation of Title VII when a disproportionate number of a protected group were laid off on the basis of low performance scores. Zia also failed, in accordance with EEOC guidelines, to

". . . *introduce evidence of validity . . . consisting of empirical data demonstrating that the test was significantly correlated with important elements of work behavior relevant to the jobs for which the appellants were being evaluated.*"

The court found that the "evaluations were based on the best judgments and opinions . . . but not on any specific performance that were supported by some kind of record."[5]

Without valid performance appraisals, the validity of such selection procedures as tests cannot be determined. The U.S. Supreme Court in *Albemarle Paper Company* v. *Moody* (1975) ruled that Albemarle's selection tests were not valid because there was

". . . *no way to determine whether the criteria actually considered were sufficiently related to the company's legitimate interests in job-specific ability to justify a testing system with a racially discriminatory impact.*" *In the process of validating their tests, Albemarle made no attempt to analyze the job to delineate the particular job skills they might require.*[6]

Thus the validity of an organization's selection procedures depends on the validity of the performance appraisal, which in turns depends on job analysis.

The results of the performance appraisal are used in many organizations to determine compensation—merit increases, incentives, and bonuses. Although only a few employees participate in incentive and bonus programs, many employees participate in merit increases. A merit increase may range as high as 16 percent of an employee's salary, the exact percentage depending on the performance evaluation. Usually the better the evaluation, the larger the percentage.

Finally, in the process of making a performance appraisal, employee weaknesses or deficiencies are often identified. Training and development programs can be designed and implemented to remedy these deficiencies. They can also be designed to give employees the skills and abilities they will need to perform effectively in future jobs.

Who's Responsible for Appraising Performance?

In almost all cases, line managers do the actual appraisal. Furthermore, it is the line managers who must tell employees how they are doing and make salary and training decisions. Personnel managers can aid line managers by providing information on how to use the performance appraisal forms and by making sure that the results of each appraisal become part of the employees' records, readily available for such management decisions as determining who to promote.

Especially in decentralized organizations, personnel managers should be responsible for ensuring that all subordinates are appraised fairly and consistently. To fulfill this responsibility, personnel managers may have to get all divisions of the organization to use the same appraisal form. They may even have to design an entire performance appraisal system for the organization.

PERFORMANCE APPRAISAL AS A SYSTEM

You may have gotten the impression so far that performance appraisal is a single activity—the superior appraises the performance of the subordinate, and that's it. Actually, performance appraisal is much more complex. Exhibit 9.1 shows performance appraisal as a system.

Criteria and Standards

To serve the organization's purposes and meet legal challenges, a performance appraisal system must appraise current employee performance. If the appraisal system is to uncover employees' potential for greater responsibilities and promotion, it must also provide accurate data about such potential. And the system must yield consistent data (be reliable) about what it is supposed to be concerned with (be valid).[7]

A valid performance appraisal system must specify performance criteria that are job-related and important, criteria that can most easily be determined through job analysis. Then employees' contributions to the organization can be evaluated based on the degree to which they perform those behaviors and attain those results specified in the job analysis. For example, if selling 100 units per month is the only important result of an employee's job, then the appraisal system should only measure the number of units sold. In this case, there is only one performance criterion.

Generally, job analysis identifies several performance criteria that determine em-

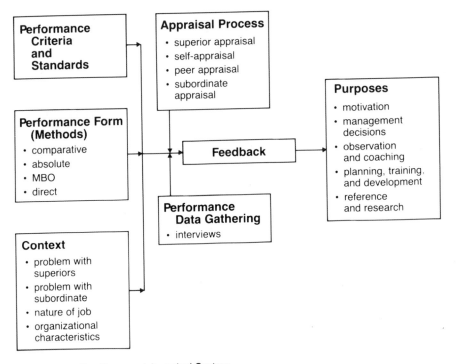

Exhibit 9.1 The Personnel Appraisal System

ployees' contributions.[8] Thus selling 100 units per month may be accompanied by such criteria as effects of remarks to customers, consistency in attendance, and even effects on co-workers. All these should be measured by the performance appraisal.

If the form used to appraise employee performance lacks the job behaviors and results important and relevant to the job, the form is said to be deficient. If the form includes appraisal of anything neither important nor relevant to the job, it is contaminated. Many performance appraisal forms actually used in organizations measure some characteristics and behaviors of employees unrelated to the employee's job. These forms are contaminated and in many cases also deficient.

In addition to performance criteria, standards are necessary to measure how well employees are performing. By using standards, performance criteria take on a range of values. For example, selling 100 units per month may be defined as excellent performance, and selling 80 units may be defined as average. This is referred to as an **absolute standard**. Sometimes employees are evaluated by comparing them to other employees. Thus selling 100 units a month may be only average if several other employees sell 125 units. This is referred to as a **comparative standard**.

Performance Appraisal Forms

There are four major forms or approaches to performance appraisal: comparative, absolute standards (quantitative and qualitative), management by objectives or goals, and direct or objective indexes.[9]

The Comparative Approach.   There are several **comparative methods** of evaluation, all comparing one subordinate to the others. The first is the straight ranking, in which a superior lists the subordinates in order from best to worst, usually on the basis of overall performance. The second method is the alternative ranking, which takes place in several steps. The first step is to put the best subordinate at the head of the list and the worst subordinate at the bottom. In the second round, the superior selects the best and worst from the remaining subordinates. Of these two, the best is placed second on the list and the worst is placed next to last. The superior chooses the best and worst until all subordinates are ranked. As you can see, the middle position on the list is the last to be filled by this method.

The remaining two comparative methods are more time-consuming but may provide better information. One is the paired comparison method, in which each subordinate is compared to every other subordinate, one at a time, on a single standard or criterion, such as overall performance. The subordinate with the second-greatest number of favorable comparisons is ranked second, and so on.

The three comparative methods discussed so far give each person a unique rank. This suggests that no two subordinates perform exactly alike. Although this may be true, many superiors say that subordinates' performances are too close to differentiate. The fourth method—the forced distribution method—was designed to overcome this complaint and to incorporate several factors or dimensions (rather than a single factor) into the ranking of subordinates. The term *forced distribution* is used because the superior must assign only a certain proportion of subordinates to each of several categories on each factor. A common forced distribution scale may be divided into five categories. A fixed percentage of all subordinates in the group fall within each of these categories. A problem with this method is, of course, that a group of subordinates may not conform to the fixed percentage. In fact, all four comparative methods assume that there are good and bad performers in all groups. You may know from experience, however, of situations where all the people in a group actually perform identically. If you encountered such a situation, how would you evaluate these people?

Absolute Standards.   In the comparative approach to performance evaluation, the superior is forced to evaluate each subordinate in relationship to the other subordinates, often based on a single overall dimension. In contrast, the absolute standard approach allows superiors to evaluate each subordinate's performance independent of the other subordinates and often on several dimensions of performance. However, there is still an element of force in the absolute standard approach, particularly in the qualitative category (the other major category is the quantitative).

When the qualitative method of evaluation is used, the superior simply indicates whether the selected performance dimensions do or do not apply to a particular subordinate. This method of evaluation does not reflect the extent to which a given dimension applies—just whether it exists. There are three general methods of qualitative evaluation: critical incidents, weighted checklist, and forced choice.

In the **critical incidents** format, superiors must indicate which of a number of incidents of performance (successful and unsuccessful) were exhibited by each subordinate. Usually these incidents—regarded as critical by the organization, subordinates, and superiors—are grouped into several categories representing separate dimensions of performance. Initially, the concept of critical incidents implied that some incidents were unique and relatively important. Superiors kept "little black books" of good, bad, and typical incidents for each subordinate. Thus the original method weighted incidents. But it was time-consuming to provide what amounted to a unique form for each subordinate, so now one form is used for all subordinates doing the same job.

The **weighted checklist** method combines some of the old and new aspects of the critical incidents method. Weighted checklists are developed by individuals familiar with the jobs of the subordinates to be evaluated, such as the personnel manager. The weighted checklist represents the relative (weighted) importance of good and bad aspects of performance. The checklists are given to the superiors, but they don't know how the items are weighted. An example of such a checklist, with the weightings, is shown in Exhibit 9.2.

The **forced choice** method is also developed by someone who is familiar with the jobs of the subordinates, such as the personnel manager—but not by the superiors. The forced choice method differs from the weighted checklist because it forces superiors to evaluate each subordinate by choosing which of two items better describes the subordinate. Usually, it has an evaluation form containing numerous pairs of statements, and these are frequently grouped into clusters representing

Exhibit 9.2 Sample Weighted Checklist for Bakeshop Managers

Item	Scale Value
_____ Occasionally buys some of the competitor's products	6.8
_____ Never consults with the head salesperson when making a bake order	1.4
_____ Belongs to a local merchants' association	4.9
_____ Criticizes employees unnecessarily	0.8
_____ Window display is usually just fair	3.1
_____ Enjoys contacting customers personally	7.4
_____ Does not know how to figure costs of products	0.6
_____ Lacks a long-range viewpoint	3.5
_____ Products are of uniformly high quality	8.5
_____ Expects too much of employees	2.2
_____ Weekly and monthly reports are sometimes inaccurate	4.2
_____ Does not always give enough thought to bake orders	1.6
_____ Occasionally runs a selling contest among salespeople	6.8
_____ Baking in the shop continues until 2 p.m. or later	8.2
_____ Has originated one or more workable new formulas	6.4
_____ Sometimes has an unreasonably large inventory of certain items	3.3
_____ Employees enjoy working for the manager	7.6
_____ Does not delegate enough responsibility to others	2.8
_____ Has accurately figured the costs of most of the products	7.8
_____ Wishes he or she were just a baker	0.8
_____ Shop is about average in cleanliness	4.4
_____ Is tardy in making minor repairs in the salesroom	1.9
_____ Periodically samples all of the products for quality	8.1

From *Performance in Organizations* by L. L. Cummings and Donald P. Schwab, p. 87. Copyright © 1973 by Scott, Foresman and Company. Reprinted by permission.

performance dimensions. The statements in each pair have two important characteristics useful for evaluation: desirability and discrimination (between good and bad performance). The statements in a pair should have equal desirability but should clearly differentiate good performers from bad performers. The indexes of desirability and discrimination are initially developed by individuals familiar with the jobs. An example of two pairs of statements with the two indexes is shown in Exhibit 9.3. Note again that the indexes are not shown to superiors before they evaluate subordinates.

Quantitative methods are different from the qualitative methods in that they do not force the superiors to make yes-or-no choices. There are two quantitative methods: the conventional or graphic rating and the behavior anchored rating scale.

The **conventional rating** is the most widely used method of performance evaluation (see Exhibit 9.4). Conventional forms vary in the number of dimensions of performance they measure. However, the term *performance* is used advisedly, because many conventional forms use personality characteristics rather than actual behaviors as indicators of performance. Frequently used traits are aggressiveness, independence, maturity, and sense of responsibility. Many conventional forms also use dimensions of performance similar to those used in the comparative approach, such as overall job performance or quality of performance. Conventional forms also vary on the range or degree of each dimension used. Some forms may have only four levels of performance, whereas others may have as many as twenty-five. Conventional forms are easy and quick and very popular, but the results are sometimes difficult to convey to subordinates, especially if the results are unfavorable. In addition, the results fail to indicate how subordinates could do better.

The **behavior anchored rating scale** (BARS) was developed to provide results subordinates could use to improve performance. They were also designed so superiors would be more comfortable giving feedback. The development of a BARS generally corresponds to the first steps in the critical incidents method. Then individuals familiar with the jobs of the subordinates evaluate the incidents in terms of goodness and badness. Incidents that the individuals agree on are arranged in order of goodness and placed in clusters. Exhibit 9.5 shows a BARS for appraising nurses' organizational ability. A disadvantage with BARS is the cost and time to develop them, which are more than required for conventional rating forms. BARS are often tailored for each job, whereas conventional forms apply to many jobs. However, a comprehensive BARS has in fact been developed using ten dimensions of performance: interpersonal relationship, organization and planning, reaction to problems,

Turns in work assignment promptly	OR	Is at ease in any situation		Almost always reports for work on time	OR	Makes friends with others easily
Desirability Index				Desirability Index		
4.75		4.72		3.27		3.30
Discrimination Index				Discrimination Index		
4.21		0.82		3.69		0.91

Exhibit 9.3 Sample Forced Choice Clusters
Adapted from L. L. Cummings and D. P. Schwab, *Performance in Organizations* (Glenview, Ill.: Scott, Foresman, 1973), p. 88.

Name of Employee _____

Job Title _____

Division _____

Department _____

Anniversary Date _____

INSTRUCTIONS

Evaluate the employee on the job now being performed. For each factor, place a check mark in the block that most clearly expresses your overall judgment. The care and accuracy with which this appraisal is made will determine its value to you, the employee, and the organization.

Factor					
JOB KNOWLEDGE Performance of required duties as outlined in the position description	☐ Understands and is capable of performing all phases of job	☐ Understands and is capable of performing almost all phases of job	☐ Has adequate grasp of essential duties of job; can proceed without special instructions on all regular work	☐ Fair knowledge but lacks knowledge of some important aspects of job content	☐ Poor job knowledge; does not understand job duties
DEPENDABILITY Degree of supervision required to perform job functions	☐ Requires very close supervision	☐ Requires regular checking to be sure work will be done on time and in accordance with instructions	☐ On only a few tasks is it necessary to check up to be sure of deadlines or following of instructions	☐ Regularly follows instructions; requires little followup	☐ Always follows instructions: you can be absolutely sure you will get just what you want when you want it
QUANTITY Ability to meet performance quota required to maintain department standards under normal conditions	☐ Seldom gets work done in required time	☐ Work output is below established requirements	☐ Turns out normal amount of work but seldom more output than is satisfactory	☐ Output of work exceeds amount deemed necessary for normal departmental operations	☐ Output of work is ordinarily high; regularly produces above and beyond the established requirements of position
QUALITY Neatness and accuracy of the individual's work	☐ Mistakes are extremely rare	☐ Very few errors, usually minor in nature; work seldom has to be done over	☐ Most work done well, usually acceptable in both accuracy and neatness	☐ Work often unacceptable; frequent errors or rejections	☐ Work constantly rejected because of inaccuracies and mistakes
ADAPTABILITY Speed with which the employee masters new methods or duties and grasps explanations	☐ Exceptionally fast to learn and adjust to changed conditions	☐ Learns easily; adjusts to changes rapidly	☐ Adjusts to changes in methods or duties on request, with average amount of instructions	☐ Adjusts to changes in methods or duties, but adjustment is slow and requires detailed instructions	☐ Unable or unwilling to adjust to new methods or duties
APPLICATION TO WORK Ability of the employee to effectively use available work time	☐ Spends much time away from desk; often interrupts work for idle talk	☐ Spends more time than necessary in talk or away from desk; sometimes causes delays in work output	☐ Spends no more time than necessary in talk or away from desk; shows fair planning to avoid delays	☐ Usually on job at all times; very little idle time; industrious	☐ Energetic; loses no time in starting and works right to last minute; plans work in advance so as to avoid delays
Comments					

Exhibit 9.4 Sample Conventional Rating Form for Nonexempt Salaried Employees

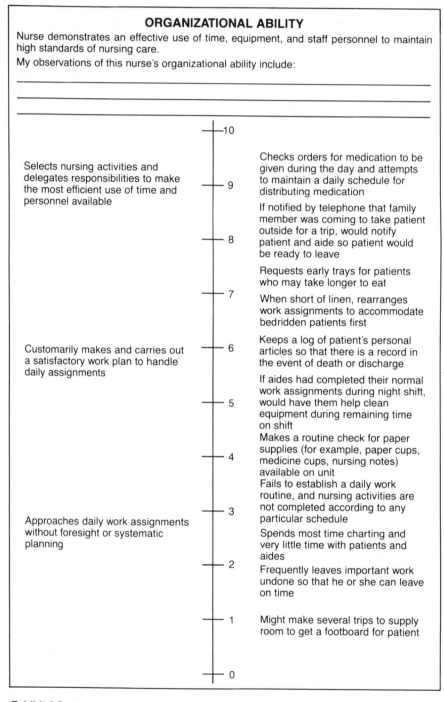

Exhibit 9.5 Sample Behavior Anchored Rating Scale for Nurses

From "Measurement of Job Performance in Nursing Homes," final report submitted to Health Resources Administration under grant No. 5R01 NU00612-02. Provided to John Sheridan, March 1980.

reliability, communication, adaptability, growth, productivity, quality of work, and teaching.[10] Perhaps the revised BARS will see increased use, especially in comparison with conventional forms.

Management by Objectives. The **management by objectives** (MBO) or goal-setting method has four steps.[11] The first step is to establish the goals each subordinate is to attain. In some organizations, superiors and subordinates work together to establish goals; in others, superiors establish goals for subordinates. The goals can refer to desired outcomes to be achieved, means (activities) for achieving the outcomes, or both.

The second step involves the subordinates' performance in a previously arranged time period. As subordinates perform, they know fairly well what there is to do, what has been done, and what remains to be done.

The third step is a comparison of the actual level of goal attainment against the agreed-on goals. The evaluator explores reasons for the goals not being met and for goals being exceeded. This step helps determine possible training needs. It also alerts the superior to conditions in the organization that may affect a subordinate's performance but over which the subordinate has no control.

The final step is to decide on new goals and possibly new strategies for goals not previously attained. At this point, subordinate and superior involvement in goal setting may change. Subordinates who successfully reach the established goals may be allowed to participate more in the goal-setting process the next time.

MBO was originally devised to help develop subordinates. It was applied especially to individuals who worked in jobs for which there were no objective measures of performance, such as managerial positions. There are many jobs, however, for which direct measures of performance are available and where, it is argued, MBO may be even more appropriate.

An approach similar to MBO, the **work standards** approach, does use more direct measures of performance and is usually applied to nonmanagerial employees. Instead of asking subordinates to set their own performance goals, as in MBO, organizations determine the goals. Organizations may, however, bring in outside consulting firms to establish the performance goals, thus avoiding the cynical question occasionally asked of the MBO goal-setting process: "Management by Whose Objectives?"[12]

To give you the flavor of what the work standards approach can be, here's a statement by a management representative from a hospital with a union:

Through observation and time studies the work load is broken down into identifiable components measured in units of time. The sum of these components represents the standard requirements for performing the tasks comprising the employee's work load. Work measurement determines the frequency, volume and time of occurrence of the task comprising the work load. These data form the basis for defining the individual work assignments, or job entities, and provide criteria for determining that no single employee is overloaded or underloaded.

On the basis of the work standards thus established, a method of monitoring and controlling manpower utilization is developed. This system provides constant feedback to the administrator in the form of weekly reports which show, department by department, actual hours worked in comparison to the measured hours required.

Data obtained provide a sound basis for fair job descriptions and wage and salary evaluations. . . .

Under the contract now in effect, the union agrees to accept and abide by the criteria established through work measurement as the essential qualification for a given position. . . .

. . . while the hospital's number of patient days has increased (by 15 percent over the past four years) it employs 10 percent fewer employees than hospitals in the same classification and size category.[13]

Direct Index Approach.   This approach differs from the first three primarily in how performance is measured. The first three approaches, except the work standards approach, depend on a superior evaluating a subordinate's performance. There is a certain amount of subjective evaluation in these cases. However, the **direct index** approach measures subordinate performance by objective, impersonal criteria, such as productivity, absenteeism, and turnover. For example, a manager's performance may be evaluated by the number of employees working for that manager who quit or by the absenteeism rate of that manager's employees. For nonmanagers, measures of productivity may be more appropriate. Measures of productivity can be broken into measures of quality and measures of quantity. Quality measures include scrap rates, customer complaints, and number of defective units or parts produced. Quantity measures include units of output per hour, new customer order, and sales volume.

Other Approaches.   The four major approaches to performance evaluation reviewed so far represent some of those most frequently used in organizations. The conventional evaluation or rating scale still appears to be the most widely used of these methods for both managers and nonmanagers. But when it is used, it is often supplemented with the **essay method**, which requires the evaluator to describe, generally in summary form, the strengths and weaknesses of a particular subordinate. Martin Marietta Corporation, for example, requires supervisors in its Aero Space Divison to write broad essays describing an individual's strengths and weaknesses. This often can be done in conjunction with one of the four forms already described.

The preceding approaches appraise current performance. Occasionally it is necessary and useful to be able to appraise how employees would perform on a future job (generally one they would be promoted to). The **assessment center** method, which is used to determine the performance potential of managers, evaluates individuals on a large number of activities. It is conducted in a relatively isolated environment and is designed to measure managerial skills and abilities. In a typical assessment center, a manager may spend two or three days going through a series of activities, which may include management games, leaderless group discussions, and in-basket exercises. A format for a typical assessment center is shown in Chapter 7.

The product of assessment centers, whether they are based on a day of activities or a week, are a series of judgments or ratings made by staff members. Typically this involves rating on behavior dimensions as well as a summary judgment or recommendation about the [managerial] candidate's potential.[14]

See Chapter 14 for a further discussion of the assessment center.

The Context of Performance Appraisal

Regardless of the form used and how valid and reliable it is, organizational influences may reduce the effectiveness of even the finest performance appraisal system.[15] One aspect of this problem is the relationship between superior and subordinate.

Superior-Subordinate Relationships. Important aspects of the superior-subordinate relationship are personal characteristics of the superior, characteristics of the superior in relation to those of the subordinate, the superior's knowledge of the subordinate and the job, and the subordinate's knowledge of the job.[16] For ease of discussion, these can be grouped into problems with the superior and problems with the subordinate.[17]

There are basically four problems with the superior that may arise. The first is that superiors may not know what employees are doing or may not understand their work well enough to appraise it fairly. This particular problem occurs more frequently when a manager has a large span of control—a large number of responsibilities and possibly a large number of employees working in different areas. This problem also occurs when the tasks of the employees are varied and technically complex or changing.

The second problem is that even when superiors understand and know how much work subordinates do, they may not have performance standards for evaluating that work. As a result, subordinates may receive unfair (invalid) evaluations because of variability in standards and ratings. This unfairness may be particularly obvious when comparing the evaluations of subordinates working for different superiors. This problem can occur in any organization, regardless of size, complexity, or the amount of change going on.

The third problem is that superiors may use inappropriate standards: They may allow personal values, needs, or biases to replace organizational values and standards. The general result is any one of several errors in evaluation. The most common errors occur when superiors rate an employee or group of subordinates on several dimensions of performance. Frequently a superior will evaluate a subordinate similarly on all dimensions of performance just on the basis of the evaluation of one dimension, the one perhaps perceived as most important. This effect is the halo error. When superiors tend to give all their subordinates favorable ratings, they are said to be committing an error of leniency. An error of strictness is just the opposite. An error of central tendency represents a tendency to evaluate all subordintes as average. A recency-of-events error is a tendency to evaluate total performance on the last or most recent part of the subordinate's performance. This error can have serious consequences for a subordinate who performs very well for six months or a year but then makes a serious or costly error in the last week or two before evaluations are made.

These errors may occur intentionally or unintentially. Some superiors, for example, may intentionally evaluate their best performers as slightly less than excellent to prevent them from being promoted out of the superior's group. On the other hand, some superiors may unintentionally evaluate certain subordinates less favorably than others merely because they "don't look like good performers." A female subordinate, for instance, may be perceived by a male superior as having such traditional female qualities as dependence, passiveness, and kindness—in unfortunate contrast to the qualities he perceives as required to be a good performer such as independence, initiative, and impersonalism. Thus this superior may evaluate this subordinate less favorably. [18]

Even the most valid and reliable appraisal forms cannot be effective when superiors commit these all-too-common errors. But many of these errors can be minimized if

- *Each performance dimension addresses a single job activity rather than a group of activities*
- *The rater on a regular basis can observe the behavior of the ratee while the job is being accomplished*
- *Terms like "average" are not used on a rating scale, since different raters have various reactions to such a term*
- *The rater does not have to evaluate large groups of employees*
- *Raters are* trained *to avoid such errors as leniency, strictness, halo, central tendency and recency of events*
- *The dimensions being evaluated are meaningful, clearly stated and important*[19]

The last major problem related to the superior, although important in itself, is also important because it often leads to some of the errors listed above, particularly the halo and leniency errors: Superiors do not like and where possible resist making ratings, especially negative ones. The result is often inadequate or inaccurate evaluations. Superiors may consider performance appraisals a conflict. For example, they may perceive that appraisals take time away from their "real job." It may also be the case that superiors fail to see how performance appraisals really fit into the mainstream of knowledge about the behavior of people in organizations.[20] Halo and leniency errors are easy to make when superiors do not take time to consider each performance criterion separately for each subordinate. The leniency error is often committed by superiors who resist evaluating subordinates because it is difficult for them to give negative feedback.

The problems for superiors in performance appraisal are difficult indeed. However, subordinates also present problems. For one thing, they may not know what's expected of them. This is true regardless of the level of difficulty of their jobs and whether they work in hospitals, government agencies, or private organizations.

The second problem is that subordinates may not be able to do what's expected. Of course, this may be corrected by training or job matching. But it is not always easy to spot performance inabilities. People may not be performing well just because they don't know what's expected. It's not that they don't have the ability; they just don't know how to apply it. The personnel manager can play an important role in these cases, working with superiors to spot reasons for performance deficiencies.

The Nature of the Job. "To a considerable extent, the potential value of any performance appraisal system is dependent upon the nature of the subordinate's job."[21] On many jobs, the quality or quantity of performance may be outside the subordinate's control. This is particularly true on very routine jobs and where the pace of the jobs is controlled by machines. And when jobs are highly interdependent, it is difficult to separate the individual's performance from that of the group.[22]

A SLICE OF LIFE

Not only is it important to separate an individual's contributions from those of the groups, but distinguishing the relationship between departments is critical. For example, suppose there are three departments in an organization—production, sales, and finance. It would seem that setting standards for appraising these divisions would be straightforward. For the production department, quantity, quality, time, and cost can be considered. The sales department is concerned with total sales. The finance department can be evaluated on amount lost to bad debts and the like. The difficulty here is that the performances of these departments are not independent. For example, the production department could operate most efficiently with a limited product line with little variation in size or color. The sales department, of course, wants as much variety as possible, and these are mutually exclusive needs. Similarly, the sales department could, through very large sales, overtax the production department, which would increase equipment fatigue, increase overtime payments, and so on. To be effective, the finance department requires sound fiscal policies. So for large sales, finance would request a relatively high down payment and a reasonably accelerated payback period. The sales department, on the other hand, would prefer to sell at a dollar down and a dollar per week forever.

The point is that if you appraise the performance of just one department, you may undermine the efforts of another. Thus the performance of all divisions, departments, and groups must be reasonably congruent. And appraisal systems must tap the performance of individuals and groups without encouraging behaviors and attitudes that are dysfunctional to the organization as a whole. These considerations are a major responsibility and a serious challenge for higher-level management.

Organizational Characteristics. If employees are unionized, performance appraisals may not even be used. Unions have traditionally favored the use of seniority to determine wage increases, promotions, transfers, and demotions.

The Appraisal Process and Gathering Data

The appraisal process is primarily a matter of gathering data. Its major elements are someone to gather data and a situation for gathering data. Appraisals can come from several different sources, each with its own advantages and disadvantages.

Appraisal by Superiors. The superior is the immediate boss of the subordinate being evaluated. It is assumed that the superior is the one who knows best the job of the subordinate and the performance of the subordinate. But there are drawbacks to appraisal by the superior:

● Since the superior may have reward and punishment power, the subordinate may feel threatened.

● The evaluation process often is a one-way process that makes the subordinate feel defensive. Thus little coaching takes place; justification of actions prevails.

● The superior may not have the necessary interpersonal skills to give good feedback.

● The superior may have an ethical bias against "playing God."

● The superior, by giving punishments, may alienate the subordinate.

Because of the potential liabilities, organizations may invite other people to share in the appraisal process, even giving the subordinate greater input.

Self-Appraisal. The use of self-appraisal, particularly through subordinate participation in setting goals, was made popular as an important component of MBO. Subordinates who participate in the evaluation process may become more involved and committed to the goals. It appears that subordinate participation may also help clarify employees' roles and reduce role conflict.[23]

At this time it would appear that self-appraisals are effective tools for programs focusing on self-development, personal growth and goal commitment. On the other hand, it would also appear that self-appraisals are subject to systematic biases and distortions when used for evaluative purposes.[24]

These biases and distortions, however, may be important topics of discussion in the performance appraisal session between superior and subordinate.

Peer Appraisal. Peer appraisals appear to be useful predictors of subordinate performance.[25] They are particularly useful when superiors lack access to some aspects of subordinates' performance. However, the validity of peer appraisals is reduced somewhat if the organizational reward system is based on performance and is highly competitive, and if there is a low level of trust among subordinates.[26]

Appraisal by Subordinates. Perhaps many of you, particularly as students, have had the chance to evaluate an instructor. How useful do you think this evaluation process is? A significant advantage of appraisal by students is that many instructors are unaware of how they are being perceived by their students. They may not realize that students fail to understand most of their instructions. It is the same in a work setting: Subordinates' appraisals can make superiors more aware of their impact on their subordinates.

Sometimes, however, subordinates may evaluate their superiors solely on the basis of personality or serving the needs of subordinates rather than the needs of the organization. Of course, there are times when subordinates may inflate the evaluation of the superiors, particularly if they feel threatened by the superiors and have no anonymity.

Characteristics of Effective Interviews

Another method of gathering data for performance appraisals is the interview with the subordinate being appraised. As you might guess, there are good ways and not-so-good ways to conduct an interview. There are six characteristics of performance appraisal interviews that make them particularly effective:

1. Interview Climate . . . *specifically determines whether the purpose of the interview is stated, whether the session is rushed and whether the employee is given sufficient opportunities to respond to issues raised during the interview.*

This factor is important in that it can affect employees' perceptions of the importance of the session and their receptivity to ideas generated during the session. It is not implied that a higher degree of formalization is necessarily more effective, but it is suggested that employees should regard the performance appraisal interview as an integral component of employee development.

2. Invitation to Participate *is the extent to which the supervisor encourages the subordinate to discuss factors that are influencing performance. This includes a discussion of why tasks are difficult, work aspects preventing high-quality performance, grievances and on-the-job performance.*

Inviting subordinate participation may enhance the level of candid discussion in the appraisal interview and increase the likelihood that conflicts will be resolved. Furthermore, by encouraging subordinates to make inputs to the interview discussions, goals and objectives are more likely to be accepted because of increases in the level of subordinate commitment.

3. Participation in Goal Setting *is the degree to which the supervisor encourages the mutual establishment of specific goals for the coming period. It also connotes the supervisor's willingness to assist the employee in meeting those objectives.*

Goal setting is increasingly recognized as an effective planning and motivational technique. It creates "traction" and permits a focusing on the efficient goal achievement. Participation in setting goals increases the likelihood that goals will be accepted and subsequently achieved.

4. Job Responsibilities *assess whether the supervisor reviews major job responsibilities during the performance appraisal interview. This includes a review of job description, a clarification of any misunderstandings about job duties, and an agreement on actual duties and responsibilities of the job.*

Agreement on an employee's role within an organization is essential to effective supervision and organization efficiency. The performance appraisal interview provides an occasion to review position requirements and to resolve any differences, since these requirements often form the basis for development of evaluative criteria.

5. Career Development *is a composite which measures the degree to which a supervisor engages in a discussion of an employee's personal goals and aspirations. This factor includes an honest discussion of employee goals and related career alternatives. It should be understood that it is very difficult for supervisors to constructively discuss career development with employees, since this requires a higher level of interviewer skill and a more complete knowledge of career alternatives than most supervisors possess.*

Career development discussions can be important for several reasons. Employees should have some understanding of opportunities available to them in their company, as well as in other organizations. Unrealistic advancement expectations can lead to dissatisfaction and turnover. A discussion of career opportunities may enhance the employee's belief that the company and the supervisor are concerned about his well-being. Furthermore, promotional and career opportunities, where available and appropriate, function as motivators and incentives. It should also be noted that current concern over the advancement of women and minorities has increased the importance of such discussions.
6. Praise *determines the extent to which a supervisor effectively transmits verbal recognition of an employee's past accomplishments and strengths during the performance appraisal interview. It measures a supervisor's inclination to give praise in a supportive manner for work performed exceptionally well.*

Existing research concludes that the use of well-timed and sincere praise is an effective technique for reducing subordinate defensiveness during the appraisal interview, reinforcing effective behaviors and encouraging the continued development of the employee. Quality interviews are dependent upon supportive behavior, which includes the appropriate administration of praise.[27]

Thus performance appraisal interviews can also be an important part of the ongoing relationship between supervisors and employees.

Feedback of Performance Appraisal Results

Feedback is an integral part of any learning experience.[28] **Feedback** in the appraisal process means telling subordinates how to improve performance through an objective assessment of their present position. Performance feedback is most effective when given immediately after the performance (behavior or result) itself. Thus the appraisal interview represents an excellent opportunity to summarize the past year's performance by citing incidents of success and failure. But this is easier said than done, particularly when discussing failures.

Negative Feedback.   Superiors often face two problems in giving negative feedback. First, performance appraisals, if communicated to the subordinate, can boomerang. Negative feedback can lead to poorer performance rather than better. Many superiors fear that negative appraisals or even negative portions of otherwise favorable appraisals will discourage rather than motivate subordinates. Their uncertainties appear quite justified. A study at General Electric found that
- *Criticism had a negative effect on achievement of goals.*
- *Praise had little effect one way or the other.*
- *The average subordinate reacted defensively to criticism during the appraisal interview.*
- *Defensiveness resulting from critical appraisal produced inferior performance.*
- *The disruptive effect of repeated criticism on subsequent performance was greater among those already low in self-esteem.*
- *The average G. E. employee's self-estimate of performance before appraisal placed him at the 77th percentile.*

● *Only 2 out of 92 participants in the study estimated their performance to be below average.*[29]

The second problem with negative feedback is that superiors often fail to distinguish between criticism and feedback. If they provide either, they usually provide criticism. But **criticism** is evaluative, implying "goodness" or "badness"; feedback is descriptive. Feedback provides the subordinate with information, data to be used in performing self-evaluations. If subordinates are not being evaluated or criticized, they are not so likely to react defensively.

Effective Feedback.   Whether negative or positive, feedback is not always easy to provide. Fortunately, several characteristics of effective feedback have been determined. First, effective feedback is specific rather than general. Telling someone that he or she is dominating is probably not so useful as saying, "Just now you were not listening to what the other said, but I felt I either had to agree with your arguments or face attack from you."

Second, effective feedback is focused on behavior rather than on the person. It is important to refer to what a person does rather than to what that person seems to be. Thus a superior might say that a person talked more than anyone else at a meeting rather than that he or she is a loudmouth. The former allows for the possibility of change; the latter implies a fixed personality trait.

Effective feedback also takes into account the needs of the receiver of the feedback. Feedback can be destructive when it serves only the evaluator's needs and fails to consider the needs of the person on the receiving end. It should be given to help, not to hurt. Too often, feedback makes the evaluator feel better or allows him or her to "cut a person down to size."

Effective feedback is directed toward behavior that the receiver can do something about. Frustration only increases when people are reminded of some shortcomings they have no control over or a physical characteristic they can do nothing about.

Feedback is most effective when it is solicited rather than imposed. To get the most benefit, receivers should formulate questions for the evaluator to answer and actively seek feedback.

Effective feedback involves sharing information rather than giving advice. Thus receivers are free to decide for themselves on the changes to make in accordance with their own needs.

Effective feedback is well-timed. In general, immediate feedback is most useful— depending, of course, on the person's readiness to hear it, the support available from others, and so on.

Effective feedback also involves the amount of information the receiver can use rather than the amount the evaluator would like to give. Overloading a person with feedback reduces the possibility that he or she will use it effectively. An evaluator who gives more than can be used, is more often than not satisfying some need of his or her own rather than helping the other person.

Effective feedback concerns what is said or done and how—not why. Telling people what their motivations or intentions are tends to alienate them and contributes to a climate of resentment, suspicion, and distrust; it does not contribute to learning or development. It is dangerous to assume knowledge of why a person says or does something. If evaluators are uncertain of receivers' motives or intent, the uncertainty itself is feedback and should be revealed.

Finally, effective feedback is checked to ensure clear communication. One way of doing this is to have the receiver try to rephrase the feedback, to see if it corresponds to what the evaluator had in mind. No matter what the intent, feedback is often threatening and thus subject to considerable distortion or misinterpretation.

Matching Purpose with Method

The final step in the performance appraisal system is personnel action, which includes the developmental and evaluative decisions that are made on the basis of the performance appraisal results. As indicated in Exhibit 9.1, the purposes that the organization wants to serve by its performance appraisal system determine which method it uses.[30] For ease of discussion, all of the purposes discussed at the beginning of the chapter can be condensed into five broad categories:

- Motivating subordinates to perform well
- Providing data for management decisions, such as compensation, promotion, and transfer
- Helping in human resource planning, training, and development
- Encouraging superiors to observe and coach their subordinates and
- Providing reference and research data

Only the methods and approaches that best match a given purpose are discussed here. Other methods of appraisal may also help achieve a particular purpose, although they may be less effective.

Management by objectives and the work standards method appear to be quite useful in motivating subordinates to do well. Both clarify the goals and roles of subordinates and provide the opportunity for feedback in the form of knowledge of results. There is an important difference, however. MBO allows participation in the goal-setting process, which may lead to an inner commitment to improve performance. Work standards allow no participation.

Presumably, an important element in motivation is feedback. MBO and critical incidents are the two most effective methods for directly involving superiors in the feedback process, in either the written or oral form. These methods focus on performance or goals attained. This approach makes it easier for subordinates to accept feedback and improves future performance as well, because it avoids feedback based on traits or ranking of overall performance.

Many personnel decisions—for example, on salary, promotion, and job assignments—require comparison of people doing different kinds of work. Techniques like MBO or work objectives, which apply to specific jobs, are therefore not appropriate for this purpose. They must at least be supplemented by more global methods that equally include all subordinates, regardless of their jobs. The most realistic method might be a conventional form combined with an essay form and supplemented with evaluations of a given subordinate by several levels of superiors. This is called the **field review** technique. Then the superiors could rank all of the subordinates, thus producing an order-of-merit list. The superiors could even rank the subordinates by category, as in the forced distribution method.

MBO, critical incidents, and the essay method of performance evaluation are useful for identifying short- and long-range training and development needs and for helping to spot reasons for performance deficiencies. They also link the deficiencies to organizational action, such as recruitment, training, or job matching programs. This is especially true if the organization has a good job analysis system.

The critical incidents, weighted checklist, and behavior anchored rating scales are especially useful here, because they require superiors to observe subordinate behaviors and provide a log of evaluated behaviors by the time of the performance review session. However, the evaluation of the subordinates' behaviors should also be provided to the subordinates as soon as each behavior has been exhibited. This provides more meaningful and useful information to the subordinates, which they may then use to improve performance before the review session.

These methods also help superiors organize their approach to performance appraisals, because they provide a record of specific incidents and give superiors a basis for giving a high or low performance rating. More importantly, subordinates can learn which activities are valued by the organization. Overall, this process removes some of the pressures that superiors often experience when judging subordinates. It also provides them an opportunity to coach subordinates who have performance deficiencies in some areas. They can at the same time give praise for the strong points of subordinates' performances.

For reference purposes, a simple essay and conventional rating form should be effective. Order-of-merit rankings are also useful in developing criteria for good and poor performance. This means defining a standard against which performance can be measured. In order for the measures to be useful, valid appraisal methods must be used when determining the order-of-merit rankings.

Monitoring a Performance Appraisal System

In actuality, the appraisal systems in many organizations are not nearly so elaborate as the system presented in this chapter, although the trend is toward being as extensive as necessary to serve several purposes of performance appraisal. Because the design and installation of a totally new system is extremely complex, costly, and challenging, it pays to monitor the consistency of its application and its health.

As discussed previously, some superiors commit errors in their appraisals of subordinates. There's little problem if all superiors commit the same error, but superiors usually commit different errors. For example, two employees may perform identically, but if one superior commits a strictness error and one superior commits a leniency error, one of the employees will appear to be far less competent than the other. These errors are common in organizations using rating forms. If the organization is to treat all its employees fairly, it must try to reduce these errors, perhaps by monitoring the lack of consistency in the way superiors complete appraisal forms.[31]

Monitoring for consistency is important, but it is only one influence on the effectiveness of a performance appraisal system. An organization must check several other aspects of its system to see if it serves all its stated purposes in an efficient and acceptable way. System health is determined by analyzing five separate matters:

● What purposes does the organization want its performance appraisal system to serve?

- Do the appraisal forms really elicit the information to serve these purposes? Are these forms compatible with the jobs for which they are being used—are they job-related?
- Are the processes of the appraisal effective. For example, are the appraisal interviews done effectively? Are goals established? Are they developed jointly? Do superiors and subordinates accept the appraisal process?
- Are the appraisals being implemented correctly? What procedures have been set up to ensure that the appraisals are being done correctly? What supporting materials are available to aid superiors in appraising their subordinates? Have the superiors been trained in using the form and in such techniques as interviewing and providing feedback?
- Do methods exist for reviewing and evaluating the effectiveness of the total system? Are there goals and objectives for the system? Are there systematic procedures for gathering data to measure how well the goals and objectives are being met?[32]

By addressing these matters and taking corrective action where needed, the personnel manager can help maintain the health of the performance appraisal system. These five steps constitute a diagnosis of the system. The diagnosis may indicate that the entire system needs to be changed or that only parts need to be changed. Whichever is necessary, the changes should be made. In today's environment, an organization can ill afford a less than effective and healthy performance appraisal system.

MANAGING INEFFECTIVE PERFORMANCE

Unfortunately, employees do not always perform the way the organization wants them to. Sometimes their ineffective performance is a reaction to the work environment, and sometimes it is the result of being prevented from attaining their career goals. Regardless of the cause, telling people the truth about their ineffective performance is difficult and therefore often avoided.

One of the biggest problems with ineffective performance is determining what it is. For example, a superior might evaluate employees on sense of responsibility, decisiveness, and friendliness and on the number of goods sold per month (a direct index of performance). A particular employee may do well on number of goods sold, but not so well on sense of responsibility, decisiveness, and friendliness. Is this employee an effective or ineffective performer? Perhaps the employee is just moderately effective and could use some improvement.

One way to determine whether the employee is an effective performer is to conduct a job analysis and incorporate the results into the performance evaluation form. Then both employee and manager know what the criteria are, and the manager can rather easily label the performance as effective or ineffective. But sometimes the employee's performance is the result of circumstances outside the employee's control. For example, how well the employee does may depend on how well others do or even on what the employee thinks he or she is supposed to do.

Sources of Ineffective Performance

The first thing managers should do when they see ineffective performance is to try to locate its sources. The four primary sources that should be diagnosed are individual qualities, personnel and human resource functions and activities, the internal environment, and the external environment. A more detailed list of possible sources is shown in Exhibit 9.6. Two of the most important primary sources are discussed below.

Individual Qualities. Lack of motivation is one important quality commonly ascribed to ineffective performers:

"We're not getting motivated workers these days like we used to." Never was a man more earnest as he talked with us about the 1600-man production department he supervised, a department all too visible within his organization because of a stubborn 10 to 15 percent production deficit.[33]

Is this organization not getting motivated workers, or is it not providing the appropriate work environment for workers to be motivated? If it is true that workers were more motivated to perform in the past than they are today, one or several of the key ingredients for employee motivation has changed. Even though technology has

Exhibit 9.6 Sources of Ineffective Performance

Highly Significant Sources	Very Significant Sources	Significant Sources
Physical problems • physical illness or handicap, including brain disorders • physical disorders of emotional origin • inappropriate physical characteristics • insufficient muscular or sensory ability or skill	**Problems of intelligence and job knowledge** • insufficient verbal ability • insufficient special ability • insufficient job knowledge • defects of judgment or memory	**Emotional problems** • frequent disruptive emotion (anxiety, depression, anger, excitement, shame, guilt, jealousy) • neurosis (with anxiety, depression, anger, and so on predominating) • psychosis (with anxiety, depression, anger, and so on predominating) • alcohol and drug problems
Family-related problems • family crises (divorce, death, severe illness, and the like) • separation from family and isolation • predominance of family considerations over work demands	**Problems caused in the work group** • negative consequences associated with group cohesion • ineffective management • inappropriate managerial standards or criteria	**Motivational problems** • strong motives frustrated at work (pleasure in success, fear of failure, avoidance, dominance, desire to be popular, social motivation, need for attention, and so on) • unintegrated means used to satisfy strong motives • excessively low personal work standards • generalized low work motivation
Problems stemming from society and its values • application of legal sanctions • enforcement of societal values by means other than the law (including the use of inappropriate value-based criteria) • conflict between job demands and cultural values (equity, freedom, moral and religious values, and so on)	**Problems growing out of the work context and the work itself** • negative consequences of economic forces • negative consequences of geographic location • detrimental conditions in the work setting • excessive danger • problems in the work itself	**Problems originating in company policies and higher-level decisions** • insufficient organizational action • placement error • organizational overpermissiveness • excessive spans of control • inappropriate organizational standards and criteria

Adapted from *The Challenge of Managing* by John B. Miner. Copyright © 1975 by the W. B. Saunders Company. Reprinted by permission of Holt, Rinehart and Winston.

become much more complex during the past fifty years, the average level of employee education has never been higher. Supervisors probably still communicate with at least the same ability as before, thus giving little reason to expect that employees do not know what to do. So any decline in motivation must be due to either a change in working conditions or a change in the value of those conditions. In reality, both of these ingredients have changed. For example, many younger employees are attaching more value to being able to make decisions on the job and are becoming less satisfied with the close supervision and rule-oriented behavior of the boss. In addition, supervisors claim they are less able to reward performance today: "These days productivity often cannot be a factor in deciding how workers are to be managed even if, for example, seniority and productivity are inversely related to one another."[34]

It has been claimed that today neither the boss nor the organization has as much control over the employee or the employee's work environment as before the days of elaborate regulations. Previously, the organization or supervisor exercised control through rewards and punishments and threats of job dismissal. Unfortunately, this power encouraged bosses to deal arbitrarily with employees on occasion, which is one of the reasons for the current lack of controls.[35] In many organizations, such as the federal government, all workers in each grade-step, regardless of output, receive the same pay. Alternative work schedules, job enrichment, and quality of work life programs are being used in part to get employees to work for the goals of the organization, but they are being used in only a fraction of the organizations in the United States. There are, of course, some organizations that retain control and reward workers for performance, but these are more the exception than the rule.[36]

Another important individual quality contributing to ineffective performance is aggressive behavior, which manifests itself in wildcat strikes, deliberate production slowdowns, sabotage, violence on the picket line, fights, verbal assaults, and theft. Since the results of the aggressive behavior are so detrimental to the organization and because it is on the rise, managers and supervisors must learn to manage it.[37] There is disagreement on whether aggressive behavior is innate or learned, but the consensus is that aggression is often preceded by frustration, a tension- or anxiety-producing state. And frustration is "the emotion generated by interference with a person's progress toward a goal."[38] The key to managing aggressive behavior is to understand that the behavior following frustration will be directed toward reestablishing an equilibrium or finding an outlet.

Internal Environment. In response to increased government regulation of the use of human resources, organizations have increasingly centralized their human resource management activities in the personnel department. Thus many personnel managers now have the responsibility for promulgating (to the extent determined by top management) many of the rules and regulations governing relationships between the organization and its employees. Much of this centralization is intended to ensure that employees are treated fairly, but it also limits supervisors' opportunities to influence and manage their employees. At least this is what many supervisors say.

Here's a comparison of two different ways to treat employees, illustrating the impact supervisors can have.

Fred and Paul are two managers in the same large corporation. Fred is a friendly sort of guy. He spends lots of time rapping with his subordinates, and prides himself on being warm and sympathetic. If an employee were to ask for time off to take care of a personal problem, Fred would worry about the rules but probably give in.

Paul, on the other hand, loves to be a boss and spends his time nudging subordinates to do their jobs. Although his manner is amiable, it is distinctly less personal and warm than Fred's. His primary loyalty is to the organization. If an employee asked him for time off because of a personal problem, Paul would suggest that he use up some vacation days or take an unpaid leave of absence.

Who is the better manager? Many people would quickly choose generous, friendly Fred. He is humane, equalitarian and understanding. But our research shows that nice guys like Fred are often bum bosses. Compared to Paul, he gets less work out of his people and creates lower morale.[39]

Fred is an **affiliative manager**—he likes people and does not want to hurt their feelings. But this desire to be liked leads him to make wishy-washy decisions, the results of which may be nice for an individual but are inconsistent and unfair for the group. This inconsistency and unfairness result in low group morale and productivity. Paul, on the other hand, is an **institutionalized-power manager** who is successful at creating a good climate for work. (There are two kinds of power: Personal power is used for personal gain; institutionalized or social power is used for the benefit of the organization.) Paul's employees have both a sense of responsibility and a clear knowledge of the organization. They stick to the work rules, not because they are hit over the head with them but because they have become loyal to the institution.[40]

Responses to Ineffective Performance

With this variety of reasons for ineffective performance, it is not surprising that there are also several responses to ineffective performance. These responses can be grouped into typical ways to deal with employee shortcomings—ignoring them, taking disciplinary action, and firing—and into less typical ways, which essentially try to change the internal environment of the organization.

Ignoring It. A typical response to ineffective performance is to ignore it. Managers and supervisors generally find it difficult to tell employees that they are ineffective and then take action to correct the problem. This is particularly true for new managers. In fact, managers may find it more trouble than it is worth to even evaluate an employee as an ineffective performer. Another reason for managers to avoid evaluating employees as ineffective is the possibility that the managers' competency will be questioned. For example, if an instructor gives out many low grades, the department chairperson or college dean might blame the instructor—not the students.

A related organizational reality is that organizations may refuse to fire employees because doing so is an admission of incompetence at selecting good employees. As a result, many organizations create conditions to encourage undesirable employees to resign, such as attractive retirement programs.

Taking Disciplinary Action.   Because supervisors and managers often have little control over such rewards as pay increases, promotions, fringe benefits, and even job assignments, particularly in organizations that are unionized, discipline frequently provides managers the only leverage they have to manage ineffective performance.[41] But administering discipline can itself result in ineffective performance:

A significant problem in both public and private organizations is the intra-organizational disciplinary structure. Inconsistencies and inequities in the disciplinary structure tend to create counterproductive actions on the part of the subordinates within the organization.[42]

Consequently managers must be concerned with making disciplinary action corrective—not punitive.

Disciplinary action involves the administration of outcomes an individual perceives as aversive or unpleasant, such as assigning a particularly dirty job, withholding a promotion, recommending a disciplinary layoff, or criticizing the employee. These outcomes can be administered as either negative reinforcement or punishment, both of which are contingent on the employee's performance (see Chapter 13). A **negative reinforcer** is used to increase the probability of a behavior by removing an aversive stimulus. For example, a supervisor may be able to increase productivity by letting good performers work at the more desirable jobs. Poor performers would in effect be disciplined by remaining in the unpleasant jobs. A **punishment**, on the other hand, is used to decrease the likelihood of a behavior. For example, workers may be docked pay for being late. The effect of the punishment is to reduce the behavior of being late.[43]

Disciplinary action can have undesirable side effects, but their likelihood can be diminished by incorporating several "hot stove principles" into the displinary procedures:

● Provide ample and clear warning. Many organizations have clearly defined disciplinary steps. For example, the first offense might elicit an oral warning; the second offense a written warning; the third offense, a disciplinary layoff; the fourth offense, discharge.

● Administer the discipline as quickly as possible. If a long time elapses between the ineffective behavior and the discipline, the employee may not know what the discipline is for.

● Administer the same discipline for the same behavior for everyone, every time. Discipline has to be administered fairly and consistently.

● Administer the discipline impersonally. Discipline should be based on a specific behavior, a specific person.[44]

Because it is the immediate supervisor or manager who plays the integral role in administering discipline, to increase its effectiveness the organization should

● Allow managers and supervisors to help select their own employees

● Educate managers and supervisors about the organization's disciplinary policies and train them to administer the policies

- Set up standards that are equitable to employees and that can easily and consistently be implemented by managers and supervisors[45]

Firing Employees.   Often the final step in a disciplinary program is dismissal, termination, separation, disengagement, removal, forced retirement, or just plain firing or displacing an employee. Displacing employees, particularly top-level managers, is often the only way an organization can survive a crisis. "You can't change organizations merely by reorganizing, by restructuring functions. Ultimately you have to make key personnel changes if you want to improve an organization."[46]

But firing can be exceedingly painful, even though it is well organized and planned. And many individuals are capable of effective performance but only in certain types of situations. Thus some organizations reassign employees to different parts of the organization and trade top-level managers to other organizations.[47] These alternatives may not be available, however, particularly if the organization needs to reduce its labor force by layoffs or if it believes that certain employees would be ineffective any place. Consequently increasing numbers of organizations have adopted counseling and outplacement services for employees being terminated for whatever reason.[48]

Outplacement is the removal of ineffective or unnecessary performers by helping them find a new job, which produces minimal disruption to the organization and maximum benefit to the individual. "One thing is important to remember: outplacement assistance is just as important to the employees who are terminated as it is to those who are not."[49] Outplacement activities help separated employees successfully present their capabilities to other organizations with professional assistance. Often managerial employees are allowed the use of an office, secretary, and telephone for up to six months after termination.

Counseling services for employees are an important part of outplacement, although they can be provided independent of other outplacement activities. A vital function in counseling is to ensure that the individual leaves the organization with as positive an attitude as possible. This if often a challenging task. "When the employee relations counselor faces an involuntarily terminating employee, he or she is likely to find someone who is either bitter, antagonistic, defensive or sullen."[50]

The task is easier if the counselor understands the psychological stages an employee may go through after being dismissed. Employees may also go through these stages when they are told that their performance is ineffective and that they must shape up. Here's an example of how an employee might react to being told that she is becoming obsolete:

She might be shocked (stage 1) at such a suggestion and deny that it is true. Sometime later she might become angry (stage 2) and argue that you have no basis for such an accusation. Next, she may plead with you to give her one more chance to show her stuff (stage 3).

Not succeeding at this stage will probably throw her into a depression (stage 4). After a period of time, according to the model, you might find that she is becoming more aware of herself and is finally able to accept (stage 5) the reality of change (in this case, obsolescence of skills).[51]

A SLICE OF LIFE

The failure of many supervisors to evaluate the performance of their employees effectively causes a great deal of consternation in personnel departments. Employees who have been terminated from their position for cause almost inevitably have a right to appeal. This right to appeal may be a function of a collective bargaining agreement or of a variety of administrative appeal processes. At an appeal hearing, the organization must prove that the termination of the employee was justified.

Suppose you as a supervisor have an employee whose performance leaves a great deal to be desired. Perhaps the quantity or quality of work is below standard; perhaps the employee wastes too much material; perhaps there is an absenteeism problem. The point is that you are not dismissing this employee for a given incident but rather for a pattern of conduct over a length of time.

Now imagine yourself at the hearing. You testify as to the facts, stating that essentially this is an unsatisfactory employee and has been for some time. The employee's spokesperson asserts that the issue is not unsatisfactory performance but a personality conflict between the dismissed employee and yourself. You, of course, vehemently deny this charge. The employee's spokesperson asks that the proceedings temporarily be recessed and requests that the dismissed employee's evaluation forms for the last several years be obtained. These evaluation forms have been made out by you and your predecessors over the past several years.

The files arrive at the hearing. It should be no surprise to learn that all the evaluations, including your own, are skewed toward good performance. Because nobody likes to tell employees that they are unsatisfactory, they rarely do. Instead, the minimum that any employee ordinarily receives is "satisfactory." Such is the case for your dismissed employee, whose evaluations for the past several years are "satisfactory" or better.

Let's review this case for a moment. Remember, you are asserting that this is an unsatisfactory employee and that no personality conflict is involved. Yet the records clearly indicate that no single supervisor before you has ever noted any of this employee's deficiencies. The analytical point, of course, is that you are going to lose this case. The employee will be reinstated, probably with full back pay and seniority. You may want to bear this in mind the next time you fill out an employee's evaluation form. Not only are you doing yourself a disservice by giving good evaluations, but you may be burying the generation of supervisors that follows you.

It is only at stage 5 that employees are ready for positive change. Thus employee relations counselors must try to get terminated employees to stage 5 before they leave the organization.

Analyzing the Environment. The typical responses to ineffective performance are aimed at the employee, but several other, untypical responses are aimed at changing the environment in which the employee works. Many organizations are beginning to realize that individual qualities (personality and ability), are not the only cause of ineffective performance. If the performance environment is the source of ineffective performance, then the solution may be to change certain aspects of the environment.

The critical aspects of the employee's performance environment are the consequences of effective and ineffective performance, feedback to the employee, task and role interference, and goals and performance standards.[52] These four major aspects are closely associated with employee motivation. Thus by analyzing these aspects of the performance environment, managers and supervisors are really analyzing the likelihood of an employee being motivated to perform. Organizations have used such analyses to help correct a variety of behavior problems, including absenteeism and performance.[53] The results have ranged from improving feedback to attempting to change environmental aspects off the job.

Improving Leader Behavior.   Over the years, people develop routines, patterns, and predictable ways of viewing situations. Managers often develop a style or set of behaviors that encourage (or at least don't discourage) ineffective performance on the part of their employees.

Managing Ineffective Performance in Reverse.   Much of the discussion on managing ineffective performance takes the position of the manager.

Managers often feel that managing people effectively is just a matter of using common sense. Nevertheless, some managers seem to be better than others, perhaps because they have better common sense—or just use it. For example, a manager may begin to assume that her employees know what's expected and that if they don't, they'll ask her. Although this sounds reasonable, employees are generally reluctant to tell their boss that they don't understand something and are even more reluctant to indicate that anything is wrong. Consequently, managers must assume responsibility for finding out how well they are managing, whether they are creating situations for ineffective performance or not.

One way for managers to analyze how they are doing is for them to use checklists like the one shown in Exhibit 9.7. Many of the items shown in this checklist relate to employee motivation; all indicate daily behaviors that will help managers improve performance. There are times, however, when you as the employee will need to know how to manage the ineffective performance (or general incompetence) of your boss. Here are a few tips based on the fundamental idea that "the one thing incompetent people in business fear most is the competence of the people under them."[54]

Although the natural tendency is for you to resent your boss or to make sure others in the organization know about his or her incompetence, these are rather foolish actions. Instead, if, say, you work on a project that your boss eventually takes credit for, swallow hard and give full credit to your boss. The boss has the power. By trying to take credit, you threaten your boss, who then has no choice but to use that power. You may even be wise to praise the boss for selling the project or idea to those higher up in the organization. Don't forget that if your boss looks good, he or she will be in a better position to make you look good. In the long run, your boss may end up being your lifelong supporter.

What if the boss is competent, but abrasive?

Leadership Checklist

YES NO

☐ ☐ 1. Have I made it clear what is expected in terms of results? Do I discuss these results with employees?

☐ ☐ 2. Have I let the employees know where they stand?

☐ ☐ 3. Do employees know how to do the work?

☐ ☐ 4. Have I done a good job of training and development?

☐ ☐ 5. Do I give employees all the support I can?

☐ ☐ 6. What have I done or not done to cultivate positive personal relationships?

☐ ☐ 7. Do the employees know why their jobs are important, how they fit into the overall company structure, and the ramifications of poor performance?

☐ ☐ 8. Are employees kept informed on what is going on in the department and the company? Not just "need to know" items, but "nice to know"?

☐ ☐ 9. Do employees have adequate freedom in which to work?

☐ ☐ 10. Are employees too often put in a defensive position regarding performance?

☐ ☐ 11. What have I done to get employees mentally and emotionally involved in their jobs?

☐ ☐ 12. Have employees been allowed to participate in setting goals and deciding means of achieving them?

☐ ☐ 13. Have good aspects of performance received adequate and periodic recognition?

☐ ☐ 14. Do I accentuate the positive instead of the negative?

☐ ☐ 15. Have I shown adequate concern for employees as individuals? For their personal goals?

☐ ☐ 16. Am I flexible about listening to employees and giving them a chance to implement ideas and suggestions?

☐ ☐ 17. Have I ever consciously assessed employees' strengths and weaknesses with the idea of structuring the work to capitalize on the former?

☐ ☐ 18. Are employees adequately and reasonably challenged?

Exhibit 9.7 Leadership Checklist
From "Management Leadership in Perspective: Getting Back to Basics," by B. Scanlon, p. 171. Reprinted with permission *Personal Journal*, Costa Mesa, CA, copyright March 1979.

● As Jimmy Carter did with Admiral Rickover, endure the person as long as you are benefiting in some ways;
● If you're angered or depressed by the situation, tactfully discuss the effect your boss is having on you;
● Or just leave and look for another job.

One thing for sure: It usually does not help to go over the boss's head. Remember, the boss still has the power.[55]

SUMMARY

Appraising employee performance is a critical personnel and human resource activity. This chapter examines performance appraisal as a system consisting of criteria specification, forms, context, process, results, personnel action, and feedback. To ensure the effectiveness of performance appraisal, personnel managers must be concerned with implementation and monitoring of all these aspects of the performance appraisal system.

Because of information presented in this chapter, you should now be in a position to analyze the effectiveness of an organization's appraisal system within the constraints of organizational realities. You should also be able to understand more thoroughly the events and processes surrounding the performance appraisals you will be receiving.

This chapter also examines what organizations can do about employees' ineffective performance. There are many options open to organizations, just as there are many sources of ineffective performance. Increasingly, organizations are more carefully diagnosing the sources of ineffective performance in order to respond more appropriately.

PERSONNEL PROBLEM
A Waste of Time

"I've been looking over the personnel records for your division, Alice, and I notice that you are quite behind on many of them," said the regional manager with some concern. "We ordinarily do the formal evaluations of employees once a year. Some of your people haven't been evaluated in over two years. Is there some kind of trouble?"

"I wouldn't say we're having any trouble. Frankly, I find those evaluations to be a waste of my time, and I am especially frustrated when I have to give a bad review to an employee," Alice replied. "It's been my experience, and the experience of other managers I have spoken to, that neither criticism nor counseling leads to improvement for a lot of employees. In fact, I feel that they just get worse after discussing areas they could improve," Alice went on. "I hate giving the evaluations and the employees hate getting them. They don't improve bad performance, and they don't especially affect good performance. So I suppose that's why my evaluations are not up to date," she concluded.

1. What is your reaction to Alice's statements?

2. What would you suggest to Alice if you were the regional manager?

3. Can you suggest an alternative way to evaluate employees?

4. Are there alternative methods for improving employee deficiencies?

KEY CONCEPTS

absolute standard
affiliative manager
assessment center
behavior anchored
    rating scale (BARS)
comparative methods
comparative standard
conventional rating
critical incidents format

criticism
direct index
disciplinary action
essay method
feedback
field review
forced choice
institutionalized-power
    manager

management by
    objectives (MBO)
negative reinforcer
outplacement
performance
performance appraisal
punishment
weighted checklist
work standards approach

DISCUSSION QUESTIONS

1. What are the major purposes of performance appraisal? Are these purposes contradictory?

2. Explain in detail the methods of performance appraisal. What are the characteristics, strengths, and weaknesses of each?

3. How can an organization attain all the purposes of performance appraisal? In other words, what are the best matches between the appraisal method and the purposes of appraisal?

4. What problems in performance appraisal are due to characteristics of the manager, the employee, and the organization?

5. How can the problems in performance appraisal be minimized?

6. Discuss the feedback process in performance appraisal. What are the characteristics of effective feedback?

7. What is validity? What methods of performance appraisal are most valid?

8. Describe an assessment center. In what ways

does it differ from other performance appraisal methods?

9. What is the role of the personnel manager in assisting other managers with performance appraisals?

10. What are the "hot stove principles" of applying discipline? Give an example of applying discipline that is not so "hot."

11. What aspects of the performance

environment can influence employee behavior? Explain how they do so.

12. Do you think activities like counseling and outplacement represent too much coddling of employees and therefore should be avoided?

13. How would you feel about having an incompetent boss? What would you do if you had one?

ENDNOTES

1. L. L. Cummings and D. P. Schwab, "Designing Appraisal Systems for Information Yield," *California Management Review,* Summer 1978, p. 19.

   For an extensive discussion of performance appraisal, also see

   Bureau of National Affairs, "Employee Performance, Evaluation and Control," *Personnel Policies Forum* No. 108, February 1975.

   K. J. Lacho, G. K. Stearns, and M. F. Villere. "A Study of Employee Appraisal Systems of Major Cities in the United States," *Public Personnel Management,* March/April 1979, pp. 111–124.

   R. I. Lazer and W. S. Wikstrom, *Appraising Managerial Performance: Current Practice and Future Directions* (New York: Conference Board, Inc., 1977).

   A. H. Locher and K. S. Teel. "Performance Appraisal: A Survey of Current Practices," *Personnel Journal,* May 1977, pp. 245–247, 254.

   Personnel Practices in Factory and Office: Manufacturing, Studies in Personnel Policy 194 (New York: National Industrial Conference Board, 1964).

2. L. W. Porter, E. E. Lawler, III, and J. R. Hackman, *Behavior in Organizations* (New York: McGraw-Hill, 1975), p. 315. © 1975 McGraw-Hill, New York, N.Y. Reprinted with permission.

3. R. E. Lefton, V. R. Buzzotta, M. Scerberg, B. L. Karraker, *Effective Motivation Through Performance Appraisal* (New York: Wiley, 1977), p. 7.

4. Lazer and Wikstrom.

5. Schneier, p. 27.

   See also

   Brito v. *Zia Company,* 478 F. 2d. 1200 (1973). *Albemarle Paper Company* v. *Moody,* U.S. Supreme Court Nos. 74–389 and 74–428, 10 FEB Cases 1181 (1975).

6. Lazer and Wikstrom, p.4.

   See also the following court cases involving performance appraisal:

   Rowe v. *General Motors Corporation* 457 F. 2d 358 (1972).

   Baxter v. *Savannah Sugar Refining Corporation,* 350 F. Supp. 139 (1972).

   Hill v. *Western Electric Co.,* U.S. District Court (Eastern District of Virginia) No. 75-375-A, 12 FEP Cases 1175 (1976)

   Wakins v. *Scott Paper Co.,* Fifth Circuit Court of Appeals, No. 74-1001, 12 FEP Cases 1191 (1976).

7. Lazer and Wikstrom.

8. For an excellent discussion of the criteria issue, see S. Zedeck and M. R. Blood, *Foundations of Behavioral Science Research in Organizations* (Monterey, Calif.: Brooks/Cole, 1974), pp. 75–94.

   For an excellent discussion of the criteria used to evaluate the entire performance appraisal system (in contrast to the criteria used to evaluate employee performance discussed by Zedeck and Blood), see J. S. Kane and E. E. Lawler III, "Performance Appraisal Effectiveness: Hs Assessment and Determinants," in B. M. Staw (ed.), *Research in Organizational Behavior,* vol. 1 (Greenwich, Conn.: JAI Press, 1979), pp. 425–478.

   P. C. Smith, "Behavior, Results, and Organizational Effectiveness," in M. Donnette (ed.), *Handbook of Industrial and Organizational Psychology* (Chicago: Rand McNally, 1976), pp. 745–776.

9. L. L. Cummings and D. Schwab, *Performance in Organizations* (Glenview, Ill.: Scott, Foresman, 1973).

10. J. Goodale and R. Burke, "BARS Need Not Be Job Specific," *Journal of Applied Psychology,* 60 (1975), pp.. 389–391.

11. For arguments for and against MBO, see

S. J. Carroll and H. L. Tosi, "Goal Characteristics and Personality Factors in a Management by Objectives Program," *Administrative Science Quarterly*, 15 (1970), 295–305.

J. P. Muczyk, "A Controlled Field Experiment Measuring the Impact of MBO on Performance Data," *Journal of Management Studies*, 15 (1978), pp. 318–329.

A. P. Raia, *Managing by Objectives* (Glenview, Ill.: Scott, Foresman, 1974).

H. L. Tosi, J. R. Rizzo, and S. J. Carroll, Setting Goals in Management by Objectives," *California Management Review*, 12 (1970), pp. 70–78.

12. H. Levinson, "Appraisal of *What* Performance," *Harvard Business Review*, 54 (July/August 1976), pp. 125–134.

13. W. Oberg, "Make Performance Appraisal Relevant" (working paper, Michigan State University, 1970), p. 10.

14. R. J. Klimoski and W. J. Strickland, "Assessment Center: Valid or Merely Prescient," *Personnel Psychology*, 20 (1977), p. 354.

15. K. N. Wexley, "Performance Appraisal and Feedback," in S. Kerr (ed.), *Organizational Behavior* (Columbus, Ohio, Grid, 1979), pp. 241–262.

16. For a more complete review of research in sex differences in performance appraisal, see F. J. Landy and J. L. Farr, "Performance Rating," *Psychological Bulletin*, January 1980, pp. 72–107.

17. Oberg.

18. R. S. Schuler "Male and Female Routes to Managerial Success," *Personnel Administrator*, May 1979, pp. 35–46.

19. J. L. Gibson, J. J. Ivancevich, and J. H. Donnelly, *Organizations: Behavior, Structure, Processes*, 3rd ed. (Dallas, Texas: Business Publications, Inc., 1979), p. 361.

20. Cummings and Schwab, 1973, p. 7.

21. Wexley, p. 256.

22. Wexley.
For a discussion on the context of performance appraisal, see Cummings and Schwab, 1978.

23. R. S. Schuler, "A Role and Expectancy Perception Model of Participation in Decision Making," *Academy of Management Journal*, June 1980, p. 338.

24. Cummings and Schwab, 1973, p. 106.

25. J. S. Kane and E. E. Lawler III, "Methods of Peer Assessment," *Psychological Bulletin*, 3 (1978), pp. 555–586.

26. Cummings and Schwab, 1973, p. 105.

27. *The Components of Effective Performance Appraisal*, Special Release No. 5. © 1977, Life Office Management Association, New York, N.Y. Reprinted with permission.
See also
R. J. Burke, W. Weitzel, and T. Weir, "Characteristics of Effective Employee Performance Review and Development Interviews: Replications and Extensions," *Personnel Psychology*, 4 (1978), pp. 903–919.

28. J. Annett, *Feedback and Human Behavior: The Effects of Knowledge of Results, Incentives, and Reinforcement on Learning and Performance*, (Baltimore: Penguin, 1969).
C. Camman, D. A. Nadler, and P. H. Mirvis, *The Ongoing Feedback System: A Tool for Improving Organizational Management* (Ann Arbor: Survey Research Center, University of Michigan, 1975).

29. For a more thorough discussion of the conflicts between appraisals for developmental and evaluational purposes, see
Cummings and Schwab, 1973.
H. H. Meyer, E. Kay, and J. R. P. French Jr., "Split Roles in Performance Appraisal," *Harvard Business Review*, January/February, 1965, pp. 123–129.

30. B. McAfee and B. Green, "Selecting a Performance Appraisal Method," *Personnel Administrator*, June 1977, pp. 61–64.
Oberg.

31. M. E. Schick, "The Refined Performance Evaluation Monitoring System: Best of Both Worlds," *Personnel Journal*, January 1980, pp. 47–50.

32. R. R. Ball, "What's the Answer to Performance Appraisal?"
M. Beer, R. Ruh, J. A. Dawson, B. B. McCaa, and M. J. Kavangh, "A Performance Management System: Research, Design, Introduction and Evaluation," *Personnel Psychology*, 3 (1978), pp. 505–535.
V. R. Buzzotta and R. E. Lefton, "How Healthy Is Your Performance Appraisal System?" *Personnel Administrator*, August 1978, pp. 48–51.
Personnel Administration, July 1978, pp. 43–46,
J. M. McFillen and P. G. Decker, "Building Meaning into Appraisal," *Personnel Administrator,* June 1978, pp. 75–84.

33. H. R. Smith, "Protecting Workers from Work," p. 59. Reprinted with permission from the March 1978 issue of the *Personnel Administrator*, copyright 1978, The American Society for

Personnel Administration, 30 Park Drive, Berea, OH 44017.

34. Smith, p. 60.

35. Smith, p. 61.

36. D. D. Steinbrecher, "Roundup: Incentive Strategies Boost Worker Productivity," *Personnel*, November/December 1979, pp. 57–58.

37. For a more extensive discussion on the issues related to the aggressive employee, see
R. H. Bailey, *Violence and Aggression* (New York: Time-Life Books, 1976).
L. Berkowitz, *Aggression* (New York: McGraw-Hill, 1962), p. 1.
K. Lorenz, *On Aggression* (New York: Harcourt Brace Jovanovich, 1966).

38. Bailey.

39. D. C. McClelland and D. H. Burnham, "Good Guys Make Bum Bosses," *Psychology Today*, December 1975, pp. 69–70. Reprinted from *Psychology Today* Magazine. Copyright © 1975 Ziff-Davis Publishing Company.

40. McClelland and Burnham, p. 70.

41. W. R. Flynn and W. E. Stratton, "Dealing with the Aggressive Employee," *Personnel Administrator*, February 1978, pp. 53–47.

42. J. A. Belohav and P. O. Popp, "Making Employee Discipline Work," p. 21. Reprinted with permission from the March 1978 issue of the *Personnel Administrator*, copyright 1978, The American Society for Personnel Administration, 30 Park Drive, Berea, OH 44017.

43. For an excellent discussion of the application of discipline in organizations, see
R. D. Arvey and J. M. Ivancevich, "Punishment in Organizations: A Review, Propositions, and Research Suggestions," *Academy of Management Review*, 5 (1980), pp. 123–132.
W. C. Hamner and D. W. Organ, *Organizational Behavior: An Applied Psychological Approach* (Dallas, Texas: Business Publications, Inc., 1978), pp. 73–88.
R. J. Hart, "Crime and Punishment in the Army," *Journal of Personality and Social Psychology*, 36 (1978), pp. 1456–1471.
J. P. Muczyk, E. B. Schwartz, and E. P. Smith, *First and Second Level Supervision* (Indianapolis: Bobbs-Merrill, 1980).
H. P. Sims Jr. "Further Thought on Punishment in Organizations," *Academy of Management Review*, 5 (1980), pp. 133–138.

44. G. Strauss and L. R. Sayles, *Managing Human Resources* (Englewood Cliffs, N.J.: Prentice-Hall, 1977), pp. 311–321.

45. Belohav and Popp.

46. C. F. Smart and W. T. Stanbury (eds.), *Studies in Crisis Management* (Toronto: Butterworth, 1978), p. 9.

47. R. A. Brooks, "Don't Fire Your Executives: Trade Them," *Personnel Journal*, May 1979, pp. 308–310.

48. For example, see
W. J. Broussard and R. J. DeLargey, "The Dynamics of the Group Outplacement Workshop," *Personnel Journal*, December 1979, pp. 855–857.
C. H. Driessnack, "Outplacement: A Benefit for Both Employee and Company," *Personnel Administrator*, January 1978, pp. 24–29.
S. S. Kaogen, "Terminating People From Key Positions," *Personnel Journal*, Febuary 1978, pp. 96–98.
D. J. Kravetz, "Counseling Strategies for Involuntary Terminations," *Personnel Administrator*, October 1978, pp. 49–53.
Organizations and unions are becoming increasingly concerned with assisting workers who are displaced because of such major organizational changes as plant closings. For an excellent discussion of union contract provisions and state and federal statutes related to this, see B. H. Millen, "Providing Assistance to Displaced Workers," *Monthly Labor Review*, May 1979, pp. 17–22.

49. Driessnack, p. 24.

50. Kravetz.

51. R. A. Morano, "How to Manage Change to Reduce Stress," *Management Review*, November 1977 (New York: AMACOM, a division of American Management Associations, 1977), p. 22.

52. These four sets of environmental performance factors are essentially those outlined by R. F. Mager and P. Pipe, *Analyzing Performance Problems* (Belmont, CA.: Fearon, 1970).

53. See W. Nord, "Improving Attendance through Rewards," *Personnel Administration*, 34 (1971), pp. 41–47.
E. Pedalino and V. Gamboa, "Behavior Modification and Absenteeism: Intervention in One Industrial Setting," *Journal of Applied Psychology*, 59 (1974), pp. 694–698.
C. E. Schneier, "Behavior Modification in Management: A Review and a Critique," *Academy of Management Journal*, 17 (1974), pp. 528–548.

54. R. R. Conarroe, "How to Handle an Incompetent
     Boss," *The Walden Company Newsletter*, August
     1975 (Westport, Conn.: The Walden Company,
     1975).

55. Based on the work reported in H. Levinson,
     "The Abrasive Personality at the Office,"
     Psychology Today, May 1978, pp. 81–84.

CHAPTER OUTLINE

COMPENSATION AND ITS OBJECTIVES
The Pay-for-Performance Dilemma
Satisfaction with Pay
  Pay Equity
  Pay Level
  Pay Administration Practices
Compensation's Relationships with Other Personnel Activities

THE BASIC PAY STRUCTURE
Job Evaluation
  Ranking Method
  Job Classification Method
  Point Rating Method
  Hay Plan
  Factor-Comparison Method
Determining Job Classes
Wage and Salary Surveys
Individual Wage Determination

CONSTRAINTS ON BASIC WAGES
Federal and State Regulations
Federal Mandates
Unions and Associations

ISSUES IN WAGE AND SALARY ADMINISTRATION
Participation Policies
Pay Secrecy
Merit versus Cost-of-Living Increases
Merit Pay Plan

PERSONNEL PROBLEM   What's My Motive?

OBJECTIVES

- To explain the relationships between pay and performance and pay and satisfaction

- To discuss the components of a good compensation system

- To discuss in detail the steps in determining the basic wage

- To explain the contemporary issues in wage and salary administration

THOUGHT STARTERS

- What is compensation?

- Why is compensation so important?

- What forms of compensation can an organization provide employees?

- Are merit pay plans better than cost-of-living plans?

CHAPTER TEN
Compensation: The Basic Wage

T he Jay Lumber Products Company manufactures molding products that are used for trim on residential and commercial constructions of all types. Jay B., the owner, inherited the operation from his father, who had built the company from a three-man work force to a work force of 175 employees. Jay has shown great ability as a manager. Plant productivity has increased steadily. In fact, through the use of capital equipment innovations, he has been able to double output with a work force no larger than that which existed when he became president and chief operating officer of the company.

Jay's philosophy of managing is simple: "We should do better each year than we did last year. Each employee should be more productive at the end of the year than at the beginning, and he should be paid more. If we continuously innovate, we will stay ahead of competition." For some five years, Jay's company has enjoyed unprecedented growth, and his wages are the highest in the local market.

Part of Jay's competitive advantage is a result of assistance he received from a friend of his who manages a metal products plant that produces specialty items. He is a mechanical genius, and he freely assisted Jay in the development of more productive machinery; however, he did not approve of the high wages Jay was paying

because "those dummies haven't done a thing to deserve the increases." In a rather heated discussion, he even suggested that Jay's employees were inferior. "Every employer in this county is mad at you for paying these shiftless, worthless sons of guns more than they deserve." Jay countered with the statement. "You and those other birds who think they are so damned smart should have enough guts to look at what my men are doing. We've had to send people back to school, and we spend one hour every day per man on training. I believe you should pay a man for the job he is doing."

In the course of the discussion, they decided they would compare jobs, and they tried to do this. Their jobs were so different, however, that it was difficult to make a comparison. Although the jobs were different, they did discover that the main requirements were somewhat similar. Reluctantly, Jay agreed to meet with all the local employers and attempt to work out some method of coding all jobs so that wage rate might be compared in a more meaningful manner. He felt that the employers wanted to fix the price of labor, and he wondered whether this was legal.

Excerpt from J. D. Dunn and F. M. Rachel, Wage and Salary Administration: Total Compensation Systems, *p. 50. Copyright © 1971 by McGraw-Hill Book Company. Reprinted with permission.*

T his scenario illustrates several important questions that most organizations face every day: What wage rates should we be paying—the same as everyone else, slightly less, or slightly more? How can we compare our jobs with those of other companies so we can fairly compare our wage rates? How can we find out what other companies are paying? Should we pay people for the job, for personal factors such as age or seniority, or for performance on the job? What are the constraints on how we pay people and give raises? Should employees get raises on the basis of their performance only, or should all employees receive raises based on the increase in the cost of living? The way an organization deals with these and other important questions may mean the difference between an efficient organization with productive and satisfied employees and an inefficient one with unproductive and dissatisfied employees. Because the range of questions about compensation is so large, three chapters are devoted to the subject.

Total compensation for employees includes monetary and nonmonetary rewards and direct and indirect rewards. As Exhibit 10.1 indicates, there are two categories of direct compensation—the basic wage and incentives—and three categories of indirect compensation—protection programs, pay for time not worked, and employee services and perquisites. Direct compensation is discussed in this chapter and the next; indirect compensation, in Chapter 12.

Employees are often willing to join an organization and to perform in it for more than just the money.

Employees are probably more conscious than employing organizations of the many non-financial rewards that become available through the employment exchange. But employees differ widely on the rewards they want and how much value they place on each.[1]

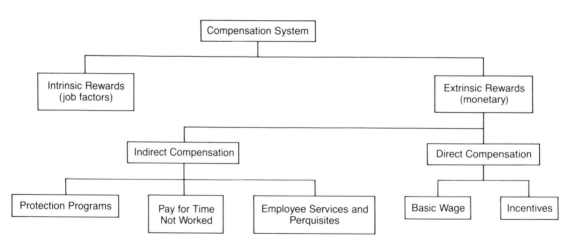

Exhibit 10.1   Components of Compensation
Adapted from J. F. Sullivan, "Indirect Compensation: The Years Ahead," © 1972 by the Regents of the University of California. From *California Management Review* vol. XV, no. 2, p. 65, table 1 by permission of the Regents.

And monetary rewards have their limits:

It is possible that other rewards to some extent can substitute for higher pay. Once pay is about a certain minimum, it will probably be important only if it is seen as a satisfier of esteem and recognition needs and these needs can be satisfied by other rewards.[2]

Some of the nonmonetary rewards an organization can provide are job status and prestige, safety, job responsibility, and variety. These three chapters on compensation primarily discuss monetary rewards, which are usually regarded as the major part of compensation in most organizations. But keep in mind the value of nonmonetary rewards, especially when the limits of monetary rewards become apparent.

Most organizations reward employees on the basis of the employment exchange, at the heart of which are contributions.

Contributions represent outputs from employees to the organization in exchange for inputs from the organization in terms of rewards. To the organization, contributions represent inputs from employees in exchange for outputs to employees in the form of rewards.[3]

The contributions of the organization are direct and indirect compensation; the contributions of the employee are job performance and personal experience. The employee's minimum contributions are described in the job analysis process. It is important to determine employee contributions accurately so that they can be matched with organizational contributions to arrive at a fair employment exchange.

COMPENSATION AND ITS OBJECTIVES

What, specifically, is compensation? **Compensation** is the activity by which organizations evaluate the contributions of employees in order to distribute fairly direct and indirect monetary and nonmonetary rewards, within the organization's ability to pay and legal regulations.

To use compensation effectively, particularly pay, its importance to employees must be known. The purpose that an organization hopes to accomplish through compensation must also be known. If the organization wants to attract more potential employees, its compensation program will be quite different from what it would be if the organization wanted to motivate employees to perform or to retain good employees. This compensation can serve several purposes for the organization as well as the individual.

The three major organizational needs that compensation serves are to attract potential employees to the organization, to motivate employees to perform, and to retain the good employees. The importance of compensation to the organization is highlighted by the fact that approximately 50 percent of an organization's costs are those of compensation. Furthermore, an ever-growing percentage of these compensation costs is going to indirect rather than direct compensation.

The importance that money has to an individual is related to the needs it serves. Because money has the potential to serve several needs and because individuals differ in the importance of their needs, money can take on varying degrees of importance. This difference is illustrated in this example from a gypsum company:

Money meant something *different to miners than it did to surfacemen. To surface workers, money* connoted security, advantage, and the wherewithal to live according to middle-class standards. *To the miner, however, money was a* source of *"independence" and an* instrument *for satisfying desires often forbidden by middle-class values. If the surfaceman wanted to compete with and impress his neighbors by buying a new car, the miner preferred "to set one up for the boys." He wanted to be a good fellow, not a better one.*[4]

The Pay-for-Performance Dilemma

If pay is going to influence employee performance it must do so by influencing the employee's motivation to perform. To direct behavior toward high performance the employee must believe that high performance will be rewarded by pay.[5]

That is, employees must perceive a close relationship between performance and pay. Pay, of course, must also be important to employees, and they must be able to perform. Being able to perform means they must have the ability, know what's expected, and perceive minimal conflicts in performing the rewarded behaviors.

Organizations have several ways to influence employee motivation through systems used. There are four frequently used systems. The first is a fixed system, with a basic single salary or wage for the job. For example, regardless of the performance or personal contribution of an individual on a job, the job pays $400 a week or $10 an hour. The job will pay essentially the same next year, except perhaps for cost-of-living adjustments. Many nonmanagement people work under a fixed system.

The alternative to the fixed system is to set a minimum wage for each job classification and then provide scheduled increases to the maximum rate for each job. These scheduled increases are provided regardless of performance. The individual in this case is rewarded merely for sticking around.

Third is the merit pay system. This system rewards people for superior contributions. Almost all management people in large organizations are covered by merit pay plans. Like the fixed system with scheduled increases, this plan typically sets a standard level of pay for all employees on the same job. Those who perform well increase their standard level, so that employees in the same job may be paid a slightly different level to reflect past performance. However,

Most salary administrators will admit that a merit pay plan is very difficult to administer properly. Typically, managers are inclined to make relatively small discriminations in salary treatment between individuals in the same job, regardless of the perceived differences in performance.[6]

The final system is the incentive pay plan (see Chapter 11). Compensation is based on the units produced rather than the time worked or an incremental merit payment. Although the relationship between performance and pay is strongest under the incentive plans, less than 15 percent of the work force is covered by them.

Incentive plans greatly increase output or productivity, but the conditions under which they can work are very restrictive. As a result, the merit pay plan (time worked plus an incremental merit payment) is the most common form of pay-for-performance plan. Note that use of the fixed pay plan or the fixed plan with scheduled increases implies either that there are no performance differences among employees or that performance differences are not rewarded.

Satisfaction with Pay

If organizations want to minimize absenteeism and turnover, they must make sure that employees are satisfied with their pay. And since satisfaction with pay and motivation to perform are not necessarily highly related, it is necessary to know the determinants of pay satisfaction. With this knowledge, organizations can develop pay practices more likely to result in satisfaction with pay. Perhaps the three major determinants of satisfaction with pay are pay equity, pay level, and pay administration practices.

Pay Equity. **Pay equity** refers to the relationship between what people feel they should be receiving and what they feel they are receiving. If they regard this comparison as fair or equitable, they will be satisfied.

An important part of determining what employees feel they should be receiving is their contributions relative to the contributions of others. Most people feel that the greater their contributions, the more they should receive. You might conclude that incentive pay plans might be more satisfying, because they directly relate individual contribution (at least in regard to performance) and pay. But this conclusion is based on the assumption that pay is more important than other rewards, such as group acceptance, and that everyone has the same opportunity to benefit from such plans. Incentive pay plans are not likely to be very satisfying, however, for individuals who feel they have to work twice as hard as the next person to get the same amount of money.

Pay Level. **Pay level** is an important determinant of the perceived amount of pay, which is compared to what should be received. The result of the comparison is satisfaction with pay if the "should" level of pay equals the action level of pay. Pay dissatisfaction results only if the actual level is less than the "should." Note that when people are overpaid, the result is often guilt. Some research has indicated that if people who are working under an incentive pay plan believe they are overpaid, they will reduce their output. Why? Because this results in less total pay. How do people reduce guilt from the feeling of being overpaid under an hourly wage rate?

Pay Administration Practices. What does this suggest for **pay administration practices**? First,

If the employer is to attract new employees and keep them satisfied with their pay, the wages and salaries offered should approximate the wages and salaries paid to other employees in comparable organizations.[7]

Second, the pricing of jobs can enhance pay satisfaction when it is perceived as embodying a philosophy of equal pay for equal work. The determination of equal pay for equal work can be aided by sound job evaluations. But the worth of jobs must be evaluated according to the factors considered most important by the employees and the organization.

Third, pay-for-performance systems must be accompanied by a method for accurately measuring the performance of employees and must be open enough so employees can clearly see the performance-pay relationship. However, as noted above, there are many personal difficulties in getting the performance-pay system to really work: "even employees who favor the principle of merit pay and see their employers' systems as well run seldom feel that performance is the only personal input for which they should be paid."[8] Therefore, such other contributions as education, seniority, and experience, as well as cost of living, should also be included in pay administration practices.

A closely related factor is the form in which the rewards are distributed. The quality and size of indirect compensation must serve the needs of employees and compare favorably with that in other organizations. Furthermore, the package of compensation benefits must be communicated clearly and accurately to the employees.

A SLICE OF LIFE

There are two aspects of compensation, particularly executive compensation, that are important when determining salary scales: external competitiveness and internal consistency. External competitiveness means that to attract and retain employees one organization's compensation program must be competitive with that of other organizations in the field. If it is not reasonably competitive, it will have difficulty acquiring staff. Internal consistency refers to reasonably equitable salary scales within the firm.

Consider the following salary scales for two hypothetical organizations:

	Company A	Company B
Chief executive officer	$100,000	$150,000
Vice president	70,000	60,000
Regional manager	49,000	22,000
Plant manager	34,000	21,000

Notice that the total salary expense for these executives is equal in the two companies but that the distribution of compensation is decidedly different. Company A is characterized by reasonable internal consistency, whereas Company B is not. In Company A, each level of management receives approximately 30 percent less than the next higher level. (The 30-percent difference is the general rule for industry. There are exceptions, of course, but many organizations stay close to this guideline.) Company B may have some problems because of the large difference in compensation between the chief executive officer and vice president and the small difference between

A final pay administration practice is trust and consistency. Employees must perceive that the organization is looking out for their interests as well as its own. Without trust and consistency, pay satisfaction is not only low, but pay also becomes a target for complaints regardless of the real issues.[9]

Although the relationships between pay and satisfaction and pay and motivation are not always clear or consistent, pay satisfaction can be attained and pay can result in performance motivation. This suggests that organizations should try to design and administer compensation systems that increase the chances of getting both pay satisfaction and performance motivation. Serving these two outcomes helps meet the concerns of the organization as well as the individual. There are, of course, other considerations for compensation administration, but these can be served while pursuing pay satisfaction and motivation for performance.

Compensation's Relationships with Other Personnel Activities

Employees differ in the value they put on pay. If personnel departments can determine how important pay is to individuals, they can recruit people to fill specific jobs with specific pay policy options. Some jobs could be very interesting but pay

the regional and plant managers. Presumably, the regional manager has more responsibility than the plant manager.

A responsible wage and salary schedule should have both external competitiveness and internal consistency, but at times this may be difficult to achieve. For instance, Company A wants to hire a new vice president, and a very capable person is available. In fact, this person is seen as a critical addition to the staff. There is a problem, however: The prospective vice president wants $95,000 as an annual salary, which is $25,000 more than that position has been paid in the past. Unquestionably, if Company A pays the $95,000, it will be more than competitive with similar organizations in the field. Indeed, several other organizations will pay this salary to this person if Company A doesn't.

Is this person worth $95,000? What about internal consistency? Carefully review Company A's salary scale if it were to pay the $95,000:

Chief executive officer	$100,000
Vice president	95,000
Regional manager	49,000
Plant manager	34,000

It is possible that Company A will have to revise its entire salary scale from top to bottom. This change may be entirely justified, but it will be costly.

Professional athletics provides another example of external competitiveness and internal consistency in wage and salary administration. What is the effect of having one player making a lot more money than any other player on the team?

little, whereas other jobs could be very dull but pay well. Individuals could be recruited and selected on the basis of their job and pay values.

Wage levels and individual wage determinations can be influenced greatly by the existence of a union or association in the organization. A union can also play an important role in the job evaluation process and may determine whether an organization will have a merit or incentive pay plan.

Compensation also plays an important part in human resource planning. If the planning activity identifies shortages of personnel, or at least potential shortages, the compensation level may have to be raised to attract more individuals.

From the individual's point of view, a compensation policy clearly identifying the levels of pay and pay ranges for jobs can be a valuable aid in deciding which career path to take and whether to stay with the organization.

Job analysis and compensation are also integrally related. The job evaluation process that determines the relative worth of jobs is based in large measure on how the job is described in the formal job description and specifications.

Perhaps the most important relationship for individuals in the organization is that between compensation and performance evaluation. Especially where merit pay exists, the results of the performance evaluation are significant. Where promotions are available, the performance evaluation system can have added significance to the extent promotion is a reward for performance.

THE BASIC PAY STRUCTURE

Exhibit 10.1 shows two groups of monetary rewards—indirect and direct. Direct compensation is subdivided into incentive and basic wages. (This section examines basic wages; Chapter 11 examines incentive wages; Chapter 12 examines indirect compensation.) Among the basic wage issues are three that represent most activities in many compensation departments: determination of the pay structures in the organization, setting of pay levels, and individual wage determinations.

Pay structures are important when organizations are concerned about establishing internal equity among the different jobs in the organization. The amount paid for a job could be decided on the basis of a manager's impression of what the job should pay or is worth, but to help ensure internal equity, more formal methods are often used. After jobs are formally evaluated, they are grouped into classes or grades. Within each class, jobs are then arranged in order of importance, and ranges of pay are established with the aid of wage surveys.

Job Evaluation

Organizations offer rewards to individuals on the basis of their job performance and personal contributions. "Organizations implicitly recognize job-related contributions by assigning pay in accordance with the difficulty and importance of jobs."[10] Most organizations also use some type of formal job evaluation or informal comparisons of job content for determining the relative worth of job-related contributions. It is usually only in the formal job evaluation process, however, that job-related contributions are explicitly specified. **Job evaluation** is the comparison of jobs by the use of formal and systematic procedures to determine their relative worth within the organization.

There are four essential steps in job evaluation. The first is a thorough job analysis (see Chapter 4). This step provides information about the job duties and responsibilities and about employee requirements for successful performance of the job.

The second step in job evaluation is deciding what the organization is paying for—that is, determining which factors will be used to evaluate jobs (although not all methods of job evaluation explicitly use factors). The factors are like yardsticks used to measure the relative importance of jobs. Since these factors help determine what jobs are paid, they are called **compensable factors**. The factors used by organizations vary widely, but they all presumably reflect job-related contributions. Such factors might include accountability, know-how, problem-solving ability, and physical demands. After the determination of compensable factors, their relative importance must be decided.

The third step is to choose and adapt a system for evaluating jobs in the organization according to the compensable factors chosen in the second step. There are many basic methods of job evaluation that organizations can adapt to their own needs.

Since the fourth step in the process of job evaluation is to decide who will do the job evaluation and then actually use the evaluation methods, it is important to examine the operation of job evaluation methods in detail. There are two common nonquantitative methods of job evaluation—ranking and job classification. The point rating method, Hay plan, and factor-comparison method are more quantifiable.

Ranking Method.   Job analysis information can be used to construct a hierarchy or ladder of jobs, which reflects their relative difficulty or value to the organization. This is the core of the **ranking method.** Although any number of compensable factors could be used to evaluate jobs, the job analyst often considers the whole job on the basis of just one factor, such as difficulty or value.

This method is convenient when there are only a few jobs to evaluate and when one person is familiar with them all. As the number of jobs increases and the likelihood of one individual knowing all jobs declines, job analysis information becomes more important and ranking is often done by committee. Especially with a large number of jobs to be ranked, key or benchmark jobs are used for comparison.

One of the difficulties in the ranking method is that jobs are forced to be different from others. Often it is difficult to make fine distinctions between similar jobs, and thus disagreements arise. One way of avoiding this difficulty is to place jobs into classes or grades.

Job Classification Method.   The **job classification method** is similar to the ranking method, except that classes or grades are established, and then the jobs are placed into the classes. Jobs are usually evaluated on the basis of the whole job, often using one factor such as difficulty or an intuitive summary of factors. Again, job analysis information is useful in the classification, and benchmark jobs are frequently established for each class. Within each class or grade, there is no further ranking of the jobs.

Although many organizations use job classification, the largest is the U.S. government, which has eighteen distinct classifications from GS 1 to GS 18 (*GS* stands for "general schedule"). GS 11 and above usually denote general management and highly specialized jobs; while GS 5 to GS 10 are assigned to management trainee and lower-level management positions; GS 1 to GS 4 are for clerical and nonsupervisory personnel.

A particular advantage of this method is that it can be applied to a large number and wide variety of jobs. As the number and variety of jobs in an organization increase, however, the classification of jobs tends to become more subjective. This is particularly true when an organization has a large number of plant or office locations, and thus jobs with the same title may differ in content. Because it is difficult to evaluate each job separately in such cases, the job title becomes a more important guide to job classification than job content is.

A major disadvantage of the job classification method is the basis of job evaluations. Evaluations either use one factor or an intuitive summary of many factors. The problem with using one factor, such as difficulty (skill), is that it may not be important on all jobs. Some jobs may require a great deal of skill, but others may require a great deal of responsibility. Does this mean that jobs requiring much responsibility should be placed in a lower classification than jobs requiring much skill? Not necessarily. Perhaps both factors could be considered together. Thus each factor becomes a compensable factor, valued by the organization. Jobs would be evaluated and classified on the basis of both factors. However, "this balancing of the compensable factors to determine the relative equality of jobs often causes misunderstandings with the employees and the labor leaders."[11] To deal with this disadvantage, many organizations use more-quantifiable methods of evaluation.

Point Rating Method.   The most widely used method of job evaluation is the **point rating method**, which consists of assigning point values for previously determined compensable factors and adding them to arrive at a total. The advantages of the point rating method are several:

1. The point rating plan is widely used throughout industry, permitting comparisons on a similar basis with other firms.
2. The point rating plan is relatively simple to understand. It is the simplest of quantitative methods of job evaluation.
3. The point values for each job are easily converted to job and wage classes with a minimum of confusion and distortion.
4. A well-conceived point rating plan has considerable stability—it is applicable to a wide range of jobs over an extended period of time. The greatest assets here are consistency and uniformity and its widespread use throughout industry.
5. The point rating method is an objective, definitive approach requiring several separate and distinct judgement decisions. Thus errors tend to cancel one another.[12]

The limitations of the point rating method are few, but an especially critical one is the assumption that all jobs can be described with the same factors. Many organizations avoid this limitation by developing separate point rating methods for different groups of employees. In Exhibit 10.2 there are eleven compensable factors used in one organization to evaluate the jobs in supervisory, nonsupervisory, and clerical categories. Exhibit 10.2 also shows a description of the skills associated with one of the factors (basic knowledge) and sets forth the specifications for the degrees or levels within that factor. Some factors are more important than others, as shown by the different point values. For example, the second degree of practical experience is worth four times as much as the second degree of job conditions. In essence, each job is evaluated on its compensable factors. The personnel department determines which degree of a factor is appropriate for the job, and then the points assigned to each degree of each factor are totaled. Levels of compensation are determined on the basis of the point totals.

Exhibit 10.2   Sample of Point Rating Method

Compensable Factor	1st Degree	2nd Degree	3rd Degree	4th Degree	5th Degree
Basic knowledge*	15	30	45	60	—
Practical experience	20	40	60	80	—
Complexity and judgment	15	30	45	60	—
Initiative	5	10	20	40	—
Probable errors	5	10	20	40	—
Contacts with others	5	10	20	40	—
Confidential data	5	10	15	20	25
Attention to functional detail	5	10	15	20	—
Job conditions	5	10	15	—	—
For Supervisory Positions Only					
Character of supervision	5	10	20	—	—
Scope of supervision	5	10	20	—	—

*Basic Knowledge

This factor appraises the minimum fundamental knowledge or special training an individual must have to be eligible for employment on this job. It is knowledge that can be acquired through some plan of schooling but need not be. For convenience, it is measured in terms of equivalent formal education. In considering this factor disregard progression to more responsible positions, knowledge that can be obtained only through practical experience, and the formal education of the person or persons on the job.

1st degree

Equivalent to four years' high school; considered the minimum job requirement. Requires basic training in mathematics, English, and grammar; accuracy in checking, posting, filing, etc.; mental alterness and adaptability to office or laboratory routines; and sufficient typing ability to type reports, memos, and letters from rough drafts.

2nd degree

Equivalent to four years' high school plus specialized training of up to one year. Requires ability to handle such functions as stenography or bookeeping; opera-

tion of office equipment for which special training is necessary (bookkeeping machines, tabulating equipment, PBX boards, etc); or simple mechanical drawing, blue print reading, repetitive laboratory testing, etc.

3rd degree

Equivalent to four years' high school plus extensive specialized training, such as night, trade, extension, or correspondence school work in specific subjects; long-term apprenticeship training in manufacturing methods, trades work, laboratory techniques, foremanship, etc.; or two years' college training of the type usually given preparatory to professions in accounting and finance, law, business administration, etc. Requires knowledge of such specialized fields as cost accounting, commercial art, nursing, statistics, time study, foreign language, personnel practices, etc.

4th degree

Equivalent to four years' college or university training that if formally acquired would lead to a bachelor's degree in such fields as accounting and finance, business administration, library science, etc. Requires broad knowledge of a general technical field.

Hay Plan.   A method with only three factors is shown in Exhibit 10.3. This method, generally known as the **Hay plan**, is the most widely used method for evaluating managerial and executive positions. The three factors—know-how, problem solving, and accountability—are used because they are assumed to be the most important aspects of managerial and executive positions. Although the Hay plan appears to use only three factors, there are for all practical purposes eight: three subfactors in know-how, two in problem solving, and three in accountability. In deriving the final point profile for any job, however, only the three major factors are assigned point values.

Factor-Comparison Method.   The point rating method, regardless of the number of factors and degrees of each factor, derives a point total for each job. Several very different types of jobs can have the same total points. After the total points are determined, jobs are priced—often according to groups or classes, similar to the job classification method. The **factor-comparison method** avoids this step between point totaling and pricing by assigning dollar values to factors and comparing the amounts directly to the pay for benchmark jobs. In short, factor-comparison is similar to point rating in that both use compensable factors. But the point method uses degrees and points for each factor to measure jobs, whereas factor-comparison uses benchmark jobs and money values on factors.

Exhibit 10.3   Hay Plan Compensable Factors

Mental Activity (problem solving)	Know-How	Accountability
The amount of original, self-starting thought required by the job for analysis, evaluation, creation, reasoning, and arriving at conclusions Mental Activity has two dimensions: • The degree of freedom with which the thinking process is used to achieve job objectives without the guidance of standards, precedents, or direction from others • The type of mental activity involved; the complexity, abstractness, or originality of thought required Mental Activity is expressed as a percentage of Know-How for the obvious reason that people think with what they know. The percentage judged to be correct for a job is applied to the Know-How point value; the result is the point value given to Mental Activity.	The sum total of all knowledge and skills, however acquired, needed for satisfactory job performance (evaluates the job, not the person) Know-How has three dimensions: • The amount of practical, specialized, or technical knowledge required • Breadth of management, or the ability to make many activities and functions work well together; the job of company president, for example, has greater breadth than that of a department supervisor • Requirement for skill in motivating people Using a chart, a number can be assigned to the level of Know-How needed in a job. This number—or point value—indicates the relative importance of Know-How in the job being evaluated.	The measured effect of the job on company goals Accountability has three dimensions: • Freedom to act, or relative presence of personal or procedural control and guidance; determined by answering the question, "How much freedom has the job holder to act independently?"; for example, a plant manager has more freedom than a supervisor under his or her control • Dollar magnitude, a measure of the sales, budget, dollar value of purchases, value added, or any other significant annual dollar figure related to the job • Impact of the job on dollar magnitude, a determination of whether the job has a primary effect on end results or has instead a sharing, contributory, or remote effect Accountability is given a point value independent of the other two factors.

The total evaluation of any job is arrived at by adding the points for Know-How, Mental Activity, and Accountability.

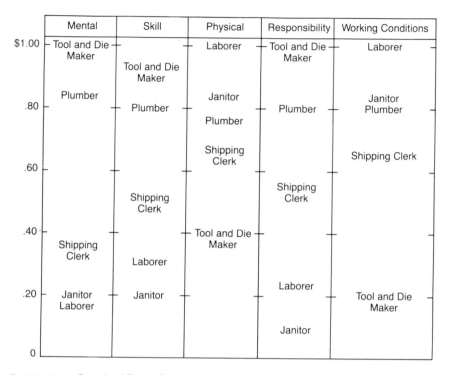

Exhibit 10.4 Sample of Factor Comparison for Key Jobs
From J. D. Dunn and F. M. Rachel, *Wage and Salary Administration: Total Compensation Systems*, p. 182. Copyright © 1971 by McGraw-Hill Book Company. Reprinted with permission.

The jobs shown in Exhibit 10.4 are the benchmark jobs in one company and the dollar value for each factor in each job. These dollar values were determined by individuals familiar with those jobs. Other jobs with the same compensable factors are then measured against these benchmark jobs, and their dollar values are determined immediately. This method tends to produce internal equity, but external equity may be more difficult to achieve, because other companies may use different benchmark jobs or assign different dollar amounts to different factors of benchmark jobs. In addition, the vast majority of organizations use the point method, so there are fewer organizations using the factor-comparison method for comparison.

Determining Job Classes

Since most organizations use the point method, it is necessary to look at the next step in determination of the salary structure. Determining job classes means grouping together all jobs of nearly the same difficulty. The jobs within the same class may be quite different, but they must be about equal in value to the organization. All jobs in each class are assigned one salary or range of salaries.

Why group jobs into classes? For efficiency of salary administration, for one thing. Also, it is hard to justify the small differences in pay that would exist without classes of jobs, and small errors that occur in evaluating the jobs can be eliminated in the classification process. Of course, employees can also find fault with the classification if their jobs are grouped with what they feel are less important jobs. Sometimes the jobs that are grouped together are too dissimilar. This may occur because there are too few classes of jobs. Few classes are appropriate, however, if many of the jobs in the organization are of similar value. It is when there is a wide range of job difficulty that too few job classes may lead to employee complaints of inequity.

How are job classes usually established? With a simple ranking method, discrete categories of jobs are automatically established. These categories conveniently separate jobs with different value to the organization. Sometimes it is unnecessary to classify jobs, especially if there are only a few and if wage survey information can be obtained for each. It is also possible to rely on wage survey information, without job classifications, when the job titles from organization to organization describe almost exactly the same work.

The job classification method also establishes its own classes or grades and thus does not really require a separate step in establishing job classes. There is a tendency in using the factor-comparison method to price jobs directly. The procedures used in establishing classes for the common point rating method begin with plotting assigned point values and current wage rates for jobs in the organization.

You may have noticed by now that although job classes are determined for the purpose of establishing wage rates, job classes are often based on wage rates that have already been established. This practice may seem somewhat bizarre, but it is typical in most organizations. Most organizations are already paying their employees and thus need to determine job classes only when many new jobs are introduced or if it has never really had a sound job analysis program. In addition, if the organization has grown and incorporated many more jobs, it may need to group them into classes for purposes of salary administration. On the other hand, an organization that is just being established is most likely small, and the price of its jobs would be determined by surveys of what other organizations are paying.

One way of establishing job classes is to plot the point value of jobs and their respective wage rates (see Exhibit 10.5). If there are several wage rates for the same job, the median rate or the average rate is plotted. After these data have been plotted, a line is drawn through them to establish the mean of all the job rates. This line highlights the differences in pay between jobs with the same point values.

Exhibit 10.6 shows how job classes can be established from the data that are plotted. This organization established seven job classes around existing wage rates (it used one evaluation system for the entire organization) with some overlap in pay between adjacent job classes.

There are many other wage structures that an organization could establish. The percentage of overlap could vary, the width of point values per job class could be different, and the range of each class could be changed. All are designed to help make the organization's internal salary structure consistent and equitable and to offer some incentive for higher performance. But organizations also need to attract and retain good employees.

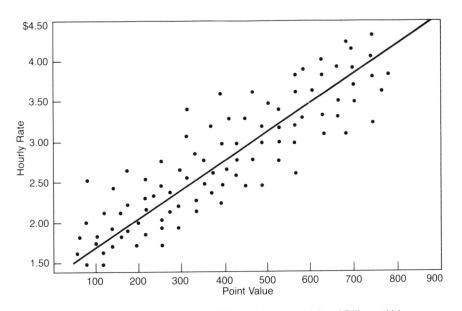

Exhibit 10.5   Method for Determining Pay Differentials among Jobs of Different Value
From J. D. Dunn and F. M. Rachel, *Wage and Salary Administration: Total Compensation Systems*, p. 223. Copyright © 1971 by McGraw-Hill Book Company. Reprinted with permission.

Wage and Salary Surveys

In order to attract and retain adequate employees, the salary structure must not only be internally equitable but also externally equitable. Wage surveys of other organizations in the same labor market provide the information for establishing external equity. An illustration of the importance of wage surveys and the notion of external equity:

A national manufacturing firm with production facilities in California, Arkansas, and New Jersey built a new plant in Michigan to serve its growing market in the Middle West and Canada. The new plant required unskilled, semiskilled, and skilled labor. A surplus of unskilled and semiskilled labor existed in the labor market adjacent to the new plant. Skilled labor, in contrast, was in short supply.

In view of the fact that unskilled labor costs constituted the bulk of total labor costs, the firm's management decided that local market rates, rather than company-wide and industry rates, should exert a strong influence on the wage levels for all unskilled jobs in the new plant. This decision forced the managers to gather wage data. A comprehensive set of wage facts was collected from selected plants within a 50-mile radius of the new plant. Information about occupations, as well as information about specific jobs, was gathered. These data provided a sound base for the wage and salary decisions that were subsequently made about the level of wages for the plant.[13]

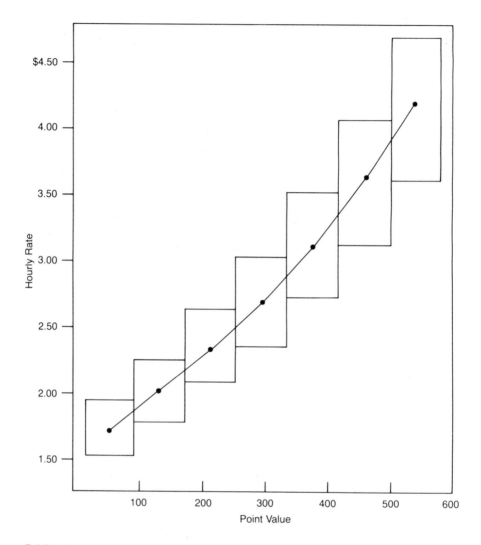

Exhibit 10.6 Method for Determining Job Classes
From J. D. Dunn and F. M. Rachel, *Wage and Salary Administration: Total Compensation Systems*, p. 226. Copyright © 1977 by McGraw-Hill Book Company. Reprinted with permission.

Wage surveys can be used to develop compensation levels, wage structures, and even payment plans (the amount and kind of direct and indirect compensation). Survey results can also be used to indicate compensation philosophies of competing organizations. For example, a large electronics company may have a policy of paying 15 percent above the market rate (the average of all rates for essentially the same job in an area); a large service organization may choose to pay the market rate; a large bank may decide to pay 5 percent less than the market rate.

Most organizations use wage surveys extensively. Separate surveys are published for different occupational groupings; thus many larger organizations subscribe to several surveys. For example, there are surveys for clerical workers, professional workers, managers, and executives. Separate surveys are conducted not only because there are such wide differences in skill levels but also because labor markets are so different. An organization surveying clerical workers may need only to survey companies within a 10-mile radius, whereas a survey of managerial salaries may cover the entire country.

Individual Wage Determination

Once the job analysis and job evaluation have been completed, the job classes have been established, and the pricing structure has been determined, the question is, How much do we pay Anne and John, both of whom work on the same job? If the rate range were $1,500 to $2,000 per month, Anne might be paid $2,000 and John $1,750. What difference might account for the pay differential? Although performance seems like the best criterion, seniority, sex, age, size of family, experience, and appearance have also been found to influence individual wages. Age and seniority, in fact, are frequently perceived to be rather important factors.

In actuality, the individual wage determinations combine both personal contributions and performance. Thus age and seniority as well as their performance may influence Anne's and John's pay. However, many managers would argue that pay differences based on performance are more equitable than those based on such personal contributions as seniority.

But if performance is the criterion, is it past, current, or future performance? Many employees are given raises on the basis of their performance potential although athletes are usually paid on the basis of the last year's performance (this is not true for certain sports, such as race-car driving, tennis, and horse racing). There are several difficulties in giving merit raises based on past performance, however. One of those difficulties is employees' perceptions of their performance. Anne and John, like many people, are apt to rate themselves in at least the top 50 percent in terms of performance. Thus both may perceive that they perform well. Using performance as the sole criterion may therefore upset John—unless he has a significantly lower level of performance, knows it, and accepts it.

The answers to the question of how much to pay Anne and John can be as varied as the number of people answering the question. Compensation managers should also ask questions like "What does the rest of my compensation program look like?"; "What was the initial understanding or contract with Anne and John?"; and "Can I defend my decision?" Defensibility and consistency are perhaps the two most important aspects of compensation management. Regardless of the method used or the decision reached, there will always be criticism from others. But being able to defend the decision and show that it is consistent with others goes a long way in reducing criticism.

CONSTRAINTS ON BASIC WAGES

The three basic wage issues—determination of pay structures, setting of pay levels, and individual wage determinations—are not handled in a vacuum. Several constraints face most organizations in making decisions related to these issues. Perhaps the most extensive are legal regulations and mandates from federal and state government.

Federal and State Regulations

The federal government has imposed several laws influencing the level of wages employers may pay, pay structures, and individual wage determinations. (Other federal laws influencing other aspects of compensation are discussed in the next two chapters.) The first federal law to protect the amount of pay employees received for their work was the Davis-Bacon Act of 1931, which requires that organizations holding construction contracts with federal agencies pay laborers and mechanics the prevailing wages of the locality in which the work is performed. The Walsh-Healey Public Contracts Act of 1936 extended the Davis-Bacon Act to include all federal contracts exceeding $10,000 and specified that pay levels conform to the industry minimum rather than the area minimum, as specified in Davis-Bacon. The Walsh-Healey Act also established overtime pay at one and one-half times the hourly rate. The wage provisions do not include administrative, professional, office, custodial, and maintenance employees or beginners and handicapped persons.

Partially because Davis-Bacon and Walsh-Healey were limited in their coverage of employees, the Fair Labor Standards Act of 1938 (or the Wage and Hour Law) was enacted. The FLSA set minimum wages, maximum hours, child-labor standards, and overtime pay provisions for all workers except domestics and government employees. A 1974 amendment extended FLSA coverage to domestic and government employees. In 1976, however, the Supreme Court ruled that state and local government employees are covered only by state minimum wage laws. The 1974 amendment also revised the minimum wage, which was 25 cents per hour in 1938, to $3.35 in 1981. Small businesses whose sales do not exceed $362,500 are exempt from all FLSA requirements.

The overtime pay provisions of the FLSA established who is to be paid overtime for work and who is not. Most employees covered by the FLSA must be paid time-and-a-half for all work exceeding forty hours per week. There are special regulations for employees in such organizations as hospitals, nursing homes, and bowling alleys. In hospitals, for example, the computation for overtime is based not on a forty-hour work week but on an average of forty hours per week over two consecutive weeks. These special regulations have been designed to recognize the needs of the organization as well as the individual.

Several groups of individuals are exempt from both overtime and minimum-wage provisions. These include employees of firms not involved in interstate commerce, employees in seasonal industries, and outside salespeople. Three other employee groups—executives, administrators, and professionals—are also exempt from overtime pay and minimum-wage laws in most organizations. In fact, they are called **exempt employees,** meaning that they may not be paid overtime for work after forty hours per week. All employees subject to being paid for overtime work are called **nonexempt employees**. Although nonexempt employees are usually paid less than exempt employees, practices and policies regarding their treatment are much more clearly defined than they are for exempt employees.[14]

Several federal antidiscrimination laws passed since 1960 also influence individual wage determination. They are the Equal Pay Act of 1963, the Civil Rights Act of 1964, and the Age Discrimination Act of 1967. All are meant to ensure that employees with similar seniority, performance, and background doing the same work are paid the same, regardless of sex, age, race, national origin, or religion. Although the laws are on the books, the practice in organizations suggests that employees are still being paid differentially because of sex and race. Employees who feel they are not being paid equally for the same work may contact the Wage and Hour Division of the Department of Labor, which enforces the Equal Pay Act and the Age Discrimination Act, or the Equal Employment Opportunity Commission, which may soon do the enforcing.

Three other federal laws influence how much employers may deduct from employee paychecks. The Copeland Act of 1934 authorized the Secretary of Labor to regulate wage deductions for contractors and subcontractors doing work financed in whole or part by a federal contract. Essentially, the Copeland Act was aimed at illegal deductions. Protection against a more severe threat from an employer with federal contracts was provided in the Anti-Kickback Law of 1948. The Federal Wage Garnishment Law of 1970 also protects employees against deductions to pay for indebtedness. It provides that only 25 percent of one's disposable weekly earnings or thirty times the minimum wage, whichever is less, can be deducted for repayment of indebtedness.

Several state laws also influence wages paid to employees and the hours they can work. Thirty-nine states have minimum-wage laws covering intrastate employees and other employees not covered by federal minimum-wage laws. Although many states at one time had laws limiting the number of hours women could work, the number of states with these laws has now declined to about ten.

Federal Mandates

The most extensive form of mandates influencing the level of pay and individual wage determinations has been the federal wage and price guidelines, or wage-guidepost policies. Guidelines have been used during the last four military confrontations engaging the United States, the last being the Vietnam War. With Executive Order 11615, President Nixon prohibited any changes in wages and prices during the period from August 15, 1971 to November 15, 1971. In October of that year, the Pay Board and Price Commission was established by Executive Order 11627 to help hold annual wage increases to 5.5 percent. (At that time, productivity was increasing about 3 percent per year and inflation at 2.5 percent per year.)

Enforcement of the 5.5 percent increase was the responsibility of the Internal Revenue Service (IRS). The Pay Board established three categories of organizations as a function of size. The larger organizations (those with more than 5,000 employees and those in the construction industry) needed to get approval from the Pay Board prior to wage adjustments, but the smaller organizations were subject only to spot checks by the IRS. Because enforcement was so difficult, in April 1972 all firms with sixty or fewer employees became exempt from the regulations. This exemption affected 5 million small firms with about 19 million employees.

Needless to say, the regulations engendered charges of unfairness, unenforce-ability, and ineffectiveness. There was also a great deal of uncertainty in many of the regulations. "For example, it was not clear whether upgrading an entire job or promoting employees into new job classes with the effect of giving raises in excess of the guidelines was permissible."[15]

According to the wage and price standards published for 1978 and 1979 by the Council on Wage and Price Stability, the average wage increase that an organization could provide was limited to 7 percent. Individuals might receive more than a 7-percent increase, but the total amount an organization allocated to salaries could not be increased by more than 7 percent. This implied that if a company gave cost-of-living increases of 7 percent, it could not grant any merit increases. For merit increases to be given, cost-of-living increases had to be less than 7 percent, even though the rate of inflation was in excess of 10 percent.

There were exceptions to this general rule, however. For example, if a company had a collective bargaining agreement with a union, the annual pay increase was limited to 8 percent in any year of a multiyear agreement. Pay increases could also exclude the effects of legitimate promotions and qualification increases.

The Council on Wage and Price Stability is currently gathering information from organizations across the country for the determination of new guidelines for 1981. Most likely similar guidelines will be established, although there may be a provision allowing the percentage of wage increases to be determined by an average of two-year increases. Thus if the wage limit is established at 16 percent for a two-year period, an organization could use the entire 16 percent in one year but not be able to grant any wage increases the following year.

Although wage guidelines present problems of interpretation, compliance, and implementation to most organizations, it is possible that such guidelines will con-tinue for the next several years.

Unions and Associations

Another major constraint on the three basic wage issues is the process of collective bargaining. Unions and associations have had a major impact on wage structures, wage levels, and individual wage determinations regardless of whether specific organizations organized or not.[16] This impact is present from the early stages of job analysis and job evaluation to the final determination of specific wage rates and the selection of the criteria used to set those roles. Although unions generally do not conduct job evaluation programs, in many instances they do help design or modify company programs. Even if union interests are not completely served in the job evaluation process, they can be served at the bargaining table. In fact, serving the interests of members at the bargaining table puts job evaluation into perspective for the union as well as the management.

Both union and management base final wage rates and levels on far more than the results of job evaluation and wage surveys, although both often rely on surveys.[17] The surveys are used to determine wage rates for comparable work in other sections of the industry and wages paid in the locality. Other criteria for wage determinations are labor market conditions (the number of people out of work and looking for work), traditions and past history of the organization's wage structure, fringe benefits, indexes of productivity, company profit figures or turnover data, and the Consumer Price Index and the Urban Workers' Family Budget figures, both of which help determine cost-of-living increases.

Final wage levels are reached on the basis of these wage criteria and the relative power of the union and management. It is important to note that individual wage determinations are generally not of concern to the union. It is the union philosophy that all employees on the same job are doing essentially the same work and therefore should be paid the same. That philosophy and collective bargaining appear to have paid off, however, for individual members. Their wages have generally been higher than without collective bargaining, especially where the unions are strong.[18] Unions that are not strong appear to be no better at getting high wage levels than employees without the benefit of a union. In fact, some companies may pay a higher wage rate than nearby unionized organizations in order to attract qualified personnel or make unionization less attractive to current employees. And in organizations with a unionized blue-collar labor force, management generally passes along the benefits negotiated with the union to nonunion white-collar employees. "In June, 1978, some 135,000 white collar workers not covered by the company's bonus plan received a $292 catch-up payment. The payment is based on increases mandated under GM's contract with the United Auto Workers."[19] This policy helps preserve equity and maintain company loyalty among the white-collar workers. Thus the effects of the union are both direct and indirect. A more complete discussion of the impact of unionization is in Chapters 15 and 16.

ISSUES IN WAGE AND SALARY ADMINISTRATION

There are several contemporary issues in wage and salary administration, but three have particular importance: To what extent should employees be able to set their own wages? What are the advantages and disadvantages of pay secrecy? And are merit pay plans preferable to cost-of-living adjustments for determining individual wage rates?

Participation Policies

For many employees, total compensation generally represents a mixture of direct salary and indirect benefits. These indirect benefits may represent as much as 45 percent of total compensation, but employees generally have no choice as to what indirect benefits they receive. Management defends this policy on the grounds that it ensures that employees have the proper benefits and there is a cost advantage in buying the same benefits for all employees.[20] Yet the proliferation of indirect pay arrangements has created a kind of smoked-glass effect through which the attitudes and desires of the recipient can be seen only darkly, if at all. Employees often receive costly benefits they neither want nor need and, in many cases, do not even know about. And even in cases where employees know they are receiving particular forms of compensation, they tend to undervalue the benefits.[21]

What are the alternatives? The popular form of participation for executive-level employees is the **cafeteria approach**, in which individuals select from a variety of compensation "entrees" those items they want. Another form incorporates employee-management negotiations on compensation levels and forms.

The cafeteria approach tends to be favored by a majority of executives, even if the administrative costs are deducted from their annual pay.[22] If given the choice, executives would also select heavier doses of supplemental (indirect) compensation than they are now receiving.

Because the cafeteria approach allows individuals to make some pay decisions, they are more likely to be satisfied with their compensation package. Allowing employees to participate in the compensation package also helps increase their understanding of what they are actually receiving from the organization.

Although the cafeteria approach appears to have several positive benefits, it has generally been limited to executives and has also generally restricted participation to initial decisions on the proportion and type of direct and indirect benefits.

Pay Secrecy

Ask anyone who works for a living how much money he or she makes, and you are likely to encounter a range of responses from evasion to outright hostility. Such responses, however, should not be surprising. According to organizational etiquette, it is generally considered gauche to ask others their salaries. In a recent study of E. I. du Pont de Nemours, all employees were asked if the company should disclose more payroll information so that everyone would know everyone else's pay. Only 18 percent voted for an open pay system.

Organizations should probably continue to support pay secrecy, especially if there is inequity in the pay structure. But employees always have ways of finding out about the salaries of others, and if there is inequity, pay dissatisfaction is a likely result. Yet several studies indicate that even if there is not salary inequity, pay dissatisfaction may still be a result. Why? Because people in fact do not always find out the correct information on salaries, and even if they do, they tend to believe what they want. People generally believe that their own pay is too low and that the pay of people above and below them is too close to their own pay, although it is closer to those below than those above. Managers also tend to underestimate the pay of those above them and overestimate the pay of those below them, although managers from government (where open pay is the stated policy) tend not to underestimate the pay of those above them.[23]

These results are important, because individuals tend to determine the equity of their own pay by comparing their contributions and rewards with those of other people in the organization (often called reference groups). When employees overestimate the pay of those below them and underestimate the pay of those above them, they become dissatisfied because of the perceived inequities. In addition, they lose the motivation to do well because they believe that it is not worth the effort to be promoted: "You only end up doing more work for relatively less pay." Studies suggest, however, that perceived inequities and pay dissatisfaction due to the inequities are less with more open pay plans (public organizations) than with secret pay plans (private organizations).

Organizational policies and practices often support the concept of salary confidentiality. Most companies limit the circulation of individual pay scales. Wide rate ranges not only provide room for merit pay but also make it difficult to guess the salary of an individual in any job classification. Most paychecks are delivered in sealed envelopes. There is a limit, however, on the organizational policies that can be used to maintain or enforce salary confidentiality. The National Labor Relations Board prohibited Blue Cross–Blue Shield of Alabama from inserting in its employee handbook a statement telling employees that their salary is a private matter and that they should not tell others what pay they are receiving.

This is not to say, however, that salaries of employees may not be kept secret. The Supreme Court of California ruled that information on salaries paid to executives is a business secret and that it is disloyal for an employee to disclose those salaries to others. Be careful not to read this as saying that a potential employer cannot find out what salary you are currently earning. Recently the New Jersey Employment Commission prevented an individual from collecting unemployment benefits because he had lied to his new employer at the time of hire about the salary he was making with his previous employer.

Merit versus Cost-of-Living Increases

Many large organizations grant **cost-of-living adjustments** (COLAs) to their employees, especially firms in which unions have written COLAs into their contracts. And where unionized workers have COLA guarantees, the pressures are great to provide the same benefits to nonunion, often white-collar, employees. But many firms are trying to eliminate their COLAs in favor of merit pay plans,[24] primarily because they aren't "getting any bang for their buck." In addition to not getting performance from pay, COLAs often take some salary control out of the hands of the organization and the compensation manager. Since most COLAs are tied to the Consumer Price Index (CPI), all the organization can do is watch salaries increase as the CPI does. The more the CPI increases, the more the organization must pay. The more the COLA budget, the smaller the pot for merit increases. And as some argue, for merit increases to really work, they must be pretty big.[25] Thus the issue is really whether the salary budget should be used for COLAs or merit increases.

Where unions have written COLAs into negotiated contracts, organizations have no choice but to pay COLAs to their unionized employees. The choice remains, however, for their nonunionized employees. Where organizations are not unionized, the COLA-versus-merit question applies to all employees.

For merit plans to work, employees must be convinced that good performance will lead to higher pay, value higher pay, believe that the negative consequences of higher performance are minimal, and believe that there are other desired rewards related to good performance. Having a merit pay plan helps relate performance and pay, but there are other requirements: Employees must know what good performance consists of, accept the performance measures as valid and inclusive, and see that the better performers actually get higher pay.[26] If these conditions exist, many of the issues raised in the earlier section of the pay-for-performance dilemma become less important. If these six conditions do not exist, merit plans are unlikely to work. It might be better to pay COLAs until some of the conditions for merit plans can be established.

Merit Pay Plan

Because most large private organizations have some type of merit plan, it may be useful to look at a specific example of such a plan. This merit plan tends to be rather typical. As shown in Exhibit 10.7, the pay increments depend not only on employee performance but also on employee position in the salary range. Position is determined by expressing the employee's current salary as a percentage of the salary that is the midpoint of the range of salaries for that job. The lower the position in the range (the first quartile is the lowest), the larger the percentage of the merit raise.

An important component of compensation administration is monitoring the number of people in each quartile. Although the percentage of merit increases is greater in the lower quartiles, the absolute size of increases is often larger in the higher quartiles. The more people in the higher quartiles, the larger the budget necessary for merit increases. Therefore, the compensation manager must monitor the line managers, who attempt to get their employees pushed to the top of the ranges in each job as a way to offer more rewards to their employees. The compensation manager ends up playing the role of police officer, especially in a highly centralized operation. Unpleasant as it may be, this role is necessary for budget purposes and to assure equity for all employees in the organization. Employees who perform equally well should not be paid different salaries and given different merit increases.

SUMMARY

Compensation is, without doubt, one of the most important activities for personnel administrators. Compensation includes those rewards—monetary and nonmonetary, direct and indirect—that an organization exchanges for the contributions of its employees—job performance and personal contributions. Direct compensation consists of the basic wage and the incentive wage. Determination of the basic wage includes establishing pay levels, pay structures and ranges, and individual wage rates within the ranges. The basic wage rate often reflects payment for both personal and performance contributions.

Exhibit 10.7   Sample Merit Pay Plan

Performance Rating	Current Position in Salary Range			
	First Quartile	Second Quartile	Third Quartile	Fourth Quartile
Truly outstanding	13–14% increase	11–12% increase	9–10% increase	6–8% increase
Above average	11–12% increase	9–10% increase	7–8% increase	6% increase or less
Good	9–10% increase	7–8% increase	6% increase or less	delay increase
Satisfactory	6– 8% increase	6% increase or less	delay increase	no increase
Unsatisfactory	no increase	no increase	no increase	no increase

An important issue in the determination of individual wage rates is that of merit pay versus cost-of-living increases. Merit pay attempts to recognize individual performance in determining individual wage rates. Cost-of-living increases recognize such personal contributions as staying with the organization and performance contributions. Cost-of-living raises are often determined on the basis of the movement of a national economic index, such as the Consumer Price Index.

Although all the conditions under which merit pay plans are most effective rarely exist in organizations, most organizations use merit plans. Cost-of-living plans are also found in most organizations. Compensation managers, however, are increasingly preferring merit pay plans because of their potential incentive value. That is, merit plans can be effective in motivating performance. But most of the merit pay plans, which essentially are used to determine raises and move individuals in their wage range, are of limited value in motivating performance. This is because possible raises are rather limited, thus limiting the payoffs for performance.

PERSONNEL PROBLEM
What's My Motive?

Select from the following list, in order of importance, the three conditions or inducements that you feel would motivate each individual in the cases below to better performance.

1. The threat of discharge

2. A raise

3. More fringe benefits

4. Less supervision

5. Recognition for achievement

6. More status (for example, title or own office)

7. A group profit-sharing plan

8. An individual incentive plan

9. More participation in managerial decisions

10. Job enlargement (for example, opportunity for creativity or wider range of activities)

11. Personal friendship and guidance

Case A

Bob Baker is office manager for a medium-size firm. He is forty-one, unmarried, and lives in an uptown apartment in New York City. He has been office manager for three years and earns $38,200 per year. He started in the mailroom and has been with the company for nearly twenty years.

Case B

Frank Folley is an automobile insurance investigator. He is fifty-eight years old, widowed, and has three married children. His annual salary is $40,000. He has been with the company for eleven years. Previously, he worked for two other insurance companies as an investigator and as an agent.

Case C

Sue Stoner is purchasing agent for a small machine tool company. She is twenty-seven and started with the company four years ago as a shipping clerk. After one year, she became a material requisition clerk. Last year, she assumed her present position under Tom Garvey, the purchasing agent, who is forty-two years old. Sue is now earning $17,200 per year. She is getting married next month.

KEY CONCEPTS

cafeteria approach
compensable factor
compensation
cost-of-living adjustment
   (COLA)
exempt employee

factor-comparison method
Hay plan
job classification method
job evaluation
nonexempt employee

pay administration practices
pay equity
pay level
point rating method
ranking method

DISCUSSION QUESTIONS

1. What is the employment exchange, and how can it influence an organization's compensation program?

2. What are the components of total compensation? What are the components of a good compensation system?

3. What are the relationships between job evaluation, job analysis, and wage surveys? What are the common methods of job evaluation?

4. What are the constraints on determination of the basic wage?

5. Do you favor employee participation in compensation issues? Which issues and why?

6. Is a system of pay openness or pay secrecy

better for the organization? Are there any conditions influencing your answer? Which ones?

7. What conditions are necessary for a merit pay plan to work? Why do so many organizations have merit pay plans?

8. When should a company have a cost-of-living plan instead of a merit pay plan?

ENDNOTES

1. D. W. Belcher, *Compensation Administration* (Englewood Cliffs, N.J.: Prentice-Hall, 1974), p. 383.

2. E. E. Lawler III, *Pay and Organizational Effectiveness: A Psychological View* (New York: McGraw-Hill, 1971), p. 35.

3. Belcher, p. 85.

4. A. Gouldner, *Patterns of Industrial Bureaucracy* (New York: Free Press, 1954), p. 125.

5. D. P. Schwab and H. G. Heneman III, "Pay: A Road to Motivation and Satisfaction?" p. 20. Reprinted with permission from the January/ February 1974 issue of the *Personnel Administrator*, copyright 1974, The American Society for Personnel Administration, 30 Park Drive, Berea, OH 44017.

6. H. M. Meyer, "The Pay-for-Performance Dilemma," *Organizational Dynamics*, Winter 1975, (New York: AMACOM, a division of American Management Associations, 1975), p. 40.

7. L. Dyer, D. P. Schwab, and J. A. Fossum, "Impacts of Pay on Employee Behaviors and Attitudes: An Update," p. 56. Reprinted with permission from the January 1978 issue of the *Personnel Administrator*, copyright 1978, The American Society for Personnel Administration, 30 Park Drive, Berea, OH 44017.

8. Dyer, Schwab, and Fossum, p. 56.

9. W. F. Whyte (ed.), *Money and Motivation: An Analysis of Incentives in Industry* (New York: Harper & Row, 1955).

10. Belcher, p. 175.

11. J. D. Dunn and F. M. Rachel, *Wage and Salary Administration: Total Compensation Systems,* p. 175. Copyright © 1971 by McGraw-Hill Book Company. Reprinted with permission.

12. Dunn and Rachel, p. 177.

13. Dunn and Rachel, p. 192.

14. W. G. Hoke, "Equity for Exempt Personnel," *Personnel Administrator*, July 1976, pp. 41–46.

15. A. N. Nash and S. J. Carroll Jr., *The Management of Compensation* (Monterey, Calif.: Brooks/Cole, 1975), p. 20.

16. H. D. Janes, "Union Views on Job Evaluation: 1971 vs. 1978," *Personnel Journal*, February 1979, pp. 80–85.

17. B. Shiskin, "Job Evaluation: What It Is and How It Works," *American Federationist*, July 1947, pp. 8, 9, 30, 31.
    B. Shiskin, "Job Evaluation: What It Means to Unionists," *American Federationist*, August 1947, pp. 20–22.
    B. Shiskin, "Job Evaluation: What Unions Should Do About It," *American Federationist*, September 1947, pp. 22–23.

18. R. S. Stockton, *Wages, Policies and Wage Surveys* (Columbus, Ohio: Bureau of Business Research, Ohio State University, 1959).

19. "Fewer Firms Grant Whitecollar COLAs," *Industry Week*, August 21, 1978, p. 18.

20. E. E. Lawler III, "Workers Can Set Their Own Wages—Responsibly," *Psychology Today*, February 1977, pp. 109–112.

21. W. G. Lewellen and H. P. Lanser, "Executive Pay Preferences," *Harvard Business Review*, September/October 1973, p. 115–123.

22. Lawler, 1977, p. 110.

23. E. E. Lawler III, "Managers' Perceptions of Their Subordinates' Pay and of Their Supervisors' Pay," *Personnel Psychology*, no. 18 (1965), pp. 413–422.

24. "Fewer Firms Grant Whitecollar COLAs," pp. 17–19.

25. S. W. Gellerman, *Management by Motivation* (New York: American Management Association, 1968).

26. Belcher, p. 297.

CHAPTER OUTLINE

OBJECTIVES

- To explain the purposes of incentive pay plans

- To discuss several plans within each of the three types of incentive plans

- To explain the problems in the administration of incentive pay plans

- To explain how to evaluate the effectiveness of incentive pay plans

THOUGHT STARTERS

- How many organizations use incentive pay plans?

- Would you prefer to work under an incentive or nonincentive plan?

- Are incentive plans applied only to profit-oriented organizations?

- What do employees think of incentive pay plans?

CHAPTER ELEVEN
Incentive Compensation Systems

Often there seems to be an undercurrent of surprise when these kinds of things surface—as if a stupidity assumption really is operating. Note yet another recent exchange:

"How," one supervisor wanted to know, "do you motivate a man who doesn't want money?" Of course I asked, "What makes you think he doesn't want money?" The answer came quickly back, "Because he could make a lot more of it than he does, but he won't do it." He then elaborated by saying that this man was so good on his machine that he could make 150 percent on incentive instead of the 115 percent he was averaging.

My next question was almost as obvious. "If," I said, "he started regularly making 150 percent, how long would you let him do that?" I was not prepared for what happened next. The entire group burst out laughing.

In retrospect it is clear enough what they thought was funny. Even to these quite low-level bosses, it was immediately evident that a consistent 150 percent incentive payment would be seen by the company as a "bad bargain"—to be forthwith worked out differently. It is not, then, worth particular note that they evidently did not see a similar "bad bargain" for the worker who vigorously increases his output only to lose much of what he thought he would gain?

Excerpt from H. R. Smith, "Brother to the Ox," Management Review, *November 1975 (New York: AMACOM, a division of American Management Associations, 1975), p. 6.*

T he questions from the supervisor in this situation illustrate several important points about the behavior of people in organizations. They also illustrate common assumptions about people's motivations to make money. The supervisor believes that because the employee is not working hard to earn more, he does not want money. What the supervisor fails to realize is the conflict that the reward system creates for the employee. The employee perceives that although he may earn a large incentive rate in the short run, in the long run he may be out a job. This is known as short-run reward and long-run punishment. There are also many conflicts and problems for the organization in establishing and administering an incentive system.

But incentive systems can work. They can increase the efficiency and profitability of organizations and the take-home pay and satisfaction of individuals far beyond that provided by nonincentive pay systems. This chapter examines the uses and purposes of incentive systems along with the types of incentive plans and the problems, issues, constraints, and results associated with them.

INCENTIVE PAY PLANS

Although there are many types of incentive pay plans, they all link rewards with performance. Performance is often, but not always, measured by standards of productivity and direct indexes of individuals, groups, or organizations. By contrast, merit pay plans generally use less direct measures of performance, such as rankings or ratings made by supervisors. Another aspect of many incentive pay plans is that the major portion of an individual's compensation is from **incentive pay**. Since the level of compensation varies with performance, the level of an individual's compensation can vary greatly. Merit pay plans, on the other hand, affect a relatively small percentage of an individual's total salary, because **merit pay** is generally used only to move an individual's compensation within a rate range (and this adjustment is made only once a year). Traditionally, incentive pay plans have used only money as a reward. More recently, such nonmonetary rewards as praise, participation, and feedback are also being tied to performance.

To sum up: **Incentive pay plans** are methods of monetary and nonmonetary compensation related to direct indexes of performance for the individual, group, or organization and generally represent a substantial proportion of an individual's direct compensation, but they must be administered within legal regulations.

Purposes and Importance of Incentive Pay Plans

Incentive pay plans can serve several purposes for both the organization and the employee. Incentive pay plans can result in higher earnings for employees and more perceived equity in the compensation system, since pay is tied to performance. These in turn can result in increased satisfaction with pay and a higher motivation to perform. The organization benefits because several of the purposes of compensation (mentioned in the early part of Chapter 10) are served by incentive pay plans. Namely, organizations are more likely to motivate their employees to perform and more likely to retain good employees.[1] Since satisfaction with pay can increase under incentive pay plans, employee absenteeism may decrease. As a result, organizations can realize substantial increases in productivity and greatly diminished costs while maintaining acceptable levels of quality.

Incentive pay plans are not cure-alls for organizational ills, however. They may provide several benefits to the organization, but they may also lead to increased employee earnings with no increase in performance. They may also increase costs and cause numerous employee relations problems.[2]

A SLICE OF LIFE

The relationship between the amount of pay people receive and their attendance at work presents an interesting problem. Presumably, the more pay people receive, the less likely they are to quit the organization. Indeed, research done in this area supports this conjecture. Absenteeism, however, is a somewhat more complex phenomenon.

Does more money lead to more or less absenteeism? For example, as income increases (as a function of basic wage increases, incentive pay, and the like), an employee may be able to "buy" leisure by being absent. This is often referred to as the substitution effect. Simply put, the employee can afford to be absent. Conversely, it could be argued that as employee income (especially incentive income) increases, absenteeism is less likely. This phenomenon is normally referred to as the income effect. In this case, absenteeism is relatively expensive, because the employee must forego a relatively large amount of money to be absent.

Of course, the existence of the substitution effect or income effect among a given group of employees may depend on other factors as well. Be aware, however, that increasing employee wages through incentives or basic wage increases does not necessarily lead to less absenteeism. As a practical note, how often have you heard of a person who works overtime for a few days and then takes the rest of the week off?

Prevalence of Incentive Pay Plans

In the United States, most incentive plans are either piecework or standard hour plans, although small-group plans and plantwide incentives are increasingly being used. Yet fewer than 15 percent of the work force is paid under an incentive plan. A survey by the U.S. Bureau of Labor Statistics showed that only about 20 percent of plant employees in manufacturing worked under incentive plans.[3] In most other industries, the percentage is smaller; it is almost zero for office employees. There is a great deal of variation in these percentages, however—by type of industry and area of the country. For example, over 60 percent of the employees in the textile, clothing, cigar, and steel industries are covered by incentive plans, but fewer than 10 percent are covered in the aircraft, bakery, beverage, chemical, and lumber industries. In addition, almost no public employees are paid under an incentive plan. "In some cities in the Northeast and North Central areas, from 35 to 40 percent of plant employees work under incentive plans; in the South some cities range from 20 to 25 percent; and on the West Coast the percentage is less than ten."[4] In general, it is more likely that incentive plans will be used if labor costs are large, the market is cost-competitive, technology is not advanced, and an employee's output is relatively independent of another employee's.[5]

TYPES OF INCENTIVE PLANS

There are numerous types of incentive plans. The easiest way to discuss them is by the level at which they are applied—individual, group, or organization. Each type of plan is generally unique to a specific level. Regardless of the level at which a plan is implemented, the intended beneficiaries are always the organization and the individuals covered by the plan.

The performance measure used to determine incentive pay varies by level. As the level goes from the individual to the organization, the relationship between pay and an individual's performance diminishes greatly and thus motivation to perform also diminishes. This is one reason why individual-level incentive plans are more common than group or organizational plans. However, group or organizational plans do reduce the need to measure the performance of each worker. The determination of which performance measure to use, regardless of level, is often a crucial ingredient in making the incentive plan a success or failure.

Individual-Level Incentive Plans

Most incentive plans are based on the performance of individuals. They represent "an effort to reward the employee more effectively for his efforts and services rendered to the firm by developing an incentive compensation system which brings into homogeneous focus the objectives of management and the employee."[6] Traditionally, this purpose was attained by using incentive plans accompanied by changes in work methods. Industrial engineers organized the tasks more systematically and efficiently, and the employees were more motivated to perform because of the incentives. The industrial engineers also helped to establish rates and standard times for the determination of incentive pay. The engineers had several methods for determining the best ways of doing the tasks as well as the rates and standard times. One of the more popular methods is referred to as time-and-motion studies (see Chapter 4). One of the most popular individual-level incentive plans using the time standards established by industrial engineers is the piecework plan.

The Piecework Plan.   Piecework is the most common type of incentive pay plan. Under this plan, employees are guaranteed a standard pay rate for each unit of output. The pay rate per unit is frequently determined by the time-and-motion studies and the current base pay of the job. For example, if the base pay of a job is $20 per day and the employee can produce at a normal rate twenty units a day, the piece rate may be established at $1 per unit. Thus the incentive pay rate is based on the standard output and the base wage rate. The "normal" rate obviously is more than what the time-and-motion studies indicate. However, it is supposed to represent 100-percent efficiency. The final rate also reflects the bargaining power of the employees, economic conditions of the organization and community, and what the competition is paying.

Although piecework plans imply a direct relationship between pay and output, in practice many piecework plans have a guarantee. For example, using the rate of $1 per unit, employees may be guaranteed $20 a day even if they do not make twenty units. But for production in excess of twenty units, employees would receive the $1 rate times the number of units produced. For eighteen units employees would be paid $20, but for twenty-five units they would be paid $25. In either case, however, employees can make more money under the incentive rate by working harder or at least by producing more than the normal rate, which may be attained by working smarter, not harder.

The advantages of the piecework plan are its simplicity of calculation, understandability, and incentive value. Employees can benefit from increased wages. Companies can benefit from increased productivity and constant labor costs. The primary disadvantages stem from the fact that standards are expressed in monetary terms. As a result, any change in wage rates or standards implies a change in the piece rates, and there is often much resistance to changing the piece rate. A minor disadvantage results from the desire for equity. Equity demands that every employee receive rewards in proportion to his or her contributions. But in piecework plans only an employee's performance contribution is rewarded. There is no provision for rewarding such contributions as seniority, cooperation, or experience. Thus employees are not treated equitably on those contributions.

Measured Day Work. An individual-level incentive plan that removes some of the relationship between rates and standards is measured day work. Again, formal production standards are established, and employee performance is judged against these standards. But with measured day work, the typical standards are less precise. For example, standards may be determined by the results of a rating or ranking procedure rather than by an objective index such as units produced. On the basis of these performance results, employees are placed into pay categories and are paid that rate until the next review. Employee performance is reviewed much more frequently than in the merit pay system, and pay rates can be adjusted up or down after each review. However, the connection between actual productivity and pay rates is much less than under the piecework plan.

As a result of the diminished relationship between pay and performance, measured day work has several disadvantages: limited incentive value; failure to reflect sufficiently differences in performance, which may discourage high performance; and less motivation for management to maintain correct standards. However, employees can easily understand this plan, better performers are still paid more than poor performers, and effective supervision is encouraged because more frequent performance reviews are necessary.[7]

The Standard Hour Plan. This plan is the second most-used incentive plan. It is essentially a piecework plan, except that standards are denominated in time per unit of output rather than money per unit of output.[8] Tasks are broken down by the amount of time it takes to complete them. This can be determined by historical records, time-and-motion studies, or a combination of both. The time to perform each task then becomes a "standard time."

Earnings under this plan can be determined in two ways. First, the employee can work against the standard time. The less time it takes to do the task, the more the incentive pay. Second, the amount of incentive pay can be calculated as a percentage of efficiency.

In the first arrangement, the worker is paid at his base rate for time taken and time saved. In the second, standard time divided by actual time yields an efficiency percentage. Multiplying the efficiency percentage by the base rate yields earnings for the job.[9]

The advantages of the standard hour plan are the same as those of the piecework plan. In addition, the standards are made in time units rather than monetary units. Thus it is easier to change the standard than when the standards and rates are inseparable, as in piecework. The disadvantages of the plan are the same as those of the piecework plan. Although both piecework and standard hour plans do have important differences, they both work best when the work is standardized, repetitive, measurable, and not subject to frequent change.

Sales Incentive Plans.   All the incentive plans discussed thus far share an important characteristic: They are usually applied to blue-collar employees and in some cases office employees. This is not to say that other employees do not participate in incentive programs with similar characteristics or incentive values. To the contrary, there are many managerial employees and salespeople who participate in incentive plans that have rather large incentive values. Incentive plans for salespeople are referred to as commissions.

About two-thirds of all salespeople are paid a salary plus commission.[10] In real estate sales, however, almost 75 percent of the people are paid straight commissions; straight commissions are paid to only 22 percent of all salespeople. As with the individual incentive plans for blue-collar and office employees, very few salespeople (11 percent) work without some guaranteed minimum pay.[11]

Although salespeople may prefer the incentive value of commissions (which varies with the size of the commission and the ability of the salesperson to influence sales), there is often a high turnover rate of people on straight commission. In addition, regardless of commission type, "customers are alienated by the 'hard sell' approach, accounts are inadequately serviced, insufficient time is allocated to non-selling activities and long-run sales considerations are neglected."[12] On the assumption that most people do not react favorably to the "hard-sell" approach, a large Midwestern retail jewelry company decided to pay its employees a salary rather than the traditional commission. The results were a sales force that did not use the hard sell and total sales and profits that increased at a rate above the industry average. This does not suggest that organizations paying commission would be better off paying only salaries. It does illustrate, however, the importance of the method of compensation and the need to examine its effect on the organization. Using a method of compensation because other companies use it does not always produce the best results.

Managerial Incentive Plans.   Incentive plans for managers generally take the form of cash bonuses for good performance of the department, division, or organization as a whole.

> *The trouble with incentive pay, as many companies have discovered, is that if the performance of an executive skyrockets beyond all expectations, so does his compensation. Thus Suave Shoe Corp., a Miami importer and manufacturer of footwear with sales last year of $67.5 million, rather shamefacedly admitted in a proxy statement last month that a senior vice-president whose salary is $33,000 annually earned an additional $438,290 bonus last year, and that his bonus this year may be even larger.*
>
> *The officer so rewarded is Robustiano Puga, general manager of Suave's manufacturing division, which accounts for about half of the company's sales and, before Puga arrived, for the lion's share of some hefty corporate losses. Suave, founded in 1961 by Chairman David Egozi, a Cuban refugee, went from a loss of $830,000 on sales of $69.8 million in fiscal 1973 to a profit of $3.1 million on revenues of $67.5 million last year.*[13]

In order to receive such a large bonus, Puga struck up a deal under which he would receive 10 percent of pretax earnings between $1.1 million and $1.5 million, 15 percent of earnings between $1.5 million and $2 million, and 20 percent of anything in excess of $2 million.

This example illustrates the potential size of managerial bonuses and how they can be determined. Not all managers, however, are able to participate in such lucrative incentive plans. In fact, plans of this size are usually applied only to top-level managers and executives. Managers of public organizations generally do not participate in any bonus plans. First-line supervisors and middle-level managers in private organizations may participate in bonus plans, but the potential size of their bonus is usually a much smaller percentage of their salary than for top-level managers.

Other forms of compensation that can be used as managerial incentives are stock options and performance shares. A **stock option** is an opportunity for a manager to buy stocks of the organization at a later date but at a price established when the option is granted. The idea is that managers will work harder to increase their performance and the profitability of the company (thus increasing the price of the company's stock) if they can share in the profits over the long run. If the market price of the stock increases over time, managers can use their options to buy the stock at a lower price and to realize financial gain.

Performance shares provide a very close connection between individual performance (as reflected in company profitability) and rewards. This is because the manager or executive is rewarded only if established goals are met. The goals are usually stated in earnings per share (EPS). Furthermore, if the EPS goal is met, the manager receives shares of stock directly. Usually the manager receives cash (called bonus units) as well as stock in order to pay taxes on the equity (stock) reward. Receipt of just the shares, however, can result in a substantial reward.

*The **Suggestion System***. This form of incentive compensation, which rewards employees for money-saving or money-producing suggestions, is important because it is used so extensively. The 1,000 members of the National Association of Suggestion Systems (NASS) realized aggregate savings from useful suggestions of $470 million in 1975 alone.[14] The organizations belonging to NASS represent only a fraction of the organizations using suggestion systems. The average award per suggestion in 1973 was $78.65, and for every dollar spent to run these systems, companies saved approximately $5.70.[15] The total value of these awards can really add up quickly. In 1969 alone, General Motors paid out $17 million in awards for suggestions.

Nevertheless, suggestion systems generally do not have a very favorable reputation, often because individual awards are too small. Also, employees sometimes never learn the results of their suggestions, and companies often save much more than the individual receives. Occasionally, an individual's suggestion is at first discarded but is then put in operation by management later—with no reward to the employee. This increases hostility, resentment, and distrust between management and nonmanagement. In turn, the use of the suggestion system, particularly the suggestion box, may become an object of ridicule and games.

Although most suggestion systems are designed to elicit and reward individuals' suggestions, some systems are designed for groups of employees. Such a system is part of the Scanlon plan, which is discussed in the section on plant incentives.

The suggestion system is unique in that it is an incentive system to increase the number of good ideas rather than the output of products. Yet it is similar to other plans in that the rewards are monetary.

*The **Positive Reinforcement System***. The **positive reinforcement system** lets employees know how well they are meeting specific goals and rewards improvements with praise and recognition. In this it is a unique incentive system.

To establish a positive reinforcement program, the employer must define the behavioral requirements of the work to be done and evaluate how well it is being done. Job performance goals must be formulated in measurable terms, such as the meeting of deadlines, quality levels, and volume. Once these are established, employees must be provided with timely data on their goal performance.[16]

One of the basic premises of positive reinforcement is that behavior such as performance or absenteeism can be understood and modified by its consequences. Of course, all incentive systems are based on this premise. That is, performance (or any behavior) is elicited because of the consequence of getting rewards. In many organizations, the consequences of behaving well are not monetary.

By recording the attendance of a group of employees on a weekly rather than monthly basis, a Michigan Bell Telephone positive reinforcement program reduced absenteeism significantly. "Within six weeks the absenteeism rate in the pilot group dropped from 11% to 6.5%."[17] The change reduced absenteeism because previously employees who were absent early in the month would forfeit their chances for recognition for the whole month. With the weekly system, employees who missed a day in the first week still had a chance for recognition in the second week.

In addition to being a form of compensation for increasing performance, reinforcement systems are also used in training and development. This use of reinforcement is examined in Chapter 13.

Group-Level Incentive Plans

As organizations become more complex, a growing number of jobs become interdependent with other jobs in either of two senses. Some jobs are part of a sequence of operations so that performance on jobs that precede them and follow them affect their performance. Other jobs require joint efforts to achieve results.[18]

In either case, measurement of individual performance is difficult at best and often impossible. Individual-level incentives are not appropriate under these conditions because they fail to reward cooperation. Group-level incentives can do this. Thus individual-level incentive plans may become less common if changing technologies make jobs even more interdependent and individual performance more difficult to measure.[19] However, most group-level incentive plans are adaptations of individual incentive plans. The standard hour and sharing plans are frequently used, but in group applications, base rates are paid for a group standard output and group performance above this standard determines the premium for the individuals in the group.

For group-level incentive systems to effectively motivate performance, they should have an objective measure of performance for the group. The individuals in the group must believe that they can affect the measure by their performance. Also, the system must be perceived as rewarding cooperation as well as group performance.

The success of group incentives depends on group size, stability, and the extent of cooperation needed. Group incentives can encourage cooperation. Stability and small size help build cohesiveness and enhance the relationship between individual effort and group reward. But the relationship between individual performance and reward are far from perfect. In many group projects, some people do much more work than other group members, and yet they all receive the same reward. This may be one of the reasons why group incentive systems are not used very extensively (fewer than 5 percent of the work force is paid this way). Another reason is the possibility of intergroup friction. Groups may restrict output, sabotage the production of other groups, and attempt to gain at the expense of other groups. Thus if intergroup cooperation is necessary, and in many organizations it is, group incentive systems can be detrimental to the organization as well as to each group. As a result, organizations use plantwide or organizational-level incentive systems.

Organization-Level Incentive Plans

Many organizations need high levels of cooperation among their employees and so provide some form of incentive on an organizationwide basis. Approximately 7 percent of the firms in the United States have either plantwide bonus plans or profit-sharing arrangements.[20] The bonus is typically a percentage of the base wage rate of the employee if the organization reaches some goal. Employees receiving the same base wage or salary rate therefore receive the same incentive. Profit-sharing plans are often not considered a form of incentive compensation because individual employees have only partial and indirect control over organizational profits. However, since the extent of employee control over performance in a profit-sharing plan is a matter of degree rather than kind, profit-sharing plans are included here as an organization-level incentive.

The Scanlon Plan.   The Scanlon plan represents as much a philosophy of management-employee relations as it does a companywide incentive system. It emphasizes employer-employee participation and sharing in the operations and profitability of the company. The plan is used in union as well as nonunion plants.

The **Scanlon plan** reflects the fact that efficiency of operations depends on companywide cooperation and that bonus incentives encourage cooperation. The bonus is determined on the basis of savings in labor costs, which are measured by comparing the payroll to the sales value of production on a monthly or bimonthly basis. Previous months' ratios help establish expected payroll costs for future months. The difference between actual costs and expected costs is shared by employees (75 percent) and employer (25 percent). Because all employees share in the savings, one group does not gain at the expense of another. Each employee's bonus is determined by converting the bonus fund to a percentage of the total payroll and applying this percentage to the employee's pay for the month.

A main ingredient in labor cost savings is increased efficiencies from employee suggestions. Thus the number and quality of employee suggestions are vital to the success of the plan. A production committee from each work group or department, composed of the supervisor and elected employee representatives, evaluates the suggestions initially.

The Scanlon plan has several beneficial results:
- Employee willingness to provide large numbers of useful, cost-saving ideas
- Employee willingness to accept technological change and to make new equipment and methods work
- A better work pace and a work climate hostile to loafing
- Greater interest in quality
- Greater willingness of workers to help one another and to share knowledge of shortcuts
- More flexible administration of seniority clauses in promotion, transfer, and recall to aid efficiency
- Less overtime
- Employee insistence on efficient management
- Greater awareness on the part of employees of company sales problems and problems of meeting competition
- More realistic contract negotiations
- Fewer grievances
- Productivity increases of 60 percent have been reported, as well as increases in employee earnings of over 50 percent.[21]

The MERIT Incentive Plan.   Most of the incentive plans presented thus far have been applied in profit organizations, but the MERIT plan can work without the profit incentive. (The Scanlon plan can also be applied to nonprofit organizations.) MERIT stands for Memorial Employees Retirement Incentive Trust. The size of the incentive is based on savings in budgeted expenses. The incentives are put into a trust, and employees may withdraw the entire sum at retirement or draw an annuity.

MERIT is based on these five steps:

1. Base performance years and a standard efficiency percentage are established. The standard efficiency percentage is the controllable expenses divided by total operating revenue in the base period.
2. Current year efficiency percentage is determined in the same manner and is subtracted from the performance base percentage. This deviation is limited to 5 percent maximum and cannot turn negative. It is called the efficiency improvement percentage.
3. The employer's contribution involves applying the efficiency improvement percentage to the current period's payroll. This total cannot exceed one-half of the total operating profit or be less than 1 percent of the current payroll.
4. The final contribution amount is limited to 15 percent of the figure calculated in the preceding step—considering the limitations.
5. The contribution to individual employees is determined by the ratio of their earnings to the total earnings of all participants. [22]

Profit-Sharing Plans. Profit-sharing plans are the most prevalent type of organization-level incentive system, possibly because they are the easiest to administer. Most of the previously discussed organization-level incentive plans include some aspect of profit sharing. In fact, Joseph Scanlon called the Scanlon plan a profit-sharing plan. However, the Scanlon plan is more appropriately called a cost-savings sharing plan because it pays off regardless of whether the organization makes a profit. Profit-sharing plans pay off only when the organization makes a profit. Thus there may be times when employees work harder and smarter but receive no increase in rewards—because the economy is slow and sales and profits are down. The result is a smaller relationship between individual performance and pay.

Profit sharing is "any method of raising output and lowering costs through human cooperation which is brought about through sharing (in addition to their regular wage) in the total results of the enterprise as measured by profits." [23] The objectives of profit sharing plans are to instill a sense of partnership, to serve as a group incentive, to provide employee security, to be fair, to provide benefits beyond basic wages without incurring fixed commitments, to attract desirable employees and reduce turnover, and to encourage employee thrift.

All profit-sharing plans must be approved by the Internal Revenue Service to comply with current tax laws. There are two major types of profit-sharing plans that organizations can use. **Cash plans** provide for payment of profit shares at regular intervals, typically ranging from monthly to yearly. The percentage of profits distributed ranges from 8 to 75 percent. [24] If profits are not realized by the company, no cash payments are made to employees. Wage-dividend plans (a special type of cash plan) set the percentage of profits paid to employees according to the amount of dividends paid to stockholders. These plans are assumed to increase understanding between employees and stockholders and are often perceived as more fair to employees than regular cash plans.

In **deferred plans** the profits to be shared are put in accounts for each employee (which may also contain contributions from the employees themselves). These accounts release the money on such occasions as retirement, death, disability, layoff, and severance. Deferred plans are becoming a feasible and attractive alternative for companies that want to avoid the administrative complexities of setting up a retirement plan to meet the standards of the Employee Retirement Income Security Act of 1974 (ERISA). Deferment of profit sharing is also good for employees, especially those in high tax brackets, who often have a reduced tax rate later in life.

ADMINISTRATION OF INCENTIVES

There are several problem areas that influence the administration of incentive plans. A general problem is getting employees to be more productive within reasonable cost constraints so that the organization can be more profitable. But this general problem must take into account other aspects of the work environment.

Employee Beliefs

Employee beliefs are a major obstacle in the implementation of an incentive system. A large number of negative beliefs have been reported:
- Incentive plans result in work speedup.
- Rates are cut if earnings under the plan increase too much.
- Incentive plans encourage competition among workers and the discharge of slow workers.
- Incentive plans result in unemployment through "working yourself out of a job."
- Incentive plans break down crafts by reducing skill requirements through methods study.
- Workers don't get their share of increased productivity.
- Incentive plans are too complex.
- Standards are set unfairly.
- Industrial engineers are out to rob workers.
- Earnings fluctuate, making it difficult to budget household expenditures, and even to obtain home mortgages.
- Incentive plans are used to avoid a deserved pay increase.
- Incentive plans increase strain on workers and may impair their health.
- Incentive plans increase the frequency of methods changes.
- Incentive plans ask workers to do more than a fair day's work.
- Incentive plans imply a lack of trust in workers by management.[25]

The last belief, that incentive plans imply a lack of trust in workers by management, pervades most of the other beliefs as well. This lack of trust has immediate implications for the establishment of rates and standards that incentive systems are based on. Workers may play elaborate charades for the benefit of time-study engineers, but these maneuvers do not entirely fool them. They know that workers might try to be misleading but not how much. Thus they plug in estimates of how much they are being fooled, combining scientific observation and measurement with a guessing game.[26] The result may be inaccurate or unfair rates, which reduce the incentive value of the system, the profitability of the company, or both.

The Organizational System and Incentives

"The supervisor-employee relationship is the place to begin working out incentive problems."[27] This relationship, however, is just one of the many relationships involved in incentive problems. For example, the relationship between lower-skilled and higher-skilled employees often becomes strained when lower-skilled employees are on an incentive plan and are making more than higher-skilled employees. The result may be that the higher-skilled workers will prevent the success of the plan for the lower-skilled workers. They may also reduce their own performance.

The relationship between top management and their employees can also affect the success of bonus incentives and performance evaluations. When employees fail to see their performance reflected in the bonus check, the success of the plan is in jeopardy, as shown in this example:

The chief executive of a steel company accomplished his review of proposed bonus payments for 200 executives in just under two hours. His only criterion for changing recommended individual bonuses (which he did in perhaps 30 or 40 cases) was what he thought of the executive involved. He had no written evidence of the man's performance during the previous year—just the retained image of past impressions. Needless to say, executives in this company had long since recognized how little top-level attention their efforts received, and the "incentive" program had serious problems.[28]

These examples illustrate the necessity of viewing any incentive system in terms of the organization as a larger system.

A SLICE OF LIFE

In recent years, a very large West Coast public utility has faced a very distressing problem regarding overtime and other special benefits. Over the years, the base pay for employees was approximately $20,000 a year. However, because of the special expertise of some of these people, they were often called on to work overtime. Aside from overtime pay, these people received a variety of additional incentives, like meal and travel allowances. Incidentally, hundreds of individuals were affected, and they regularly earned not $20,000, but up to $34,000 a year. At this rate, base-level employees made about 15 percent more than top-paid craft employees, who made around $23,000 per year because they were salaried people who could receive no overtime allowances.

Aside from the obvious problem of having low-level employees making a great deal more money than their supervisors, another more serious problem was soon evident: Virtually none of the most qualified people would take a promotion. Very few of us would take a "promotion" with an implicit $10,000 per year decrease in pay.

Incentive programs often have similar drawbacks. Certainly, some people fare exceedingly well under most incentive programs. But if people can earn more by staying where they are, where can an organization find outstanding talent for promotion?

The Value of Incentive Pay Plans

Regardless of organizational conditions and constraints, incentive plans can be measured by how well they relate motivation to performance.[29] The three criteria for judging incentive plans are (1) the relationship between performance and pay—that is, the time between performance and the administration of the pay (actual and as perceived by employees); (2) how well the incentive plan minimizes the perceived negative consequences of good performance, such as social ostracism; and (3) whether it contributes to the perception that rewards other than pay (such as cooperation and recognition) stem from good performance. A plan's incentive value increases the more closely it ties pay to performance, the more it minimizes the perceived negative consequences, and the more it contributes to the perception that other good rewards are also tied to performance. Exhibit 11.1 presents an evaluation of individual, group, and organizational incentive plans based on these three criteria.

Four objective measures used to determine the level of performance to be rewarded are sales, units made, cost effectiveness, and savings below budget; subjective measures include things like traditional supervisor ratings. The more objective measures generally have higher credibility, are more valid, and are more visible and verifiable than the subjective measures. As shown in Exhibit 11.1, the objective measures (productivity and cost effectiveness) are more likely to link pay to performance than they are to minimize negative side effects. This evaluation is based on the notion that people do what's rewarded. More objective measures tend to make

Exhibit 11.1   Effectiveness of Incentive Plans

	Type of Plan	Performance Measure	Tie Pay to Perfor- mance	Minimize Negative Side Effects	Tie Other Rewards to Perfor- mance
SALARY REWARD	Individual plan	Productivity	+2	0	0
		Cost effectiveness	+1	0	0
		Superiors' rating	+1	0	+1
	Group	Productivity	+1	0	+1
		Cost effectiveness	+1	0	+1
		Superiors' rating	+1	0	+1
	Organizationwide	Productivity	+1	0	+1
		Cost effectiveness	+1	0	+1
		Profit	0	0	+1
BONUS	Individual plan	Productivity	+3	−2	0
		Cost effectiveness	+2	−1	0
		Superiors' rating	+2	−1	+1
	Group	Productivity	+2	0	+1
		Cost effectiveness	+2	0	+1
		Superiors' rating	+2	0	+1
	Organizationwide	Productivity	+2	0	+1
		Cost effectiveness	+2	0	+1
		Profit	+1	0	+1

it very clear what's rewarded and what's not. This may produce more keen competition with other workers, result in more social ostracism, and lead workers to perceive that good performance may reduce the work available to them.

The overall evaluation of incentive plans suggests that group and organization-wide incentive plans, although not high in relating individual performance with pay, result in no negative side effects (the exception is with intergroup competition with group-level incentives). These plans are also perceived as tying other rewards to good performance besides pay, such as esteem, respect, and social acceptance from other employees.

In short, if a person feels he can benefit from another's good performance, he is much more likely to encourage his fellow worker to perform well than if he will not benefit, and might even be harmed.[30]

Among the three levels of incentive pay plans there are no clear winners by all criteria. Any one of the plans, however, has more incentive value than stock-option plans, seniority increases, across-the-board raises, and even merit pay plans. Thus the situation for motivating performance with pay is not hopeless. But remember that these evaluations disregard the problems, conditions, and constraints in administration. Therefore, it may be imprudent to conclude that more organizations should adopt incentive pay plans. This is true even though examples can be cited showing that after only three months of operation, an individual incentive plan resulted in a 14 percent decrease in unit labor costs, a 29 percent increase in production, and a 15 percent increase in wages. Many other successfully administered incentive pay plans can be found, but so can many unsuccessfully administered ones.

One of the major factors influencing success is employee participation in the plan. The more participation at more stages in the plan, the better. That is one main reason why the Scanlon plans often perform better than imposed group and companywide incentive plans and even the individual incentive plans designed and controlled by the organization. If the use of incentive pay plans in organizations increases in the future, it will most likely be due largely to the adoption of Scanlon-type plans.

SUMMARY

Although incentive compensation plans are used in relatively few organizations, they continue to attract the attention of many personnel managers, and line managers continue to ask whether pay can be used as a motivator with their employees. And yet their experiences with nonincentive plans, such as merit pay, convince them that pay cannot motivate. The success of many incentive plans indicates, however, that pay can motivate performance, although there can of course be many problems.

Implementation of incentive pay plans requires an effective performance appraisal program. The more objective the measures of performance, the more value incentive plans have. But many organizations do not have effective appraisal programs. As a result, pay is not based on performance (even though some people may actually be doing more work than others) but rather on nonperformance factors, such as the cost of living or seniority. To retain some appearance of rewarding performance, some organizations may use merit pay plans. Consequently, most organizations do not or are not able to provide the full incentive value of pay. Nevertheless, a few organizations are attempting to change the incentive plans, generally organization-wide plans that allow a great deal of employee participation in implementation and administration. The future for this type of plan looks much more promising than for any other type of incentive plan because of its wider applicability.

Even when organizations adopt some type of incentive plan, they still need to provide employees with indirect compensation, such as pension and retirement benefits, holidays, and other benefits related only to organization membership.

PERSONNEL PROBLEM
Do You Reap What You Sow?

"You set the standards, so how can you fire her?" asked the union steward vehemently.

"She's a problem, and you know it," countered the plant manager. "She's late half the time and makes up for it by leaving early. She has as bad an attitude as I've ever seen, and nobody on the line likes her."

"I think perhaps you miss my point," said the steward. "Within the last few months you have introduced an incentive system. Anyone who produces more than eight units with less than a 2 percent return rate, at a unit cost of under 71 cents, is supposed to receive incentive pay."

"So what's your point?"

"Presumably, anyone who meets the standards meets your minimum expectations for performance, and the lady you are trying to fire has averaged twelve units with virtually no returns at 63 cents a unit. Based on that, you can't fire her."

1. Does the steward have a valid point?

2. When an incentive standard is set, does it automatically include a minimum performance standard?

3. Organizations presumably offer incentives in areas crucial to their operations. If a person meets those crucial standards, how important are matters of behavior?

4. Must high-performance employees abide by the same rules as average employees?

KEY CONCEPTS

cash plan
deferred plan
incentive pay
incentive pay plan

managerial incentive plan
merit pay
performance share
positive reinforcement system

Scanlon plan
stock option
suggestion system

DISCUSSION QUESTIONS

1. How do incentive pay plans differ from nonincentive and even merit pay plans?
2. What are the common managerial incentive pay plans?
3. How can nonmonetary rewards be used to increase performance? Explain the application of reinforcement principles.
4. What is the Scanlon plan? Why is the plan so effective?
5. How can nonprofit organizations apply an incentive pay plan? Could school teachers be paid by an incentive plan? Explain.

6. What are some important employee beliefs that can influence the administration of incentives?
7. What are some organizational factors influencing the effectiveness of incentive pay plans? How many organizations have factors favoring incentive plans?
8. How can incentive pay plans be evaluated? On the basis of one type of evaluation plan, what incentive plans have the most value?

ENDNOTES

1. E. E. Lawler III., *Pay and Organizational Effectiveness: A Psychological View* (New York: McGraw-Hill, 1971).

2. S. H. Slichter, J. J. Healy, and E. R. Livernash, *The Impact of Collective Bargaining on Management* (Washington D.C.: The Brookings Institution, 1960).

3. D. W. Belcher, *Compensation Administration* (Englewood Cliffs, N.J.: Prentice-Hall, 1974), p. 401.

4. Slichter, Healy, and Livernash, p. 301.

5. R. B. McKersie, C. F. Miller Jr., and W. E. Quarterman, "Some Indicators of Incentive Plan Prevalence," *Monthly Labor Review,* March 1964, pp. 271–276.

6. J. D. Dunn and F. M. Rachel, *Wage and Salary Administration: Total Compensation Systems* (New York: McGraw-Hill, 1971), p. 236.

7. Belcher, p. 312.

8. Dunn and Rachel, p. 247.

9. D. W. Belcher, *Compensation Administration,* © 1974 Prentice-Hall, p. 317.

10. *Incentive Plans for Salesmen*, Studies in Personnel Policy 217 (New York: National Industrial Conference Board, 1970).

11. *Compensating Field Sales Representatives,* Studies in Personnel Policy 202 (New York: National Industrial Conference Board, 1966).

12. A. N. Nash and S. J. Carroll, Jr., *The Management of Compensation* (Monterey, Calif: Brooks/Cole, 1975), p. 198.

13. "This Bonus Is a Real Incentive," p. 54. Reprinted from the March 14, 1977 issue of *Business Week* © 1977 by McGraw-Hill, Inc., 1221 Avenue of the Americas, New York, N.Y. 10020. All rights reserved.

14. M. A. Tather, "Turning Ideas into Gold," *Management Review*, March 1975, pp. 4–10.

15. V. G. Reuter, "A New Look at Suggestion Systems," *Journal of Systems Management,* January 1976, pp. 6–15.

16. W. J. Kearney, "Pay for Performance? Not Always," p. 6, *MSU Business Topics,* Spring 1979. Reprinted by permission of the publisher, Division of Research, Graduate School of Business Administration, Michigan State University.

17. "Where Skinner's Theories Work," *Business Week*, December 2, 1972, p. 64.

18. Belcher, pp. 323–324.

19. Belcher, p. 325.

20. J. Corina, *Forms of Wage and Salary Payment for High Productivity* (Paris: Organization for Economic Cooperation and Development, 1970).

21. R. W. Davenport, "Enterprise for Everyman," *Fortune*, January 1950, pp. 55–59, 152, 157–159.

22. Dunn and Rachel, p. 257. *Wage and Salary Administration: Total Compensation Systems,* p. 257. Copyright © 1971 by McGraw-Hill Book Company. Reprinted with permission.

23. B. L. Metzger, *Profit Sharing in Perspective,* 2nd ed. (Evanston, Ill.: Profit Sharing Research Foundation, 1966), p. vi.

24. Metzger, p. 45.

25. S. Barkin, "Labor's Attitude Toward Wage Incentive Plans," *Industrial and Labor Relations Review,* July 1948, pp. 553–572.

26. W. F. Whyte, "Skinnerian Theory in Organizations," *Psychology Today*, April 1972, pp. 67, 68, 96, 98, 100.

27. G. Strauss and L. R. Sayles, *Personnel: The Human Problems of Management*, 4th ed. (Englewood Cliffs, N.J.: Prentice-Hall, 1980), p. 63.

28. Reprinted by permission of the *Harvard Business Review*. Excerpt from "Why Incentive Plans Fail" by Arch Patton (May/June 1972), p. 63. Copyright © 1972 by the President and Fellows of Harvard College; all rights reserved.

29. Lawler, pp. 157–177.

30. Lawler, pp. 166–167.

CHAPTER OUTLINE

OBJECTIVES

- To specify the purposes of indirect compensation

- To describe the three major categories of indirect compensation

- To explain the current state of private and public protection programs

- To discuss how many indirect benefits an organization should provide to its employees

THOUGHT STARTERS

- What is indirect compensation?

- Is there really such a thing as "rugged individualism"?

- Does government intervention into an organization help or hinder the employee?

- If you had your choice, how much of your compensation would you choose as direct and how much as indirect?

CHAPTER TWELVE
Indirect Compensation

The Christmas season always made John Gorman, security director of a Rochester, New York, department store, tense and nervous. Usually he calmed down by January, but in January 1971 his anxiety and depression deepened. When a colleague was fired, Mr. Gorman became more withdrawn.

His twenty-seven year old secretary, Diana Wolfe, was close to him, protected him, and shouldered some of his responsibilities. But this time she was unable to cheer him up. On June 9 Mr. Gorman came to the office as usual. A few minutes later, he telephoned Mrs. Wolfe and told her to send the police to his office one floor away. She did, then rushed there herself. She found him lying dead in a pool of blood, the result of a self-inflicted gunshot wound in the head.

The shock of the experience contributed to a serious depression. Mrs. Wolfe was unable to work. She lost twenty pounds. She spent hours in bed staring at the ceiling, silent and withdrawn. She was hospitalized twice, eventually receiving electroshock therapy which finally eased her depression.

Mrs. Wolfe also left her mark on the field of occupational stress. She recovered after a year but still faced $20,000 worth of hospital bills. Her insurance company would not pay and she was told that Worker Compensation did not cover mental illness in New York State. She went to court, however, and finally, in May 1975, she won: the New York Court of Appeals ordered her hospital bills paid by Worker Compensation, ruling that crippling mental illness is as real in the eyes of the law as physical injuries and illnesses.

From A. McLean, Work Stress, © *1979, Addison-Wesley Publishing Company, Inc., pp. 7–8. Reprinted with permission.*

Willie Brice Worked 24 Years at a Nonunionized Plant: His Pension Is $14.56 Per Month

Adapted from the Cleveland Plain Dealer, *September 17, 1979, p. A-1.*

The new contract has brought the union close to another of its goals—a four-day workweek—by granting an additional 13 paid personal holidays to produce a total which in effect gives the GM worker two months off a year. In the same contract signed between the United Auto Workers and General Motors in 1979, pension benefits were raised substantially. In contrast to Willie Brice, employees at GM who retire with 30 years of service, regardless of age, will receive $533.50 a month plus a $381.50 per month supplement until they start receiving Social Security benefits.

Adapted from the Cleveland Plain Dealer, *September 20, 1979, pp. A-1, A-2.*

Thiese examples illustrate some of the many qualities of indirect compensation: the size of the benefits can vary greatly, benefits can be very lucrative to the employee and costly to the organization, and the trend is to expand benefits. Other aspects of indirect compensation are the large number of benefits that are being provided by organizations; the growing involvement of federal and state government, resulting in mandates for increased coverage and scrutiny of benefit administration; and the complexity of administering an effective indirect compensation program.

There are several important questions pertaining to indirect as well as direct compensation. For example, do employees perceive indirect benefits as a right or as a reward? Do increases in indirect compensation offset employee demands for increased direct compensation? Do all employees value the same indirect benefits? What are the costs to the organization of providing indirect benefits? What are the laws within which indirect compensation programs must be administered? Should employees be allowed to choose what benefits they want? What are all the benefits included in indirect compensation, and what purposes do they serve? Since these questions are directed at the heart of indirect compensation, they will form the basis of this third and final chapter on compensation.

INDIRECT COMPENSATION

Almost all organizations offer some form of indirect compensation—also known as fringe benefits or supplemental compensation. For some of these organizations, indirect compensation may make up as much as 50 percent of the cost of total compensation. Furthermore, the percentage of total compensation devoted to indirect compensation is expected to increase. Since the cost of indirect compensation is becoming so significant, it is important to ask whether organizations are getting their money's worth. The answer depends on the purposes or objectives of indirect compensation and its definition.

Indirect compensation is defined here as those rewards provided by the organization to employees for their membership or participation (attendance) in the organization. The rewards consist of protection programs, pay for time not worked, and employee services and benefits. Although several of these rewards are mandated by federal and state governments and must therefore be administered within the boundaries of laws and regulations, many others are provided voluntarily by organizations. Indirect rewards are much more diverse than direct compensation and as a result are not always valued or seen as a reward by all employees. It is only when indirect compensation is seen as a reward, however, that many of the purposes of indirect compensation can be attained.

The Purposes and Importance of Indirect Compensation

Statistics collected by the U.S. Chamber of Commerce indicate that the average organization spends over 35 percent of its total payroll dollars in indirect compensation.[1] In return, organizations expect to fulfill several purposes, including
- Attracting good employees
- Increasing employee morale

- Reducing turnover
- Increasing job satisfaction
- Motivating employees
- Enhancing the organization's image among employees
- Making better use of compensation dollars
- Keeping the union out[2]

These objectives are listed in order of importance; attracting good employees is thus the most important.

Only rarely are all these purposes attained. "There is ample research to demonstrate that these purposes are not being attained, largely because of inadequate communication."[3] The argument can be made, however, that some of these purposes cannot be attained with indirect compensation. For example, it is possible to motivate employees with incentives because the rewards are tied closely to performance, but the rewards of indirect compensation are tied only to organizational membership. Thus there is no direct reason why employees should be more motivated to perform because of increased indirect compensation. Because of this very fact, it has been recommended that organizations tie indirect compensation to performance.[4]

Another important reason why some of the purposes of indirect compensation are not attained is that employees may regard compensation benefits not as rewards but as conditions (rights) of employment. They may also think of indirect benefits as safeguards against insecurity provided by the organization as a social responsibility because they are not provided by society.[5]

Even when indirect compensation is regarded as a reward, its importance relative to other aspects of the organization is low. "Indirect benefits were ranked *last* by [a sample of MBA students across the country], behind opportunity for advancement, salary, geographic location, job responsibilities and prestige on the job as a factor in job selection."[6] Needless to say, the importance of indirect benefits varies from one employee to another and also from one organization to another. In addition, particular types of indirect benefits are seen as more important to protection programs; younger employees attach more importance to pay for time not worked.[7] The relative importance of indirect benefits for all workers is shown in Exhibit 12.1.

The Growth of Indirect Compensation

The Depression of the 1930s gave the necessary impetus for the beginning of extensive indirect benefits. The Social Security Act, passed in 1935, provided old age, disability, survivor's, and health benefits and the basis for federal and state unemployment programs. The unions have also had a significant impact on indirect benefits, and their growth was enhanced by the National Labor Relations Act of 1935. There were indirect benefits before 1930, but the rapid growth of federally mandated benefits began then, which in turn sparked the growth of voluntary benefits. In fact, in 1929 indirect benefits were less than 5 percent of the cost of total compensation. By 1949, after the Depression, World War II, and two court cases, this cost rose to 16 percent.

During World War II, wages and salaries were frozen by the federal government. Benefits, particularly pensions, were exempt from the freeze. With a strong demand for labor and strong demands from unions, pension benefits were increased and

"Which of the fringe benefits you get are most important to you?"

Benefit	Percentage
Medical surgical, or hospital coverage for any illness or injury that occurs off the job (1,506)*	83.9
Sick leave with full pay (1,193)	59.1
Retirement program (1,288)	50.3
Paid vacation (1,550)	47.0
Life insurance covering death unrelated to job (1,218)	41.2
Dental benefits (569)	35.5
Profit sharing (378)	33.1
Eyeglass or eyecare benefits (416)	25.5
Work clothing allowance (330)	18.5
Skill-training or education program (941)	18.3
Stock options (333)	16.2
Free or discounted meals (313)	14.7
Legal aid or services (193)	13.5
Thrift or savings plan (757)	13.1
Maternity leave with full reemployment rights (513)	12.7
Maternity leave with pay (197)	10.7
Free or discounted merchandise (669)	10.5
Child-care services while parents are working (42)	9.5

Percentage   0   10   20   30   40   50   60   70   80   90   100

Exhibit 12.1 Perceived Importance of Indirect Benefits

Adapted from R. P. Quinn and G. L. Staines, *The 1977 Quality of Employment Survey* (Ann Arbor, Mich.: Survey Research Center, University of Michigan), p. 60.

*The numbers in parentheses indicate how many employees in the sample receive this benefit.

extended to new employees. And because employers saw that employees valued indirect benefits as much as direct wages, they reasoned that increasing indirect benefits was just as useful as direct wages for rewarding employees. Furthermore, the benefits could be treated as an expense for tax purposes, just as wages and salaries.

After the War, two court cases helped to expand benefit coverage by declaring pension and insurance provisions were bargainable issues in union and management relations. The right to bargain over pensions was decided in *Inland Steel* v. *National Labor Relations Board* (1948), and the right to bargain over insurance was decided in *W. W. Cross* v. *National Labor Relations Board* (1949).

These economic and legal changes were accompanied by rapid changes in technological conditions. Technological changes increased employee productivity but also created many jobs that were repetitive and unattractive to many employees, even though well paid. As a consequence, employees demanded more time away from the job (such as shorter work weeks), more variation, and holidays with pay.

From the 1950s to the present, indirect benefits have expanded significantly in terms of both percentage of payroll and dollars per employee. The percentage of total payroll has gone from 22.7 percent in 1955 to as much as 42 percent in 1980, and the yearly dollar amount has gone from $970 to approximately $5,500.[8]

PROTECTION PROGRAMS

Protection programs of indirect compensation are designed to protect the employee and family if and when the employee's income (direct compensation) is terminated and to protect the employee and family against the burden of health care expenses. Protection programs required by federal and state governments are referred to as public programs, and those voluntarily offered by organizations are called private programs. An outline of typical private and public protection programs appears in Exhibit 12.2.

Public Protection Programs

Many public protection programs are for the most part direct products of the Social Security Act of 1935. The protection programs of Social Security were initially funded by Old Age, Survivor's, and Disability Insurance. The Act initially set up systems for retirement benefits, disability, and unemployment insurance. Health insurance, particularly Medicare, was added in 1966 to provide hospital insurance to almost everyone sixty-five and older.

The Social Security System. Funding of the Social Security system is provided by equal contributions from employee and employer. Employees' contributions are deducted from paychecks under the terms of FICA (Federal Insurance Contribution Act). Initially, employee and employer each paid 1 percent of the employee's income up to $3,000. The rate is scheduled to go to 7.15 percent by 1987 on a base income up to $42,500. This amounts to employee and employer contributions of $3,045 each per year.

Exhibit 12.2   Protection Programs

Hazard	Private Plans	Public Plans
Old age	• Pensions • Deferred profit sharing • "Thrift" plans	• Social Security old age benefits
Death	• Group term life insurance (including accidental death and travel insurance) • Payouts from profit-sharing, pension, and/or thrift plans • Dependent survivors' benefits	• Social Security survivors' benefits • Worker's compensation
Disability	• Short-term accident and sickness insurance, sick leave • Long-term disability insurance	• Worker's compensation • Social Security disability benefits • State disability benefits
Unemployment	• Supplemental unemployment benefits and/or severance pay	• Unemployment benefits
Medical/dental expenses	• Hospital/surgical insurance • Other medical insurance • Dental insurance	• Worker's compensation • Medicare

Adapted from J. S. Sullivan, Indirect Compensation: The Decade Ahead, *California Management Review*, Winter 1972, Vol XV, no. 2, p. 65.

The much-publicized financial troubles of the Social Security system stem from several purposes and assumptions. The original purpose was to provide retired people with income to supplement their savings and support from such other sources as family members. Individuals were to receive payments from the system in proportion to what they put into the system. When the system was enacted, approximately fifteen to twenty people were working for every individual receiving Social Security benefits. Furthermore, it was assumed that the rate of inflation would remain low, that the population would keep increasing at the same rate, that productivity would continue to increase, and that people would continue to view Social Security only as a supplement.

However, the birth rate has declined significantly since the 1930s, and the life span has increased, leaving fewer people in the work force to support those receiving benefits from Social Security. There are currently seven employed people for every beneficiary, with a projected ratio of 3 to 1 by the end of the decade. This reduction has been aided by increasing dropouts from the Social Security system. Federal, state, and local government employees are among those most conspicuously excluded from the system. The notion of individuals receiving in proportion to what they contributed has also long since been discarded. Now payments are made to survivors, dependents, and persons over seventy-two who have never contributed to the system. Many people who never contributed are eligible for Medicare, especially those who retired before 1966.

In light of these problems, the Social Security Advisory Council (which meets only once every four years) is considering recommending to Congress a reduction in the present 6.13 percent contribution rate to 5.6 percent until 2005 and a somewhat slower rate of increase in the current base income of $22,900. In addition, the

Council is also proposing that half of a person's Social Security benefits (the employer's share) be subject to U.S. income tax for the first time. The tax revenue to the Treasury would be $1.5 billion to $2 billion yearly. Another recommendation is that the entire income from the proposed 5.6 percent rate be used to fund old-age and disability trust funds. Medicare would be funded by general revenues from U.S. income taxes and business taxes imposed specifically for Medicare.

Social Security Pension Benefits.   The average pension check from Social Security is now about $255 per month. In 1972 Congress passed a law providing that increases in pension benefits be determined by an inflation escalator clause. As a result, recipients receive increases in benefits greater than the inflation rate of the preceding year. Individuals receiving pension benefits can now earn up to $5,000 per year; in 1982 this will be raised to $6,000. Presently federal employees are not eligible for Social Security coverage, but other employees, including self-employed individuals, are eligible. Passage of the Council's recommendations could, however, expand eligibility and make enrollment less voluntary.

Unemployment Compensation Benefits.   In order to control the pension provisions of Social Security, the unemployment provisions dictate that benefits from unemployment compensation be determined jointly through federal and state cooperation. As a result, employer costs and employee benefits can vary from state to state. The unemployment compensation fund is supported solely by employers, except in Alabama, Alaska, and New Jersey, where employees also contribute. The base rate for employer contributions varies depending on the number of unemployed people an organization has drawing from the state's unemployment fund. Thus it pays for an organization to maintain relatively stable employment and to avoid layoffs.

The current rate an employer has to pay into the unemployment fund is 3.4 percent of each employee's salary, up to $6,000 per year. The employer, however, can obtain a credit of 2.7 percent, thus paying only 0.7 percent. The credit can be obtained by making payments to the state unemployment fund through the company's experience rating (the more people on layoff, the higher the rating). Thus a company with a good rating may pay only 1 percent of employee's salaries to the state fund and 0.7 percent to the federal fund. The remaining 2.7 percent is not paid, because it is a bonus for having a good rating. The exact percentages assigned for good experience ratings varies from state to state, but the potential savings for stable employment and good human resource planning are significant.

The purpose of unemployment compensation is to provide income to an individual who is employed but not currently working (indefinite layoff) or who is seeking a job. To be eligible for benefits, an employee must first have worked a minimum number of weeks (exact number set by the state), currently be without a job, and be willing to accept an appropriate job offered through the State Unemployment Compensation Commission. It was recently declared in New York that even individuals on strike may collect unemployment benefits. Although the typical period of time a person may receive unemployment benefits is twenty-six weeks, the period has often been extended. These benefits generally represent no more than half of an employee's regular earnings, but again, the exact amount varies greatly from state to state.

Disability and Worker's Compensation Benefits. These benefits are provided in public programs by the Social Security system and by state systems. At both the state and federal level, compensation benefits are administered to assist workers who are ill or injured and cannot work due to work or occupational injury or ailment. Totally disabled employees can receive payments from Social Security until retirement. Usually these payments are minimal (less than $100), but state compensation benefits can add substantially to that amount. State compensation benefits are usually paid for permanent partial, temporary total, partial, or permanent total disability.[9]

The exact benefits received depend on the state the individual works in, the individual's earnings, and the number of dependents. Payment for total disabilities is generally in the form of weekly or monthly payments. Permanent partial disability payments are often lump sums for a predetermined value—for example, $10,000 for the loss of an eye or a leg. Payments are also made for medical and hospital costs related to work-related injury or illness and for survivor benefits in the case of death.[10]

Until recently, most compensation benefits were provided for injury or illness resulting from a physical cause—lifting heavy boxes, falling from a ladder at work—or from the physical environment of the work—such as black lung disease from working in a coal mine. But just because a disease or ailment is associated with a specific work environment does not mean it will be covered or covered adequately by worker's compensation. A case in point is described in this story about Ed London:

Standing outside a chain link fence, he looked over at the old brick plant where he worked for 30 years and where he was slowly poisoned by lead.

London calls himself a survivor of an occupational disease, but his voice lacks any jubilation. Instead, he speaks of surviving as if he were serving a prison sentence.

London's wife, Mollie, said he still suffers poor health from decades of lead poisoning. "The doctors told me his kidneys and lungs could go at any time," she confided in an interview outside their Chicago home.

Looking back, London, 67, has few fond memories of his career with NL Industries Inc. (formerly National Lead Co.) where he produced lead oxide to be used in batteries. He retired two years ago, but he feels anger, not nostalgia, toward his work. Now he knows that his job ruined his health.

By breathing the fumes of melting lead and from constant exposure to powdered lead oxide, London took a daily dose of poison.

Last year, London received $17,000 in workers' compensation for being poisoned. But unlike the taste of beer, the money left him with a bitter taste. He had to use $12,000 of it to pay medical bills, Another $3,000 went for legal fees. At this point the remaining $2,000 is gone and the Londons now live on his $100 a month pension and Social Security.[11]

In addition to physical injury, work environments may produce mental or psychological injuries, often caused by psychological and interpersonal conditions. An example of this is provided by the story of Mrs. Wolfe at the beginning of the chapter.

Medical and Hospital Benefits.   The major public program providing medical and hospital benefits is Medicare. This program is now funded by Social Security, although the recommendation of the Social Security Council is to move it out of Social Security. Such a move, however, may increase the total contributions of an organization for support of public programs. If the proposed recommendation is adopted by Congress, each organization would continue to pay its Social Security contributions for every employee, although at a lower rate, and pay an additional tax for Medicare.

Medicare applies only to people over sixty-five, but the Health Maintenance Organization Act of 1973 is an attempt to provide medical and hospital benefits for younger people as well. The Act established and regulates health maintenance organizations (HMOs), which incorporate the services of hospitals, clinics, doctors, nurses, and technicians at a single monthly rate.[12] The Act also requires employers of at least twenty-five persons to offer an HMO plan option if they offer traditional health benefits. If HMOs organized for both group and individual practice operate in an employer's area, the employer is required to offer enrollment in both types.[13]

Private Protection Programs

Private protection programs are those offered by organizations (private and public) that are not required by law, although their administration may be regulated by law. The programs provide benefits for health care, income after retirement, and insurance against loss of life and limb. Almost all employers provide them for their employees. In contrast, only about 2 million employees, or about 2 percent of the work force, are covered by programs providing income before retirement in the form of supplemental unemployment benefits and guaranteed pay and work programs.

Retirement Benefits.   About 78 percent of all plant workers and 85 percent of all office workers are covered by private pension programs, none of which are required by law. Although these percentages may appear to be rather high, only about one-third of the entire U.S. work force is covered. This proportion, however, does represent a significant gain in coverage since the 1940s, when pension programs became a bargainable issue according to *Inland Steel* v. *National Labor Relations Board*. In addition, pension coverage varies widely by type of industry, size of firm, and whether the employees are unionized. Pension coverage is most likely to exist for unionized employees in manufacturing firms with over 500 employees.[14]

Most private pension programs are noncontributory, except those covering public employees; public employees are covered by contributory programs.[15] A **contributory program** is one in which employees and the organization contribute to their retirement fund. Public employees contribute about 7 percent of wages or salary to the retirement fund. As a result, pension benefits for public employees are one-third greater than those for private employees.[16] This difference has helped make employment in public organizations (federal, state, and local government agencies) much more attractive than ever before. At the same time, however, this difference has led to a crisis. The gap between yearly benefits paid and contributions keeps widening, and the amount of unfunded liabilities keeps growing.

ERISA and Private Employees' Pensions.   ERISA (Employees' Retirement Income Security Act) was enacted to protect employees covered by private pension programs. Before ERISA, employees in such plans often found themselves without any real benefits by the time they reached retirement. Sometimes employees who left an organization after working there many years would receive no retirement benefits or only a small proportion of the benefits due to them because they had no **vested rights.** If vested employees quit, they still receive a pension when they reach retirement age; without vesting, employees who quit must remove their pension contribution and may not receive the employer's contribution. Sometimes the pension programs were not adequately funded or were mismanaged.

ERISA specified numerous minimum requirements for private employee pension programs if organizations chose to have them at all. Organizations with existing programs can either comply with these requirements or drop their programs, which many have done. Between the enactment of ERISA (in 1974) and 1977, about 18,000 private pension programs were terminated by organizations.[17] Critics of ERISA say this is primarily due to the requirements of ERISA; its supporters claim that this many would have been dropped with or without ERISA. Thus the real effect of ERISA on the number of pension programs is unclear.

Much more clear are the benefits gained by those in organizations whose pension programs went defunct. ERISA established the Pension Benefit Guarantee Corporation (PBGC) to take over defunct pension programs and assume their liabilities. Thus individuals receiving retirement benefits continued to do so, and those still working were guaranteed their pension benefits. The liabilities assumed by the PBGC were so large, however, that it is now unfunded. Continued funding is under the control of Congress. Employer contributions per employee to help provide money for the PBGC have recently been raised in order to support the Corporation's liabilities.

Insurance Benefits.   There are three major types of insurance programs: life, health, and disability. These insurance programs are provided by most organizations at a cost far below what would be charged to employees buying their own insurance. They are essential benefits, although employees do not always recognize them as being very important. Nevertheless, these programs have grown substantially, both in the dollar amount of benefits and the percentage of employees covered.

Life insurance programs cover almost all employees. The benefits are equal to about two years' income, but this tends to be more true for managerial employees than nonmanagerial employees.[18] Nonmanagerial, clerical, and blue-collar employees are generally covered for an amount less than one year's income. After retirement the benefits continue for most employees, but they may be reduced by as much as two-thirds.[19] A majority of the life insurance programs offered by organizations are noncontributory—the employee does not pay into the program. The trend is toward more noncontributory programs, even though there is also a trend toward providing more coverage, especially coverage to family members. Despite the cost, organizations are doing this to keep up with other organizations.

A similar philosophy dictates the offering of health insurance programs. The extent of health coverage has increased greatly over the past few years. Some organizations now offer, in addition to the typical hospital (Blue Cross), surgical (Blue

Shield), and major medical coverage, insurance for eyeglasses, dental care, prescription drugs, and hearing aids. As with life insurance programs, almost all employees are provided with the typical health insurance package (hospital, surgical, and major medical), although managerial employees have slightly more extensive coverage.[20] Often health programs for managerial employees also have a deductible feature, which obligates employees to pay the first $50 to $100 of their health expenses for each sickness or accident before receiving the benefits of the insurance coverage. Nonmanagerial employees, especially those who are unionized, generally do not pay a deductible.

Benefits received under health insurance programs are rather well defined by the organization. For example, the benefits paid for hospital expenses may be a maximum of $3,000 per year or per sickness, and surgical expenses may be covered up to $1,000 per operation. Particular operations may be reimbursed at very specific rates—say, $450 for an appendectomy. Major medical benefits are provided to defray expenses not covered by hospital and surgical benefits. Again, limits may be set, such as $10,000 per sickness.

Health insurance programs generally cover short-term absences from work due to sickness, whereas short-term absences due to disability are covered by short-term disability insurance offered by the employer. Longer-term absences due to sickness or disability are covered by long-term sickness and disability insurance. Both types of disability insurance generally supplement state and federal disability programs. However, short-term disability protection is generally offered by more organizations than is long-term disability protection. About 70 percent of all organizations provide short-term sickness and accident protection, but only 60 percent provide long-term coverage.[21] Long-term sickness and disability coverage for nonmanagerial employees is often a set sum, such as $10,000; for managerial employees, reimbursement is often a percentage of salary and therefore increases with the level of manager. Another form of payment is reimbursement for a fixed percentage of the expenses due to the sickness or disability.

Supplemental Unemployment Benefits. A small number of organizations offer employees protection against loss of income and loss of work before retirement. **Supplemental unemployment benefits** (SUB) are for people laid off from work. When SUB benefits are combined with unemployment compensation benefits, laid-off employees can receive as much as 95 percent of their average income.[22] The size of these benefits makes it easier for employees with more years of service to accept layoffs, thus allowing employees with less service, often younger, to continue working. SUB programs exist in a limited number of industries, and all are the product of labor-management contracts. The industries in which they are found include the automotive, steel, rubber, glass, ceramic, and ladies' garment industries.[23]

PAY FOR TIME NOT WORKED

Pay for time not worked is not so complex to administer as benefits from protection programs, but it is almost as costly to the organization. Pay for time not worked continues to grow, in amount as well as in kind.[24] For example, in 1955 the average number of paid holidays per year was approximately six; in 1978 it was ten. During the same period, the average number of weeks of paid vacation went from three to four.[25]

There are two major categories of **pay for time not worked.** Holidays and vacations belong to the off-the-job category; the other category is on-the-job.

Off the Job

Payments for time not worked (and those referred to primarily as off-the-job benefits) constitute a major portion of the total cost of indirect compensation. Approximately 22 percent of total benefit costs are for protection programs. Almost 16 percent is pay for time not worked; about 11 percent of the total is for off-the-job payments. The most common paid off-the-job components are vacations, sick leave, holidays, and personal days.

On the Job

Paid benefits for time not worked on the job include rest periods, lunch periods, wash-up time, and clothes-change and get-ready times. Together these benefits are the fifth most expensive indirect compensation benefit. Two of these benefits are particularly important. Many organizations do not currently offer them, but they are gaining in popularity and even necessity. Paid time for physical fitness is clearly pay for time not worked on the job, but flexible time and condensed work week arrangements could also be considered pay for time not worked off the job.

Physical Fitness Benefits.   With increased awareness of the relationship between job stress and coronary heart disease and other physical and mental disabilities, organizations have become more concerned with finding ways to alleviate stress whenever possible. People who are in good physical condition can often deal with stress better and suffer fewer negative symptoms than people in poor physical condition. In addition, physical exercise is a good way to cope with stress and reduce its effects. Consequently, organizations are encouraging their employees to be physically fit and to engage in exercise by providing athletic facilities on company premises. These facilities are essentially a service to employees.

Flextime and Condensed Work Weeks.   These arrangements are discussed in Chapter 8 as methods of accommodating employees rather than as forms of indirect compensation. But many organizations regard them as such.[26] These arrangements are seen as giving employees more time off, but not without pay.

EMPLOYEE SERVICES AND PERQUISITES

The third and final component of indirect compensation is employee services and **perquisites,** which may consist of
- Food service costs or losses
- Employee discounts
- Day-care centers

- Employer-sponsored scholarships (or tuition assistance) for employees and their dependents
- Employee counseling and advisory services (legal, tax, and personal problems)
- Low-cost loans
- Company-leased or -owned vehicles for business and personal use
- Service/suggestion awards

Primarily for top executives are such perquisites as

- Annual company-paid physical examinations
- Company-paid memberships in country, athletic, and social clubs
- Use of company expense accounts to cover personal travel, meals, and entertainment
- Business and personal use of corporate aircraft[27]

Although this component represents the smallest percentage of indirect compensation, services and perquisites are rewarding as well as necessary for many employees. To some, they represent an important element in the status system of the organization; to others, they represent a means by which working is made possible. For example, day-care centers make it more practicable for some individuals to start working and make it more feasible for them to continue working and with less absenteeism.[28] For another example, expense accounts, club memberships, carpeting in the office, and free trips are designed to give a status boost to managers.[29]

Many of the services and perquisites listed above have been provided by organizations for many years. But a few have been recent additions, so recent that many organizations still have not included them in their compensation programs. In addition, a few services and perquisites formerly offered only to managers are now also available to nonmanagers.

Counseling and Assistance Services

Although counseling in organizations is not new, what is discussed and what is done as a result are new. Employee counseling services now include advice and information regarding legal concerns, tax matters, and more personal problems such as drinking and absenteeism.[30]

Discussion and recognition, especially of personal problems, is being combined with action-oriented programs to help employees deal with problems they have. As a matter of fact, the establishment of these programs is a recognition that an employee's problem is also the organization's problem, whether the organization caused the employee's problem or not. Recognition is due in part to two views: The employee is a valuable resource to the organization, and organizations have a social responsibility to assist their employees in dealing with problems related to their performance.

Relocation

What used to be a service offered mainly to managers is now offered to nonmanagers as well. The current contract between General Motors and the United Auto Workers contains a provision for increasing moving allowances by as much as $400 to make the movement of union members to new or other plants easier.[31]

The costs of employee relocation are not insignificant. In 1980 alone, the estimated cost of relocation by American industry was almost $4 billion. No longer do companies reimburse only expenses for the movement of household goods and transportation of the employee and family to the new work location.[32] Relocation reimbursements may now cover

- *At least one and perhaps two trips to the new location for the executive and spouse (limit of seven days)*
- *Selling costs on old residence plus guaranteed disposal of old home*
- *Closing costs on new residence*
- *Duplicate housing cost if necessary*
- *A relocation allowance ranging from a low of $500 to a high of $2,000 . . . [often] figured as a percentage of salary (one-half to one month) or on sale price of old home (10 percent)*
- *A mortgage differential allowance to offset the recent rise in loan rates*
- *A no- or low-interest loan to cover down payment on new residence*
- *All moving expenses including moving of auto and small pets*
- *Temporary lodging at new location for 30 days (seven days with family)*[33]

ADMINISTRATION OF INDIRECT COMPENSATION

Although indirect compensation is often used and seen as a reward, it is not used or seen as a reward by everyone. Some benefits, in fact, may be used by only a few employees. It is estimated, for example, that only 3 percent of the eligible employees take advantage of company-sponsored tuition refund programs.[34] But if the benefits of indirect compensation are not seen as rewards, the organization is getting nothing for something. Because organizations prefer to get at least something for something, they become concerned with their package of indirect compensation benefits and how they are administered.

There are three necessary aspects of the administration of indirect compensation—each requiring considerable attention to detail in development and implementation. The three aspects are assuring that the indirect compensation programs and benefits are consistent with legal requirements; determining which programs and benefits will best serve the purposes of indirect compensation; and communicating and evaluating the benefits package so that employees will see indirect compensation as a reward. In addition, the administrator of indirect compensation should be aware of the trends and future developments in indirect compensation.

Legal Requirements

Many of the legal requirements for indirect compensation have been indicated in earlier sections of this chapter, such as those related to the mandatory provision of unemployment compensation, contributions to Social Security for pension benefits, Medicare costs and disability allowances, payments for worker's compensation, and voluntary benefits programs, particularly for retirement. There are two legal areas, however, that should be mentioned here. Discrimination in the administration of indirect compensation has had particular impact on two areas: pregnancy and mandatory retirement.

There has been a trend in recent years to treat pregnancy as a disability. Opponents of this trend argue that pregnancy is a voluntary condition, not an involuntary sickness, and therefore should not be covered by disability benefits. The Pregnancy Discrimination Act of 1978, however, states that pregnancy is a disability and furthermore must receive the same benefits as any other disability.

Although the Social Security Act allows women to retire earlier than men (at age sixty-two as opposed to age sixty-five), the U.S. Supreme Court, by refusing to hear a lower-court ruling, affirmed that it is illegal to require women to retire earlier than men. On the issue of mandatory retirement, neither men nor women can now be forced to retire before the age of seventy if they are working for a private business with at least twenty persons on the payroll. Federal workers cannot be forced to retire at any age. These provisions, which are contained in a 1978 amendment to the 1967 Age Discrimination Act, took effect January 1, 1979. Employees, however, may still choose to retire at sixty-five and receive full benefits. This five-year latitude provides further uncertainty in the administration and costs of indirect compensation. It is also forcing organizations to take a hard look at the performance of employees who previously may have been allowed to coast to retirement, especially if they were only a couple of years away from sixty-five.

Determining the Benefits Package

The benefits package should be selected on the basis of what's good for the employee as well as the employer. Often what is good for the employee can help determine what is good for the employer.

Employee Preferences. Indirect compensation programs and benefits are often provided without any specific knowledge of what employees really want or prefer. Employees, however, have indicated strong preferences for certain benefits over others, regardless of cost considerations. Employees in one company indicated a strong preference for dental insurance over life insurance, even though dental insurance was only one-fourth the cost of life insurance to the company.[35] The most desired benefit appears to be time off from work in large chunks.[36] There are, of course, differences in employee preferences. As workers get older, there is a consistent increase in the desire for increased pension benefits. This is also the case for employees with rising incomes. Employees with children prefer increased hospitalization benefits compared to those without children.[37]

Benefits and Costs to the Organization. An organization can determine the costs of indirect compensation in four ways:
- Total cost of benefits annually for all employees
- Cost per employee per year divided by the number of hours worked
- Percentage of payroll divided by annual payroll
- Cost per employee per hour divided by employee hours worked[38]

Using these four cost bases, the organization can figure out the benefits-to-cost ratio and competitiveness of its indirect compensation program in six steps:

1. Examine the internal cost to the company of all benefits and services, by payroll classification, by profit center, and for each benefit.

2. Compare the company's costs for benefits to external norms. For example, compare its costs to average costs, averages by industry, and so on, as reported in surveys such as those conducted by the Chamber of Commerce, for the package as a whole and for each benefit.

3. Prepare a report for the decision maker contrasting steps 1 and 2 and highlighting major variances.

4. Analyze the costs of the program to employees. Determine what each employee is paying for benefits, totally and by benefit.

5. Compare the data in step 4 with external data such as Chamber of Commerce data.

6. Analyze how satisfied the individual is with the organization's program—and as compared to competitors' programs.[39]

These steps highlight the cost and benefit considerations of indirect compensation to an organization as well as the strategic choices for remaining competitive with other organizations.

A SLICE OF LIFE

A very large West Coast organization uses a "second paycheck" as an effective tool for communicating benefits packages to its employees. Every year, every employee receives a piece of paper that lists each indirect benefit that the employee has received and specifies the exact amount of money that the company has paid for these benefits. It lists the exact amount spent on

- Social Security paid by the employer
- State disability insurance
- State unemployment insurance
- The pension fund
- Medical insurance
- Medical benefits
- Federal unemployment insurance
- Life insurance
- Sick pay
- Holiday pay
- Vacation pay
- Tuition aid
- Dental insurance
- Dental benefits
- A host of miscellaneous payments

Most people are not impressed when told that the company has spent some $40 million in indirect compensation for its employees, because they cannot relate to that amount of money. But the second paycheck is meaningful, because it is personalized and because it ordinarily amounts to over 35 percent of employees' yearly income. Most employees have no idea how much these "fringe benefits" cost and are genuinely surprised to see the amount in dollars and cents.

Communicating the Benefits Package

Many employees are not only unaware of the costs of the benefits they are receiving but also unaware of which benefits they are receiving.[40] If employees have no knowledge of their benefits, then there is little reason to believe that the organization's benefit program objectives will be attained. Many organizations indicate that they assign a high priority to telling employees about their benefits, although a majority spend only $10 per employee per year.[41] Recall that the average benefits package costs over $5,000 per employee.

Benefits communication programs often have several specific objectives: to enhance awareness of benefits, to enhance understanding of benefits, to enhance awareness of the costs of the benefits, to encourage full use of benefits, to create good will among employees, and to demonstrate how competitive the benefit program is.[42] Although most organizations (60 percent) have these objectives, many still find it difficult to assess the effectiveness of their communication programs. Nevertheless, it is these objectives against which such evaluations must be made.

Considering that most benefits program objectives are not currently attained, it is likely that assessment of communication effectiveness would produce unfavorable results.[43] This may in part be due to the communication techniques used. Almost all organizations use impersonal, passive booklets and brochures to convey benefits information; only a few use more personal, active media, such as slide presentations and regular employee meetings.

SUMMARY

Chapters 10, 11, and 12 address what are often the most frequently asked questions in organization orientation programs: "How much do I get paid?" and "How much and when is my vacation?" Although most organizations have been responding to both questions with "More than ever before," the growth in indirect compensation has been double that of direct compensation. This doubling has occurred despite the lack of evidence that indirect compensation is really helping to attain the purposes of total compensation. Money, job challenge, and opportunities for advancement appear to serve the purposes of compensation as much as, if not more than, pension benefits, disability provisions, and services, especially for employees aspiring to managerial careers.

This is not to say, however, that employees do not desire indirect benefits. It is in part because employees desire them that organizations are offering them at such a rapid rate. The specific indirect benefits offered by an organization are, however, not always valued by all employees, nor do all employees know what benefits are offered. As a result, some organizations solicit employee opinions about their preferences for compensation programs. Organizations are also becoming more concerned with the communication of their benefits programs, partly because of the requirements of ERISA. The current evidence suggests that employees' lack of awareness of benefit programs and their value may partially explain why they are not perceived as valuable. Increased communication and more employee participation in the benefits packages may, therefore, increase the likelihood that organizations will receive some benefit from providing benefits.

PERSONNEL PROBLEM
Indirect Compensation and Overtime

"Did you realize that our indirect compensation package for employees is now over 40 percent?" asked the second shift supervisor, Joanne Ames.

"I didn't know the exact figures, but I knew it was increasing," answered the first shift supervisor, Pat McFall. "I'll bet these new expenses will increase the pressure to use less overtime. The company probably won't allow it now, or they'll be very careful with it."

"I don't think it will work like that. I think we will be encouraged to use more overtime, but we'll have a harder time hiring new employees," Ms. Ames responded.

1. Do you agree with Pat McFall's opinion on the effect of indirect compensation costs on overtime?

2. Do you agree with Ms. Ames's opinion on the effect of indirect compensation costs on overtime?

3. What is the relationship between indirect compensation payments and overtime?

4. If the trend continues to pay higher and higher percentages of indirect compensation to employees, would there be pressure to reduce the hiring of new employees?

KEY CONCEPTS

contributory program
ERISA (Employees'
   Retirement Income Security Act)
indirect compensation

pay for time not worked
perquisite
protection program

supplemental unemployment
   benefit (SUB)
vested rights

DISCUSSION QUESTIONS

1. What are the purposes of indirect compensation? Are they being met?
2. Describe public and private protection programs. What has been the trend in the growth of each of these?
3. Describe ERISA and its impact on private pension plans. Has its impact been good?
4. Should organizations provide time off with pay for such things as physical fitness programs? Why or why not?
5. Should organizations give employees a chance to improve before firing them? How far should

the organization go to help employees with free services?
6. What are the pros and cons of considering employee preferences in benefit administration? How should they be considered?
7. What are the legal requirements and constraints on indirect compensation administration?
8. Why do organizations fail to communicate their benefits package to employees? Does this help explain why benefits are not important to many employees? What can be done about the communication of benefits?

ENDNOTES

1. R. C. Huseman, J. D. Hatfield, and R. W. Driver, "Getting Your Benefit Programs Understood and Appreciated," *Personnel Journal*, October 1978, pp. 560–566, 758.
2. Huseman, Hatfield, and Driver. Reprinted with permission *Personnel Journal*, Costa Mesa, CA, copyright October 1978, p. 562.
3. Huseman, Hatfield, and Driver, p. 560.
4. D. W. Belcher, *Compensation Administration*, (Englewood Cliffs, N.J.: Prentice-Hall, 1974).
5. Belcher, p. 376.
6. Huseman, Hatfield, and Driver, p. 562.
7. R. Tilove, "Pensions, Health and Welfare Plans," in L. Ulman (ed.), *Challenges to*

Collective Bargaining (Englewood Cliffs, N.J.: Prentice-Hall, 1967), pp. 37–64.

8. *Employee Benefits 1975* (Washington D.C.: Chamber of Commerce of the United States, 1976).

9. A. Davis, "Workmen's Compensation," in J. Famularo (ed.), *Handbook of Modern Personnel Management* (New York: McGraw-Hill, 1972), chapter 51.

10. R. M. McCaffery, *Managing the Employee Benefits Program* (New York: American Management Associations, 1972).

11. E. Price, "Jobs That Kill," *Cleveland Plain Dealer*, September 23, 1979, sec. E, p. 1. Reprinted with permission.

12. R. I. Henderson, *Compensation Management: Rewarding Performance in the Modern Organization* (Reston, Va.: Reston Publishing Company, 1976).

13. *Congressional Quarterly Almanac*, 29 (Washington D.C.: Congressional Quarterly Service, 1973), p. 507.

14. D. R. Bell, "Prevalence of Private Retirement Plans," *Monthly Labor Review*, 98 (1975), pp. 17–20.

15. H. G. Heneman Jr. and D. Yoder, *Labor Economics* (Cincinnati: Southwestern, 1965).

16. *Employee Benefits 1975* (Washington, D.C.: Chamber of Commerce of the United States, 1976).

17. P. S. Greenlaw and W. D. Biggs, *Modern Personnel Management* (Philadelphia: Saunders, 1979), p. 513.

18. M. Meyer and H. Fox, *Profile of Employee Benefits* (New York: Conference Board, 1974).

19. *Employee Health and Welfare Benefits*, Personnel Policies Forum Survey 122 (Washington D.C.: Bureau of National Affairs, 1978).

20. Meyer and Fox.
Employee Health and Welfare Benefits.

21. *Employee Health and Welfare Benefits*, p. 10.

22. "The Labor Month in Review," *Monthly Labor Review*, 1 (1968), pp. III–IV.

23. "The Labor Month in Review."

24. *Employee Benefits 1975*, p. 28.

25. Adapted from *Basic Patterns in Union Contracts*, 9th ed. (Washington D.C.: Bureau of National Affairs, 1979).

26. *Wage Survey for the Columbus Metropolitan Area* (Columbus, Ohio: City National Bank, 1979).

27. J. Sullivan, "Indirect Compensation: The Years Ahead," © 1972 by the Regents of the University of California. Reprinted from *California Management Review*, vol. XV, no. 2, p. 67, Table 3 by permission of the Regents.

28. G. Milkovich and L. Gomez, "Day Care and Selected Employee Work Behaviors," *Academy of Management Journal*, March 1976, pp. 111–115.

29. Arthur Young and Co., "Compensating Executives: Meeting the Needs of Management Today," *Financial Executive*, July 1974, pp. 46–47.

30. T. N. McGaffey, "New Horizons in Organizational Stress Prevention Approaches," *Personnel Administrator*, November 1978, pp. 26–32.

31. "UAW Looks Like Dixie Winner in GM Pact," *Cleveland Plain Dealer*, September 20, 1979, sec. A-1.

32. P. J. DiDomenico Jr., "Current Trends in Employee Relocation," *Personnel Administrator*, February 1978, pp. 17–20.
W. E. Edwards, "Tackling the $2 Billion Employee Relocation Problem," *Personnel Administrator*, January/February 1974, pp. 45–48.

33. L. W. Foster and M. L. Liebrenz, "Corporate Moves: Who Pays the Psychic Costs?" *Personnel*, November/December 1977, (New York: AMACOM, a division of American Management Associations, 1977), pp. 69–70.

34. "Employees Shun Free Education," *Small Business Report*, September 1979, p. 17.

35. S. Nealey, "Pay and Benefit Preferences," *Industrial Relations*, October 1963, pp. 17–28.

36. A. N. Nash and S. J. Carroll Jr., *The Management of Compensation* (Monterey, Calif.: Brooks/Cole, 1975), p. 241.

37. Nash and Carroll.

38. B. Ellig, "Determining the Competitiveness of Employee Benefits Systems," *Compensation Review*, 1st quarter, 1974, (New York: AMACOM, a division of American Management Associations, 1974), p. 9.

39. Ellig, pp. 8–34.

40. J. A. Gilden, "What's Happening in Employee Benefit Communications?" *Pension and Welfare News*, March 1972, pp. 31–38.
W. H. Holley Jr. and E. Ingram III, "Communicating Fringe Benefits," *Personnel Administrator*, March/April 1973, pp. 21–22.
Huseman, Hatfield, and Driver.

41. Huseman, Hatfield, and Driver, p. 563.

42. Huseman, Hatfield, and Driver, p. 563.

43. Huseman, Hatfield, and Driver, p. 578.

SECTION FIVE

Training and Developing Employees

CHAPTER OUTLINE
TRAINING AND DEVELOPMENT
The Importance and Purposes of Training and Development

Who's Responsible for Training and Development?

Relationships of Training and Development
Human Resource Planning
Performance Appraisal and Job Analysis
Recruitment
Compensation

DETERMINING TRAINING AND DEVELOPMENT NEEDS
Organizational Needs Analysis
Job Needs Analysis
Person Needs Analysis

IMPLEMENTING TRAINING AND DEVELOPMENT PROGRAMS
Principles of Learning
Learning Curves and Plateaus
Reinforcement, Knowledge of Results, and Goals
Transfer of Training

Training and Development Programs
On-the-Job Programs
Off-the-Job Programs

Selecting a Program

Problems and Mistakes in Training and Development Efforts

EVALUATION OF TRAINING AND DEVELOPMENT PROGRAMS
PERSONNEL PROBLEM   Within or Without?

OBJECTIVES
- To describe the relationships between training and other personnel activities

- To explain thoroughly how to determine training and development needs

- To discuss the principles of learning as they relate to training

- To describe off-the-job and on-the-job training and development programs

THOUGHT STARTERS
- Who should be responsible for an employee's level of training

- What role should the federal government play in training individuals?

- How can you select the best training program?

- Is there a "best" training program?

CHAPTER THIRTEEN
Employee Training and Development

Comparing the business environments of two areas, Bronx businessman Harry Katz has concluded: "If you're running a profitable business, and you compare New York with Pennsylvania, you find that real estate, taxes, and the cost of labor are about the same. *But what really kills you in New York is that the productivity is so low*. A laborer gets angry, he just walks off the line. The absenteeism is phenomenal. On Mondays during the summer, 30 percent of our work force would call in sick. You pay the same wage in New York that you'd pay in Pennsylvania, But you get 70 percent of the work."

Compounding the problems for employers are the city's public shools—so wretched that the high-school dropout rate is 45 percent. Employers who draw their workers from this system naturally find them expensive to train. The low quality of public education, and the high cost of private schools, also make it difficult to attract middle managers to the city. In short, the educational system is robbing New York business of talent from the lowest levels all the way to the top.

The *added costs of training* and *of inducing middle managers to relocate are two of the difficulties* gnawing at Dan Golomb, a partner in Everlast Sporting Goods Manufacturing Co.—the outfit that boxing made famous. (The original Everlast was a bathing suit; Golomb's father, an avid sports fan, started the sporting-goods factory after Jack Demsey complained to him about the poor quality of boxing equipment.) Everlast is a big employer—400 workers in a 150,000-square-foot factory in the South Bronx.

Golomb describes the situation this way: "We're sitting on top of the largest unskilled labor pool outside Calcutta, and this pool has enormous potential. But we've got to train them, and that costs money. We've got to infuse a work ethic in them, and that costs even more money." Golomb spends $2,000 to train a worker in New York, but only $200 in Missouri, where he has been making some of his products since 1966. This year he is planning to discontinue a line that employed fifty people in New York, and to add fifty new workers in Missouri.

Golomb is feeling the press of competition from countries like Taiwan, where labor is cheap. He has tried to counter the high cost of training here by taking part in the federally funded *Comprehensive Employment and Training Act (CETA)* program. But he gave up after two months. For many years Everlast has run its own training program. The company takes on trainees—almost all of them "gate hires"—and pays them the minimum wage, $2.90 per hour. They're trained by a company supervisor, and when they qualify for a specific job, they are moved into that position and paid that job's wage, commonly $3.50 per hour.

But CETA would have required Everlast to pay $3.50 per hour to the trainee, which "was totally destructive of morale," Golomb says. "My regular worker comes to me and says, *'I got pride. Don't take in someone who doesn't know what he's doing and pay him my wage.'* Sure a CETA worker only costs me $1.75 an hour (the federal government pays half the cost), but I'm better off paying the full $2.90 because the CETA system destroys my organization."

Nowadays visitors to Golomb's office are confronted with evidence that he is exploring the idea of taking his business elsewhere: his office is littered with correspondence and reports from practically every southern and midwestern state.

He finds the southern training programs particularly enticing, especially those in Charleston, South Carolina, where training schools provide off-the-premises training for such specialized jobs as sewing-machine mechanics. "The fantastic thing here used to be that you could get any kind of machine fixed immediately. If you needed an attachment, you just called up. Now you can't hire a sewing-machine mechanic here, but you can get them by the dozen in Charleston because Charleston trains them for you."

From J. Vitullo-Martin, "The Real Sore Spot in New York's Economy,"Fortune, November 19, 1979, pp. 99–100. Courtesy of Fortune *Magazine; ©1979 Time Inc.*

T his scenario illustrates not only the importance of training but also its complexities. What would appear to be a straightforward decision—to train or not to train—becomes a complex set of decisions involving wage levels, fairness of pay to employees in training, methods of using the human resources of the nation's largest city, and even whether to move the organization. The company must decide if it will take part in the federal government's Comprehensive Employment and Training Act (CETA) program, with its stipulations regarding wage rates for trainees. Or perhaps the company can take advantage of training programs provided by cities to develop pools of skilled labor that will entice organizations to relocate in their areas.

This chapter, then, examines in detail several issues presented by the scenario: the importance of employee training and development to organizations, the complexities of determining the organization's need for training and development, and implementation of effective training and development programs.

TRAINING AND DEVELOPMENT

Employee training and development is any attempt to improve current or future employee performance by increasing through learning an employee's ability to perform, usually by changing the employee's attitudes or increasing his or her skills and knowledge.[1] The need for training and development is determined by the employee's performance deficiency, computed as

Standard or desired performance − Actual (present or potential) performance = Training and development need[2]

The goal of training and development programs, therefore, is to remove performance deficiencies, whether current or anticipated, that are the result of the employee's inability to perform at the desired level.

The Importance and Purposes of Training and Development

Employee training and development is useful because it can, when done correctly, remove performance deficiencies. As a consequence, employees will perform better and organizations will be more effective. Improving employee ability may also result in enhanced feelings of self-esteem, lower employee turnover and absenteeism, and improved quality and quantity of work.

There is little doubt that training and development is important today. A recent estimate puts U.S. spending on training and development by industry and government at $100 billion annually.[3] In the future, training and development will have even greater significance, because of the demands of society and the pace at which these demands are changing:

The march into the post-industrial society has drawn the working population of the United States through a dramatic shift from blue- to white-collar occupations, with the vanguard position taken by employees in the professional and technical classes. Concomitantly, the requirements for coordination and control of increasingly differentiated organizations have swollen the numbers of managers and administrators from about 1.5 million at the turn of the century to some 7 million today.[4]

These changes in the demands of our postindustrial society have resulted in large part from the development of a new intellectual technology. This new technology not only requires the training and retraining of key personnel, particularly managers,[5] but it also demands a shift in emphasis from blue-collar to white-collar employees.

In 1950, there were 23.3 million blue-collar workers and 22.4 white-collar workers. By 1975, the blue-collar ranks increased to only 27.2 million, whereas the white-collar group reached 42.1 million. This gap will continue to widen. By the end of the next decade, there will be a 73% increase in professional and technical jobs, a 52% increase in clerical jobs and a 59% increase in service workers, but the number of blue-collar workers will expand only 30%.[6]

Although the emphasis may shift from blue-collar to white-collar, training for blue-collar workers is and will continue to be extremely important, as the scenario of Everlast indicates. This fact is recognized by employees at Everlast and emphasized by the existence of federal and state programs like CETA. Just as training and development can benefit organizations, it is increasingly recognized that society can benefit by enabling individuals to be productive and contributing members of organizations.

Who's Responsible for Training and Development?

If training and development is so essential, it is necessary that it be done effectively. This requires that someone assume responsibility for these programs. It has been noted that failure to run effective training and development programs results in part from the "failure to adhere to the principle that it is each *line* manager's responsibility to develop and utilize his human resources to get the results for which he is held directly accountable . . . and that staff [the personnel department] can/should really only assist him in this."[7] Staff specialists can help line managers serve the training and development needs of their employees by conducting interviews with employees and gathering performance data, analyzing performance requirements for each position, comparing employee skill and performance levels with those requirements, recommending and designing training and development programs to improve employee skill levels and to remove any unfavorable discrepancies, and conducting training and development programs where appropriate.

The success of any program, however, requires that employees take a role in their own training. After all, "development cannot occur unless there is a conscious desire for it to occur on the part of the employee."[8] In addition,

No business enterprise is competent . . . [or] obligated to substitute its efforts for the self-development efforts of the individual. To do so would not only be unwarranted paternalism, it would be foolish pretension.[9]

This does not suggest, however, that all individuals should be totally responsible for their own training. Individual responsibility should be limited by the extent to which a worker is able to take the lead in the training and development effort. Top-level managers have traditionally been able to exercise the most initiative in their own training. At lower levels, the supervisor and the organization become increasingly responsible for the implementation of training and development programs. Although individual responsibility is never eliminated, there may be a shift from being responsible for initiating training to being responsible for using and applying available programs.

A SLICE OF LIFE

In the western states, there are three major organizations primarily involved in communication services to the public. There is a startling contrast in their policies toward training prospective and continuing employees, especially in the more technical areas. Two of the organizations have relatively sophisticated training programs that are very expensive and thorough. In some technical areas, employees receive the equivalent of a college degree in electronics, or computer technology.

The third company operates quite differently. It essentially buys the talent it needs. What is the primary source for this company? The well-trained employees of the other two companies. This pirating of talent has been going on for years. All prospective employees of this third company are given a grueling examination to determine if they are in fact qualified. If they are, they receive higher salaries and more lucrative fringe benefits than either of the other companies offers.

Professional athletics provides another example of differences in training and development philosophies. Who, after all, is a draft choice? Presumably, it is a person with high potential but no track record. As a manager, would you prefer to have a seasoned veteran with proven ability or an individual with high potential whom you would have to train?

Relationships of Training and Development

Two aspects of the employee training and development activity—the determination of training and development needs and the implementation of training and development—have an extensive set of relationships with other personnel activities. In addition, there are several individual and organizational conditions that influence the implementation of training and development programs.

Human Resource Planning. The determination of the organization's training and development needs depends initially on its human resource planning requirements. These requirements are derived from the organization's overall plans and objectives, its projected human resource needs (by skill type and number), and the anticipated supply of human resources to fill these needs. As shown in the Everlast scenario, organizations are finding it increasingly difficult to fill some of their human resource needs with already-trained employees. As a result, they find it necessary to do more of their own training.

Performance Appraisal and Job Analysis.   Training and development needs are also determined by comparing the current performance of employees with the desired levels of performance. Job analysis helps establish the desired performance and skill levels for a job. This analysis helps to determine what training is needed by new employees. Performance appraisal describes the current performance of employees. It is important in the appraisal of an employee's performance to ascertain whether there is a training problem or a motivational or organizational problem.

Recruitment.   Although an organization may determine that it has need for training and development, it may still choose to recruit trained individuals rather than train its current employees. By "going outside," an organization may get somebody who is already trained, but it does so at the expense of reducing the promotional rewards that could be used as incentives for its current employees. The many organizations that do promote from within have training and development programs both for employees needing abilities for future jobs and for those needing abilities for current jobs. But occasionally these organizations need a uniquely skilled individual and therefore go outside to recruit.

Compensation.   It is important for rewards to be attached to any training and development activity, because an employee may not be interested in performing better if there are no monetary or promotional rewards for doing so. For instance, to encourage managers to train their employees, organizations often evaluate managers on how well they perform this function. The use of incentives is important not only for getting employees into training and development programs but also for maintaining the effects of these programs. Employees will revert to the old performance if that is the one that is rewarded.

   Thus the successful implementation and maintenance of training and development programs depend on establishing a compensation system that will motivate employees to perform. The quality of the methods used in the training and development programs, the leadership climate, and the organizational climate and culture are also important elements. Success, however, begins with the proper determination of training and development needs.

DETERMINING TRAINING AND DEVELOPMENT NEEDS

The three major phases of any training and development program are the **assessment phase,** which determines the training and development needs of the organization; the **implementation phase** (actual training and development), in which certain programs and learning methods are used to impart new attitudes, skills, and abilities; and the **evaluation phase**. The relationships among these three phases are shown in Exhibit 13.1.

   This section focuses on the assessment phase, which consists of the analysis of the organization's needs, the job's needs, and the person's needs. [10]

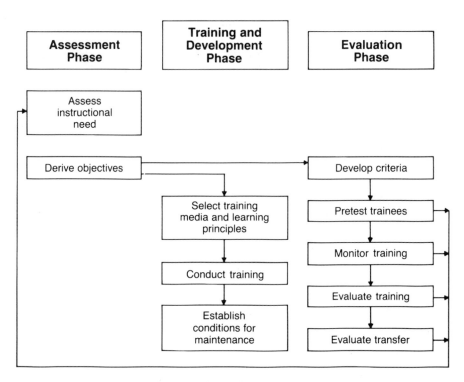

Exhibit 13.1 Model for an Instructional System*
Adapted from *Training: Program Development and Evaluation*, by I. I. Goldstein, p. 8. Copyright ©
1974 Wadsworth, Inc. Reprinted by permission of the publisher, Brooks/Cole Publishing Company,
Monterey, California.

*There are many other models for instructional systems in the military, in business, and in education.
Some of the components of this model were suggested by these other systems.

Organizational Needs Analysis

Organizational needs analysis begins with an examination of the short-term and
long-term objectives of the organization and the trends that are likely to affect these
objectives.[11] According to one expert "organizational objectives should be the ultimate concern of any training and development effort."[12] In addition to examining
the organization's objectives, the organizational needs analysis also consists of human resource analysis, analysis of efficiency indexes, and analysis of the organizational climate.[13] Although analysis of the efficiency indexes and the organizational
climate help to locate training needs, they are primarily useful in the evaluation of
training and development programs. Thus they are discussed in the last section of
this chapter.

Human resource analysis consists of the activities of translating the organization's
objectives into the demand for human resources, skills required, and programs for
supplying the needed skills and human resources. Training and development programs play a vital role in matching the supply of human resources and skills with
the demands.

Analysis of efficiency indexes provides information on the current efficiency of
work groups and the organization. Efficiency indexes that can be used include costs

of labor, quantity of output, quality of output, waste, equipment use, and repairs.[14] The organization can determine standards for these indexes and then analyze them to evaluate the general effectiveness of training programs and to locate training and development needs in the group or organization.

The analysis of the organizational climate is the final aspect of the organizational needs analysis. Like the analysis of efficiency indexes, it can help identify where training and development programs may be needed and provide criteria against which to evaluate the effectiveness of the programs that are implemented. Measures of the quality of the organizational climate include absenteeism, turnover, grievances, productivity, suggestions, attitude surveys, and accidents.[15]

Although these three aspects of the organizational needs analysis present only a broad definition of the organization's need for training and development, they are extremely important in isolating where the training and development programs should be focused and in providing some criteria against which to evaluate the effectiveness of the programs. Many organizations, however, fail to do this analysis, preferring to jump in and train because everyone else is doing it.

Job Needs Analysis

Just as important as analyzing the organization's needs, and perhaps just as frequently overlooked, is the second phase of any needs analysis. The organizational needs analysis is too broad to spot training and development needs for specific jobs, so it is necessary to conduct a **job needs analysis**.[16] Essentially, this analysis provides information on the tasks to be performed on each job (the basic information contained in job descriptions), the skills necessary to perform those tasks (from the job specifications or qualifications), and the minimum acceptable standards (information that is often not a part of the traditional job analysis).[17] These three pieces of information are gathered independently from current employees or job applicants.

The skills necessary to perform a task are next ranked by one or more people in order of their importance to the task. Only when all the people rating the task agree that the skills are related to an independent measure of performance is the job needs analysis validated.

As an example of job skills identification, consider the three common skills needed for managerial jobs.[18] As shown in Exhibit 13.2, managers at all levels need managerial and administrative, interpersonal, and technical and professional skills:
- *Managerial and administrative:* Includes understanding the complexities of the organization, being able to set objectives and goals, solving problems, and controlling results
- *Interpersonal:* Includes understanding of motivation, effectiveness of relationships with co-workers, sensitivity, and communication skills
- *Technical and professional:* Covers knowledge of the area of the business the employee works in and of its methods and techniques, as well as the ability to use them.

After the information about the necessary skills and their importance and the minimal acceptable standards of proficiency has been collected, only the person needs analysis remains to be done before the potential training and development needs can be determined.

Level of Management

	Technical and Professional	Interpersonal	Managerial and Administrative
Top			
Middle			
First			

Exhibit 13.2 Training and Development Skills Needed by Managers
Adapted from "A Basic Model of Manager Development," by E. Mandt, p. 298. Reprinted with permission *Personnel Journal*, Costa Mesa, CA, copyright March 1979.

Person Needs Analysis

The **person needs analysis** can be accomplished in two different ways. Employee performance discrepancies may be identified either by comparing actual performance with the minimal acceptable standards of performance or by comparing an evaluation of employee proficiency on each required skill dimension with the proficiency level required for each skill. Notice that the first method is based on the actual, current job performance of an employee; therefore, it determines training and development needs for the current job. The second method, on the other hand, really identifies training and development needs for future jobs.

A relevant training question for the first method is, Can the employee do his or her current job? For the second method, the relevant question is, Can this employee or new job applicant do some job he or she has yet to do? Both these questions have important implications for equal employment opportunity and affirmative action. To ensure equal opportunity and affirmative action, the basis for the above answers must be a validated set of measures that will enable the organization to determine current performance or future performance potential.

A final aspect of the person needs analysis is the determination of the level to which the needed skills should be developed. Three basic levels have been identified. At the lowest level, the employee or potential employee must develop fundamental knowledge, which means developing the basic understanding of a field and getting acquainted with the language, concepts, and relationships involved in it. The goal of the next-highest level is skill development, or acquiring the ability to perform in a particular skill area. The highest level aims for increased operational proficiency, which means obtaining additional experience and improving skills that have already been developed.[19]

The level at which training must be targeted thus combines with the other information from needs analysis of the person, job, and organization to determine what training and development programs should be offered, to whom they should be provided, and on what criteria they should be evaluated. The next important step is to decide how these programs should be implemented.

IMPLEMENTING TRAINING AND DEVELOPMENT PROGRAMS

Successful implementation of training and development programs depends on selecting the right programs for the right people at the right time. Needs analysis helps identify the right people and the right time. An effective program can then be developed by using the principles of learning to tailor the content, design, and methods of the program to the needs of individuals.

Principles of Learning

As previously stated, training and development programs improve current or future performance by increasing employee ability through learning. "Learning may be thought of as a process by which an individual's pattern of behavior is changed by experience . . . of exposure to the training activity."[20] Although the term *behavior* can include any aspect of human activity, thoughts, or feelings, only behavioral changes that result in increased employee ability to perform are generally considered important in training and development programs. However, "where the balance of outcomes leans too heavily toward the exclusive benefit of organizational objectives (such as employee performance), training efforts will lose their effectiveness, and vice versa."[21] This means that considering the individual in the implementation of training and development programs will increase the likelihood of the training being effective, because it increases the chances of the individual actually learning a new behavior. "A behavior becomes learned when one experiences a new way of acting, thinking, or feeling, finds the new pattern gratifying or useful, and incorporates it into the repertoire of behaviors."[22] Thus training and development programs should aim at changing behaviors to benefit both the organization and the individual.

Learning Curves and Plateaus.   Learning does not always progress at the same rate during a training program. Differing rates of learning can be described by learning curves and plateaus, which illustrate the relationship between the time an individual spends learning the task for which he or she is being trained and the rate of success in acquiring that skill. Often the skills for complex tasks are acquired at a much slower rate than for simple tasks. Have you noticed that the amount you can learn per hour decreases rapidly the longer you study? That pattern of learning is described as a **decreasing returns curve**. An **increasing returns curve** illustrates a situation in which learning progresses very slowly at first and then accelerates dramatically. Another learning curve, the **S-shaped curve**, is a composite of the decreasing and increasing returns curves. "Many psychologists believe that if we could measure a response (successful learning) from the very first stages of learning to the asymptote, we would always come up with an S-shaped curve."[23]

The S-shaped curve is typical of the rate of learning in many situations, but somewhere along the S-curve there is generally a **plateau**, a temporary leveling-off. Plateaus can occur for several reasons. After the initial excitment of learning, motivation may decline for a while and then pick up again. Or the individual may need to synthesize what has been learned so far, and until synthesis takes place, little new learning may occur. Or the individual may be taking time to sort out and eliminate incorrect learning.[24]

Consider the implications of these learning curves and plateaus. If you have been studying for a while and doing well, but begin to slow down, it may be very reasonable to ride out this plateau in a favorite spot, just thinking about what you have already learned. Moreover, knowing that there will be peaks and valleys in learning can alert you when you should work hardest and when you should take a break.

Reinforcement, Knowledge of Results, and Goals. According to the principles of **reinforcement**, people will do what's rewarded and avoid doing what is not rewarded or what is punished. And although learning can be rewarding for its own sake, it is generally regarded as "a difficult and distasteful process which must be rewarded extrinsically to ensure its effectiveness."[25] This fact may be useful for training and development programs, because extrinsic rewards are often at the disposal of the organization and the trainer. For example, managers may praise their employees for learning a new skill, and the organization may provide promotional opportunities for those who successfully complete a training and development program. These extrinsic rewards are said to reinforce an individual's behavior (for example, learning a new skill) because they are given on the basis of that behavior. Another term used to describe these extrinsic rewards is *contingent rewards*. Because the principles of reinforcement are so important in learning, the implementation and maintenance of effective training depend in part on the effective management of contingent rewards.[26]

Effective management of contingent rewards depends on knowing when to give them. Although reinforcement should be given immediately following the desired behavior, it need not be given after each behavior.[27] Indeed, an individual who is reinforced only after a certain number of desired behaviors will perform vigorously

---

Here are some descriptions and examples of schedules of reinforcement:

- *Continuous schedule:* Rewards are administered after every desired behavior, and punishment is administered after every incorrect behavior. An example would be giving praise after every sale that is made.
- *Fixed-interval schedule:* Reinforcement or punishment is provided after a certain fixed period of time. A monthly paycheck is an example of a typical fixed-interval reward.
- *Fixed-ratio schedule:* Reinforcement or punishment is provided after a certain predetermined number of behaviors have been observed. For example, punishment may be administered only after a worker has been absent for five consecutive days.
- *Intermittent or variable-ratio schedule:* Reinforcement or punishment is provided after a number of behaviors have been observed. Unlike the fixed-ratio schedule, however, the number of observed behaviors constantly changes and is therefore not known by the person being observed. For example, a supervisor may give an employee an afternoon off for one excellent report and then not provide one again until three or four more good reports have been submitted. The employee never knows how may good reports will earn an afternoon off.

and quickly until the required number of behaviors is achieved. In addition, the behaviors learned under such a **partial reinforcement** schedule are much more resistant to extinction than those learned under conditions of continuous reinforcement.[28] The advantages of the partial reinforcement schedule are important to managers who want to change the behavior of their employees or maintain a change that has occurred. In addition, partial reinforcement schedules are a benefit to the manager, because they do not require the manager to observe and be ready to administer rewards to employees every time they perform. Instead, they allow the manager to observe employees' behavior only intermittently.[29]

Although the evidence indicates that contingent rewards and punishments are effective if they are administered properly, managers occasionally claim that there are few rewards to give. Yet they often fail to provide what is probably the single most important reinforcement and incentive: knowledge of results.[30] In learning a new behavior, people sometimes cannot judge whether they are behaving correctly. Managers can play an important role at this point simply by telling employees how well they are doing. Adding rewards for properly performed behaviors and imposing punishments for improper behaviors accelerates learning considerably.

Goal setting can also accelerate learning, particularly when it is accompanied by knowledge of results.[31] Individuals generally perform better and learn more quickly when they have goals, particularly if the goals are specific and reasonably difficult. Goals that are too easy or too difficult have little motivational value. It is only when people have some chance of reaching the goal that they can really become motivated.[32] The motivational value of goal setting may also increase when employees participate in the goal-setting process.[33] When the manager or trainer and the employee work together to set goals, the employee's unique strengths and weaknesses can be identified. Then aspects of the training and development program can be tailored to specific employees, which may increase the effectiveness of the training program.

Transfer of Training.   One serious mistake in designing training and development programs is the "failure to provide definite systems, policies and/or follow-up programs to ensure the learners' effective use of their newly acquired knowledge, skills and attitudes *on the job*."[34] As a result, what an employee learns in a training program may never be tried in the actual job situation. Or if the newly learned behavior is tried, it may quickly be extinguished due to lack of support. It is therefore important that provisions be made in training programs for the positive transfer to the job of the behaviors learned in training. There are two ways to do this. One is to have conditions in the training program identical to those in the job situation. The second is to teach principles for applying the behaviors learned in the training program to the job situation.[35]

Although it is desirable to incorporate these principles of learning, many training and development programs do not have them or are designed without consideration of individual differences, motivation, learning curves and plateaus, and reinforcement, feedback, and goal setting.[36] Nevertheless, application of these principles of learning can increase the chances of successfully implementing a training and development program. Successful implementation, however, also depends on selecting the correct programs.

Training and Development Programs

There are a multitude of training and development programs for both managers and nonmanagers. Although other characteristics may be used, these programs are most often distinguished by who participates (for example, managers or nonmanagers); where the programs are conducted (on-the- job or off-the-job); and what employee ability is being changed (technical skills and knowledge, interpersonal skills and attitudes, or conceptual skills and knowledge). The abilities gained by the employee in any of these programs can be used to reduce current or future performance deficiences.

On-the-Job Programs. As shown in Exhibit 13.3, several programs can be conducted on the job. These programs are often formally developed and implemented by the organization, but some training and development is informal. One such informal method is supervisory assistance, which can be provided for both non-managerial and managerial employees.

Generally, on-the-job training programs are used by organizations because they provide "hands-on" learning experience that facilitates learning transfer and because they can fit into the organizations' flow of activities. Separate areas for training and development are thus unnecessary, and employees can begin to make a contribution to the organization while still in training.[37] On-the-job training programs, however, are not without their disadvantages. For example, have you ever been waited on by a trainee in a restaurant? Or have you ever had to wait in line a particularly long time because the bank was "breaking in" two teller trainees? On-the-job programs may result not only in customer dissatisfaction but also in damage to equipment, costly errors, and frustration for both the trainer (most likely a co-worker or supervisor) and the trainee.

The disadvantages of on-the-job training can be minimized by making the training program as systematic and complete as possible. **Job instruction training (JIT)** represents such a systematic technique. JIT was developed "to provide a guide for giving on-the-job skill training to white- and blue-collar employees as well as technicians."[38] Since JIT is a technique rather than a program, it can be adapted to training efforts for all employees in off-the-job as well as on-the-job programs.

JIT consists of four steps: (1) careful selection and preparation of the trainer and the trainee for the learning experience to follow; (2) a full explanation and demonstration by the trainer of the job to be done by the trainee; (3) a trial on-the-job performance by the trainee; and (4) a thorough feedback session between the trainer and trainee to discuss the trainee's performance and the job requirements.[39]

Another method for minimizing the disadvantages of on-the-job training is combining it with off-the-job training. Apprenticeship training, internships, and assistantships are programs based on this combination. **Apprenticeship training** is mandatory for admission into many of the skilled trades, such as plumbing, electronics, and carpentry. These programs are formally defined by the U.S. Department of Labor's Bureau of Apprenticeship and Training and involve a written agreement "providing for not less than 4,000 hours of reasonably continuous employment . . . and supplemented by a recommended minimum of 144 hours per year of related classroom instruction."[40] To be really effective, the on- and off-the-job components of the apprenticeship program must be well integrated and appropriately planned, recognize individual differences in learning rates and abilities, and be flexible enough to meet the changing demands and technology of the trades.[41]

Somewhat less formalized and extensive than apprenticeship training are the internship and assistantship programs. **Internships** are often part of an agreement between schools and colleges and local organizations. As with apprenticeship training, individuals in these programs earn while they learn but at a rate that is less than that paid to fulltime employees or master craftworkers. The internships, however, function not only as a source of training but also as a source of exposure to job and organizational conditions. Students on internship programs are often able to see the application of ideas taught in the classroom more readily than students without any work experience. **Assistantships** involve fulltime employment and expose an individual to a wide range of jobs. However, since the individual only assists other workers, the learning experience is often vicarious. This disadvantage is eliminated by programs of job or position rotation and multiple management.

Both job rotation and multiple-management programs are used to train and expose employees to a variety of jobs and decision-making situations. Although **job rotation** does provide employee exposure, the extent of training and long-run benefit it provides may be overstated. This is because the employees are not in a single job for a long enough period to learn very much and are not motivated to dig in because they know that they will move on in the near future.[42] As a personal career strategy, you may want to avoid job rotation and opt instead for job assignments that are more fixed but that provide a greater challenge.[43] This choice is discussed more fully in Chapter 14, which deals with career management.

In **multiple-management** programs, lower- and middle-level managers participate formally with top management in the planning and administration of corporate affairs.[44] In essence, the top level of management makes decisions with the advice of the middle and lower levels. Using multiple managers provides an opportunity for top management to identify and select top-management candidates. In a sense, it becomes an on-the-job assessment process. Being part of multiple-management program can be an important step in an individual's career. Because of a relatively limited number of positions in the multiple-management program, competition for them can be great, but the potential rewards are even greater. If such an opportunity is provided, you may not wish to pass it up.

The final and most informal program of training and development is **supervisory assistance**. This method of training is a regular part of the supervisor's job. It includes day-to-day coaching and counseling of workers on how to do the job and how to get along in the organization. The effectiveness of coaching and counseling as a technique for training and development depends in part on whether the supervisor creates feelings of mutual confidence, provides opportunities for growth to employees, and effectively delegates tasks.[45]

Off-the-Job Programs. Exhibit 13.3 lists five categories of off-the-job training and development programs. The first two—formal courses and simulation—are applicable to both nonmanagerial and managerial employees; the last three are primarily for managerial employees.[46]

The **formal course method** of training and development can be accomplished

	On-the-Job	Off-the-Job
Managerial	internship assistantship job rotation multiple management supervisory assistance job instruction training	internship job instruction training formal courses simulation case discussion role playing sensitivity training
Nonmanagerial	job instruction training apprenticeship training supervisory assistance	apprenticeship training job instruction training formal courses simulation

Exhibit 13.3 Major Options for Training and Development Programs

either by self-training, which is facilitated by programmed instruction, computer-assisted instruction, and reading and correspondence courses, or by others-training, as in formal classrooms and lectures. Although many training programs use the lecture method, because it efficiently conveys large amounts of information to large groups of people at the same time, it does have several drawbacks:

● It perpetuates the authority structure of traditional organizations and hinders performance because the learning process is not self-controlled.[47]

● Except in the area of cognitive knowledge and conceptual principles, there is probably limited transfer from the lecture to the actual skills and abilities required to do the job.

● The high verbal and symbolic requirements of the lecture method may be threatening to people with low verbal or symbolic experience or aptitude.

● The lecture method does not permit individualized training based on individual differences in ability, interests, and personality.[48]

Because of these drawbacks, the lecture method is often complemented by self-training methods based on auto-instructional technologies.

The two predominant auto-instructional methods are the linear programming method and the branch programming method, both of which are types of **programmed instruction (PI)**. In each, the learning material is broken down into "frames." Each frame represents a small component of the entire subject to be learned, and each frame must be learned successfully before going on to the next. To facilitate the learning process, feedback about the correctness of the response to a frame is provided immediately.

The successful use of PI requires that the skills and tasks to be learned be broken down into appropriate frames. Once this is done, the probability of an individual learning by PI is high, because PI allows individuals to determine their own learning pace and to get immediate and impersonal feedback.[49] Nevertheless, there are many skills and tasks that are impossible to break down into appropriate frames. Thus other methods, such as simulation, are used for off-the-job training and development.

Simulation, a training and development technique that presents participants with situations that are similar to actual job conditions, is used for both managers and nonmanagers. A common technique for nonmanagers is the vestibule method, which simulates the environment of the individual's actual job. Since the environment is not real, it is generally less hectic and safer than the actual environment; as a consequence, there is the potential for adjustment difficulties in going from the simulated training environment to the actual environment. Because of this, some organizations prefer to do the training in the actual job environment. But the arguments for using the simulated environment are compelling: It reduces the possibility of customer dissatisfaction that can result from on-the-job training; it can reduce the frustration of the trainee; and it may save the organization a great deal of money, because fewer training accidents occur. Even though these arguments may seem compelling, however, not all organizations, even in the same industry, see the situation the same way. Some banks, for example, train their tellers on the job, whereas others train them in a simulated bank environment.[50]

An increasingly popular simulation technique for managers is the assessment center method. The assessment center is discussed in Chapter 7 as a device for selecting managers. However, certain aspects of the assessment center, such as the management games and in-basket exercises, are excellent for training and do not have to be confined to assessment center programs.

Business games may be thought of as simulations of the operation of an enterprise. Depending upon the degree to which they mirror real life organizations, they should provide for considerable transfer from the training to the job situation.[51]

Regardless of where they are used, management games almost always entail various degrees of competition between teams of trainees. In contrast, in-basket exercises are more solitary. The trainee sits at a desk and works through a pile of papers that would be found in the in-basket of a typical manager, prioritizing, recommending solutions to any problems, and taking any immediate action necessary according to what is contained in the papers.

Although the in-basket tends to be an enjoyable and challenging exercise, the extent to which it improves a manager's ability depends in part on what takes place after the trainee has gone through the in-basket. The debriefing and analysis of what happened and what should have happened in both the business games and the in-basket exercise, when done by upper-level managers in the organization, should help the trainee to learn how to perform like a manager. Without the debriefing and analysis, however, the opportunity for improvement may be drastically reduced since it is left to the trainee to decide what to transfer from the game or exercise to the job.[52]

Another method of training that is a part of many managerial training programs is the **case discussion**, or conference. This method emphasizes individual or group analysis of a case that describes an organization and its sometimes not-so-apparent problems. Based on the information in the case, the individual trainee or group of trainees presents a solution to the problems faced by the organization.

Whereas the simulation exercises and case discussions may be useful for developing conceptual and problem-solving skills, there are two types of human relations or process-oriented training that are used by organizations to develop in its managers "interpersonal insights—awareness of self and of others—for changing attitudes and for practice in human relations skills, such as leadership or the interview."[53] These two types are role playing and sensitivity training.

Role playing, in comparison with the simulation and case discussion methods, generally focuses on emotional (that is, human relations) issues rather than on factual ones. The essence of role playing is to create a realistic situation, as in the case discussion method, and then have the trainees assume the parts of specific personalities in the situation.[54] The usefulness of role playing depends heavily on the extent to which the trainees really "get into" the parts they are playing. If you have done any role playing, however, you know how difficult this can be and how much easier it is to do what amounts to just "reading" the part. But when the trainee does get into the role, the result is a greater sensitivity on the part of the trainee to the feelings and insights that are presented by the role.[55]

A method of training and development that has been quite popular is **sensitivity training**, or laboratory training. Individuals in an unstructured group exchange thoughts and feelings on the 'ere-and-now" rather than the "there-and-then." Although the experience of being in a sensitivity group often gives individuals insight into how and why they and others feel and act the way they do,[56] critics claim that these results may not be beneficial:

Do we really want to rip off the "executive mask," which hides from the individual his true feelings, desires, and knowledge of self? Most people have taken many years to build up this "mask" or to build up their psychological defenses. While it can be very enlightening to find out that nobody loves you and that some people think that you have undersirable traits, this can also be a very shocking experience to individuals and not necessarily a beneficial one.[57]

This criticism is just one of many, and behind much of the criticism is a concern for the psychological safety of participants in these groups. Because of this concern, and because there has been no consistent proof that sensitivity training benefits on-the-job performance, the use of it in training and development has declined. Nevertheless, there are still a great many training programs to select from, and the problem of determining which one should be selected still remains.

Selecting a Program

A knowledge of the principles of learning, the three categories of skills needed by individuals in organizations, and the methods of training and development available provides the necessary information to select the training and development programs that are most appropriate for a specific organization. Program selection is based on the answers to three questions:
- What skills do the employees need to learn?
- At what level do these skills need to be learned?
- What training and development programs are most appropriate for the required skills and level?

The answers to the first two questions are determined by the results of the needs analyses. Referring back to Exhibit 13.2, you can see that the question of what skills employees need to learn can be answered in part by knowing what types of employees need the training. For example, if there are performance deficiencies among the supervisory and nonsupervisory employees, most of the training should be aimed at increasing technical and professional skills; on the other hand, interpersonal skills would be the primary need of middle-management employees, and top-level managers would most be in need of conceptual or managerial and administrative skills.[58] These matches between type of employee and the predominant type of skill training needed are useful guides to training employees for their current jobs and for future jobs they might assume. Thus knowledge of these matches can be used to facilitate employee career development and the organization's planning of what training and development programs it will need to offer.

But to use these matches for the benefit of the individual and the organization, it is still necessary to know the appropriate level of skill training: increased operational proficiency, skill development, or fundamental knowledge. The results of the job and person needs analyses determine the necessary level, particularly for current job training. The levels required for future job training depend on the organizational needs analysis as well as on the job and person needs analyses.

The final step is to determine which programs are most appropriate for the skill and level of training needed. A guide for this determination is shown in Exhibit 13.4.[59] For example, apprenticeship training is appropriate for those who need to increase their operational proficiency in technical skills, whereas the case discussion method is appropriate for conceptual or managerial and administrative skill training at all three levels.

Unfortunately, selection of the appropriate program does not ensure the success of a training and development effort. Success also depends on effective use of the principles of learning (such as reinforcement and feedback), provisions for learning transfer, well-trained trainers, and systematic and supportive organizational policies for the training and development of employees.[60] In an organization with systematic and supportive policies, training and development

> . . . becomes an integral part and parcel of the business plan and cycle, and its importance is not diminished as organizations become more profitable or less profitable. The key to a successful management development system is its continuity and its relevance to today as well as the future. It must not be looked upon as one-shot effort to hype morale but rather a well-planned, well-implemented, action-oriented, practical program headed up by a professional who believes in his charter.[61]

Problems and Mistakes in Training and Development Efforts

This training and development stuff is all good, but it's my boss who really needs it.—Middle- and lower-level managers

If top management would only show active support of the program, it would be a certain success.—The staff training specialist

Skills Required		
Technical and Professional	**Interpersonal**	**Managerial and Administrative**

Level of Skill Required

	Technical and Professional	Interpersonal	Managerial and Administrative
Fundamental Knowledge	job rotation multiple management apprenticeship training job instruction training	role playing sensitivity training formal courses	job rotation multiple management simulation case discussion
Skill Development	job rotation multiple management simulation supervisory assistance	role playing sensitivity training job rotation multiple management simulation	job rotation multiple management simulation case discussion
Operational Efficiency	job rotation multiple management apprenticeship training job instruction training simulation internship and assistantship supervisory assistance	role playing job rotation multiple management apprenticeship training job instruction training simulation	job rotation multiple management simulation case discussion

Exhibit 13.4   Selecting a Training and Development Program
Adapted from T. J. Von der Embse, "Choosing a Management Development Program: A Decision Model," *Personnel Journal*, October 1973, p. 911.

> The use of the term training and development *effort* refers to the total set of training and development activities and programs an organization uses for its employees. The term *program* refers to just one technique or method of training in the total training and development effort.

Management development? Active support? Why I'm doing that all the time.—
Top management[62]

As shown by these three quotations, misperceptions and the tendency to assign blame and responsibility to others are typical when talking about training and development in organizations. These are also good reasons for the lack of success of training and development efforts. But there are other reasons for failure as well, including:

● Performing hasty and shallow needs analyses and thus failing to define what the real training needs are and who should receive the training

- Substituting training for selection and relying too heavily on the "magic" of training to increase the ability of individuals who lack the capability
- Limiting the training and development effort to only formal courses and ignoring all other methods
- Lumping together all training and development needs and thus failing to implement programs appropriate for different needs
- Failing to give consistent attention to the entire training and development effort
- Failing to provide for practical application and organizational support systems for the newly learned behaviors[63]

The critical element is organizational support and a general willingness to make the changes necessary to the training and development effort. To provide support, the organization may need to change its philosophy regarding the development of human resources, to encourage managers to have positive attitudes toward training and to adapt to employees with newly learned behaviors, and even to change the compensation system to reward those newly learned behaviors.[64]

EVALUATION OF TRAINING AND DEVELOPMENT PROGRAMS

If we cannot judge whether an action has led forward or backward, if we have no criteria for evaluating the relation between effort and achievement, there is nothing to prevent us from making wrong work habits. Realistic fact-finding and evaluation is a prerequisite for any learning.[65]

And yet,

. . . historically very little evaluation of employee training has been carried out in industry, business or government. Managers, needless to say, expect their manufacturing and sales departments to yield a good return and will go to great lengths to find out if they have done so. When it comes to training, however, they may expect the return but rarely do they make a like effort to measure the actual results.[66]

Evaluation of employee training and development programs may be lacking for several reasons. The organization may be willing to accept the programs at face value, or it may be unaware of the importance and value of evaluation. Managers may be fearful of finding out that the programs really are not working. There may be a lack of understanding of the methods of evaluation and a lack of agreement on the bases or criteria of evaluation. The people in the organization may not be totally committed to the support of any training or change. Finally, a general design or framework for planning the evaluation of training and development programs and organizational change programs may be lacking.[67]

Nevertheless, the importance and necessity for evaluating the impact of any program remains. Evaluation is necessary to determine how well a program achieves its goals, the efficiency with which the goals were attained by the program, and the extent to which the changes that occurred were due to the program.[68] Evaluation should therefore be regarded as a necessary aspect of any employee training and development program.

The potential effectiveness of the evaluation process is enhanced when it is regarded as an integral part of the training and development program. There are many ways to emphasize the relationship between program development and implementation and program evaluation. The organizational decision makers can be identified at the program's inception and involved in the definition of program objectives and criteria. An impact model that specifies the logic of change and sequence of events should underlie each change effort. Plausible rival hypotheses should be examined and any irrelevant hypotheses ruled out in order to use the minimum, but appropriate, evaluation design. Results can be corroborated through multiple criteria, multiple methods of measurement, and systematic tapping of both quantitative and qualitative data sources. Finally, analytical procedures that are consistent with the data to be collected and the kinds of change anticipated should be used.[69] Implementation of these considerations will help to ensure that a program is evaluated effectively and fairly.

SUMMARY

The training and development of employees is becoming an increasingly important and necessary activity of personnel and human resource management. Rapidly changing technologies increase the potential obsolescence of employees more quickly today than ever before. And as reflected in the initial scenario of this chapter, some skills are just dying off, so that in some areas of the nation, local, state, and federal governments are entering into training and development.

As employee training and development becomes more important, it also becomes more necessary that the training and development be done effectively. This requires careful attention to the three phases of training and development: assessment or needs analysis, program development and implementation, and evaluation. The three types of needs analysis discussed in this chapter are a careful and systematic diagnosis of the short- and long-range human resource needs of the organization; a determination of the skills and abilities necessary for specific jobs in the organization; and an analysis of the current and expected performance levels of employees in the organization compared with the performance levels desired of them. It is really this difference between actual and desired employee performance (either present or expected) that defines a training and development need. This performance deficiency, however, only becomes a training and development need when it is the result of employee ability.

Although removing performance deficiencies is vital to the organization, training and development must consider the needs of the employees. Recognition of this fact helps make employee training and development a mutual process between the organization and the individual.

PERSONNEL PROBLEM
Within or Without?

The production department has been allotted four new positions. There is a difference of opinion between the personnel department and the production department about what type of people should be hired.

The production manager insists that four fully trained people be hired. She has indicated that her department has neither the time nor the inclination to train people. Besides, during the time of their training, they would be nonproductive, and their presence would decrease the productivity of the regular employees.

The personnel manager takes a different view. He wants to hire people who are not trained, because they can be paid less than fully trained workers. Moreover, they would be trained in the specific techniques appropriate for the

organization, and under these circumstances, the new employees would presumably be more committed to and more likely to remain with the organization. The personnel manager also feels that since fully trained people would have to quit other jobs to come here, they might be inclined to do so again at a later date.

1. Evaluate the position of the production department.

2. Evaluate the position of the personnel department.

3. Are there other factors that would make the choice easier?

4. Given the information in this case, which position do you support?

KEY CONCEPTS

apprenticeship training
assessment phase
assistantship
case discussion
decreasing returns curve
employee training and
   development
evaluation phase
formal course method

implementation phase
increasing returns curve
internship
job instruction training (JIT)
job needs analysis
job rotation
multiple management
organizational needs analysis
partial reinforcement

person needs analysis
plateau
programmed instruction (PI)
reinforcement
role playing
S-shaped curve
sensitivity training
simulation
supervisory assistance

DISCUSSION QUESTIONS

1. Why is training and development so important in organizations? Is this importance growing? Why?

2. What role should the federal government play in the training of people so that they are able to work?

3. How is training and development related to other personnel activities?

4. Why is it important to do an analysis of the organization in order to determine employee training and development needs?

5. How can principles of learning be applied to employee training and development?

6. What are some types of on-the-job and off-the-job training and development programs?

7. How can selection of the most appropriate training and development program be ensured?

8. What are some of the problems and mistakes often found in training and development programs?

ENDNOTES

1. R. J. House, *Management Development: Design, Evaluation and Implementation* (Ann Arbor, Mich.: Bureau of Industrial Relations, Graduate School of Business, The University of Michigan, 1967).

2. T. F. Gilbert, "Proxeconomy: A Systematic Approach to Identifying Training Needs," *Management of Personnel Quarterly*, Fall 1967, pp. 20–33.
   J. R. Hinrichs, "Personnel Training," in M. D. Dunnette (ed.), *Handbook of Industrial and Organizational Psychology* (Chicago: Rand McNally, 1976), pp. 829–860.
   R. F. Mager and P. Pipe, *Analyzing Performance Problems* (Belmont, Calif.: Fearon, 1970).
   G. S. Odiorne, *Training by Objectives: An Economic Approach to Management* (New York: Macmillan, 1970).

3. Gilbert.

4. J. F. Guyot, "Management Training and Post-Industrial Apologetics," © 1978 by the Regents of the University of California. Reprinted from *California Management Review*, vol. XX, no. 4, p. 84, by permission of the Regents.

5. Guyot, p. 84.

6. E. Mandt, "Managing the Knowledge Worker of the Future," *Personnel Journal*, March 1978, p. 139.

7. "Ten Serious Mistakes in Management Training Development" by J. W. Taylor, pp. 357–362. Reprinted with permission *Personnel Journal*, Costa Mesa, CA, copyright May 1974.

8. E. Mandt, "A Basic Model of Manager Development," *Personnel Journal*, June 1979, p. 395.

9. P. F. Drucker, *The Practice of Management* (New York: Harper & Row, 1954), p. 187.

10. I. L. Goldstein, *Training: Program Development and Evaluation* (Monterey, Calif.: Brooks/Cole, 1974).
    W. McGehee and P. W. Thayer, *Training in Business and Industry* (New York: Wiley, 1961).
    M. L. Moore and P. Dutton, "Training Needs Analysis: Review and Critique," *The Academy of Management Review*, July 1978, pp. 532–545.

11. Goldstein.

12. "Choosing a Management Development Program: A Decision Model," by T. J. Vonder Embse, p. 908. Reprinted with permission *Personnel Journal*, Costa Mesa, CA, copyright October 1973.

13. McGehee and Thayer.

14. Moore and Dutton.

15. Moore and Dutton.

16. McGehee and Thayer.
    Goldstein.

17. L. A. Berger, "A DEW Line for Training and Development: The Needs Analysis Survey," *Personnel Administrator*, November 1976, pp. 51–55.

18. Mandt, 1979, p. 396.

19. Von der Embse, p. 908.

20. Hinrichs, p. 832.

21. Hinrichs, p. 833.

22. Hinrichs, p. 833.

23. B. M. Bass and J. A. Vaughan, *Training in Industry: The Management of Learning* (Belmont, Calif.: Wadsworth, 1966), p. 44.

24. Bass and Vaughan.

25. Bass and Vaughan, p. 62.

26. C. W. Hamner, "Worker Motivation Programs: Importance of Climate, Structure and Performance Consequences," in W. C. Hamner and F. L. Schmidt (eds.), *Contemporary Problems in Personnel* (Chicago: St. Clair Press, 1977).
    T. C. Mawhinney and J. D. Ford, "The Path-Goal Theory of Leader Effectiveness: An Operant Interpretation." *Academy of Management Review*, July 1977, pp. 398–411.

27. H. P. Sims Jr., "The Leader as a Manager of Reinforcement Contingencies: An Empirical Example and a Model," in J. G. Hunt and L. L. Larson, (eds.), *Leadership: The Cutting Edge* (Carbondale, Ill.: Southern Illinois University Press, 1977), pp. 121–137.
    W. C. Hamner and D. W. Organ, *Organizational Behavior: An Applied Psychological Approach* (Dallas, Texas: Business Publications, Inc., 1978), see especially pp. 237–70.

28. Goldstein.

29. Sims.

30. Bass and Vaughan, p. 66.

31. D. R. Ilegan, C. D. Fisher, and M. S. Taylor, "Consequences of Individual Feedback on Behavior in Organizations," *Journal of Applied Psychology*, 64 (1979) pp. 349–371.
    E. A. Locke, "Effects of Knowledge of Results, Feedback in Relation to Standards, and Goals on Reaction-Time Performance," *American Journal of Psychology*, 81 (1968), pp. 566–75.

32. Bass and Vaughan.
    Locke.

33. R. Likert, "Motivational Approach to Management Development," *Harvard Business Review*, 37 (1959), pp. 75–82.

34. Taylor, p. 362.

35. See
    Bass and Vaughan, pp. 38–40.
    Goldstein, pp. 105–111.

36. Some of the principles of learning that have not been included here, such as massed versus spaced practice, are more fully discussed in Goldstein and in Hamner and Organ.

37. Goldstein.
    Bass and Vaughan.

38. Bass and Vaughan, p. 88.

39. P. S. Greenlaw and W. D. Biggs, *Modern Personnel Management* (Philadelphia: Saunders, 1979), pp. 270–272.
    Goldstein.

40. Bureau of National Affairs, "Planning the Training Program," *Personnel Management: BNA Policy and Practice Series*, no. 41 (Washington, D.C.: The Bureau of National Affairs, 1975), p. 205. Reprinted by special permission from BNA Policy and Practice Series, copyright 1975 by The Bureau of National Affairs, Inc., Washington, D.C.
    See also, Bass and Vaughan, pp. 89–90.

41. Bass and Vaughan.
    Goldstein.

42. Hinrichs, p. 854.

43. D. T. Hall, *Careers in Organizations* (Santa Monica, Calif.: Goodyear 1976).

44. K. B. Watson, "The Maturing of Multiple Management," *Management Review*, 63 (1974), p. 5.

45. M. Mace, "The Supervisor's Responsibility Toward His Subordinates," *Developing Executive Skills* (New York; American Management Association, 1958), pp. 89–135.

46. For further discussion of these programs, see
    W. F. Glueck, *Personnel: A Diagnostic Approach*, revised ed. (Dallas, Texas: Business Publications, Inc., 1978).
    Greenlaw and Biggs.

47. A. K. Korman, *Industrial and Organizational Psychology* (Englewood Cliffs, N.J.: Prentice-Hall, 1971).
    S. C. Pressey, "Two Basic Neglected Psychoeducational Problems," *American Psychologist*, 20 (1965), pp. 391–395.

48. Hinrichs, p. 849.

49. Goldstein.
    Hinrichs.

50. These results are from a survey I conducted in Summer 1979 of Columbus, Ohio area banks regarding their personnel functions, particularly training and development.

51. Hinrichs, p. 853.

52. R. B. Finkle, "Managerial Assessment Centers," in M. D. Dunnette (ed.), *Handbook of Industrial and Organizational Psychology* (Chicago: Rand McNally, 1976), pp. 861–888.
    D. L. Warmke, "Effects of Accountability Procedures upon the Utility of Peer Ratings of Present Performance" (Ph.D. dissertation, The Ohio State University, 1979).

53. Hinrichs, p. 855.

54. Hinrichs, p. 855.

55. Goldstein, p. 194.

56. J. P. Campbell, M. D. Dunnette, E. E. Lawler III, and K. E. Weick Jr., *Managerial Behavior, Performance and Effectiveness* (New York: McGraw-Hill, 1970).

57. W. K. Kirchner, Review of *Behind the Executive Mask* by A. J. Morrow, in *Personnel Psychology*, 18 (1965), pp. 211–212.

58. Mandt.

59. Note that Von der Embse suggested a table for the selection of training programs for managerial employees only. I revised the table, adding more training programs and adapting it to cover nonmanagerial as well as managerial employees.

60. Taylor.
    House.

61. "A Systems Approach to Management Development," by J. D. Somerville, p. 371. Reprinted with permission *Personnel Journal*, Costa Mesa, CA, copyright May 1974.

62. House, pp. 9–10.

63. Taylor.

64. House, pp. 1–19.

65. K. Lewin, "Feedback Problems in Social Diagnosis and Action," in W. Buckley (ed.), *Modern Systems Research for the Behavioral Scientist* (Chicago: Aldine, 1968), pp. 441–444.

66. "An Organized Evaluation of Management Training, by M. H. Steel, p. 724. Reprinted with permission *Personnel Journal*, Costa Mesa, CA, copyright October 1972.

67. P. Horst, J. N. Nay, J. W. Scanlon, and J. S. Wholey, "Program Management and the Public Evaluator," *Public Administration Review*, 34 (July/August 1974), pp. 300–308.

E. A. Suchman, *Evaluative Research* (New York: Russell Sage, 1967).

68. R. Lippitt, J. Watson, and B. Westley, *The Dynamics of Planned Change* (New York: Harcourt, Brace and World, 1958). Suchman.

69. J. M. Nicholas, "Evaluation Research in Organizational Change Interventions: Considerations and Some Suggestions," *Journal of Applied Behavioral Science*, 1 (1979) pp. 23–40.

CHAPTER FOURTEEN
Career Management

I have been identified as a "winger" because I have never formally laid out my career goals. The only career decision I ever made, both before and after obtaining my engineering degree, was not to make sales my career. I accepted a position as a sales engineer, since nothing else was available at the time, and found the job so rewarding and enjoyable that I decided to make it my life's work. Some time later, my lack of knowledge of basic management principles became apparent and, with no thought of moving into management, I decided an M.B.A. would be advantageous. This background has been valuable and has contributed greatly to my past achievements, but it certainly was not planned.

The label of winger obviously applies to me. but not 100 percent, since planning is a must if I am to complete my daily workload and meet my many deadlines. But in "planning" my career, my top priority goal has been to enjoy my work, and, therefore, no specific career plan has been necessary. Enjoyment of the job results in enthusiasm, a necessary ingredient to success. Enthusiasm is contagious among coworkers and associates. This in turn produces a successful operation.

The major advantage of winging it is that it provides maximum flexibility with the least amount of personal stress. If you have worked out a positive career plan that allows no deviation, any detour or delay over which you have no control can cause severe mental problems. There is no question that if you have a specific career goal in mind, you will probably reach it sooner with a definite plan than without one. But are the sacrifices that have to be made worth the cost?

To decide whether you should be a winger or a planner, follow these steps. First, honestly analyze who you are, your capabilities, and what you want out of life. Next, determine your goals and priorities. Doing this enables you to define what you mean by success. From there, the path should be obvious. If success to you is reaching the top job, you have a better chance of achieving it if you do some formal planning. If success to you is to enjoy what you are doing, then become a winger, relax, and savor it to the fullest.

—Raymond R. Dirksen
General Plant Manager
Airflex Plant
Industrial Drives Division
Eaton Corporation

Reprinted by permission of the publisher, from "Is Career Planning a Useless Exercise?" H. Cleveland, Society for Advancement of Management, Advanced Management Journal, *Summer 1975,* © *1975 by Society for Advancement of Management, a division of American Management Associations, pp. 60–61. All rights reserved.*

Do you regard yourself as a "winger" like Raymond Dirksen? If, as Mr. Dirksen states, some formal planning will probably increase one's chances of making it to the top, why, then, do people just wing it? Is it really more relaxing? Does it really keep options open? Perhaps for you it does. For many, however, career planning is an effective way of helping to ensure that one gets out of a career and a life what one really wants.

Career planning involves identifying what is really important, what is really worth going after. People generally avoid this identification process because it tends to be difficult and can often reveal things they would rather not know. Once they do it, however, they know where their career is going and why. The rewards of career planning attest to its importance.

Career success is not necessarily seen as "making it to the top"; for many, it is simply being given the opportunity for growth and development. Organizations that fail to provide this opportunity risk losing good employees, and so many companies are now offering an extensive array of career development programs to their employees.

This chapter discusses the purposes and importance of career management, identifies several critical relationships between career management and other personnel and human resource activities, and discusses who is responsible for managing careers. Then it examines a few types of career development programs and also looks at several important aspects of planning one's own career.

MANAGING CAREERS

Career Management is a joint activity between the organization and the individual that identifies the individual's needs, abilities, and goals and the organization's job demands and job rewards. Successful career management thus requires the efforts of both the individual and the organization.

Career management has two essential components: career planning and career development programs. Together these two constitute a career management system.

Career Planning

Until recently, an individual's career was decided by the organization. If the organization needed someone in another location, someone was transferred. The success of one's career was often indicated by the number of moves that were made, since these moves were generally rewarded by promotions to more important and better-paying jobs. The organization was rarely concerned with whether the new job was really what the individual wanted, and the individual had very limited control over his or her career.

Today career planning has taken on a new meaning. Individuals are still transferred, and for many this still constitutes career success. But to a greater degree than ever before, employees now have a real choice about transferring. Organizations are becoming more concerned about what's best for the individual—not only in terms of whether the individual can do the job but also in terms of whether the job offers what the individual wants. That is, organizations are becoming concerned about whether an individual's abilities and needs are really matched to the job. Organizations have also begun to accept the fact that not all people want to be promoted. As a result, it has become more legitimate to have a successful career without climbing to the top of the organization. With more options now open within organizations, individuals are becoming more involved in their own career planning.

Most career planning programs offered by organizations are based on the premise that both the employee and the organization must be responsible for career planning. The individual must continually evaluate personal strengths and weaknesses, needs, values, interests, and motivations and be responsible for seeking out and taking advantage of opportunities afforded by the organization's career development programs.

Career Development Programs

When an organization becomes committed to having a career management system, it prepares to offer **career development programs (CDPs)** to its employees. These programs can range in complexity from posting jobs to developing multiple career paths. A listing of some specific career development programs is provided in Exhibit 14.1.

Career development programs are most effective when they are tied to the realities of the organization, when they evaluate the skills of employees as perceived by others, and when they encourage employees to identify needs and goals and to develop career plans. In addition, the programs should be applicable to all employees, not just managerial employees, and should allow for counseling if an individual wants it. Finally, they should be offered on a regular and continuous basis and should provide for feedback and followup for the employees.[1]

The Purposes and Importance of Career Management

The general purpose of career development programs is to match an employee's needs, abilities, and goals with current or future opportunities and challenges within the organization. In other words, the purpose of career development programs is to increase the employee's likelihood of achieving personal fulfillment and to ensure that the organization places the right people in the right place at the right time. Career development programs are therefore aimed at satisfying the two matches that were discussed in the recruitment and selection chapters: the match between individual ability and job demands and the match between individual needs and job rewards.

In addition to this general purpose, there are several specific purposes for conducting career management programs. "For the organization, career programs serve to assure maximum contributions from individual employees, as well as reduce underemployment."[2] In addition, these programs enable organizations to identify pools of talent and to practice a policy of promotion from within. They enable organizations to fulfill equal employment obligations by developing female and minority employees. They also help reduce absenteeism and turnover to the extent that they are successful in meeting the individual need-job reward match. "Overall, organizations encourage these career programs, hoping to improve performance and

Exhibit 14.1   Career Development Programs

Career Counseling
Career counseling during the employment interview
Career counseling during the performance appraisal session
Psychological assessment and career alternative planning
Career counseling as part of the day-to-day supervisor/subordinate relationship
Special career counseling for high-potential employees
Counseling for downward transfers

Career Pathing
Planned job progression for new employees
Career pathing to help managers acquire the necessary experience for future jobs
Committee performs an annual review of management personnel's strengths and weaknesses
and then develops a five-year career plan for each
Plan job moves for high-potential employees to place them in a particular target job
Rotate first-level supervisors through various departments to prepare them for upper-
management positions

Human Resources
Computerized inventory of backgrounds and skills to help identify replacements
Succession planning or replacement charts at all levels of management

Career Information Systems
Job posting for all nonofficer positions; individual can bid to be considered
Job posting for hourly employees and career counseling for salaried employees

Management or Supervisory Development
Special program for those moving from hourly employment to management
Responsibility of the department head to develop managers
Management development committee to look after the career development of management
groups
In-house advanced management program

Training
In-house supervisory training
Technical skills training for lower levels
Outside management seminars
Formalized job rotation programs
Intern programs
Responsibility of manager for on-the-job training
Tuition reimbursement program

Special Groups
Outplacement programs
Minority indoctrination training program
Career management seminar for women
Preretirement counseling
Career counseling and job rotation for women and minorities
Refresher courses for midcareer managers
Presupervisory training program for women and minorities

From M. A. Morgan, "Career Development Strategies in Industry: Where Are We and Where Should We
Be?" *Personnel*, March/April 1979 (New York: AMACOM, a division of American Management
Associations, 1979), p. 16.

profitability."[3] And in order for organizations to attain these purposes, they need to
offer a diverse range of CDPs.

For the individual, career development programs can result in increased responsibility, mobility, and acquisition of new skills. CDPs also help an individual to
adjust to significant life and career changes whether they be positive (such as a new

promotion) or negative (such as being passed over for promotion). They can also increase an individual's life and job satisfaction, involvement, exposure, and visibility and provide a better understanding of self and the organization.[4] In order for individuals to receive the benefits of a complete career management system, they must take the following steps with the aid of organization:

- Understand themselves and their current job performance (Where am I now?)
- Set reasonable goals for personal development and career growth (Where do I want to go?)
- Develop methods of acquiring skills and job information (How will I get there?)
- Plan alternative career paths (What do I do if . . . ?)[5]

Several significant changes are occurring that make career management important. One change is that more than ever before, employees are challenging or rejecting traditional career paths and traditional definitions of career success. Nonwork concerns such as family, job location, and recreation are becoming more important. And at the same time, individuals are also demanding and expecting more challenge and responsibility on the job. Career success, however, is no longer indicated exclusively by number of promotions. Other factors—happiness, growth, doing what one wants to do, and having control over one's life—also mark career success. Another change is that those still seeking career success through traditional paths are finding opportunities for promotions more limited. Thus it is necessary to develop alternative career paths that will enable these individuals to attain success without promotion. If organizations fail to develop these alternatives, the result will be employee dissatisfaction, lack of fulfillment, and job withdrawal. Finally, increased rates of change in technology are making employees' potential for obsolescence greater. At the same time, it is becoming more difficult and costly to fire and hire employees. Consequently, CDPs aimed at preventing obsolescence benefit the employee as well as the organization.[6]

Relationships of Career Management

Career development programs and career planning opportunities have important relationships with several other personnel and human resource activities. Among the most important are relationships with human resource planning and programming, job analysis, staffing activities, and performance appraisal.

Human Resource Planning and Programming.   Until recently, the HRPP activity was the traditional way an organization dealt with career management.[7] That is, potential job demands were forecast, and then supplies of employees were forecast to fill those needs. The primary concern was making sure that the job demands were filled, and thus one match—between individual ability and job demands—received much attention. Now, however, with the increased necessity of accommodating employees (see Chapter 8), HRPP must also consider the individual needs–job rewards match. Since a critical part of career management is the identification of and accommodation to individual needs and values, it is an activity that complements HRPP. Organizations such as Nationwide Insurance Company, XEROX Corporation, and IBM have recognized this relationship by adding personal data, such as employee preferences regarding promotion and transfer, to their HRISs.

Job Analysis.   Sears, Roebuck and Company has an extensive job-based career development program that depends heavily on its job analysis. As Chapter 4 explains, job analysis identifies the critical job dimensions and necessary employee qualifications. At Sears this information is used to develop career paths or routes of job progression. Career paths are constructed to provide employees with an increase in at least one skill area on each new assignment, an increase of at least 10 percent in total points (based on the Hay job evaluation plan) on each new assignment, and assignments in several different functional areas.[8] The Sears program is based on the Hay Plan, but that plan could be supplemented by an analysis of what new skills employees can expect to acquire.

Staffing Activities.   An organization is more successful in recruiting qualified job applicants if it has a career development system. The system itself is important, but it also represents the organization's concern for the individual. An effective system suggests that the organization regards its relationship with the individual as mutually beneficial.

In spite of these benefits, however, organizations are reluctant to have career development systems for fear they will actually lose rather than gain employees as a result of the employees finding out that they really belong in some other line of work. Organizations like the Cleveland Trust, however, have found that even if this happens, it is probably in the best interests of both the organization and the employee.[9]

Performance Appraisal.   Many organizations use performance appraisals to find out employees' career aspirations and to provide an outside assessment of employees' abilities. Performance appraisal is also an important part of a career development system, since it identifies how well and, with the job analysis, under what conditions an employee performs. This information can then be used to map that employee's career path.

Who's Responsible for Career Management?

Both employees and the organization have responsibility for managing careers. Employees must engage in self-evaluation and be responsible for identifying and taking advantage of career opportunities. Organizations must provide those opportunities by offering career development programs and establishing an environment that is favorable to career planning.

[Organizations] must provide challenging jobs, systematic performance appraisal systems, equitable salary administration, and training and incentive for managers to adequately deal with the development of their subordinates.[10]

The personnel manager and the line manager or supervisor carry out the organization's responsibility. The supervisor, who frequently can have more impact on a worker's career than any other person, seldom has the time or the skill necessary to develop programs or even to counsel employees adequately. The personnel manager can aid supervisors in these activities. The personnel manager in turn relies on supervisors to encourage employees to engage in career planning activities and to identify their career management needs whenever possible.

ORGANIZATIONAL CAREER DEVELOPMENT PROGRAMS

Career development programs are offered by organizations to assist employees in career planning and development. Of the many career development programs shown in Exhibit 14.1, only a few can be examined here.[11] These few, however, illustrate the diversity of needs that are filled by the programs and the wide range of concerns that are considered by organizations to be important in career management.[12] The first three CDPs can serve the interests of all employees, and the remaining programs are aimed at the needs of specific groups of employees.

CDPs for All Employees

Job Progression.   The job progression program at Sears, mentioned earlier, was developed to enhance the relationship between career planning and development and to serve the practical needs of the employees and the organization. To do this, Sears focuses on the job as the vehicle for career development. There are four principles on which Sears bases its approach:

- The most important influences on career development occur on the job.
- Different jobs demand the development of different skills.
- Development can occur only when a person has not yet developed the skills demanded by a particular job.
- By identifying a rational sequence of job assignments for a person, the time required to develop the necessary skills for a chosen target can be reduced.[13]

The essence of the Sears job progression program is the identification of job demands or dimensions. Sears uses the Hay plan to analyze their jobs on three basic dimensions: know-how, problem solving, and accountability. Since these dimensions require different employee skills, a rational sequence of job assignments for an employee's career development would consist of jobs with different dimensions. As a consequence, Sears can use its program to identify rational paths to target jobs (those that represent the end of the employees' path); to classify paths according to speed and level of development obtained; to justify and identify lateral moves and even downward moves; and to assess training needs and provide input into a human resource planning program.

Used appropriately, such a job program can be very helpful in aiding an organization's equal employment efforts and in opening up career opportunities. "This kind of system can lift career planning out of the informal corporate 'old boy' network and reduce the employee's dependence upon a well-informed boss.[14]

Career Information Systems.   Carborundum's career development program is more modest than Sears's, yet it is more typical of career management programs offered by many organizations. Carborundum's program has four major ingredients.[15]

First, although the company helps provide job opportunities, it is the responsibility of the employees to invest in themselves. This means, for example, that employees must decide whether they want to compete for jobs open in other areas of the company besides their own or if they want to stay where they are.

Carborundum's second ingredient is that everyone has the right to explore job opportunities. To facilitate this search, the company has established extensive job-posting and job-bidding systems. Job posting alerts current employees to what jobs are open; job bidding gives those who are qualified the chance to become applicants for the open jobs. An important aspect of these two systems is that they are in effect throughout the organization. Thus an employee at a plant on the East Coast can hear about job opportunities in a plant on the West Coast.

To assist employees in realistically assessing what kind of career they can expect in the organization, several sources of feedback are available. This is the third ingredient. Thus employees can get realistic information about their skills and abilities from their supervisors and the human resource manager.

As the fourth ingredient, employees are provided with an opportunity to discuss what the needs of the organization are likely to be in the next several years. This career discussion also gives employees a chance to express their preferences for types of work, location, and other job conditions. A record of these preferences then goes into a data bank, which is tied into a more complete HRIS.

One key provision in Carborundum's career management program is that there are no restrictions on the frequency of job mobility:

Initially there was a great demand to put time-on-job restrictions on the system. But since management wants flexibility to staff new businesses, we believe that individuals should also have flexibility. We don't want our employees locked into jobs because they haven't served a one- or two-year sentence.[16]

Career Planning Models. The two CDPs just examined may appear rather simple. They involve the analysis of jobs, but they are basically programs that systematically make available more opportunities for employees to match their abilities and needs with jobs in the organization. But how does an employee's need for training fit into career planning? How can employees get involved in career development programs? How can a nonmanager develop into a manager? These are all critical questions for employees.

One way an organization may address these concerns is by developing a career planning model. The model is not a CDP in itself but is instead a framework linking together several CDPs (for instance, career counseling, career pathing, and training programs).

Although a career planning model has many components, three are of particular importance. One is that CDPs should be used to assess employees early in their career. This assessment helps the organization to determine its human resource needs and provides employees with the chance to learn if their careers with the organization will move upward or stay at the same organization level. An important and successful method used by organizations to assess individuals is the assessment center.[17] Although it is generally used to select management candidates, the assessment center is also good for career development because of several features:

● *Reliance on an employee's exhibited behavior:* This technique provides a more objective evaluation of the individual's skills and abilities, thus giving employees more realistic information about the likelihood of success at various upper-level jobs within the organization.

● *Use of simulation exercises to represent the work activities of the actual job:* This permits an evaluation of behaviors that are relevant to the job and of their possible impact on future jobs within the organization.

● *Determination of relative strengths and weaknesses in skills:* This helps an individual to identify those areas that need the most development and that are relevant to effective performance in certain jobs.

● *Relatively objective feedback to an individual about strengths and weaknesses:* Such feedback, based on exhibited behaviors recorded by several trained evaluators, confronts the employee with more factual, and therefore more palatable, evaluations. Objective, job-relevant feedback encourages employees to initiate developmental activities, since they can readily see the link between improved skills and success in higher-level jobs.[18]

The second component of a career planning model is that there are dual routes for participation in career planning activities: Employees can either nominate themselves or wait to be nominated by the organization.

The third component of a career planning model is the potential savings to an organization that implements such a systematic and extensive career management system. These savings may result from more efficient use of human resources, improved performance of incumbents in key jobs, decreased turnover because of increased opportunities for development within the organization, and more efficient achievement of affirmative action goals.[19]

CDPs for Specific Employee Groups

Organizations also provide CDPs that are targeted to the specific needs that employees will have at different points in their careers.

The New Recruit. As discussed in Chapter 8, the first job is critical in determining how well a new recruit performs and how long that person will stay with the organization. Because of the importance of the first job, the question of how to treat the recruit in the first year should be answered carefully. The individual should be given a meaningful first job, one that is seen as permanent and not as part of a training program. The temporary, look-see job assignments may provide an individual with some visibility and exposure, but unless they are viewed as serious and realistic job challenges, they will do little good for either the organization or the individual.

The organization should also provide training and realistic expectations for the managers of new recruits.[20] The managers should be able to provide recruits with useful information in their performance reviews. In addition, managers should be alerted to the career aspirations and goals of new recruits, so as to be able to aid in their career planning. New recruits' nonwork changes, including life stage and family cycle, should be considered as potential influences on the recruits' on-the-job performance.[21] The organization's reward system should be reevaluated to determine if performance is clearly defined and if valued rewards are provided to recruits.

The Nonpromotable Employee.   Due to gradual technical obsolescence or promotion to the level of one's incompetence,[22] many employees become nonpromotable. Thus organizations have been establishing programs to update systematically the skills of their midcareer managers.[23] Organizations are also trying to establish a climate that stimulates employees to change and learn.[24]

For managers who have been promoted to their level of incompetence, the organization has several choices: termination, transfer, demotion, training, restructuring of the situation, or restructuring of the job.

Termination of a subordinate may sometimes appear a simple solution, but it can be costly and is rarely uncomplicated. The actual monetary loss includes termination benefits, which can be quite high for long-term employees, in addition to the cost of recruiting and training replacements. For instance, an employee who earns $25,000 a year with 15 years' time with the same company might get over $12,000 in termination benefits. And the cost of recruiting and training a replacement could easily exceed that amount.

Less readily quantifiable, but nevertheless of significant value, are the nonmonetary costs—the effects of termination on others closely related to the person fired, as well as on the manager forced to fire a long-term employee. Such costs are rarely short term.[25]

An alternative to termination is returning the employees to previous jobs they were successful in. But getting employees to accept demotions (or "downward transfers") is not always easy and may take considerable career counseling. However, it can be done:

An outstanding salesman in one manufacturing organization had performed at exceptional levels for many years. Two years after promotion to district manager, he was referred to the personnel department for career counseling by his supervisor because of his poor performance. After a series of counseling sessions, the manager decided he would like to take the "demotion" and return to the job of salesman. He liked sales work and he was good at it, but he recognized that he was not a manager. He is now back among the ranks of the top sales force. This cooperative effort on the part of an individual and an organization has brought about increased levels of satisfaction for both parties.[26]

The Preretirement Employee.   In the years just prior to retirement, many employees become apprehensive about the anticipated removal of an activity—work—that has probably served many functions.[27] It is important to recall that career activities have significant psychological and physiological influences that may continue even after retirement. Retirement, however, can be viewed in a very positive sense as a time to do what one has always wanted to do to escape from an undesirable job condition. For some, it may be the start of a very exciting personal venture.

Individuals can ease the transition from preretirement to retirement with parttime work and hobbies. In addition, self-evaluation to determine when to retire and what to do after retirement is extremely crucial in preparing for this important life change.

To help preretired employees through this often difficult time, the organization and government agencies can take steps to assure that these people are aware of the benefits and support they will receive on retirement. Organizations may offer counseling services to assist retiring employees in identifying their personal goals and determining how they may best be attained, either through current activities or preretirement activities.

CDP Effectiveness

Regardless of whether the organization is implementing CDPs for all employees or for specific employees, their effectiveness depends on six factors:
● Line managers must have expertise in identifying career problems and counseling employees:

Great strides can be made in employee career development simply by giving supervisors training in certain basic skills: employee counseling and coaching, performance appraisal and feedback, mutual goal setting (both job performance goals and career goals) and job redesign (to provide subordinates with more skill-building activities with the present job.)[28]

● The program must have the strong support and endorsement of the organization's top management. Without this support, a comprehensive, integrated, and continuous approach to career management is unlikely.
● The organization's human resource planning and programming activity, job analysis activity, employee training and development activity, and the entire staffing function must be well coordinated.
● CDPs should not focus solely on advancement but also concern themselves with lateral transfers, demotions, job rotations, and job enrichment.
● CDPs should reflect the needs of the employees as identified by their career stage.
● Realistic career opportunity information must be provided and realistic expectations on the part of the employees developed. It is critical here that an accurate assessment be made of each employee's strengths and weakness and needs and goals. If realistic information regarding job demands and rewards is available, this assessment enables both matches to be made.

PLANNING YOUR CAREER

Since we spend one-third of our lives preparing for or working at our jobs, and the other two-thirds are greatly affected by how satisfying that one-third is, it seems logical to give some thought to career planning. In fact, career decisions cannot be avoided. "No decision" is actually a decision not to make a decision. And there's nothing wrong with that it you're willing to live with the results. But from the decision on, career planning is a matter of depth and degree of planning.

Career plans can be as varied as careers themselves, but some elements should be considered in all plans. To begin with, every plan must start with a goal or objective. In addition to a primary goal, we should set interim or secondary goals that we would settle for if we find our primary goal is beyond our reach or not worth the sacrifice. (A case can be made for setting one firm, far-reaching goal that we singlemindedly strive to reach; although the odds for success are greater, the price of failure is also great.)

The goal we set must relate to our potential. Therefore, we must assess our inherent and acquired strengths and weaknesses and, as a result of our evaluation, select the general direction that plays to our strengths and minimizes our weaknesses. Although we should attempt to be realistic in our assessment, we must remember that time and experience will thrust wisdom upon us and our potential will grow.

Since most of us do not have complete control of our destinies, our plan should be flexible in direction and in timing. Just about every organization has some key bench marks by which we can measure our progress. If we're hitting the bench marks, our planning must be right. If we're missing them, we're receiving a signal that must be answered. Because many circumstances can temporarily retard the progress of a highly regarded person, an executive should not overreact if his plan falls behind schedule. But the evaluation of our potential is largely subjective and certainly subject to error; and if the evaluation of our potential by others differs substantially from our self-evaluation, a complete review of the situation is necessary.

If we conclude that we're really not as good as we thought we were, we make peace with ourselves and find satisfaction in our present jobs. If, on the other hand, we feel we can still go further, we must resolve the disagreement. If we do not, it could lead to bitterness. In some instances, the best resolution may be a completely new environment with new evaluators.

In planning his career, a manager should start with one objective: outstanding performance in every position. To demonstrate on the current job how well we can do the general manager's job, or to regard the present job as just another step in our career plan, is deadly. The best guarantee for the future is outstanding performance in the present.[29]

—David E. Leibson
   Vice President and Director
   Manufacturing and Engineering Division
   Corning Glass Works

David Leibson's comments express the basic idea of this section: By actively managing your career, you'll do better than by not managing it. "Better" is measured by any standard you choose—personal fulfillment, climbing to the top of the organization, happiness, salary level. By planning and managing, you'll increase your chances of getting whatever you realistically identify as most important.

Getting into an Organization

To choose the right organization, you must first know what you want from yourself and life. You must evaluate your skills, abilities, experience, and aptitudes. You must know what you want, what you have to offer, and how the organization fits into your overall, long-run career strategy.

Exhibit 14.2 outlines one strategy for getting into the right organization. To obtain the most from this model, you should carefully review and do each step.[30]

Step 1: Identifying Career Objectives.   To begin with, realize that you are considering a sequence of jobs and job experiences as part of your career planning. Also make a point of eliminating several common career misconceptions.[31] The following interview between a career counselor and a client (a student) whô was seeking assistance in deciding on a career reveals several misconceptions:
● *The misconception of exactitude:*

Client: I would like some help in choosing a career.
Counselor: Why don't you begin by telling me about the decisions that confront you.
Client: Well, it's very important that I make the right choice. You see, I don't want to make any mistakes. I want to be sure that what I choose will turn out right.

Perhaps you can see this student has a misconception that career choice is an exact science. The counselor will need to convince the client that this is not the case.
● *The misconception of singularity and finality:* There is no such thing as *the* career decision, made once and for all. The client must be convinced by the counselor that people are always in the process of making career decisions.
● *The misconceived expectations of career jobs:*

Client: I'd like to take some of those tests that tell a person what to do or that would tell me what I'm suited for.

Tests cannot reveal everything about a person. Furthermore, tests can only partially indicate what job a person is suited for.
● *The misconceived relationship between interests and abilities:*

Client: I would like to find out what I would be good at—you know, what I can be happy with and succeed at.

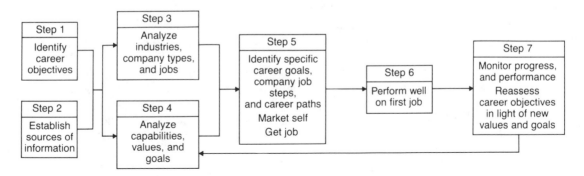

Exhibit 14.2 Career Strategy Model
Adapted from B. Greco, *How to Get a Job That's Right for You* (Homewood, Ill.: Dow Jones-Irwin, 1975), p. 22.

The evidence suggests that the relationship between interest and ability is not strong. In addition it's rather difficult to determine all abilities that are needed for a job or occupation today, not to mention what abilities may be needed in the future.

● *The misconception of taking a year off to find oneself:* Unless one actively engages in self-analysis and gathers career information, the year off will only delay the moment of truth.

Step 2: Establishing Sources of Information.

Step 2: Establishing Sources of Information.   This step is really a process. That is, you set up the methods of collecting information about jobs or occupations, organizations, and yourself or become aware of where you can go for information. You may consider getting together with close friends to review one another's skills, values, and perceptions.

Step 3: Analyzing Industries, Companies, and Jobs.   Summer work experience, internships, and parttime work are valuable ways to gain exposure to new work environments. Although some work experiences may be boring to you, it sometimes helps if you look at them as learning experiences, ways of getting to know yourself better. Other sources of information are newspapers and professional magazines, school placement offices, libraries, direct mail, job-search firms, friends, and family. A part of this step is reviewing such things as the organizations you value most, the products you prefer, the importance of a company's location, and your preference for working in private industry or government.

Step 4: Analyzing Capabilities, Values, and Goals.   Analyze your own strengths, weaknesses, personality characteristics, needs, and values, and determine what personal contacts you and your family already have with others in organizations. You should realize that education, family connections, and personal characteristics may be important in determining how much money you will make in your lifetime and what occupational status you will attain. The relative importance of these factors is shown in Exhibit 14.3. Although you may have no influence over some of these qualities, consider those you do have influence over—and then use them.

One thing you should realize is that most organizations expect new employees to have certain characteristics:

● *Competence to get a job done:* To identify the problem and see it through to solution

● *Ability to accept organizational realities:* To recognize such nontechnical values as the need for stability and survival, group loyalties, informal power arrangements, and office politics

● *Ability to generate and sell ideas:* To have, in effect, a whole range of skills, such as the ability to translate technical solutions into practical, understandable terms; the ability to diagnose and overcome sources of resistance to change; the patience and perserverance to gaining acceptance for new ideas; the ability to work through or around organizational realities; and the interpersonal skills or ability to influence others

● *Loyalty and commitment:* To place the goals and values of the organization ahead of one's own selfish motives and, if necessary, to sacrifice some parts of one's personal life

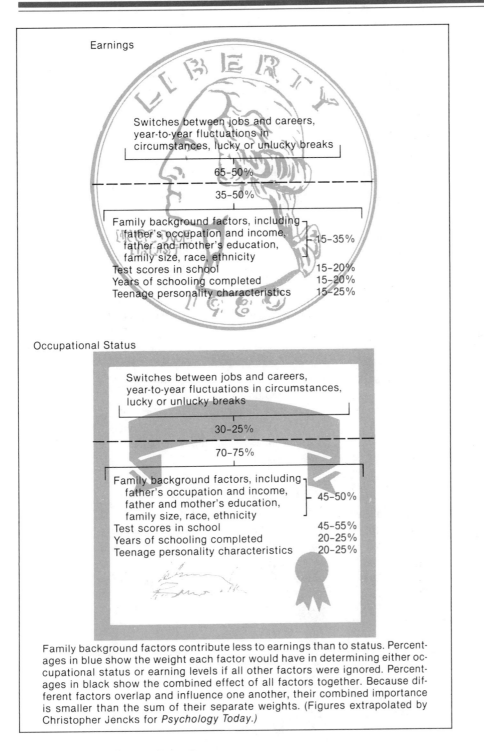

Earnings

Switches between jobs and careers,
year-to-year fluctuations in
circumstances, lucky or unlucky breaks

65–50%

35–50%

Family background factors, including
father's occupation and income,
father and mother's education,
family size, race, ethnicity — 15–35%
Test scores in school — 15–20%
Years of schooling completed — 15–20%
Teenage personality characteristics — 15–25%

Occupational Status

Switches between jobs and careers,
year-to-year fluctuations in circumstances,
lucky or unlucky breaks

30–25%

70–75%

Family background factors, including
father's occupation and income,
father and mother's education,
family size, race, ethnicity — 45–50%
Test scores in school — 45–55%
Years of schooling completed — 20–25%
Teenage personality characteristics — 20–25%

Family background factors contribute less to earnings than to status. Percentages in blue show the weight each factor would have in determining either occupational status or earning levels if all other factors were ignored. Percentages in black show the combined effect of all factors together. Because different factors overlap and influence one another, their combined importance is smaller than the sum of their separate weights. (Figures extrapolated by Christopher Jencks for *Psychology Today.*)

Exhibit 14.3 Influences on Career Success
From D. Yankelovich, "Influences on Success," *Psychology Today,* July 1979, p. 33. Reprinted from *Psychology Today* Magazine. Copyright © 1979 Ziff-Davis Publishing Company.

- *High personal integrity and strength:* To stick to one's own point of view without, however, being a deviant or a rebel; to know how to compromise when necessary
- *Capacity to grow:* To learn from one's experiences (mistakes are expected, but the repetition of mistakes is not tolerated); to demonstrate the ability to take on increasing responsibility and maturity in the handling of interpersonal relationships[32]

Step 4 has great value as preparation for job interviews. If you know yourself inside and out, you will find it easier to "sell" yourself to potential employers. Here are six suggestions for participating in job interviews:

- "Sell" yourself to the recruiter with the same determination you would use in selling a product or service to a customer. Remember that the interview period is brief. Yet a favorable impression of your appearance, sense of purpose, and clarity of self-expression will probably weigh more heavily with the recruiter than your transcript, your resume, or your references.
- Familiarize yourself ahead of time with the employer to be interviewed—know what the company does and what products or services it offers. Ask only pertinent questions during the interview, and suggest how your skills and abilities may benefit the organization.
- Develop your ability to communicate, but do not come on too strong or be overly confident.
- Cite academic achievements, especially if they appear to relate to the job area you are interested in. Remember that recruiting companies often view your college work as a preparatory period. Hence, cite your academic efforts as evidence that you can attain long-range goals and objectives.
- Mention extracurricular activities that demonstrate your leadership or initiative.
- Learn the art of interviewing by accepting as many interview opportunities as you can, even with organizations you think you may not prefer. Enroll in psychology and management courses where interviews are practiced by role playing.[33]

A SLICE OF LIFE

You may have spent years educating yourself and gaining the proper experience for the job you want. Possibly, all this preparation will be distilled down to one interview for the job of your choice with the company of your choice. Volumes of advice have been written for this time, but remember this: YOU NEVER GET A SECOND CHANCE TO MAKE A GOOD FIRST IMPRESSION.

Preparation for a job interview must also include making up a resume. An example of a well-written resume can be found in Appendix D.

If you are sure of your interest in an organization after the initial interview, pursue a visit or a followup interview. If you receive an offer of employment, gather as much information as you can before accepting it. And if you decide you do not wish to join the organization, notify the appropriate person immediately. It is really not necessary to provide detailed reasons. Similarly, most organizations prefer not to give you specific reasons if they reject you.

Step 5: Implementing a Career Strategy.   Decide what jobs or occupations you wish to occupy and the organizations and locations you would prefer. Keep in mind, however, that these decisions are tentative and subject to change. As a tool for developing your career strategies, consider using a **career balance sheet**. On this you enter positive and negative aspects of each job available to you. A balance sheet is a good way to organize job information and to weigh various alternatives. Exhibit 14.4 is an example of a balance sheet written by a manager considering a job change.

Exhibit 14.4   A Manager's Career Balance Sheet

The grid lays out the pros and cons of one alternative facing a production manager at a large manufacturing plant who is contemplating a job change: whether or not to remain in the present position. Balance sheets would be filled out as well for all other alternatives—for example, whether to seek a lateral transfer within the company.

	Positive Anticipations	Negative Anticipations
Tangible gains and losses for self	1. Satisfactory pay 2. Plenty of opportunities to use my skills and competencies 3. For the present, my status in organization is OK (but it won't be for long if I am not promoted in the next year)	1. Long hours 2. Constant time pressures—deadlines too short 3. Unpleasant paperwork 4. Poor prospects for advancement to a higher-level position 5. Repeated reorganizations make my work chaotic 6. Constant disruption from high turnover of other executives I deal with
Tangible gains and losses for others	1. Adequate income for family 2. Spouse and children get special privileges because of my position in the firm.	1. Not enough time free to spend with my family 2. Spouse often has to put up with my irritability when I come home after bad days at work
Self-approval or self-disapproval	1. This position allows me to make full use of my potentialities 2. Proud of my achievements 3. Proud of the competent team I have shaped up 4. Sense of meaningful accomplishment when I see the products for which we are responsible	1. Sometimes feel I'm a fool to continue putting up with the unreasonable deadlines and other stupid demands made by the top managers.
Social approval or disapproval	1. Approval of men on my team, who look up to me as their leader and who are good friends 2. Approval of my superior who is a friend and wants me to stay	1. Very slight skeptical reaction of my spouse who asks me if I might be better off in a different firm 2. A friend in another firm who has been wanting to wangle something for me will be disappointed

From I. Janis and D. Wheeler, "Thinking Clearly About Career Choices," *Psychology Today*, May 1978, p. 75. Reprinted from *Psychology Today* Magazine. Copyright © 1978 Ziff-Davis Publishing Company.

Staying in an Organization

The first five steps of this career planning model are important in making yourself attractive to organizations. After going through these steps, you should know what you want and what your capabilities and interests are, and you should be confident that you are seeking the organization that suits you. The final steps help you to stay attractive once you get your job.[34]

Step 6: Performing Well on the First Job.   Although "who you know" is important for career success, doing well is also important. Occasionally the best performers may not be promoted, but your chances of progressing in the organization are increased substantially by being an outstanding performer.

Step 7: Monitoring Career Progress.   People tend to seek low energy states—that is why they like to establish routines, find shortcuts, and resist change or innovation. As a result, they tend to avoid looking at themselves or reassessing and evaluating themselves, because the consequences imply change. But without such reassessment, you risk letting yourself become obsolescent in your job or never attaining your personal and career goals.

There are several techniques that you can use to help prevent career obsolescence. One, the **marketing model**, casts you as a supplier of goods and services with a price on them. The organization is a customer offering a price for your goods and services. Essentially, this model emphasizes the importance of knowing the demands of the organization. The job analysis, discussed in Chapter 4, reveals the organization's formal demands. But you must know the informal demands as well—what the boss likes, when and how to help the boss, what your place is in the organization, and what the importance is of the informal power system in the organization. The following example shows how significant these informal aspects of organizations really are for your career, especially if you want to get to the top:

Do you get to the top of a corporation by knowing more about your speciality than anyone else? You certainly do not unless your specialty is knowing how to make a favorable impression on those who are now top executives.

"In the corporate world," says C. Wright Mills in The Power Elite, *"one is drawn upward by the appraisals of one's superiors.* Fortune *magazine observers have remarked, even how the man looks as an executive, becomes more important than technical ability."*

To climb higher you must fit in with those already at the top.

"This means," explains Mr. Mills, "that he must meet the expectations of his superiors and peers; that in personal manner and political view, in social ways and business style, he must be like those who are already in, and upon whose judgment his own success rests. If it is to count in the corporate career, talent, no matter how defined, must be discovered by one's talented superiors. It is the nature of the morality of corporate accomplishment that those at the top do not and cannot admire that which they do not and cannot understand."

Fitness may not mean formal competence at all. It may mean only conformity with the criteria of those who have succeeded.

The nonconforming individualist, the disturber of the status quo, is likely to have a difficult time. His ideas, because of their value, may be put into operation, but the chances are, not by the creator of them.

"To be compatible with the men at the top," says Mr. Mills, "is to act like them, to look like them, to think like them: to be of and for them—at least to display oneself to them in such a way as to create that impression."

All that may make you doggone mad. But isn't it the truth? There are exceptions, of course, but aren't they as scarce as hen's teeth? [35]

The marketing model also emphasizes the importance of knowing your price. Your price reflects your values, needs, and goals. You can begin estimating your price by analyzing which of the following alternatives you would choose: a job paying $32,000 with an 80-percent chance for promotion to the next job (paying $60,000 and with a great deal more responsibility) or a job paying $45,000 with a 20-percent chance for promotion to the next job.

Not So Fast: Reality Shock

Based on all the information in this chapter, and all that you have done in response to the seven steps, you might think that your career will progress rapidly. Let's hope it does. There is, however, one more thing you should know. It's called **reality shock**, and it results from things not happening the way you think they will. Reality shock is less likely if you accept a job based on realistic job and organizational expectations.

There are several common aspects of reality shock:

● *Low initial job challenge:* Although some findings have indicated the usefulness of giving new recruits a challenging initial job, many organizations continue to ease the new recruit into the organization. This, of course, is consistent with the organization's perception of the new recruit as a novice.

● *Low self-actualization and need satisfaction:* The new recruit may fail to experience the autonomy and challenge necessary to grow and to develop self-esteem and competency. Some researchers have suggested that an individual may actually lose competency on the job if not given the opportunity to advance in the direction of the growth and independence characteristic of mature adults.

● *The vanishing performance appraisal, or inability to determine what the real criteria are:* New recruits come on board with the expectation of receiving clear and unambiguous evaluations of their performance. In reality, new recruits report having little feedback on their performance, although their supervisors may claim the opposite.

● *Unrealistically high aspirations:* As it turns out, most recruits have higher expectations of being able to use their skills and abilities than actually occurs. The gap between an individual's skills and the skills actually used on the job is probably increased because of the manager's belief that the new recruit really is not capable of assuming responsibility.

● *Inability to create challenge:* Although new recruits may not be given challenging assignments, they are also often incapable of creating their own challenge. They have been conditioned to receive well-defined projects from others. As a result, they find it more difficult to create challenge from an ill-defined or unstructured situation.

● *Source of threat to the boss:* A new recruit's first boss plays a critical role for the recruit's future in the organization. This role tends to be negative, especially if the boss feels threatened. The threat may occur to the supervisor who is in a terminal position and can't go any further in the organization. The new recruit may be seen as a "comer" with a great deal more potential than the boss. In addition, the new recruit is probably younger and has different values and styles. As a result, the supervisor may not be very supportive of the new employee and may not provide many positive experiences.[36]

● *Amount of conflict and uncertainty in the organization:* New recruits think that rules and procedures, directions, and communications will be clear, crisp, and without conflict. The reality in many situations is just the opposite.

These and other problems are illustrated in this actual case study:

I'm quitting! I can't stand this job. Every morning I drag myself out of bed and force myself to drive to work. It's hard to believe that nine months ago I thought taking this job was the smartest move I had ever made.

It was last May, when I was a month away from graduation, that I had narrowed my choices down to three companies. I knew exactly what I was looking for in a company. The ideal company had to be a small division of a national organization, provide good advancement opportunities, and offer a high salary. I even had the interviewing processs down to a science. My philosophy was to have a good resume and to tell them what they wanted to hear. Salesmanship was the key to interviewing. After weeks of interviews and a second visit with Electronics, Inc., I knew what job to take. I was wined and dined at their corporate headquarters in New York for three days, during which they told me of the management training program and success stories of young managers. They met all of my criteria, and the people were professional and friendly. I felt I would fit in.

I had no way of knowing at the time that the person who previously occupied my job had resigned after three months and that the position had been left vacant for six months. Mary, one of the nonmanagerial workers, had been trying to perform the job in the interim. Another bit of information they neglected to tell me at the headquarters was that my future boss, Mr. Durbin, was not meeting his profit plan and would be terminated one month after I started the job. It wasn't until I had moved from the West to the Midwest and had settled into the regional office that I got my first insight into a job that didn't appear to even closely resemble what had been described to me in New York. My job was to manage inventory, which required more paperwork and knowledge of rules and procedures than it did intelligence. I was to supervise a staff of twelve "clerical" employees (all of whom had college degrees). My scheduled training was canceled because they needed a manager in my position immediately.

During the short time I had with Mr. Durbin, I was given a project that was not related to my job responsibilities, so that upon the arrival of Mr. Kent, my new boss, I had not yet been exposed to the functions of my job.

My relationship with Mr. Kent has probably been the single most frustrating aspect of this job. He expected me to know my job when he arrived, and my explanation of the situation didn't matter. He recommended that I have Mary train me, a suggestion I found uncomfortable to implement since I was her boss and in theory was supposed to evaluate her on her performance. How could I manage her and still rely heavily on her advice and instruction? Not liking me very much, Mary is reluctant to train me in a position she feels she should occupy. Mr. Kent tends to go directly to Mary for information, and she has become a key informal leader of the office staff. The other workers won't cooperate with me unless Mary gives them the go-ahead. So here I am watching my boss bypass me to conduct business with one of my subordinates. The other workers don't follow me, and Mr. Kent yells at me for lacking leadership ability. Mary really should have been given this job, but I can't help that.

Last week I was so fed up that I marched into Mr. Kent's office and explained my frustration with this situation. He agreed that the lack of training was unfortunate and that he frequently violated the line of authority, but he explained that he was under constraints to make the regional office profitable. He went on to say that he had had to work his way up the ladder from a clerical position with little guidance, so I shouldn't need any hand-holding. I told him that I was working from 7:30 a.m. to 9:00 p.m. and was trying hard to learn on my own. He just smiled and shrugged his shoulders.

At this point I see few alternatives to the existing situation. Mary is still reluctant to provide me with information. Mr. Kent doesn't have time to help me. There isn't even another person in the region with a job similar to mine that I can talk to. I'm losing my self-confidence, my subordinates have little respect for me, and I don't even like the kind of work I'm doing.

My problem is that I can't quit. I'm two thousand miles from my family and friends, I just bought a car, and I really need the money. Besides, Mr. Kent probably wouldn't give me a good reference anyway. I thought I knew what I was doing when I took this job; all I know now is that I want out.[37]

Summary for Management of Your Career

A. Develop basic career competencies
   1. Appraise yourself
   2. Obtain occupational information
   3. Select career goals
   4. Plan
   5. Solve problems
B. Choose an organization carefully
C. Get a challenging initial job
D. Be an outstanding performer
E. Develop professional mobility ("executive chess")
   1. Maintain the widest set of options
   2. Don't be blocked by an immobile superior
   3. Become a crucial subordinate to a mobile superior

   4. Be prepared to practice self-nomination
   5. Leave an organization at your own convenience
   6. Rehearse before quitting
   7. Plan for your career to consist of a sequence of jobs (a "multicareer")
F. Plan your own and your spouse's careers collaboratively
G. Get help in career management[38]

EVALUATION OF CAREER MANAGEMENT

Evaluating the effectiveness of career management must be done from the individual and the organizational perspectives. Although the overall purpose of career management is to match individual ability to job demands and individual needs to job rewards, there are several specific purposes that relate primarily to the individual or the organization.

The Individual Perspective

From the individual's perspective, effective career management should result in several beneficial outcomes:
- A more realistic awareness of one's skills, abilities, and weaknesses
- An awareness of one's needs, values, and goals
- An awareness of realistic job and career opportunities that match one's abilities and needs
- A greater sense of self-worth and self-esteem from doing what one is able to do and wants to do
- A more satisfied and productive individual

   There is, however, little evidence to indicate how well career management activities actually help to attain these outcomes.[39] The evidence that does exist suggests that employees are more satisfied as a result of job placement activities that match them on needs as well as abilities (see Chapter 5). More informal evidence indicates, however, that the initial stages of gaining self-awareness and career awareness are often difficult and even frustrating if appropriate opportunities are not available. People who gain greater self-awareness may even leave an organization in search of better matches. How do organizations respond to this? If they offer career programs for their benefit as well as for that of the individual, organizations often wish the individual well.[40]

The Organizational Perspective

From the organization's perspective, effective career management should also result in several beneficial outcomes, including
- More effective use of its current work force
- Reduced absenteeism, since employees are better fitted to their job situation
- Reduced turnover after employees go through career planning and find an appropriate job in the current organization
- Improved morale among employees who decide to remain

- A work force with lower potential for obsolescence and a higher level of flexibility and adaptability to changing circumstances
- More employees suitable for potential promotion
- A better "image" as an organization to work for and, as a result, a larger pool of job applicants to select from
- A greater likelihood of fulfilling equal employment obligations and using the skills of all employees
- And last but not least, improved performance

Again the evidence on how well career management provides these outcomes is limited. However, those organizations that have them—for instance, Sears, Roebuck and Company, IBM, Cleveland Trust, Standard Oil (Ohio), J. C. Penney Company and Procter & Gamble—indicate that they are able to identify more potentially promotable employees and have an easier time attracting qualified candidates because of being known for offering career development opportunities. Career development is becoming more and more necessary in order for companies to remain effective.

SUMMARY

Career management is an important activity that provides benefits to both organizations and individuals. The benefits include better use of human resources, more satisfied and productive employees, and more personally fulfilling careers.

Organizations have only recently become involved in career management activities. Previously, organizations were concerned only with matching an employee's abilities to the demands of the job. Now they are also concerned with matching an employee's needs to the rewards of the job. The result of this dual concern is in recruitment and selection is reduced absenteeism and turnover and increased performance. In addition, when organizations are concerned with employee needs, it becomes easier for them to attract new employees.

It is important for any prospective employee to become attractive to organizations. This involves several steps that must be followed in order to manage one's career effectively. Once hired by the company, the individual must then know how to remain attractive. One aspect of this task is always knowing what your goals and needs are. What are yours now?

PERSONNEL PROBLEM
Evaluating an Organization's CDP

"Our career development program has been in effect for two full years," said vice president of personnel Jane Winslow. "What is your opinion of the program so far?"

"I think we are providing a service to our managerial employees and to some extent, to our hourly employees," answered the eastern division manager, Lyn Elliot. "However, I don't think we're serving the organization. Our career development program places a limit on the number of people we can promote, and we can't promote most people at the time they are ready. Often the promotion must wait for an available job opening, so we are essentially preparing people for other organizations. Our employees leave us for organizations that do have available job openings."

1. What is your reaction to the eastern division manager's opinion?

2. What is your recommendation?

3. Can a career development program be developed that does not result in this attrition problem?

KEY CONCEPTS

career balance sheet
career development program (CDP)

career management
marketing model

reality shock

DISCUSSION QUESTIONS

1. What are the benefits to an organization in offering career development programs to its employees?

2. What are the benefits you receive from managing your own career?

3. What things can you do to manage your career?

4. Why do new recruits experience reality shock? What is reality shock?

5. What career development programs can organizations offer employees? Are these programs effective?

6. Should nonpromotables be terminated? What are the costs of termination? What other courses of action are available to the company?

7. Who should be responsible for managing an employee's career—the individual or the organization?

8. What are your career goals? What are your strengths and weaknesses in relation to these goals?

ENDNOTES

1. For an extensive discussion of these issues, see
   S. L. Cohen and H. H. Meyer, "Toward a More Comprehensive Career Planning Program," *Personnel Journal*, September 1979, pp. 611–615.
   D. T. Hall, *Careers in Organizations* (Santa Monica, Calif.: Goodyear, 1976)
   M. A. Morgan, D. T. Hall, and A. Martier, "Career Development Strategies in Industry: Where Are We and Where Should We Be?" *Personnel*, March/April 1979, pp. 13–30.

2. Morgan et al., p. 14.

3. Morgan et al.

4. J. C. Aplin and D. K. Gerster, "Career Development: An Integration of Individual and Organizational Needs," *Personnel*, March/April 1978, pp. 23–28.
   Cohen and Meyer.
   Morgan et al.

5. P. G. Benson and G. C. Thornton III, "A Model Career Planning Program," *Personnel*, March/April 1978, p. 34.

6. Benson and Thornton, pp. 30–45.

7. Benson and Thornton.

8. M. Jelinek, *Career Management for the Individual and the Organization* (Chicago: St. Clair Press, 1979).
   J. W. Walter, "Let's Get Realistic About Career Paths," *Human Resource Management*, Fall 1976, pp. 2–7.
   H. L. Wellbank, D. T. Hall, M. A. Morgan, and W. C. Hamner, "Planning Job Progression for Effective Career Development and Human Resources Management," *Personnel*, March/April 1978, pp. 54–64.

9. R. E. Hastings, "Career Development: Maximizing Options," *Personnel Administrator*, May 1978, pp. 58–61.

10. Benson and Thornton, p. 39.

11. For an extensive discussion of CDPs and career issues related to males and females in organizations, see
    Personnel Administrator, April 1980.
    R. S. Schuler, "Male and Female Routes to Managerial Success," *Personnel Administrator*, February 1979, pp. 35–38.

12. J. Van Maanen and E. Schein, "Career Development," J. R. Hackman and J. L. Suttle (eds.), in *Improving Life at Work* (Santa Monica, Calif.: Goodyear, 1977).

13. Wellbank et al., p. 55.

14. Wellbank et al., p. 55.

15. "Symposium: Employee Career Planning," *Personnel*, March/April 1978, pp. 10–22.

16. "Symposium: Employee Career Planning," p. 17.

17. For a discussion on the use of the assessment center as a development program, see
    J. Fitz-enz, K. E. Hards, and G. E. Savage, "Total Development: Selection, Assessment, Growth," *Personnel Administrator*, February 1980, pp. 58–62.
    J. C. Quick, W. A. Fisher, L. C. Schkade, and G. W. Ayers, "Developing Administrative Personnel Through the Assessment Center Technique," *Personnel Administrator*, February 1980, pp. 44–46, 62.

18. Cohen and Meyer, p. 614.

19. Cohen and Meyer, p. 615.

20. Hall.

21. For an excellent discussion of career stages, see
    Hall.
    D. T. Hall and M. Morgan, "Career Development and Planning," in W. C. Hamner and F. Schmidt (eds.), *Contemporary Problems in Personnel*, Revised ed. (Chicago: St. Clair Press, 1977).
    Van Maanen and Schein.

22. L. J. Peter and R. Hull, *The Peter Principal* (New York: Morrow, 1969).

23. Morgan et al.

24. H. J. Horgan and R. P. Floyd Jr., "MBO Approach to Prevent Technical Obsolescence," *Personnel Journal*, September 1971, pp. 687–693.
    R. L. Shearer and J. A. Steger, "Manpower Obsolescence: A New Definition and Empirical Investigation of Personal Variable," *Academy of Management Journal*, 18 (1975), pp. 263–275.

25. E. Roseman, *Confronting Nonpromotability* (New York: AMACOM, 1977), pp. 136–137.

26. Morgan et al., p. 18.

27. F. H. Cassell, "The Increasing Complexity of Retirement Decisions," *MSU Business Topics*, Winter 1978, pp. 15–24.

28. Morgan et al., p. 24.

29. Reprinted by permission of the publisher, from "Is Career Planning a Useless Exercise?", H. Cleveland, S.A.M. *Advanced Management Journal*, Summer 1975, © 1975 by S.A.M., a division of American Management Associations, pp. 59–60. All rights reserved.

30. S. A. Culbert, *The Organization Trap and How to Get Out of It* (New York: Basic Books, 1974).

31. For an extensive discussion of career
     misconceptions, see
     A. P. Thompson, "Client Misconceptions in
     Vocational Counseling," *Personnel and
     Guidance Journal*, September 1976, pp.
     30–33.

32. E. H. Schein, "How to Break in the College
     Graduate," *Harvard Business Review*, 42 (1964),
     p. 70.

33. J. H. Conley, J. M. Hueghi, and R. L. Minter,
     Perspectives on Administrative Communication
     (Dubuque, Iowa: Kendall/Hunt, 1976), p. 172.

34. J. Rago, "Career Management and
     Obsolescence" (The Cleveland State University,
     1979).

35. *The Wright Line* (Worcester, Mass.: The Wright

Line, Inc., 1970), p. 1, Reprinted with
permission.

36. D. E. Berlew and D. T. Hall, "Some
     Determinants of Early Managerial Success,"
     Working paper #81-64 (Cambridge, Mass.:
     Sloan School of Management, MIT, 1964).
     R. A. Webber, "Career Problems of Young
     Managers," *California Management Review*, 4
     (1976), pp. 19–33.

37. This case was written expressly for this chapter
     by Cathy Enz, Ph.D. student at The Ohio State
     University. This story is based on her personal
     job experiences. All names have been changed.

38. Hall.

39. Morgan et al.,

40. Hastings.

SECTION SIX

Establishing and Maintaining Effective Labor Relations

CHAPTER 15
Collective Representation
CHAPTER 16
Interactions between Union and Management

THIS SECTION PREPARED BY
William D. Todor

CHAPTER OUTLINE

OBJECTIVES

- To explain why individual employees join unions

- To discuss the history and development of the labor movement

- To explain the laws governing labor relations

- To describe the process by which a union becomes the bargaining representative of a work group

THOUGHT STARTERS

- How do you feel about unions, and why might you join one?

- Why have union-management relations been so turbulent and adversarial?

- What is the future of unions? Have unions outlived their usefulness?

- Why are increasing numbers of public employees unionizing?

CHAPTER FIFTEEN
Collective Representation

Brenda C. is a nursing aide at a nursing home. She has been a diligent employee there for two-and-one-half years and enjoys her work. She has been considered a good worker by her supervisor. Recently she has become increasingly concerned with the pay and the working conditions at the home.

Although the nursing aides often work extra to help a patient and as a group are dedicated to their work, the pay scale is significantly below that of other homes in the area. In addition, the nursing aides and other hospital staff have no area where they can get away from the patients for a break; in fact, the nursing home does not provide for a coffee break at all. The nursing staff does, however, take informal breaks whenever they can get a few minutes, and Brenda has found that these help her function better in the sometimes hectic work situation. Since the staff is not allowed to eat in the cafeteria, they must provide for their lunch by eating out or bringing a bag lunch. This has also caused problems, because sometimes the staff is delayed at the restaurant when they go out for lunch.

It seems to Brenda that providing a lounge area for coffee and lunch breaks would make the job much easier for the staff and would result in

better care for the patients. She approached her supervisor about the matter, but he was not receptive and suggested that she concentrate on her job. Brenda persisted and was told that the budget is too tight and space is too limited.

Brenda knows that her nursing aide friends in other homes have such facilities, and she is fairly certain that those homes are no better off financially than hers. She feels she can get no further on her own, so she contacts the union that represents nursing aides in some of the other homes and arranges for a meeting after work on Friday, expecting a good turnout. She discusses the situation with her co-workers and many of them are very interested.

On Friday afternoon the manager of the nursing home calls her into his office and tells her that her performance has recently been inadequate (although her last review was good), that her attitude toward the patients has changed, and that he is terminating her employment as of that day. Brenda is shocked. She tells her co-workers what has happened, and they are also very surprised. Four people attend the union meeting that night. They soon leave expressing fear for their jobs.

his scenario highlights some features of union-management relations that unions have reported during attempts to organize employees. First, it indicates the main concerns that cause workers to think about organizing—pay, working conditions, and management behavior[1] In addition, although the union may actively solicit employees to join, there generally has to be interest among the members of the organization for the organizing process to get underway. Third, the opposition to unionization shown by the organization in the scenario is typical.

Organizing, or **collective bargaining**, is the effort by employees and outside agencies (unions or associations) to band together and act as a single unit when dealing with management over issues related to their work. The most common form for organizing employees is the **union**, an organization with the legal authority to negotiate with the employer on behalf of the employees—over wages, hours, and other conditions of employment—and to administrate the ensuing agreement. In the public sector, employees are sometimes represented by **employee associations** like the National Education Association. Although employee associations may not be involved in as many functions as a union (they may not bargain with the employer, for example), most of the large associations do engage in the same activities and have become very similar to private-sector unions. Consequently, in this chapter associations and private-sector unions will be treated as equivalent.

Understanding the organizing process, its causes, and its consequences is an important part of personnel and human resource management. The personnel department can play a key role in designing the organization and management structure to prevent unionization of employees. If unionization occurs, personnel managers will probably be given the task of dealing with the organizing effort: presenting management's view to the employees; responding to statements or behaviors of the unions, such as boycotts or picketing; and representing management at the certification proceedings. The personnel department may even need to create a labor relations department to deal with the union.

The following sections examine the reasons why employees join unions, the history of union development, the laws and regulations that govern union activities, the organizing process, and union-management relations.

EMPLOYEES AND UNIONIZATION

Unions were originally formed as a response to management's exploitation and abuse of employees. Today over 23 million employees belong to unions or employee associations, and the number continues to grow.[2] To understand the union movement, it is necessary to consider the attraction that unions have for employees.

The Decision to Join a Union

When an individual takes a job, certain conditions of employment (wages, hours, type of work) are specified in the **formal contract**. There is also a **psychological contract** between employer and employee, which consists of the unspecified expectations of the employee—expectations about reasonable working conditions, requirements of the work itself, the level of effort that should be expended on the job, and the amount and nature of the authority the employer has in directing the employee's work.[3] These expectations are related to the employees' desire to satisfy certain personal needs in the workplace. The degree to which the organization fulfills these needs determines the employees' level of satisfaction.[4]

Dissatisfaction with either the formal or the psychological contract will lead employees to attempt to improve the work situation, often through unionization. A major study has found a very strong relationship between level of satisfaction and the proportion of workers voting for a union.[5] Almost all workers who were highly dissatisfied voted for a union, but almost all workers who were satisfied voted against the union (see Exhibit 15.1).

Unionization, however, is seldom the first recourse of employees who are dissatisfied with some aspect of their job. The first attempt to improve the work situation is usually made by an individual acting alone. Someone who has enough power or influence can effect the necessary changes without collaborating with others. The features of a job that determine the amount of power the job holder has in the organization are essentiality, or how important or critical the job is to the overall success of the organization, and exclusivity, or how difficult it is to replace the person.[6] An employee with an essential task who is difficult to replace will be able to force the employer to make changes. If, however, the individual task is not critical

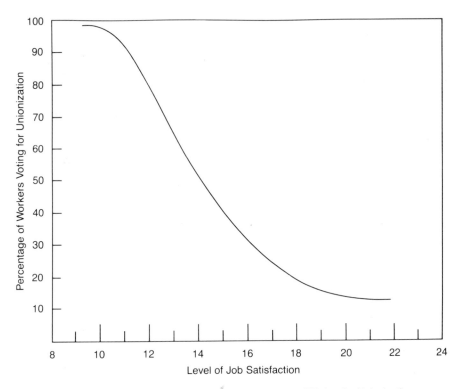

Exhibit 15.1 Relationship between Employee Satisfaction and Voting for Unionization
Adapted from J. G. Getman, S. B. Goldberg and Jeanne B. Herman. *Union Representation Elections: Law and Reality* (New York: Russell Sage Foundation, 1976), p. 55.

and the employee can easily be replaced, employees are likely to consider other means, including collective action, to increase their power to influence the organization.

To summarize, there are two factors on which the decision or motivation to unionize is based: dissatisfaction with the employer's fulfillment of the written or psychological contract, which impairs satisfaction of needs, and the individual's lack of ability or power to change the situation or to influence the employer to change the situation.[7]

Although it has been suggested that unions are attractive because they directly satisfy people's social or growth needs, this function does not appear to be so important as the union's influence in changing the work setting. A national survey of workers by the University of Michigan Survey Research Center indicates that workers perceive the union's goals to be related primarily to job context factors. Of all the goals listed, 80.5 percent were related to wages, benefits, working conditions, or job security; 1.3 percent were concerned with job content; 6.5 percent had to do with union power, such as dominating business or obtaining political power, and 11.7 percent had negative associations, such as hurting employees, business, or the country. The same survey showed that 89 percent of the workers felt unions have power to improve wages and working conditions, 87 percent felt they had power to improve job security, and 80 percent felt they could protect workers.[8]

Although employees have most often been concerned with wages, job security, and working conditions, there are indications that other factors will become more important in the future. As work values change and individuals look to the job for meaningful work, a sense of achievement, and the opportunity to grow, unions will have to pay more attention to these needs and increase their efforts to change the nature of work itself. The facts that less than one-fourth of the work force is unionized and that the proportion of unionized workers is steadily declining may indicate that the unions are already feeling the impact of changing work values on membership.

The processes involved in the decision to unionize are summarized in Exhibit 15.2. The expectation that work will satisfy personal needs may induce satisfaction or dissatisfaction with work. As the level of dissatisfaction increases, individual workers seek to change their work situation. If they fail, and if the positive consequences of unionization seem to outweigh the negative consequences, individuals will be inclined to join the union.   .

Management Behavior Affecting the Decision to Join

Management and the personnel department can contribute to the level of work dissatisfaction in several ways:
- Unrealistic job interviews can mean that a new recruit's expectations are not likely to be met.
- The design of the job affects how the individual responds to it.
- Day-to-day management and supervisory behaviors, such as poor supervisory practices, unfair treatment, and lack of upward communication, can lead to unionization.[9]

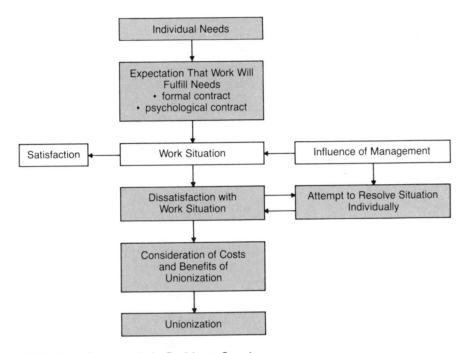

Exhibit 15.2 Processes in the Decision to Organize

The Decision Not to Join a Union

The question of whether to join a union involves an assessment of the negative consequences of unionization. Employees may have misgivings about how effectively a union can improve unsatisfactory work conditions. Collective bargaining is not always successful; if the union is not strong, it will be unable to make an employer meet its demands. Even if an employer does respond to union demands, the workers may be affected adversely. The employer may not be able to survive when the demands of the union are met, and thus the company may close down, costing employees their jobs. The organization may force the union to strike, inflicting economic hardship on employees who may not be able to afford being out of work, or it may in some cases attempt reprisals against pro-union employees, although this is illegal.[10]

Beyond perceptions of unions as ineffective in the pursuit of personal goals, employees may also resist unionization because of general attitudes toward unions. Employees may identify strongly with the company and have a high level of commitment to it. They would therefore tend to view the union as an adversary and would be receptive to company arguments against unions. Employees may also perceive the goals of the union to be objectionable, intending to harm the company and the free enterprise system in general. They may object to the concept of seniority or even to the political activities of the unions. Moreover, certain employees—for example, engineers or college professors—view themselves as professionals and find collective action to be contrary to such professional ideals as independence and self-control.[11] The decision not to unionize can be influenced by management as well. Many companies successfully avoid unionization through good management practices: fostering employee participation in planning and decision making, opening channels of communication, setting up processes for handling employee problems and grievances, developing employee trust, and offering competitive wages.[12]

SOME FACTS ABOUT UNIONS

In 1978 the number of employees belonging to unions or employee associations was 23,307,000.[13] The distribution of these members among unions and employee associations is shown in Exhibit 15.3 Membership grew to a peak of 23.4 million in 1974 but has leveled off since then.

The proportion of the labor force represented by unions has been declining steadily since the mid-1960s. In 1978, only 22.2 percent of nonagricultural workers were represented by unions, the lowest proportion since the mid-1930s. Factors that contribute to this decline include the increase in public sector employment and white-collar jobs, both of which have historically had a low proportion of union members, and the decline in employment in industries that are highly unionized. In the future, however, economic conditions and legislation may make unionization more feasible in white-collar and public sector jobs. Indeed, most organizing activities today are focused on government and the public sector.

Historically, membership has been concentrated in a small number of large unions.[14] In 1976, sixteen unions represented 60 percent of union membership, and eighty-five unions represented just 2.4 percent. Similarly, the National Education Association accounted for 62 percent of all association members. Many employee associations are small because they are state organizations; their membership potential, therefore, is limited. Moreover, unions have been acquiring members at the expense of some associations.[15] Exhibit 15.4 lists the ten largest unions and six largest employee associations and their membership as of 1976.

Exhibit 15.3 Union and Association Membership in the United States, 1978 (in thousands)

National unions	20,085	
Locals affiliated with AFL-CIO	42	
Single-firm and unaffiliated unions	332	
Total union membership		20,459
Professional and state employee associations	2,623	
Municipal employee associations	235	
Total employee association membership		2,858
Total union and association membership		23,307

Adapted from Eugene Becker, Bureau of Labor Statistics, U.S. Department of Labor, Washington, D.C., May 1980, personal communication.

Exhibit 15.4 Union and Employee Association Membership, 1976

Union	Membership (in thousands)	Employee Association	Membership (in thousands)
Teamsters	1,889	Teachers (National Education Association)	1,887
Automobile workers	1,358		
Steelworkers	1,300	Civil service employees	207
Electrical workers (Internal Brotherhood of Electrical Workers)	924	Nurses	200
		Police	135
Machinists	917	California employees	112
Carpenters	820		
State, county and municipal employees	750	Classified school employees	109
Retail clerks	699		
Laborers	627		
Service employees	575		

Adapted from U.S. Department of Labor, Bureau of Labor Statistics, *Director of National Unions and Employee Associations, 1977*, Bulletin No. 2044 (Washington D.C.: Government Printing Office, 1979), p. 65.

It is interesting to examine the distribution of union membership by industry. Manufacturing accounted for 33.4 percent of union and association membership in 1978, nonmanufacturing for 41.8 percent, and government for 34.8 percent. There has been a steady drop in the proportion of union membership in manufacturing—from 48.2 percent in 1958 to 33.4 percent in 1978—and a steady increase in government—from 5 percent in 1958 to 34.8 percent in 1978.

The proportion of employees in different industries is presented in Exhibit 15.5. Many of the major industries—transportation, construction, mining, telephone and telegraph—have over half their employees unionized, whereas service, finance, agriculture and fishing, and trade are the least represented. Since the effectiveness of unions depends on their ability to increase membership, unions in industries that are highly unionized have begun to look to these less-organized industries for members.

Unions today are exhibiting a substantial and increasing amount of diversification of membership. For example, in 1958, 73 percent of the unions had at least four-fifths of their members in a single industry; this had dropped to 55 percent in 1976. The most pronounced diversification has occurred in manufacturing. For example, of the twenty-nine unions that represent workers in chemicals and allied products, twenty-six presently have less than 20 percent of their membership in a single industry.

Structure

The basic unit of labor unions in the United States is the **national union** (or international union), a body that organizes, charters, and controls member **union locals**. The national union develops general policies and procedures by which locals operate

Exhibit 15.5 Proportion of Employees Unionized, by Industry

75 percent and over	50 percent to 75 percent
Transportation	Telephone and telegraph
Contract construction	Transportation equipment
	Primary metals
	Petroleum
	Food and kindred products
	Apparel
	Tobacco manufactures
	Stone, clay, and glass products
	Mining
	Fabricated metals
	Electrical machinery
	Federal government
	Paper
	Manufacturing

25 percent to 50 percent	Less than 25 percent
Rubber	Chemicals
Machinery	Nonmanufacturing
Lumber	Textile mill products
Leather	Instruments
Electric and gas utilities	Service
Furniture	Finance
Federal government	Agriculture and fishing
Local government	Trade
Printing and publishing	
State government	

Adapted from U.S. Department of Labor, Bureau of Labor Statistics, *Directory of National Unions and Employee Associations, 1977*, Bulletin No. 2044 (Washington, D.C.: Government Printing Office, 1979), p. 70.

and provides assistance to them in such areas as collective bargaining. National unions provide clout for the locals because they control a large number of employees and can influence large organizations through national strikes or slowdown activities.

The major umbrella organization for national unions is the **AFL-CIO**—the American Federation of Labor and Congress of Industrial Organizations. It represents about 77 percent of the total union membership and contains 106 national unions. Although several major unions are not members, including the two biggest (the Teamsters and United Auto Workers), the AFL-CIO is an important and powerful body.

Every two years the AFL-CIO holds a convention to develop policy and amend its constitution. Each national union is represented in proportion to its membership. Between conventions, an executive council (the governing body) and a general board direct the organization's affairs; a president is in charge of day-to-day operations. The executive council's activities include evaluating legislation that affects labor and watching for corruption within the AFL-CIO. Standing committees are appointed to deal with executive, legislative, political, educational, and other activities.

The Department of Organization and Field Services, for instance, focuses its attention on organizing activities. Outside of headquarters, three structures exist to organize the local unions. Many of the craft unions are organized into the Trade Department and the Industrial Department, which represent them to the national union. The remaining locals are organized directly into national unions, which are affiliated with headquarters but retain their independence in dealing with their own union matters.

Sixty-three national unions, representing 4.5 million workers, operate independently of the AFL-CIO. This separation is not considered desirable by the AFL-CIO, and at its 1980 convention Lane Kirkland, the AFL-CIO president, indicated that affiliation talks were underway with the Teamsters, the largest independent union.

At the heart of the labor movement are the 70,000 or so local unions, varying in size up to 40,000 members. The locals represent the workers at the workplace, where much of the day-to-day contact with management and the personnel department takes place. Most locals elect a president, a secretary-treasurer, and perhaps one or two other officers from the membership. In the larger locals, a business representative is hired as a fulltime employee to handle grievances and contract negotiations. The other important member of the union local is the **steward**, an employee elected by his or her work unit to act as the union representative on the work site and to respond to company actions against employees that may violate the labor agreement. The steward protects the rights of the worker by filing grievances where the employer has acted improperly.

Operations

Activities of union locals revolve around collective bargaining and handling grievances. In addition, locals hold general meetings, publish newsletters, and otherwise keep their members informed. Typically, however, the membership is apathetic about union involvement. Unless a serious problem exists, attendance at meetings is usually very low, and often even elections of officers draw votes from less than one-fourth of the membership.

At headquarters, the AFL-CIO is involved in a variety of activities. Staff and committees work on a wide range of issues, including civil rights, community service, economic policy, education, ethical practices, housing, international affairs, legislation, public relations, research, safety, social security, and veterans' affairs. There is also a publication department, which produces a variety of literature for the membership and outsiders.

National union headquarters also provide a variety of specialized services to regional and local bodies. Specialists in organizing, strikes, legal matters, public relations, and negotiations are available to individual unions.

Another important role for national unions and the AFL-CIO is in the political arena. Labor maintains a strong lobbying force in Washington, D.C. and is also involved at the state and local level. A recent development is the international political activities of some of the large national unions. The United Auto Workers have held discussions with Japanese car manufacturers concerning the level of imports into the United States and the construction of assembly plants here. They have threatened to lobby in Washington to restrict imports of cars in an attempt to bolster

U.S. auto makers and to increase jobs. Thus, in an attempt to help their membership, unions are expanding their activities on all levels, and in some cases they work with organizations to attain mutual goals.

A Historical View of Labor

The study of labor unions is enhanced a great deal by an appreciation of their historical context.[16] You may also better understand some of the attitudes and behaviors of both unions and management through a knowledge of past labor-management relations.

The Early Days.　Labor unions in the United States can be traced back to the successful attempt of journeymen printers to win a wage increase in 1778.[17] By the 1790s, unions of shoemakers, carpenters, and printers had appeared in Boston, Baltimore, New York, and other cities.[18] The Federal Society of Journeymen Cordwainers, for example, was organized in Philadelphia in 1794, primarily to resist employers' attempts to reduce wages. Other issues of concern to these early unions were union shops (companies using only union members) and regulation of apprenticeship to prevent the replacement of journeymen employees.

The early unions had methods and objectives that are still in evidence today. Although there was no collective bargaining, the unions did establish a price below which members would not work. Strikes were used to enforce this rate. These strikes were relatively peaceful and for the most part successful.

One negative characteristic of early unions was their susceptibility to depressions. Until the late 1800s, most unions thrived in times of prosperity but died off during depressions. Part of this problem may have been related to the insularity of the unions. Aside from sharing information on strikebreakers or scabs, the unions operated independently.

The work situation at the end of the nineteenth century was not yet oppressive to employees. Some important changes had occurred, however. Transportation systems (canals and turnpikes) expanded the markets for products and increased worker mobility. Increases in capital costs prevented journeymen from reaching the status of master craftworker (that is, from setting up their own businesses), thereby creating a class of skilled workers. Unionism found its start in these skilled occupations, largely because "the skilled worker . . . had mastered his craft and was no longer occupationally mobile" and the alternatives were "to passively accept wage cuts, the competition of nonapprentice labor and the harsh working conditions, or to join in collective action against such employer innovations."[19]

Employers reacted to the unions by forming employers' associations and taking court action. The major legal tool was the conspiracy law, which was used to prosecute workers' organizations as illegal conspiracies in restraint of trade. The Cordwainers of Philadelphia were found guilty of such a conspiracy in 1806, and the courts established a "conspiracy doctrine" that was used against unions in the ensuing decades. This doctrine, along with a depression in 1819, successfully repressed the union movement.

The unions continued to experience highs and lows that were largely tied to economic conditions. Employers took advantage of the depressions to combat unions: In "an all out frontal attack . . . they engaged in frequent lockouts, hired spies . . . summarily discharged labor 'agitators,' and [engaged] the services of strike breakers on a widespread scale."[20] These actions, and the retaliations of unions, established a tenor of violence and lent a strong adversarial nature to labor-management relations, the residual of which is in evidence today.

The AFL-CIO. The American Federation of Labor began in 1886 and quickly assumed a leading role in the union movement. Much of its early success can be traced to the pragmatic approach of its president, Samuel Gompers, and to the principles he adopted:

- The national unions were to be autonomous within the AFL.
- Only one national union would be accepted for each trade or craft.
- The AFL would focus on the issues of wages, hours and working conditions and avoid reformist goals.
- The AFL would avoid permanent political alliances.
- The strike would become a key weapon for achieving union objectives.

The AFL also accepted and endorsed the free enterprise system, choosing to operate within it rather than to change the whole system. The policy of giving national craft unions substantial control over their own affairs successfully attracted these unions and allowed the AFL to grow substantially despite employer campaigns to inhibit growth. Legislation passed in the 1930s made the legal climate more conducive to union growth.

The Congress of Industrial Organizations (CIO) was formed in 1935 as a rival union organization that focused on industrywide unions rather than craft unions. The competition between the AFL and the CIO intensified unionizing efforts, and by 1941, 10.2 million workers were union members. The labor movement had become "not only a major force to be reckoned with but, for the first time, was to a great extent representative of the full spectrum of American workers."[21]

Eventually the CIO and the AFL, realizing that their competition was not in the best interests of labor, merged into the AFL-CIO. The merger of these organizations eliminated jurisdictional squabbles and gave union leaders a stronger voice. The new organization had great expectations for a significant growth in membership.

In spite of these expectations, the AFL-CIO lost membership over the next two decades. Several factors accounted for this decline: The Teamsters and the United Auto Workers left the organization, corruption among unions tarnished their image, and increasingly high wage demands resulted in a lack of public confidence. Changing attitudes among employees and the public also reduced the appeal of labor unions. Membership today continues to grow at a slow pace, and hopes for large-scale unionization seem to be fading.

THE LEGAL FRAMEWORK FOR LABOR RELATIONS

The federal government entered the labor scene in an attempt to stabilize the rather violent and disruptive labor situation in the 1920s and 1930s.[22] Court actions and efforts by employers appeared to be suppressing the rights of workers to act collectively and to protect their interests. The first legislation was aimed at restoring a balance of power between labor and employers.

Federal legislation specifically addressing labor relations dates back to 1926, when the Railway Labor Act was passed. Since then, several statutory labor laws (listed in Appendix B) have become the basis for today's labor relations.

Railway Labor Act

The **Railway Labor Act (RLA)** was passed by Congress to prevent the serious economic consequences of labor unrest in the railway industry. It has since been expanded to include air carrier employees as well.

The RLA was the first act to protect "the fundamental right of workers to engage in labor organizing actively without fear of employer retaliation and discrimination."[23] Other objectives of the act were to avoid service interruptions, to eliminate any restrictions on joining a union, and to provide for prompt settlement of disputes and grievances.[24]

The act specified that employers and employees would maintain an agreement over pay, rules, working conditions, dispute settlement, representation, and grievance settlement. A Board of Mediation (later to be called the National Mediation Board) was created to aid in the settlement of disputes through encouragement of, first, negotiation, then arbitration, and finally the President's emergency intervention. A second Board—the National Railway Adjustment Board—was created in 1934 to deal with grievances. This board has exclusive jurisdiction over questions relating to grievances or the interpretation of agreements concerning pay, rules, or working conditions; it makes decisions and awards that are binding on both parties.

National Labor Relations Act

The success of the Railway Labor Act led Congress to enact a comprehensive labor code in 1935. The purpose of the National Labor Relations Act (NLRA), also known as the **Wagner Act**, was to "restore the equality of bargaining power arising out of employers' general denial to labor of the right to bargain collectively with them."[25] Such employer refusal resulted in poor working conditions, depression of wages, and a general depression of business.

The NLRA affirmed employees' rights to form, join, or assist labor organizations, to bargain collectively, and to choose their own bargaining representative through majority rule. The second significant portion of the act identified five unfair labor practices on the part of employers:
- Interference with the efforts of employees to organize
- Domination of the labor organization by the employer
- Discrimination in the hiring or tenure of employees to discourage union affiliation
- Discrimination for filing charges or giving testimony under the act
- Refusal to bargain collectively with a representative of the employees

Court interpretation of these unfair labor practices has made it clear that bribing, spying, blacklisting union sympathizers, moving a business to avoid union activities, and other such employer actions are illegal.[26]

The **National Labor Relations Board (NLRB)** was established to administer this act. Its major function is to decide all unfair labor practice suits. It also has authority over the election of bargaining representatives.

Labor-Management Relations Act

Employer groups criticized the Wagner Act on several grounds. They argued that the act, in addition to being biased toward unions, limited the constitutional right of free speech of employers, did not consider unfair labor practices on the part of unions, and caused employers serious damage when there were jurisdictional disputes.

Congress responded to these criticisms in 1947 by enacting the Labor-Management Relations Act, often called the **Taft-Hartley Act**. This act revised and expanded the Wagner Act in order to establish a balance between union and management power and to protect the public interest. Among the changes it introduced:

● Employees were allowed to refrain from union activity as well as to engage in it.
● The closed shop was outlawed, and written agreement from employees was required for deducting union dues from workers' paychecks.
● Unions composed of supervisors did not need to be recognized.
● Employers were ensured of their right to free speech and they were given the right to file charges against unfair labor practices. The unfair practices that were identified were coercing workers to join the unions, causing employers to discriminate against those who do not join, refusing to bargain in good faith, requiring excessive or discriminatory fees, and engaging in featherbedding activities.
● Certification elections (voting for union representation) could not be held more frequently than once a year.
● Employees were given the right to initiate decertification elections.[27]

These provisions indicated the philosophy behind the act—as Senator Taft put it, "simply to reduce the special privileges granted labor leaders."

Labor-Management Reporting and Disclosure Act

Although the Taft-Hartley Act included some regulation of internal union activities, abuse of power and the corruption of some union officials led to the passage of a "bill of rights" for union members in 1959. The Labor-Management Reporting and Disclosure Act, or the **Landrum-Griffin Act**, provided a detailed regulation of internal union affairs. Some of the provisions include

● Equality of rights for union members in nominating and voting in elections
● Controls on increases in dues
● Control of suspension and fining of union members
● Union elections at least every five years
● Restriction of the use of trusteeship to take control of a member group's autonomy for political reasons
● Definition of the type of person who can hold union office
● Filing of yearly reports with the Secretary of Labor

The intention of this act was to protect employees from corrupt or discriminatory labor unions. By providing detailed provisions for union conduct, much of the flagrant abuse of power was eliminated, and the democratic rights of employees were protected to some degree. The United Mine Workers, for example, held their first election of international officers in 1969. This event would not have been likely to occur even then without the provisions of the Landrum-Griffin Act.

Federal Employee Regulations

These labor laws were enacted to govern labor relations in the private sector. In fact, the Wagner Act specifically excludes the U.S. government, government corporations, states, and municipal corporations in its definition of employer. Therefore, for a long time government employees lacked the legislative protection afforded private-sector workers. Until recently, federal employee labor relations were controlled by executive orders issued by the President.

The government's view of its employees differs from its view of private-sector employees. Several of the rights of unions in the private sector are not included in public-sector regulations, although the content of these regulations often is lifted from private-sector acts.

Executive Orders.   The first set of regulations for federal employee labor relations was Executive Order 10988, introduced by President John Kennedy in 1962. This order forbade federal agencies from interfering with employee organizing or unlawful union activity and provided for recognition of employee organizations. Employee organizations were denied the right to strike, however, and economic issues were not part of the bargaining process, since these are fixed by the Civil Service classification system. Agency heads were made the ultimate authority on grievances, and managers were excluded from the bargaining units.

Executive Order 11491, issued in 1969 and amended in 1971 (EO 11616) and 1975 (EO 11838), addressed some of the difficulties presented by the first executive order. It created a Labor Relations Council to hear appeals from the decisions of agency heads, prescribed regulations and policies, and created a Federal Services Impasses Panel to act on negotiation impasses. The Council and the employee representatives could meet and discuss personnel practices and working conditions, but all agreements had to be approved by the Council head. Unfair labor practices by both agency management and labor organizations were delineated. The Council was restricted from interference, discrimination, and sponsorship of union discipline against an employee for filing a complaint and was required to recognize or deal with a qualified union. Labor organizations also were restrained from interfering, coercing management or employees, discriminating against employees, calling for or engaging in a strike, or denying membership to an employee.

These controls on employers and labor organizations are similar to those found in private-sector legislation. Yet federal employees do not have the same bargaining rights. They lack rights in four areas:

- No provision is made for bargaining on economic issues.
- Although the parties can meet and confer, there is no obligation to do so.
- The ultimate authority is the agency head rather than a neutral party.
- There is no provision for union security through the agency shop, which requires all employees to pay dues but not to join the union.

Civil Service Reform Act.   In 1978 the Federal Service Labor-Management Relations Statute was passed as **Title VII of the Civil Service Reform Act,** which has been referred to as "the most significant change in federal personnel administration since the passage of the Civil Service Act in 1883."[28] Several significant changes were made by the statute, prime among them the following:

• Passage of the statute removed the President's ability to change the act through executive order and in general made it more difficult to change the legislation.

• It established the **Federal Labor Relations Authority (FLRA)**, modeled after the NLRB, as an "independent, neutral, full-time, bipartisan agency"[29] created, as President Jimmy Carter said, "to remedy unfair labor practices within the Government."[30] Interpretation of the act is the province of the FLRA and the courts. Agency heads, including the President, cannot define the meaning of the act.

• An aggrieved person may now seek judicial review of a final order of the FLRA. The FLRA may also seek judicial enforcement of its order.

• Negotiated grievance procedures, which must be included in all agreements, must provide for arbitration as the final step.

State and Local Employee Regulations

Employee relations regulations at the state and local level are varied. Not all states have legislation governing their employees, but some states have legislation covering municipal employees as well. One widespread regulation can be noted: Collective bargaining is permitted in most states, and it covers wages, hours, and other terms and conditions of employment. The other terms and conditions have caused the most difficulty in interpretation. Managerial prerogatives are usually quite strong, especially for firefighters, police, and teachers. The requirement to bargain over certain issues in the private sector is not so stringent at the state or local level. In addition, some twenty states have passed "right-to-work" laws, which prohibit union membership as a condition of employment.

Although the rights and privileges of public-sector labor organizations are not so extensive as those in the private sector, the greatest growth in unionization in recent years has come in the public sector. This will become an increasingly important area of labor relations in the 1980s.

THE ORGANIZING CAMPAIGN

The process by which a single union is selected to represent all employees in a particular unit is crucial to the American system of collective bargaining. If a majority vote for union representation, all employees are bound by that choice and the employer is obligated to recognize and bargain with the chosen union.[31]

One of the major functions of the National Labor Relations Board is to conduct the selection of unions to represent nongovernment employees. This is accomplished through a **certification election** to determine if the majority of employees want the union. From 1966 to 1975, 85,000 elections were held, affecting 5 million employees.[32] Under American labor law, the union that is certified to represent a group of employees has sole and exclusive right to bargain for that group. Because unions thereby acquire significant power, employers are anxious to keep them out. To add to this potentially turbulent situation, there may be more than one union attempting to win certification as representative of a group of employees, creating competition between unions.

Several stages in the certification process can be identified: (1) a campaign to solicit employee support for union reprsentation; (2) the determination of the appropriate group the union will represent; (3) the preelection campaign by unions and employers; (4) the election itself; and (5) the certification of a union. These steps are outlined in Exhibit 15.6. The next stage of the organizing process—negotiation of a collective bargaining agreement—is discussed in Chapter 16.

The Campaign to Solicit Employee Support

Establishing Contact between the Union and Employees.   Contact between the union and employees can be initiated by either party. National unions usually initiate contact with employees in industries or occupations that they have an interest in or are traditionally involved in. The United Auto Workers, for example, would be likely to contact nonunion employees in automobile plants and have done so for the new plants that have been built in the South. Another prominent example of union initiative was the attempt by two competing unions—the United Farm Workers and the Teamsters—to organize the agricultural workers in California. Often these unions were aggressive, even violent, during their campaigns for worker support. One consequence of their precertification activities, which included national boycotts of grapes and lettuce, was the California Agricultural Relations Act, passed in 1975. The purpose of this Act is to regulate union-management relations in the agriculture industry.

In many cases the union is approached by employees interested in union representation, and the union is usually happy to oblige. Employees may have strong reasons for desiring union representation—low pay, poor working conditions, and other factors relating to dissatisfaction.[33] Since workers tend to be apathetic toward unions, their concern generally becomes quite serious before they will take any action.[34]

Authorization Cards and the Request for Elections.   Once contact has been made, the union begins the campaign to get sufficient **authorization cards**, or signatures of employees interested in having union representation. This campaign must be carried out within the constraints set by law. If the union collects cards from 30

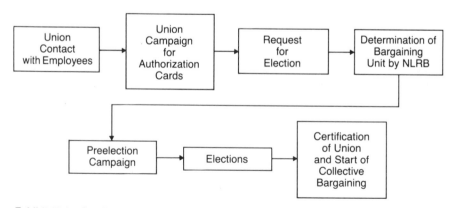

Exhibit 15.6 Certification Process

percent of an organization's employees, it can petition the National Labor Relations Board for an election. (Procedures in the public sector are similar.) If the NLRB determines that there is indeed sufficient interest, it will schedule an election. If the union gets more than 50 percent of the employees to sign authorization cards, it may petition the employer as the bargaining representative. Usually employers refuse, whereupon the union petitions the NLRB for an election.

The employer usually resists the union's card-signing campaign. For instance, companies usually prohibit solicitation on the premises. However, employers are legally constrained from interfering with an employee's freedom of choice. Union representatives have argued that employers ignore this law because the consequences for doing so are minimal—and they can effectively discourage unionism. One employer that has been very aggressive in resisting unionization is the J. P. Stevens Company, a large textile manufacturer. The Amalgamated Clothing and Textile Workers Union has been trying since 1963 to organize its employees. As of early 1980, only eleven of eighty-four J. P. Stevens plants had been organized. Much of this lack of success is attributed to unfair labor practices by J. P. Stevens and "wholesale violations of the rights of workers to join a union."[35] The company has been found guilty of many violations over the years and has been accused of being the "most flagrant labor law violator in this country."[36]

Unfair labor practices, when identified, generally cause the election being set aside. Severe violations by the employer can result in certification of the union as the bargaining representative, even if it has lost the election.

Determination of the Bargaining Unit

When the union has gathered sufficient signatures to petition for an election, the NLRB will make a determination of the **bargaining unit**, the group of employees that will be represented by the union. This is a crucial process, for it can determine the quality of labor-management relations in the future:

At the heart of labor-management relations is the bargaining unit. It is all important that the bargaining unit be truly appropriate and not contain a mix of antagonistic interests or submerge the legitimate interests of a small group of employees in the interest of a larger group.[37]

In order to assure "the fullest freedom of Collective Bargaining,"[38] there are legal constraints and guidelines for the unit. Professional and nonprofessional groups cannot be included in the same unit, and a craft unit cannot be placed in a larger unit unless both groups agree to it. Physical location, skill levels, degree of ownership, collective bargaining history, and extent of organization of employees are also guidelines that are considered.

From the union's perspective, the most desirable bargaining unit is one whose members are pro-union, so that they can win certification. The unit must also have sufficient influence over the operations of the employer to give the union some power once it wins representation. Employers generally want a bargaining unit that is least beneficial to the union; this will help to maximize the likelihood of failure in the election and to minimize the power of the unit.

The Preelection Campaign

After the bargaining unit has been determined, both union and employer embark on a **preelection campaign**. Unions claim to provide a strong voice for employees, emphasizing improvement in wages and working conditions and the establishment of a grievance process to ensure fairness. Employers emphasize the costs of unionization—union dues, strikes, and loss of jobs.

The impact of preelection campaigns is not clear. A study of thirty-one elections showed very little change in attitude and voting propensity after the campaign.[39] People who will vote for or against a union before the election campaign generally vote the same way after. Severe violations of the legal constraints on behavior, such as using threats or coercion, could be effective, but the NLRB watches the preelection activity carefully to prevent such behavior.

Election, Certification, and Decertification

The NLRB conducts the election and certifies the results. If a majority vote for union representation, the union will be certified. If the union does not get a majority, another election will not be held for a least a year. The NLRB holds about 9,000 elections a year involving about 500,000 employees. Generally about a third to a half of the elections certify a union, with less union success in larger organizations. Once a union has been certified, the employer is required to bargain with that union.

The NLRB also conducts **decertification elections**, which remove a union from representation. If 30 percent or more of the employees request such an election, it will be held. These decertification elections most frequently occur in the first year of a union's representation, when the union is negotiating its first contract. Union strength has not yet been established, and employees are readily discouraged about union behavior. Recently there has been a substantial increase in decertification elections and actual decertification (849 elections were held in 1977, five times the number in 1955). However, the impact on the union movement is small, with less than 1 percent of union members being affected.[40] Decertification is not a direct threat to union success at present, but it may be an indication that unions will be facing problems in the future.

UNION-MANAGEMENT RELATIONS

The relationship between unions and management at the organizational level is represented in Exhibit 15.7. The labor relations system is composed of three subunits—employees, management, and the union—with the government influencing the interaction among the three. Employees may be managers or union members, and some of the union members are part of the union management system (local union leaders). Each of the three interrelationships in the model is addressed by specific government regulations: union and management (by the National Labor Relations Act); management and employees (by the National Labor Relations Act, and Title VII of the Civil Rights Act); and union and employees (by the Labor-Management Reporting and Disclosure Act and Title VII of the Civil Rights Act).

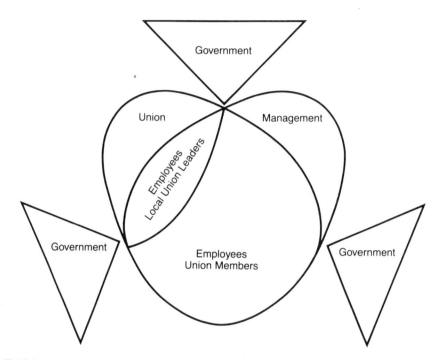

Exhibit 15.7   Labor Relations System
From J. M. Brett, "Behavioral Research on Unions and Union Management Systems," p. 190.
Reprinted from Research in Organizational Behavior, Vol. 2 (1980). JAI Press, Inc., Greenwich, Conn.

The Adversarial System

*For the first 150 years of this country's independence, the American worker was
free politically, but a virtual slave industrially. A look backward at management
practices such as company-owned housing, water supplies, stores, etc., with
their inflated prices, the payment of workers in company scrip, the unsafe and
unhealthy working conditions, the unbelievably long work week, the ridiculously
low wages which made it impossible for most families to live on the earnings of a
single breadwinner, the completely arbitrary employment and personnel
practices, and the company police forces, to mention only a few—in fact the
complete lack of consideration of the worker as a human being—puts the
remarkable growth of labor unions in the early 1900's in a different light.
Certainly at this point in U.S. history, workers were ready to support any type of
organization that promised them relief from their miserable industrial existence.
Thus, labor unions filled a real need: they brought humanitarianism to the work
place and a degree of dignity to the American worker.*

*Yet ironically enough, because of their success, unions have eradicated
most of the conditions that led to their foundation. Thus, an often heard
argument today is that while unions were necessary once, they are no longer
necessary now.*

While there is much support for this point of view, the author must take exception to it. Laws and subsequent conditions of employment may have changed, but basic human nature has not. While it may be a pessimistic assessment of mankind, and one with which the reader will likely disagree, I firmly believe that a high percentage of humanity will still take advantage of their fellows if the price is right.

The biggest single deterrent, besides the law, to the reduction of standards in the work place is the combined action of the workers—call it a "union" or any other name you wish. This action does not even have to come to pass to serve its purpose, for in many instances, the mere possibility of such action is sufficient. (there can be no doubt that the level of benefits received by many nonunion workers is in part buttressed by their employers' desire to reward them at such a level that they remain unorganized.)

Thus, while unions may have outlived their usefulness in terms of their original objectives, they are still needed because of what I have been referring to as their "deterrent" effect. This fact alone, in my opinion, continues to make unions what they've always been—an absolute necessity to the well-being of the work place.[41]

Each of the groups identified in the labor relations model has different goals, as shown in Exhibit 15.8. Workers are interested in improved working conditions, wages, and opportunities; unions are interested in their own survival, growth, and

Exhibit 15.8   Traditional Goals of Parties to the Labor Relations System

Workers

Good extrinsic working conditions—wages, benefits, fair supervisor, safe and pleasant working conditions, job security
Good intrinsic working conditions—interesting work that provides a sense of accomplishment
Participation in decisions which affect work and working conditions
System for redressing grievances

Unions

Achievement of members' goals for working conditions
Survival and growth
Political security for union leaders

Management

Profitability
Preservation of management's prerogative to direct the work force
Job security/advancement

Government

Democratic unionism
Healthy economy
Safe working conditions
Profitable firms
Fair wages
Fair and nondiscriminatory employment
Noninflationary wage agreements and pricing policies

From J. Brett, "Behavioral Research on Unions and Union Management Systems." In *Research in Organizational Behavior*, vol. 2, eds. Staw and Cummings. Copyright 1980. JAI Press Inc. Reprinted with permission.

acquisition of power, which depend on their ability to maintain the support of the employees by providing for their needs. Management has overall organizational goals (profit, market share, growth, and others), and it also seeks to preserve managerial prerogatives to direct the work force and to attain the personal goals of the managers (promotion, achievement). Government is interested in a stable and healthy economy, protection of individual rights, and safety and fairness in the work place.

These goals are not compatible in most cases. Conflict arises when two groups, typically union and management, attempt to achieve incompatible goals simultaneously. Thus an adversarial system has emerged, with labor and management attempting to get a bigger cut of the pie while government looks on to protect its interests. Success for labor and management is measured by their relative gains.

The Cooperative System

In an adversarial system of union-management relations, the union's role is to gain concessions from management during collective bargaining and to preserve those concessions through the grievance procedure. The union is an outsider and critic. In a cooperative system, the union's role is that of a partner, not a critic, and the union becomes jointly responsible with management for reaching a cooperative solution. Thus, a cooperative system requires that union and management engage in problem solving, information sharing, and integration of outcomes. [42]

Cooperative systems have not been a major component of labor relations in the United States. Other countries—Sweden, Yugoslavia, and West Germany, for example—have built a cooperative mechanism (codetermination is discussed in Chapter 20) into the labor system. There have been occasions, however, when American management and labor have worked together to solve a problem. Most changes and job redesign projects undertaken by management need the acceptance of the union to be successful. [43] Active involvement of the union is one of the best ways to gain this acceptance.

Successful projects like the Tarrytown, New York, plant of General Motors and the Rushton Mining plant in Pennsylvania involve the union in a cooperative effort to solve problems of concern to both parties. [44] Another example of a cooperative approach is the use of an in-house factfinder appointed by mutual agreement of management and union to develop and suggest alternative solutions to problems associated with labor relations. The factfinder is a neutral party who has the trust and confidence of both labor and management and whose primary concern is employee participation in decision making. The factfinder is often able to alter an adversarial relationship between union and management. [45]

Although there are obstacles to union-management cooperation—a history of adversarial relations, hesitancy on the part of the union to give up the traditional roles of labor, and both parties' fear of losing power—present economic conditions and the threat of an influx of foreign products are prompting many organizations to act for their mutual benefit. In one notable example, the president of the United Auto Workers lobbied in both Washington and Japan to reduce imports, which would aid the auto companies by lessening competition and the union by preserving jobs. The success of such cooperative activities can be measured first by the attainment of specific goals and second by the effect they have on labor-managment relations in general. The need for cooperation has been recognized by some union leaders who recommend more decision-making participation with management.[46] It appears that cooperation may become more common in the future as unions reexamine their role.

Effective Relations

The effectiveness of union-management relations could be measured by the extent to which each party attains its goals, but there are difficulties associated with this approach. Because goals are incompatible in many cases and can therefore lead to conflicting estimates of effectiveness, a more useful measure of effectiveness is the quality of the system used to resolve conflict. Conflict is most apparent in the collective bargaining process, where failure to resolve the issues typically leads to strikes.[47] Another measure of effectiveness is the success of the grievance process, or the ability to resolve issues developing out of the bargaining agreement.[48]

The Office of Labor-Management Relations of the U.S. Office of Personnel Management has identified eleven other elements essential for effective union-management relations:

- Acceptance of collective bargaining
- Balance of power between union and management
- Respect for each other's goals
- Recognition of common goals
- Well-organized labor relations program set up by management
- High level of communication
- Sincere negotiations
- Effective administration of the labor contract
- Comprehensive grievance process
- Evaluation by both parties of their relationship
- Sense of participation in their own welfare on the part of employees[49]

Deficiencies in these factors have been associated with increased conflict and a greater number of problems between unions and management.[50]

ISSUES FACING UNIONS AND MANAGEMENT

In recent years, several issues have replaced the traditional concerns of unions and management. Two, in particular, are direct results of the changing social environment in the United States.

Equal Employment Opportunity and Seniority

The union's cherished principle of seniority rights is today facing a challenge from affirmative action requirements. The seniority principle of "last hired, first fired" means that, in a period of recession and large-scale layoffs, minority and female employees are the first to go. Thus there is a "face-off between internal job equity

A SLICE OF LIFE

Effective labor-management relations, particularly at the local level, require an understanding of the fabled "cry wolf" syndrome. Recall the little boy who often yelled for help when none was required. One day, when he really needed help, no one heeded his cries. Everyone thought the child, once again, was calling for no reason.

Labor unions are often accused of "crying wolf" when they file grievances. It is true that grievances have a certain nuisance value, and this fact is not lost to the leaders of labor unions. Still, this strategy is one that should be used sparingly. Pursuing grievances without regard to their merit has at least two attendant problems.

First, the credibility of the union may be lost. If the union continually files nonviable grievances (grievances that cannot be won), a legitimate grievance may not receive the hearing it is entitled to. Arbitrators are aware of the reputation that certain unions have for the judicious or nonjudicious use of the grievance process.

Second, rank-and-file members of the union are likely to notice if it wins very few of its grievances. This outcome is to be expected when a series of grievances are filed that have almost no chance of winning. If you, as a rank-and-file union member, realized that very few grievances were ever adjudicated in favor of the grievant, would you file one?

Because of these two problems, the very process that rank-and-file members use to express grievances can make a fair hearing less likely.

The same admonitions apply to the organization as well. Very often, companies develop reputations for being intractable. Very few grievances are resolved informally, because the company won't give an inch even when the grievance is viable. Again, a strategy like this soon becomes known to arbitrators. True, by insisting on higher and higher levels of grievance resolution, a company can postpone the final decision on a grievance, even in cases where it is fairly sure to lose. Justice delayed may be justice denied in such cases. On the other hand, the result may be that the grievant receives higher rewards by arbitration than if the company had resolved the grievance itself. Even if the case does not eventually reach arbitration, the union's demands may escalate.

Both the union and management are best served by a responsible use of the grievance process.

in the form of seniority and external job rights associated with equalized employment opportunity."[51] The issue of which right takes precedence—the contractual right of seniority or the civil right of equal access to jobs—is now being examined in the courts. The apparent tendency is for equal employment and affirmative action to override seniority status. This poses a difficult problem for unions, for they can no longer ensure job security through seniority at a time when job security is of primary concern to many workers. Attempts to move women and minorities into managerial positions also conflict with seniority provisions for promotion and transfer of employees. The recent Weber case, discussed in Chapter 7, emphasized that in the Supreme Court's view, affirmative action takes priority over seniority.

Women in Unions

The 6.6 million women who belong to unions and employee associations comprise 22 percent of union membership and 59 percent of association membership. In spite of this, representation of women in union governing bodies has been extremely low.[52] In 1976 only 8 percent of union board members were women. The membership of the International Ladies Garment Workers, for example, is 80 percent female, but only one woman sits on that union's board of directors. Increased attention to equal and fair representation for women could put pressure on the unions to reduce this disparity.

Political Power

National unions and the AFL-CIO wield substantial political power. The endorsement of labor is an important factor for politicians, and many workers see unions as influential in electing government officials, passing laws, and otherwise influencing government.[53] However, recent indications are that the lobbying clout of unions in Washington has diminished substantially when compared to business. Most large unions have always had political action committees in Washington, but the number of business committees has increased tenfold from 1974 to 1980.[54] This increase in activity and a concern for the abuse of influence by big business has encouraged labor, consumer, and public-interest groups to unite to curb the power of business.

The Changing Union Role

Historically, unions have adopted an adversarial role in their interactions with management. Their focus has been on wages and working conditions as they have attempted to get "more and better" from management. This approach works well in economic boom times but becomes difficult when the economy is not healthy. High unemployment and the threat of continued job losses have recently induced unions to expand their role, especially since many of their traditional goals—better pay and working conditions—have been achieved. Many unions have begun to enter into new, collaborative efforts with employers. Cooperation in improving productivity and the quality of the work life is one example. Another is the political lobbying done by such unions as the United Auto Workers to protect the industry from foreign competition and thereby save jobs. The declining proportion of union members in the work force and the dramatically increasing number of decertification elections may indicate that changes like this are necessary.

SUMMARY

A labor union is attractive to employees when the union is perceived as being able to reduce dissatisfaction at work by providing for their needs. The attractiveness of unions is therefore related to management's behavior. If the company is able to deal successfully with employee dissatisfaction, employees will be less likely to unionize.

Unions represent about a fifth of the work force. They have obtained a good deal of power through organizing important industries. Currently the greatest opportunity for union growth is in the public sector. The labor union structure includes union locals, which deal with the work organization on a daily basis, national unions, which are the source of power in the union movement, and the AFL-CIO, an association of most of the national unions.

Labor-management relations are regulated by a series of labor laws governing the interactions between unions, management, and employees in both the public and private sectors. These laws attempt to maintain stable relations by facilitating collective bargaining and the settlement of disputes.

Historically, labor and management have operated as adversaries, because many of their goals are in conflict. But since conflict is detrimental to both management and labor, effective labor relations have been established to reduce this conflict. For instance, unions and management have begun to cooperate to achieve mutual goals. Although cooperation is not widespread, it may be the style of labor-management relations in the future.

PERSONNEL PROBLEM
That's Hard to Say

Western Manufacturing is a medium-size assembly plant in the Midwest. Until recently, the employees have not been interested in unionizing. The pay and fringe benefits are competitive with comparable unionized plants in the vicinity and Western Manufacturing has a fairly successful grievance process.

However, several employees have concluded that a labor union might be a good idea and have begun a drive to receive union representation. Soon they intend to collect authorization cards and make a formal request for election.

The management of Western Manufacturing is not pleased with these developments and has begun a campaign to influence employees not to vote for the union. Within the last six weeks, the company has called three meetings between the shift supervisors and their employees to explain the company's position. It has been pointed out

that wages, benefits, and working conditions are competitive with comparable union plants.

The employees who are campaigning for union representation have complained bitterly that these meetings called by management during company time are unfair and are a clear case of unfair labor practices. Not surprisingly, the company disagrees.

1. Comment on the pro-union employees' opinion of the meetings.

2. Comment on the management's opinion of the meetings.

3. Is calling the meetings on company time an unfair labor practice? Why or why not?

4. Are these meetings the fundamental issue?

KEY CONCEPTS

AFL-CIO	**formal contract**	**steward**
authorization card	**Landrum-Griffin Act**	**Taft-Hartley Act**
bargaining unit	**National Labor Relations**	**Title VII of the Civil Service**
certification election	**Board (NLRB)**	**Reform Act**
collective bargaining	**national union**	**union**
decertification election	**preelection campaign**	**union local**
employee association	**psychological contract**	**Wagner Act**
Federal Labor Relations	**Railway Labor Act (RLA)**	
Authority (FLRA)		

DISCUSSION QUESTIONS

1. In Europe, unions are often strongly involved in politics. Should unions in the United States be more involved politically?

2. Should unions change from a focus on wages and benefits in their bargaining to one that emphasizes the nature of the job itself?

3. Can unions survive if they develop a cooperative relationship with management, or should they maintain an adversarial position?

4. Do you think that the average employee is being well served by the labor union?

5. Management is almost always opposed to unions. Why? Under what circumstances might it not be?

6. Do unions still provide an essential "deterrent" to management practices, or are they becoming obsolete with the advent of more humanistic management techniques and increased

government legislation protecting the rights of workers?

7. Large national unions, like the Teamsters, represent a broad spectrum of occupations. What are the advantages and disadvantages for the employees?

8. Do you think professional groups or managers will ever unionize? What might prompt them to do so? Which professional groups are most likely to unionize? Why?

ENDNOTES

1. J. H. Hopkins and R. D. Binderup,"Employee Relations and Union Organizing Campaigns," *Personnel Administrator*, March 1980, pp. 57–61.
   R. P. Quinn and G. L. Staines, *The 1977 Quality of Employment Survey* (Ann Arbor, Mich.: Institute for Social Research, Survey Research Center, University of Michigan, 1979).

2. U.S. Department of Labor, Bureau of Labor Statistics, *Directory of National Unions and Employee Associations*, Bulletin No. 2044. (Washington, D.C.: Government Printing Office, 1979), p. 60.

3. E. H. Schein, *Organizational Psychology* (Englewood Cliffs, N.J.: Prentice-Hall, 1965).

4. For a discussion of the concept of met expectations and satisfaction, see A. C. Kalleberg, "Work Values and Job Rewards: A Theory of Job Satisfaction," *American Sociological Review*, 42 (1977), pp. 124–143.
   E. A. Locke, "What Is Job Satisfaction?" *Organizational Behavior and Human Performance*, 4 (1969), pp. 309–335.

5. J. G. Getman, S. B. Goldberg, and J. B. Herman, *Union Representation Elections: Law and Reality* (New York: Russell Sage Foundation, 1976).
   See also, J. M. Brett, "Behavioral Research on Unions," in B. M. Staw and L. L. Cummings (eds.), *Research in Organizational Behavior*, Vol. 2 (Greenwich, Conn.: JAI Press, 1980) p. 182.

6. R. Dubin, *The World of Work* (Englewood Cliffs, N.J.: Prentice-Hall, 1958).

7. Brett.

8. Quinn and Staines.

9. S. D. Hatkoff, "To What Lengths Should Medical Institutions Go in Preventing Unionizations?" *Personnel Administrator*, March 1978, pp. 17–18, 29.
   Hopkins and Binderup.

10. Getman.

11. F. Bairstow, "Professionalism and Unionism: Are They Compatible," *Industrial Engineering*, April 1974, pp. 40–42.
    P. Feville and J. Blandin, "Faculty Job Satisfaction and Bargaining Sentiments," *Academy of Management Journal*, December 1974, pp. 678–92.
    B. Husaini and J. Geschwender, "Some Correlates of Attitudes Toward and Membership in White Collar Unions," *Southwestern Social Science Quarterly*, March 1967, pp. 595–601.
    L. Imundo, "Attitudes of Non-Union White Collar Federal Government Employees toward Unions," *Public Personnel Management*, January/February 1974, pp. 87–92.
    A. Kleingartner, "Professionalism and Engineering Unionism," *Industrial Relations*, May 1969, pp. 224–235.
    A. Vogel, "Your Clerical Workers Are Ripe for Unionism," *Harvard Business Review*, March/April 1971, pp. 48–54.

12. Hopkins & Binderup.

13. Data in this section is compiled from the U.S. Department of Labor's *The Directory of National Unions and Employee Associations*, *The Bureau of Labor Statistics News* (September 1979), and information provided to the author by the Bureau of Labor Statistics, May 1980.

14. U.S. Department of Labor, 1979, p. 63.

15. Data supplied to the author by the offices of The Bureau of Labor Statistics, Washington, D.C., May, 1980.

16. Interesting discussions of early American labor history can be found in R. B. Morris, "A Bicentennial Look at the Early Days of American Labor," *American Labor Monthly Labor Review*, May 1976, pp. 21–26.
    E. Ressen, Labor from the Revolution to the Civil War," *Monthly Labor Review*, June 1976, pp. 17–24.

17. J. A. Fossum, *Labor Relations: Development, Structure, Process* (Dallas, Texas: Business Publications, Inc., 1979), p. 10.

18. L. G. Reynolds, *Labor Economics and Labor Relations*, 7th ed. (Englewood Cliffs, N.J.: Prentice-Hall, 1978).

19. A. Sloan and F. Whitney, *Labor Relations,* 3rd ed. (Englewood Cliffs, N.J.: Prentice-Hall, 1977), p. 59.

20. Sloan and Whitney, p. 64.

21. Sloan and Whitney, p. 83–84.

22. A good discussion of earlier contributions to Labor Law can be found in D. P. Twomey, *Labor Law and Legislation*, 6th ed. (Cincinnati, Ohio: Southwestern, 1980).

23. H. B. Frazier, II, "Labor-Management Relations in the Federal Government," *Labor Law Journal*, March 1979, p. 131.

24. Twomey,

25. Twomey, p. 77.

26. Sloan and Whitney.

27. Fossum, pp. 395–396.

28. Frazier, p. 133.

29. Frazier, p. 133.

30. Getman, Goldberg, and Herman, p. 1.

31. Getman, Goldberg, and Herman, p. 1.

32. Getman, Goldberg, and Herman, p. 55.

33. Getman, Goldberg, and Herman.

34. Hopkins and Binderup.

35. K. A. Kovach, "J. P. Stevens and the Struggle for Union Organization," *Labor Law Journal*, May 1978, p. 307.

36. Twomey, p. 137.

37. Twomey, p. 134.

38. Getman, Goldberg, and Herman.

39. W. Imberman, "How Expensive Is an NLRB Election?" *MSU Business Topics*, Summer 1975, pp. 13–18.
    J. Krislov, "Decertification Elections Increase but Remain No Major Burden to Unions," *Monthly Labor Review*, November 1979, p. 31.

40. Krislov, p. 31.

41. K. A. Kovach, "Do We Still Need Labor Unions?" *Personnel Journal*, December 1979, pp. 849–850.

42. Brett, p. 200. Reprinted from *Research in Organizational Behavior*, vol. 2 (1980). JAI Press, Inc., Greenwich, Conn., p. 200.

43. E. E. Lawler III and J. A. Drexler Jr., "Dynamics of Establishing Cooperative Quality of Worklife Projects," *Monthly Labor Review*, March 1978, 23–28.

44. R. H. Guest, "Quality of Worklife: Learning from Tarrytown," *Harvard Business Review*, July/August 1979, pp. 76–87.

45. T. Mills, "Altering the Social Structure in Coal Mining," *Monthly Labor Review*, October 1976, pp. 3–10.
    R. P. Nielson, "The Problem-Solving Model for Cooperative Labor Relations," *Labor Law Journal*, April 1978, pp. 236–240.

46. *The Changing World of Work* (Institute of Industrial Relations, University of California, Berkeley, September 1974).

47. Brett, pp. 189–192.

48. J. Anderson, "The Grievance Process in Canadian Municipal Relations," paper presented to the Annual Meeting of The Academy of Management, Atlanta, Georgia, August, 1979.

49. L. L. Biasatti and J. E. Martin, "A Measure of the Quality of Union-Management Relations," *Journal of Applied Psychology*, 64 (1979), pp. 387–390.

50. Biasatti and Martin.

51. B. J. Offerman, "Legal Update: Seniority and Affirmative Action" (unpublished manuscript, Cleveland State University, October 1977), p. 18.

52. U.S. Department of Labor, Bureau of Labor Statistics, *Directory of National Unions and Employee Associations, 1975*, Bulletin No. 1937 (Washington, D.C.: Government Printing Office, 1977).

53. Kovach.

54. P. Shabecoff, "Days of Wine and Roses," *Cleveland Plain Dealer*, December 9, 1979, p. 2-F.

OBJECTIVES

● To explain the issues that most commonly arise in collective bargaining

● To understand a model of the bargaining process and some of the bargaining strategies used by management and union negotiators

● To describe the methods of resolving impasses and conflicts arising out of collective bargaining

● To understand the grievance process used to resolve employee complaints

THOUGHT STARTERS

● How do union and management negotiators decide what to ask for and what to offer in negotiations?

● Is the strike a necessary part of collective bargaining, and should all employees have the right to strike?

● How can employees protect their rights under the collective bargaining agreement?

● How can the effectiveness of the collective bargaining process be determined?

CHAPTER SIXTEEN
Interactions between Union and Management

The collective bargaining contract between the Metropolitan Transportation Authority (MTA), which operates the buses and subways in New York City, and the Transport Workers Union (TWU), which represents 31,000 bus drivers and subway workers, and the Amalgamated Transportation Union (ATU), which represents another 2,000 workers, expired March 31, 1980. Negotiations on a new contract had been underway for some time and had had the help of a three-member mediation panel since February 29. Negotiations were difficult. The MTA was facing a serious financial crisis: Its deficit for 1980–1981 was estimated at $200 million, and there was little hope for additional financing from the various governments. Inflation had been reducing the real wages of the employees, with some workers needing a 31 percent increase to stay even with 1974 wages.

The MTA demanded changes in work rules, increased productivity, and a shift from fringe benefits as an exchange for wage increases. Productivity increases were viewed as essential (the MTA suggested that only 47 percent of the time spent on some jobs was productive), and the MTA negotiators would not talk about wages until the unions agreed to these conditions. The TWU, the principal union negotiator, faced disgruntled members who had seen their position as some of the highest-paid transit workers drop to some of the lower-paid. Internal political strife added to the union negotiators' problems. The union was after a 30 percent wage increase and some improved fringe benefits.

The expiration date approached with no progress. The union told its members to prepare for a strike on April 1. On March 30, the MTA made its initial offer: a 3.5 percent increase in each of three years. The union countered with its demand for a 15 percent increase in each of two years. The day prior to the strike deadline was filled with intense negotiations. The union demanded 15 percent the first year and 10 percent the second. Thirty minutes before the strike deadline, the MTA made a final offer of 6 percent increases in each of two years. The union rejected the offer. Efforts by the mediators were futile. The strike was on.

The strike stranded the 95,000 commuters who use the buses and subways daily, causing massive traffic jams and disrupting business in the city. The cost to the city in lost revenue was estimated at $3.1 million per day. Both negotiating teams faced pressure from their constituents. The mayor and the businesses in the city wanted the MTA to be tough. Union members wanted the union to hold out for their demands, and union leadership faced contempt-of-court charges for calling the strike.

After eleven days of disruption of business and traffic congestion in the city, the strike ended. The parties agreed to increases of 9 percent and 8 percent over two years with a cost-of-living adjustment. Both negotiating teams faced criticisms. The mayor assailed the agreement as too expensive. The union board was split evenly over the agreement, and the president cast the deciding vote. Many union members were unhappy; some attempted to have another board vote. The task of getting union members to accept the agreement was not easy. While the workers went back to work, the ratification vote was taken. The vote was completed by the second week of May, and the collective bargaining session came to an end.

ach year a large number of collective agreements are negotiated. In 1980, over 876 agreements affecting 3.7 million workers were made. Besides the New York City transportation service, major bargaining took place in the street, telephone, shipping, and aerospace industries. But the New York City transit negotiations and strike are good examples of the complexities of negotiations and of the conflicts that can arise when attempting to reach agreement on a labor contract. Fortunately, not all negotiations involve this much hostility or disagreement, and most are resolved without resorting to the strike.

Collective bargaining is the core of union-management relations. It may include two types of interaction. The first is the negotiation of work conditions that, when written up as the collective agreement, becomes the basis for employee-employer relationships on the job. The second is the activity related to interpreting and enforcing the collective agreement and the resolution of any conflicts arising out of it. This is often referred to as the administration of the collective agreement.

This chapter discusses both of these interactions. First the actual bargaining process, including the nature of a collective agreement and the bargaining process that is involved, is discussed. Then the problems that arise under a collective agreement are examined. The grievance process and forms of resolution are also considered.

NEGOTIATING THE AGREEMENT

Once a union is certified as the representative of a work unit or bargaining unit, it becomes the only party that can negotiate an agreement with the employer for all members of that work unit, whether or not they are union members. This is, therefore, an important and potent position. The union is responsible to its members to negotiate for what they want, and it has the "duty to represent all employees fairly."[1] The union is a critical link between employees and employer. The quality of its bargaining is an important measure of union effectiveness.

Negotiating Committees

The employer and the union select their own representatives for the **negotiating committee**. Neither party is required to consider the wishes of the other. Management negotiators, for example, cannot refuse to bargain with representatives of the union because they dislike them or do not think they are appropriate.

Union negotiating teams typically include representatives of the union local, often the president and other executive staff members. In addition, the national union may send a negotiating specialist, who is likely to be a labor lawyer, to work with the team. The negotiators selected by the union do not have to be members of the union or employees of the company. The general goal is to balance bargaining skill and experience with knowledge and information about the specific situation.

At the local level, when a single bargaining unit is negotiating a contract, the company is usually represented by the manager and members of the labor relations or personnel staff. Finance and production managers may also be involved. When the negotiations are critical, either because the size of the bargaining unit is large or because the effect on the company is great, such specialists as labor lawyers may be included on the team.

In national negotiations, top industrial relations or personnel executives frequently head a team made up of specialists from corporate headquarters and perhaps managers from critical divisions or plants within the company. Again, the goal is to have expertise along with specific knowledge about critical situations.

The Negotiating Structure

Most contracts are negotiated by a single union and a single employer. In some situations, however, different arrangements can be agreed on. When a single union negotiates with several similar companies—for instance, the construction industry or supermarkets—the employers may bargain as a group with the union. At the local level this is called **multi-employer bargaining**, but at the national level it is referred to as **industry-wide bargaining**. Industry-wide bargaining occurs in the railroad, coal, wallpaper, and men's suits industries.[2] National negotiations result in contracts that settle major issues, such as compensation, whereas issues relating to working conditions are settled locally. This split bargaining style is common in Great Britain and has been used in the auto industry in the United States. When several unions bargain jointly with a single employer, they engage in **coordinated bargaining**. Although not so common as the others, coordinated bargaining appears to be increasing, especially in public-sector bargaining,[3] as in the example at the beginning of the chapter.

The incentive to use these bargaining structures usually is related to efficiency and the relative strength of union and management. In multi-employer bargaining, the companies negotiate very similar contracts to eliminate the time and cost of individual negotiations. Since it too will save time and money, the union may be willing to accept this type of bargaining if its own bargaining position is not weakened. Where local conditions vary substantially, there may be a need for splitting the bargaining between the national and local levels—settling the major issues at the national level and leaving specific issues for the local level, where they can be adjusted to meet local needs.

BARGAINING ISSUES

The issues that can be discussed in collective bargaining sessions are specified by the Labor-Management Relations Act (which is discussed in Chapter 15). The act differentiates among three categories: mandatory issues, permissive issues, and prohibited issues.[4]

Employers and employee representatives (unions) are obligated to meet and discuss "wages, hours, and other terms and conditions of employment." These are the **mandatory issues**. Historically there has been a debate over what specific topics fall into this category. The Supreme Court's decision in the Borg Warner case (1958) suggests that the distinction between mandatory and permissive bargaining issues is based on whether the topic regulates the relations between the employer and its employees.[5] Any issue that changes the nature of the job itself or compensation for work must be discussed in collective bargaining. Mandatory issues therefore include subcontracting work, plant closings, changes of operations, and other actions management might take that will have an impact on employees' jobs.

Permissive issues are those that are not mandatory but are not specifically illegal. They are issues not specifically related to the nature of the job but still of concern to both parties. For example, issues of price, product design, and decisions about new jobs may be subject to bargaining if the parties agree to it. Permissive issues usually develop when both parties see that mutual discussion and agreement will be beneficial. Management and union negotiators cannot refuse to agree on a contract if they fail to settle a permissive issue.[6]

Prohibited issues are those concerning illegal or outlawed activities, such as the demand that an employer use only union-produced goods or, where it is illegal, that it employ only union members. Such issues may not be discussed in collective bargaining sessions.

Mandatory bargaining issues, therefore, are the critical factors in the bargaining process. They are the issues that may affect management's ability to run the company efficiently or clash with the union's desire to protect jobs and workers' standing in their jobs.[7]

A SLICE OF LIFE

When listing the issues most often discussed in collective bargaining, one issue is often conspicuous by its absence. Employees today are seeking autonomy, greater participation in decision making, job enrichment, and job enlargement. Possibly, these issues could increase cooperation between labor and management and thus improve the quality of work life for employees and the productivity of the organization. But rarely are these types of issues part of the collective bargaining agenda.

Does this mean that labor unions are not receptive to, or are perhaps unaware of, the needs of their membership? Or could it be that even though these items may be of interest to the rank-and-file employee, they are not sufficiently important to become collective bargaining issues? It is interesting that items of such great importance to workers have not found their way into the collective bargaining process.

Wages

"Probably no issues under collective bargaining continue to give rise to more difficult problems than do wage and wage-related subjects."[8] The wage issues involved in the New York City transit negotiations are a good example of these problems. Wage conflicts are the leading cause of strikes. Difficulties here are understandable: A wage increase is a direct cost to the employer.

Wages are one general category of payment to employees. The other is **economic supplements**, or fringe benefits. Collective bargaining deliberations may include discussion of how an increase in compensation will be split between these two types of payments. This is an important question, because the cost to the company of wages and fringe benefits may differ.

The wages that an employee is paid are primarily determined by the basic pay rate for a certain job. Then this pay may be increased by several other factors. All of these payments are subject to collective bargaining.

Basic Pay.   Although management would prefer that basic pay be related only to productivity, this is seldom the case. Three additional standards are frequently used: comparative norm, where rate of pay is influenced by the rates provided for similar jobs in other companies within an industry or even by comparative rates between industries; ability to pay, where the pay rate is influenced by the financial capability of the company and especially the amount of its profit; and standard of living, where changes in the cost of living influence the rate of pay.[9]

Job Evaluation and Job Comparison.   The related pay rates for jobs within a bargaining unit is an important issue. Different jobs are paid differently, based on their worth or their contribution to production. This is determined by various job requirements: skill, responsibility, mental effort, physical effort, and working conditions, as discussed in Chapter 4. Based on these factors, jobs are graded and assigned some level that determines their relative pay (refer to Chapter 10). The pay rate an individual receives is also influenced by seniority. Within a basic job classification, an individual with many years of service will usually be paid more than a person who is new to the company.[10]

Cost-of-Living Adjustments.   Another wage issue is the **cost-of-living adjustment (COLA)**, which ties wages to the Consumer Price Index (CPI).[11] The typical COLA clause provides for a 1-percent increase for each 0.3-percent rise in the CPI. This results in an average yearly wage increase of 5.4 percent for workers covered by these agreements. Contracts with COLA clauses generally provide for a larger total wage change than contracts without such clauses.

COLA clauses have become more popular as inflation has eroded employees' paychecks. In 1980, for example, 5.5 million workers were covered by COLA clauses, and 60 percent of the contracts negotiated had COLA provisions.[12]

Wage Differentials.   In companies where employees work different shifts, the labor contract often provides that those working the afternoon and night shifts receive more pay. Virtually all plants with multiple shifts have such a provision.[13] On occasion, organizations with workers spread over a large geographic area negotiate with the union over regional wage differentials, based on variations in the cost of living in different areas. Bell Telephone and the Communication Workers of America have made such arrangements. Differential wages may also be paid for extra duties, for supervisory or instructional activities, or for temporary or probationary workers.

Overtime.   Collective agreements establish the standard number of hours per day and per week that employees are expected to work, the most common being an eight-hour day and a forty-hour week. For work in excess of either of these established amounts, the agreement may specify overtime compensation. Rates of one-and-one-half times the regular pay are common, although this may vary. Scheduling overtime and making overtime mandatory are also bargaining issues. For instance, agreements may specify that overtime be scheduled so that it is distributed among workers as much as possible. Recently the right to refuse overtime has become an important bargaining issue, since unions may perceive overtime as a management strategy to reduce the number of employees and ultimately reduce labor costs. Unions have thus sought to reduce overtime or to limit its use.

Pay for Reporting. Occasionally workers who have been asked to report to work find little or no work to do. Thus some collective bargaining negotiations have involved a determination of the minimum amount of pay employees will receive for coming to work. For example, workers may receive a minimum of four hours' pay if called in to work, even if there is no work when they arrive.

Economic Supplements

An increasingly important part of the pay package is the section covering **economic supplements**, or such fringe benefits as vacations, holidays, pensions, and insurance. These benefits run as high as 45 percent of the cost of wages and are now a major factor in collective bargaining.

It is important to realize that provisions written into the bargaining agreement are very difficult to remove. If the union wins a new medical plan, for example, management will not be able to negotiate for its removal at the next bargaining session. Since management has less control over fringe benefits than over wages, it tends to be cautious about agreeing to costly benefits.

Occasionally, economic circumstances are so extreme that the union will agree to reductions in fringe benefits. The response of the United Auto Workers to the financially troubled Chrysler Corporation is a case in point. The union agreed to a reduction in paid personal holidays, a modification of the sick-pay provisions, and smaller increases in pension benefits to help the ailing company survive.[14] The general rule, however, is that once something becomes part of the agreement, it is difficult to eliminate.

Some of the more common economic supplements:

• *Pensions:* Once management has decided to provide a pension plan, the conditions of the plan must be determined (when the benefits will be available, how much will be paid, and whether they become available according to age or years of service). Finally, the organization must decide how long employees must work for the company in order to receive minimum benefits (vesting) and whether the organization will pay the whole cost or whether employees or the union will be asked to help.

• *Paid vacations:* Most agreements provide for paid vacations. The length of vacation is usually determined by length of service, up to some maximum. The conditions that qualify an individual for a vacation in a given year are also specified. Agreements occasionally specify how the timing of vacations will be determined. For example, employees may be given their choice of vacation time according to seniority.

• *Paid holidays:* Most agreements provide time off with pay on Independence Day, Labor Day, Thanksgiving, Christmas, New Year's Day, and Memorial Day. Several others may also be included.

- *Sick leave:* Unpaid sick leave allows the employee to take time off for sickness without compensation. Paid sick leave is usually accumulated while working. Typically one-half to one-and-one-half days of paid sick leave are credited for each month of work.
- *Health and life insurance:* The employer may be required to pay some or all of the costs of health and life insurance plans.
- *Dismissal or severance pay:* Occasionally employers agree to pay any employee who is dismissed or laid off due to technological changes or business difficulties.
- *Supplemental unemployment benefits:* In the mid-1950s, the United Auto Workers negotiated a plan to supplement state unemployment benefits and to make up the difference when these state benefits expired. Most contracts with this provision are found in the auto and steel industries, where layoffs are common, but workers in other industries are beginning to negotiate them as well.

Institutional Issues

Some issues are not directly related to jobs but are nevertheless important to both employees and management. Institutional issues are those that affect the security and success of both parties.

- *Union security:* About 63 percent of the major labor contracts stipulate that employees must join the union after being hired into its bargaining unit. However, twenty states that traditionally have had low levels of unionization have passed "right-to-work" laws outlawing union membership as a condition of employment.
- *Checkoff:* Unions have attempted to arrange for payment of dues through deduction from employees' paychecks. By law, employees must agree to this in writing, but about 86 percent of union contracts contain this provision anyway.
- *Strikes:* The employer may insist that the union agree not to strike during the life of the agreement, typically when a cost-of-living clause has been included. The agreement may be unconditional, allowing no strikes at all, or it may limit strikes to specific circumstances.
- *Managerial prerogatives:* Over half the agreements today stipulate that certain activities are the right of management. In addition, management in most companies argues that it has "residual rights"—that all rights not specifically limited by the agreement belong to management.

Administrative Issues

The last category of issues is concerned with the treatment of employees at work.

- *Breaks and cleanup time:* Some contracts specify the time and length of coffee breaks and meal breaks for employees. Also, jobs requiring cleanup may have a portion of the work period set aside for this procedure.
- *Job security:* This is perhaps the issue of most concern to employees and unions. Employers are concerned with restriction of their ability to lay off employees. Changes in technology or attempts to subcontract work are issues that impinge on job security. A typical union response to technological change was the reaction of the International Longshoremen's Association in the late 1960s to the introduction of containerized shipping: The union operated exclusive hiring halls, developed

complex work rules, and negotiated a guaranteed annual income for its members. Job security continues to be a primary issue for longshoremen, telephone workers, and most other blue-collar occupations.

● *Seniority:* Length of service is used as a criterion for many personnel decisions in most collective agreements. Layoffs are usually determined by seniority. "Last hired, first fired" is a common situation. Seniority is also important in transfer and promotion decisions. The method of calculating seniority is usually specified to clarify the relative seniority of employees.

● *Discharge and discipline:* This is a touchy issue, and even when an agreement addresses these problems, many grievances are filed concerning the way employees are disciplined or discharged.

● *Safety and health:* Although the Occupational Safety and Health Act specifically deals with worker safety and health, some contracts have provisions specifying that the company will provide safety equipment, first aid, physical examinations, accident investigations, and safety committees. Hazardous work may be covered by special provisions and pay rates. Often the agreement will contain a general statement that the employer is responsible for the safety of the workers so the union can use the grievance process when any safety issues arise.[15]

● *Production standards:* The level of productivity or performance of employees is a concern of both management and the union. Management is concerned with efficiency, but the union is concerned with the fairness and reasonableness of management's demands. This was a key issue in the New York City transit negotiations.

● *Grievance procedures:* This is a significant part of collective bargaining, and is discussed in more detail later in this chapter.

● *Training:* The design and administration of training and development programs, and the procedure for selecting employees for training, may also be bargaining issues.

● *Duration of the agreement:* Agreements can last for one year or longer, with the most common period being three years.

THE COLLECTIVE BARGAINING PROCESS

Collective bargaining is a complex process in which union and management negotiators maneuver to win the most advantageous contract. As in any complex process, a variety of issues come into play.

A Model of the Bargaining Process

The most widely used model of the bargaining process incorporates four types of bargaining in contract negotiation: distributive bargaining, integrative bargaining, attitudinal structuring, and intraorganizational bargaining.[16]

Distributive Bargaining. **Distributive bargaining** takes place when the parties are in conflict over an issue and the outcome represents a gain for one party and a loss for the other. Each party tries to negotiate for the best possible outcome. The process is outlined in Exhibit 16.1.

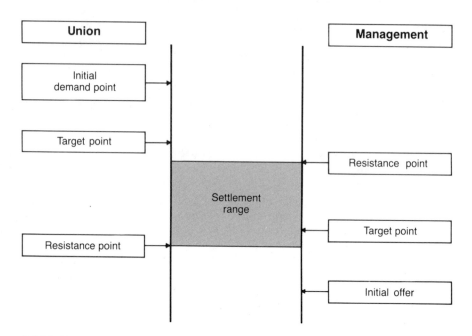

Exhibit 16.1 Distributive Bargaining Process
From U.S. Department of Labor, Bureau of Labor Statistics, *Occupational Safety and Health Statistics: Concepts and Methods*, BLS report 438 (Washington D.C.: Bureau of Labor Statistics, 1975), p. 2.

On any particular issue, union and management negotiators each have three identifiable positions. The union has an initial demand point, which is generally more than they expect to get; a target point, which is their realistic assessment of what they may be able to get; and a resistance point, which is the lowest acceptable level for that issue. Management has three similar points: an initial offer, which is usually lower than the expected settlement; a target point, which is the point it would like to reach agreement at; and a resistance point, which is its upper acceptable limit. If, as shown in Exhibit 16.1, management's resistance point is greater than the union's resistance point, there is a positive settlement range where negotiation can take place. The exact agreement within this range depends on the bargaining behavior of the negotiators. If however, management's resistance point is below the union's, there is no common ground for negotiation. In such a situation, there is a negative settlement range, and a bargaining impasse exists.[17]

Using wages as an example, the union may have a resistance point of $5.40 per hour, a target of $5.60, and an initial demand of $5.75. Management may offer $5.20 but have a target of $5.45 and a resistance point of $5.55. The positive settlement range is between $5.40 and $5.55, and it is very likely that this is where the settlement will be. Note, however, that only the initial wage demand and offer are actually made public at the beginning of negotiations.

Since many issues are involved in a bargaining session, the process becomes much more complicated. Although each issue may be described by the above model, in actual negotiations there is an interaction among issues. Union concessions on one issue may be traded for management concessions on another. Thus the total process is dynamic.

The ritual of the distributive bargaining process is well established, and deviations are often met with suspicion. The following story illustrates this point:

A labor lawyer tells the story of a young executive who had just taken over the helm of a company. Imbued with idealism, he wanted to end the bickering he had seen take place during past negotiations with labor. To do this, he was ready to give the workers as much as his company could afford. Consequently he asked some members of his staff to study his firm's own wage structure and decide how it compared with other companies, as well as a host of other related matters. He approached the collective bargaining table with a halo of goodness surrounding him. Asking for the floor, he proceeded to describe what he had done and with a big smile on his face made the offer.

Throughout his entire presentation, the union officials stared at him in amazement. He had offered more than they had expected to secure. But no matter, as soon as he finished, they proceeded to lambaste him, denouncing him for trying to destroy collective bargaining and for attempting to buy off labor. They announced that they would not stand for any such unethical maneuvering, and immediately asked for 5 cents more than the idealistic executive had offered.[18]

Integrative Bargaining.　**Integrative bargaining** is the situation in which management and the union work to solve a problem to the benefit of both. For instance, issues of work crew size may be addressed or union concerns for job security. Most quality-of-work life changes involve integrative bargaining. The new work setting will benefit employees as well as the employer. Given the adversarial nature of labor-management relations, integrative bargaining is not common, although the recent interest in cooperative relations may change that.

Attitudinal Structuring.　The relationship between labor and management results in **attitudinal structuring**, or the shaping of attitudes toward one another. Four dimensions of this relationship have been identified: motivational orientation, or tendencies that indicate whether the interaction will be competitive and adversarial or cooperative; beliefs about the legitimacy of the other, or how much a party believes the other has a right to be bargaining; level of trust in conducting affairs, or belief in the integrity and honesty of the other party; and degree of friendliness, or whether the interactions are friendly or hostile. As the bargaining process proceeds, these attitudes may be altered. The attitudes emerging from the negotiations will have a serious impact on the administration of the contract and on future negotiations.

Intraorganizational Bargaining.　During negotiations, the bargaining teams from both sides may have to engage in **intraorganizational bargaining**, or conferring with their constituents over changes in bargaining positions. Management negotiators may have to convince management to change its position on an issue—for instance, to agree to a higher wage settlement. Union negotiators must eventually convince their members to accept the negotiated contract, so they must be sensitive to the demands of the membership but be realistic as well. When the membership votes on the proposed package, it will be strongly influenced by the opinions of the union negotiators. Recall that in the New York City transit negotiations, both management and union leaders experienced difficulties in convincing their respective constituents to accept the contract.

Management Strategies

Prior to the bargaining session, management negotiators prepare by developing the strategies and proposals they will use. Four major areas of preparation have been identified:

- Preparation of specific proposals for changes in contract language
- Determination of the general size of the economic package that the company anticipates offering during the negotiations
- Preparation of statistical displays and supportive data that the company will use during negotiations
- Preparation of a bargaining book for the use of company negotiators, a compilation of information on issues that will be discussed, giving an analysis of the effect of each clause, its use in other companies, and other facts[19]

An important part of this preparation is calculation of the cost of various bargaining issues or demands. The relative cost of pension contributions, pay increases, health benefits, and other provisions should be determined prior to negotiations. Other costs should also be considered. For instance, what is the cost to management, in terms of its ability to do its job, of union demands for changes in grievance and discipline procedures or transfer and promotion provisions? The goal is to be as well prepared as possible by considering the implications and ramifications of the issues that will be discussed and by being able to present a strong argument for the position management takes.

An example of preparation to the extreme is the bargaining practice called **Boulwarism**, in which management presents the union with an offer early in the negotiations and holds firm to that offer. This practice, used successfully by General Electric in the 1960s and early 1970s, involves preparing for negotiations by effecting what company representatives describe as "the steady accumulation of all facts available on matters likely to be discussed." This information will be modified only on the basis of "any additional or different facts" the company is made aware of, either by its unions or from other sources, before or during the negotiations. The company offers at an "appropriate" but invariably very early point during the bargaining "what the facts from all sources seem to indicate that we should," and it changes this offer only if confronted with "new facts."[20]

Along with these bargaining strategies, GE engaged in a massive communication program aimed at convincing workers that GE was looking out for their interests. During the 1960 negotiations and subsequent strike, GE sent out 246 written communications to its employees.[21] Using these tactics, GE was able to have its proposal accepted by the International Brotherhood of Electrical Workers. Union leaders protested that these tactics constituted an unfair labor practice because the company refused to bargain.[22] To be sure, this bargaining approach made the union look bad and further weakened its position with union members. (The union had already been relatively weak due to internal problems and conflicts with other unions.)

GE is having less success in getting its offers accepted in recent negotiations, because the union has since become stronger and better prepared. Other companies have not adopted GE's strategy, partly because the issue of refusing to bargain in good faith has not been settled and partly because they do not want to give up potential gains at the bargaining table or risk higher costs when a strong union responds to this strategy.

A final component of management strategy is the decision about how to respond to a threatened strike. The costs of a strike have to be set against the costs of the demands so that a position can be taken.

Union Strategies

Like management, unions need to prepare for negotiations by collecting information. More and better information gives the union the ability to be more convincing in negotiations. Since collective bargaining is the major means by which a union can convince its members that it is effective and valuable, this is a critical activity.

Unions should collect information in at least three areas:

- The financial situation of the company and its ability to pay
- The attitude of management toward various issues, as reflected in past negotiations or inferred from negotiations in similar companies
- The attitudes and desires of the employees

The first two areas give the union an idea of what demands management is likely to accept. The third area is important but is sometimes overlooked. The union should be aware of the preferences of the membership. For instance, is a pension increase preferred over increased vacation or holiday benefits? The preferences will vary with the characteristics of the workers. Younger workers are more likely to prefer more holidays, shorter work weeks, and limited overtime, whereas older workers are more interested in pension plans, benefits, and overtime. The union can determine these preferences by using a questionnaire to survey its members, as discussed in Chapter 19.

Productivity Bargaining

A relatively recent procedure in negotiations is **productivity bargaining**. Labor agrees to scrap old work habits for new and more effective ones desired by management, and in exchange management returns some of the gains of modernization and increased efficiency to labor in the form of new and better work incentives.[23]

Some unions have been hesitant to agree to this approach, because they fear that their members will lose jobs, that the company will require excessive work, or that technological change will eventually eliminate more jobs. Despite this hesitancy, productivity bargaining has been used successfully.[24] One of the notable changes is that the bargaining process changes from distributive to integrative. "Labor and management work together, not only to create the agreement itself, but to create an atmosphere of ongoing cooperation."[25]

Continuous Bargaining

As affirmative action, safety and health, and other government regulations continue to complicate the situation for both unions and employers, and as the rate of change in the environment continues to increase, some labor and management negotiators are turning to **continuous bargaining**. A joint committee meets on a regular basis to explore issues of common interest. These committees have appeared in retail food, over-the-road trucking, nuclear power, and men's garment industries.[26]

Several characteristics of continuous bargaining have been identified:

- Frequent meetings during the life of the contract
- Focus on external events and problem areas rather than internal problems
- Use of outside experts in decision making
- Use of a problem-solving (integrative) approach[27]

The intention is to develop a union-management structure that is capable of adapting to sudden changes in the environment in a positive and productive manner. This continuous bargaining approach is different from, but an extension of, the emergency negotiations that unions have insisted on when inflation or other factors have substantially changed the acceptability of the existing agreement. Continuous bargaining is a permanent arrangement intended to help avoid the crises that often occur under traditional collective bargaining systems.

CONFLICT RESOLUTION

Although the desired outcome of collective bargaining is agreement on the conditions of employment. there are many occasions when negotiators are unable to reach such an agreement at the bargaining table. In these situations several alternatives are used to resolve the impasse. The most visible response is the strike or lockout, but third-party interventions such as mediation and arbitration are also used.

Strikes and Lockouts

When the union is unable to get management to agree to a demand it feels is critical, it may resort to a strike. A **strike** may be defined as the refusal by employees to work at the company. Management may refuse to allow employees to work, which is called a **lockout**, but this is not a frequent occurrence. In 1979 there were 4,788 strikes involving 1,735,000 workers.[28] This was lower than the rate for previous years, which had peaked at 6,074 strikes in 1974. The frequency of strikes is affected by a variety of circumstances, including the general health of the economy, union-management relations, and internal union affairs.

In order to strike, the union usually holds a strike vote to get its members' approval for a strike if the negotiations are not successful. Strong membership support for a strike strengthens the union negotiators' position. If the strike takes place, union members picket the employer, informing the public about the existence of a labor dispute and preferably, from the union's point of view, convincing them to avoid this company during the strike. A common practice is the refusal of union members to cross the picket line of another striking union. This gives added support to the striking union.

Employers usually attempt to continue operations while the strike is in effect. They either run the company with supervisory personnel and people not in the bargaining unit or hire replacements for the employees. Although the company can legally hire these replacements, the union reacts strongly to the use of "scabs," and they may be a cause of increasingly belligerent labor relations. The success of a strike depends on its ability to cause economic hardship to the employer. Severe hardship usually causes the employer to concede to the union's demands. Thus it is paramount, from the union's point of view, that the company not be able to operate successfully during the strike and that the cost of this lack of production be high. The union is therefore very active in trying to prevent replacement employees from working. In addition, the timing of the strike is often critical. The union attempts to hold negotiations just prior to the period when the employer has a peak demand for its product or services, when a strike will have maximum economic impact.

Although strikes are common, they are costly to both the employer, who loses revenue, and employees, who face loss of income. If the strike is prolonged, it is likely that the cost to employees will never fully be recovered by the benefits gained. Moreover, public interest is generally not served by strikes. They are often an inconvenience to the public and can have serious consequences to the economy as a whole. Conflict resolution that avoids work stoppage—especially third-party interventions like mediation and arbitration—is therefore desirable from several perspectives.

Mediation

Mediation is a procedure in which "a neutral third party assists the union and management negotiators in reaching voluntary agreement."[29] Having no power to impose a solution, the mediator attempts to facilitate the negotiations between union and management. The mediator may make suggestions and recommendations and perhaps add objectivity to the often emotional negotiations. To have any success at all, the mediator must have the trust and respect of both parties and have sufficient expertise and neutrality to convince the union and employer that he or she will be fair and equitable. The U.S. government operates the Federal Mediation and Conciliation Service to make experienced mediators available to unions and companies.

Arbitration

Arbitration is a procedure in which a neutral third party studies the bargaining situation, listening to both parties and gathering information, and then makes recommendations that are binding on the parties. The arbitrator, in effect, determines the conditions of the agreement.

Two types of arbitration have developed.[30] The first is an extension of bargaining; the arbitrator attempts to reach a rational and equitable decision acceptable to both parties. The second type is called final-offer arbitration. It involves the arbitrator choosing between the final offer of the union and the final offer of the employer. The arbitrator cannot alter these offers but must choose one as it stands. Since the arbitrator chooses the offer that appears most fair, and since losing the arbitration decision means settling for the other's offer, there is pressure to make as good an offer as possible. The intention of final-offer arbitration is to encourage the parties to make their best offer and to reach an agreement before arbitration becomes necessary.

Effectiveness of Negotiations

Since the purpose of negotations is to achieve an agreement, this becomes an overall measure of bargaining effectiveness. A healthy and effective bargaining process encourages the discussion of issues and problems and their subsequent resolution at the bargaining table. In addition, the effort required to reach agreement is a measure of how well the process is working. Some indications of this effort are the duration of negotiations, the outcome of member ratification votes, the frequency and duration of strikes, the use of mediation and arbitration, the need for government intervention, and the resulting quality of management relations (whether conflict or cooperation exists).[31]

The success of arbitration is often judged by the acceptability of the decisions, the satisfaction of the parties, innovation, and the absence of biases in either direction.[32] The effectiveness of any third-party intervention rests in part on its ability to reduce or avoid strikes, since the motivation for third-party intervention is the realization that strikes are not a desirable form of conflict resolution.

ADMINISTERING THE AGREEMENT

The collective agreement, once signed, becomes "the basic legislation governing the lines of the workers."[33] That is, the daily operation and activities in the organization are subject to the conditions of the agreement. Since it is impossible to write an unambiguous agreement that will anticipate all the situations occurring over its life, there will inevitably be disputes over interpretation and application of the agreement. The most common method of resolving these disputes is a **grievance procedure**. Virtually all agreements negotiated today provide for a grievance process to handle employee complaints.

Grievance Procedures

Basically a grievance is a "charge that the union-management contract has been violated."[34] A grievance may be filed by the union for employees or by employers, although management rarely does so. The grievance process is designed to investigate the charges and to resolve the problem.

Five sources of grievances have been identified:
- Outright violation of the agreement
- Disagreement over facts
- Dispute over the meaning of the agreement
- Dispute over the method of applying the agreement
- Argument over the fairness or reasonableness of actions[35]

In resolving these sources of conflict, the grievance procedure should serve three separate groups: the employers and unions, by interpreting and adjusting the agreement as conditions require; the employees, by protecting their contractual rights and providing a channel of appeal; and society at large, by keeping industrial peace and reducing the number of industrial disputes in the courts.[36]

Grievance procedures typically involve several stages. The collective bargaining agreement specifies the maximum length of time that each step may take. For example, it may require the grievance to be filed within five days of the incident that is the subject of dispute. The most common grievance procedure, shown in Exhibit 16.2, involves four steps, with the final step being arbitration.[37] An employee who feels that the labor contract has been violated usually contacts the union steward, and together they discuss the problem with the supervisor involved. If the problem is simple and straightforward, it is often resolved at this level. Many contracts require the grievance to be in written form at this first stage. However, there may be cases that are resolved by informal discussion between the supervisor and the employee and therefore do not officially enter the grievance process.

If agreement cannot be reached at the supervisor level, or if the employee is not satisfied, the complaint can enter the second step of the grievance procedure. Typically, an industrial-relations representative of the company now seeks to resolve the grievance.

If the grievance is sufficiently important or difficult to resolve, it may be taken to the third step. Although contracts vary, top-level management and union executives are usually involved at this step. These people have the authority to make the major decisons that may be required to resolve the grievance.

If a grievance cannot be resolved at the third step, most agreements require the use of an arbitrator to consider the case and reach a decision. The arbitrator is a neutral, mutually acceptable individual who may be provided by the Federal Me-

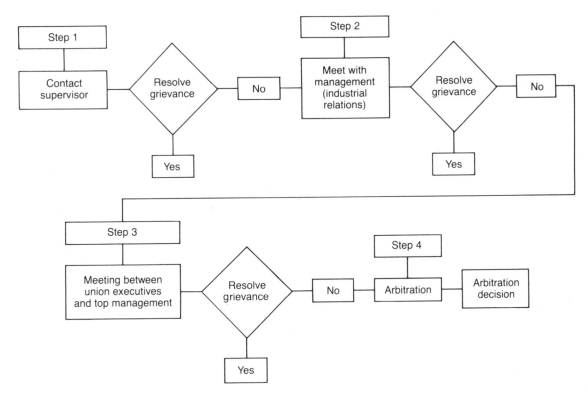

Exhibit 16.2 Typical Grievance Procedure

diation and Conciliation Service or some private agency. The arbitrator holds a hearing, reviews the evidence, then rules on the grievance. The decision of the arbitrator is usually binding.

Since the cost of arbitration is shared by the union and employer, there is some incentive to settle the grievance before it goes to arbitration. The average fee for each arbitration case is $1,434, and there are other expenses involved. An added incentive in some cases is the requirement that the loser pay for the arbitration.[38] The expectation is that the parties will screen or evaluate grievances more carefully, because pursuing a weak grievance to arbitration will result in a loss and the costs of arbitration.

Occasionally the union will call a strike over a grievance in order to resolve it. This may happen when the issue at hand is so important that the union feels it cannot wait for the slower arbitration process, which takes an average of 223 days.[39] This "employee rights" strike may be legal, but if the contract specifically forbids strikes during the tenure of the agreement, it is not legal and is called a **wildcat strike**. Wildcat strikes are not common, since most grievances are settled through arbitration.

Grievance Issues

Grievances can be filed over any issue relating to the workplace that is subject to the collective agreement, or they can be filed over interpretation and implementation of the agreement itself. The most common type of grievance reaching the arbitration stage is concerned with discipline and discharge, although many grievances are filed over other issues. Exhibit 16.3 presents a list of common categories of grievances.

It is generally conceded that management has the right to discipline employees. The grievance issue usually relates to "just cause" for the discipline and the fairness and consistency of the action taken. No firm rule exists that defines these issues, so discipline and discharge are prone to grievances.

Although it is accepted that absenteeism can be grounds for discharge, the critical issue is the determination that the absenteeism in question is excessive.[40] Insubordination usually is either failure to do what the supervisor requests or the more serious problem of outright refusal to do it. If the supervisor's orders are clear and explicit and if the employee is warned of the consequences, discipline for refusal to respond is usually acceptable. The exception is when the employee feels that the work endangers health.

Since seniority is usually used to determine who is laid off, bumped from a job to make way for someone else, or rehired, its calculation is of great concern to employees. Promotions and transfers also use seniority as one of the criteria to determine eligibility, so management must be careful in this area so as to avoid complaints and grievances.

Compensation for time away from work, vacations, holidays, or sick leave is also a common source of grievances. Holidays cause problems because there are often special pay arrangements for people working on those days.

Wage and work schedules may also lead to grievances. Disagreements often arise over interpretation or application of the agreement relating to such issues as overtime pay, pay for reporting, and scheduling.

Exhibit 16.3 Types of Grievances

Discipline and discharge	**Vacation**
Absenteeism	Eligibility
Insubordination	Scheduling
Misconduct	Pay
Poor Work	**Holidays**
Seniority	Eligibility for pay
Calculating seniority	Pay for holiday work
Layoffs	**Wages and hours**
Bumping	Incentive pay plans
Worksharing	Job evaluation
Rehiring	Overtime
Leave of absence	Premium pay
Paid sick leave	Pay for reporting (call-in pay)
Personal leave	Scheduling
Union business	Wage guarantee and SUB plans
Promotion	**Management rights**
Posting and bidding	**Union rights, union security,**
Basis for promotion	**and the checkoff**
Measurement of ability	**Administration of benefits**
Transfer	

Adapted from Bureau of National Affairs, *Grievance Guide*, 4th ed. (Washington, D.C.: Bureau of National Affairs, 1972).

Grievances have been filed over the exercise of management rights—that is, its right to introduce technological changes, use subcontractors, or change jobs in other ways. This type of behavior may also be the source of charges of unfair labor practices, since these activities may require collective bargaining.

The Taft-Hartley Act gives unions the right to file grievances on their own behalf if they feel their rights have been violated. This act also gives unions access to information necessary to process the grievance or to make sure the agreement is not being violated. In addition, unions may file grievances for violations of union shop or checkoff provisions.

Occasionally other activities prompt grievances. Wildcat strikes or behavior that is considered to be a strike (mass absences from work, for example) may result in a management grievance. The major focus of grievances, however, is in the administration of the conditions of the agreement.

Management Procedures

Management can significantly affect the grievance rate by adopting proper procedures when taking action against an employee. One of the most important areas for such procedures is discipline and discharge. Since the issue of just cause and fairness is central to most discipline grievances, employers must ensure that the employee is adequately warned of the consequences, that the rule involved is related to operation of the company, that a thorough investigation is undertaken, and that the penalty is reasonable. The following activities have been identified as being useful in meeting these conditions:

- Explanation of rules to employees
- Consideration of the accusations and facts
- Regular warning procedures, including written records
- Involvement of the union in the case
- Examination of the employee's motives and reasons
- Consideration of the employee's past record
- Familiarization of all management personnel, especially supervisors, with disciplinary procedure and company rules[41]

In areas outside of discipline and discharge, management can avoid some grievance problems by educating supervisors and managers about labor relations and about the conditions of the collective agreement. It has been found that supervisors with labor knowledge are an important factor in the reduction of grievances.[42]

Union Procedures

The union has an obligation to its members to represent them fairly in the grievance process. Thus it should have a grievance-handling procedure that will aid in effectively processing grievances.

Unions may have an additional interest in grievances as a tool in collective negotiation. They may attempt to increase grievance rates to influence management as collective bargaining approaches. Grievances may also be a way to introduce or show concern for an issue in negotiations. In some cases, grievances may be withdrawn by unions in exchange for some management concessions, although this may be dangerous, since it may be an unfair representation of the employee.[43]

Unfair representation, according to the National Labor Relations Board, is usually related to one of four types of union behavior:

- *Improper motives or fraud:* The union cannot refuse to process a grievance because of the employee's race or sex or because of the employee's attitude toward the union.
- *Arbitrary conduct:* The union must investigate the merits of the grievance. Unions cannot dismiss a grievance without investigating it.
- *Gross negligence:* The union cannot display a reckless disregard of the employee's interests.
- *Union conduct after filing the grievance:* The union must process the grievance to a reasonable conclusion.[44]

Because the employer can also be cited for unfair representation, management should attempt to maintain a fair grievance process. Company labor-relations managers should avoid taking advantage of union errors in handling grievances lest this action affect fair representation.

Another important influence on the grievance process is the union steward. Since the union steward is generally the first person to hear about an employee's grievance, the steward has substantial influence on the grievance process.[45] A steward can encourage an employee to file a grievance, can suggest that the problem is really not a grievance, or can informally resolve the problem outside the grievance procedure. The steward, being in such a key position, can have a profound effect on the situation. Personality characteristics of stewards may, in fact, influence the number of grievances filed.[46] Since stewards are selected from the ranks of employees and may have little knowledge of labor relations, the union should provide training to improve their effectiveness. The company, since it may also be liable in a fair-representation suit, should support such training.

Effectiveness of the Grievance Procedure

How successful a grievance procedure is may be assessed from different perspectives. Management may view the number of grievances filed and the number settled in management's favor as measures of effectiveness. Unions may also consider the number of grievances, but from their point of view, a larger number, rather than a smaller number, would be considered more successful.

Although the views of management and the union may differ, an overall set of measures to gauge grievance procedure effectiveness may be related to the disagreements between managers and employees. Some of the measures that might be included are frequency of grievances; the level in the grievance procedure at which grievances are usually settled; the frequency of strikes or slowdowns during the term of the labor agreements; the rates of absenteeism, turnover, and sabotage; and the necessity for government intervention.[47]

PUBLIC-SECTOR COLLECTIVE BARGAINING

Collective bargaining in the public sector differs somewhat from that in the private sector. Federal employees do not have the right to strike, and management can "meet and confer" but does not have to bargain. The recently passed Civil Service Reform Act has changed the situation somewhat by creating an independent agency to remedy unfair labor practices, yet federal employees still do not have the same collective bargaining rights as other workers.

Arrangements for collective bargaining at the state and local level vary considerably. All but fourteen of the states have collective bargaining provisions.[48] There is a wide range of coverage among states: Some include municipal employees, some include state employees, and some include both. Special legislation for police officers, firefighters, and teachers are also often found.

One distinctive characteristic of public-sector collective bargaining is the tendency to have multilateral bargaining.[49] **Multilateral bargaining** occurs when more than two parties are involved in the negotiation and there is no clear union-management dichotomy. Governments tend to have so many levels of authority that unions can sometimes go outside the government negotiating team to higher authorities to seek a settlement. However, such actions tend to disrupt the bargaining process and can lead to distrust and difficulties in future negotiations. The New York City transit negotiations are a good example of multilateral bargaining. The mayor, the governor, and the MTA authorities were all involved in the negotiations.

The frequency of strikes in the public sector is increasing,[50] partly because the penalty for striking has rarely been enforced in the public sector.[51] The success of strikes or work stoppages in the public sector depends on both the political clout of the union and its ability to impose economic costs. Since many public-sector services are not essential and strikes can mean a cost savings in unpaid wages to the government involved, strikes of teachers or public employees have a lower success rate for unions. However, when a strike does have economic and political impact, as did the New York City transit strike, it can be effective in achieving union demands.

Arbitration procedures for bargaining impasses have been effective in reducing the incidence of strikes in police and firefighter negotiations.[52] Mediation and arbitration are becoming common methods for resolving difficulties in the public sector as a whole.

The new Civil Service Reform Act requires a grievance procedure with arbitration to be included as the last step in all agreements. Thus the mechanism for grievance settlement is similar to that in the private sector. However, unlike the private sector, the collective bargaining process in the public sector appears to provide higher wages and greater final benefits to union employees than to nonunion employees. In addition, personnel practices are more formalized, and the discretion of management in discipline, promotions, transfers, and work assignments is reduced.[53]

NONUNION EMPLOYEE RELATIONS

Since unions represent only one-fourth of the work force, the majority of employees do not have unions or collective agreements to protect their rights. Instead, many nonunion companies have their own rules of conduct and complaint procedures for employees. A recent survey showed that 82 percent of the nonunion companies have written rules of conduct, and 80 percent have discipline complaint procedures.[54] Moreover, 90 percent of the surveyed companies have an informal complaint procedure for employees, and 80 percent of the employees rated that procedure as excellent or good. Formal complaint procedures, typically with three or four steps, are found in 44 percent of the companies. Thus there is some evidence that many nonunion employees enjoy some of the benefits found in union companies. In fact, many companies are now offering "pay and benefit packages which top even union demands."[55] This may be attributable primarily to the desire of these companies to remain nonunionized.

SUMMARY

Collective bargaining is a key activity for unions and management. Each selects a bargaining committee to negotiate the new agreement. The negotiations may be between a single union and a single company or multiple companies or between multiple unions and a single company.

Bargaining issues are either mandatory, permissive, or prohibited. Mandatory issues must be discussed, permissive issues can be discussed if both parties agree, and prohibited issues cannot be discussed. The issues can be grouped into wage issues, economic supplements issues, institutional issues, and administrative issues.

Both management and the union should be well prepared for bargaining negotiations by collecting information and evaluating possible solutions. A management strategy that has been used is Boulwarism, where management makes an offer and then refuses to budge from this position. Productivity bargaining is an attempt to encourage increased effectiveness in the workplace by passing some of the economic savings of modernization or increased efficiency on to the employees. A recent innovation is continuous bargaining, where a joint union-management committee meets on a regular basis to deal with problems.

Almost all labor contracts outline grievance procedures for handling employee complaints. The most common grievance is related to discipline and discharge, although wages, promotions, seniority, vacations, holidays, and management and union rights are also sources of complaints.

Management can influence the results of grievances by developing a procedure that ensures their actions are for just cause and are fair. Written records of actions taken are useful for potential arbitration. Unions have a legal responsibility to represent the employee fairly in grievances; therefore, they also need a grievance-handling procedure.

The effectiveness of collective bargaining and contract administration is usually assessed by measures of how well the process is working. Bargaining can be evaluated using such measures as the duration of negotiations, the frequency of strikes, use of third-party intervention, and the need for government intervention. The effectiveness of the grievance process can be assessed by number of grievances, level in the grievance process that settlement occurs, frequency of strikes or slowdowns, rate of absenteeism, turnover, and sabotage, and need for government intervention.

PERSONNEL PROBLEM
Arbitration or Justice?

A grievance filed by an employee of a large southeastern manufacturing company progressed through various administrative levels before being settled by arbitration. The arbitrator ruled for the company and denied the employee the relief she sought. Immediately after the judgment of the arbitrator was rendered, it was discovered that the arbitrator had made an error of law and that the decision should have been in favor of the grievant.

1. Does the decision of the arbitrator stand?
2. Can the decision of an arbitrator be appealed?
3. If the judgment had been in favor of the grievant under similar circumstances, could the company have appealed?

KEY CONCEPTS

arbitration
attitudinal structuring
Boulwarism
continuous bargaining
coordinated bargaining
cost-of-living adjustment
   (COLA)
distributive bargaining
economic supplement

grievance procedure
industrywide bargaining
integrative bargaining
intraorganizational bargaining
lockout
mandatory issue
mediation
multi-employer bargaining
multilateral bargaining

negotiating committee
permissive issue
productivity bargaining
prohibited issue
strike
unfair representation
wildcat strike

DISCUSSION QUESTIONS

1. It has been suggested that bargaining negotiations are merely a ritual, with the outcome known in advance. Do you agree? If so, what function does the negotiation process serve?
2. How much influence do you think the members of a union have in determining the demands of the union in negotiations? How much should they have?
3. What personal characteristics are important for negotiators?
4. Is it possible for the same negotiators to engage in both distributive and integrative bargaining? Could this be a reason why integrative bargaining is not more prevalent?

5. Will collective bargaining remain primarily distributive, or will integrative bargaining become more prominent in the future?
6. Under what conditions might the membership of a union reject a contract negotiated by the union leaders?
7. What societal factors tend to make public-sector collective bargaining more difficult than private-sector bargaining?
8. What attitudes and behaviors of management and union officials influence the level at which grievances are resolved? Why might either party want to take a grievance all the way to arbitration?

ENDNOTES

1. *1979 Guidebook to Labor Relations*, 18th ed. (Chicago: Commerce Clearing House, 1978), p. 282.

2. D. Greenberg, "The Structure of Collective Bargaining and Some of its Determinants," Proceedings, Industrial Relations Research Association, Albany, N.Y., December 1966.

3. A. Leonard, "Collective Bargaining with Multinational Firms by American Labor Unions," *Labor Law Journal*, December 1974, pp. 746–59.
   R. Mansfield, "The Advent of Public Sector Multi-Employer Bargaining," *Personnel Journal*, May 1975, pp. 290–294.

4. J. Fossum, *Labor Relations: Development, Structure and Process* (Dallas, Texas: Business Publications, Inc., 1979), p. 171.

5. E. Platt, "The Duty to Bargain as Applied to Management Decisions," *Labor Law Journal*, March 1968, p. 145.

6. Fossum, p. 173.

7. Platt, p. 144.

8. A. A. Sloan and F. Whitney, *Labor Relations*, 3rd ed. (Englewood Cliffs, N.J.: Prentice-Hall, 1977), p. 275.

9. Examples of these are discussed in *Business Week*, "The Oil Workers Vow to Catch Up on Wages," December 31, 1979, p. 34 and *Business Week*, "Taking Aim at Union-Busters," November 26, 1979, pp. 67–72.

10. Note that this does not violate equal pay for equal work because individuals with more seniority can be expected to contribute more to the job than individuals with less seniority.

11. P. Farish, "American Wage Gains," *Personnel Administrator*, March 1980, p. 17.

12. M. A. Andrews, and W. Tillery, "Heavy Bargaining Again in 1980," *Monthly Labor Review*, December 1979, pp. 20–28.
    E. Wasiewski, "Scheduled Wage Increases and Escalator Provisions in 1980," *Monthly Labor Review*, January 1980, pp. 9–13.

13. Sloan and Whitney, p. 298.

14. "The Price of Peace at Chrysler," *Business Week*, November 12, 1979, pp. 93–96.

15. T. A. Kochan, *Collective Bargaining and Industrial Relations* (Homewood, Ill.: Irwin, 1980a).

16. R. E. Walton and R. B. McKersie, *A Behavioral Theory of Labor Negotiations* (New York: McGraw-Hill, 1965).

17. T. A. Kochan, "Collective Bargaining in Organizational Research," in B. M. Staw and L. C. Cummings (eds.), *Research in Organizational Behavior*, vol. 2 (Greenwich, Conn.: JAI Press, Inc., 1980b).

18. Reprinted by permission of the *Harvard Business Review*. Excerpt from "Collective Bargaining: Ritual or Reality?" by A. A. Blum (November/December 1961). Copyright © 1961 by the President and Fellows of Harvard College; all rights reserved.

19. M. S. Ryder, C. M. Rehmus, and S. Cohen, *Management Preparation for Collective Bargaining* (Homewood, Ill.: Dow Jones-Irwin, 1966).

20. A. A. Sloan and F. Whitney. pp. 211–212.

21. D. E. Callen, *Negotiating Labor-Management Contracts*, Bulletin 56 (Ithaca, N.Y.: New York State School of Industrial and Labor Relations, Cornell University, 1968), p. 23.

22. For the company's view, see H. R. Northrop, "The Case for Boulwarism," *Harvard Business Review*, September/October 1964, pp. 86–97.

23. J. M. Rosow, "Now Is the Time for Productivity Bargaining," *Harvard Business Review*, January/February 1972, p. 78.

24. Rosow, pp. 78–79.

25. Rosow, p. 78.

26. J. W. Driscoll, "A Behavioral Science View of the Future of Collective Bargaining in the United States," *Labor Law Journal*, July 1979, pp. 433–438.

27. Driscoll, p. 435.

28. "Current Labor Statistics," *Monthly Labor Review*, March 1980, p. 103.

29. Kochan, 1980b, p. 144.

30. Kochan, 1980b, p. 151.

31. J. M. Brett, "Behavioral Research on Unions," in B. M. Staw, and L. L. Cummings, (eds.), *Research in Organizational Behavior*, vol. 2 (Greenwich, Conn.: JAI Press, 1980).

32. Kochan, 1980b, p. 151.

33. A. Cox, "Rights Under a Labor Agreement," *Harvard Law Review*, 69 (February 1956):601–57.

34. S. H. Slichter, J. J. Healy, and E. R. Livernash, *The Impact of Collective Bargaining on Management* (Washington, D. C.: The Brookings Institution, 1960), p. 694.

35. Slichter, Healy, and Livernash, pp. 694–696.

36. Kochan, 1980a, pp. 385–386.

38. B. R. Skelton and P. C. Marett, "Loser Pays Arbitration," *Labor Law Journal*, May 1979, pp. 302–309.

39. G. W. Bohlander, "Fair Representation: Not Just a Union Problem," *Personnel Administrator*, March 1980, p. 39.

40. Bureau of National Affairs, *Grievance Guide*, 4th ed. (Washington, D.C.: Bureau of National Affairs, 1972), p. 18.

41. Bureau of National Affairs, 1972, pp. 8–9.

42. J. C. Anderson, "The Grievance Process in Canadian Municipal Labor Relations," paper presented to the Annual Meeting of the Academy of Management, Atlanta, Georgia, August 1979.

43. Bohlander, p. 28.

44. Memorandum 79-55, National Labor Relations Board, July 7, 1979.

45. D. R. Dalton and W. D. Todor, "Manifest Needs of Stewards: Propensity to File a Grievance," *Journal of Applied Psychology*, 64 (1979), pp. 654–659.

46. Dalton and Todor.

47. Brett.

48. Kochan, 1980a, p. 452.

49. Kochan, 1980a, p. 460.

50. J. T. Barrett and I. B. Lobel, "Public Sector Strikes: Legislative and Court Treatment," *Monthly Labor Review*, September 1974, p. 19.

51. Sloan and Whitney, p. 44.

52. Kochan, 1980a, p. 471.

53. Kochan, 1980a, p. 472.

54. Bureau of National Affairs, *Policies for Unorganized Employees,* Survey No. 125 (Washington, D.C.: Bureau of National Affairs, April 1979).

55. J. N. Draznin, "Why Unions Are Declining," *Personnel Administrator*, December 1978, p. 39.

Improving and Analyzing the Work Environment

CHAPTER OUTLINE

THE PHYSICAL WORK ENVIRONMENT
Who's Responsible for the Work Environment?
The Work Environment's Relationships with Other Personnel Activities

SAFETY AND ACCIDENTS
Accident Rates
Causes of Occupational Accidents
  Organizational Qualities
  Safety Programs
  The Unsafe Employee?
Organizational Responses to Safety and Accidents
  The Environmental Response
  The People-Oriented Response
Government's Response to Safety and Accidents

HEALTH AND ILLNESS
Causes of Occupational Illness
Categories of Occupational Illness
Occupational Groups at Risk
Solutions to Occupational Health Hazards
  OSHA's Policy
  Organizational Approaches

PERSONNEL PROBLEM The Reluctant Employee

OBJECTIVES

- To describe the important aspects of the work environment

- To discuss the causes of occupational accidents and diseases

- To suggest ways to prevent occupational accidents and diseases

THOUGHT STARTERS

- Should employees be at all responsible for their own health and safety?

- Why does OSHA place the responsibility for safety and health on the employer?

- What can organizations do to make their work environments safer?

- Should programs that seek to create healthy and safe working conditions be cost-justified?

CHAPTER SEVENTEEN
Health and Safety in the Workplace

Diseases developed on the job are insidious, not dramatic. They begin with a cough, a wheeze, a headache or chronic fatigue, and they rarely go away.

When a worker gets too sick, he stays home. When he dies, he does so quietly—the victim of a time bomb that has ticked away inside him for years.

Accidents at work held center stage for a long time, but in recent years, occupational diseases are getting more attention from federal officials because of their enormous cost, in terms of dollars and human lives.

"Last year, 5.5 million workers were injured on the job. Untold thousands were struck down by deadly and debilitating toxic substances.

. . . This is an annual toll that is clearly larger than the toll of Americans killed and injured in the Vietnam conflict," said Secretary of Labor F. Ray Marshall at a recent conference on occupational diseases in Chicago.

The National Safety Council estimates that last year, $15 billion was spent on occupational diseases, counting lost wages, medical expenses, insurance claims and productivity delays.

But because of the insidious nature of disease, people are rarely aware that they are developing, often until it is too late to cure.

Marshall noted, "Perhaps because workplace deaths are diffused throughout our society and because the individual victims often die quietly many years after their workplace exposure, there are no marches in the streets or mass rallies calling for an end to on-the-job disease."

Many concerned scientists, labor leaders, workers and government officials wish there was more public concern.

It is, however, such a complicated problem that even accurate statistics are elusive. Yet most people familiar with the problem agree on one point: workers' health is being jeopardized every day by what they do for a living.

People who hold white-collar jobs can become victims of stress-related illnesses.

Blue-collar workers are potential victims of cancer, of infertility or genetic damage, of chronic lung diseases and of other organ diseases.

Exposures to chemicals on the job not only can trigger diseases, but when combined with other environmental hazards of poor lifestyles, they can make disease unavoidable.

Lung cancer, for example, can begin with a brief exposure to asbestos, according to medical experts. But it may not show up until years later. Since cigarette smoking also causes lung cancer, it is difficult to sort out how an asbestos worker who smokes developed lung cancer.

The elusiveness of the problem of job-related, or occupational, diseases does not make them any less real to the thousands of people stricken and killed by them each year. Nor does it make them any less urgent to concerned scientists, labor leaders and government officials.

Controversy centers on the size of the problem and over who should take responsibility for it.

Cancer is an especially controversial issue. Government scientists estimate that at least 20% of all cancer cases can be linked to the workplace, but industry spokesmen hotly dispute that figure.

"Most independent scientists agree that workplace cancer amounts to less than 5% of the total," said Dr. William J. McCarville, director of environmental affairs of Monsanto Co. in St. Louis.

From E. Price, "Occupational Diseases: The Scope," Cleveland Plain Dealer, 3 September 1979, p. E-2. Reprinted with permission.

A s gloomy as this scenario is, it represents only part of the story. The workplace hazards associated with employee accidents are just as important as the conditions that endanger health. In 1978 alone, the total costs of these accidents were estimated by the National Safety Council as $23 billion.[1]

In this chapter, these two aspects of the work environment—safety/accidents, and health/illness—are discussed in detail. The causes of injuries and diseases are considered, as well as organizational and government efforts to reduce their occurrence. The role of the Occupational Safety and Health Administration is scrutinized especially carefully.

THE PHYSICAL WORK ENVIRONMENT

Although some occupational injuries and illnesses result from emotional and behavioral factors, most—from minor cuts and sprains to loss of limb and even life—can be traced directly to the physical work environment. In an average year, over 10,000 deaths and 6 million lesser injuries occur in the workplace. Characteristics of the work environment associated with these injuries are called **safety hazards**. Efforts by organizations to reduce accidents often involve removing these safety hazards—for example, by putting guards on cutting machines. Organizations also try to reduce accidents by making people more safety conscious.

More costly to organizations and more harmful to their employees are diseases related to the work environment. The Public Health Service reports that every year over 100,000 deaths and over 390,000 cases of disabling illness can be connected to the workplace. **Health hazards**—those characteristics of the work environment associated with employee illness—are far more subtle than safety hazards. Often an occupational illness may appear only after several years of exposure to a health hazard. Moreover, it is often difficult to determine a single cause of the illness and to eliminate it. As a consequence,

The very nature of the differences between health and safety hazards has resulted in a pervasive safety bias that has affected legislation, the setting of standards, enforcement, manpower development, employer and employee education and technology development. The relative overemphasis on safety has fostered complacency and has thus prevented much needed progress in the more neglected area of occupational health.[2]

Whereas the consequences of safety hazards are solely physical injuries, hazards associated with occupational disease result not only in physical illnesses but also in debilitating mental and emotional conditions. As illustrated in the scenario at the beginning of this chapter, occupational illnesses affect both white-collar employees, who become victims of stress-related diseases, and blue-collar workers, who become victims of cancer, infertility, and other organic diseases. However, stress-related illnesses may almost be more prevalent among blue-collar employees than among white-collar employees. Indeed, the incidence of stress-related illness is increasing dramatically for all categories of employees, due in part to the fact that more illnesses are being associated with work stress.[3] This subject is discussed more thoroughly in Chapter 18.

Who's Responsible for the Work Environment?

Safety and health should be the concern of everyone in the organization. In a formal sense, however, the top management of the organization often has the responsibility for ensuring that employees are aware of health and safety and that the organization meets federal and state health and safety requirements. This is especially true in smaller organizations. In organizations with over 2,000 employees, the responsibility shifts to the personnel department or line managers.[4] There may even be a safety director or even an industrial engineer directly responsible for safety and health who reports to the personnel manager or the plant or office manager. In most organizations, however, the day-to-day enforcement of safety rules falls into the hands of the supervisor. The personnel manager or safety director then plays the role of assisting that supervisor, often by providing administrative research and advice. The personnel department often relies on experts in safety and health. To provide this expertise and to establish standards regarding health and safety at the federal level, the Occupational Safety and Health Act established the **National Institute for Occupational Safety and Health (NIOSH)**.

Another trend in the development and administration of safety and health programs is employee involvement and participation, which is most directly seen in the use of health and safety committees.

The Work Environment's Relationships with Other Personnel Activities

To the extent that an organization can provide a safe, healthy, and comfortable work environment, it may increase its success in staffing and maintaining the human resource needs of the organization. Obviously, when organizations have high rates of accidents, particularly fatal ones, they need to recruit more employees. And if organizations develop reputations for being death traps, they will find it extremely difficult to recruit and select qualified employees.

The administration of indirect compensation is also affected by characteristics of the work environment. Worker's compensation benefits increased from $2.6 billion in 1969 to $8.5 billion in 1977.[5] As the costs for indirect compensation rise, so do the costs of the total compensation package. This in turn may make it necessary for the organization to hold down the rate of increase in direct compensation, and organizations that cannot offer good salaries will not be able to attract and retain able employees or to motive the work force.

In sum, the health and safety aspects of the work environment play an important role in personnel management and the effective management of human resources. In addition, these aspects of the work environment have an impact beyond the organization. What happens to employees on the job cannot help but affect them off the job. Consequently, the concern of the organization for the physical environment has great potential payoffs—for itself, its employees, and society.

SAFETY AND ACCIDENTS

The safety and accident aspect of the work environment has been the most visible in terms of its effects, and therefore it is the one that gets the most attention. Even the Occupational Safety and Health Administration (OSHA), which was created to deal with both accidents and illnesses, has given more attention to safety and accidents.[6] But faced with visible injuries, organizations and OSHA alike have made it their priority to determine why these accidents occur and how the work environment can be made safer.

Accident Rates

Accidents are described in terms of their frequency, severity, and incidence. Although organizations are required by OSHA to maintain records only of the incidence of accidents, for comparison purposes, many organizations also maintain frequency and severity records. Exhibit 17.1 is an OSHA guide to determining what constitutes an accident that must be recorded. Note, however, that illnesses are included as well.

The **incidence rate** is most explicit in combining both illnesses and injuries, as shown by this formula:

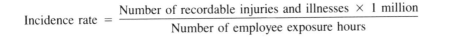

$$\text{Incidence rate} = \frac{\text{Number of recordable injuries and illnesses} \times 1\text{ million}}{\text{Number of employee exposure hours}}$$

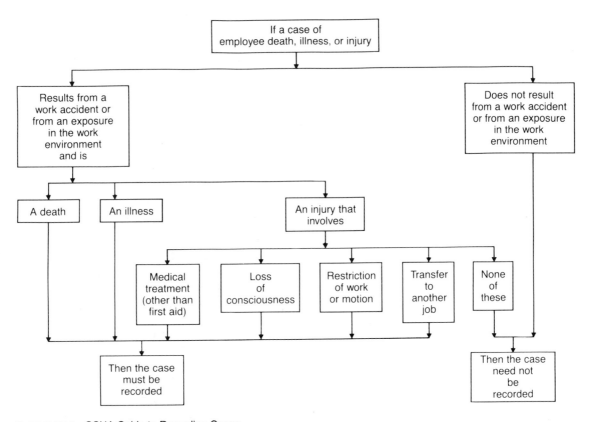

Exhibit 17.1   OSHA Guide to Recording Cases

Suppose an organization had 10 recorded injuries and illnesses and 500 employees. To get the number of exposure hours, it would multiply the number of employees by forty hours and by fifty work weeks—500 × 40 × 50 = 1 million. In this case, the incidence rate would be 10. In 1977, the average incidence rate for all private organizations was 9.3. That is, there were 9.3 recorded injuries and illnesses for each 100 employees.

The **severity rate** reflects the hours actually lost due to injury or illness. It recognizes that not all injuries and illnesses are equal. Four categories of injuries and illnesses have been established: deaths, permanent total disabilities, permanent partial disabilities, and temporary total disabilities. OSHA assigned each category a specific number of hours to be charged against an organization. The severity rate is calculated by this formula:

$$\text{Severity rate} = \frac{\text{Total hours charged} \times 1 \text{ million}}{\text{Number of employee hours worked}}$$

Obviously, an organization with the same number of injuries and illnesses as another but with more deaths would have a higher severity rate. However, because OSHA decided the assignment of hours charged for each type of accident and illness was arbitrary, it dropped the idea of using a severity rate.

The **frequency rate** is similar to the incidence rate except that it reflects the number of injuries and illnesses per million hours worked rather than per year:

$$\text{Frequency rate} = \frac{\text{Number of disabling injuries} \times 1 \text{ million}}{\text{Number of employee hours worked}}$$

Causes of Occupational Accidents

Certain organizations, and even certain departments within the same organization, have higher accident rates than others. There are several factors that explain this difference.

Organizational Qualities.   Accident rates vary substantially by industry. For example, firms in the construction and manufacturing industries have higher incidence rates than firms in services, finance, insurance, and real estate.

Small and large organizations (those with fewer than 100 employees and more than 1,000) have lower incidence rates than medium-size organizations. This may be because supervisors in small organizations are better able to detect safety hazards and prevent accidents than those in medium-size organizations. And larger organizations have more resources than medium-size organizations to hire staff specialists who can devote all their efforts to safety and accidents.[7]

Although data on incidence, severity, and frequency rates by type of industry and size of organization are important, these rates often veil differences between same-size organizations in the same industry. For example, Du Pont's accident rate in 1974 was only a tenth that of the chemical industry average and a twentieth that of all industry. These differences can in part be attributed to the effectiveness of Du Pont's safety programs.

Safety Programs.   Organizations differ in the extent to which they develop techniques, programs and activities to promote safety and prevent accidents. The effectiveness of these techniques and programs varies by the type of industry and size of organization. For example, in large chemical firms, greater expenditures for off-the-job safety, medical facilities and staff, safety training, and additional supervision are associated with decreased work-injury costs.[8] On the other hand, work-injury costs have actually increased with additional expenditures for correction of unsafe physical conditions, for safety staff, for employee orientation, and for safety records if these expenditures are applied ineffectively. As a result, some organizations in the same industry may have higher injury costs per employee than others. And of course, those organizations that have no safety programs generally have higher injury costs than similar companies that have implemented such programs.

The Unsafe Employee?   Although organizational factors play an important role in occupational safety, many experts point to the employee as the cause of accidents. Accidents depend on the behavior of the person, the degree of hazard in the work environment, and pure chance.

The degree to which the person contributes to the accident is often regarded as an indicator of proneness to accidents. Accident proneness cannot be considered as a stable set of personal traits that always contribute to accidents; "the traits that contribute to accidents may differ from one situation to another since there are a great variety of ways in which to have accidents."[9] Nevertheless, there are certain psychological and physical characteristics that make some people more susceptible to accidents. For example, employees who are emotionally "low" have more accidents than those who are emotionally "high," and employees who have had fewer accidents have been found to be more optimistic, trusting, and concerned for others than those who have had more accidents.[10] Employees under greater stress are likely to have more accidents than those under less stress, and those with better vision have fewer accidents than those with poorer vision. People who are quicker in recognizing differences in visual patterns than in making muscular manipulations are less likely to have accidents than those who are faster in muscular manipulation than in recognition of visual patterns.[11] Many psychological conditions that may be related to accident proneness—for instance, hostility and emotional immaturity—may be temporary states. Thus they are difficult to detect until after at least one accident.

Since none of these characteristics are related to accidents in all work environments, and since none are ever-present in employees, selecting and screening job applicants on the basis of accident proneness is difficult. But even if it were possible, aspects of the organization—such as its size, technology, management attitudes, safety programs, and quality of supervision—would still be important sources of accidents for those job applicants who are actually hired.

Organizational Responses to Safety and Accidents

Organizations can respond to safety and accidents in either of two general ways: by dealing with the physical aspects of the organization or by dealing with the people aspects, particularly through line and staff activities.

The Environmental Response.   Designing the work environment to make accidents difficult is perhaps the best way to prevent accidents and increase safety. Among the safety features that can be designed into the physical environment are guards on machines, handrails in stairways, safety goggles and helmets, warning lights, self-correcting mechanisms, and automatic shutoffs. The extent to which these features will actually reduce accidents depends on employee acceptance and use. For example, eye injuries will be reduced by the availability of safety goggles only if employees wear the goggles correctly. The effectiveness of any safety regulation depends on how the regulation is implemented and whether there is a conflict in complying with it. If employees are involved in the decision to make some physical change to improve safety, they are more likely to accept the decision than if they are not part of the decision-making process.

Another way of altering the work environment to improve safety is to make the job itself more comfortable and less fatiguing.[12] This approach is generally referred to as **ergonomics**. Ergonomics considers changes in the job environment in conjunction with the physical and physiological capabilities and limitations of the employees. As a result, employees are less likely to make mistakes due to fatigue and tiredness.

Whereas ergonomics focuses on the physical and physiological, another approach focuses on the psychological. Job redesign, although not aimed primarily at accident prevention, attempts to increase employee motivation and reduce boredom. The result may be increased alertness and fewer accidents. Because of the importance of job redesign, it is discussed more thoroughly in Chapter 18.

The People-Oriented Response.   There are several people-oriented responses to accidents that can be made by the personnel department, by supervisors and managers, and by both groups working together. One response that is carried out by both groups is the recording of accidents. These records can highlight the sources of accidents and their severity and frequency, and this information can then be used in the selection of safety strategies and the evaluation of their success. Accident rates that are determined from these records can be compared to the rates in other organizations, and such a study may point out more effective safety strategies to the organization with the higher rate.

Another strategy for accident prevention is the use of the safety committee. The personnel department can serve as the coordinator of a committee composed of several employee representatives. Where unions exist, the committees should have union representation as well. Often organizations have several safety committees at the department level for implementation and administration purposes and one larger committee at the organizational level for the purpose of policy formulation.[13]

The personnel department can be instrumental in accident prevention by assisting the supervisors in their training efforts and by implementing safety motivation programs, such as contests and communications. Many organizations display signs indicating the number of days or hours worked without an accident. Many organizations display posters saying "Safety First." In safety contests, prizes or awards are given to individuals or departments with the best safety record. These programs seem to work best when employees are already safety conscious and when physical conditions of the work environment provide no extreme safety hazards.[14]

Government's Response to Safety and Accidents

So far, the federal government's main response to the issue of safety in the work place has been the **Occupational Safety and Health Act** of 1970, which prescribed inspections of organizations for safety and health hazards; reporting by employers; and investigations of accidents and allegations of hazards.[15] Although this act was well-intentioned, it soon was perceived as emphasizing minor safety matters while overlooking major ones and, even more vital, of failing to focus attention on health standards.[16] Actually, this perception developed around one of the three organizations established by the act, the **Occupational Safety and Health Administration (OSHA)**. The other two organizations are NIOSH, mentioned earlier, and the Occupational Safety and Health Review Commission (OSHRC).

OSHA was given responsibility for establishing and enforcing occupational safety and health standards and for inspecting and issuing citations to organizations that violate these standards. The fact of the matter is, however, that there are over 5 million organizations and a very limited number of OSHA inspectors, so that "the typical business establishment will see an [OSHA] inspector every 77 years, about as often as we see Halley's comet."[17]

OSHA inspectors were given the right to enter at reasonable times any factory, plant, establishment, construction site, or other area, workplace, or environment where work is performed.[18] However, this inspection mandate was changed by the Supreme Court's decision in **Marshall v. Barlow's, Inc.** handed down in May 1979. According to this decision, employers are not required to let OSHA inspectors enter their premises unless the inspectors have search warrants.[19] Thus OSHA inspectors must now justify site selection by "showing that a specific business has been chosen for an [OSHA] search on the basis of a general administrative plan."[20] This has reduced some of the discretion of the local OSHA officials, who previously were able to determine their own inspection sites. In December 1978, OSHA's "directive to the field offices for the first time explicitly outline[d] the steps to take to insure that planned inspections include[d] a number of high-hazard industries."[21]

Regardless of whether organizations are inspected, they are required to keep safety and health records so that OSHA can

. . . compile accurate statistics on work injuries and illnesses which shall include all disabling, serious or significant injuries and illnesses, whether or not involving loss of time from work, other than minor injuries requiring only first aid treatment and which do not involve medical treatment, loss of consciousness, restriction of work or motion, or transfer to another job.[22]

The records must contain information on the accidents and illnesses occurring in the organization. (Refer back to Exhibit 17.1 for a definition of what OSHA considers a recordable accident or illness.) Falsification of records results in a fine of up to $10,000, imprisonment for up to six months, or both.

How effective has OSHA been? According to one General Motors spokesperson,

We had a good safety program going long before anybody ever heard of OSHA, and we haven't seen any effect from all the money ($79 million in 1974 alone) that's been spent, so far as any reduction in our accident rate is concerned.

Judging from this statement, it would appear that OSHA is not effective. But consider the result of OSHA's requirement that trenches in construction projects be shored adequately:

> . . . until 1973 Massachusetts alone had a 40-year average of five workers killed in trench accidents each year. Then OSHA selected this standard [of shoring trenches] for concentrated enforcement. The result: only two fatalities in Massachusetts in more than 30 months.[23]

Unfortunately, such successes occur only in selected organizations. Meanwhile, in 1980 alone, the estimated cost to organizations of implementing OSHA requirements was approximately $4 billion. In fact, it is often more cost-effective for an organization to comply with OSHA regulations only when forced to by an OSHA inspector, since there is such a slight change that an inspection will ever occur.

Yet what are the alternatives to OSHA? Many would argue that employees should assume more of the responsibility for their own health and safety. This may be

---

A SLICE OF LIFE

It has been noted that OSHA administrators face the monumental task of monitoring organizations for compliance with safety and health regulations and that the penalties organizations face for noncompliance often cost much less than the cost of compliance. The safety and health of employees is a commendable goal and a legitimate concern, but the practical realities of corporate policy, especially where a large amount of money is involved, must be taken into account.

Consider the following scenario. Suppose that the board of directors of a large manufacturing company is faced with these two alternatives: to spend $500,000 to install safety apparatus required by OSHA or to ignore the OSHA specifications, an action clearly in violation of the law, and take a chance of being fined $10,000 plus having to buy the required safety equipment. The probability of the organization being discovered noncompliant is probably far less than 1 percent. The number of inspectors that OSHA has is not even remotely adequate to make periodic examinations of all organizations that fall under the OSHA guidelines.

What would you expect the board of directors to do given this circumstance? What would you do? The choice is this: Do you approve an expenditure of $500,000, or do you take a slight chance of having to spend $510,000? Of course, if you are not caught, you spend nothing. Suppose the organization has an adequate, even exemplary safety program and does not believe that the OSHA guidelines will actually reduce the incidence or severity of industrial injury. Apparently, many organizations do feel this way, and there is some evidence that OSHA regulations have not decreased accidents or injury. Under these circumstances, would you change your decision about implementation of the OSHA standards?

possible to the extent that employees contribute to their own accidents, but "how can employees be responsible for diseases such as lung cancer, cancer of liver and brain and kidney disease from exposure to arsenic, radiation and asbestos, vinyl chloride and lead?"[24] Perhaps OSHA's most effective role is to reduce the incidence of such diseases.

HEALTH AND ILLNESS

The U.S. Public Health Service estimates that there are approximately 400,000 new cases of occupational disease annually and that as many as 100,000 workers die each year as a result of occupational diseases. Although these figures are frightening, they only reflect illnesses that are actually detected. Unlike safety hazards, the effects of health hazards are often slow, cumulative, irreversible, and complicated by nonoccupational factors. It may be almost impossible to perceive the danger from brief exposure to a potential carcinogen that may take years to cause a tumor or death. As OSHA head administrator Evla Bingham has noted,

Early tests on the drug diethylstilbestrol (DES) indicated that it was probably not very carcinogenic, and in the 1940's, thousands of pregnant women took the medication. Now, many of the offspring of these women have developed cancer.[25]

She therefore believes that tough regulations for health hazards such as carcinogens are appropriate.

Causes of Occupational Illness

The potential sources of work-related illness are distressingly varied:

Typical health hazards include toxic and carcinogenic chemicals and dust, often in combination with noise, heat and other forms of stress. Other health hazards include physical and biological agents. The interaction of health hazards and the human organism can occur either through the senses, by absorption through the skin, by intake into the digestive tract via the mouth or by inhalation into the lungs.[26]

Ten major health hazards are described in Exhibit 17.2 In addition, worker illness can be caused by sociopsychological conditions in the job environment. Since these conditions are usually identified with employee stress, they are discussed in Chapter 18.

Categories of Occupational Illness

The fastest-growing category of occupational disease includes illnesses of the respiratory system. "Chronic bronchitis and emphysema are the fastest growing diseases in the country, doubling every five years since World War II, and [they] account for the second highest number of disabilities, under Social Security."[27] Cancer, however, tends to receive the most attention, since it is a leading cause of death in

Exhibit 17.2   Ten Suspected Hazards in the Workplace

As cited by federal agencies, here are some of the major agents linked to on-the-job diseases—

Potential Dangers	Diseases That May Result	Workers Exposed
Arsenic	Lung cancer; lymphoma	Smelter, chemical, oil refinery workers; insecticide makers and sprayers—estimated 660,000 exposed
Asbestos	White-lung disease (asbestosis); cancer of lungs and lining of lungs; cancer of other organs	Miners; millers; textile, insulation, and shipyard workers—estimated 1.6 million exposed
Benzene	Leukemia; aplastic anemia	Petrochemical and oil refinery workers; dye users; distillers; painters; shoemakers—estimated 600,000 exposed
Bischloromethylether (BCME)	Lung cancer	Industrial chemical workers
Coal dust	Black-lung disease	Coal miners—estimated 208,000 exposed
Coke-oven emissions	Cancer of lungs, kidneys	Coke-oven workers—estimated 30,000 exposed
Cotton dust	Brown-lung disease (byssinosis); chronic bronchitis; emphysema	Textile workers—estimated 600,000 exposed
Lead	Kidney disease; anemia; central-nervous-system damage; sterility, birth defects	Metal grinders; lead-smelter workers; lead storage-battery workers—estimated 835,000 exposed
Radiation	Cancer of thyroid, lungs, and bone; leukemia; reproductive effects (spontaneous abortion, genetic damage)	Medical technicians; uranium miners; nuclear-power and atomic workers
Vinyl chloride	Cancer of liver, brain	Plastic-industry workers—estimated 10,000 directly exposed

Reprinted from *U.S. News & World Report*, February 1979. Copyright 1979 U.S. News & World Report, Inc.

the United States (after heart disease). Many of the known causes of cancer are physical and chemical agents in the environment. And because physical and chemical agents are theoretically more controllable than human behavior, OSHA is placing increasing emphasis on eliminating them from the workplace.[28]

OSHA's emphasis on health, however, is not aimed solely at eliminating cancer and respiratory diseases. OSHA is concerned with all seven categories of occupational diseases and illnesses that employers are required to keep records of:

- Occupational skin diseases and disorders
- Dust diseases of the lungs
- Respiratory conditions due to toxic agents
- Poisoning (systemic effects of toxic materials)
- Disorders due to physical agents
- Disorders associated with repeated trauma
- All other occupational illnesses[29]

Occupational Groups at Risk

"Miners, construction and transportation workers and blue-collar and lower-level supervisory personnel in manufacturing industries experience the bulk of both occupational disease and injury."[30] In addition, large numbers of petrochemical and oil refinery workers, dye users, textile workers, plastic-industry workers, and industrial chemical workers are also particularly susceptible to some of the most dangerous health hazards (See Exhibit 17.2). Interestingly enough, skin diseases are the most common of all reported occupational diseases, with the group most affected being leather workers.[31]

Health hazards, however, are not a monopoly of industrial and manufacturing workers. For example, dentists are routinely exposed to radiation, mercury, and anesthetics, and cosmetologists suffer from high rates of cancer and respiratory and cardiac diseases connected with their frequent use of chemicals.[32]

Solutions to Occupational Health Hazards

OSHA's Policy. OSHA's policy regarding solutions to health hazards is illustrated by its approach to cancer. If a substance is shown to cause cancer in a long-term mammal test and in two short-term tests, it is labeled as a category I carcinogen. Industry must then reduce employees' exposure to the carcinogen to the "lowest level possible."[33] Thus OSHA's policy is based on the assumption that a **threshold level**—a level below which exposure to the agent is safe—does not exist. However, it has been found that "there are safe levels to which a biological organism will not respond. It's a matter of concentration exposure, duration exposure and susceptibility."[34] If this is the case, carcinogens or other suspected agents do not need to be reduced to the lowest possible level, which is desirable to organizations because of the great costs involved in reducing the concentration of substances below a certain level. By controlling the job environment instead, many substances could be used safely in the work environment.[35]

Needless to say, organizations are not opposed to industrial health, but they believe that the facts on which OSHA bases its policies should be correct and that the costs and benefits of policy should be considered. OSHA generally does not weigh health against costs or inconvenience to industry.

Organizational Approaches. Organizational approaches to health hazards are often determined by OSHA standards and requirements, unless, of course, an organization chooses to ignore them. One OSHA requirement is that organizations measure the chemicals in the work environment and keep records on these measurements. The records must include the date, number of samples taken, length of period over which the sampling was done, procedure used, analytical method, the employee's names, social security numbers, and job classifications, where the employees work in the organization, and the protective equipment used. Often a physician is involved in the process of gathering this information, but the responsibility for having the information lies with the organization.

The organization is required to keep this information "for as long a period as is associated with the incubation period of the specific disease—it could be 40 years of medical surveillance of the environment."[36] If the organization is sold, the new owner must assume responsibility for storing the old records and continuing to gather the required data. If the organization goes out of business, the administrative director of OSHA must be informed of the whereabouts of the firm's records.

OSHA's purpose in having these records is to contribute to the knowledge of epidemiology in order to determine how to improve future work environments. And although organizations find this goal commendable, they often only keep these records because they are required to comply with OSHA regulations or because they may have to defend their behavior in negligence suits.

Compliance with OSHA standards and requirements is not the only approach organizations can take to occupational health hazards. They can also become more active in the process by which OSHA establishes those standards. OSHA must publish its intent to review or establish standards, and it must hold a hearing. At this hearing, organizations can contribute information regarding what they believe the standard should be. A past administrator of OSHA, Morton Corn, advised organizations that

When the government promulgates some regulations then it is too late—you are coming from behind. Use your facts to maneuver what the government is doing so that good standards result, otherwise your evidence will not be accepted to put down a standard. They can't regulate every industry because they don't know every industry. You know the industry.[37]

SUMMARY

The physical aspects of an organization's work environment can have a significant influence on its employees. In fact, the physical work environment is the cause of illness and injury for thousands of employees each year. Because of this, the federal Occupational Safety and Health Act of 1970 was enacted. Initially, the Occupational Safety and Health Administration (OSHA), which enforces this act, was concerned about safety and accidents in work environments. Recently, however, it has shown increasing interest in occupational health and illnesses. Since death and illness due to the health aspects of the work environment are much more prevalent than accidents due to the safety aspects, the increased concern is overdue and certainly appropriate.

Organizations have shown a concern for occupational safety and health by taking steps to improve the work environment and to make employees more aware of health and safety. Often, however, changes in the physical environment are made and records of chemicals in the work environment are kept, only because of OSHA requirements. Organizations must play an active role in shaping the standards and regulations promulgated by OSHA in order to prevent excessive costs. To what extent must organizations take responsibility for preventing deaths and accidents? According to OSHA, the answer is to the greatest extent possible—regardless of cost.

PERSONNEL PROBLEM
The Reluctant Employee

Sharon Hawkins is plant manager of Dalton Manufacturing's eastern facility. Just after noon she was approached by a production supervisor who told her of a problem he had encountered earlier in the day. One of the production employees had refused to do an assigned job that he had never done before. The employee argued that the job was unsafe and that he was therefore not obligated to perform it.

The production supervisor told Ms. Hawkins that he called the employee aside and explained that other employees routinely performed the job without complaining about safety. As he told Ms. Hawkins, this refusal seemed a clear case of insubordination, and since it had taken place in front of several other employees, he was concerned that it had eroded his authority.

The job in question, like many in an automated plant, does have an element of risk to it; however, every reasonable safety precaution is regularly followed by employees. Moreover, the equipment is periodically inspected for both operation and the integrity of its many safety features.

Ms. Hawkins has several concerns: First, if the employee performs the job and is injured, there is an issue of contributory negligence. Second, given that the job is reasonably safe and that precautions are taken, there is an issue of insubordination. Third, who should judge the safety of this or any operation? Should this decision be made by management or by individual employees? Most jobs in manufacturing plants carry an element of risk. Therefore, any employee could refuse to work most jobs if the only criterion for refusal were the existence of some risk.

1. What would you advise Ms. Hawkins to tell the supervisor to do about the reluctant employee?

2. Should the employee receive disciplinary action for refusing to follow orders?

3. Suppose that the job is reasonably safe. Would your judgment change if you knew that the employee was genuinely afraid?

4. Suppose that the employee agrees to work the job and is injured. Could the company argue the doctrine of contributory negligence to relieve its liability?

KEY CONCEPTS

ergonomics
frequency rate
health hazard
incidence rate
Marshall v. *Barlow's, Inc.*

National Institute for
  Occupational Safety
  and Health (NIOSH)
Occupational Safety
  and Health Act

Occupational Safety and
  Health Administration (OSHA)
safety hazard
severity rate
threshold level

DISCUSSION QUESTIONS

1. Who is responsible for health and safety in organizations? Who should be responsible?
2. Describe in detail the two most important aspects of an organization's physical work environment.
3. What are the causes of occupational accidents? What can be done to reduce the incidence rate of accidents?
4. Is the job situation or the employee more responsible for accidents? Why do some employees have more accidents than others in the same situations?

5. Should OSHA be given more power by Congress to force organizations to comply with its safety standards? Why or why not?

6. What are the causes of occupational illness? Why is it difficult to pinpoint these causes?

7. Describe the differences in causes and effects between occupational accidents and illnesses.

8. What is OSHA's policy regarding health hazards? With what parts of its policy do you agree or disagree?

ENDNOTES

1. P. E. O'Brien, "Health Safety and the Corporate Balance Sheet," *Personnel Journal*, August 1973, p. 726.

2. N. A. Ashford, "The Nature and Dimension of Occupational Health and Safety Problems," p. 47. Reprinted with permission from the August 1977 issue of the *Personnel Administrator* copyright 1977, The American Society for Personnel Administration, 30 Park Drive, Berea, OH 44017.

3. A. Brief, R. Schuler, and M. Van Sell, *Managing Job Stress* (Boston: Little, Brown, 1981).

4. J. Gardner, "Employee Safety, " in J. Famularo (ed.), *Handbook of Modern Personnel* (New York: McGraw-Hill, 1972).

5. P. S. Greenlaw and W. D. Biggs, *Modern Personnel Management* (Philadelphia: Saunders, 1979), p. 588.

6. Ashford.

7. J. V. Frimaldi and R. H. Simonds, *Safety Management* (Homewood, Ill: Irwin, 1975).

8. F. C. Rineford, "A New Look at Occupational Safety," *Personnel Administrator*, November 1977, pp. 29–36.

9. N. R. F. Maier, *Psychology in Industrial Organizations* 4th ed. (Boston: Houghton Mifflin 1973), p. 461.

10. R. B. Hersey, "Emotional Factors in Accidents," *Personnel Journal*, May 1936, pp. 59–65.
    R. B. Hersey, "Rates of Production and Emotional State," *Personnel Journal*, April 1932, pp. 355–364.

11. A. Divids and J. T. Mahoney, "Personality Dynamics and Accident Proneness in an Industrial Setting," *Journal of Applied Psychology*, no. 41 (1957), pp. 303–306.

12. V. Reinhart, "Ergonomic Studies Improving Life on the Job," *Job Safety and Health*, December 1975, pp. 16–21.

13. G. R. Carnehan, "Using Safety Committees Effectively," *Personnel Administrator*, no. 19, (1974), pp. 46–49.

14. A. Czernek and G. Clark, "Incentives for Safety," *Job Safety and Health*, October 1973, pp. 7–11.
    D. Hampton, "Contests Have Side Effects, Too," *California Management Review*, no. 12 (1970), pp. 86–94.

15. American Federation of Labor and Congress of Industrial Organizations, *The Occupational Safety and Health Act*, Publication No. 149 (Washington, D. C.: American Federation of Labor and Congress of Industrial Organizations, September 1971).

16. W. Hammer, *Occupational Safety Management and Engineering* (Englewood Cliffs, N.J.: "Why Nobody Wants to Listen to OSHA," *Business Week*, June 14, 1976, p. 64. Prentice-Hall, 1976).

17. "Why Nobody Wants to Listen to OSHA," p. 65.

18. *The Occupational Safety and Health Act*, Public Law 91–596, December 29, 1970, Sec. 2, p. 1.

19. "Now OSHA Must Justify Its Inspection Targets," *Business Week*, April 9, 1979, p. 64.

20. "Now OSHA Must Justify Its Inspection Targets," p. 64.

21. "Now OSHA Must Justify Its Inspection Targets," p. 64.

22. *The Occupational Safety and Health Act*, Public Law 91–596, December 29, 1970, Sec. 12, p. 6.

23. "Why Nobody Wants to Listen to OSHA," *Business Week*, June 14, 1976, p. 76, copyright 1976, McGraw-Hill. Reprinted with permission.

24. E. Price, "Occupational Diseases: The Scope," *Cleveland Plain Dealer*, 3 September 1979, Z–E. Reprinted with permission.

25. "Dubious Tactics in the War on Cancer," *Business Week*, August 27, 1979, pp. 46E–46T. Copyright 1979, McGraw-Hill. Reprinted with permission.

26. Ashford, p. 46.

27. Ashford, p. 48.

28. M. Corn, "An Inside View of OSHA Compliance," pp. 39–42, 44. Reprinted with permission from the November 1979 issue of

Personnel Administrator, copyright 1979, The American Society for Personnel Administration, 30 Park Drive, Berea, OH 44017.

29. C. L. Wang, "Occupational Skin Disease Continues to Plague Industry," *Monthly Labor Review*, February 1979, pp. 17–22.

30. Ashford, p. 48.

31. Wang.

32. Wang.

33. "Dubious Tactics in the War on Cancer," p. 46P.

34. "Dubious Tactics in the War on Cancer," p. 46P.

35. "Dubious Tactics in the War on Cancer," p. 46P.

36. Corn, p. 42.

37. Corn, p. 42.

OBJECTIVES

● To explain the sociopsychological environment of organizations

● To discuss why organizations should be concerned with quality of work life (QWL)

● To explain the impact of stress in organizations

● To identify the techniques of QWL projects and explain their effects on work culture

● To describe two strategies for dealing with stress

THOUGHT STARTERS

● What is quality of work life (QWL)?

● What is stress in organizations?

● Why be concerned with QWL?

● Do people expect too much from their jobs?

CHAPTER EIGHTEEN
Sociopsychological Aspects of the Workplace

Without work all life goes rotten. But when work is soulless, life stifles and dies.

Albert Camus

Working for a living is one of the basic activities in a man's life. By forcing him to come to grips with his environment, with his livelihood at stake, it confronts him with the actuality of his personal capacity—to exercise judgment, to achieve concrete and specific results. It gives him a continuous account of his correspondence between outside reality and the inner perception of that reality, as well as an account of the accuracy of his appraisal of himself. . . . In short, a man's work does not satisfy his material needs alone. In a very deep sense, it gives him a measure of his sanity.

No less dramatic. . . are those questions of identity which present themselves to the self-employed. These identity crises and situations usually come packaged in little episodes which occur when others find that they have encountered a bona fide weirdo without a boss. . . . You are stopped by a traffic policeman to be given a ticket and he asks the name of your employer and you say that you work for yourself. Next he says, "Come on, where do you work? Are you employed or not?" You say, "Self-employed." . . . He, among others you meet, knows that self-employment is a tired euphemism for being out of work. . . . You

become extremely nervous about meeting new people because of the ever-present question, "Who are you with?" When your answer fails to attach you to a recognized organization . . . both parties to the conversation often become embarrassed by your obscurity.

From Elliot Jacques, Equitable Payment *(New York: John Wiley & Sons, 1961), p. 25.*

Traditionally management has called upon labor to cooperate in increasing productivity and improving the quality of the product. My view of the other side of the coin is more appropriate; namely, that management should cooperate with the worker to find ways to enhance the dignity of labor and to tap the creative resources in each human being in developing a more satisfying work life, with emphasis on worker participation in the decision-making process.

From Irving Bluestone, vice president, General Motors Department of the United Auto Workers, "A Changing View of Union-Management Relationship," Vital Speeches, *December 11, 1976.*

Executives are more likely than secretaries or garment workers to think their work is stressful—but it's the secretaries and garment workers who are more likely to suffer the mental and physical symptoms of stress.

This is one of the findings of a survey of six occupational groups carried out under the sponsorship of the American Academy of Family

Physicians. The survey, covering executives, secretaries, physicians, farmers, teachers and garment workers, was aimed at determining the relations among stress, work and home life, particularly in view of the increasing separation between Americans' home life and their work life.

Surveyed by questionnaire were members of the American Management Association, the National Grange, the International Ladies Garment Workers Union, the National Secretaries Association, the American Federation of Teachers and members of the family physicians' academy.

The survey found that 81% of the executives believed their work environment was stressful, compared with about two-thirds of the physicians, secretaries and teachers. Less than half of the garment workers considered their work stressful and only 38% of the farmers thought so, even though these two groups had the lowest incomes.

The executives rated deadlines as being the biggest source of stress, followed by workload and pressure from superiors. The garment workers rated salary as a main source of stress while the other four groups checked workload as the biggest cause of their stress.

Despite their feelings of job stress, the executives seemed happier and more optimistic than the secretaries and garment workers. "Family physicians, business executives and farmers don't tend to worry or feel blue, only 10% indicating such a mental state 'much of the time'," the report said. "For teachers and secretaries this rate doubles and for garment workers it triples," the survey found.

Among medical problems, only a fifth to a quarter of the executives reported having muscle aches, tension, headaches and backaches in the previous month. However, about a third of the garment workers, secretaries and teachers reported such recent problems. In addition, these last three groups reported a higher incidence of anxiety and nervousness.

About half of the executives and physicians said they exercise to cope with stress while "talking with a friend" was the main means of coping cited by the garment workers, secretaries and teachers.

From "Stress, Work, Home Relations Examined in Job Groups Study," Wall Street Journal, June 14, 1979, p. 1. Reprinted by permission of Wall Street Journal, © Dow Jones & Company, Inc. 1979. All Rights Reserved.

Together these quotes illustrate several facts about the sociopsychological aspects of the work environment. One is that work plays an important role in the lives of most individuals. Another is that concern for the quality of work life is increasing, due in part to the changing needs and values of individuals. To address this concern, management, unions, and employees are taking steps to improve the quality of work life in a way that will fulfill those needs and values. A final fact revealed by the last quote is that stress is being recognized as an important sociopsychological aspect of the work environment, one that may be experienced in different ways in different occupations.

Issues related to the quality of work and stress in organizations are becoming increasingly important in the management of human resources. It is therefore necessary for the manager of human resources to be aware of these issues and to be able to solve the organizational problems and employee conditions that are increasingly associated with them.

Interest in the quality of work life usually focuses on techniques for changing the organization's culture in order to improve employee satisfaction and job performance and to reduce turnover and absenteeism. In the words of Gundy Gundvaldson, the late president of the Northwest Region of the International Woodworkers of America,

The workers see many ways of improving the quality of a product and improving productivity at the same time. If a management climate can be developed in which workers are encouraged and rewarded for taking an interest in worksite improvement; if communication structures are set up to invite meaningful participation in arriving at work-related decisions; if it stimulates a reduction in absenteeism; if the quality of the product improves; if the safety record improves; if the worksite becomes more pleasant; if the workers begin to feel a sense of ownership, then a quality of work life project is a success.[1]

The interest in stress in organizations, on the other hand, tends to focus on organizational and individual characteristics that give rise to stress in workers; symptoms associated with stress, especially physiological ones like coronary heart disease, ulcers, and hypertension; and ways of reducing or managing stress.

Although different in specific concerns, the interest in both quality of work life and stress is centered on the mental and physical health of workers as a consequence of the sociopsychological aspects of the work environment. (The physical aspects of the work environment are discussed in Chapter 17.) These sociopsychological aspects include employees' perceptions and interpretations of the work environment, the supervisor, job design, policies and procedures, communications, and status symbols. These perceptions and interpretations describe the **work culture** of the organization, which partially determines how employees feel and behave.

A challenge in dealing with quality of work life and stress in organizations is that employees do not always perceive the work environment the same way. And even if they do, they may not all respond to it in the same way. "The stressors in the work setting are pervasive but are perceived differently by each person exposed to a given situation. Some react; some don't. One person's stressor seems to be another person's stimulus."[2] One person may see a job as repetitive, and another may see it as nonrepetitive, yet both may express a great deal of job satisfaction.

This chapter's emphasis on the sociopsychological aspects of the work environment does not imply that the physical aspects play no role—just that their role is diminished. It is how the employee perceives and interprets aspects of the physical environment, in addition to such other aspects of the work environment as supervision, that is of concern here. Although the sociopsychological aspects of the work environment are potentially as detrimental to employees and organizations as the physical aspects, the sociopsychological aspects and their effects on employees are often difficult to determine exactly. As a result, they have generally been neglected. As concern with employee health and illness grows, however, this neglect is rapidly diminishing.

This chapter discusses quality of work life and stress in organizations and presents techniques for improving jobs and reducing or managing stress.

QUALITY OF WORK LIFE AND STRESS IN ORGANIZATIONS

Quality of work life (QWL) is the degree to which employees or a work organization are able to satisfy important personal needs and values through their experiences in the organization.[3] Thus, the quality of a person's work life improves as more and more needs and values are satisfied by that person's job.

Since employees attach different levels of importance to the same needs and values, some employees respond positively to such QWL techniques as job enrichment while others reject the same techniques. It follows that attempts to improve the quality of work life should begin with an assessment of the importance that each employee attaches to needs and values and the degree to which these important needs and values are being satisfied. Then the organization should engage in techniques to increase the level of satisfaction of those important needs and values. This approach to improving the quality of work life recognizes the interaction of individuals who have certain needs and values, and the organization, as a source of satisfaction of those needs and values.

Stress in organizations is a dynamic situation in which an employee is uncertain about how to deal with a situation but knows that resolution of the condition will bring important outcomes.[4] Stress may occur, for example, just before an exam, when meeting a person for the first time, or when confronting one's boss. These situations are stressful because they involve some uncertainty. For instance, an instructor may not provide information about the exam or a student may be uncertain about being able to learn the material by exam time. This uncertainty can be reduced or eliminated if the student is well prepared for the exam or doesn't care about doing well on it. In addition, these situations are stressful because they may bring important outcomes. Since doing well on an exam will result in several important outcomes—passing the course, feeling good about having met the challenge of the exam, gaining praise from others for doing a good job[5]—a stressful situation does exist.

As with the quality of work life, stress depends on the situation and the individual. A situation that one person may find stressful may not bother another at all. Another aspect of stress is that it can be associated with positive as well as negative situations.

Meeting a person for the first time may be stressful even though it presents an opportunity to develop a friendship or to impress a potential boss. Stress is associated with any situation that involves uncertainty and is related to something significant to the person.

The Importance and Purposes of QWL and Stress

The attention now being paid to the quality of work life and stress reflects the growing importance being attached to each of these concerns.

It is clear that a substantial number of workers are unhappy with their jobs and are demanding more meaningful work. Workers are beginning to demand improvements in both economic and noneconomic outcomes from their jobs. The importance of noneconomic rewards is increasing relative to the importance of economic ones, especially among white-collar and highly educated workers. Thus, there is a need for *improvement, and considerable* room for *improvement, in the quality of work life of many contemporary American workers.*[6]

The importance of QWL is reflected in the effects of its absence.[7] Some people attribute part of the present productivity slowdown in the United States to deficiencies in the quality of work life and to changes in the needs and values that employees consider important. Young people want high pay and good fringe benefits, but they also want chances for promotion and training. They don't want to be treated as a cog in a machine. When these needs are not satisfied, employees may lose interest in their jobs, and productivity decreases.

The evidence suggests that the influence of stress in organizations is significant:

Among the diseases or symptoms most frequently related to stress in organizations are peptic ulcers, cardiovascular disorders and high blood pressure. It is estimated that the economic cost of peptic ulcers and cardiovascular disease alone in the United States is about $45 billion annually. Cardiovascular disease is the major contributing factor to disability and hospital care in the United States. For every employee killed in an industrial accident, 50 suffer from cardiovascular disease.[8]

Approximately 600,000 people die from cardiovascular disease annually in the United States, and only 25 percent of these deaths can be explained by such known causes as age and smoking. Of the 75 percent left unexplained, stress may be a primary cause.[9]

Projects to improve the QWL and to manage or reduce stress in organizations serve a very useful purpose. In fact, this has been attested to by organizations:

"[General Motor's quality of work life] program was initially explained to us that it would make a worker feel as important when he walked through the door of a plant as he felt before he walked in there. It dignified him. It made him feel important where he's working as well as in his community. Why should walking

through the door of a factory—or whatever—change you suddenly into a nothing, when you're someone?" [10]

But not all QWL projects are meant exclusively to improve conditions for the employee:

The "blue collar blues" may promote the adoption and diffusion of innovative work designs in a wide range of industries, from blue collar manufacturing work to white collar and service work and in both the private and the public sectors, but a major reason companies are trying work improvement projects is competition. Another is the changing expectations of workers, whose consciousness of quality of work life issues continues to rise. Another is the implicit threat of legislation that might set new, more embracing quality of work environment standards or that might require workers to participate in the governance of private industry. [11]

Relationships of QWL and Stress

QWL and stress have a significant influence on several personnel activities. The consequences of a low QWL are aptly illustrated by these quotes about the Tarrytown, New York plant of General Motors before its QWL program began:

In the late 1960s and early 1970s, the Tarrytown plant suffered from much absenteeism and labor turnover. Warnings, disciplinary layoffs and firings were commonplace. At certain times, as many as 2,000 labor grievances were on the docket. [12]

Naturally, the recruitment and selection activities of the plant were directly affected by these occurrences. "Because of the high labor turnover, the plant was hiring a large number of young people," who were not so conscientious about their work as older employees. Labor relations were difficult at best in this environment of mistrust. Union officers and committee members battled constantly with management. As one union officer describes it,

"We were always trying to solve yesterday's problems. There was no trust and everybody was putting out fires. The company's attitude was to employ a stupid robot with hands and no face." [13]

All of these consequences eventually prompted the company to employ management and organizational development, which greatly improved the sociopsychological aspects of the work environment there.

The consequences of stress also have important implications for other personnel activities. The Occupational Safety and Health Administration (OSHA) has classified stress-related disease as one of seven categories of occupational illness (see Chapter 17). Thus organizations are liable for disabilities that stem from the work setting. "Worker compensation laws now make an employer legally liable for an employee's mental illness." [14]

To the extent that job enrichment techniques are used to improve QWL, job analysis and job evaluation are affected.[15] After working in a job enrichment program, one employee commented,

"I like branch coding but because you get such a variety of work, it is hard to make your efficiency. I think the [basic job classification] should be raised."[16]

QWL and stress projects also influence human resource planning. Since turnover and absenteeism may be reduced by these projects, human resource needs may also be reduced. Training needs may increase, however, at least initially. Of course, a change in any human resource activity will influence the overall plan for using human resources effectively. For example, if an organization desires to implement a strategy for career management or to open up opportunities for women and minorities in management and nontraditional jobs, it must carefully plan who will be involved, how many, when, what this will mean for the rest of the employees in the organization, and how support for these changes can be obtained from top management. Thus QWL and stress involve not only most of the other personnel activities but practically all levels of management.

Who's Responsible for QWL and Stress in Organizations?

In the early 1970s it was plant and division-level managers who sought educational and consultative assistance for potential QWL projects, but today top corporate managers are also interested in understanding and supporting QWL projects.[17] However, it is often the first-level supervisor whose cooperation is most needed to ensure the success of QWL projects and whose role is often most changed by them:

Suddenly we asked foremen to develop a rather different set of skills. We wanted them to be "good managers of people." Instead of people receiving discipline from the supervisor, the new climate emphasized self-discipline. We redefined the foreman's role rapidly, and this created problems during the change. The problems were exacerbated by the fact that formal training for foremen was traditionally less important than on-the-job training, so they tended to be reluctant to take courses at first.

Yet in the new circumstances foremen needed considerable training to regard themselves as information-gatherers, as aides to the employees, as teachers and consultants, rather than as bosses. And in many cases the attitude change was only partial, stimulated and, at the same time, hampered because it was forced by pressure from employees and management, rather than from the foremen's own convictions.[18]

Although first-line supervisors may be regarded as the key people in the day-to-day success of many QWL projects, the plant manager and the manager of human resources, with or without the initial assistance of an outside consultant, must support and facilitate the projects. Anyone in the organization may conceivably initiate these projects, but the lead may fall into the hands of a few management or labor representatives.

The personnel manager must be alert to the necessity for changes in order to play the role of facilitator adequately. Facilitation may begin with an analysis, in cooperation with management and labor, of employees' attitudes, needs, values, and behaviors. The results of this analysis can aid management and labor in defining techniques to implement their QWL project. Based on the techniques selected, the personnel manager must be ready to adapt the affected human resource activities to facilitate implementation of the techniques. The activities most likely to be affected are job analysis, recruitment, selection, training and development, career management, compensation, and labor relations. QWL projects may require not just that these personnel activities be changed or modified to fit the situation but also that they be shared with line managers, supervisors, employees, and employee representatives. For example, work groups may begin to make some recruitment, selection, and compensation decisions. The personnel manager must be there to assist the work groups with these decisions, even though the work group may initially seem to be reducing the power and responsibility of that manager.

Unions also have an important responsibility in QWL projects:

We as a union knew that our primary job was to protect the worker and improve his economic life. But times had changed and we began to realize we had a broader obligation, which was to help the workers become more involved in decisions affecting their own jobs, to get their ideas, and to help them to improve the whole quality of life at work beyond the paycheck.[19]

Not all unions, however, embrace the notion that workers are concerned with QWL issues or that unions should be a party to QWL projects with management. As Thomas Donahue, executive assistant to the past AFL-CIO president George Meany, said:

We do not seek to be a partner in management, to be, most likely, the junior partner in success and the senior partner in failure. We do not want to blur in any way the distinction between the respective roles of management and labor in the plant.[20]

You may be concluding from these statements that there is no uniform union position or that not all unions represent the best interests of the workers. This may be true, but you should remember that many job enrichment projects have been less than successful, although some for reasons unrelated to worker acceptance of QWL principles and ideals.[21] Also consider that of the more than 5 million organizations in the United States, there have been only about 500 QWL projects.[22] Thus it becomes apparent that there is no uniform management position on QWL programs either. Moreover, since unions represent only 25 percent of all employees, the responsibility for initiating and implementing QWL projects rests more directly on management.

QUALITY OF WORK LIFE

QWL programs have appeared in organizations in the United States under several labels—humanization of work, work reform, work restructuring, work design, sociotechnical systems, and work improvements.[23] Although different in name and technique, all these programs generally share the same goal: to create a work culture that fulfills employees' needs and values and benefits the organization. Exhibit 18.1 outlines the common components of programs to improve QWL.

Not all QWL projects place equal emphasis on employee and organizational benefits, but the most successful of them simultaneously enhance business performance and the quality of the human experience.[24] Thus many of the intended results shown in Exhibit 18.1 are attained through implementation of any one of the techniques shown in the exhibit. Many QWL programs, however, employ several of the techniques in order to ensure that as many individual and organizational results are attained as possible. Two of the most popular techniques for improving QWL—job design and participation in decision making—are discussed in detail in the following sections.

Job Design

Job design is the deliberate and purposeful planning of the job, including all its structural and social aspects and their effects on the employee.[25] As discussed in Chapter 4, job design can be important in matching job rewards with individual needs. Unfortunately, however, the effects of the job on the employee have not always been of primary importance in the design of many jobs. The resulting symptoms have been called the "blue-collar blues":[26]

If you were in a plant you'd see—everybody thinks that General Motors workers have it easy, but it's not that easy. Some jobs you go home after eight hours and you're tired, your back is sore and you're sweatin'. All the jobs ain't that easy. We make good money; yeah, the money is real good out there, but that ain't all of it—cause there's really a lot of bad jobs out there.[27]

And these problems are not confined to blue-collar jobs. Symptoms of the "white-collar woes" have also been identified:

Exhibit 18.1 Components of Programs to Improve Quality of Work Life

Techniques	Work Culture Ideals	Intended Results
Job design	High skill levels and flexibility in using them	For organization:
Participation in decision making		Low cost
Equal treatment of women and minorities	Identification with product	Quick delivery
	Problem solving, not finger pointing	High quality
Upgraded compensation	Freedom	Low turnover
Job performance standards	Mutual influence	Low absenteeism
Communication	Openness	For individual:
Leadership	Trust	Self-esteem
Status symbol removal	Responsiveness	Satisfaction
Career development	Egalitarian climate	Security
Environmental improvements	Equity	Involvement
Adaptations in supervisor's role		Participation
Training		Growth
Feedback		

Adapted from R. E. Walton, "Work Innovations in the United States," *Harvard Busiiness Review*, July/August 1979, p. 90.

Lack of positive feedback and feeling of connection between the individual worker and the centers where decisions affecting him are made are inevitable to some degree in any large organization, but there is every reason to believe that they are especial hazards in government departments.[28]

Spurred by increased recognition of the importance of the effects of jobs on the employee, several different approaches to job design have been implemented, including job rotation and enlargement, job enrichment, and sociotechnical job design.

Job Rotation and Enlargement.   **Job enlargement** seeks to expand employees' jobs in order to add variety. However, job enlargement can be perceived as a management ruse to get more work out of employees without increasing their pay. Thus adding activities to employees' jobs may meet with more resistance than acceptance, particularly if the activities are no more interesting or meaningful than their current duties.

Job rotation, like job enlargement, seeks to add variety to jobs, but job rotation does so by sending employees from job to job instead of increasing the number of job activities. For example, an employee may work in the paint department one month and in the packaging department the next. Therefore, variety is introduced as an intermittent rather than a daily occurrence, as in job enlargement.

The biggest problem with both job enlargement and job rotation is that employees may feel they are doing more for less. They may also become more fatigued from doing more. Moreover, these techniques may still not satisfy many important needs, and employees may even prefer the lack of variety and new challenge, which allows them opportunities to daydream. A potential remedy to these ill effects is job enrichment.

Job Enrichment.   **Job enrichment** seeks to please employees by satisfying several of their important psychological needs. For example, by changing certain aspects of a job, an employee's needs for responsibility, achievement, and knowledge of results might be met.[29]

Exhibit 18.2 presents a model of job enrichment that describes specific job characteristics, psychological needs, and personal and work outcomes. This model indicates several things about the relationships between job characteristics and psychological needs. First, the more skill variety, identity, and significance a job has, the more meaningfulness, sense of achievement, and variety the employee will experience. Next, the more autonomy there is in a task, the greater will be the employee's sense of responsibility, self-control, and self-esteem. Finally, the more intrinsic feedback there is in the task, the more knowledge of results the employee will have. In turn, the more these psychological needs are fulfilled by the job, the greater the employee's satisfaction with work and the higher the employee's internal motivation and quality of work performance.[30]

According to the job enrichment model, then, in order for the employee to experience favorable outcomes, the job must offer the following:

● *Variety:* The job should require the use of a number of different skills and abilities.

- *Identification with a whole job:* For example, an employee could build an entire radio rather than install only one section of it.
- *Significance or importance:* The employee should feel that the rest of the organization or people outside the organization need him or her. For example, a garbage collector in New York City on a hot summer day probably perceives a high level of job significance.
- *Autonomy or freedom:* The employee should be able to make some decisions about how and when to do the job. Traditionally, managers make most decisions for nonmanagers, a feature that in part distinguishes the two groups.
- *Intrinsic feedback:* The most enriched jobs provide information on how well the employee is doing, without requiring that he or she be told by some other person. For instance, carpenters know how well they are doing by just looking at the work they have completed, but most office jobs provide little feedback of this type.

The relationships shown in Exhibit 18.2 between core job characteristics, psychological needs, and outcomes may not apply to everyone, since not all employees value these needs. But for those who do, increasing the core characteristics of the job is beneficial.[31] However, there are limits to both the impact of job enrichment and the extent to which jobs can be enriched. These limitations result from the fact that the job is embedded in the social and technological network of the organization, as discussed in Chapter 4. This network acts as a constraint on the redesign of individual jobs. In addition, job enrichment is limited in its impact on employees because it can serve only some needs and values.

Sociotechnical Job Design.   **Sociotechnical job design** overcomes some of the limitations of job enrichment. It arose as a response to two views: that jobs, as organizational units, are not conceptually appropriate bases for the analysis, design, or redesign of work systems and that jobs are not practical or appropriate units for making changes in organizations to enhance organizational effectiveness and im-

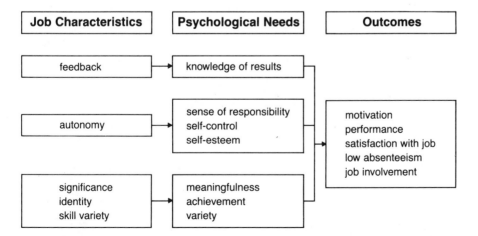

Exhibit 18.2   Job Enrichment Model
Adapted from R. J. Hackman and G. R. Oldham, *Work Redesign* (Reading, Mass.: Addison-Wesley, 1980), p. 77.

prove the quality of work life.[32] Instead, it is the social and technical systems surrounding jobs that must be changed.

Many organizations claim that it is impossible to change the technology used to make their products, but this is true only in the short run. The implementation of a new and different technology by Volvo in its famous Kalmar plant is an example of how a product—the automobile, in this case—can be produced in an extremely different way. The classic assembly line gave way to a system that made a team of workers responsible for an entire car. In considering which technology to use, Volvo responded to the needs of the employees:

Like other auto manufacturers, at its inception Volvo had a production system that was technically oriented and planned in detail. When labor unrest became visible in 1969, it became necessary to adapt the way we controlled production to new attitudes in the work force.[33]

As a result, Volvo selected a technological system that would adapt to the needs of the people and yet still serve the needs of production.

Similarly, the organization's social system can be altered so that employee needs and values are satisfied by the actual design of the jobs and the social network in which they are embedded. This approach to job design thus enlarges the way that jobs should be analyzed and redesigned. Sociotechnical job design is illustrated in detail in the section of this chapter that examines the Tarrytown QWL project.

Participation in Decision Making

The decision to improve the quality of work life by letting employees participate in management decisions that affect their jobs is based on the assumption that doing so helps fulfill employees' needs and values.[34] The effectiveness of participation depends on several factors. First, the employees must have a need to participate in decision making. Second, the type and extent of decisions in which they participate must be appropriate. For instance, employees may decide issues related to their jobs, which they possess sufficient information about, rather than issues related to the total organization, which they may have insufficient information about. Third, the organization must be willing to share with employees information that will allow them to make better decisions. Sharing information also conveys a sense of trust. Fourth, supervisors and managers must be willing to allow their employees to participate in decision making. And fifth, there must be problems and situations for which decisions are necessary. Some organizations are stable, facing the same situations day after day. Fewer decisons need to be made when the organization can write rules and procedures describing what should be done in almost every situation. But as organizations begin to encounter change, rules and procedures often become deficient or inappropriate. In this case, increased participation may be seen as the best and fastest way to make increasingly frequent decisions.

Because these five conditions do not always exist, it is apparent that participation is not always effective for either the organization or the employee. Nevertheless, participation is often an important part of many QWL projects.

Improving QWL: The Tarrytown Project

The Tarrytown project is a QWL program at a General Motors car assembly plant in Tarrytown, New York, that employs more than 3,800 employees.[35] This cooperative project between the union and management began in 1970, when the plant had one of the poorest labor and production records at GM. The project was initiated by the plant manager because it was necessary to make substantial changes in the operations of the plant. The plant workers were asked to participate in making the necessary changes. Although top management was behind the project, many supervisors doubted that the workers could produce useful ideas. Yet according to those supervisors, "We found they did know a lot about their own operations. They made hundreds of suggestions and we adopted many of them."[36]

Management, the union, and the workers continued to cooperate. In 1973, the United Auto Workers and GM explicitly addressed QWL in their contract agreement. This reflected a new atmosphere of trust between the union and the plant management. In 1974 a professional consultant was brought in to conduct joint training programs in problem solving for supervisors and workers, because the project was expanding. Although participation in the project was voluntary, out of 600 workers in two volunteering sections, 95 percent said they wanted to be involved in the project. In 1977 the participation and problem-solving training sessions were launched plantwide. "Each week, 25 different workers reported to the training rooms on Tuesdays, Wednesdays and Thursdays, for nine hours a day."[37] Included in these sessions were discussions of the QWL concept, plant operations, and problem-solving skills. While the employees were in training, the company continued to pay their regular hourly rate of about $7.

Although the Tarrytown project cost approximately $1.6 million, the quality of performance improved substantially, and absenteeism fell from 7¼ percent to between 2 and 3 percent. In December 1978 there were 32 grievances on the docket, in contrast to 2,000 in 1971.[38]

The principles learned from the Tarrytown project are numerous. They are described thoroughly in Exhibit 18.3. It is clear from this project that workers do not desire to take over the management of the operations but that they do want to become involved in pragmatic, immediate, and localized problems and issues.

STRESS IN ORGANIZATIONS

John R. is a 38-year-old middle-level sales manager in a large corporation. He is considered hard-working, dependable, loyal, and productive by his superiors, who nevertheless feel that he does not have executive suite potential. This belief was formalized eight months ago when a key promotion was given to one of John's subordinates, instead of John. Since then his on-the-job behavior has gradually changed. His attention to detail has slipped. He has become withdrawn and seems to have lost enthusiasm for his superiors, who view his changed behavior as confirmation of their decision not to promote him.[39]

Not all employees are exposed to the midcareer stress experienced by John R., and even if they were, they would not all react as he did. Nevertheless, many employees

Exhibit 18.3   Principles of an Effective QWL Project (Tarrytown)

What generalizations or principles might one derive from the Tarrytown story? The list below combines those of the participants themselves with my own observations about quality of work life experiments here and abroad. The list is not exhaustive. The first six are limited in general to organizations with collective bargaining agreements. The others have more universal applications.

1. For quality of work life to succeed, management must be wholly competent in running the business as a profit-making enterprise. When management lacks organizational competence and adequate technical expertise, no amount of good intentions to improve worker-union-management communication will succeed. Workers will not be willing to become involved knowing management lacks the competence to do anything about their ideas.

2. The union must be strong. The members must trust their leadership, and this trust must exist within the framework of a democratic "political" process.

3. In most instances, management has to be the first party to initiate change, to "hold out the olive branch."

4. Quality of work life should never be used by either party to circumvent the labor-management agreement. The rights, privileges, and obligations of both parties should remain inviolate. Dealing with grievances and disputes can be made easier through quality of work life efforts, but at no time should management give up its right to manage nor the union its

right to protect its members on matters related to wages, hours, benefits, and general conditions of employment.

5. Top management and top union officials must make an explicit commitment to support quality of work life.

6. Even with agreement at high levels and a demonstrated concern on the part of rank-and-file employees, it is essential that middle management and front-line supervisors (and shop stewards) not only know what is taking place but also feel they have a say in the change process. Supervisors naturally feel threatened by any moves to give subordinates greater power in determining how work is to be performed. Union representatives can perceive unilateral work participation as a threat to their political position.

7. A quality of work life program is unlikely to succeed if management's intention is to increase productivity by speeding up the individual worker's work pace or, if it uses the program *as such,* to reduce the work force through layoffs. Workers will quickly see such actions as unfair exploitation. This is not to say that cost savings from better quality performance, lower absenteeism and turnover, and better production methods should not be an expected consequence of the effort.

8. A program should be voluntary for the participants.

9. Quality of work life should not be initiated with a detailed master plan. It should start on a limited scale focused on the solution of specific problems, however small.

It should be flexible.

10. At each step in developing a program, all small bottlenecks or misunderstandings must be talked out and solved on the spot. If set aside simply to get on with the "important" plans, the little misunderstandings can later explode with enough force to destroy the entire program.

11. It is not enough to expose employees to the principles of effective interpersonal communication and problem-solving skills. There must be immediate opportunities available for them to use these skills in practical ways right in the job situation itself. Further follow-up action of some kind is necessary to serve as positive reenforcement to the employees.

12. Quality of work life efforts should not be thought of as a "program" with a finite ending. There must be a built-in momentum that is dynamic, on-going, and that can continue regardless of changes in the personnel in the organization. Once employees come to believe that they can participate and do in fact become involved in solving problems, the process gains a momentum of its own.

There is an implied warning here. Management may have the *formal* power to drop quality of work life efforts summarily. Union officers may have the *political* power to scuttle such efforts. Both would be acting at their peril for, under quality of work life, the workers will have gained a unique power to influence substantially the quality of their own lives at work. To them there is no turning back.

encounter stress on their jobs every day, and many organizational conditions are associated with stress, as shown in Exhibit 18.4. Fortunately, there is growing concern about stress in organizations, and ways are being sought to manage and even reduce it.

Conditions Associated with Employee Stress

The Four Ss.   The four Ss, which are stressful for many employees, are supervisor, salary, security, and safety.[40] The two major stresses that blue-collar workers asso-

Exhibit 18.4 Organizational Stressors

Roles	**Job Qualities**
Low role awareness	Quantitative overload/underload
Role conflict	Qualitative overload/underload
Too little management support	Time pressures
Middle-management positions	Responsibility for things/people
	Work pace
Relationships	Lack of security
Relationships with supervisors	
Relationships with subordinates	**Organizational Structure**
Relationships with colleagues	Lack of participation
Inability to delegate	No sense of belonging
	Poor communications
Physical Environment	Restrictions on behavior
Temperature, noise, lights	Lack of opportunity
Spatial arrangements	Inequality in pay and performance evaluation
Crowding	Work hours
Lack of privacy	
Lack of safety	**Career Development**
	Status incongruity
Change	Underpromotion
Organizational change	Overpromotion
Individual change	Midcareer position
	Obsolescence

Adapted from C. L. Cooper and J. Marshall, "Occupational Sources of Stress: A Review of the Literature Relating to Coronary Heart Disease and Mental Ill Health," *Journal of Occupational Psychology*, no. 49, (1976), p. 12.

ciate with the supervisor are petty work rules and relentless pressure for more production. Both deny workers fulfillment of the need to control the work situation and of the needs to be recognized and accepted.

Salary is a stressor when it is perceived as being given unfairly. Many blue-collar workers feel that they are underpaid relative to their white-collar counterparts in the office. Teachers think they are underpaid relative to people with similar education who work in private industry.

Employees experience stress when they are unsure whether they will have their jobs next week, next month, or even next day. For many employees, lack of job security is even more stressful than jobs that are generally unsafe. At least the employees know the jobs are unsafe, whereas with a lack of job security, the employees are always in a state of uncertainty.

Organizational Change.   Changes made by organizations are often stressful, because usually they involve something important and are accompanied by uncertainty. Many changes are made without advance warning. Although rumors often circulate that a change is coming, the exact nature of the change is left to speculation. People become concerned about whether the change will affect them, perhaps by displacing them or by causing them to be transferred. The result is that the uncertainty surrounding a change yet to come causes many employees to suffer stress symptoms.

Work Pace.   Work pacing, particularly who or what controls the pace of the work, is an important potential stressor in organizations. Machine pacing gives control over the speed of the operation and the work output to something other than the individual. Employee pacing gives the individual control of the operations. The effects of machine pacing are severe, since the individual is unable to satisfy a crucial need for control of the situation. It has been reported that workers on machine-paced jobs feel exhausted at the end of the shift and are unable to relax soon after work because of increased adrenaline secretion on the job. In a study of twenty-three white- and blue-collar occupations, assembly workers reported the highest level of severe stress symptoms.

Symptoms of Stress

There are three major classes of symptoms associated with stress. The first two, physiological and psychological symptoms, become manifest directly in the individual. The third class, behavioral symptoms, becomes apparent in events of consequence to the organization.

It is important to note that these symptoms are only associated with stress. Research has not proved that they are caused by stress. The same is true of the relationship between stressors and stress.

Physiological Symptoms.   Short-term physiological symptoms of stress are increased heart rate and respiration, increased production of adrenaline and blood sugar, and frequent headaches. Long-term symptoms include ulcers, increased blood pressure (hypertension), and increased likelihood of coronary heart disease.[41]

With some exceptions, however, the short-term physiological symptoms are not necessarily unfavorable. These symptoms can give the energy that is needed to deal with stress, so that the situation may have a favorable outcome. However, most research on stress in organizations has thus far focused on the unfavorable physiological, as well as psychological and behavioral, symptoms.

Psychological Symptoms.   Psychological responses to stress include apathy and withdrawal, satisfaction and dissatisfaction, irritability, procrastination, forgetfulness, tunnel vision, tendency to misjudge people, and inability to organize oneself. Most of these seem reasonable, but how can both satisfaction and dissatisfaction be symptoms of stress? Recall that stress can be associated with either favorable or unfavorable circumstances, that is, with either opportunites or constraints. Satisfaction is most likely to be the result of the former, whereas dissatsifaction is likely to be the result of the latter.

Behavioral Symptoms.   Behavioral consequences associated with negative stress conditions include increased absenteeism, turnover, and accident proneness, and job performance that is low in both quantity and quality. Associated with positive stress conditions are decreased absenteeism, turnover, and proneness to accidents and high job performance. Job performance and accident proneness are affected by the increased adrenaline secretion and blood sugar production that occur in response to stress. These physiological reactions provide extra energy, which is directed toward performing well if the stress condition is a positive one. However, if the condition becomes too complex, the performance-directed energy can actually get in the way, resulting in more accidents and lowered productivity.

An Organizational Strategy for Dealing with Stress

By clarifying uncertainties, effective performance planning can reduce the stress associated with job responsibilities.[42] One company implemented effective performance planning by training its managers in management by objectives. One of the managers' objectives was to help their employees identify, and become committed to, work goals.

Before the managers received their training, the employees were surveyed on six goal-oriented job dimensions:

- Difficulty of work goals
- Clarity of work goals
- Quality of performance feedback from the supervisor
- Amount of performance feedback from the supervisor
- Employee participation in setting work goals
- Peer competition for goal accomplishment

Five months after the program began, the employees were resurveyed on the same six dimensions. Comparison of the two surveys indicated considerable improvement. And as a result, role conflict and absenteeism within the organization declined and role awareness increased.

The results of this strategy illustrate that a change in just one personnel activity—

A SLICE OF LIFE

Stress sometimes leads to very different outcomes for different people. What one person finds stressful, another may find stimulating. Similarly, one person may perform remarkably well in a very difficult situation, whereas another may fall apart under the same pressure.

The management of stress thus presents organizations with a problem. Goal setting, management by objectives, sales quotas, production quotas, and many other incentive programs have been instituted to encourage high levels of employee performance. But they all put pressure on people to perform and may therefore be stressful for some people. If the organization were to curtail these types of programs in an attempt to reduce potential stress, productivity might decrease. Must organizations choose between stress and productivity?

Suppose that the organization attempts to reduce stress by identifying the people who can handle stress and then applying pressure only to them. Stress-sensitive people would receive little or no pressure. Besides the fact that it might be quite costly and time-consuming to make this distinction, it would be difficult to justify treating two groups of employees so differently. Obviously stress management is an extremely complex issue.

in this case, performance appraisal—can be useful in reducing stress. The results also indicate that organizations should pay particular attention to their performance appraisal systems, especially to the phenomenon of the "vanishing performance appraisal"—the performance appraisal that never takes place—because of the adverse effects they can have on employees' stress levels.

An Individual Strategy for Dealing with Stress

Time pressure is one of the conditions most commonly associated with stress. Reducing the frequency of time shortages will help a person not only to reduce stress but also to accomplish more.

One technique for dealing with a time shortage is **time management**.[44] Time management consists of the following steps:

• Establishing goals—both short-term and long-term, both job and nonjob—and then setting priorities for these goals

• Determining measures and standards by which to evaluate your progress toward attaining these goals

• Identifying personal strengths and weaknesses that will help or hinder attainment of these goals and then identifying strategies for eliminating these weaknesses

• Soliciting feedback about your strengths, weaknesses, and strategies from those who know you well (friends) and from those who are a part of your goal attainment (colleagues)

• Taking steps to enhance the likelihood of attaining goals, including breaking large goals into smaller, more readily attainable goals; making sure the goals and standards are clearly stated; establishing goals with moderate levels of difficulty, neither too hard nor too easy; and making a commitment to others and yourself to attain these goals

• Continually asking "What is the best use of my time right now?" and answering that in light of the priorities you have given your goals

These activities can help a person to attain goals that reflect important personal needs and values. And because time is brought under control, the stress a person experiences will also be brought under control.

Although time management is an effective way to control stress, it is not necessary for all people. The technique is especially effective for those who have never clearly identified their important goals. Many people run out of time to do the things they want to do only because they spend time on other things that appear easy or necessary to do. They also derive instant pleasure from accomplishing even the smallest of activities, such as opening mail. For these people, the six time-managment techniques are invaluable.

SUMMARY

This chapter concludes coverage of the organization's work environment. Although both the physical and sociopsychological aspects of the environment are important in the management of human resources, more attention has been paid so far to the physical environment. This is due in large measure to its greater visibility and its more direct impact on the employee than the sociopsychological aspect of the work environment. Another important reason for greater attention to the physical environment is the need to comply with OSHA standards and regulations. Organizations, however, may run the risk of additional federal regulation if they continue their relative neglect of the quality of work life and stress in organizations. Courts are already awarding worker's compensation to employees who suffer from the effects of stress. Neglect of the sociopsychological work environment may also have serious consequences for the organization, including greater employee dissatisfaction and absenteeism and lower motivation and job performance.

To prevent these consequences, organizations need to employ QWL techniques, including job redesign and employee participation in decision making. Also, since many aspects of the organization, like the performance appraisal system, are potential contributors to employee stress, organizations need to help employees manage stress in the organization or to reduce the levels of stress that they encounter. The results will be beneficial to both individuals and the organization.

The success of QWL projects and stress-reduction and management programs depends on whether appropriate techniques are used, how well the programs are implemented, and whether their progress is monitored and evaluated to make any needed adjustment. To ensure the appropriateness of the techniques, the existing organization must be carefully surveyed and analyzed, and the criteria the organization would like to improve, such as turnover and absenteeism, must be selected. These criteria then become the standards against which the program's effectiveness can be monitored, evaluated, and modified.

PERSONNEL PROBLEM
Better Jobs for Whom?

Managerial representatives and union officials have been meeting all morning to discuss a managerial proposal to implement certain job enlargement, rotation, and enrichment programs at the Eastern Division plants. The union has no authority to block the implementation of these programs, but it has been invited to participate in the hope that it will support management's efforts to reduce stress and to improve the quality of work life for many employees. The company plans to accomplish these goals by providing more variety in jobs and by adding more responsibility and autonomy to some of the job classifications.

The union vehemently opposes these efforts. It argues, among other things, that job enlargement and job rotation programs are a ruse to get employees trained in a variety of different jobs. The employees do not receive additional pay, which is decidedly unfair. For one thing, an employee with more job skills is worth more money. For another, the work of absent employees can be done easily by other employees if they have been rotated into that position. Job enrichment programs are similarly unfair. When employees are expected to shoulder more responsibility for decision making, they should be paid more. After all, this is the main distinction between managerial and hourly employees.

1. Comment on the union's position on job enlargement and job rotation programs.

2. Comment on the union's position on job enrichment programs.

3. Comment on the company's position on both issues.

4. What would you recommend to both parties to help settle this impasse?

5. Is the union's argument that workers who can do more should be paid more correct? Are compensation levels established on the basis of evaluation of the job or evaluation of the employee's ability?

KEY CONCEPTS

job design

job enlargement

job enrichment

job rotation

quality of work life (QWL)

sociotechnical job design

stress

time management

work culture

DISCUSSION QUESTIONS

1. What are QWL and stress in organizations? Should an organization be concerned with them?
2. How do stress and QWL relate to employee needs and values?
3. What is the role of the personnel manager in QWL and stress in management?
4. Who's responsible for QWL and stress? Should nonjob concerns of an employee be of concern to the organization?
5. Do workers expect too much from their jobs? Has QWL declined, or have workers' expectations increased?
6. Explain some techniques that can be used in QWL projects. What are the purposes of these techniques?
7. What are the three classes of symptoms associated with employee stress? Give examples of each.
8. What are the results or consequences of QWL and stress programs?

ENDNOTES

1. Reprinted by permission of the *Harvard Business Review*. Excerpt from "Europe's Industrial Democracy: An American Response" by T. Mills (November/December 1978), p. 151. Copyright © 1978 by the President and Fellows of Harvard College; all rights reserved.

2. A. A. McLean, *Work Stress* (Reading, Mass: Addison-Wesley, 1979), p. 76.

3. L. E. Daves and A. B. Cherns (eds.), *The Quality of Working Life*, vols. 1 and 2 (New York: Free Press, 1975).
   J. R. Hackman and J. L. Suttle, *Improving Life at Work* (Santa Monica, Calif: Goodyear, 1977).
   R. P. Quinn and G. L. Staines, *The Quality of Employment Survey* (Ann Arbor, Mich.: Survey Research Center, Institute for Social Research, The University of Michigan, 1979).

4. R. S. Schuler, "Definition and Conceptualization of Stress in Organizations," *Organizational Behavior and Human Performance*, April 1980, pp. 184–215.

5. E. A. Locke, "The Nature and Causes of Job Satisfaction," in M. D. Dunnette (ed.), *Handbook of Industrial and Organizational Psychology* (Chicago: Rand McNally, 1976), pp. 1297–1350.

6. J. R. Hackman and J. L. Suttle, *Improving Life at Work*, p. 8. Copyright © 1977 Goodyear Publishing Company, Inc. Reprinted with permission.

7. F. Herzberg, "The Human Need for Work," *Industry Week*, July 24, 1978, pp. 49–52.
   D. C. McClelland, "N Achievement and Entrepreneurship: A Longitudinal Study," *Journal of Personality and Social Psychology*, no. 1, (1965), pp. 389–392.

8. M. Moser, "Hypertension: A Major Controllable Public Health Problem: Industry Can Help," *Occupational Health Nursing*, August 1977, p. 19.

9. M. T. Matteson and J. M. Ivanovich, "Organizational Stressors and Heart Disease: A Research Model" *Academy of Management Review*, no. 4 (1979), pp. 347–357.

10. Mills, p. 151.

11. Reprinted by permission of the *Harvard Business Review*. Excerpt from "Work Innovations in the United States" by R. E. Walton (July/August 1979), p. 93. Copyright © 1979 by the President and Fellows of Harvard College; all rights reserved.

12. Reprinted by permission of the *Harvard Business Review*. Excert from "Quality of Work Life: Learning from Tarrytown" by R. H. Guest (July/August 1979), p. 77. Copyright © 1979 by the President and Fellows of Harvard College; all rights reserved.

13. Guest, p. 77.

14. L. Levi. *Stress: Sources, Management and Prevention* (New York: Liveright, 1967), p. 7.

15. T. H. Patten Jr., "Job Evaluation and Job Enlargement: A Collison Course?" *Human Resource Management*, Winter 1977, pp. 2–8.

16. P. J. Champagne and C. Tausky, "When Job Enrichment Doesn't Pay," *Personnel*, January/February 1978, pp. 30–40.

17. Walton, p. 93.

18. Reprinted by permission of the Harvard Business Review. Excerpt from "How Volvo Adapts Work to People" by P. G. Gyllenhammar (July/August 1977), p. 112. Copyright © 1977 by the President and Fellows of Harvard College; all rights reserved.

19. Guest, p. 79.
    See also,
    M. Beer, and J. W. Driscoll, "Strategies for Change," in J. R. Hackman and J. L. Suttle (eds.), *Improving Life at Work* (Santa Monica, Calif.: Goodyear, 1977), pp. 364–447.

20. Mills, p. 148.

21. Champagne and Tausky.

22. Walton.

23. Walton.

24. Walton.

25. Hackman and Suttle.

26. *Work in America* (Cambridge, Mass.: MIT Press, 1973).

27. *Work in America* p. 37.

28. *Work in America* p. 39.

29. F. Herzberg, "One More Time: How Do You Motivate Employees?" *Harvard Business Review*, January/February 1968, pp. 56–62.

30. G. R. Oldman and J. R. Hackman, "Work Design in the Organizational Context," in B. M. Staw and L. L. Cummings (eds.), *Research in Organizational Behavior*, vol. 2 (Greenwich, Conn.: JAI Press, 1980), pp. 247–278.
    G. R. Oldham, J. R. Hackman and J. L. Pearce, "Conditions Under Which Employees Respond Positively to Enriched Work,"

Journal of Applied Psychology, no. 61 (1976), pp. 395–403.

31. A. P. Brief and R. J. Aldag, *Task Design and Employee Motivation* (Glenview, Ill.: Scott, Foresman, 1979).

32. L. E. Davis, "Job Design: Overview and Future Direction," *Journal of Contemporary Business*, Spring 1977, pp. 85–102.

33. Gyllenhammar, p. 106.

34. R. J. House and M. L. Baetz, "Leadership: Some Empirical Generalizations and New Research Directions," in B. M. Staw and L. L. Cummings (eds.), *Research in Organizational Behavior*, vol. 1 (Greenwich, Conn.: JAI Press, 1980), pp. 341–423.

    E. A. Locke and B. Schweiger, "Participation in Decision Making: One More Look," in B. M. Staw and L. L. Cummings (eds.), *Research in Organizational Behavior*, vol. 1 (Greenwich, Conn.: JAI Press, 1979), pp. 265–339.

    V. H. Vroom and E. W. Yetton, *Leadership and Decision Making* (Pittsburgh: University of Pittsburgh Press, 1973).

35. Guest.

36. Guest.

37. Guest, p. 83.

38. Guest, p. 85.

39. B. Blau, "Understanding Midcareer Stress,"

Management Review, August 1978 (New York: AMACOM, a division of American Management Associations, 1978), p. 57.

40. A. B. Shostak, *Blue-Collar Stress* (Reading, Mass.: Addison-Wesley, 1980).

41. T. A. Beehr and J. E. Newman, "Job Stress, Employee Health and Organizational Effectiveness: A Facet Analysis, Model and Literature Review," *Personnel Psychology*, Winter 1978, pp. 665–699.

    A. P. Brief, R. S. Schuler, and M. Van Sell, *Managing Job Stress* (Boston: Little, Brown, 1981).

    C. L. Cooper and J. Marshall, "Occupational Sources of Stress: A Review of the Literature Relating to Coronary Heart Disease and Mental Ill Health," *Journal of Occupational Psychology*, no. 49 (1976), pp. 11–28.

    T. Cox, *Stress* (London: Macmillan Press, Ltd., 1978).

    Schuler, 1980.

42. W. C. Duemer, N. F. Walker, and J. C. Quick, "Improving Work Life Through Effective Performance Planning," *Personnel Administrator*, July 1978, pp. 23–26.

43. Duemer, Walker, and Quick.

44. R. S. Schuler, "Time Management: A Stress Management Technique," *Personnel Journal*, December 1979, pp. 851–854.

CHAPTER OUTLINE

COLLECTING PERSONNEL DATA

The Purposes and Importance of Data Collection

Personnel Data Collectors

ANALYZING AND APPLYING PERSONNEL DATA

Determining the Costs of Absenteeism

    Gathering Data on Absenteeism

Calculating the Validity of Performance Appraisals

Conducting an Organizational Survey

    What Do We Measure?

    Purposes of an Organizational Survey

    Steps in an Organizational Survey

    A Sample Questionnaire

PERSONNEL PROBLEM   How Do You Account for It?

OBJECTIVES

- To explain the need for collecting personnel data

- To describe the methods for collecting personnel data

- To explain how to determine the costs of absenteeism

- To show how to determine the validity of a performance appraisal system

THOUGHT STARTERS

- What are personnel data?

- What are some sources of personnel data?

- Can employee satisfaction be measured? How?

- Why must personnel data be collected?

CHAPTER NINETEEN
Personnel Data Collection and Use

When I received the first letter from the president, I was surprised and hurt. I had never been told that there was any serious quality problem with our radios and I have always been proud of my work. Anyhow, during lunch breaks that next week most of us talked a lot about how we could improve our quality. We decided that the best thing to do would be to slow down a little and make sure each and every radio was put together exactly right. We agreed that we would show our president that we could do things right. After all, Hanover Radio had always taken pretty good care of us and this was the first time the president had really acted like a son-of-a-bitch.

When that second letter came things changed right away. Here we were breaking our backs trying to help the company and that old guy rewards us by cutting our pay. Some of the guys got so mad that they took a couple of sick days and went job hunting—quite a few of them even took other jobs. The rest of us decided that, if we were going to be paid less, we would work less. We also decided that it was time to listen to the people who had been talking about forming a union so that this kind of thing couldn't happen again.

From Organizational Surveys, *by R. B. Dunham and F. J. Smith, pp. 12–13. Copyright © 1979 by Scott, Foresman and Company. Reprinted by permission.*

 hat happened at Hanover Radio is an example of what can happen when personnel decisions are made and action is taken without correct and accurate information. The first letter from the president was preceded by reports that the company was incurring high costs due to returns and warranty repair work. The president confirmed these reports with information from the service records. Desiring to reverse the situation, he sent his letter informing (translated as accusing) the employees of poor quality and indicating (threatening) that 10 percent of them would be laid off if they failed to improve their performance. As a consequence of this letter, productivity not only failed to improve but actually declined from fifty radios per hour to forty. Without gathering more information to back up his feelings, the president concluded that the drop in performance represented employee resentment. In his desire to let the employees know who was boss, the president, in a second letter, told them that their "slowdown" would not be tolerated and that their wages would be cut by 10 percent until improvement occurred. In reality, productivity had declined only because the employees were trying to improve quality.

The employees' response to the second letter was predictable. Production dropped even lower, below forty radios per hour, 42 out of 375 employees quit, and 75 percent of those remaining signed authorization cards in an attempt to introduce a union to the company.[1]

This example illustrates that accurate personnel information is necessary for making decisions, but this is not its only purpose. In fact, personnel data are essential to the evaluation of each personnel function and activity and of the entire personnel department.

There are many important applications for personnel data. This chapter examines three: determining the cost of absenteeism, calculating the validity of a performance appraisal form, and conducting an organizational survey. First, however, personnel data collection and its importance and purposes are discussed.

COLLECTING PERSONNEL DATA

Personnel data collection is both a process for collecting information about employees and a procedure for using the information in making personnel decisions, evaluations, and policies. Important aspects of the collection process are who does the collecting and what methods are employed. The procedures for using the information include survey feedback sessions, evaluations, and statistical analysis.

The Purposes and Importance of Data Collection

Personnel data serve many purposes:
- To aid in development of a human resource plan by providing such information as the rates of employee turnover, absenteeism, and productivity
- To help in validation of selection procedures, through comparing test scores and performance evaluations, often using statistical techniques
- To help in validation of any device used in making personnel decisions related to firing, promotion, demotion, appraisal, compensation, and training, as well as initial hiring (especially important in meeting employment obligations)

• To identify potential or current areas of employee dissatisfaction and possible reasons for it
• To indicate employees' perceptions of the quality of work life and levels of stress in the organization
• To determine the relative worth of jobs and price them accordingly
• To measure the physical work environment so the organization can meet OSHA standards
• To serve as standards for developing, implementing, and evaluating personnel activities and programs
• To measure, where appropriate, the quality of union-management relationships

In general, the collection of personnel data helps an organization monitor and evaluate how well its human resources are being used, locate the problem areas (whether departments, divisions, or individual managers), and determine what personnel decisions have to be made.

Personnel Data Collectors

Personnel data are often gathered and supplied by people outside the personnel department. For example, line managers supply the personnel department with performance appraisal data on their employees. In some organizations, the employees contribute their own performance appraisal data. Managers generally supply the personnel department with absenteeism data. As a consequence of medical care provided to employees, doctors and nurses may supply to the personnel department such vital information as frequency of visits by an employee and costs incurred as a result of each visit. The doctors and nurses are expected to become even larger contributors of personnel data as organizations increase their concern for the physical and mental health of employees.

Personnel departments also rely on many sources of data outside the organization. These sources can be categorized as follows:
• Government agencies like the Bureau of Labor Statistics (BLS) of the U.S. Department of Labor and federal, state, and local employment offices
• Reporting services and societies such as the Bureau of National Affairs (BNA) and the American Society of Personnel Administrators (ASPA)
• Employer associations at the national, regional, or local level—for example, the U.S. Chamber of Commerce, the Northwest Industrial Council, and the Indiana Manufacturers' Association
• Consulting firms that conduct their own surveys, particularly in the compensation area—for example, Towers, Perrin, Forster, & Crosby; Hay Associates; and Sibson & Company
• Industry trade associations, such as the National Footwear Association, the American Banking Association, and the American Hospital Association[2]
Data commonly obtained from outside sources include job absence rates (from quarterly surveys conducted by the BNA in cooperation with the ASPA, the BLS, industry trade associations, and local employee councils); merit increase and salary-level data (from trade association annual surveys and consulting firms' surveys); and safety figures (from the National Safety Council, state worker's compensation boards, and the Occupational Safety and Health Administration).[3]

The personnel department, either alone or in cooperation with an outside consultant, conducts employee attitude surveys to determine the perceptions, opinions, and attitudes of employees;[4] administers preemployment selection tests; and collects data about the physical and sociopsychological environments of the organization.

ANALYZING AND APPLYING PERSONNEL DATA

Once personnel data have been collected, they must be analyzed and then applied to specific purposes. Three specific applications are discussed in this section—determining the costs of absenteeism, calculating the validity of performance appraisals, and conducting an organizational survey.

Determining the Costs of Absenteeism

One of the criteria used to evaluate the effectiveness of personnel and human resource management is employee absenteeism. Absenteeism is obviously a personnel problem; less obvious is the cost of absenteeism. "Recent estimates tag the national absence bill at somewhere between $15 and $20 billion a year."[5] Although these national estimates alert us to the cost of absenteeism, they tell us little about individual organizations. It is the duty of the personnel manager to quantify the cost for the organization.

Gathering Data on Absenteeism.   In Exhibit 19.1 Frank E. Kuzmits has prepared a clear and thorough description of the steps involved in measuring the costs of absenteeism.[6]

Exhibit 19.1   Measuring the Costs of Absenteeism

Let's assume your curiosity has been aroused to the point where you would like to estimate the cost of absenteeism to your organization for a one-year period—1978, for example. As in most research projects, the first step involves gathering information. Assuming your organization regularly computes traditional absence statistics and labor cost data, much of the information you will need should not be too burdensome or time-consuming to gather. Some estimates will involve discussions with other staff and management personnel, but the overall time you spend on this project should be well worth the effort.

As an aid in computing estimates for your organization, we'll provide examples at each step along the way. Using the hypothetical firm Acme International, a medium-sized steel manufacturer employing 1,200 people, our examples will hopefully provide a realistic portrayal of the problems and costs related to employee absenteeism. The data you'll need to collect and compute are outlined below.

1. *The organization's total man-hours lost to absenteeism for the period for all employees—blue-collar, clerical, management and professional.* Include time lost for all reasons except organizationally-sanctioned time off such as vacations, holidays, official "bad weather" days, etc. Be sure to include both whole-day and

part-day absences in computing the total hours lost. Include, for example, absences resulting from illness, accidents, funerals, jury duty, emergencies, personal time off and doctor's appointments, whether "excused" or "unexcused."

In our example, let's assume Acme International's personnel records show 9,792 days, or 78,336 total man-hours lost to employee absenteeism for all reasons except vacations and holidays in 1978. This figure represents an absence rate of 3.4 percent for the year—about average for manufacturing firms.

A great deal of confusion exists concerning the computation of absence rates, as a number of different formulas have reportedly been published and used. The formula used here is recommended by the U.S. Department of Labor and also used by the majority of firms responding to absenteeism surveys conducted by the Bureau of National Affairs (see "Employee Absenteeism and Turnover," *Personnel Policies Forum,* Survey No. 106, Washington D.C., Bureau of National Affairs, Inc., 1974). The formula is illustrated below:

$$\text{Absenteeism rate} = \frac{\text{Number of man-days lost through job absence during the period}}{\text{Average number of employees} \times \text{number of work days}} \times 100$$

This computation may not be quite as straightforward as it appears. Often, wage earners are not covered under a sick leave plan while salaried employees are. Look closely at your organization's employee benefits program to determine if your estimates should reflect differential absenteeism costs for employee groups who receive sick pay and those who do not. In addition, some organizations have policies which define the kinds of absences for which employees are not paid ("unauthorized" or "unexcused"). Should this be the case in your organization, you will need to segregate absences by "paid" vs. "unpaid" and apply the appropriate costs to each category.

2. *The weighted average hourly wage/salary level for the various occupational groups that claimed absenteeism during the period.* Note: If your organization *does not pay* absent workers, *skip this step* and go directly to step three.

For Acme International, let's assume about 85 percent of all absentees were blue collar, 13 percent clerical and two percent management and professional. And, to keep our example simple, we'll also assume all employees were paid for sick days taken under the company's employee benefits program. The average hourly wage rate per absentee is computed by applying the appropriate percentages to the average hourly rate for each major occupational regrouping. The following illustration reflects how this figure is computed:

Occupational Class	Approximate Percent of Total Absenteeism	Average Hourly Wage	Weighted Average Hourly Wage
Blue collar	85	$4.25	$3.61
Clerical	13	3.95	.51
Management and professional	2	9.85	.20
			$4.32 Total

3. *The cost of employee benefits per hour per employee.* For most organizations, employee benefits (profit-sharing, pensions, health and life insurance, paid vacations and holidays, etc.) represent a sizable portion of total employee compensation—often as much as one-quarter to one-third. One method for computing the cost of employee benefits per hour per employee is to divide the total cost of benefits per employee per week by the number of hours worked per week.

We'll assume Acme International's cost of benefits per employee is $76.00 per week. Using this figure, Acme's cost for this item is computed as follows:

$$\text{Cost of benefits/hour/employee} = \frac{\text{Cost of benefits}/week/employee}{\text{Hours worked/week}} = \frac{\$76.00}{40} = \$1.90$$

4. *The estimated total number of supervisory hours lost to employee absenteeism for the period.* This estimate will be more difficult to make compared to wage and benefits estimates, as existing records seldom provide the information necessary to compute this figure. First, estimate the average number of supervisory hours spent *per day* rectifying the myriad of problems resulting from employee absenteeism. Examples of such problems include time spent solving production problems, instructing replacement employees, checking on the performance of replacements and counseling and disciplining absentees. Perhaps the most accurate way to develop this estimate is through discussions with a sampling of supervisors. In estimating your average, be sure to take into account typically high-absence days (Monday, Friday, days before and after holidays, day after payday). After estimating this figure, compute the total number of supervisory hours lost to your organization by multiplying three figures: the estimated average number of hours lost per supervisor per day times the total number of supervisors who deal with problems of absenteeism times the number of working days for the period. Include all shifts and weekend work, if any, in your estimate.

In our example, let's assume Acme International's data in these areas are:
- Estimated number of supervisory hours lost per day: ½ hour
- Total number of supervisors who deal with absence problems: 32
- Total number of working days for the year: 240

Acme International's total supervisory hours lost to absenteeism for the year is estimated by multiplying . . . one-half hour per day per supervisor × 32 supervisors × 240 working days = 3,840 total supervisory hours lost to employee absenteeism.

5. *The average hourly wage rate for supervisors, including benefits.* In your estimate, include only the salaries of supervisors who normally deal with problems of absenteeism. Usually the first level of supervision within the manufacturing and clerical areas bears the lion's share of absenteeism problems.

We'll estimate Acme International's cost for the figure as follows:

Average hourly supervisory salary:	$7.25
Cost of benefits per hour per employee:	1.90
Total compensation per hour per supervisor:	$9.15

6. *The last estimate is a catchall—a conglomerate of costs unique to your organization that were not included in the above estimates.* Such costs may include temporary help, labor pools for absent workers, overtime premiums, production losses, machine downtime, quality problems and inefficient materials usage. Like the previous figure, the estimates will be difficult to generate and should be based on discussions with a number of management and staff personnel.

We'll assume Acme International incurred overtime premiums, production losses and inefficient materials usage problems as a result of absenteeism and these problems resulted in an estimated financial loss of $38,500 for the year. Having computed all the necessary estimates, the total cost of employee absenteeism is determined by summing the individual cost figures pertaining to wages and salaries, benefits, supervisory salaries and other costs incidental to absenteeism.

Space has been provided [in Exhibit 19.2] for your figures and we'll also put Acme International's estimates next to your estimates for illustrative purposes. (Remember that Acme International is a hypothetical firm—don't pass judgment on your figures by comparing them to Acme's!)

Are Acme's costs too high? "About right?" And more importantly, what about *your* estimates? Just what do they say about the absenteeism problem your organization may be facing? Having computed the costs of absenteeism for your organization, the next step is to evaluate the figures against some pre-determined cost standard or financial measure of performance. A comparison of the absence costs of your organization to an industry average would provide valuable information in determining whether an "absenteeism problem" does in fact exist or how significant the problem may be.

Unfortunately, absenteeism cost data are not published on a regular or periodic basis. Unlike traditional cost, revenue and profit data, where regularly published financial ratios and composite income statements and balance sheets enable one to accurately gauge the financial soundness of an individual organization, very little data are available for passing judgment upon the level of dollars and cents lost to employee absenteeism. While the costs of absenteeism to individual organizations occasionally appear in the literature, these estimates normally result from case studies of individual firms rather than surveys of specific industries.[7]

Without a sound basis for comparing the costs of absenteeism by industry category or other relevant organizational criteria, is it worth the time and effort to undertake a cost analysis of the individual organization? Yes—and at least two compelling reasons exist for doing so. Perhaps the principal reason for computing the economic costs of employee absenteeism is to call management's attention to the severity of the problem. Translating behavioral acts into dollars and cents enables managers to readily grasp the burdens of absenteeism, particularly in a firm suffering from extraordinary absence problems. The spark recognition of a five, six, or even seven figure outlay for absenteeism will likely result in a concentrated effort to combat the problem.[8]

A second reason for computing the cost of employee absenteeism is to create meaningful criteria for evaluating the effectiveness of absence control programs. Comparing the quarterly, semi-annual and annual costs of absenteeism across

> various departments and supervisory work units provides a valid and reliable information system for measuring the success—or lack of success—of methods and techniques designed to reduce the problem. Organizations with computerized absence reporting systems should find this additional information relatively easy and inexpensive to generate.

This material is graciously provided by Frank E. Kuzmits and is reprinted with permission from the June 1979 issue of the *Personnel Administrator,* copyright 1979, The American Society for Personnel Administration, 30 Park Drive, Berea, OH 44017.

Calculating the Validity of Performance Appraisals

It has become increasingly important (not only because it is legally required but also because it increases the effectiveness of personnel management) to validate the form that the organization uses to appraise how well its employees are performing.[9] After all, the performance evaluation is used to determine many things: an employee's merit raises, promotion potential, and job assignments; the validity of selection devices; the behavior of the supervisor; and even the employee's level of self-esteem and reactions to co-workers.

The validity of an organization's performance appraisal form is determined by establishing a relationship between the employee's performance evaluation and the employee's actual performance. This relationship can be established with one of the most common statistical procedures used in personnel administration—the **Pearson product-moment correlation**, which is also used to validate selection tests and training programs. The Pearson correlation coefficient provides an estimate of the relationship between two variables. In determining the validity of the performance appraisal form, the variables are the employees' appraisal scores and their output in units of production. (Examples of correlation coefficients are presented in Chapter 7.)

> Although we will use the Pearson correlation coefficient, there are other measures of correlation, including the point biserial correlation, eta (the correlation for curvilinear relationships), Spearman-Brown rank order correlation, and Kendall's tau.

Let's suppose that you have the job of analyzing the performance appraisal process at the Applegate Foundry.[10] You need to investigate the appraisals being completed by the managers in four departments. All employees in each department are doing very similar work, and the performance output measure is an accurate and objective record of the units produced by each worker. What you want to know is how well the performance appraisals reflect actual production—that is, how valid they are—

Exhibit 19.2   Total Estimated Cost of Employee Absenteeism

Item	Acme International	Your Organization
1. Total man-hours lost to employee absenteeism for the period	78,336	
2. Weighted average wage/salary per hour per employee	$4.32	
3. Cost of employee benefits per hour per employee	$1.90	
4. Total compensation lost per hour per absent employee		
A. If absent workers are paid (wage/salary plus benefits)	$6.22	
B. If absent workers are not paid (benefits only)		
5. Total compensation lost to absent employees (total man-hours lost × 4.A or 4.B, whichever applicable)	$487,250	
6. Total supervisory hours lost on employee absenteeism	3,840	
7. Average hourly supervisory wage, including benefits	$9.15	
8. Total supervisory salaries lost to managing problems of absenteeism (hours lost × average hourly supervisory wage—item 6 × item 7)	$35,136	
9. All other costs incidental to absenteeism not included in the above items	$38,500	
10. Total estimated cost of absenteeism—summation of items, 5, 8, and 9	$560,887	
11. Total estimated cost of absenteeism per employee		

$$\frac{\text{(Total estimated costs)}}{\text{(Total number of employees)}} = \frac{\$560,886}{1200} = _____ =$$

$467.41 per employee

From Frank E. Kuzmits, "How Much Is Absenteeism Costing Your Organization?" p. 31. Reprinted with permission from the June 1979 issue of the *Personnel Administrator* copyright 1979, The American Society for Personnel Administration, 30 Park Drive, Berea, OH 44017.

and how accurately each manager completes the appraisal form. You are aware that many things can interfere with the appraisal process. What you should also become aware of is how various things can affect such statistics as the correlation.

Exhibit 19.3 lists the employees' numbers, their department, their performance appraisal score, and their level of performance output. The performance appraisal score is computed by summing the manager's rating of each employee on five 5-point scales. Thus an employee's score could range from a low of 5 to a high of 25. The level of output is the number of ornamental paperweights produced during an eight-hour shift. Because of the machinery used, the maximum output per hour is ten units. Thus individual performance could range from zero to a maximum of eighty units per shift. Each person works individually and has comparable equipment and materials.

Exhibit 19.3   Applegate Foundry Employee Performance

Employee	Department	Appraisal Score	Performance Output
1	1	20	75
2	2	22	73
3	4	25	75
4	1	25	73
5	3	17	73
6	1	23	70
7	2	25	71
8	4	25	73
9	1	19	68
10	2	24	69
11	1	22	67
12	1	18	59
13	3	18	70
14	3	16	72
15	1	17	56
16	3	15	69
17	1	16	52
18	2	24	67
19	1	18	51
20	3	18	65
21	1	15	48
22	4	24	74
23	4	24	73
24	2	23	67
25	4	25	74
26	3	17	61
27	3	15	62
28	4	25	73
29	2	22	63
30	4	24	72
31	2	23	61
32	3	16	58
33	4	24	74
34	4	24	73
35	2	23	60
36	3	18	54
37	2	22	58
38	4	25	72
39	3	17	50
40	2	22	58

The first step is to determine the correlation between the employees' level of output and their performance appraisal scores. Let X be the appraisal score and Y be the performance output. The formula for determining the correlation between X and Y is

$$\text{Pearson product-moment correlation } (r) = \frac{n\Sigma XY - (\Sigma X)(\Sigma Y)}{\sqrt{[n\Sigma X^2 - (\Sigma X)^2][n\Sigma Y^2 - (\Sigma Y)^2]}}$$

For this total group, $r = .59$.

The second step is to determine the mean, the variance, the standard deviation, and the range for both the actual output and the appraisal score. For the total group these data are as follows:

	Appraisal Score	Output Level
Mean	20.88	65.83
Variance	12.63	63.69
Standard deviation	3.55	7.98
Range	10.00	27.00

The third step is to repeat the first and second steps for the subgroups. This is important, because different supervisors did the appraisals for each subgroup. Therefore, a **subgroup analysis** will reveal more about how the appraisal forms are being used. Note also that the correlation of .59 determined by the first step is not extremely high, and subgroup analysis may tell us why. Remember that the possible range of this correlation is -1.00 to $+1.00$.

The data below show the steps in computing the correlation for subgroup 1:

X	X²	Y	Y²	XY	$(X-\overline{X})^2$	$(Y-\overline{Y})^2$
20	400	75	5625	1500	.49	171.61
25	625	73	5329	1825	32.49	123.21
23	529	70	4900	1610	13.69	65.61
19	361	68	4624	1292	.09	37.21
22	484	67	4489	1474	7.29	26.01
18	324	59	3481	1062	1.69	8.41
17	289	56	3136	952	5.29	34.81
16	256	52	2704	832	10.89	98.01
18	324	51	2601	918	1.69	118.81
15	225	48	2304	720	18.49	193.21
Sums 193	3817	619	39193	12185	92.10	876.90
Means 19.3		61.9				

Range of X 15–25
Range of Y 48–75

$$SD_X = \sqrt{\frac{\Sigma (x - \overline{x})^2}{n - 1}} = \sqrt{\frac{92.10}{10 - 1}} = 3.19$$

$$SD_Y = \sqrt{\frac{\Sigma (y - \overline{y})^2}{n - 1}} = \sqrt{\frac{876.9}{10 - 1}} = 9.871$$

$$r = \frac{10 \,(12185) - 119467}{\sqrt{[10 \cdot 3817 - (193)^2]\,[10 \cdot 39193 - (619)^2]}}$$

$$= \frac{2383}{\sqrt{(921)(8769)}}$$

$$= \frac{2383}{2841.87}$$

$$= .84$$

The high correlation (.84) between the appraisal scores and actual output indicates a high validity for the performance appraisal form for subgroup 1. The results for the other three subgroups are as follows:

	Mean	Variance	Standard Deviation	Range
Appraisal score				
Subgroup 2	23.00	1.11	1.05	3
Subgroup 3	16.70	1.34	1.15	3
Subgroup 4	14.50	0.28	0.53	1
Output level				
Subgroup 2	64.70	29.57	5.44	15
Subgroup 3	63.40	60.93	7.81	23
Subgroup 4	73.30	0.90	0.95	3

The correlations for subgroups 2, 3, and 4 are .50, −.16, and .11, respectively, which do not indicate a high validity for the appraisal form.

It is important to know the reason for the level of validity that is determined by using these data. Otherwise, erroneous decisions may be made—for example, that the performance appraisal form is not useful or that supervisors commit many errors in using it. Consider the correlation for subgroup 4, which shows a low validity even though both the actual levels of output and the appraisals are high. In other words, the employees and the supervisor are actually doing well, but the correlation is low because of the **restriction in range**: The variances, standard deviations, and ranges all indicate that the range of possible scores is very limited. Thus the correlation will always be low. As discussed in Chapter 9, errors of central tendency, leniency, and strictness may also occur.

In using these validity data, it is also important to consider the effect that a decision related to the use of the appraisal method will have on a specific employee. As an example, let's look at subgroup 2. The validity of the appraisal form is moderately high. Thus whatever evaluation an employee gets by the appraisal method is a reasonably good indication of that employee's actual output. But is that a correct conclusion for all employees? The **scattergram** in Exhibit 19.4 shows that it is not the case for employee A. Employee A received a high appraisal score even though his output was actually very low. Perhaps the supervisor really liked employee A, or perhaps employee A performed very well just before appraisal time, thus benefiting from what is known as the recency effect. Note that if employee A were not in subgroup 2, the correlation would be much higher.

Conducting an Organizational Survey

What Do We Measure?   In each of the applications of personnel data discussed so far, the data gathered have been either measures of job performance itself or predictors of job performance, such as tests and background characteristics. But the personnel manager often has need of other types of data. For example, in order to develop ways to improve employee performance, the personnel manager needs to measure how the employees perceive their environment, including the consequences of job performance, qualities of feedback, task interference characteristics, and

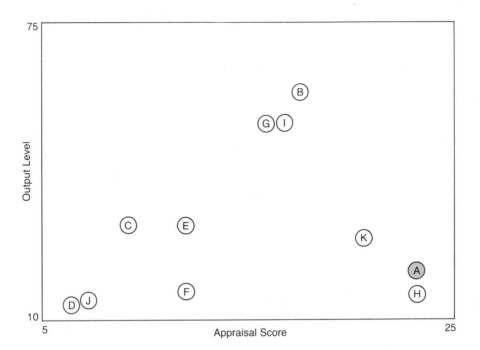

Exhibit 19.4 Scattergram Showing Actual Output of Employees in Subgroup 2

aspects of goal setting. It is equally necessary to gather data on the employee's perceptions of the quality of work life and employee stress. This is not to say, however, that the objective qualities of the job are not important. Only with at least these two pieces of data can the personnel manager begin to make useful changes in job design.[11]

It is also important to know how employees react to the environment and job qualities. Many of these reactions are symptoms of employee stress, which include such physiological measures as blood pressure and heart rate. Since one of our criteria for the effectiveness of personnel management is employee health, additional measures of employee reactions may become more common.

Thus organizational surveys can measure the following:

● *Employee perceptions:* role awareness, role conflict, qualities of the job, interpersonal qualities such as supervision and organizational characteristics

● *Employee reactions:* feelings such as satisfaction and physiological responses such as heart rate and blood pressure

● *Behaviors:* employee performance, absenteeism, and turnover

Purposes of an Organizational Survey.   An organizational survey serves several purposes. First, it determines the effectiveness of personnel functions and activities. Second, it measures the quality of the organization's internal environment and therefore helps to locate things that require improvement. Finally, the survey aids in the development of programs to make the necessary changes, and then it helps in evaluating the effectiveness of these programs.

Steps in an Organizational Survey.   There are several important steps and issues for the personnel manager—or an outside consultant—to consider when conducting an organizational survey.[12] These become necessary, however, only after top management has given its support for the survey.

As the first step, the personnel manager must consider the following:
- The specific employee perceptions and responses that should be measured
- The methods that will be used to collect the data, including observations, questionnaires, interviews, and personnel records
- The reliability and validity of the measures to be used
- The people from whom the data will be collected—all employees, managerial employees only, a sample of employees, or only certain departments within the organization
- The timing of the survey and the way to make the survey part of a longer-term effort
- The types of analyses that will be made with the data
- The specific purposes of the data—to determine reasons for the organization's turnover problem, for example

This last consideration is important, because by identifying the problem, the personnel manager can determine which models or theories will be relevant to the survey. Knowing which model or theory to use tells the personnel manager what data are needed and what statistical techniques will be necessary to analyze the data.

The next step is the actual collection of data. Three things are important here. It must be decided who will administer the questionnaire—the line manager, someone from the personnel department, or someone from outside the organization. It must also be decided where, when, and in what size groups the data will be collected. Both these considerations are influenced by the method used to gather the data. For example, if a questionnaire is used, larger groups are more feasible than if interviews are conducted. Finally, employee participation in the survey must be ensured. This can be done by gathering the data during company time and by providing feedback— for instance, by promising employees that the results of the survey will be made known to them.

The actual feedback process is the third step in the survey. As part of this process, the data are analyzed according to the purposes and problems for which they were collected. The results of the analysis can then be presented by the personnel department to the line managers, who in turn discuss the results with their employees. The feedback sessions can be used to develop solutions to any problems that are identified and to evaluate the effectiveness of programs that may already have been implemented on the basis of results of an earlier survey.

The extent to which employees actually participate in the development of solutions during the feedback process depends on the philosophy of top management. Organizations that are willing to survey their employees to ask how things are going are also usually willing to invite employee participation in deciding to make things better. It is this willingness that allows organizational surveys to be used most effectively.

A Sample Questionnaire.   "The paper-and-pencil questionnaire is the most common method of obtaining survey data."[13] Exhibit 19.5 is a questionnaire asking students to describe the degree to which they know what's expected of them (role awareness) and how much conflict they face in doing what's expected (role conflict). Measures of role awareness and role conflict have been used extensively in organizational surveys; typical items have been reworded here to apply to a classroom situation. You should complete this questionnaire according to the instructions before reading any further.

If you have completed the questionnaire, add the numbers you circled in items 1, 6, 7, 9, 10, and 12. This is your role awareness score. Now add the remaining numbers you circled to determine your role conflict score. Next, circle the response below that you think best describes your overall level of satisfaction with the class:

	Strongly Disagree	Disagree	Neutral	Agree	Strongly Agree
All in all, I am very satisfied with this class	1	2	3	4	5

How does your score on satisfaction compare with your scores on role conflict and role awareness? Are you high on all three or low on all three, or do you have a mixed pattern?

What is the importance of these scores? In most organizational surveys, employees are asked for their perceptions of and attitudes toward many aspects of the

---

Exhibit 19.5 Role Awareness and Role Conflict Questionnaire

Read each classroom characteristic, and select the scale number that best reflects your opinion.

Definitely not characteristic of this class			Definitely characteristic of this class	
1	2	3	4	5

1. I know what my responsibilities are.	1	2	3	4	5
2. I receive assignments without the time to complete them.	1	2	3	4	5
3. Part of my grade depends on a group project.	1	2	3	4	5
4. I have to go through all sorts of hassles to find out what's expected of me.	1	2	3	4	5
5. Good work or a good idea is not really recognized by the instructor.	1	2	3	4	5
6. I have been given clearly planned goals and objectives for this class.	1	2	3	4	5
7. I know how to study for this class to do well.	1	2	3	4	5
8. I do things that are apt to be accepted by the instructor at one time but not acepted at another time.	1	2	3	4	5
9. I feel certain about how much I am responsible for.	1	2	3	4	5
10. I know exactly what is expected of me.	1	2	3	4	5
11. I have to do things that can be done in different ways.	1	2	3	4	5
12. Explanations of what has to be done are clear.	1	2	3	4	5
13. I work on unnecessary things.	1	2	3	4	5
14. The amount of work I am expected to do is fair.	1	2	3	4	5

Adapted from J. R. Rizzo, R. J. House, and S. I. Lirtzman, "Role Conflict and Ambiguity in Complex Organizations," *Administrative Science Quarterly*, no. 15 (1970) p. 156.

organization. These surveys generally reveal very definite patterns. Satisfaction, for instance, tends to have a negative relationship with role conflict but a positive relationship with role awareness. Role conflict and role awareness are also frequently related to employee performance and stress. Therefore, an employee's role conflict and role awareness scores reveal a great deal more about the employee. Other variables—for example, the employee's supervisor, the job, and the extent of the employee's perceived participation in decision making—also tell a lot about the employee.

The personnel manager must collect data in order to show that employment practices and policies are valid; to demonstrate the relationship between personnel activities and employee satisfaction, health, turnover, absenteeism, and performance; and to determine the cost of these employee outcomes. Personnel data can tell the personnel manager and the organization how employees feel, where potential trouble spots are, and what the potential causes of those trouble spots are. Using this information, the personnel manager can design programs to increase the effectiveness of the organization, to the benefit of both the individual and the organization. In the 1980s, these purposes will become even more important.

SUMMARY

Personnel data collection is essential in justifying the importance of personnel activities to the organization. The personnel manager must demonstrate the relationship between these activities and employee satisfaction, health, turnover, absenteeism, and job performance. These data are also used to quantify the cost to the organization of employee dissatisfaction, illness, turnover, and absenteeism. Computing the cost of absenteeism is one example of how personnel data can be used.

Quantification is also important to the personnel manager and the organization in defending employment practices and policies. Recruitment, selection, performance evaluation, promotion, and termination decisions must be done using reliable and valid methods. The example in this chapter used statistical methods to determine the validity of an organization's appraisal form by using two types of personnel data—appraisal scores and employee output. The results of using valid methods are organizational compliance with the law and better use of human resources.

PERSONNEL PROBLEM
How Do You Account for It?

A series of research projects on many West Coast organizations has shown a correlation between the use of management by objectives (MBO) programs and very poor organizational performance. This was quite the opposite of what was expected, since it is widely believed that MBO programs are very successful. They should therefore be associated with good, not poor, organizational performance.

The research on MBO programs was conducted by professionals who were knowledgeable in the specific operations of the organizations studied. Assume that any errors in the research did not influence the findings. Also assume that the MBO programs had nothing to do with the poor performance of the organizations.

1. How do you account for the research results?

2. Based on the information in the report, what other interpretations of the results could be made?

3. How would you determine the real reasons for these results? Would you gather more data? If so, what kind and how?

KEY CONCEPTS

Pearson product-moment correlation

personnel data collection
restriction in range

scattergram
subgroup analysis

DISCUSSION QUESTIONS

1. Why is it especially important now for personnel managers to collect and analyze data?

2. Who should collect personnel data?

3. What are the procedures and data needed to determine the cost of an organization's absenteeism? How is absenteeism measured?

4. If a performance appraisal is valid for one group of employees, will it necessarily be valid for another group? Explain thoroughly.

5. What is the range of validity a performance appraisal measure can have? What is high validity?

6. What are the steps in doing an organizational survey?

7. By what methods can data be gathered in an organizational survey?

8. How can the results of an organizational survey improve a situation?

ENDNOTES

1. R. B. Dunham and F. J. Smith, *Organization Surveys* (Glenview, Ill: Scott, Foresman, 1979), p. 12.

2. "Personnel Policies: Research and Evaluation," ASPA-BNA Survey No. 37, p. 6. Reprinted by special permission from *Bulletin to Management*, copyright 1979 by The Bureau of National Affairs, Inc., Washington, D.C.

3. Bureau of National Affairs, p. 2.

4. Bureau of National Affairs, p. 2.

5. F. E. Kuzmits, "How Much Is Absenteeism Costing Your Organization?" *Personnel Administrator*, June 1979, p. 29.

6. This example is graciously provided by Frank E. Kuzmits and is reprinted with permission from the June 1979 issue of the *Personnel Administrator*, copyright 1979, The American Society for Personnel Administration, 30 Park Drive, Berea, OH 44017. The following are references used by Kuzmits:
   A. J. Gemmel, "Personnel and Line Management: Partners in Absentee Control," *Personnel Journal*, February 1973, pp. 113–115.
   F. E. Kuzmits, "Managing Absenteeism," *Personnel*, May/June, 1977, pp. 73–76.

7. Several cost estimates for individual organizations are reported in Frederick J. Gaudet, *Solving the Problems of Employee Absence*, New York, American Management Association, 1963, Chapter Four. Unfortunately, significant inflation since the report was published makes a comparison of costs incurred today to those reported by Gaudet invalid.

8. Articles concerning the prevention and control of absenteeism exist in a wide variety of publications. See *The Personnel Administrator, Personnel, Personnel Journal, Supervisory Personnel, Management Review,* and Bureau of National Affairs, reports on employee absenteeism. See also S. F. Yolles, *et al., Absenteeism in Industry,* Springfield, Illinois, Charles C Thomas, 1974.

9. R. D. Arvey, *Fairness in Selecting Employees* (Reading, Mass.: Addison-Wesley, 1979).
   S. Zedeck and M. R. Blood, *Foundations of Behavioral Science Research in Organizations* (Monterey, Calif.: Brooks/Cole, 1974), p. 69.

10. This example is provided by James McFillen and used with his permission.

11. For a discussion of the methodological issues relevant to surveys see, J. R. Hackman and G. R. Oldham, *Task Design* (Reading, Mass.: Addison-Wesley, 1980).

12. Dunham and Smith, Chapter 5, pp. 91–97.

13. Dunham and Smith, p. 13.

SECTION EIGHT

Putting It All Together

CHAPTER TWENTY
Trends and Comparisons

CHAPTER OUTLINE

THE GROWING IMPORTANCE OF PERSONNEL MANAGEMENT
Declining Productivity
Demographic Changes
Work Force Expectations
Government Regulations
Technology, the Economy, and the New Knowledge Workers

TRENDS IN PERSONNEL MANAGEMENT
Planning for Human Resource Management
Human Resource Planning and Programming
Job Analysis
Staffing
Recruitment
Selection
Socialization and Accommodation
Appraising and Compensating
Appraising
Compensating
Developing the Employee
Establishing and Maintaining Effective Labor Relations
Organizing
Labor-Management Cooperation
Improving the Work Environment
Sociopsychological Aspects of the Environment
Analysis of the Work Environment

PERSONNEL PRACTICES IN OTHER COUNTRIES
Europe
Codetermination
Quality of Work Life
Japan
The Highly Motivated Work Force
Employee Socialization and Development
Canada
Pensions
Health and Safety
Human Rights Legislation
Labor Relations

OBJECTIVES

● To explain why personnel management will become even more important in the 1980s

● To discuss the trends in each of the personnel functions

● To explain how we might benefit from the experiences of Europe and Japan

● To describe some differences in personnel management between the United States and Canada

THOUGHT STARTERS

● What are the two superordinate goals for personnel management in the 1980s?

● What is codetermination?

● Do the Japanese work harder than U.S. workers?

● How does the Canadian human rights legislation differ from equal employment legislation in the United States?

CHAPTER TWENTY
Trends and Comparisons

Certainly anyone practicing as a personnel professional in 1964 has experienced the striking changes between then and now. But there is more to come—a lot more—which will change the profession so dramatically that what has happened in the past fifteen years will seem insignificant in comparison. While some of these changes will undoubtedly bring about even greater recordkeeping and reporting requirements, most of them will affect the very core of the personnel professional's daily schedule and tax to the limit his or her ability to meet organizational needs.

From "The Intensification of the Personnel Role," by L. A. Wangler. Reprinted with permission Personnel Journal, *copyright February 1979, pp. 111–112.*

Personnel executives of the 1980s, facing increased responsibilities and new challenges, will be viewed as key decision makers. They will have to meet not only organizational goals but also individual and social goals. Moreover, all personnel activities will continue to grow in importance.

The first part of this chapter explores the reasons for this increasing importance and discusses the significant trends in personnel management in the 1980s. Then some aspects of personnel management in other countries are examined.

THE GROWING IMPORTANCE OF PERSONNEL MANAGEMENT

There are several fundamental reasons why personnel management will become more important in the 1980s, all of them related to sociocultural changes now under way.

Declining Productivity

The United States is still the most productive nation in the world in absolute terms, but the annual rate of growth has begun to slip. Between 1970 and 1980, the growth in productivity was less than 1.5 percent, down from approximately 3.2 percent in the previous decade. This decline has made top management realize that human resources are an organization's most important asset.[1] Consequently, top management will look to the personnel department for help in reversing the decline in productivity.

Demographic Changes

In the 1980s, older people will work longer because of inflation's erosion of retirement income and more flexible retirement programs.

The median age of the U.S. population will be 31.5 in 1985, which is higher than ever before. Accordingly, the number of new workers entering the labor force will decline, increasing by only 12 percent in the 1980s as compared to 21 percent in the 1970s. The greatest growth in employment will be in the South and West.

By 1985, white men will become a minority of those working.

Work Force Expectations

Workers, particularly those just entering the labor force, will continue to emphasize participation, freedom of expression, and more control over the workplace. In addition, they will continue to resist the role of authority. Some workers, however, will continue to value authority in the workplace and the right of management to direct their behavior. As a result, the biggest challenge will be to manage a work force with differing value systems.

Other expectations are also changing. "Where our cultural values once stressed equality of opportunity and the value of hard work, it appears that increasingly members of our society are demanding *equality of results* rather than *equality of opportunity*." Coupled with this is "a clear pattern of our society to place less responsibility on the individual and to assume a greater responsibility on the part of society at large for providing a minimum standard of living and a constantly increasing standard of living for all members of our society."[2]

Finally, there will be a growing desire for personal flexibility, a greater need for personal privacy and civil liberties, and a continued demand by minorities and women for equal participation at all levels of the work force.

Goverment Regulations

In contrast to the previous two decades, the regulatory trend will slow down in the 1980s, and management and labor will become more involved in the rule-making process. Two areas of potential government intervention are labor-management relations and privacy legislation. Labor-management intervention might consist of making organizing easier for unions and shortening the time organizations now have "to get their house in order" between notification and the actual election.[3]

Although some legislation guarding employee privacy already exists, more may be on the way. Eventually, employees may control employment information to the point that none is disseminated without prior authorization. In addition, organizations may be restricted from retaining certain information—for example, medical histories, performance appraisals after a certain length of time, histories of garnishments (amounts withheld from a paycheck for creditors), and even conviction records.

Equal employment opportunity and affirmative action issues will continue to have a significant impact on personnel management. Only companies that have managed to place appropriate numbers of women and minorities at all levels will be able to relax their efforts. Unfortunately, there are no such organizations today in either the public or the private sector.

The impact of the Occupational Safety and Health Act, the Employees' Retirement Income Security Act, and other laws currently on the books will expand in the 1980s. Employees will increasingly be protected from the physical and psychological hazards of the work environment.

Technology, the Economy, and the New Knowledge Workers

In the next decade, significant technological changes in the communications and data-processing industries will increase the demand for knowledge workers. These employees tend to identify primarily with their profession or occupation rather than their employer, so worker loyalties as a whole are likely to switch toward the profession. Rapid technological changes will also increase the need for highly trained individuals and increase the likelihood of employee obsolescence.

Two aspects of the economy with significant impact on personnel activities are financial uncertainties (economic fluctuations) and inflation. Financial uncertainties encourage companies to expand their product lines so that they will be less affected by declines in demand for any one product. The resulting large multidivisional organizations need varied yet centralized personnel policies and administration.

Inflationary excesses of recent years may result in a substantial recession in the 1980s. If so, organizations need to confront the issue of unemployment in order to prevent potential social disruption.[4] In addition, inflation will challenge organizations seeking to compensate employees for performance and retain a motivated work force.

TRENDS IN PERSONNEL MANAGEMENT

The same factors that are making personnel management more important are also creating new trends in this field. Although I could speculate about many of these trends, I will analyze here only those that are most significant and that have the greatest likelihood of occurring. These trends are analyzed for each personnel function presented in the preceding chapters. First, however, several trends that influence the entire area of personnel management should be examined.

The two superordinate goals of personnel departments will continue to be productivity and the quality of work life, both of which reflect a concern for the needs of the organization and the worker. Society's needs will continue to be served by equal employment and affirmative action regulations and all other laws relevant to personnel management. These laws will be used as criteria for evaluating personnel activities even more than they are now.

Another general trend of note is that human resource managers are becoming less likely to spend their entire careers in personnel work. For instance, line managers will serve in personnel roles as prerequisite training for higher management positions. But because the personnel department will increasingly be considered a profit center, it will command the best talent that the organization has to offer. Those in personnel will need to be highly educated and experienced. MBAs in general management or advanced degrees in management or the behavioral sciences will become quite common.

The new breed of personnel manager will play a highly important role in the organization: "The human resource management specialist will simultaneously be viewed as a member of the total management team, as an internal consultant to all levels of management and as a source of expertise."[5] These personnel specialists will also be charged with translating the latest personnel theory and research into practical applications.

Finally, there will be increased recognition of the internal and external environmental factors influencing the effective management of human resources. This. along with an increased recognition of the interdependence of personnel functions and activities, will bring about greater concern for human resource planning.

Planning for Human Resource Management

Human Resource Planning and Programming.   Many organizations have long engaged in various forms of planning. In most, however, human resource plans were built around decisions that had already been made.[6] This was possible when human resources were abundant and organizations had a great degree of freedom to hire and fire, but it is no longer possible. Organizations must now integrate human resource plans with the strategic plans of the total organization. This involves forecasting the human resources needed to carry out the organization's plans—for instance, for expansion or even for retrenchment or reduction in operations.

This corporate-level integration of human resource planning offers the opportunity to generate more understanding of and support for the organization's personnel objectives. Corporate-level integration is also a necessity if the human resource planning is to be effective:

When human resources issues are not included in the formal planning process, directives from top management about employee relations policy often are met by lower managers with indifference or in some instances, outright hostility.[7]

Job Analysis.   As organizations attempt to meet equal employment and affirmative action requirements, there is an increased need to justify staffing procedures and performance appraisal results. A critical basis for this justification is the job analysis, which provides adequate details of both the duties that a job entails and the skills needed to perform those duties. Thus organizations without a formal job analysis program will be likely to institute one, and those that already have such a program will review their job analyses to ensure that they are current and that the skills listed are really necessary.

In addition to having the conventional descriptions of job duties and employee skill qualifications, more job analyses will include a description of the results expected and even the rewards that are part of the job. Such a description might include design characteristics and context of the job.

Staffing

Recruitment.   Because fewer individuals will be entering the labor force in the 1980s than previously, entry positions may remain open even though there is a surplus of middle and senior managers. Consequently, recruiting efforts will have to be increased for entry-level positions and reduced at higher levels.

In addition, fewer managers will be hired from other organizations. The rare middle- and upper-level management positions that open up will be reserved for people who are already part of the organization. Because there will be fewer opportunities for upward movement, promotion will also come to include lateral movements.

Rapid technological changes and the growing potential for employee obsolescence may make demotions more necessary. The impact of obsolescence and demotion will be eased by renaming it a **downward transfer.**

Selection.   Because of the trends in recruiting, there will be a need to select more entry-level employees. And although it would appear that selection for higher-level positions will become easier because fewer positions will be available, the opposite will actually be the case. The better an organization's affirmative action program, the more employees there will be going after these scarce positions.

But an organization must still be careful to fill vacancies with qualified employees. The burden will be on the organization to defend its selection procedures, so it will have to spend more time making each selection decision. It will also need to defend and explain its decisions to those who are passed over, particularly if they are passed over because the organization is complying with a consent decree or an affirmative action program.

Both recruitment and selection will continue to be closely constrained by the need to comply with employment regulations. At least three regulatory trends are expected:

- The courts are likely to give more weight to the 1978 Uniform Guidelines on Selection Procedures than they did those of 1970.
- The courts are also likely to deal with more cases involving employment discrimination against the handicapped and the elderly.
- Content validity procedures and an insistence on sound job analysis will be more accepted by the courts.[8]

Socialization and Accommodation.   As the work force becomes more diverse in values and preferences, organizations will find it more necessary to accommodate to the needs of their employees than ever before. Indeed, to serve fairly the needs of both the organization and the individual, the entire staffing function will have to be based on realistic views of the job, supervisor, colleagues, and entire organization.

An important accommodation that organizations will provide to individuals is alternative work arrangements. Employees will be able to choose, within limitations, when they will work, what number of hours they will work, and even whether they will share a work schedule with another person. The American Management Association's Center for Management Development also predicts that there will be more nontraditional office hours to make better use of high-cost equipment and high-rent office space; that as a part of this trend there will be three-shift offices, which may call for a 25-percent salary premium for night work; and that business will be conducted from homes, automobiles, and even computer terminals. Thus employees can remain outside the actual space of business but be working nonetheless.

Appraising and Compensating

Appraising.   With the increased emphasis on fair employment practices, greater care will be taken in appraising employee performance. This care will manifest itself in the use of more objective measures of performance and a decline in the use of more subjective, less performance-related measures. In addition, the system in which an employee's performance is embedded will increasingly be taken into account.

Managing ineffective performance will become even more important in the years ahead. Thus organizations will become more concerned about feeding back the results of performance appraisals to employees as frequently as possible. However, the idea of mandatory retirement will become less popular, so it will no longer be so easy to wait for poor performers to retire. As a means of correcting poor performance, **performance contracts** will be brought into use. Employees agree to achieve clearly specified objectives within a given time period, and failure to do so results in agreed-on disciplinary procedures.

Organizations will also examine their own policies and practices for possible causes of ineffective performance. When organizations terminate employees for ineffective performance, they will make sure that it is the employee, not the organization, who is in fact at fault.

Compensating. There are several major trends in compensating employees. First is a change in the basis on which compensation is decided. Generally organizations fix the pay for jobs according to an evaluation of the job content and characteristics. In accordance with nondiscriminatory pay policies, people with the same jobs (or jobs of equal evaluation) receive equal pay. However, women still tend to earn less than men because the jobs they have traditionally held have been determined through job evaluation to be less valuable or of less worth to the organization. Some people argue that the jobs many women perform are just as important to the organization as those men perform. In other words, the job evaluation system has biased job worth in favor of traditional men's jobs. In the 1980s, then, there may well be a move to determine the pay of jobs by their intrinsic worth to the organization. The result could be substantial increases in compensation costs if many jobs are upgraded rather than downgraded to achieve equal pay for jobs of equal worth.

Another trend in compensation is **salary compression.** Leveling pressures in our economy are decreasing the spread in pay between various positions in an organization. Unions have done much to raise wages at the lower end, and salaries for middle-level jobs have remained about the same due to stable profits, low productivity, and the progressive nature of the tax and Social Security system. It appears that salary compression will increase during the 1980s, making promotion to middle-level jobs less attractive.

Since indirect compensation is becoming such a large part of the total compensation package, organizations will have to increase their communications about it. And to help make indirect compensation more appealing, organizations will increasingly adopt individualized benefit plans.

The use of indirect compensation will in general be stimulated by several factors:
- Continued pressure from organized labor
- Increased leisure time available to all workers (both a benefit and a stimulant for more benefits)
- Higher levels of affluence
- New medical advances
- Further social legislation
- Continued demands by minorities and women for equal employment benefits[9]

Specifically, "labor is expected to be very active in stimulating the accelerating benefit programs and manufacturing is the sector which will be affected most."[10] The federal government can also be expected to play a major role in benefit growth, both by providing public benefits and by encouraging the growth of private programs. Of course, organizations—with or without a union presence—will be important shapers and providers of indirect benefits, especially as they try to serve the needs of an increasingly heterogeneous work force.

Although most current benefit programs are expected to grow in terms of both the number of employees covered and the dollar value of benefits offered, some are expected to grow more than others. The greatest growth is expected in the three major areas of indirect benefits: protection programs, pay for time not worked, and employee services and perquisites.

The protection benefits provided by government are likely to increase through the continued liberalization of Social Security benefits and the expansion of worker's compensation and unemployment insurance programs. In 1978 alone, all but four states increased temporary total disability benefits. Weekly payments now range from $87.50 in Arkansas to $607.85 in Alaska. The number of workers covered also increased, and a number of changes were made to improve the administration of benefits.[11] The 1978 changes in state unemployment insurance were not so favorable, however. Only three states increased the maximum weekly benefit, and New Jersey decreased its weekly benefit.[12] However, many states did amend tax provisions to restore unemployment funds and to help individuals repay advances borrowed from the Unemployment Trust Fund Account.[13]

The trend in private protection programs has been toward increased coverage and reform in administration of the programs. In a group of 131 pension plans, the Bureau of Labor Statistics reported that benefits had increased an average of 20.6 percent between 1974 and 1978. "By 1978, all but one of the plans studied had a vesting provision [a guarantee of benefits], and all met the [Employees' Retirement Income Security Act] age and service requirements for vesting compared with only 50 percent in 1974."[14] The final settlement between the United Auto Workers and General Motors Corporation in 1979 increased pension benefits by 27 to 40 percent over three years for both future retirees and the 137,000 current GM pensioners. "By 1982, workers who retire under 30-and-out—that is, with 30 years of service, regardless of age—will receive $553.50 a month plus a $321.50 supplement to encourage them to retire early and open up jobs for new workers."[15] By the way, the total compensation base at GM is $14.28 per hour. Of this, 33.4 percent, or $4.77, represents indirect benefits.

The number of days off with pay keeps increasing, too. The GM-UAW contract increased the number of days off with pay by eleven. Another trend is the reduction in the number of hours worked, with pay remaining almost the same or even increasing. "Since 1940 the average work year has fallen by about 235 hours, or more than 10%."[16] The work week is shrinking not only because of added days off with pay but also because of compressed work weeks. In 1978, 1.4 million workers, or 2.2 percent of the work force, were on weekly schedules of less than five days. An extreme form of the compressed work week is the plan at General Tire and Rubber. It has two plants where some individuals work only two twelve-hour weekend shifts each week and are still considered fulltime employees. They receive nearly all the same indirect benefits and are paid for thirty-six hours of work.

Many companies are giving time off with pay to employees who volunteer their time and talents to public groups and organizations needing assistance. There are many different types of company-sponsored volunteer programs. For example, "employees of the Hartford Insurance Company in Hartford, Connecticut, take advantage of their lunch hours to deliver meals to the elderly and shutins."[17] The volunteering employees are often paid for the time spent doing volunteer work or are given prizes and awards at annual banquets, as at Avon Products.

A rapid increase is expected in employer-sponsored day-care centers for the dependents of employees. In addition, companies will set up more tuition-reimbursed programs and programs to provide employees with psychological counseling to help them in adjusting to both job-related and personal situations. Organizations will help employees through the psychological trauma of involuntary terminations and the arduous task of finding a new organization and a new job.[18] Counseling employees about career obsolescence and career development will also become increasingly prevalent.

Developing the Employee

In the future, organizations will provide training and development to prevent employee obsolescence. The training and development will be done less on a one-shot basis and more as part of a package of career development opportunities. This shift toward career management will demand that employees take greater responsibility for their own career development.

Second careers, reeducation, consultation, and parttime work are becoming common activities for our older population. Currently about 20 percent of the adult population is between forty-five and sixty-four years of age. By the year 2000, when that figure will reach 38 percent, incentives for retirement and the indexing of benefits will be very important.[19] Already, organizational preretirement programs are steadily improving.

Establishing and Maintaining Effective Labor Relations

Organizing. Although the proportion of the work force that is unionized has been leveling off in recent years, this trend is expected to reverse:

Over the next few years we expect the percent in unions to increase again to over 30 percent, perhaps to an historic high, primarily as a result of organization in the public sector. Compared to approximately 30 percent today, we expect that fully 75 percent of public employees will be organized by 1985, representing 40 percent of all organized labor.[20]

The two fastest-growing unions in the United States today are the American Federation of State and Municipal Employees and the United Food and Commercial Workers Union. They will continue this growth into the 1980s.

There are indications that the U.S. Congress may change the entire process of organizing. A controversial labor law (H.R. 8410–S. 2467) was presented to Congress in 1978. Although it did not pass, several of its provisions indicate the possible direction of labor law in the 1980s:

● The National Labor Relations Board (NLRB) would increase in size from five to seven members, with a high probability that the additional members would be prolabor.

● Cases before the NLRB would be reviewed and affirmed by a two-person panel. As a result, the board could "rubber stamp" decisions of administrative-law judges instead of providing proper review.

● The NLRB would be required to rewrite some of its own criteria for decision making, possibly ignoring carefully established precedents in the process.

● Unions would be allowed to organize on company time on company property. Each time an employer used company time to respond to union literature, union representatives would be allowed the same forum. Unions, but not employers, would be able to contact employees at home, by phone, or in person—and, of course, at union meetings.

● Unions would be able to call elections with only fifteen days' notice to employers or to postpone elections up to seventy-five days. Employers would have no control at all over these activities.

- Court review of NLRB decisions would be narrowly limited.
- The NLRB would be able to assess punitive damages to employers who attempt to fight union representation by disallowing them access to federal contracts for three years.
- Employers exercising their right to court review of NLRB decisions could be forced to forfeit their rights to collective bargaining.
- The NLRB would be required to seek a court injunction against any employer who fired someone during an organizing campaign, even if the employer acted in good faith.[21]

Labor-Management Cooperation. Because of the need for improved productivity, international competition, workers' rights, and industrial democracy, the European labor-relations model will become increasingly popular. Codetermination, work councils, and union-controlled funds are all ideas that are transferable to the United States. Multinational companies have been gaining experience with the European model for several years. Chrysler, for instance, already has a union representative on its board of directors. A more detailed explanation of codetermination is presented in a later section of this chapter.

Improving the Work Environment

Sociopsychological Aspects of the Environment. Eaton's chairman, E. M. DeWindt, had this to say about the quality of work life:

About ten years ago, Eaton launched a massive expansion program, a long-range project involving the building of nearly a score of new plants around the nation. We knew that each plant design would incorporate the most modern methods and machinery for productivity. And, realizing that productivity is really a function of people, we decided that our employee relations practices and policies should get as much streamlining as the plants and equipment. When we looked at our traditional practices, it was obvious that they weren't designed for rushing into the 21st century. These practices were born of mistrust, agitation and negotiation. This was apparent in the paraphernalia and terminology that went along with them. We had the tyrannical time clocks and mindless bells and buzzers. We had probationary periods, posted work rules, disciplinary proceedings and restrictive holiday-eligibility rules for production workers that stamped them as second-class members of the total team.

The building of so many new plants gave us a unique opportunity to start from scratch, and our employee relations people were challenged to break away from tradition and develop a program built on mutual trust.

They responded with vigor and enthusiasm, and today nearly 20 Eaton plants operate under the new philosophy. There are no time clocks in these plants, no bells or buzzers or whistles to remind people that Big Daddy is watching them. All employees of these plants—management, office and production—are salaried, and all participate in major decisions concerning the operation. There are no paycheck penalties for casual absences or tardiness, no segregated parking lots.

The results have been dramatic and productive. Absenteeism averages 2% in these plants and turnover is almost zero. Productivity ranges from 30 to 40% higher than in traditional plants. There is a genuine feeling of involvement and belonging throughout the plants. The program has passed the tests of good and bad times, and many of its elements are working their way into older, organized plants.

While it is true that such sweeping changes could only be made in new and unorganized plants, this is not a program to combat the unions, but rather to combat the climate of mistrust that so often and so easily pervades a manufacturing operation. It has helped bring about productive negotiations in unionized plants, and we are convinced that both management and labor will pursue the course of mutual trust at a greater degree than ever before. . . .[22]

Many organizations are adopting QWL programs. Flextime and job-sharing arrangements, participatory management, management-by-objectives projects and more work redesign projects will all become more commonplace in the 1980s.

The number of stress management programs that organizations offer will increase by a significant number. There will be greater concern for potential stress due to job assignments, travel, management practices, and a general lack of match between employee ability and job demands and between employee needs and job rewards. As one consequence, organizations will offer more physical exercise programs and even time and room for meditation.

Analysis of the Work Environment.   The trend toward collecting and analyzing personnel data is expected to continue. The two major forces making this trend a necessity are the government and top managements of organizations. Equal opportunity laws require the organization to keep extensive records of such employment practices as recruitment and selection. The organization must demonstrate that the procedures it used to select job applicants have validity. It must also provide safety and health information.

The personnel department will be given a larger role in the organization if it can show how its functions and activities influence the efficiency and effectiveness of the organization. For example, it can demonstrate how a QWL program reduces the rate of absenteeism, and it can show how much money is saved as a result of the decline in absenteeism.

PERSONNEL PRACTICES IN OTHER COUNTRIES

Human resource managers in the United States can learn valuable lessons by looking at what other nations are doing. Although many comparisons are possible, only those with Europe, Japan, and Canada are made here. The focus is on the most significant differences and, in some cases, on practices that might be adopted in the United States.

Europe

Codetermination. The philosophy of labor-management relations stating that worker interests are best served if employees have a direct say in the management of the company is known as **codetermination.** Originally conceived in Germany, codetermination now exists in Sweden, the Netherlands, France, Norway, Denmark, Luxembourg, and Austria. [23]

Codetermination provides for union seats on the boards of directors of corporations. It encourages managers to consult with unions before making major organizational changes, whether they be mergers, investments, or personnel matters like plant closings and relocations. If management disagrees with a union position, management prevails. However, unions may veto subcontracts by the company, and they have access to all company information.

Codetermination also makes it possible for unions to propose asset formation. Such proposals seek to transfer funds provided by the employer to the control of the union. At this time, however, these proposals have been rejected by management.

Nevertheless, the ideas of codetermination and union-controlled funds could be applied in the United States. Although the European framework may not be adopted in this country in the 1980s, it is likely that increased cooperation between labor and management on issues of productivity and quality of work life will occur.

Quality of Work Life. Although the Volvo QWL experiment was mentioned briefly in Chapter 18, it is useful to describe it more fully here, pointing out differences between that project and the Tarrytown project, also described in Chapter 18. The Volvo QWL projects have been implemented in several plants in Sweden, but the most famous is at Volvo's new assembly plant in the city of Kalmar. This plant, in operation since 1972, uses work teams instead of the traditional assembly line (which is used in Tarrytown) and allows employees to design and organize their own work. The plant was built in response to employees' job hopping, absenteeism, apathetic attitudes, and antagonism and to the extremely low level of unemployment in Sweden, which means that the pool of replacement workers is very small.

In contrast to the Tarrytown project, Volvo's QWL project made substantial improvements by changing the technology for assembling cars. Although changing the technology of an organization is not easy or inexpensive and entails some risk, Volvo proved that it can be done successfully. In fact, changing the technology may be the only way to satisfy the needs and values of employees.

When we started thinking about reorganizing the way we worked, the first bottleneck seemed to be production and technology. We couldn't really reorganize the work to suit the people unless we also changed the technology that chained people to the assembly line. [24]

Now car assembly is done in work groups of about twenty people. The change in technology has been accompanied by a new climate of cooperation and partnership and an improved physical working environment.

As with the Tarrytown project, employee participation through councils and committees resulted in increased employee involvement and further improvements in the work itself. In contrast to Tarrytown, however, this participation is implemented in accordance with a 1977 Swedish law calling for "full consultation with employees and full participation by their representatives in decision making from board level to the shop floor."

A QWL project has also been instituted at Volvo's "bread and butter" plant in Torslanda. Here, participation and autonomous groups are the two dominant techniques, rather than just participation, as at Kalmar. This is due mostly to the fact that Torslanda has a large-scale assembly line and employs 8,000 workers, compared to 600 at Kalmar.

A technique used in both plants at the discretion of the workers is job rotation. This is done within the relatively autonomous work groups. Today approximately 70 percent of the assembly workers engage in job rotation. "There will always be a few people, however, especially older ones, who don't want to change [jobs] at all."[25] This recognition and acceptance of employee differences, which was also characteristic of the Tarrytown program, is an important aspect of the long-run success of QWL projects in general. Without the acceptance of employee differences, changes and QWL techniques are likely to be resisted, and thus improvement in the quality of work life is less likely to take place.

Japan

The Highly Motivated Work Force. Some of us laugh at the Japanese when we read that a shift going on the job in Japan applauds the shift leaving the job. But when you examine it, the practice is not really something to laugh about. The Japanese are highly motivated—their increase in productivity clearly demonstrates that. And the Japanese appreciate and understand the dignity of work. The shift leaving the plant, having done its job well and having produced a high-quality product, is deserving of applause.[26]

Although the Japanese may be more highly motivated, they do not necessarily work any harder than Americans. There are, however, several important differences affecting the management of human resources in Japan and in the United States, as described by Masaya Hattori, a Japanese businessperson working for the World Bank in Washington D.C.:

Japanese are often characterized as workaholics, both in the Tokyo newspapers and in the international press. . . .

Is it true that Japanese work harder than others? I think not. . . .

The Japanese practice of working a half day on Saturday makes little sense [in the United States]. Since most employees commute long distances, spending two hours traveling in order to put in three hours at the office is a total waste of time.

But the five-day workweek is not as commonly adhered to in Western countries as many Japanese think it is. Of the 250 people in my department, at least a third put in regular overtime without pay. Senior officials work both Saturdays and Sundays at least once a month. A "9-to-5 man" is someone who is considered lazy and refuses to do more than the minimum.

In American companies, it is the top executives, those who make the innovative, risk-taking decisions, who put in the longest hours. Lower-level employees, those who perform routine tasks, are rarely required to work late.

In a Japanese company, heavy demands are placed on lower-level staff, and they often are given responsibilities which would be handled by a top executive in the United States. All workers are expected to be flexible enough to perform any task the department has before it, and for this reason junior staff must put in long hours.

In my opinion, younger employees in Japan are much more capable than their counterparts elsewhere. They are given responsibility much earlier in their careers because complex tasks are delegated to a much lower level. . . .

Just the opposite of Western companies, the proportion of competent people declines with seniority.

The cause of this curious reversal is the unique seniority system in Japan, which more often than not causes a retrogression of talent. Because of guaranteed lifetime employment, the less able are not weeded out through selective advancement. Quite frankly, few Japanese executives over the age of 45 would be able to handle the duties of an equivalent post in Europe or the United States.

Another difference between Japanese and Western organizations is the place of continuing education. A common Japanese misconception is that the American employee leaves his worries at the office and spends his free time in pursuit of leisure entertainment.

Nothing is further from the truth. The most able executives go to school or study on their own in order to continually upgrade their professional and technical skills.

In the Japanese lifetime employment system, a worker may undergo training during business hours at corporate expense. In the Western firm, 100% of the time on the job is devoted to work. If the employee wishes to improve his skills, he does it on his own time.[27]

Employee Socialization and Development.   The Japanese also differ substantially in how they train today's college graduate to become tomorrow's manager.[28] There are two major aspects of this training: preemployment education, or socialization and training given before the first day on the job, and initial managerial education. This training has five general aims:

● To educate new graduates as members of the company, emphasizing self-discipline and the transition from student life to company life

● To teach professionalism and the significance and meaning of work

● To provide background information about the company and to familiarize employees with distinctive management trends

● To familiarize employees with basic company procedures and fundamental business rules and etiquette

● To cultivate a spirit of harmony and teamwork among employees[29]

Preemployment education consists of communications between the company and the future employees, who are still in school. Some companies recommend to future employees what they should read before starting work. Future employees are frequently sent a directory of all new recruits, an employee handbook, a booklet on health and nutrition, and even words of encouragement from senior employees. Many companies also hold meetings that provide an opportunity for future employees to get to know one another.

[These meetings] afford an opportunity for the future employees to learn the company song, to meet senior employees who are graduates of the same university, to visit the factories and see exhibitions of the company's products and to become familiar with the company's various departments and divisions.[30]

Initial managerial education has three parts: orientation, work experience, and residency. Exhibit 20.1 shows a typical set of orientation topics. The program of work experience involves real grass-roots exposure, especially in the area of production. For example, the current president of Matsushita Electric Works spent his first six months carrying and shifting goods in the company's storage area. Most of the present executives of Japan's major companies have also passed through similar on-the-job training programs.[31]

Exhibit 20.1 Typical Japanese New-Employee Orientation

Topics	Contents
Company background	Background information
	Organizational structure, occupational hierarchy
	Long-range plans
	Operating budget and financial situation
	Employee-employer relations, labor unions
	Working conditions and regulations
	Salary structure
	Employee welfare and fringe benefits
Products	Introduction to the range of company's products
	Physical structure, working principles, price and users of company's main products, and their value as merchandise in relation to competitive products
Production	Variation, flow, preparation of operational directives
	Interpretation of production charts, blueprints
	Prnciples of production processes
	Product management and cost accounting
Sales	Performance and market share
	Future perspective and trends of competitors
	Dealer and agent relations
	Sales techniques
Basic business skills	Execises to increase proficiency with abacus, slide rule, business machines, and computers
	Business etiquette, including telephone manners, use of business cards, use of deferential language and posture, seating order in social space (restaurants, public and private transportation, meetings)
	Instruction in business letter writing, format, and expression
	Fundamental statistical knowledge pertaining to such areas as marketing research and financial statements

From "The Japanese Method of Preparing Today's Graduate to Become Tomorrow's Manager," by H. Tanaka. Reprinted with permission. *Personnel Journal,* copyright February 1980, p. 111.

During orientation and the work experience program, new employees live together in company residences. Here they learn social rules, etiquette, human relations, and punctuality, all considered necessary for an effective manager.

An important aspect of this training and development is the evaluation of how well the new employees have done. Mitsubishi Corporation and Isetan Department Stores, for example, administer a quiz, which the recruits must pass, on the essential knowledge for handling the companies' products. Immediate supervisors of these new employees also file reports, which are later used in identifying the work areas new employees should be placed in and the jobs they should be rotated through.

Canada

As in the United States, the Canadian labor force is slightly less than half of the total population. Women, however, represent only about a third of the labor force, as compared with approximately 45 percent in the United States.

Pensions. There are many similarities between the two nations. For example, Canada has the Canada Pension Plan and the Quebec Pension Plan in the province of Quebec, both of which are similar to the U.S. Social Security system. The Canada Pension Plan (CPP) is a mandatory plan for all employees except federal workers. Like the Social Security system, the CPP pays retirement benefits, disability pensions, benefits for children of disabled contributors, orphans' benefits, and pension benefits to survivors' spouses. Canada also has private pension plans, although fewer than 40 percent of all employees are covered by these plans. The administration of these plans is governed by the Pension Benefits Act, which is less extensive in its regulation of private pension plans than the Employees' Retirement Income Security Act.

Health and Safety. Employee health and safety are major concerns in Canada, as they are in the United States. In both nations safety and health are regulated at the federal level—in Canada by the Canada Labor Code and in the United States by the Occupational Safety and Health Act—and at the state or province level by standards and regulations adopted and enforced by the state or province safety and health agencies. However, whereas OSHA covers all employees regardless of the type of employer, Canada has a separate health and safety program for federal employees. In Canada the provinces generally exert more authority over health and safety issues than do the states in the United States.

Human Rights Legislation. Relatively comprehensive human rights legislation now exists at the federal level and in each of Canada's ten provinces. This legislation follows a common pattern, so that it is simplest to outline the pattern and then note deviations from the pattern.[32]

The typical Canadian human rights statute prohibits discrimination on grounds of race, color, religion, ancestry, place of origin, marital status, sex, or age, when such discrimination involves employment or trade union membership, services or accommodations that are available to the public, residential or commercial rentals, or public notices. (Some of the statutes define age so as to limit the effect of this particular ground of discrimination. Such definitions normally have an upper limit of age sixty-five, but the lower limit varies from nineteen to forty-five.) Some of the statutes also prohibit discrimination by occupational or professional associations, employer or business associations, and employment agencies. The statutes are enforced by a Human Rights Commission, which employs staff to investigate and conciliate complaints of violations of the statute. If the commission staff is unable to conciliate a complaint successfully, an ad hoc tribunal or board of inquiry may be appointed to hold a public hearing. The commission normally takes the lead in supporting the complaint at this hearing. If the tribunal finds that discrimination has occurred, it can formulate a remedial order. The legislation varies as to whether the tribunal issues the order or recommends the order to either the Human Rights Commission or a designated cabinet minister who has the authority to issue it. Normally, the order can be enforced by court proceedings and can be appealed to a court. Violations of the statutes are also subject to the ordinary penal process, although consent of either the Human Rights Commission or a designated cabinet minister is usually necessary to prosecute. In addition, recent case law supports the view that a violation of the statute may give rise to civil action.

In addition to the grounds commonly covered, the federal statute prohibits discrimination on the basis of criminal conviction if the person has been pardoned.[33] In the case of the physically handicapped, only employment discrimination is prohibited, and employers are not compelled to renovate their premises to accommodate the handicapped. The federal statute addresses sex discrimination by requiring that employers provide equal pay for work of equal value. This contrasts with provincial legislation, which does not affect pay differentials between jobs so long as there is no ongoing practice of denying access to these jobs because of sex. Penal proceedings for discrimination under the federal statute are possible only where a person violates the terms of an agreed-on settlement of a complaint. Otherwise, there must be a hearing procedure on the violation and, if necessary, court enforcement of the resulting decision.

Labor Relations. Approximately one-third of the Canadian labor force is unionized. About three-fourths of those belong to unions affiliated with the Canadian Labor Congress (CLC). As in the United States the union local is the basic labor unit. The CLC is the dominant labor group at the federal level. Its political influence may be compared to that of the AFL-CIO.

Although the labor laws of Canada are similar to those in the United States, there are several noteworthy differences.[34] Since 1925, the majority of Canadian workers have been covered by provincial, not federal, labor laws, whereas in the United States over 90 percent of the workers are covered by a federal law, the National Labor Relations Act. The Canadian federal law, the Industrial Relations and Disputes and Investigation Act, covers less than 10 percent of the labor force.

Canadian labor laws require frequent intervention by government bodies before a strike can take place. In the United States such intervention is largely voluntary. Compulsory arbitration is also more common in Canada. The most recent law requiring such arbitration is the Public Service Staff Relations Act of 1967. This law also allows nonmanagerial federal employees to join unions and bargain collectively.

The history of labor relations in Canada and the United States is similar in that it follows British common law, but there is one major difference: In Canada the provincial governments rather than the federal government developed as the center for most labor law. Since the 1925 decision in the case of *Toronto Electric Commissioners* v. *Snider,* Canadian workers have been governed primarily by provincial laws (except for employees working for the federal government and industries under federal coverage as defined by amendments to the Industrial Disputes Investigation Act of 1973—for instance longshoring, seafaring, provincial railroads, Crown corporations, and airlines). Many of the features of the U.S. Taft-Hartley Act of 1947 have been incorporated into the labor laws of the Canadian provinces.

SUMMARY

This final chapter has presented trends that are likely to occur in personnel work in the 1980s. Many of these trends are based on declining productivity, substantial demographic shifts, changing work force expectations, government regulation, new technologies, and economic conditions. Not only do these forces shape the trends in personnel management, but they also increase its importance.

Effective human resource management is considered by many organizations to be vital to organizational growth and increased productivity. The effective use of human resources requires that organizations be concerned with the needs of their employees. Consequently, the drive to increase effectiveness should benefit employees as well as organizations. Because it is likely that this drive will be made within legal constraints and equal employment legislation, society should also benefit.

Thus personnel managers will have a vital role to play in serving the organization, its employees, and society. Playing this role will be both difficult and challenging. Are you ready for the job?

KEY CONCEPTS

codetermination   performance contract   salary compression

downward transfer

DISCUSSION QUESTIONS

1. Why will personnel management continue to gain in importance in the 1980s?

2. How will work force expectations and demographic changes influence personnel management?

3. How will the entire area of personnel management change in the 1980s? What will be the criteria on which personnel activities are likely to be evaluated?

4. Why will planning become more critical for personnel managers in the 1980s?

5. How might job evaluation change in the 1980s?

6. How does the Japanese style of bringing a new recruit into the company differ from the way a U.S. organization would do it?

7. What is codetermination? Do you think it should be applied in the United States? Give reasons for your answer.

8. What are some of the differences between Canadian and U.S. personnel practices?

ENDNOTES

1. F. E. Schuster, "Human Resources Management: Key to the Future," *Personnel Administrator*, December 1978, p. 66.

2. Schuster, p. 35.

3. L. A. Wangler, "The Intensification of the Personnel Role," *Personnel Journal*, February 1979, p. 115.

4. D. Q. Mills, "Human Resources in the 1980's," *Harvard Business Review*, July/August, 1979, p. 135.

5. Schuster, p. 67.

6. M. R. Schiavoni, "Employee Relations: Where Will It Be in 1985?" *Personnel Administrator*, March 1978, p. 28.

7. Reprinted by permission of the *Harvard Business Review*. Excerpt from "Human Resources in the 1980's" by D. Q. Mills (July/August 1979), p. 160. Copyright © 1979 by the President and Fellows of Harvard College; all rights reserved.

8. R. D. Arvey, *Fairness in Selecting Employees* (Reading, Mass.: Addison-Wesley, 1979), pp. 228–232.

9. T. J. Gordon and R. E. LeBleu, "Employee Benefits, 1979–1985," *Harvard Business Review*, January/February 1979, pp. 93–107.

10. Gordon and LeBleu, p. 96.

11. G. Minor, "Worker's Compensation Laws: Key State Amendments of 1978," *Monthly Labor Review*, January 1979, pp. 43–50.

12. D. Runner, "State Unemployment Insurance: Changes During 1978," *Monthly Labor Review*, February 1979, pp. 13–16.

13. Runner.

14. R. Frumkin and D. Schmidt, "Pension Improvements Since 1974 Reflect Inflation, New U.S. Law," *Monthly Labor Review*, April 1979, pp. 32–37.

15. "Will the Auto Pact Break Pattern Bargaining?" *Business Week*, October 1, 1979, p. 92.

16. "A Full-Time Job: Weekends Only," *Business Week*, October 5, 1979, p. 150.

17. "Time Off for Good Behavior," *TWA Ambassador*, October 1979, pp. 38–39.

18. C. H. Driessnack, "Outplacement: A Benefit for Both Employee and Company," *Personnel Administrator*, January 1978, pp. 24–29.
D. J. Kravetz, "Counseling Strategies for Involuntary Terminations," *Personnel Administrator*, October 1978, pp. 49–54.

19. B. S. Murphy, "The Past Is Prologue: Building Better Industrial Relations in the '80s," *Personnel Journal*, January 1980, p. 35.

20. Schiavoni, p. 27.

21. Wangler, p. 115.

22. "A Decade of Rapid Change: The Outlook for Human Resources Management in the '80s" by J. C. Toedtman. Reprinted with permission *Personnel Journal* Copyright January 1980, p. 31.

23. R. J. Kahn, *Codetermination in Business* (New York: Praeger, 1980).

24. Reprinted by permission from the *Harvard Business Review*. Excerpt from "How Volvo Adapts Work to People" by P. G. Gyllenhammar (July/August 1977), p. 106. Copyright © 1977 by the President and Fellows of Harvard College; all rights reserved.

25. Gyllenhammar, p. 110.

26. "The Past Is Prologue: Building Better Industrial Relations in the 1980's" by B. S. Murphy. Reprinted with permission *Personnel Journal* copyright January 1980, p. 24.

27. M. Hattori, "Japanese Don't Work Harder," *Cleveland Plain Dealer,* 29 December 1979, p. 13-A. © *The Plain Dealer*. Reprinted with permission.

28. H. Tanaka, "The Japanese Method of Preparing Today's Graduate to Become Tomorrow's Manager," *Personnel Journal,* February 1980, pp. 109–112.

29. Tanaka, pp. 109–110.

30. "The Japanese Method of Preparing Today's Graduate to Become Tomorrow's Manager" by H. Tanaka. Reprinted with permission *Personnel Journal,* copyright February 1980, p. 110.

31. Tanaka.

32. This section on human rights legislation has been prepared by Robert W. Kerr, Professor of Law, University of Windsor and is gratefully used with his permission.

33. *Canadian Human Rights Act,* Statutes of Canada, 1976–1977, chapter 33.

34. D. A. Peach, and D. Keuchle, *The Practice of Industrial Relations* (Toronto: McGraw-Hill Ryerson, 1975).
   For an in-depth discussion of the personnel practices in Canadian firms see, V. V. Murray and D. E. Dimick, "Personnel Administration in Large and Middle-Sized Canadian Businesses," Study No. 25, Ottawa, Canada, Royal Commission on Corporate Concentration, November 1979.

Jobs and Career Paths in Personnel and Human Resource Management

Numerous jobs are available in the field of personnel and human resource management. As suggested in Chapter 1, people seeking a career in the field may enter directly or indirectly through an operations line job. Depending upon experience and education, new personnel employees can be specialists or generalists, managers or nonmanagers. A typical first job for someone fresh out of college and without much experience would be as a nonmanagerial specialist, say in compensation analysis or employment counseling.

Career paths in personnel depend on the company. Since most large organizations undertake all of the personnel functions discussed in this book, they often have groups or units that specialize. These groups or units are all part of the company's office, division, or department of personnel and human resources management. One could spend an entire career working in just one unit or could work in several different units. However, the health and safety group or the medical unit is less likely than the others to encourage cross-fertilization.

In large companies, the way to make it to the top of the personnel department is by coming up through just one unit or functional area or by working in another part of the organization and then coming in at a managerial level. It is common for a person on the way up to leave an area of specialty and become a generalist. Thus the trip to the top often involves a tour of duty as manager of all the personnel functions in a regional office or plant of the parent company. One may be a specialist in either the parent company (headquarters) or at the plant or regional office, then become manager in a specialty, then become manager of all personnel functions in a plant or office, and then return to headquarters. Back at headquarters, one may become a director of an entire unit (in charge of one or several functions). The next step is to become vice president of personnel for the entire company.

Here are some typical job titles found in personnel departments:

- Personnel interviewer
- Employment assistant
- Claims examiner
- Employment counselor
- Senior employee benefits counselor
- Nurse
- Training services coordinator
- Personnel administration analyst
- Senior employment supervisor
- Personnel administration senior analyst
- Personnel counselor

- Compensation analyst
- Senior compensation analyst
- Personnel compensation specialist
- Personnel development specialist
- Personnel administration specialist
- Employment and placement manager
- Junior analyst
- Regional personnel manager
- Plant personnel manager
- Physician
- Assistant medical director
- Health services coordinator
- Director of employment placement
- Vice president of personnel
- Human resource planning specialist
- Recruiter
- Job analyst
- Wage and salary specialist
- Safety specialist
- Labor relations specialist
- Director of labor relations
- Manager of affirmative action

Exhibit 1.2 (in Chapter 1) shows some other personnel job titles at Xerox Corporation.

APPENDIX B
Legislation and Court Decisions Affecting Personnel and Human Resource Management

Employment Legislation

Act	Jurisdiction	Basic Provisions
Prevailing wage laws—Davis-Bacon Act (1931) and Walsh-Healey Act (1935)	Employers with government construction projects of $2,000 or more (Davis-Bacon) and government contracts of $10,000 or more	Guarantees prevailing wages to employees of government contractors
Legally required fringe benefits		
Old Age Survivor's Disability and Health Insurance (1935 and amendments)—OASDHI	Virtually all employers	Provides income and health care to retired emplyees and income to the suvivors of employees who are disabled or die
Unemployment compensation (1935)	Virtually all employers	Provides income to employees who are laid off or fired
Worker's compensation (dates differ from state to state)	Virtually all employers	Provides benefits to employees who are injured on the job and to the survivors of employees who are killed on the job.
Fair Labor Standards Act (1938 and subsequent amendments)—FLSA	Most employers (executive, administrative, and professional employees and outside salespeople are exempt from overtime provisions)	Establishes a minimum wage; controls hours through premium pay for overtime; controls working hours for children
Equal Pay Act (1963 amendment to FLSA)	Same as FLSA, but no employees are exempt	Prohibits unequal pay for men and women with equal skills, effort, and responsibility and working under similar conditions
Civil Rights Act (1964)	Employers with twenty-five or more employees, employment agencies, and labor unions	Prevents discrimination on the basis of race, color, religion, sex, or national origin; establishes Equal Employment Opportunity Commission (EEOC)
Executive Order 11246 (1965), as amended by Executive Order 11375 (1966)	Federal contractors and subcontractors with contracts over $50,000 and fifty or more employees	Prevents discrimination on the basis of race, color, religion, sex, or national origin; establishes Office of Federal Contract Compliance

Employment Legislation *(continued)*

Act	Jurisdiction	Basic Provisions
Age Discrimination in Employment Act (1967)	Employers with more than twenty-five employees	Prevents discrimination against persons forty to sixty-five years of age
Executive Order 11478 (1969)	Federal agencies	Prevents discrimination on the basis of race, color, religion, sex, or national origin
Occupational Safety and Health Act (1970)—OSHA	Most employers	"Assures as far as possible every working man and woman in the Nation safe and healthful working conditions and to preserve our human resources"
Equal Employment Opportunity Act (1972)—EEOA	Most employers, including state and local government, educational institutions, and those who employ fifteen or more people	Amends Title VII of the Civil Rights Act; increases enforcement powers of EEOC
Rehabilitation Act (1973)	Government contractors and federal agencies	Prevents discrimination against people with physical and/or mental handicaps
Employee Retirement Income Security Act (1974)—ERISA	Most employers with pension plans (no employer is required to have such a plan)	Protects employees covered by a pension plan from losses in benefits due to mismanagement, plant closings and bankruptcies, and job changes

Privacy Legislation
See Appendix F

Labor Relations Legislation: Private Sector

Act	Jurisdiction	Basic Provisions
Railway Labor Act (1926)	Railroad workers and airline employees	Provides right to organize; provides majority choice of representatives; prohibits "yellow-dog" contracts, in which the employee agrees not to join a union; outlines dispute settlement procedures
Norris-LaGuardia Act (1932)	All employers and labor organizations	Prohibits "yellow-dog" cntracts; prohibits injunctions for nonviolent union activity (strikes, picketing, and boycotts); limits union liability
National Labor Relations Act (1935)—Wagner Act	Nonmanagerial employees in private industry not covered by Railway Labor Act (RLA)	Provides right to organize; provides for collective bargaining; requires employers to bargain; requires unions to represent all members equally
Labor-Management Relations Act (1947)—Taft-Hartley Act	Nonmanagerial employees in private industry not covered by RLA	Prohibits unfair labor practices of unions; outlaws closed shop; prohibits strikes in national emergencies; requires both parties to bargain in good faith

Labor Relations Legislation: Private Sector *(continued)*

Act	Jurisdiction	Basic Provisions
Labor Management Reporting and Disclosure Act (1959)—Landrum-Griffin Act	Labor organizations	Outlines procedures for redressing internal union problems
Amendments to Taft-Hartley Act (1974)	Labor organizations	Specifies illegal activities within unions

Labor Relations Legislation: Public Sector

Act	Jurisdiction	Basic Provisions
Executive Order 10988 (1962)	Federal employees	Recognizes employees' right to join unions and bargain collectively; prohibits strikes; requires agency to meet and confer with unions on policy, practices, and working conditions
Executive Order 11491 (1969)	Federal employees	Strengthens, coordinates, and clarifies EO 10988; establishes provisions for representation elections
Executive Orders 1166, 11636, and 11838 (1975)	Federal employees	Expands EO 11491 to cover labor-management relations; cover disputes of bargaining rights; order elections; consolidate units; limit scope of grievance and arbitration procedures
Civil Service Reform Act, Title VII (1978)	Federal employees	Defines grievance procedures
Pregnancy Discrimination Act (1978)	Female employees	Defines pregnancy as a disability; requires that pregnancy receive the same benefits as any other disability

Court Decisions

Case	Basic Provisions
Griggs v. Duke Power (1971)	Prohibits tests for hiring unless job-related; requires organization to show evidence of job relatedness; relieves defendant of need to establish intent to discriminate
Diaz v. Pan American World Airways, Inc. (1971)	Defines the primary function of an airline as transporting passengers safely from one point to another and makes the refusal to hire men as flight attendants discriminatory; establishes the principle of business necessity

Court Decisions *(continued)*

Act	Jurisdiction	Basic Provisions
Spurlock v. *United Airlines* (1972)		Permits the use of a college degree as a selection criterion because it is job-related even though no performance data are provided
Richardson v. *Hotel Corporation of America* (1972)		Finds that dismissal on grounds of conviction record results in adverse impact but permits dismissal since conviction record is argued to be related to business necessity (not job performance)
Brito v. *Zia Company* (1973)		Prohibits layoffs of a protected group because of low scores on performance measures that are not validated
Hodgson v. *Greyhound Lines, Inc.* (1974)		Allows employers to discriminate on basis of age without empirical evidence but requires good-faith effort to show older people would make less-safe drivers
Albemarle v. *Moody* (1975)		Requires organization to prove that tests are related to content of jobs but permits job analysis as evidence; aligns validation evidence with EEOC guidelines (1970)
Washington v. *Davis* (1976)		Requires that intent to discriminate must be established when a test procedure is challenged under constitutional law but need not be established if challenged under Title VII of Civil Rights Act (need only show effects)
Dothard v. *Rawlinson* (1977)		Specifies that height requirements are invalid and therefore constitute discriminatory practice
Bakke v. *Regents of the University of California* (1978)		Prohibits reverse discrimination but allows race to be considered in selection decisions; permits affirmative action programs when prior discrimination has been established
Marshall v. *Barlow's Inc.* (1979)		Allows employers to bar entry to OSHA inspectors who do not have search warrants
Marshall v. *Whirlpool* (1980)		Gives employees the right to refuse job assignments that constitute a clear and present danger to life or limb; relieves employer of responsibility to pay employees consequently sent home because of no work

APPENDIX C
Basics of an Affirmative Action Program

Many organizations must have an affirmative action plan (AAP). The basic parts of any AAP are specified in 41 CFR, Part 60, Office of Federal Contract Compliance Programs, Equal Employment Opportunity, Department of Labor. The items discussed below may be used to determine compliance with equal employment laws, but AAPs may include other items as well.

ELIGIBILITY

Employers are eligible for compliance review, according to Revised Order No. 4 (41 CFR, Part 60–2), if they employ fifty or more people and have a contract of $50,000 or more or have government bills of lading totaling $50,000 or more annually or serve as a depository for government funds or are a financial institution that issues and redeems U.S. bonds. Eligible employers must develop an AAP. In addition, federal agencies may require prime contractors, and in turn subcontractors, to file on or before March 31 of each year Standard Form 100 (EEO-1), or its replacement, unless they are exempt. The first report is due thirty days after the initial award and annually thereafter.

PURPOSE

The purpose of an AAP is to establish a "set of specific and result-oriented procedures to which a contractor commits himself to apply every good faith effort." The objective of the procedures is equal employment as guaranteed by law, and this should be indicated at the beginning of the written AAP. The written AAP should also specify an office of affirmative action and its reponsibilities and indicate what records and support data the organization needs to retain. Exhibit C.1 is a checklist of the necessary records and data.

UTILIZATION ANALYSIS

Every AAP must contain a utilization analysis, which compares a work force analysis and an availability analysis. The work force analysis lists all the job titles and wage or salary rates in the organization, ranked from lowest-paid to highest-paid within each unit or department. The total number of incumbents is listed for each job title, and the number of male and female incumbents is assessed in each of these groups. The number of blacks, hispanics, American Indians, and orientials is also assessed.

This appendix was prepared by Margaret M. Watman.

Exhibit C.1 Checklist for AAP Records and Support Data

- ☐ SF-100 (EEO-1) forms for past three years
- ☐ Applicant flow data for past twelve months, charting the following:
  —Number of applications for job groups and hires by sex and minority group
  —Hires by name, sex, minority, job, rate of pay, and recruitment source
  —College recruitment program, including list of schools, date, name, sex, and minority group
- ☐ Promotion and transfer data for past twelve-month period, including date, name, sex, minority group, previous job (department and pay), and new job (department and pay)
- ☐ Termination data for past twelve months by department, including name, sex, minority group, job, date of hire, date of termination and reason
- ☐ Training data for past twelve months, including name, sex, minority, completion date, and job and pay before and after training
- ☐ Copies of all labor agreements
- ☐ Copies of agreements pursuant to investigation of discrimination charges and copies and status of outstanding charges
- ☐ Seniority list of all employees by name, sex, minority group, date of hire, original job, date of last promotion, present job and EEO-1 category, rate of pay, and education or training, indicating the following:
  —Layoff status
  —Organization charts
  —Lines of progression
  —Promotional sequences
- ☐ Copies of AAP goals and current status
- ☐ Copies of testing materials
- ☐ Copies of job descriptions, specifications, and qualifications

An availability analysis seeks to explain whether minorities and women are underrepresented in the organization given their numbers in the local work force. An availability analysis is based on job groups, jobs with similar content, wage rates, and opportunities. Nine points must be considered in this analysis:

- Minority population of the labor area around the organization
- Extent of minority and female unemployment in the area
- Percentage of the total work force that is minority or female
- Availability of minorities and women with the requisite skills in the immediate area
- Availability of minorities and women with the requisite skills in an area where the employer can recruit
- Availability of promotable and transferable minorities and women already working for the employer
- Existence of training institutions capable of training people in the required skills
- Degree of training the employer is able to undertake as an avenue for making all job classes available to minorities and women
- Availability of minorities and women seeking employment in the labor or recruitment area

GOALS AND TIMETABLES

Next an employer must establish goals and timetables for implementing the AAP. The goals should be "significant, measurable and attainable" and should take into consideration expansion, turnover, and contraction of the work force. If deficiencies exist, specific goals and timetables for minorities and for women must be designed to correct them. Exhibit C.2 shows how availability data can be used in setting goals.

Any goals for correcting deficiencies must be accompanied by supporting data in the written AAP. Copies of the AAP and support data must be available on request to compliance agencies.

EEO POLICY

The next step is to develop or reaffirm the company's policy on equal employment opportunity (EEO). This policy statement should express the chief executive officer's attitude toward affirmative action, assign overall responsibility for EEO, and provide for reporting and monitoring procedures. Specifically, the EEO policy should state the organization's intent to recruit, hire, train, and promote people in all job titles without regard to race, color, religion, sex, or national origin and to ensure that all personnel actions are administered without regard to race, color, religion, sex, or national origin.

Department _____ EEO-1 Category _____						Person Completing Chart _____ Title _____										
Salary Group	Current Work Force					% Availability						Annual Goal		Ultimate Goal	
						80–81		81–82		82–83		Female	Minority	Female %	Minority %
	All Total	Female Total	% Female	Minority Total	% Minority	% Female	% Minority	% Female	% Minority	% Female	% Minority	Number	% of Hires	Number	% of Hires		

Affirmative Action Data Estimated Human Resource Availability																	
Department _____ EEO-1 Category _____								Person Completing Chart _____ Title _____									
Salary Group	1980–1981								1981–1982				1982–1983				
	Local (1)		National (2)		Grads 1979–1980 (3)		Total (4)		Grads 1980–1981 (5)		Total (4 + 5) (6)		Grads 1981–1982 (7)		Total (6 + 7) (8)	
	min	other	min	other	min	other	min	other	min	other	min	other	min	other	min	other
	M F	M F	M F	M F	M F	M F	M F	M F	M F	M F	M F	M F	M F	M F	M F	M F

Exhibit C.2 AAP Availability Goals

FORMAL DISSEMMINATION

Employers should develop a formal policy for disseminating information on the AAP. Internal avenues include
- The organization's policy manual
- The company newspaper, magazine, annual report, and other similar media
- Special meetings with all administrative and supervisory personnel to explain policy and individual responsibility
- Special meetings with all other employees
- Discussions of policy in orientation and management training sessions
- Meetings with union officials to inform them and ask for cooperation
- Nondiscrimination clauses in union agreements
- Articles about EEO programs, progress reports, and the like
- Statements of policy posted on the premises
- Features about and pictures of minority and nonminority men and women in such publications as advertising handbooks
- Special communications to employees

External avenues for disseminating information about an organization's AAP include
- Verbal and written statements to all recruiting sources
- An EEO clause in all purchase orders, bases, contracts, and the like
- Notices to minority and women's organizations, community agencies, community vendors, colleges, and the like
- Statements to prospective employees
- Pictures of minority and nonminority men and women in advertising
- Written notification of company policy to all subcontractors, vendors, and suppliers that requests appropriate action from them

RESPONSIBILITY FOR THE AAP

The next step is to delegate responsibility for the development, implementation, and progress of the organization's AAP. A member of top management should be appointed and given the staff to carry out the assignment. Some of this person's responsibilities are
- Developing policy statements, AAPs, and communication techniques
- Assisting in the identification of problem areas
- Assisting line management in problem solving
- Designing and implementing audit and reporting systems
- Serving as liaison between employer and enforcement agencies, community action groups, minority and women's groups, and so on
- Assisting in establishment of goals and timetables
- Auditing personnel procedures, such as hiring and promotion
- Reviewing employee qualifications in promotions and transfers
- Career counseling

IDENTIFICATION OF PROBLEM AREAS

This identification of problem areas by job group and by department is another aspect of an AAP. Some of these problems will come to light with the utilization analysis, but study of the following areas may also reveal problems:

- Composition of the organization's work force by minority group and sex
- Composition of applicant flow by minority group and sex
- The process for resolving employee problems and retaining forms and raw data
- Transfer and promotion practices
- Facilities and special programs, such as training, educational assistance and apprenticeship
- Seniority practices
- Worker attitudes

CORRECTIVE PROGRAMS

Special corrective action should take place if any of the following is discovered:
- "Underutilization" in a specific job group
- Less frequent lateral or vertical promotion of women and minorities than for nonminorities and men
- Applications and preemployment forms that do not meet federal requirements
- Position descriptions that do not reflect actual duties and functions
- Unvalidated tests and selection techniques
- Significantly lower percentage of referrals for minorities and women than for nonminority and male applicants
- Exclusion of minorities and women from company activities or programs
- De facto segregation
- Overt or inadvertent discrimination in seniority system
- Lack of support for company policy on equal employment by management or workers
- Low representation of minorities and women in training or career-development programs
- No formal process for evaluating the effectiveness of EEO programs
- Low recruitment of women and minorities through lack of access to suitable housing
- Lack of suitable transportation for women and minorities
- Lack of cooperation from labor organizations and subcontractors
- Purchase orders without EEO clause
- Low visibility of EEO posters

PROGRAM DEVELOPMENT AND EXECUTION

Once problems have been identified and goals and objectives have been set, specific programs must be designed and implemented. These programs may consist of one or more of the following:
- Doing a detailed analysis of position descriptions
- Validating job specifications
- Making position descriptions and specifications available to all managers and recruiting sources
- Making sure the employees involved in recruiting, screening, selection, discipline, and other personnel matters are carefully selected and trained to eliminate bias
- Evaluating and eliminating selection techniques (other than tests) that may be

used improperly, such as unscored interviews, unscored or casual application forms, arrest records, and credit checks
- Contacting community organizations to increase the flow of minority and female applicants
- Encouraging minority and female employees to refer applicants
- Making special efforts to include minorities and women on the personnel relations staff
- Participating in "job fairs"
- Carrying out active recruiting programs in secondary schools, junior colleges, and colleges with large minority and female enrollments
- Developing special employment programs for women and minorities
- Advertising job openings in minority news media and women's interest media
- Making sure minority and female employees are given equal opportunity for promotion

INTERNAL AUDITING

Employers need to develop a system to measure the effectiveness of their AAP. One way to do this is to monitor the records of referrals, placements, transfers, promotions, and terminations. Another way is to get reports from department managers on the degree to which goals and timetables are being met.

LOCAL AND NATIONAL PROGRAMS

Employers can foster EEO by actively supporting local and national programs designed to improve employment opportunities for minorities and women. Among the ways employers can do this is to support vocational guidance institutes, vestibule training programs, and the like; to assist secondary schools and colleges; to help publicize the achievements of minority and female employees in local and minority news media; and to appoint key members of management to serve on community relations boards or in simimlar organizations.

COMPLIANCE WITH EEO

Employers who must meet the EEO requirements specified by law must develop an AAP as well as file the standard EEO forms. Various groups publish a number of documents to assist in complying with affirmative action guidelines. Among those is 41 CFR, Part 60, which gives specific details of the affirmative action requirements. Others that may prove helpful are listed at the end of this appendix.

People who are responsible for developing and implementing an AAP may benefit by contacting other affirmative action/EEO officers. An informal network enables all members to keep current with changes and developments in the marketplace, the legal arena, and government regulations, as well as providing support. Three areas of particular interest to affirmative action/EEO officers are sex discrimination, discrimination on the basis of religion or national origin, and obligations to handicapped workers.

Sex Discrimination

To avoid sex discrimination, the AAP should incorporate the following points (among other issues):
- Employers should recruit both sexes
- Advertisements must not express a preference for either sex
- Personnel policies should stand firmly behind EEO
- Both sexes must have an equal opportunity to take any available job
- Employment opportunities, wages, hours, and benefits must be equal for both sexes
- There must be appropriate physical facilities for both sexes
- Employers may not deny female employees on the basis of state "protective" law, the right to any job they are qualified for
- Women may not be penalized because of time away from work on account of childbearing. Childbearing must be considered a reason for a leave of absence
- Seniority lists may not be based solely on sex

Discrimination on the Basis of Religion or National Origin

All equal employment policies should be sure that applicants and employees are treated without regard to religion or national origin. The following are examples of, but not all of, the actions that may be taken:
- Reviewing employment practices to determine whether members of certain religious or ethnic groups are receiving fair consideration
- Reviewing employment records to determine the availability of promotable and transferable employees
- Establishing contacts with religious and ethnic organizations for referral, education, and technical assistance
- Using religious and ethnic media for employment advertising

Obligations to Handicapped Workers

A handicapped person is defined as anyone "who (1) has a physical or mental impairment which substantially limits" a life activity, (2) has a history of such impairment, or (3) is perceived as having such impairment. Employers are required to act affirmatively to employ and promote qualified handicapped persons, as well as to modify personnel procedures where necessary. For example, employers should
- Annotate the applications or personnnel files for handicapped applicants, identifying each vacancy for which they were considered
- Identify in the personnel records of all known handicapped employees the promotion and training programs for which they were considered
- Note in the personnel files the reasons for rejecting handicapped employees or applicants for employment, promotion, or training—with a statement comparing the qualifications of the handicapped applicant or employee and the person selected as well as a description of the accommodations that were considered. Describe the accommodations they make in order to place a handicapped person on a job.

Contractors with federal agencies must also make reasonable accommodations for the physical or mental limitations of employees or applicants, unless undue hardship can be demonstrated. In addition, contractors should review their employment practices and undertake appropriate action. Of course, the scope of these efforts depends on the employer's size and resources. Some of the specific actions that may be taken:

● Developing internal systems for communicating the employer's obligations to seek qualified handicapped employees

● Developing reasonable internal procedures to ensure full implementation of AAPs to employ and promote qualified handicapped individuals

● Periodically informing all employees and prospective employees of the organization's commitment to increase employment opportunities for qualified handicapped individuals

● Enlisting the assistance and support or recruiting sources (a list of national organizations serving the handicapped, many of which have state or local affiliates, appears in the "Directory of Organizations Interested in the Handicapped," published by the Committee for the Handicapped People-to-People Program, Washington D.C.)

● Engaging in recruitment activities at educational institutions that train the handicapped, such as schools for the blind, deaf, and retarded

● Establishing meaningful contracts with organizations of and for handicapped individuals and vocational rehabilitation agencies or facilities, for such purposes as advice, technical assistance, and referral of potential employees

● Reviewing employment records to determine the availability of promotable and transferable handicapped employees and to determine whether their present and potential skills are being fully used or developed.

COMPLIANCE REVIEWS

The purpose of the compliance review is to determine whether the employer "maintains non-discriminatory hiring and employment practice and is taking affirmative action to ensure" such. A compliance investigation may be the result of a filed complaint or a review prior to a settlement.

Review Procedures

The procedures for evaluating compliance are outlined in 41 CFR, Parts 60–10 and 60–60. The evaluations include a desk audit of the AAP document, on-site review, and when necessary, off-site analysis.

The desk audit is the evaluation of a contractor's AAP and supporting data. The auditor usually pays special attention to the work force analysis. Sometimes, when good cause is shown, the agency skips this step and goes directly to the on-site review.

The on-site review is conducted when aspects of the AAP are not clear, are unsatisfactory, or do not demonstrate reasonable effort. This phase is usually scheduled after the agency desk audit.

The off-site analysis is an analysis of the information supplied during or pursuant to the on-site review. This is usually done when deficiencies or violations have been found and the reviewing agency feels the need for additional analysis before making a determination.

Time Schedule

Without extensions for good cause, the reviewing agency must either find the employer in compliance with sixty days of receipt of the AAP or issue a thirty-day notice to show cause, also within sixty days of receiving the employer's AAP.

Standard Compliance Review Report

The purpose of the standard compliance review report (SCRR) is to provide reviewing agencies with a standardized procedure. The prescribed format for an SCRR is divided into two main parts. The first part, based on the desk audit, contains

- Idenifying Information
- Work Force Analysis
- Recruitment, Hiring, Selection, and Placement
- Promotion and Transfer
- Terminations
- Analysis of Jobs with Substantial Concentrations of Minorities or Women

The second part, based on the on-site review, contains

- Identifying Information
- Community Survey
- Initial Contact with Contractor
- EEO Policies and Procedures
- Recruitment, Hiring, Selection, and Placement
- Promotion and Transfer
- Terminations
- Supervisory Positions
- Pay Practices
- Analysis of Jobs with Substantial Concentrations of Minorities or Women
- Training and Educational Opportunities
- Goals and Timetable
- Religious and National Origin Discrimination

No review is complete until the necessary information has been forwarded to the Office of Contract Compliance.

Deficiencies and Violations

Complaints about an AAP are to be filed with the Office of Contract Compliance within 180 days of the alleged violation. The agency assigned to investigate the complaint should promptly notify the complainant and the employer.

If the investigating agency determines that deficiencies do exist, it attempts to secure compliance through conciliation and persuasion. Employers must make a specific, written commitment to correct these deficiencies before they can be found in compliance.

Violations of EEO regulations may be based on any of the following, among other factors:

- Any substantial or material violation of or threat to violate EEO rules and regulations
- Results of a complaint investigation
- Analysis of an AAP
- Results of an on-site review or an employer's compliance with the order
- An employer's refusal to submit an AAP
- An employer's refusal to allow an on-site compliance review
- An employer's refusal to supply records or other required information

Compliance Status

Each employer's compliance status is determined by reviewing the contents of the AAP, the extent of adherence to the AAP, and good-faith efforts to make the program work. No employer's status is judged solely by whether the goals and timetables have been met.

BIBLIOGRAPHY

American Association of University Women, *Affirmative Action Glossary.* Washington, D.C.: American Association of University Women, 1978

Anderson, Howard J., ed. *Primer of Equal Employment Opportunity.* Washington, D.C.: The Bureau of National Affairs, Inc., 1978.

Brookmire, David, and Burton, Amy. "A Format for Packaging Your Affirmative Action Program." *Personnel Journal,* June 1978, pp. 294–304.

Office of Federal Contract Compliance Programs. Equal Employment Opportunity. Department of Labor. *41 CFR Chapter 60.* Washington, D.C.: Government Printing Office, 1978.

U.S. Equal Employment Opportunity Commission. *Affirmative Action and Equal Employment: A Guidebook for Employers.* Vols. 1 and 2. Appendices. Washington, D.C.: Government Printing Office, January 1974.

APPENDIX D
How to Prepare a Resume

The best advice is to make your resume clear, concise, easy to read, and easy to understand.

Make your resume one page—or two pages at the most. Remember, when a company needs people, it receives many resumes. Neither the technical directors nor the personnel director have time to read long, involved descriptions. Also, the general procedure is that one copy remains with personnel and a photocopy is prepared for routing. Thus you may want to send two copies.

A time-tested sequence for the contents of your resume:

- *Your name, address, and telephone number*
- *Summary, highlights, or synopsis:* Whatever it's called, employers like it. In the advertising industry, the first lesson a writer learns is that the first ten words are the most important. This is where you win or lose your audience.
- *Education:* List your most recent degree first, the date, your major(s), and the university. List your thesis title if it's relevant to the type of job you seek. Many employers also like to see a GPA. If you're proud of it, put it in.
- *Experience:* List your title, the company, the dates, and your responsibilities chronologically, with your present position first. The description of your duties or reponsibilities should highlight your accomplishments and contributions. Don't waste space decribing the functions of your company, division, or project. The reader wants to know what you did.
- *Publications:* If space permits, list only those you authored and especially those that may be relevant to the type of job you seek.
- *Personal information:* At the bottom, describe your marital status, number of children, present salary, and asking salary. Your date of birth is optional, but most employers appreciate it.

Exhibit D.1 provides an example using this format.

The biggest problem people have in preparing a resume is writing a synopsis and being concise. Before you even try to write a synopsis, build a resume in the sequence I recommend. Type up a rough draft, then abstract the highlights from your resume. It is easier to synopsize once everything is on paper.

To be concise, you should review the resume and see if you can cut it down. If you are like most people, you will find repetitions and ways to make some of your sentences say more with fewer words. Be your own editor!

As long as you've come this far, you might consider preparing two versions of your resume, each highlighting a different significant experience. You might also play with the layout to make sure your presentation is as clear as possible.

Now there is only one thing left to do—have a final type. If you have followed these procedures, you will have an eye-catching resume packed with factual data, but most importantly a resume that will be easy and inviting to read.

Prepared by Eva M. June, president, Ability Search, Inc., 1629 K Street N.W., Washington D.C. 20006. Presented at the 41st National Operations Research Society of America Meeting, New Orleans, Louisiana, April 1972. Reprinted with permission.

Exhibit D.1   Sample Resume

RICHARD L. GOODE
141 East 15th Avenue
Columbus, Ohio 43201
Telephone: (614) 291-7371

OBJECTIVE:	A challenging college internship or entry-level position offering on-the-job training in the field of accounting, finance, or economics
EDUCATION:	The Ohio State University, Columbus, Ohio Candidate for BS in Business Administration, December 1980 Major: Finance GPA: 2.8 GPA in Major: 3.5
	Oxford University, Oxford, England Summer Study Program, 1979, Curriculum: Eighteenth-Century Art, Literature, and History
	Hanover High School, Hanover, New Hampshire Graduated 1976
COLLEGE ACTIVITIES:	Phi Kappa Tau Fraternity Treasurer, 1979: Managed financial affairs of fraternity under a $90,000 annual budget; made a significant contribution in eliminating a $4,000 deficit
	Vice President of Rush, 1978: Organized and coordinated the recruitment program, which was highlighted by "formal rush" involving 500 rushees
	Scarlet Representative to Interfraternity Council, 1978: Acted as liaison between fraternity presidents and executive board
JOB EXPERIENCE:	April–June 1979 T.G.I. Friday's, 4540 Kenny Rd., Columbus, Ohio 43220 Fulltime waiter on day shift
	Summer 1977 and 1978 Chieftain Motel, Lyme Rd., Hanover, New Hampshire 03755 Manager on evening shift
	November 1973-September 1976 Mary Hitchcock Memorial Hospital, Manor St., Hanover, New Hampshire 03755 Worked in transportation department as an orderly, fulltime summers and parttime during the school year
PERSONAL:	Age: 23 Height: 5'8" Weight: 145 lbs. Health: Excellent Marital Status: Single
REFERENCES:	Available on request

APPENDIX E
Journals in Personnel and Human Resource Management

RESEARCH AND ACADEMIC JOURNALS

Administrative Science Quarterly, Graduate School of Business and Public Administration, Cornell University, Ithaca, New York. Broad coverage of management opinion and research reports, with a continuing emphasis on theory and philosophy; book reviews and abstracts.

American Journal of Sociology, published for the American Sociological Association by the University of Chicago Press, 5750 Ellis Avenue, Chicago, Illinois. Increasing attention to the broad area of industrial sociology, with frequent reports on studies of work and organizational theory.

American Management Association Research Reports, American Management Association, 1515 Broadway, New York, New York. Reports of company philosophy, policy, and practice in all phases of management.

Behavioral Sciences, Mental Health Research Institute, University of Michigan, Ann Arbor, Michigan. Articles on general theories of behavior and on empirical research.

Bulletin of Industrial Psychology and Personnel Practice, Department of Labor and National Service, Melbourne, Australia. Reports of research in Australia and abroad, book reviews, and abstracts of articles from numerous other foreign and domestic publications.

Ergonomics, Taylor and Francis, Ltd., Red Lion Court, Fleet Street, London, England. Emphasizes human engineering; combines approaches of human biology, anatomy, physiology, and psychology with mechanical engineering.

Harvard Business Review, Graduate School of Business Administration, Harvard University, Soldier's Field, Boston, Massachusetts. A review of the general field of business, with frequent articles on industrial relations.

Human Organizations, Society for Applied Anthropology, New York State School of Industrial and Labor Relations, Cornell University, Ithaca, New York. Intercultural approach to problems of human relations, including industrial relations.

Industrial and Labor Relations Review, New York State School of Labor and Industrial Relations, Cornell University, Ithaca, New York. Opinions and reports of studies on labor legislation, collective bargaining, and related subjects.

Industrial Medicine and Surgery, Industrial Medicine Publishing Company, 605 North Michigan Avenue, Chicago, Illinois. Emphasizes health programs in industry, with reports on health hazards, occupational diseases, handicapped workers, medical services, and related subjects.

Industrial Relations, Institute of Industrial Relations, University of California, Berkeley and Los Angeles, California. Ideas and opinions as well as reports of research.

Industrial Training Abstracts, Wayne State University Press, Detroit, Michigan. Abstracts articles dealing with apprentice, foreman, and supervisory safety and related types of training in industry.

Journal of Applied Psychology, American Psychological Association, 1313 Sixteenth Street N.W., Washington D.C. All phases of applied psychology, with numerous reports of personnel research.

Labor Law Journal, Commerce Clearing House, Inc., 214 N. Michigan Avenue, Chicago, Illinois. Generally presents nonlegalistic discussions of legal phases of industrial relations.

Monthly Labor Review, Bureau of Labor Statistics, U.S. Department of Labor, Washington, D.C. Summaries of staff studies on industrial relations; statistical sections include continuing series on industrial disputes, employment, payrolls, and cost of living.

TRADE JOURNALS

Advanced Management, Society for the Advancement of Management, 74 Fifth Avenue, New York, New York. Successor to *The Society for the Advancement of Management Journal,* and *Bulletin of the Taylor Society,* and *Modern Management;* reports on managerial developments and viewpoints in all phases of management.

Journal of Personnel Administration and Industrial Relations, Personnel Research Publishers, Washington D.C. Reports original studies and theoretical analyses in all phases of industrial relations.

Journal of the American Society of Training Directors, official publication of the American Society of Training Directors, 2020 University Avenue, Madison, Wisconsin. Broad coverage of the personnel field, with a special emphasis on training problems.

Management Record, National Industrial Conference Board, 247 Park Avenue, New York, New York. Numerous reports of both experience and research, surveys conducted by the NICB staff, and digests of symposia.

Management Review, American Management Association, 330 West Forty-second Street, New York, New York. General coverage of all phases of management.

Personnel, American Management Association, 330 West Forty-second Street, New York, New York. Broad interest in entire field of industrial relations, with numerous reports of surveys, studies, and experience.

Personnel Journal, published at *Personnel Journal,* 866 West Eighteenth Street, Costa Mesa, California. Covers a broad spectrum of topics in personnel and labor relations.

Personnel Management, formerly the *Journal of the Institute of Personnel Management,* Institute of Personnel Management, Management House, 80 Fetter Lane, London, England. Theory and practice in both personnel management and labor relations.

Personnel Management Abstracts, Bureau of Industrial Relations, University of Michigan, Ann Arbor, Michigan. Abstracts of books and articles in both personnel management and labor relations.

Personnel Psychology, PO Box 6965, College Station, Durham, North Carolina. Emphasizes reports on research in psychological aspects of personnel and industrial relations.

Public Personnel Quarterly, published by the International Personnel Management Association, 1850 K Street N.W., Washington D.C.

The Personnel Administrator, published by the American Society for Personnel Administrators/ACPA), 30 Park Drive, Berea, Ohio. Information on taking the ASPA's examinations for the purpose of becoming a certified personnel administrator can be obtained by writing to the ASPA.

Studies in Personnel Policy, National Industrial Conference Board, 247 Park Avenue, New York, New York. Mainly compares experience and evaluations of programs, with frequent surveys of policy and practice.

The Legality of Employment Records

Recently there have been several lawsuits brought on behalf of individuals against organizations for invasion of privacy rights. These lawsuits have been related to or responsible for four federal laws. The encompassing law is the Privacy Act of 1974, which applies only to federal agencies. It pertains to the verification of references in selection and employment decisions. This act allows individuals to determine what records pertaining to them are collected, used, and maintained; to review and amend such records; to prevent unspecified use of such records; and to bring civil suit for damages against those intentionally violating the rights specified in the act.

The second federal privacy law is the Fair Credit and Reporting Act, which permits job applicants to know the nature and content of the credit file on them that is obtained by the organization. The third law is the Family Education Rights and Privacy Act, or the Buckley Amendment. This allows students to inspect their educational records, and prevents educational institutions from supplying information without students' consent. If they do not provide this consent, potential employers are prevented from learning of their educational record. The fourth law is the Freedom of Information Act, which also pertains only to federal agencies. This act allows individuals to see all the material an agency uses in its decision-making processes.

Although these four laws apply primarily to federal agencies, private organizations will most likely face similar federal or state laws in the near future. These laws will probably establish the right of all individuals to have access to their personnel files and to be notified of the pending release of information to third parties. Several states have already enacted privacy legislation affecting the privacy of job applicants as well as that of current employees. These laws influence the use of the personnel file, access to it and its contents, and implicitly the information collected for it.

Some organizations have taken the lead by establishing their own policies regarding privacy and individuals' rights. These policies relate to hiring, placement, promotion, discipline, and discharge—the heart of the employer/employee relationship. Here is an example from Worldwide, a large private organization (the name has been changed). Note the role of the personnel department at the home office in centralizing personnel policies for all the regional offices.

WORLDWIDE'S POLICY ON PRIVACY

Recommendations

- Establish an official employee personnel file, which will be maintained in the regional personnel department or the employment and placement department in the home office.
- The unofficial, department files will contain minimal information, such as the

latest appraisal, absence reports, correspondence relating to disciplinary action, and so on.

● The office of personnel, in concurrence with the office of general counsel, will prepare a list of acceptable types of information to be kept in the department files and the official files.

● The employment and placement departments for staff offices and for each region's personnel department will schedule the purging of employees' files and establish the official personnel file.

● The personnel department will have the responsibility for auditing the contents of the department files.

● Adopt a corporate privacy policy as follows:

All employees have the right to inspect their official personnel files subject to the following requirements:

● *The request for inspection of the file must be made in writing and submitted to the employee's personnel manager in the region (or to employment and placement manager in the home office). The employee's personnel manager will schedule the date and time (during normal working hours) of the inspection and advise the employee's supervisor of the time and place. The employee may inspect the file once a year, unless the personnel manager decides it is appropriate for a particular employee to see his or her file more than once in a twelve-month period.*

● *The personnel manager shall designate a personnel representative to be present when the employee inspects the file. The employee shall be allowed a reasonable time to review the file (thirty to sixty minutes), as the personnel manager deems appropriate.*

● *The employee may not remove any information or make copies of the contents of the file but may make notes of the information it contains.*

● *If the employee requests permission to review the department file, the personnel representative will secure this file. The same procedures will be followed as outlined for review of the official personnel file.*

Expected Results

The experience of other companies that have implemented similar programs leads us to expect the following results for a formal, company-wide, fully communicated employee privacy policy:

● The costs of implementing and managing the program will be reasonable and acceptable.

● Much of the information that has been collected is personal, outdated, and not used in making management decisions. This type of information will be discarded.

● None of the basic personnel functions—hiring, appraisal, assignment, promotion, discipline, and discharge—will be adversely affected.

● The personnel department will not be swamped with requests by employees to review their files, but employees will express strong satisfaction and approval for cleaning up the files and making them available under a formal, uniform program.

● Employee privacy will become a continuing corporate activity—not a once-and-for-all event. This will cost time and manpower. However, these costs will be far outweighed by the elimination of grievances and lawsuits, not only within the parameters of privacy legislation but EEO as well.

Name Index

Subject Index